PROGRAMMING
ASSEMBLER LANGUAGE
Second Edition

Peter Abel

a *RESTON COMPUTER GROUP* book from
RESTON PUBLISHING COMPANY, INC.
a *PRENTICE-HALL* company
Reston, Virginia

Library of Congress Cataloging in Publication Data

Abel, Peter,
   Programming assembler language.

   Includes index.
   1. Assembler language (Computer program language)
2. IBM 370 (Computer)—Programming.   I. Title.
QA76.73.A8A23   1984   001.64′24   83–24668
ISBN 0–8359–5661–X

10   9   8   7   6   5   4   3   2

Interior design and production: Jack Zibulsky

Printed in the United States of America

CONTENTS

PREFACE AND ACKNOWLEDGMENTS, vii

I INTRODUCTION TO THE COMPUTER AND THE AS-SEMBLER, 1

0 BASIC COMPUTER CONCEPTS, 3

Introduction, 3/The Computer System, 4/Input/Output Devices, 7/Binary Number System, 9/Bits and Bytes, 10/S/370 Organization, 11/Operating Systems and the Supervisor, 14/Hexadecimal Representation, 15/Problems, 17

1 THE ASSEMBLER, 19

Languages, 19/The Assembler, 20/The Assembler Coding Form, 21/Directives, 25/Declaratives, 27/Coding Conventions, 28/Programming Steps, 29/The Assembled Program Listing, 30/Assembler Diagnostic Messages, 34/Addressing, 34/Instruction Format, 37/Problems, 38

2 PROGRAM EXECUTION, 41

Files and Records, 41/Program Execution Statements, 42/Sample Program: Read and Print One Record, 47/Looping, 50/Sample Program: Read and Print Multiple Records, 50/Cross Reference Listing, 52/Input Data, 53/Condition Code, 55/Flowchart Logic, 56/Job Control, 60/Problems, 61

II BASIC ASSEMBLER CODING, 63

3 PROGRAMMING FOR CHARACTER DATA, 65

Declaratives, 65/Character Instructions, 73/Storage-to-Storage Format, 74/Move Characters—MVC, 74/Duplicating Characters, 79/

Sample Program: Process Inventory Records, 80/Compare Logical Character—CLC, 82/Storage Immediate Format, 87/Logic Example, 89/Literals, 90/Equate Symbol—EQU, 91/Set Location Counter— ORG, 93/Sample Program: Read and Print Customer Records, 94/ Debugging Tips, 98/Problems, 100

4 DECIMAL DATA AND ARITHMETIC I, 103

Hexadecimal Constants, 103/Move Numeric (MVN) and Move Zones (MVZ), 104/Zoned Decimal Data, 106/Packed Decimal Data, 107/ Packed Operations, 109/Sum of Digits Calculation, 119/Formatting the Print Area, 119/Subroutines and Linkage, 122/Sample Program: Budget Statement, 125/Representation in Storage, 127/Debugging Tips, 132/Problems, 133

5 DECIMAL ARITHMETIC II, 137

Editing—ED, 137/Multiply Packed—MP, 142/Shifting and Rounding, 143/Shift and Round Packed—SRP, 145/Move with Offset—MVO, 147 /Sample Program: Loan Repayment Schedule, 148/Divide Packed— DP, 151/Sample Program: Inventory Calculation, 156/Debugging Tips, 162/Problems, 162

6 BASE REGISTERS AND INSTRUCTION FORMAT, 165

The General-Purpose Registers, 165/Base Register Addressing, 166/ Instruction Format, 170/Control Sections, 175/Assigning Base Registers, 177/Loading the Base Register, 178/OS Initialization, 181/The Assembly Process, 182/Technical Note About BCR and BC, 185/ Debugging Tips, 186/Problems, 187

7 INPUT AND OUTPUT, 189

Input/Output Control System, 189/Imperative Macros, 192/The DOS DTF File Definition Macro, 197/The OS DCB File Definition Macro, 201/Locate Mode, 204/Device Independence Under DOS, 207/Abnormal Termination, 208/Terminal I/O, 209/Debugging Tips, 210/ Problems, 210

8 STRATEGY, STYLE, AND STANDARDS, 211

Programming Objectives, 211/Programming Style, 212/Hierarchy Charts, 213/Program Documentation, 214/Debugging Tips, 229/ Problems, 229

III BINARY OPERATIONS, 231

9 REGISTERS AND BINARY PROGRAMMING, 233

Binary Data Representation, 233/Binary Constants, 235/Conversion of Decimal and Binary Data—CVB and CVD, 240/Loading Registers —L, LH, LR, LM, LA, 241/Store Register Operations—ST, STH, STM, 246/Binary Arithmetic—A, S, AH, SH, AR, SR, 248/Binary Comparison—C, CH, CR, 249/Example Use of Binary Arithmetic, 251/Multiplication—M, MH, MR, 252/Register Shift Instructions, 255/Binary Division, 258/Conversion of Double Precision Binary to Decimal Format, 261/Sample Partial Program: Finance Charge Rebates, 263/ Move Long and Compare Long—MVCL and CLCL, 264/Debugging Tips, 267/Problems, 267

10 EXPLICIT USE OF BASE REGISTERS, 269

Explicit Base/Displacement Addressing for MVC, 269/Explicit Base Addressing for Packed Instructions, 270/Operations Explicitly Using Base Registers, 272/Tables, 277/Other Table Handling Routines, 285 /Direct Table Addressing, 286/Sorting Data in Storage, 288/Binary Search, 292/Sample Program: Calculate Stock Value, 292/Debugging Tips, 302/Problems, 303

11 LOGICAL OPERATIONS AND BIT MANIPULATION, 307

Logical Operations, 307/Boolean Logic, 311/Other Operations—TM, IC, STC, EX, TR, TRT, 314/Masked Byte Operations—ICM, STCM, and CLM, 327/Binary Operations—Summary, 330/Debugging Tips, 330/Problems, 330

IV EXTERNAL STORAGE, 333

12 MAGNETIC TAPE, 335

Uses of Magnetic Tape, 335/Magnetic Tape Characteristics, 336/DOS Tape Programming Example: Creating a Tape File, 339/OS Coding for Magnetic Tape, 341/IOCS For Magnetic Tape, 347/Variable-Length Records, 349/Debugging Tips, 354/Problems, 355

13 DIRECT ACCESS STORAGE, 357

DASD Characteristics, 358/Count-Key-Data Architecture—CKD, 359 /Fixed-Block Architecture—FBA, 362/File Organization, 363/DOS Programming Example: Creating a Sequential Disk File, 364/OS Program Example, 366/Disk Labels, 366/DASD Capacity, 369/Debugging Tips, 371/Problems, 371

14 INDEXED SEQUENTIAL FILE ORGANIZATION, 373

The Prime Data Area, 373/The Track Index, 373/The Cylinder Index, 374/The Master Index, 375/Overflow Areas, 375/Processing DOS Indexed Sequential Files, 377/Processing OS Indexed Sequential Files, 384/Problems, 387

15 VIRTUAL STORAGE ACCESS METHOD—VSAM, 389

Control Interval, 390/Entry Sequenced Data Sets, 390/Relative Record Data Sets, 391/Key Sequenced Data Sets, 391/Access Method Services (AMS), 394/Accessing and Processing, 396/VSAM Macro Instructions, 396/The ACB Macro—Access Method Control Block, 398/ The RPL Macro—Request Parameter List, 399/The OPEN Macro, 400 /The CLOSE Macro, 401/The Request Macros—GET, PUT, and ERASE, 401/The EXLST Macro, 403/The SHOWCB Macro, 404/Program Example: Loading a Key Sequenced Data Set, 405/Keyed Direct Retrieval, 409/VSAM Sort, 409/VSAM Utility Print, 410/Debugging Tips, 411/Problems, 412

V SPECIAL TOPICS, 413

16 DEBUGGING, 415

Character Data, 415/Packed Decimal Data, 416/Binary Data, 418/ Endless Looping, 418/Addressing, 418/Input/Output, 419/Uncatalogued I/O Modules, 421/Storage Dumps, 421/Dump Example, 424 /Partial Dumps of Storage—PDUMP and SNAP, 429/STXIT—Set Exit, 437/Problems, 438

17 FLOATING POINT OPERATIONS, 441

Floating Point Formats, 441/Declaratives, 446/Floating Point Registers, 447/Floating Point Instructions, 448/Conversion From Packed to Float, 458/Conversion From Float to Packed, 458/Problems, 460

18 MACRO WRITING, 461

Writing Macros, 462/Conditional Assembly Instructions, 468/Other Instructions, 471/Set Symbols, 473/System Variable Symbols, 479/ Global Set Symbols, 479/Extended Example—Table Look-up Macro, 480/Problems, 481

19 SUBPROGRAMS AND OVERLAYS, 483

CSECT—Control Section, 483/DSECT—Dummy Section, 484/Subprogram Linkage, 487/Linking Two Control Sections, 489/Passing Parameters, 493/Linking Phases, 496/Overlay Considerations, 503/ Linking COBOL and Assembler, 504/Problems, 508

20 OPERATING SYSTEMS, 509

Operating Systems, 509/Multiprogramming, 515/Virtual Storage, 515 /The Supervisor, 516/The Program Status Word—PSW, 519/Interrupts, 521/Channels, 523/I/O Logic Modules, 526/Physical IOCS, 527 /Example Physical IOCS Program, 529/Problems, 532

APPENDICES, 533

A HEXADECIMAL AND DECIMAL CONVERSION, 535

B PROGRAM INTERRUPTS BY CODE, 537

C 370 INSTRUCTION SET, 541

D DOS AND OS JOB CONTROL, 545

E SPECIAL MACROS: INIT, PUTPR, DEFIN, DEFPR, EOJ, 553

F 370 CODE REPRESENTATION, 557

G SUMMARY OF ASSEMBLER DECLARATIVES, 561

H SUMMARY OF ASSEMBLER DIRECTIVES, 563

I ANSWERS TO SELECTED PROBLEMS, 567

INDEX, 573

PREFACE AND ACKNOWLEDGMENTS

Assembler language is the fundamental "low-level" language of the IBM 370-series of computers. As such, it is directly translatable into machine language; thus, one Assembler instruction typically generates one machine code instruction. "High-level" languages like COBOL and PL/I are easier to learn. Why then an emphasis on learning Assembler language? An understanding of Assembler language can help the programmer in a number of ways:

- A knowledge of Assembler can facilitate learning of any other language, including "high-level" languages and other assembly languages. And with a background in Assembler, the user can more clearly understand what the computer is doing.
- A knowledge of Assembler can help the programmer become more efficient. High-level languages like COBOL and PL/I can be deceptive, and appear to execute in some mysterious fashion. A programmer familiar with Assembler can code high-level languages with an understanding of what machine code they generate, and what is the more efficient technique. For example, why in COBOL does the use of COMPUTATIONAL, COMPUTATIONAL-3, and SYNC have considerable effect on the program's efficiency? What is the significance in PL/I of Decimal Fixed, Aligned, and Defined? With knowledge of Assembler, a programmer can examine the generated code to determine more efficient ways to write certain routines.
- Although most high-level languages provide extensive debugging aids, there are times when the programmer needs to delve into the generated machine code or examine storage dumps.
- Programs written in Assembler may be considerably more efficient in storage space and execute-time, a useful consideration if such programs are run frequently.
- Some advanced areas, such as technical support and telecommunications, require an extensive knowledge of Assembler.

Although the material in this text has been used successfully as an introduction to programming, most educational institutes would not teach Assembler as an introductory language. Generally, the concepts of logic and programming style are easier to learn when there is less need for concern with rigorous rules and field sizes. The text does not, however, assume that the reader has had much, if any, programming experience. The approach of the text is to introduce simple processing using card or terminal input and printer output, first with character data only, and then with simple decimal arithmetic, all by Chapter 4. In this way, packed (decimal) data and editing are introduced early, and the user is soon writing quite realistic programs.

The book should provide both a practical guide for the Assembler student and also may act subsequently as a useful reference. These two objectives are accomplished by:

1. A step-by-step presentation beginning with simple material through to more complex material. There are many practical examples of complete and partial programs to illustrate concepts as they are introduced.

2. Chapters organized by logical topics, such as character data, packed, binary, input/output. The user can concentrate on mastering one programming area at a time, and most related material is contained in its own chapter.

The complexities of base/displacement addressing and file definition are delayed through use of several simple macros, similar to those used in many colleges. The text drops these macros by Chapters 6 and 7, where the technical material is covered in detail. Appendix E provides a listing of the macros for those who want to catalog them on their own system.

The two major IBM operating systems are DOS and OS. The text covers the differences between them, giving examples for both.

It is possible to proceed through the text by several routes. Chapters 0 through 3 are fundamental, and the normal steps would be to continue sequentially with decimal arithmetic in Chapters 4 and 5. You could refer at any time to the material in Chapter 16 on debugging, as needed. It is recommended next to cover the important material in Chapter 6 on base/displacement addressing and the instruction format, and then the elements of input/output in Chapter 7. By this point the user should be capable of coding some quite advanced programs. Chapter 8 on Programming Strategy could be covered in part or total, perhaps the sooner the better to get the user into programming style. Following Chapter 8, the chapters need not all be covered sequentially. The following diagram indicates related chapters in boxes that may be taken in any sequence following Chapters 6 and 7:

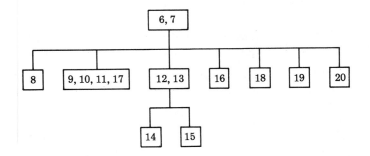

Chapters 9, 10, and 11 develop related material on processing binary data. Chapter 12 on Magnetic Tape introduces basic material required for an understanding of Disk Storage in Chapters 13, 14, and 15. To complete Chapter 18 (Macro Writing) would require some familiarity with the material in Chapter 9. Anyone interested in linking separately assembled programs or COBOL with Assembler could attempt Chapter 19 directly after Chapter 7, perhaps referencing Chapter 9 for some basic binary operations. Chapter 20 on Operating Systems is presented for general useful information, although not entirely related to Assembler programming as such.

Among the users of earlier versions of this text, many have worked ahead of the course, experimenting with binary operations, macro writing, and subprogram linkage. Such motivation is certainly commendable and should be encouraged.

The IBM manuals concerned with the material in this text require a bookshelf about five feet wide. Readers should not expect, therefore, that this or any other single book will provide all there is to know about the Assembler language and related topics. Eventually the IBM manuals have to be referenced for current detailed information. The following IBM manuals or their equivalent are especially recommended:

IBM FORM	TITLE
GA22-7000	IBM System/370 Principles of Operation. (370 system organization, machine instructions, input/output.)
GC33-4010	OS/VS-DOS/VS-VM/370 Assembler Language. (Assembler statements and macros.)
GC33-5373	DOS/VS Supervisor and Input/Output Macros.
GC28-6646	OS Supervisor Services and Macro Instructions.
GC26-3746	OS Data Management Services Guide.
GC26-3794	OS Data Management Macro Instructions.

Other useful manuals include those on job control, disk file organization, tape labels, disk labels, the operating system, and virtual storage.

NOTE ON THE SECOND EDITION

Since "Programming Assembler Language" was introduced in 1978, the computer world has changed dramatically. The most notable change has been the increase in microcomputer technology and a renewed interest in Assembler language. As well, authors evolve (or should) their thinking and approaches to programming. This second edition reflects these changes.

- An emphasis on device-independent input/output. Until recently, a lot of processing was of necessity done on punched cards. In this edition, input is as independent of devices as possible. Users may process on terminals, disk, or if need be on cards.

- An earlier introduction to programming style. Admittedly, Assembler does not lend itself readily to all structured programming conventions. One area where Assembler does meet its requirements is in program organization and subroutines. This edition introduces this subject as early as possible, in Chapter 4 instead of Chapter 8. Also, this edition has adopted the structured style of performing an input operation during initialization, and performing a repetitive loop with the repeated input operation at the end of the loop:

Initialization:
Initialize
Read first record
Process:
Process the record
Read the next record
Loop to Process
End-of-file:
Process totals
Terminate

- Full chapters on virtual storage and debugging.
- Two changes to the special macros that the text uses:

1. INIT now generates only base register initialization, and no longer generates the START directive. As a consequence, all programs start with START and end with END.

2. The previous input macro DEFCD was hardly suitable for users of terminals. The new macro is DEFIN (Define Input), and although Appendix E provides a possible macro definition, users may substitute any input device.

- More program examples and further explanations, especially at the beginning where students have the most trouble.

I hope that this revision satisfies your current needs, at least until new technology replaces the IBM 370-based Assembler.

*   *   *   *   *

The author is grateful for the assistance from all those who contributed typing, reviews, and suggestions, and to IBM for permission to reproduce some of their copyrighted materials. The following materials are printed with permission, and with modifications from publications copyrighted in 1970, 1972, 1973, and 1974 by International Business Machines Corporation as IBM form numbers GA22-7000, GX20-1850 and GC20-1649: Figures 2-2, 13-2, 16-3, Appendix A, and Appendix C.

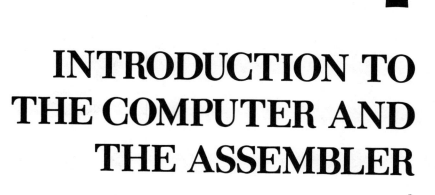

INTRODUCTION TO THE COMPUTER AND THE ASSEMBLER

1

0

BASIC COMPUTER CONCEPTS

INTRODUCTION

This chapter discusses computer concepts and systems in general terms, then introduces basic technical detail concerned specifically with the IBM 370-series of computers. The three main areas are general computer systems, the binary number system, and the S/370 organization.

The first generation of computers was introduced in the early 1950s. These computers were characterized by many vacuum tubes and relatively slow processing speed. The second generation, introduced in 1957–1958, used transistorized circuitry that permitted smaller size, higher speed storage, and lower cost. Finally, third generation computers, introduced in the early 1960s, replaced the transistorized computers with integrated circuits. These computers featured higher speed, greater storage capacity, and more facilities.

IBM introduced System/360, a third generation computer, in 1964 to replace and to improve upon a variety of then existing IBM computers. Some computers had been specialized for business applications, others for scientific purposes. The 360 provided a single computer designed to serve effectively in both fields. The 360 (and third generation computers by other manufacturers) provided many other advantages over second generation computers. It performed considerably faster and it had greater size and capacity for performing more functions. These characteristics enabled the computer to handle larger and more complex applications. The 360 also had the potential to be expanded. IBM adopted a building block concept to enable the user to increase the size of computer storage without always requiring a different computer. Similarly, because the programming languages were standardized for 360 models, little reprogramming was required when transferring to a larger system.

An important feature of the 360 (and of many other computers) was its supervisor capability. It contained a *control program* that permitted error recovery, storing of programs and data on disk storage or magnetic tape for subsequent processing, continuous job processing with limited operator intervention, and multiprogramming (concurrent processing of several data-processing jobs).

In 1970, IBM introduced System/370 with significant improvement in computing performance over the 360. Although the 370 has some additional instructions and capabilities, it was designed for compatibility with the 360, with the same languages and control programs. This text covers differences where applicable.

In 1977, the 370 was further extended into a more complex processor system: the 3031, 3032, and 3033. In 1979, IBM announced the 4300 series and subsequently the 308X series in the early 1980s. Through all the various improvements, the basic Assembler language remained the same.

THE COMPUTER SYSTEM

Although computers have evolved radically since the 1940s and there are many manufacturers and models, their basic structure remains the same. Figure 0-1 illustrates the four main components: input/output, storage or memory, arithmetic/logic and control. Arithmetic/logic and control together form what is called the *central processing unit* (CPU).

INPUT/OUTPUT.   A computer must be able to access new data. The computer "reads" data into its storage from such input devices as terminals, card readers, and magnetic tape. Because the computer must communicate its results to the user, it "writes" data from storage onto such devices as printers and tape.

STORAGE OR MEMORY.   We write a program using computer instructions to solve a specific problem. The program consists of *instructions* (such as read, add, and compare) and data (numbers used in calculations and areas to develop answers and to read input data). The instructions and data area which may be on disk storage are read (loaded) into the computer storage.

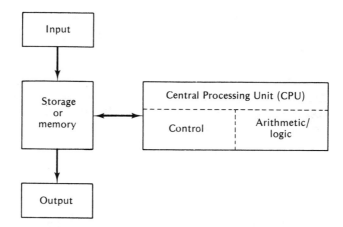

FIGURE 0-1 Basic computer components.

This program in storage is the *stored program* that reads input data, makes calculations, and writes output according to the program instructions. Another program loaded in storage can replace the previous program to work on a different problem and data. Figure 0-2 depicts a layout of instructions and data areas.

The size of storage varies considerably by computer model, from as little as a few thousand storage positions to millions. Storage size in an installation depends generally on the volume of data and the complexity of the

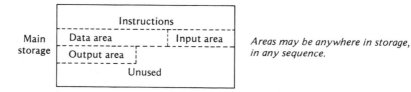

FIGURE 0-2 Simplified map of main storage.

problems. Each storage location is numbered, the first position being *zero*, the second *one*, etc. An instruction may require only a few locations. An area for data may require from one position to hundreds.

Here is a simple example using an imaginary computer that is to add the number '005' to '125'. Assume the '005' is in storage locations 1338, 1339, and 1340, and that the '125' is in storage locations 1263, 1264, and 1265:

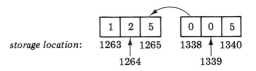

Assume that an add operation is the letter 'A'. The instruction to add the *contents* of locations 1338–1340 to the *contents* of locations 1263–1265 could be the following:

A	1	2	6	3	1	3	3	8

Locations 1263–1265 now contain '130'. Locations 1338–1340 still contain '005', unchanged by the add operation. This instruction would itself require nine storage locations consisting of three parts. A is the *operation,* telling the computer what function to perform; '1263' and '1338' are respectively *operand-1* and *operand-2* that specify which storage positions to process. An add instruction on the 370 is similar to this example.

CENTRAL PROCESSING UNIT.   The CPU consists of an arithmetic/logic unit and a control unit.

ARITHMETIC/LOGIC.   In order to solve problems, the computer must be able to perform arithmetic and make decisions. Computers add and subtract, and most can multiply and divide. With these basic functions, the computer can be programmed to perform, for example, square roots, trigonometric functions, and calculus.

Also, a program generally must make tests and comparisons. For example, does a divisor have a zero value? If so, then a division cannot be performed. Is a value negative? If so, we cannot calculate its square root. Similarly, we may have to check if a value is greater than, less than, or equal to another. The ability to make such decisions is the computer logic.

CONTROL.   The computer requires a component to control its actions. The control device that performs this function does the following:

- Causes the computer to execute each instruction in the stored program, step-by-step. Typically, each instruction is stored and executed one after another, such as "READ", "ADD", "MOVE", "PRINT".
- Involves control of the input/output devices.
- Handles the transfer of data between storage positions.
- Handles the transfer of data between storage and arithmetic/logic.

The time required to transfer data is known as *access time*. Access time is measured in thousandths of a second, millionths (microseconds), or even billionths (nanoseconds). The number and type of input/output devices, the size of storage, the type and complexity of arithmetic/logic circuitry, and the access time vary considerably by computer model.

INPUT/OUTPUT DEVICES

There are many types of input/output devices of various capacities and speeds. This section discusses the three basic common ones, the terminal, the card reader, and the printer. Later chapters cover magnetic tape and disk storage devices.

THE VIDEO DISPLAY TERMINAL. The ubiquitous video display terminal typically contains a typewriter-like keyboard and an 80-column screen. Many installations are equipped to facilitate programmers entering their programs onto the terminal. Most installations also require that users "log on" to the terminal using a special password, and "log off" when they have finished a session.

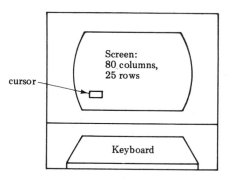

FIGURE 0-3 Video display terminal.

If your installation operates under a system such as IBM's CMS (Conversational Monitor System), you should be able to key in your programs, test them, store them on disk, and recover them for further changes and tests. The CMS system has an associated screen editor, XEDIT, that facilitates full screen editing. You can develop a program on the terminal by entering each program instruction one after another, and you can move the cursor about freely to change any instruction on any line.

When you fill the screen (about 25 lines), some systems require that you enter a special command to continue on a fresh screen, whereas other systems automatically scroll up the lines so that the top lines seem to disappear off the top of the screen.

Presumably your system provides for tab stops which you can set at convenient columns. Desirable tab stops for an Assembler program are the following:

1   10   16   41   72

Column 1 is actually a "return" column rather than a tab stop. Column 41 could be a different column—you can resolve that choice later.

THE PUNCHED CARD.   The punched card is still a common source of input although terminals have replaced it in most installations. The card represents data by means of small rectangular holes punched by a keypunch machine. The holes in the card, when read by a card reader, are translated into electrical impulses and transferred into storage.

The punched card normally has 80 vertical *columns* (numbered columns 1 through 80) for storing data. Each column represents one character of data by means of the punched holes in any of its twelve horizontal *rows*. The rows are numbered as in Figure 0-3. Digits 0 through 9 are punched as a single hole, from row 0 through row 9. Alphabetic and special characters are punched with multiple holes: the 0-9 *numeric* rows and the *zone* rows, 10, 11 and 12. (Note that the numeric row 0 is the same as zone row 10.) For example, the letter A in column 11 consists of zone 12 and numeric 1.

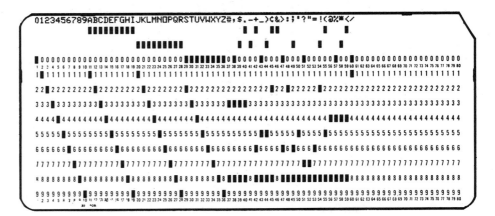

FIGURE 0-4 Punched card featuring keypunch codes.

The punched card has served two main purposes, to record *programs*, and to record *data*. Information for data processing is supplied to the keypunch department on *source documents*. Examples are customer payments, sales, and employee hours worked. These data are punched according to a predesigned card format. The cards are then submitted as input to the computer department for processing.

A group of records that contains related information is called a *file*, or *data set*.

THE PRINTER.   There are many different types of printers, but all have certain common features. They print at speeds ranging from a few hundred to several thousand lines per minute. Many can print 60 or more different characters, including the numbers 0 through 9, letters A through Z, and various characters such as $, #, *, and +. Typical printers print 10 characters to the inch, and 120, 132, or 160 characters on a line.

The paper used for printing is called *continuous forms*. The forms are perforated horizontally so that each sheet may be separated after printing. Manufacturers supply the forms in various widths, such as 11" and 15", and lengths such as 8½. This length at six lines per inch permits up to 60 lines of print per page. It is available in single-part or, with carbon inserts, two or more parts. The forms may be preprinted according to the user's design (e.g., customer bills), or they may contain only horizontal lines or bars *(stock tab forms* or *continuous printout).*

BINARY NUMBER SYSTEM

Binary numbers provide the basic numbering system of computers. Whereas a decimal (base 10) number has ten digits, a binary (base 2) number has two: 0 and 1. For both decimal and binary, the position of the digit determines the value. Consider the decimal number 1111:

$$\text{decimal } 1111$$
$$= (1 \times 10^3) + (1 \times 10^2) + (1 \times 10^1) + (1 \times 10^0)$$
$$= 1000 + 100 + 10 + 1$$

Whereas a decimal number uses the base of ten, a binary number uses the base of two. Consider the same number, 1111, this time expressed as binary:

$$\text{binary } 1111$$
$$= \text{decimal } (1 \times 2^3) + (1 \times 2^2) + (1 \times 2^1) + (1 \times 2^0)$$
$$= 8 + 4 + 2 + 1 = 15 \text{ (or } 2^4 - 1)$$

As another example, the value of the decimal number 1010 is determined as:

decimal 1010
$= (1 \times 10^3) + (0 \times 10^2) + (1 \times 10^1) + (0 \times 10^0)$
$= 1000 + 0 + 10 + 0$

A decimal digit zero as shown above has no value, nor has a binary digit zero. The number 1010 expressed in binary is:

binary 1010
$=$ decimal $(1 \times 2^3) + (0 \times 2^2) + (1 \times 2^1) + (0 \times 2^0)$
$= 8 + 0 + 2 + 0 = 10$ (decimal)

Through the use of digits 0 and 1, binary numbers can represent any decimal value. For example, the binary number 101101 equals:

$2^5 + 0^4 + 2^3 + 2^2 + 0^1 + 2^0$
$=$ decimal $32 + 0 + 8 + 4 + 0 + 1 = 45$

A binary value may also have a *binary point*, equivalent to the decimal point. You can calculate a binary number with a point such as 101.1101 as:

$2^2 + 0^1 + 2^0 + 2^{-1} + 2^{-2} + 0^{-3} + 2^{-4}$
$= 4 + 0 + 1 + 1/2^1 + 1/2^2 + 0/2^3 + 1/2^4$
$= 4 + 1 + 1/2 + 1/4 + 0 + 1/16$
$= 5 + .5 + .25 + .0625$
$= 5.8125$

Later chapters cover binary representation and binary arithmetic in detail.

BITS AND BYTES

In computer terminology, a binary digit is called a *bit*. A storage location, or *byte*, consists of a specified number of bits, and can be related to binary digits, since a computer bit can be OFF (zero) or ON (one). The number of bits in a byte varies by computer (the 370-series uses nine bits). Assume a byte that contains only five bits. Four bits represent data and the other is a *parity bit*:

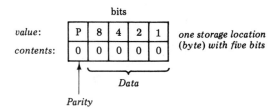

In the diagram, each bit is indicated by a '0', with the binary value of the bit above it. Each bit can contain the value 0 or 1, so if the bit numbered 1 on the right is ON, the contents of the byte are 00001, and the value is 1. If only bit 2 (second from the right) is ON, the contents are 00010, and the value is 2. Both bits 1 and 2 ON (00011) represent 3, and combinations of ON bits provide values 1 through 9. All bits OFF means zero.

The bit on the left is the parity bit. The typical byte must have "odd parity"; i.e., the number of bits ON must always be an odd number. For example, the value in a byte is 7; bits 4, 2, and 1 are ON. Because this is an odd number of bits, the computer sets the parity bit OFF:

P	8	4	2	1
0	0	1	1	1

value = 7, odd parity

Assume that the value in a byte is 9: bits 8 and 1 are ON. To force odd parity, the computer sets the parity bit ON:

P	8	4	2	1
1	1	0	0	1

value = 9, parity bit ON for odd parity

Setting bits ON and OFF is entirely an automatic process over which we have no control. When processing the contents of a byte, the computer automatically checks its parity. If the parity is not odd, the computer circuitry may require servicing; the computer signals a warning to the operator and may stop processing.

On the 370-series, the configuration in a byte is eight data bits and one parity bit. A hardware malfunction such as losing odd parity causes a "machine interrupt," as explained in Chapter 16.

S/370 ORGANIZATION

As Figure 0-1 illustrated, the computer system consists of the central processing unit (CPU) which contains the arithmetic/logic unit and the control section, input and output devices and facilities, and main storage or memory. In addition, the 370-series has a special unit called *general-purpose registers* that serve such purposes as arithmetic and addressing. Another unit contains *floating point registers* that perform floating point arithmetic. Another feature, *program status word (PSW)*, controls the sequence of instructions executed by the program and records the current status of the program. The next sections briefly describe the CPU, input/output (I/O), storage, the general registers, and the PSW.

THE CENTRAL PROCESSING UNIT (CPU).   The CPU is the control center of the computer system. It consists of two sections, control and arithmetic/logic, and provides facilities for the following features:

1.   Addressing of main storage locations.
2.   Accessing data from storage and storing data in storage.
3.   Arithmetic and logical processing of data.
   - Arithmetic operations (add, subtract, multiply, and divide) can be performed on data in three different formats: ordinary decimal (packed), fixed point binary, and floating point. This text covers each format.
   - Logic operations include comparing, testing, translating of characters, and editing (sign and punctuation control).
4.   Executing instructions in main storage in the required sequence.
5.   Initiating communications between main storage and the input/output (I/O) devices.

INPUT AND OUTPUT (I/O) DEVICES.   There are various models of each input/output device, providing different capabilities and I/O speeds. Disk and magnetic tape, for example, supply external data storage of practically unlimited capacity. I/O devices include the following:

DEVICE	INPUT	OUTPUT	TYPICAL USES
Direct access storage devices (disk)	X	X	Large external storage of data.
Magnetic ink character readers (MICR)	X		Processing checks in banks.
Magnetic tape	X	X	Large external storage of data.
Manual controls (console typewriter)	X	X	Communication between the computer operating system and the human operator
Optical readers	X		Reading bills printed by a computer, and cash register tapes.
Printers		X	Printing reports, programs, and diagnostic messages.
Punched card devices	X	X	Reading and punching cards.
Visual display terminals	X	X	Used to enter data into the computer and to make inquiries.

MAIN STORAGE.   Each 1,024 bytes of main storage is called 1K. Addressable storage varies from a minimum of 8,192 (8K) bytes to a maximum of 16,777,216 (16,384K).

The basic building block of main storage is the byte, which represents a single storage location. Each byte consists of nine bits. Eight bits represent data and the ninth is the parity bit to ensure odd parity, and is not a programming consideration. The eight data bits are "split" into two portions of four bits (half-bytes), a *zone* and a *numeric* portion:

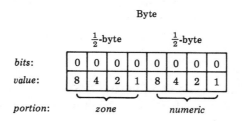

The value represented in a byte varies from zero (all bits OFF, 0000 0000) through 255 (all bits ON, 1111 1111). The CPU normally executes a program by accessing bytes or groups of bytes. Bytes serve different purposes and may represent:

1. *Instructions.* A 370 instruction is always 2, 4, or 6 bytes, depending on the type of instruction. Every instruction begins on an even-numbered storage location.

2. *Data.* Although some instructions can access individual bits or half-bytes, for most purposes a byte is the smallest data length. A group of one or more related bytes is a *field,* such as an inventory item number or quantity on hand. You may define data in order to represent it as bytes in the following formats:

CHARACTER FORMAT. A character field (such as the letters A through Z, the numbers 1 through 9, and special characters as $ or * or &) requires one byte for each character. The eight bits in a byte can represent 256 (2^8) possible characters. For example, the ON bits 1100 0001 represent the letter A. The character code is called the *"extended binary-coded-decimal-interchange code" (EBCDIC).*

DECIMAL, OR PACKED, FORMAT. For ordinary decimal arithmetic, the digits 0 through 9 are "packed" two digits per byte. For example, the digits 4 and 7 appear in a byte as the bits 0100 0111. Whereas a character '1' requires a full byte (11110001), a packed digit '1' uses a half-byte (0001).

BINARY FORMAT. For binary arithmetic, addressing, and special features, each bit represents a binary 0 or 1. The binary value 01000111 equals the decimal value 71.

FLOATING POINT FORMAT. An arithmetic format used to represent extremely small or large values.

GENERAL-PURPOSE REGISTERS. The 370-series has 16 general-purpose registers (GPRs), numbered 0 through 15. Instead of being part of main storage, they are special circuitry. Each register consists of 32 bits. The two main uses of registers are:

1. Addressing storage positions, by means of "base displacement addressing." Every reference to a location in main storage is by means of a "base address" in a register and a "displacement" from that address.
2. Performing binary arithmetic in the registers, done at extremely high speed.

PROGRAM STATUS WORD (PSW). The program status word (PSW) is a 64-bit hardware feature in the control section of the CPU. The PSW contains the current status of the computer and controls the sequence of instructions being executed.

One PSW feature important to the programmer is the 2-bit *condition code* that indicates the result of an arithmetic test (minus/zero/plus) or a logical comparison (low/equal/high). Another field, the 24-bit *instruction address,* contains the address of the next instruction to be executed.

OPERATING SYSTEMS AND THE SUPERVISOR

Computer manufacturers supply various programs (software) to support the computer system. These programs include language translators such as Assembler, COBOL, and PL/I, and "utility" programs to facilitate disk and tape processing. Except for the smallest models, the 370-series computers are supplied with a set of related programs called an *operating system* to provide for preparation and execution of the user's programs and to minimize operator intervention. The two major IBM operating systems are Disk Operating System (DOS) for medium-sized users, and Operating System (OS) for large users. The operating system programs are stored on disk, and the heart of the operating system, the *supervisor,* is at all times stored in the lower part of the computer's main storage, as indicated in Figure 0-5.

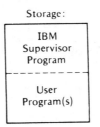

Storage:

IBM
Supervisor
Program

User
Program(s)

FIGURE 0-5 Supervisor and user programs.

Among the functions of the supervisor are to

- determine the sequence in which programs will be executed,
- "load" a program into main storage prior to its execution,
- generally control and coordinate the various programs being executed,
- handle all input/output operations,
- provide error message and error recovery where possible.

Both the programmer and the computer operator can request the supervisor to perform certain actions. For example, if you want the system to "assemble" a program, enter a *job control statement* such as // EXEC AS-SEMBLY that tells the supervisor to arrange for the assembling of the program following.

PROGRAM INTERRUPTION. The program status word contains bits that record the status of the program. Among these conditions are bits to record "program interrupts." An interrupt occurs when your program asks the supervisor to perform some special task, such as input/output. Basically, your program is "interrupted," and control is passed to the supervisor program. An interrupt also occurs, for example, when a serious processing error occurs —such as invalid data in an arithmetic operation. The supervisor may have to "flush" the interrupted program and resume processing with the next job waiting to be run.

HEXADECIMAL REPRESENTATION

A hexadecimal numbering system uses base-16. Hexadecimal (or hex) numbers are 0 through 9 and A through F, for the decimal values 0-15. *The purpose of hexadecimal numbers is to represent the contents of storage.* Hexadecimal is only a representation of storage—at no time does the computer actually work in base-16 as such. One hex digit depicts four bits of a byte, and two hex digits represent all eight bits in a byte. Figure 0-6 lists the equivalent decimal, binary, and hexadecimal numbers.

Two hex digits can represent the contents of any storage location, regardless of the data format that it contains. For example, a byte contains the character 'A'. The binary representation of A in main storage is 1100 0001, and its hex representation is 'C1', or as commonly notated, X'C1'. Thus, if an input record contains the letter 'A' in a certain position, when read into storage, the 'A' appears in a byte as 1100 0001. You can represent the contents of the storage location as either character A or as hex 'C1'.

Since there are 256 possible bit configurations in a byte, there is no way to represent each possibility as a single character (there are only about 60 different print characters). Assume that a byte contains the packed digits 4

Decimal	Binary	Hexadecimal	Decimal	Binary	Hexadecimal
0	0000	0	8	1000	8
1	0001	1	9	1001	9
2	0010	2	10	1010	A
3	0011	3	11	1011	B
4	0100	4	12	1100	C
5	0101	5	13	1101	D
6	0110	6	14	1110	E
7	0111	7	15	1111	F

FIGURE 0-6 Decimal, binary, and hexadecimal representation.

and 5. The binary representation of the byte's contents is 0100 0101. There is no single character that can represent this 8-bit code, but we can represent it with two hex digits as X'45'.

A byte used for binary data could contain 0101 1011 (which equals decimal value 91). The hexadecimal representation is X'5B'. In this way, hex format can represent all 370 data formats, such as character, packed, and binary, one hex digit for each half-byte (four bits). The computer supervisor and the Assembler both use hex extensively to display the contents of storage, although only the programmer knows that the specific contents of bytes and fields are in a particular format.

Among the uses of hexadecimal format are the following:

1. The Assembler converts your symbolic program to machine code. It prints the locations of instructions and their object code entirely in hex format.

2. To facilitate tracing program errors, you can instruct the supervisor to print a *storage dump*. The dump prints the contents of storage, two hex digits per byte.

3. Some special purpose characters, for example, control the printer carriage (spacing lines, skipping to a new page), and "edit" data fields with punctuation and sign (as $1,250.00CR). Many of these special characters are bit configurations that cannot be printed. You can represent them, however, in your Assembler program with hex numbers.

Since the supervisor and the Assembler print storage addresses in hex, a knowledge of hexadecimal arithmetic is quite useful (and so would be 16 fingers for doing it). Note how X'F' overflows when you add 1 to it:

DECIMAL VALUE		HEX VALUE
15	=	F
$+\underline{1}$		$+\underline{1}$
$\underline{16}$	=	$\underline{10}$

Thus, X'10' equals the decimal value 16. Also, note that X'5' + X'5' = X'A', and X'8' + X'8' = X'10'. The following examples illustrate more hex addition:

$$
\begin{array}{cccc}
\text{X'21'} & \text{X'385'} & \text{X'412A'} & \text{X'53A6'} \\
\underline{+\ 15} & \underline{+\ 385} & \underline{+\ 94} & \underline{+\ 92A} \\
\text{X'36'} & \text{X'70A'} & \text{X'41BE'} & \text{X'5CD0'}
\end{array}
$$

Appendix A provides conversion of hexadecimal numbers to decimal, and decimal to hex, a useful reference. Understanding hex notation is extremely important in Assembler programming, and you are urged to grasp it fully.

• *Now complete the remaining problems in this chapter.* •

PROBLEMS

0-1. What are the basic components of a digital computer? What is the function of each one?

0-2. Distinguish between instructions and data.

0-3. What holes are punched in a card for the letters READ?

0-4. Define the following: (a) stored program; (b) access time; (c) field; (d) file or data set; (e) alphameric data.

0-5. What is the decimal value of binary (a) 1110; (b) 11001; (c) 101101?

0-6. What is a "bit?" What is a bit's relationship to a "byte?"

0-7. The left four bits of a byte are the_____portion; the right four bits are the_____portion. The ninth bit is called_____; what is its purpose?

0-8. What are the two main purposes of the general registers?

0-9. What is the purpose of an "operating system?"

0-10. Where is the supervisor stored? What are its main functions?

0-11. What is a "program interrupt?"

0-12. What action does the system take when a serious processing error occurs?

0-13. What is the purpose of hexadecimal representation?

0-14. Give the hexadecimal representation for the following binary values: (a) 1110; (b) 0101 1101; (c) 1011 0011; (d) 1111 0010 1100 1110.

0-15. Convert the following decimal values to hexadecimal (refer to Appendix A): (a) 10; (b) 16; (c) 24; (d) 32; (e) 275; (f) 2048; (g) 4096.

0-16. Convert the following hex values to decimal: (a) F; (b) 10; (c) 2D; (d) 4F; (e) 80; (f) 800; (g) 1000.

0-17. Add the following hex values: (a) 24 + 6; (b) 3A + 7; (c) AAA + 555; (d) FFF + 1; (e) 437B + 2A4B; (f) 6EBD + 5CAE.

1

THE ASSEMBLER

The previous chapter examined the organization of a computer and hardware features. This chapter covers the Assembler translator program, a software feature, and the requirements for coding and assembling a program in Basic Assembler Language (BAL). In order to make computer programs more comprehensible and more easily maintained, this text advocates standard coding practices, such as naming conventions for fields and for files.

LANGUAGES

The 370-series computers come equipped with a set of executable machine instructions similar in all models. Instructions include the ability to read input data, to move data in storage, to add and subtract the contents of storage locations, to compare, and to print or display output data.

MACHINE LANGUAGE. The computer executes only instructions that are in main storage and are in machine language. You provide a special job control command to instruct the supervisor to enter or "load" the machine instructions from disk into main storage, where they become the "stored program." Each storage location (byte) has a unique numeric address; the "operands" of the instructions reference the addresses of storage locations by their number. For example, we earlier showed a hypothetical machine instruction as A 1263 1338 that adds the contents of storage locations 1338–1340 to the contents of 1263–1265.

On the earliest computers, programmers coded at this basic level; on modern computers, however, coding in machine language is far too complex.

SYMBOLIC LANGUAGE. Because of the complexity of machine language, programmers code in "symbolic languages." These are special languages that the manufacturers design to facilitate program coding. The above machine language instruction could be coded in a symbolic language as:

ADD ACCUM, AMOUNT

You then use a *translator program* such as Assembler, COBOL, PL/I, or Pascal to translate the operation ADD into a machine code instruction and the symbolic addresses to machine language addresses.

ASSEMBLER LANGUAGE. The Assembler is a *low-level* language that translates symbolic code into machine code. Each symbolic instruction translates directly into one machine instruction, on a one-for-one basis. (A compiler such as COBOL and PL/I may generate dozens of machine instructions for one symbolic statement.)

Assembler is directly related to a particular computer and its architecture. Consequently, a program written in IBM Assembler language will not run on most other computers. But since there are many similarities among computer designs, there are many similarities among Assembler versions.

MACRO INSTRUCTIONS. Assembler is close to the level of machine language and translates one symbolic instruction into one machine language instruction. But the Assembler also has provision for macro instructions, which are specially written instructions that the Assembler recognizes. Depending on its requirements, *a macro causes the Assembler to generate one or more machine language instructions.* IBM supplies special macros such as CALL, GET, and RETURN to facilitate supervisor and input/output operations.

In contrast to the low-level Assembler language are *high-level* languages such as COBOL, PL/I, and Pascal which you code entirely with macro instructions. Chapter 18 describes how you can write and execute your own macro instructions.

THE ASSEMBLER

Basic Assembler Language (BAL) with which this text deals is the fundamental language for the 370-series, and is reasonably standardized for all models. But although you code programs in Assembler language, the computer cannot execute such instructions. You require an Assembler translator program to "assemble" or translate symbolic language into computer machine language.

Every Assembler program begins with the Assembler directive START (or CSECT) and terminates with the Assembler directive END, as follows:

```
Column     1              10              16
           |              |               |
           progname       START           blank or a machine location
           instructions—executable code
           declaratives—defined constants and work areas
                          END             progname
```

A convention is to begin names in column 1, instructions and directives in column 10, and operands in column 16. In this case, both START and END are directives that begin in column 10. Column 1 of START also includes the name of the program which may be any unique name beginning with a letter (A through Z) up to eight characters long. A later section provides more details of name conventions.

The END directive contains the same name as the START directive, but in this case the name is in the operand field beginning in column 16.

START tells the Assembler that this point is the beginning of the assembly, and END tells the Assembler that this point is the end of the assembly. The program name in the END operand informs the system where the program is to begin execution—normally but not necessarily at the start.

An Assembler program typically consists of executable instructions and declaratives coded in separate sections. The declaratives contain the various constants, workareas, and input/output areas that the instructions process.

THE ASSEMBLER CODING FORM

Figure 1-1 depicts an example of an Assembler coding form used for coding Assembler programs. The top of the form contains space for the program name, programmer name, date, and page number.

On the form, statements that begin with an asterisk (*) in column 1 are comments. The program consists of two sections: "program execution" that contains executable instructions, and "declaratives" for the defined printer device and constants.

This is a simple program that skips to the top of a new page and prints two headings—that's all! Under DECLARATIVES are the name of the printer device, PRINTER, and two heading lines named PRHEAD1 and PRHEAD2 that the executable instructions print. Beginning in column 41 are various comments that explain the action of the executable instructions. The rest of this chapter and the next will make the details clearer.

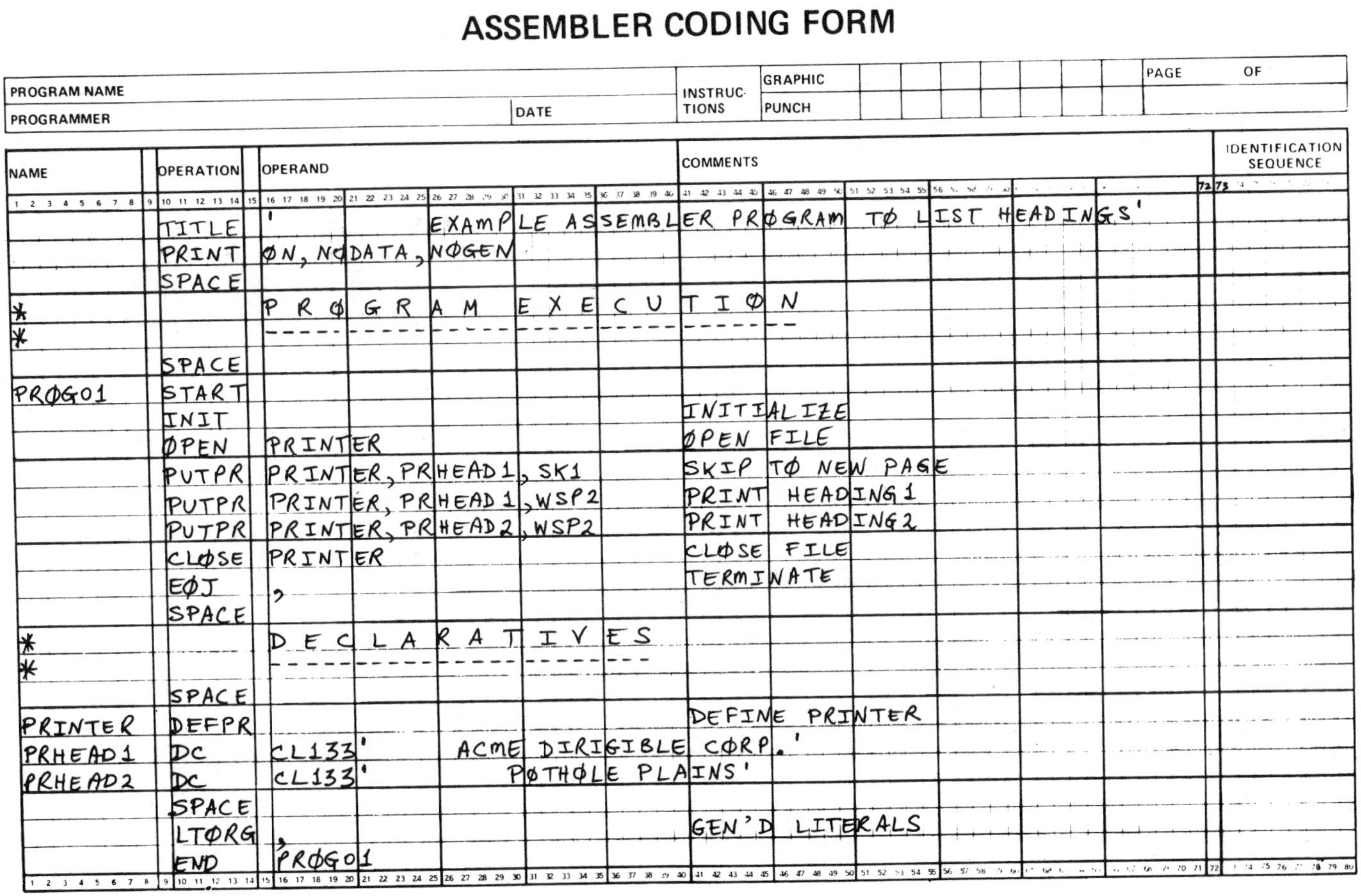

ASSEMBLER CODING FORM

PROGRAM NAME | DATE | INSTRUCTIONS: GRAPHIC / PUNCH | PAGE OF
PROGRAMMER

NAME | OPERATION | OPERAND | COMMENTS | IDENTIFICATION SEQUENCE

```
         TITLE '          EXAMPLE ASSEMBLER PROGRAM TO LIST HEADINGS'
         PRINT ØN,NØDATA,NØGEN
         SPACE
*              P R Ø G R A M   E X E C U T I Ø N
*              ---------------------------------
         SPACE
PRØG01   START
         INIT                                   INITIALIZE
         ØPEN  PRINTER                          ØPEN FILE
         PUTPR PRINTER,PRHEAD1,SK1              SKIP TØ NEW PAGE
         PUTPR PRINTER,PRHEAD1,WSP2             PRINT HEADING1
         PUTPR PRINTER,PRHEAD2,WSP2             PRINT HEADING2
         CLØSE PRINTER                          CLØSE FILE
         EØJ   ,                                TERMINATE
         SPACE
*              D E C L A R A T I V E S
*              -----------------------
         SPACE
PRINTER  DEFPR                                  DEFINE PRINTER
PRHEAD1  DC    CL133'     ACME DIRIGIBLE CØRP.'
PRHEAD2  DC    CL133'          PØTHØLE PLAINS'
         SPACE
         LTØRG ,                                GEN'D LITERALS
         END   PRØG01
```

FIGURE 1-1 Assembler coding form.

The Assembler accepts coding that is "free-form"—that is, although the form has predefined columns for name, operation, and operand, you do not have to begin these fields in the defined columns. However, there is usually little need to vary from the defined columns, and there is a need for standardized, legible programs. The examples in this text use only the defined columns.

CODING FORMAT.   There are four types of Assembler coding statements:

1. *Instructions* such as move, add, and compare that the Assembler converts to executable object code.

2. *Directives* such as TITLE, START, and END that notify the Assembler to take special action and generate no object code.

3. *Declaratives* such as accumulators and constants defined by DS and DC and referenced by instructions. Technically, a declarative is a special type of directive with one difference: a DC generates an object code constant.

4. *Comments* that you code as documentation to make your program clearer. The Assembler includes comments on the assembled listing but deletes them from the executable object code program.

CODING FIELDS.   The following is a description of each field on the coding form.

COLUMN   1–8   NAME.   Assign a name to each instruction and declarative that you intend to reference in your program. For example, in Figure 1-1 PROG01 is the name of the program. The rules governing the name (or label) of an instruction or a declarative are:

- The name must be unique in the program—defined only once.
- The name may be one to eight characters long. The first character must be a letter A through Z (and $, #, or @, although these special characters are not recommended). Remaining characters in the name may be letters or digits, such as PROG25. A name may not contain blank characters.

If column 1 is blank, the Assembler assumes that the instruction or declarative has no name, and if column 1 contains an asterisk (*), the Assembler assumes that the entire line is a comment. Figure 1-1 illustrates both unnamed instructions and comment lines.

COLUMN   10–14   OPERATION.   This field provides the symbolic (mnemonic) operation code for an instruction, declarative, directive, or macro. The Assembler must be able to recognize it. Figure 1-1 shows operations such as TITLE and PRINT. There must be at least one blank position between operation and the next field, operand.

16–71   OPERAND.   The operand identifies data on which the operation is to act. Depending on the operation, there may be none, one, or more operands. A comma separates each operand, with no blank spaces either within operands or between them; the Assembler assumes that a blank ends the operands. In the following instruction, the name is A20ADD, the operation is AP (add), and the operand is ACCUM,FIVE (add FIVE to ACCUM):

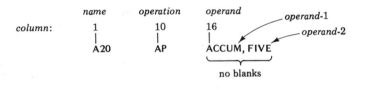

72   CONTINUATION.   Operands and comments may not continue past column 71. If you require more positions, then do the following:

- Code any nonblank character in column 72. This text uses a plus (+) sign, although many others use an X.
- Continue coding the statement on the next line beginning in column 16. Depending on the Assembler version, one or more continuations are permitted.

73–80   IDENTIFICATION SEQUENCE.   For programs on cards, you can use this optional field to identify your program with a name and a sequence number. For example, columns 73–76 could contain the program identification such as P023 for Payroll program 023, and columns 77–80 could contain a sequence number. A common practice is to number the sequence in intervals of 10, such as 0010, 0020, and 0030, so that you can insert instructions between them if necessary. You may instruct the Assembler to check the sequence of columns 73–80 by coding the Directive ISEQ (Input Sequence Checking), as discussed in the later section Assembler Directives.

On terminal systems such as IBM's CMS, the editor can automatically assign and reassign sequence numbers.

1   COMMENTS.   An asterisk in column 1 means that the entire line is a comment. You may also code a comment on a line following an instruction, with at least one blank between the operand and the comment. For readabil-

ity and to facilitate data entry, the coding in Figure 1-2 aligns comments beginning in column 41. For example:

```
Column    10                16                41 comments
          |                 |                 |
          MP                HOURS,RATE        MULTIPLY HOURS × RATE
```

DIRECTIVES

The Assembler translates instructions such as AP (Add) or MVC (Move) into machine language executable code. But the Assembler recognizes directives such as START, TITLE, and END as requests to perform certain operations only during the assembly, and generates no machine code. Included next are some of the more common Assembler directives:

NAME	*OPERATION*	*OPERAND*
(symbol)	TITLE	1–100 characters, within apostrophes
program name	START	blank or a numeric value
omit	EJECT	blank
omit	SPACE	blank or a number
omit	PRINT	one, two, or three operands
omit	ISEQ	blank, or 2 digits of the form, l, r
omit	END	blank or program name

FIGURE 1-2 Assembler directives.

TITLE. The purpose of the TITLE directive is to identify an assembly listing, as shown in Figure 1-2. The name field is optional.

The operand field contains any descriptive title that you want printed at the top of each page of the assembled listing (see the top line of Figure 1-1). You enclose the title in apostrophes to denote its start and end. The maximum length is 100 characters. But, if the title exceeds 56 characters, you have to continue it on the next line. Code a continuation character (any nonblank character) in column 72, and continue the title on the next line in column 16.

When used in a directive, the apostrophe (') and the ampersand (&) have special meaning to the Assembler. If you need to use them in your title, code them as two adjacent apostrophes (' ') or ampersands (&&). The Assembler stores and prints only one. The following example contains both apostrophes and ampersands:

```
Column      10              16
            |               |
            TITLE           'JEAN && SAM''S PROGRAM'
```

START. The START directive designates the beginning of an assembly, although technically you may code TITLE, EJECT, and SPACE directives before START. The name field contains the name of the program, and must match the entry in the operand of the END directive. Some systems load programs from disk into storage for execution beginning at fixed, predictable locations; other systems load programs into one of a number of locations, depending on where there is sufficient space—check the requirements for your own system.

```
1               10      16
|               |       |
progname        START   numeric value   (fixed starting address)
progname        START   0 or blank      (unknown starting address)
```

EJECT. After printing a full page of a program listing, the Assembler automatically ejects to the top of the next page. However, you may want to eject a page before it is full, for example, to start printing a new major routine or a section of declaratives. To cause the Assembler to eject the forms to a new page of the program listing, code EJECT in the operation columns.

SPACE. The SPACE directive tells the Assembler to space one or more blank lines on the program listing. Code the number of lines to be spaced (up to three) in the operand field. If you leave the operand blank, the Assembler assumes a space of one line:

```
Column      10              16
            SPACE                       Space 1 line
            SPACE           1           Space 1 line
            SPACE           2           Space 2 lines
            SPACE           3           Space 3 lines
```

Note: The Assembler acts on EJECT and SPACE but does not print them. It does, however, increment the statement (STMT) number on the listing; see for example missing statement number 87 in Figure 1-3.

PRINT. The PRINT directive controls the general format of a program listing, and contains any or all of the following three operands, in any sequence. A common requirement is

PRINT ON,NOGEN,NODATA

ON   Print the program listing from this point on.
OFF   Do not print the listing.
GEN   Print all statements that macros generate.
NOGEN   Suppress statements that macros generate.
                    In Figure 1-1, OPEN is a macro; since its generated code is seldom of interest, you normally suppress its listing.
DATA   Print the full hexadecimal contents of constants (on the left side of the listing, under OBJECT CODE).
NODATA   Print only the leftmost eight bytes (or 16 hex digits) of constants. Since the full printed hex contents of constants are of little interest, a common practice is to code NODATA.

ISEQ. The ISEQ directive causes the Assembler to sequence-check your input source statements. The two operands specify the leftmost and rightmost columns of the sequence field, normally the "Identification Sequence" between columns 73 and 80, coded as ISEQ 73,80. Since each Assembler statement checked must contain a higher sequence value than the previous one, the Assembler generates an error message for low, equal, or blank fields. ISEQ with a blank operand terminates sequence-checking.

END. The END directive must be the last statement of an Assembler program, and causes termination of the assembly. You may code the operand with a symbolic address, such as END PROG25. The operand PROG25 in this case designates an address in the program where execution is to begin, and is therefore normally the program's first executable instruction.

     Remember that these directives simply tell the Assembler how to handle your source program, and generate no machine code. This section provides the most commonly required information. Later chapters cover other directives such as EQU, LTORG, and USING. Appendix H summarizes all the Assembler directives.

DECLARATIVES

A declarative is a nonexecutable statement that defines constants, counters, and input/output areas. There are two types of declaratives, DS and DC:

1	10	16
[name]	DS	operand denoting type and length
[name]	DC	operand denoting type, length and constant

     For both DS and DC, the name entry is optional, but must contain a name if your program references the field. An operand such as CL5 means a character (C) field five bytes long (L5).

DS (DEFINE STORAGE).   A DS declarative defines an area of storage within a program, such as an input/output area. The following declarative

```
RECDIN DS CL80
```

defines a field named RECDIN, character (C) format, and a length of 80 bytes (CL80). When a program first executes, the contents of a DS are unpredictable, and could contain "garbage." (Actually, a DS contains the contents of the last program that happened to occupy the same storage locations.) It is up to you to move data into the area as required in the program. For example, your program could read data into this area using the macro instruction

```
GET FILEIN,RECDIN
```

The GET macro reads an 80-byte record from a file named FILEIN into RECDIN in main storage, and erases any previous contents.

DC (DEFINE CONSTANT).   A DC declarative defines an area containing an initial constant. For example, the declarative

```
HEADING DC C'PHASAR ELECTRONICS'
```

defines a field named HEADING containing a character constant used for a report heading. In this example, a program would not normally change the contents of HEADING during its execution. But a program would change other constants, such as an accumulator initialized to zero and used to count the number of lines displayed on a screen.

For any declarative, the name, if any, references the leftmost byte. In effect, any name that you use in an operand must be defined with a unique name. However, a name is optional, and, as you will see, there are situations where a program never references a field, and you may omit the name.

Appendix G summarizes all the Assembler declaratives.

CODING CONVENTIONS

This text uses clear and meaningful conventions to define the names of declaratives and instructions.

DECLARATIVE NAMES.   Always assign unique, descriptive names to declaratives. Since a name (or label) may be up to eight characters long, it is more meaningful, for example, to assign a name such as EXPENSE rather than EXP. Also, it is often helpful to identify a packed field with a suffix PK, such as RATEPK, and a binary field with a suffix BIN, such as RATEBIN. You may assign an input area with a descriptive name such as RECDIN and an output area with a name such as PRINT or DISPLINE (display line).

In the case of the *declarative* PRINT, do not confuse it with the *directive* PRINT that controls the assembled listing. This example illustrates how you can legally use the same symbol for both an operation and a declarative name; the Assembler can tell from your use of the symbol whether it references a declarative or a directive.

ADDRESS NAMES.   Give an instruction a name if you reference it elsewhere in your program. This text uses a convention in which the first character of an instruction label is an alphabetic letter, A through Z. The next two or three characters are digits, for example A20, D35, and P200. In the first main logical section of the program, labels begin with A. Instruction labels, where required, are numbered within this section starting with A10, then increasing by intervals of 10, such as A20, A30, and so forth.

The next logical section of the program and all others begin with a letter higher than the previous, such as B10, E10, and R10. Each section uses digits starting with 10 and increasing by intervals of 10. The first label of a section has a descriptive name, such as C10TAX or E10PENSN. This practice facilitates the following:

- Since all labels are sequential, they are easy to locate.
- There is less chance of using duplicate labels in a program.
- You can easily insert additional labels where required, such as B12 and B16.

An examination of the programs throughout this text should make clear the advantages of such coding conventions. Note, however, that there are other methods, and you should adopt the convention of your own installation.

PROGRAMMING STEPS

The following explains the steps in programming, from coding through assembling and execution.

CODING.   Based on your definition of the problem and the required output, code your *source program* in symbolic language on special Assembler coding forms. The program consists of Assembler instructions and data areas.

Watch carefully for coding characters that are similar. Although there is no universal standard, you could use the following to distinguish among certain easily confused characters:

- Code the digit zero as 0, and the letter O with a slash (some use the opposite convention).

- Code the digit one and letter I clearly.
- Code the letter Z with a bar to distinguish it from the digit 2.
- There is often confusion between the digit 5 and letter S, between the left parenthesis and the letter C, and between the letters U and V.

KEYING. Key the symbolic instructions from the coding forms onto disk via a terminal or onto punched cards.

ASSEMBLY. Request the supervisor (through a job control command) to assemble your source program. For this purpose, the supervisor loads the Assembler translator program from disk into main storage. The Assembler translator then reads your source program as data into the computer and performs the following:

- Accounts for the amount of storage that each instruction and data area requires, and assigns storage locations to them in the sequence in which you have coded them.
- Supplies messages for programming errors, such as the invalid use of an instruction and spelling errors.
- Converts the source program to machine object code.
- Prints the original symbolic coding and the translated machine language on a printer form. This printout is useful for "debugging" a program and for making subsequent changes.

The Assembler uses a *location counter* to account for the length of each data field and instruction. If the Assembler has just assigned a four-byte instruction starting at location 10,024, the location counter now contains 10,028, the starting address of the next instruction. The Assembler always assigns an address to the leftmost byte of a data field or an instruction.

ERROR CHECKING. Correct any errors that the Assembler signals, reassemble your program, and execute it using special job control commands. Supply input data that thoroughly tests your program.

Note: The Assembler cannot recognize errors in your program logic. You must locate these errors through testing and debugging.

THE ASSEMBLED PROGRAM LISTING

Figure 1-1 showed the coding for a small program that simply prints two heading lines. Assume that the instructions on the coding sheet were keyed as a source program into a storage medium such as a terminal or cards, and that special job control commands requested that the program be assembled. The system's supervisor program loads the Assembler translator program from disk into main storage. The Assembler program then reads the source program, translates it into machine-executable object code, and prints a listing of the assembled program.

Figure 1-3 shows the listing of the assembled program. The first page lists an EXTERNAL SYMBOL DICTIONARY (ESD) containing information about "external symbols" that the program has used. The first entry, PROG01, is the actual name of the program; the supervisor must know this name in order to transfer to its address in main storage to begin execution of the program.

The second strange-looking entry, IJDFYZIW, is the name of a printer module contained in the system disk library. The system automatically includes a special module for each input/output device that the program references. To perform an input/output operation, the program temporarily exits to the supervisor which performs all I/O including printing. You don't have to know the names of these I/O modules.

You will seldom, if ever, have to refer to the ESD. If you are processing under full OS, you will get a lot of additional diagnostics that you can safely ignore for now.

The next page of the Assembler listing in Figure 1-3 is overlapped with page 1 to save space. It contains the listing of the assembled program. The first line lists the contents of the TITLE statement (if any) at the top of each page (there could be more than one page), and the page number to the right.

The second line contains the following information:

LOC (for location, or technically Assembler Location Counter) is the location or address of the leftmost byte of each instruction. The notation is in hexadecimal format. Note for example that the address of PRHEAD1 begins at X'0001BA'. The program actually "begins" at location X'000000' and the macros INIT, OPEN, PUTPR, CLOSE, and EOJ occupy the locations up to X'1AA'. Since PRHEAD1 is defined as 133 bytes (CL133), then PRHEAD2 should begin 133 (X'85') bytes following PRHEAD1:

Location of PRHEAD1	X'0001AA'
Add 133	X'000085'
Location of PRHEAD2	X'00022F'

If you check the listing in Figure 1-3, you will see that the location of PRHEAD2 is indeed at X'00022F'.

You are probably wondering why there are no entries under LOC before PRHEAD1. Every preceding statement is a macro instruction. For macros, the directive PRINT NOGEN causes the Assembler to omit listing their generated object code. PRINT GEN causes the generated object

EXTERNAL SYMBOL DICTIONARY   PAGE   1

SYMBOL   TYPE   ID ADDR   LENGTH LD-ID

PROG01   SD (CSECT)   001 000000 0002D4
IJDFYZIW ER (EXTRN)   002

EXAMPLE ASSEMBLER PROGRAM TO LIST HEADINGS   DOS/VSE ASSEMBLER 19.08 86-02-23   PAGE   2

LOC   OBJECT CODE   ADDR1 ADDR2 STMT SOURCE STATEMENT

                                         2   PRINT ON,NODATA,NOGEN

                                                     P R O G R A M   E X E C U T I O N
                                                     ───────────────────────────────
                                         5 **
                                         7 PROG01 START   INITIALIZE
000000   8   INIT   OPEN FILE
                                        14   OPEN   PRINTER

                                        23   PUTPR   PRINTER,PRHEAD1,SK1   SKIP TO NEW PAGE
                                        30   PUTPR   PRINTER,PRHEAD1,WSP2   PRINT HEADING1
                                        37   PUTPR   PRINTER,PRHEAD2,WSP2   PRINT HEADING2

                                        45   CLOSE   PRINTER   CLOSE FILE
                                        53   EOJ   ,   TERMINATE

                                        57 *   D E C L A R A T I V E S
                                        58 *   ─────────────────────────

                                        60 PRINTER DEFPR   DEFINE PRINTER

0001AA 4040404040C1C3D4   85 PRHEAD1 DC CL133'   ACME DIRIGIBLE CORP.'
00022F 404040404040404040   86 PRHEAD2 DC CL133'   POTHOLE PLAINS'

0002B8   88   LTORG ,   GEN'D LITERALS
0002B8 5B5BC2D6D7C5D540   89   =C'$$BOPEN '
0002C0 5B5BC2C3D3D6E2C5   90   =C'$$BCLOSE'
0002C8 00000070   91   =A(PRINTER)
0002CC 000001AA   92   =A(PRHEAD1)
0002D0 0000022F   93   =A(PRHEAD2)

00000   95   END   PROG01   END OF ASSEMBLY

DIAGNOSTICS AND STATISTICS   PAGE   3

NO ERRORS FOUND

Output:-

ACME DIRIGIBLE CORP.

FIGURE 1-3 Assembler program listing.

code to print, and you may want to experiment with this feature, although at this point you won't find the generated code very useful.

OBJECT CODE shows the contents of instructions (but not macros in this case) and defined constants. In the case of constants, the directive PRINT NODATA causes only the first eight bytes (16 hex digits) to print. PRHEAD1, for example, begins with five blanks (X'40') and the three letters ACM:

```
40  40  40  40  40  C1  C3  D4
 b   b   b   b   b   A   C   M
```

To print the entire contents of constants (not recommended because of the added space required to list the program), code PRINT DATA.

ADDR1 AND ADDR2 refer to the addresses that instructions reference. No addresses appear here because PRINT NOGEN has suppressed the generated code for all the macro instructions. Subsequent programs, however, will all contain conventional instructions and will show addresses under LOC, OBJECT CODE, ADDR1, and ADDR2.

STMT provides the number that the Assembler has assigned to each statement, and accounts for all entries including code that macros generate. TITLE is actually the first statement. Statement 3 does not show because it contains the directive SPACE that tells the Assembler to space one line.

SOURCE STATEMENT shows the original instructions in the source program, exactly as keyed in. But there is one exception: immediately following the directive LTORG are some addresses such as =C'$$BOPEN' that the Assembler has generated to facilitate input/output. Technically, these addresses are *literals* which for now you may ignore. Note, however, that the Assembler automatically generates these literals—don't code them yourself!

To the right of PAGE 2 at the top is an entry specifying DOS/VSE ASSEMBLER 22.53 which indicates the operating system (DOS/VSE in this case) and its "release" (22) and "version" (53) numbers. These entries will vary according to the operating system installed. At the extreme right is the date of the assembly.

A special job control command would instruct the supervisor to execute this program as a job. The object program (not the source program) loads into main storage and execution begins at the address of PROG01—wherever it happens to be located in storage. The computer executes the instructions generated by the macros INIT, OPEN, PUTPR, CLOSE, and EOJ. EOJ causes termination of the program's execution and return to the supervisor which then checks for the next job to process.

Admittedly, in order to examine even a simple program there is a lot of miscellaneous detail to cover. However, the next sections and Chapter 2 explain this material, and furthermore, most of it is common to all the Assembler programs in this text.

ASSEMBLER DIAGNOSTIC MESSAGES

Figure 1-4 provides the assembled program listing, similar to the previous example, with a random assortment of coding errors. Immediately following the program is a list of errors that the Assembler has identified, along with a statement number and an explanation. (The code numbers under ERROR NO. can also help locate further explanations in the IBM Assembler manual, but you will rarely find this necessary.) Check this section immediately on receiving a listing of your assembled program.

The Assembler denotes some (but not all) errors to the left of an invalid statement with ***ERROR***. Before reading the following explanation, try to identify the cause of each error message.

STATEMENT	CAUSE
7	The directive should be coded START.
20	The message refers to the OPEN macro in which the undefined name PRTR appears. (Statement 67 defines the printer device as PRINTER.) The use of PRINT NOGEN has caused the Assembler to suppress printing statements generated by macros.
38	Since PRHEAD2 is invalidly defined in statement 86, the Assembler generates an error message for any reference to it.
56	The directive should be coded as SPACE.
86	A DC instruction must contain a defined constant within apostrophes.
93	The PUTPR macro at statement 37 has generated the address of PRHEAD2, but the instruction that defines PRHEAD2 is invalid. This is a common case of one error causing another error.
95	The operand should be PROG1A to match the program name in the START directive. In this case, the one error has generated two diagnostic messages.

If the computer attempts to execute this program, it will "bomb" on an unpredictable error. Before executing the program, be sure to correct all error diagnostics and reassemble.

ADDRESSING

The first location in main storage is numbered zero, with subsequent bytes numbered consecutively from that address. Therefore, a storage size of

EXAMPLE ASSEMBLER PROGRAM TO LIST HEADINGS

```
LOC     OBJECT CODE     ADDR1 ADDR2  STMT    SOURCE STATEMENT

                                      2      PRINT ON,NODATA,NOGEN

                                      4  *            P R O G R A M   E X E C U T I O N
                                      5  *            -----------------------------------

                                      7  PROG1A  STRAT

                *** ERROR ***

                                      8          INIT                                  INITIALIZE
                                     14          OPEN  PRTR                            OPEN FILE

                                     23          PUTPR PRINTER,PRHEAD1,SK1             SKIP TO NEW PAGE
                                     30          PUTPR PRINTER,PRHEAD1,WSP2            PRINT HEADING1
                                     37          PUTPR PRINTER,PRHEAD2,WSP2            PRINT HEADING2

                                     45          CLOSE PRINTER                         CLOSE FILE
                                     53          EOJ   ,                               TERMINATE
                                     56          SAPCE

                *** ERROR ***

                                     57  *              D E C L A R A T I V E S
                                     58  *              -----------------------------

                                     60  PRINTER DEFPR                                 DEFINE PRINTER

0001AA 40404040C1C3D4                85  PRHEAD1 DC    CL133'      ACME DIRIGIBLE CORP.'
                                     86  PRHEAD2 DC    CL133

                *** ERROR ***

000230                               88          LTORG ,                              GEN'D LITERALS
000230 5B5BC2D6D7C5D540              89                =C'$$BOPEN '
000238 5B5BC2C3D3D6E2C5              90                =C'$$BCLOSE'
000240 00000070                      91                =A(PRINTER)
000244 000001AA                      92                =A(PRHEAD1)
000248 00000000                      93                =A(PRHEAD2)

                *** ERROR ***

                                     95          END   PROG01                         END OF ASSEMBLY

                *** ERROR ***
```

DIAGNOSTICS AND STATISTICS

```
STMNT  ERROR NO.  MESSAGE
   7   IPK097     UNDEFINED OP CODE 'STRAT', OR MACRO NOT FOUND
  20   IPK156     SYMBOL 'PRTR' UNDEFINED
  38   IPK156     SYMBOL 'PRHEAD2' UNDEFINED
  56   IPK097     UNDEFINED OP CODE 'SAPCE', OR MACRO NOT FOUND
  86   IPK128     CONSTANT FIELD MISSING OR PRECEDED BY INVALID FIELD, ' '
  93   IPK156     SYMBOL 'PRHEAD2' UNDEFINED
  95   IPK144     INVALID END OPERAND
  95   IPK149     SYMBOL 'PROG01' NOT PREVIOUSLY DEFINED
```

FIGURE 1-4 Assembler diagnostic messages.

65,536 bytes has addresses numbered zero through 65,535. The amount of storage in this case would be 64K, where 1K equals 1024 bytes.

The computer performs its addressing by means of the rightmost 24 bits of a register. These 24 bits provide a capacity of 2^{24} or 16,777,216 addressable bytes of storage. Machine code uses a two-address system for addressing, consisting of:

1. A *base register* (an available general-purpose register). The base register contains the beginning address of an area in storage where the program resides, and provides a reference point for 4096 bytes of storage. Programs larger than 4096 bytes (4K) may require more than one base register.

2. A *displacement*, or the number of bytes from zero to 4095, from the first byte of the storage area. Thus, the first byte of a program has a displacement of zero, the second byte has a displacement of one, and so forth.

At this point you do not have to understand base/displacement addressing, and Chapter 6 provides a full discussion.

When you code an Assembler program, you do not know, or need to know, where in storage your instructions and declaratives will reside. You code in symbolic language, assigning names to the various instructions and data fields. For example, an instruction may have the name B20CALC, and an accumulator that counts the number of pages printed may have the name PAGECTR. The name you give refers only to a single storage location, the leftmost byte of the field.

For example, the contents of PAGECTR may be three bytes long, and the Assembler assigns it to locations 10516, 10517, and 10518. A reference to PAGECTR is to a three-byte field beginning in location 10516:

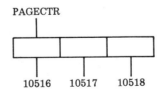

RELATIVE ADDRESSING.   You may reference a storage position *relative* to a symbolic address. For example, you could define an area of 80 bytes named RECDIN for reading and storing 80-byte records. The following definition uses the declarative DS (Define Storage) to define this 80-byte area:

```
RECDIN DS CL80
```

The name RECDIN refers to the first (leftmost) byte of the area. You may reference the second byte as RECDIN+1, the third byte as RECDIN+2, and the 80th byte as RECDIN+79:

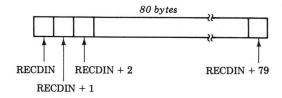

You can reference any location in a program by similar relative addressing.

INSTRUCTION FORMAT

The Assembler translates your symbolic instructions into machine čode object instructions, with correct format and length. The Assembler aligns the first byte of every instruction on an even-numbered storage location. The first byte is the operation code, such as add, move, or compare, and provides for 256 possible operations. When the computer executes a machine instruction, it accesses the operation code (the first byte) from main storage and analyzes it for the instruction's format and length.

There are five basic instruction formats, with lengths of two, four, and six bytes. An instruction usually contains one or more operands which involve a reference to a storage location or a register. An instruction, depending on its format, may transfer data between registers, between a register and storage, and between storage locations.

The five main instruction formats are RR (Register-to-Register), RX (Register-to-Indexed-Storage), SI (Storage Immediate), and SS (Storage-to-Storage), as Figure 1-5 shows. A special sixth format called S-format (not on the 360) is mainly used by the operating system and uses two bytes for the op-code.

For example, you can use an RR format instruction, AR, to add the contents of register-8 to register+6, coded in Assembler language as:

```
          AR                    6, 8 ◄———operand-2
          |                      ▲
    operation code           operand-1
```

Length in bytes	Format		Typical use
2	RR	Register-to-Register	Data movement between registers.
4	RX	Register-to-Indexed Storage	Data movement between a register and storage.
4	RS	Register-to-Storage	Data movement between a register and storage.
4	SI	Storage Immediate	Data movement from one-byte constant in the instruction to storage.
6	SS	Storage-to-Storage	Data movement between two areas in storage.

FIGURE 1-5 Assembler instruction formats.

The machine code for AR is X'1A'. The Assembler translates the symbolic instruction AR to two bytes of object code, in hexadecimal as |1A|68|. This instruction is relatively simple because it addresses only registers. The object code for instructions that reference storage is more complex because the Assembler has to convert their addresses to base/displacement format, as Chapter 6 explains.

PROBLEMS

1-1. Explain (a) machine language instruction; (b) symbolic instruction; (c) macro instruction.

1-2. On the coding form, what does an asterisk in column 1 indicate? What would it indicate in column 72?

1-3. Comment on the validity of the following Assembler names (labels): (a) W25; (b) START-UP; (c) READDEVICE; (d) $AMT; (e) TOT AMT; (f) *TOTAL; (g) 25CENTS.

1-4. What is the first statement required in an Assembler program?

1-5. Does the EJECT directive cause the printer to skip to the top of a page during an assembly, during program execution, or both?

1-6. What statement causes an assembled program listing to space three lines?

1-7. How can you cause the Assembler to check the sequence of a source program?

1-8. How can you cause the generated code for a macro to appear on an assembled listing?

1-9. What statement terminates assembly of a program?

1-10. What is a declarative? How do DS and DC differ?

1-11. How does the Assembler account for the address of each instruction and declarative?

1-12. What steps are required to assemble a program? Where does the system store the assembled object program?

1-13. Distinguish between "source program" and "object program."

1-14. What do the following mean on an assembled program listing: (a) LOC; (b) OBJECT CODE; (c) ADDR1 and ADDR2; (d) STMT?

1-15. Indicate which instruction formats that you use to move data (a) between registers; (b) between storage locations; (c) between registers and storage.

1-16. Refer to the IBM Assembler manual. Define in your own words (a) self-defining terms; (b) absolute and relocatable expressions.

2

PROGRAM EXECUTION

Chapter 1 covered the requirements for coding an Assembler program. This chapter covers the basic instructions for executing an Assembler language program: initialization, the defining of files, and the input/output macros. You will also examine the input of a data record and its format in main storage. Now that you are close to coding a program, you also examine a conventional analytical tool for program design, the flowchart. The next chapter provides enough information so that you can write programs that use character data.

FILES AND RECORDS

A *field* consists of one or more related bytes. A *record* consists of one or more related fields. Fields may also contain *subfields:* a date field for example could contain subfields month, day, and year. Some fields, such as customer name, contain *alphabetic* (or *character*) data. Other fields such as customer number or billing amount contain *numeric* data. A field such as address contains mixed alphabetic and numeric data, known as *alphameric.* A record may also contain unused spaces, available for future expansion.

Figure 2-1 portrays an 80-byte record containing the fields for a customer. This record could be kept on any type of device such as disk, tape, or card, and is viewable on a terminal.

customer number	customer name	address-1	address-2	balance due	unused
1 — 5	6 — — — — 27	28 — — — — 49	50 — — — — 71	72 — — 78	79 — — 80

FIGURE 2-1 Example input record.

In order to print or display the contents of this customer record, you normally design a print layout. As Figure 2-2 shows, the output fields are spaced apart for readability. Note that the balance owing field in the print layout is two characters longer to allow for a comma and a decimal point.

customer number	customer name	address-1	address-2	balance due
xxxx	x — — — x	x — — — — — x	x — — — — x	xx,xxx.xx
7 — 11	15 — — 36	41 — — — 62	67 — — — 88	93 — — 101

FIGURE 2-2 Example output layout.

PROGRAM EXECUTION STATEMENTS

An Assembler program requires certain special coding for program execution. It is necessary initially to "load base registers" for addressing, to define the input and output files, to activate these files, and to provide for termination of program execution and for termination of the assembly. This section describes the simple macros used for these complex functions. It is desirable for the beginning programmer to write a program as soon as possible; thus, this text uses four macros that have been specially written for introducing Assembler programming, INIT, DEFIN, DEFPR and PUTPR. They handle some complex coding and enable the beginner to get started quickly. All other macros used in this text are standard IBM macros.

INITIALIZATION. The first statements in an Assembler program may vary depending upon the Assembler version being used or requirements of the computer installation. The INIT macro's main function is to "load base registers."

NAME	OPERATION	OPERAND
blank	INIT	blank

Under Disk Operating System (DOS), you would normally code (at least) the following instructions to initialize addressing for a program:

```
BALR   3,0     (not necessarily register-3)
USING  *,3
```

Under Operating System (OS), you would have to code not only the above instructions, but also a number of others concerned with returning to the supervisor program at the end of execution.

Chapter 6 covers the precise methods of initializing an Assembler program and explains the requirements for both DOS and OS.

DEFINING INPUT AND PRINTER FILES. This text begins with the simplest processing of input/output files: terminal or card input, and terminal or printer output. A program must define the names of the input and output files. At the beginning of this text, two special macros handle this definition: DEFIN (Define Input) and DEFPR (Define Printer). These macros generate some complex Assembler code. (Chapter 7 covers the standard IBM file definition macros DTFCD, DTFPR, and DCB.) The imperative macros such as OPEN and GET reference these files by their defined names.

NAME	OPERATION	OPERAND
inputfile	DEFIN	end-of-file address
printfile	DEFPR	blank

DEFIN defines an input file with any valid unique name, preferably descriptive. The operand specifies an address in your program where the system is to link on encountering the end of input data. Under DOS, the last record of input data for cards or CMS terminals is a job control entry containing /* in columns 1-2. As it reads each data record, the system checks the first two positions. If they contain /*, the system directs your program to your end-of-file address, typically the name of a routine that may print final totals and terminate program execution.

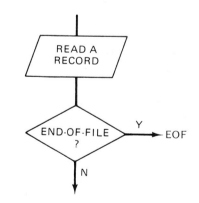

DEFPR defines the name of the printer file with any unique name. The printer is an output file and has no associated "end-of-file."

OPENING AND CLOSING FILES. Many programming languages require the programmer to code statements that "activate" (OPEN) the files at the start of program execution and "deactivate" (CLOSE) them at the end. The normal function of OPEN is to make the file available to the program (it may be damaged or in use by another program). At the end of the program execution, CLOSE releases the file for use by other programs. For both macros, the operands are the input and printer file names defined by DEFIN and DEFPR. (Under many large systems, the programmer may omit the OPEN and CLOSE of input, printer, and terminal files.)

Under DOS, OPEN and CLOSE are coded as:

	OPEN	inputfile,printfile
	CLOSE	inputfile,printfile

Under OS, code OPEN and CLOSE with the operands in brackets. Also OPEN must specify if the file is INPUT or OUTPUT; CLOSE may omit the references.

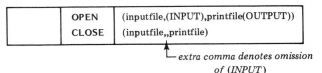

	OPEN	(inputfile,(INPUT),printfile(OUTPUT))
	CLOSE	(inputfile,,printfile)

extra comma denotes omission of (INPUT)

For either DOS or OS, you may OPEN or CLOSE one or more files with one statement. The advantage of a separate OPEN statement for each file is that you may more easily identify which file is invalid if an OPEN fails.

READING INPUT RECORDS. The GET macro reads input records. There are two operands: Operand-1 designates the file name defined by DEFIN (or by the IBM macro DCB or DTFCD); Operand-2 is the name of an 80-byte input area in main storage.

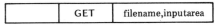

	GET	filename,inputarea

GET causes the input device to read a record and store its contents in the input area, erasing the previous contents of the area. The input area may have any unique name. Prior to storing in the input area, the operation checks the record; if it is the end-of-file record (/*), the program branches to the end-of-file address defined in the DEFIN macro. An example:

```
        OPEN    READER              Open input file
        GET     READER,INAREA       Read record into INAREA


D10END  CLOSE   READER              End-of-file, CLOSE READER

READER  DEFIN   D10END              Define file as READER
INAREA  DS      CL80                Define 80-byte input area
```

An OS program would OPEN and CLOSE the file named READER as follows:

```
        OPEN    (READER(INPUT))
        CLOSE   (READER)
```

PRINTING LINES. Printing lines during program execution requires special treatment, because you may want to space on a page without printing, or print and space one or more lines. To simplify the requirements involved in spacing the print forms, in the early chapters this text uses a special macro, PUTPR. (Do not confuse this printing during execute-time with the SPACE or PRINT statements that control the printing of the program listing during assembly-time.)

```
┌──────────┬────────────────────────────────────────┐
│   PUTPR  │  printfile,printarea,print-command      │
└──────────┴────────────────────────────────────────┘
```

For PUTPR, operand-1 is the name of the printer file defined by DEFPR (or by the IBM macros DCB or DTFPR). Operand-2 is the name of the print area that contains data that is to be printed. The print area may have any unique name, and there may be more than one print area. Operand-3 specifies the forms control:

```
WSP0    Write, no space        SK1    Skip to new page
WSP1    Write, space 1 line     SP1    Space 1 line
WSP2    Write, space 2 lines    SP2    Space 2 lines
WSP3    Write, space 3 lines    SP3    Space 3 lines
```

For example, the instruction PUTPR PRINTER,PRINT,WSP1 causes the program to print the contents of an area, PRINT, and to space to the next line on the page. WSP0 may be used occasionally for underlining important information. SK1, SP1, SP2, and SP3 simply move the printer; nothing prints on the page, regardless of the contents of the print area. PUTPR uses the first byte of the print area to insert a special forms control character; any character that you may have already stored there will be erased. If the print area is defined as PRINT DS CL133, then PRINT+0 is the position that the control character uses. The remaining positions, PRINT+1 through PRINT +132, are available for storing your printable data. (The standard IBM macro, PUT, requires the programmer to define and insert the control character, as discussed in Chapter 7.)

Note: PUTPR does not clear the print area. Because unwanted data may still be in the area from the previous print operation, it is usually desirable to clear the print area to blanks after printing so that the next printing does not contain "garbage." Also, if the print area is a DS, then it may contain garbage from some previous program. It is useful to define the print area as a DC as in PRINT DC CL133' ', to initialize the print area to blanks.

TERMINATING EXECUTION. After closing the files, you terminate program *execution* under DOS with the EOJ macro, which causes a return to the supervisor program. Under OS, termination involves the RETURN macro.

	EOJ	blank	(normal termination)
	CANCEL	, or ALL	(abnormal termination)

More advanced programs are written to check if input records contain invalid data, and you may want to cancel the run if the input is invalid. The CANCEL macro also terminates processing, but as well it "flushes" any remaining input records. The beginning programmer may want to delay using CANCEL until becoming more advanced. Under OS, the macro equivalent to CANCEL is ABEND.

END OF ASSEMBLY. EOJ and CANCEL are concerned with terminating a program's execution, and may be coded in any logical place within the program. To terminate program *assembly,* the last statement in the program must be END, which tells the Assembler that there are no more statements.

The operand of the END directive stipulates the address of the first executable statement in the program. Through most of this text, this address is the program name, as:

PROG07	START		Start of program
	·		
	·		
	·		
	END	PROG07	End of program

The END directive is not a macro and generates no executable code; it does, however, provide the starting address for the supervisor to begin execution of the program.

SAMPLE PROGRAM: READ AND PRINT ONE RECORD

Figure 2-3 combines the preceding Assembler macros into a program that prints a heading, reads one record, prints its contents, and terminates execution. The GET macro reads a record from the file named FILEIN and transfers the record into an 80-byte field defined as RECORDIN. The instruction following GET is MVC (Move Characters) that moves (actually copies) the contents of RECORDIN to the print area:

```
MVC DATAPR,RECORDIN
```

DATAPR is defined *within* PRINT. Note that PRINT is defined as 0CL133, the zero indicating that the Assembler is not to increment its location counter. Consequently, the following 10-byte field (unnamed) is aligned at the same location as PRINT and all the fields are defined within PRINT:

```
| —— 10 —— | —————————— 80 —————————— | —————— 43 —————— |
|          |
PRINT    DATAPR
```

In effect, PRINT is a *record* consisting of three fields which total 133 bytes. A reference to PRINT is to the entire 133-byte record.

In this program, the end-of-file address is A90END, although since there is only one input record, the system never has to test for end-of-file.

The program was coded to run under DOS. An OS program would code the OPEN and CLOSE macros as follows:

```
OPEN    (FILEIN,(INPUT),PRINTER,(OUTPUT))
CLOSE   (FILEIN,,PRINTER)
```

Now, there are two considerations:

1. What if the program was run with no input data? The program would open the files, print the heading, and attempt to read a record. Assum-

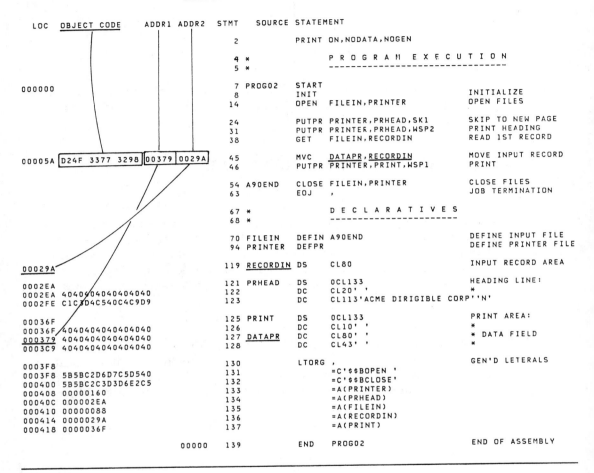

EXAMPLE ASSEMBLER PROGRAM TO LIST ONE INPUT RECORD

```
  LOC    OBJECT CODE        ADDR1 ADDR2   STMT    SOURCE STATEMENT
                                            2              PRINT ON,NODATA,NOGEN

                                            4  *                    P R O G R A M   E X E C U T I O N
                                            5  *                    ---------------------------------
000000                                      7  PROG02  START                              INITIALIZE
                                            8          INIT                               INITIALIZE
                                           14          OPEN   FILEIN,PRINTER              OPEN FILES

                                           24          PUTPR  PRINTER,PRHEAD,SK1          SKIP TO NEW PAGE
                                           31          PUTPR  PRINTER,PRHEAD,WSP2         PRINT HEADING
                                           38          GET    FILEIN,RECORDIN             READ 1ST RECORD

00005A  D24F 3377 3298   00379 0029A        45          MVC    DATAPR,RECORDIN            MOVE INPUT RECORD
                                           46          PUTPR  PRINTER,PRINT,WSP1          PRINT

                                           54  A90END  CLOSE  FILEIN,PRINTER              CLOSE FILES
                                           63          EOJ    ,                           JOB TERMINATION

                                           67  *                    D E C L A R A T I V E S
                                           68  *                    -----------------------
                                           70  FILEIN  DEFIN  A90END                     DEFINE INPUT FILE
                                           94  PRINTER DEFPR                              DEFINE PRINTER FILE

00029A                                     119  RECORDIN DS    CL80                       INPUT RECORD AREA

0002EA                                     121  PRHEAD  DS     0CL133                     HEADING LINE:
0002EA  40404040404040                     122          DC     CL20' '                    *
0002FE  C1C3D4C540C0C9D9                   123          DC     CL113'ACME DIRIGIBLE CORP''N'

00036F                                     125  PRINT   DS     0CL133                     PRINT AREA:
00036F  40404040404040                     126          DC     CL10' '                    *
000379  40404040404040                     127  DATAPR  DC     CL80' '                    * DATA FIELD
0003C9  40404040404040                     128          DC     CL43' '                    *

0003F8                                     130          LTORG  ,                           GEN'D LETERALS
0003F8  5B5BC2D6D7C5D540                   131                 =C'$$BOPEN '
000400  5B5BC2C3D3D6E2C5                   132                 =C'$$BCLOSE'
000408  00000160                           133                 =A(PRINTER)
00040C  000002EA                           134                 =A(PRHEAD)
000410  00000088                           135                 =A(FILEIN)
000414  0000029A                           136                 =A(RECORDIN)
000418  0000036F                           137                 =A(PRINT)

                              00000        139          END    PROG02                      END OF ASSEMBLY
```

Output:-

ACME DIRIGIBLE CORP'N

WORLD'S GREATEST BLIMPS

FIGURE 2-3 Read and print one record.

ing that the job control entries were correct, the system would signal end-of-file, and the program would immediately link to its end-of-file address A90END where it closes the files and terminates. In effect, although the program does not read or print a record, there is no error.

2. What if the program was run with two input records? The program would open the files, print the heading, read the first record, and print it. The program then closes the files and EOJ terminates execution and returns to the supervisor. The supervisor would expect a job control entry at this point in the job stream, but instead would encounter a data record. Since the data record would be incomprehensible to the supervisor, it would print (or display) a warning message such as:

INVALID STATEMENT

OBJECT CODE. Let's now examine the generated machine object code for this program. Since the MVC (Move Character) instruction is not a macro, the Assembler has listed its object code to the left, as follows:

```
LOC          OBJECT CODE        ADDR1  ADDR2

00005A       D24F 3377 3298     00379  0029A
```

The instruction begins at location X'00005A'—that is, the first byte containing X'D2'. The actual machine code is six bytes and consists of operation, length code, and two operands. Note that this explanation applies to an MVC instruction and not necessarily to other Assembler instructions.

D2	The machine code for MVC. MVC will always generate this code for its first byte.
4F	The length in hex of this move operation. Actually, X'4F' is decimal value 79, not 80 (look it up!), but the Assembler always deducts 1 from the length, and the computer when executing always adds 1.
3377	The address of operand-1 (DATAPR) in terms of the computer's addressing scheme.
3298	The address of operand-2 (RECORDIN) in terms of the computer's addressing scheme.

These two operand addresses consist of a reference to a base register and a displacement. A full discussion of this topic is delayed until Chapter 6; there's enough to wrestle with learning symbolic code first.

Under ADDR1 and ADDR2 are two values that the Assembler lists for informative purposes, and are not part of the actual machine code. The value 00379 indicates the location (LOC) of operand-1, DATAPR, and the value 0029A indicates the location of operand-2, RECORDIN. If you trace down the column under LOC, you will find these two values, and sure enough, they are the lines that define DATAPR and RECORDIN respectively.

That's enough machine code for now. You may want to examine a few other op-codes, lengths, and addresses in your own programs, but don't expect to fully understand this material until Chapter 6.

Let's now find out how to process any number of input records.

LOOPING

Most programs involve reading and processing a number of input records. The program has to perform *looping*, or repetitive processing, until reaching end-of-file, as follows:

```
              GET    first-record            Initialization
— — — — — — — — — — — — — — — — — — — — — — — — —
A10LOOP        .
               .      (process record)       Processing
               .
              GET    next-record             If end-file, exit
              B      A10LOOP                    to A90EOF
— — — — — — — — — — — — — — — — — — — — — — — — —
A90EOF        ...                            End-of-file processing
```

This text has adopted a programming style that involves an initial GET instruction that reads only the first record. The program then processes the record (including perhaps an output operation), then executes another GET. The GET is followed by a *branch* (B) instruction that says in effect: Branch to the address A90LOOP, which is coded *after* the initial GET. The loop processes and reads continuously until a GET senses the end-of-file condition. At this point, the program automatically links to the end-of-file address, in this case assumed to be A90EOF.

SAMPLE PROGRAM: READ AND PRINT MULTIPLE RECORDS

Figure 2-4 provides an example that combines the program in Figure 2-3 that reads one record with the preceding material on looping. In this example, the program reads and processes any number of records. For this purpose, the only new instruction is B A10LOOP, and the MVC instruction contains the name A10LOOP.

Basically, the program in Figure 2-4 is a model for the remaining programs in this text, although defined names may differ by example.

```
LOC   OBJECT CODE        ADDR1 ADDR2   STMT    SOURCE STATEMENT

                                        3              PRINT ON,NODATA,NOGEN

                                        5 *                   I N I T I A L I Z A T I O N
                                        6 *                   ---------------------------
000000                                  8 PROG02     START
                                        9            INIT                        INITIALIZE
                                       15            OPEN   FILEIN,PRINTER        OPEN FILES

                                       25            PUTPR  PRINTER,PRHEAD,SK1    SKIP TO NEW PAGE
                                       32            PUTPR  PRINTER,PRHEAD,WSP2   PRINT HEADING
                                       39            GET    FILEIN,RECORDIN       READ 1ST RECORD

                                       46 *                   R E A D  &  P R I N T   R O U T I N E
                                       47 *                   ----------------------------------------
00005A D24F 339F 32C0 003A1 002C2      49 A10LOOP    MVC    DATAPR,RECORDIN       MOVE INPUT RECORD
                                       50            PUTPR  PRINTER,PRINT,WSP1    PRINT
                                       57            GET    FILEIN,RECORDIN       READ NEXT RECORD
000084 47F0 3058         0005A         63            B      A10LOOP              LOOP

                                       65 *                   E N D - O F - F I L E   R O U T I N E
                                       66 *                   -----------------------------------------
                                       68 A90END     PUTPR  PRINTER,PRINT,SK1     SKIP PAGE
                                       75            CLOSE  FILEIN,PRINTER        CLOSE FILES
                                       84            EOJ    ,                     TERMINATE JOB

                                       88 *                   D E C L A R A T I V E S
                                       89 *                   -----------------------
                                       91 FILEIN     DEFIN  A90END               DEFINE INPUT FILE
                                      115 PRINTER    DEFPR                        DEFINE PRINTER FILE
0002C2                                140 RECORDIN   DS     CL80                  INPUT RECORD AREA

000312                                142 PRHEAD     DS     0CL133               HEADING LINE:
000312 4040404040404040               143            DC     CL10' '              *
00031C C3D6D4D7C1D5E840               144            DC     CL123'COMPANY NAME AND ADDRESS'

000397                                146 PRINT      DS     0CL133               PRINT AREA:
000397 4040404040404040               147            DC     CL10' '              *
0003A1 4040404040404040               148 DATAPR     DC     CL80' '              * DATA FIELD
0003F1 4040404040404040               149            DC     CL43' '              *

000420                                151            LTORG                       GEN'D LITERALS
000420 5B5BC2D6D7C5D540               152                   =C'$$BOPEN '
000428 5B5BC2C3D3D6E2C5               153                   =C'$$BCLOSE'
000430 00000188                       154                   =A(PRINTER)
000434 00000312                       155                   =A(PRHEAD)
000438 000000B0                       156                   =A(FILEIN)
00043C 000002C2                       157                   =A(RECORDIN)
000440 00000397                       158                   =A(PRINT)

                        00000        160            END    PROG02               END OF ASSEMBLY
```

FIGURE 2-4 (partial)

CROSS-REFERENCE

```
SYMBOL    LEN   ID  VALUE   DEFN    REFERENCES

A10LOOP   00006 001 00005A  00049   0063
A90END    00004 001 000088  00069   0107
DATAPR    00080 001 0003A1  00148   0049
FILEIN    00006 001 000CB0  00094   0021   0081  0156
IJCX0016  00008 001 0000D0  00108   0097        ⎫  IBM modules
IJJC0013  00004 001 0000A0  00080               ⎬  generated by
IJJ00002  00004 001 000014  00020               ⎭  input/output
IJJZ0016  00001 001 0000E2  00111
IJJZ0018  00001 001 0001B8  00135
INBUFF1   00080 001 0000E2  00113   0108        ⎫  Input and
INBUFF2   00080 001 000132  00114   0105        ⎬  output
PRBUFF1   00133 001 0001B8  00137   0129        ⎭  buffers
PRBUFF2   00133 001 00023D  00138   0134
PRHEAD    00133 001 000312  00142   0026   0033  0155
PRINT     00133 001 000397  00146   0051   0069  0158
PRINTER   00006 001 000188  00118   0022   0082  0154
PROG02    00001 001 000000  00008   0160
RECORDIN  00080 001 0002C2  00140   0049   0157
=A(FILEIN)
          00004 001 000438  00156   0041   0059
=A(PRINTER)
          00004 001 000430  00154   0028   0035  0053  0071
=A(PRHEAD)
          00004 001 000434  00155   0029   0036                 ⎫  literals
=A(PRINT)                                                       ⎬  generated
          00004 001 000440  00158   0054   0072                 ⎭  by the
=A(RECORDIN)                                                        Assembler
          00004 001 00043C  00157   0042   0060
=C'$$BOPEN '
          00008 001 000420  00152   0019
=C'$$BCLOSE'
          00008 001 000428  00153   0079
```

Output:-

COMPANY NAME AND ADDRESS

ACE ELECTRONICS CORPORATION
4325 SUNNYHILL ROAD
FONZDALE, CALIFORNIA

FIGURE 2-4 Processing multiple records.

CROSS REFERENCE LISTING

The program in Figure 2-4 supplies one additional feature: a Cross Reference Listing of the defined symbols in alphabetic sequence. In this case, assume that "symbol" means any declarative and name in the program. The listing is useful for more complex programs where you want to locate quickly all the instructions that reference a particular declarative.

Some of the symbols are not immediately recognizable. For example, symbols beginning with IJC and IJJ are special entries that the system has included to handle reading and printing. Immediately following are four entries for "buffers" that are generated to facilitate input/output. Also, the Assembler has generated literals for addresses concerned with I/O. These begin with equal signs, such as =A(FILEIN) meaning the address of the input file. You may cheerfully ignore these entries.

The column headed LEN provides the length in decimal notation of instructions and declaratives. For example, the instruction at A10LOOP, the MVC, is six bytes long. Of more relevance is the length of declaratives; the length for example of PRHEAD is 133.

The column headed VALUE contains the location of the symbol. For example, the "value" of A10LOOP is X'00005A' which relates directly to the LOC column in the Assembler listing.

The column headed by DEFN indicates the statement number of the symbol. For example, the DEFN of A10LOOP is 00049, which agrees with its number under STMT in the assembled listing.

REFERENCES identifies all the other statements in the program that refer to the symbol. For example, A10LOOP is defined in 49 and referenced in 63. PRHEAD is defined in 142 and referenced in 26, 33, and 155.

INPUT DATA

An input record, such as a Customer Balance, is divided into fields of data, as customer number, name, and balance owing. A collection of related records, such as all the Customer Balance records, comprises a file, or, in OS terminology, a "data set."

Many records contain a unique code in a specified position to identify the file to which they belong. Thus, Customer Balance records could all contain '01' in the first two positions, and programs that read this file can check each record to ensure that the correct records are being entered. Also, the records are normally in ascending sequence by control field, in this case, customer number. If the program prints reports in sequence, a user can quickly locate any required customer number. Because the file may be submitted in an incorrect sequence, it is common practice for the program to *sequence-check* input records by their control fields.

You may define a field that contains character data: the numbers 0 through 9, the letters A through Z, and other characters as $, *, and @. Character data, like all other data, use binary representation through the bit on/off condition. One byte (8 bits) represents one character. The combinations of eight bits in a byte provide 256 (2^8) possible characters. The typical printer, however, can print about 60 different characters. Figure 2-5 depicts some of the standard printable characters.

As can be seen, the representation of a blank character is binary 0100 0000, or hex 40. The letter A would appear in storage as 1100 0001, or X'C1', and the numbers 0 through 9 are 1111 0000 through 1111 1001, or X'F0'–X'F9'.

You need not memorize these representations. When necessary, refer to this Figure or to Appendix F which provides the representation of all 256 codes from X'00' through X'FF'.

DEC	HEX	BINARY	SYMBOL
64	40	0100 0000	BLANK
75	4B	0100 1011	. (DEC POINT)
91	5B	0101 1011	$ (DOLLAR SIGN)
92	5C	0101 1100	* (ASTERISK)
107	6B	0110 1011	, (COMMA)
193	C1	1100 0001	A
.	.		.
.	.		.
201	C9	1100 1001	I
209	D1	1101 0001	J
.	.		.
.	.		.
217	D9	1101 1001	R
226	E2	1110 0010	S
.	.		.
.	.		.
232	E9	1110 1001	Z
240	F0	1111 0000	0 (ZERO)
.	.		.
.	.		.
249	F9	1111 1001	9 (NINE)

FIGURE 2-5 Representation of selected codes.

A keyboard and a card deliver input data into storage normally only in *character* format. A terminal screen and printer display output also in this format. An input record containing alphabetic and numeric data reads into an 80-byte area, defined anywhere in available storage, entirely in character format. You may also accept individual fields from a terminal keyboard, but they are also in character format. (Note that to perform arithmetic on a numeric field, you must translate it into packed or binary format.) The following lists the contents of an input record:

COLUMN	FIELD	CONTENTS
1–2	Record code	01
3–5	Account number	123
6–18	Name	JP MCKINNON (Alphabetic data is entered beginning on the left in column 6, with blanks filled to the right up to column 18.)
19–25	Balance	0125000 (The balance is $1,250.00—do not enter dollar sign or comma, nor usually the decimal point.)
26–80	Unused	Blank

Assume that the name of the 80-byte input area is RECDIN, and the name of the input file is FILEIN. The relevant instructions to read the record are:

```
                          GET       FILEIN,RECDIN
                            .
                            .
                            .
           FILEIN         DEFIN      .  .  .
           RECDIN         DS         CL80
```

The GET instruction reads the 80-character input record into the 80-byte RECDIN area in main storage, byte-for-byte, as shown in Figure 2-6.

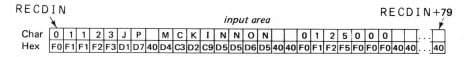

RECDIN   *input area*   RECDIN+79

| Char | 0 | 1 | 1 | 2 | 3 | J | P | | M | C | K | I | N | N | O | N | | | 0 | 1 | 2 | 5 | 0 | 0 | 0 | | . . . | |
| Hex | F0 | F1 | F1 | F2 | F3 | D1 | D7 | 40 | D4 | C3 | D2 | C9 | D5 | D5 | D6 | D5 | 40 | 40 | F0 | F1 | F2 | F5 | F0 | F0 | F0 | 40 | 40 | . . . | 40 |

Figure 2-6 Character and hex representation.

Compare the character and the hexadecimal representation, two hex digits for each character read. Note especially that any *blank* position appears in storage as X'40' (binary 0100 0000). Also, the numbers 0 through 9 become X'F0' through X'F9'. You may assign symbolic names to each field within the input area. You then process the data by referring to each field's symbolic name. For example, you may check that a record code (01) is correct. You may move the account number (123) and the name to another storage area in order to print them. Also, you may convert the balance field (1,250.00) into packed decimal format in order to add it to an accumulator. In order to perform these tasks, you must be able to do the following:

- Reference areas and fields in storage. For this purpose use *declaratives* to tell the Assembler each field's name, length, and format (e.g., character, binary, packed).
- Instruct the computer step-by-step what is to be done. Use Assembler symbolic *instructions* in order, for example, to move, add, and compare data.

CONDITION CODE

Computers must have logic: the ability to compare the contents of one field to that of another, and to check if a value is positive, negative, or zero. On the 370-series, comparing or checking fields sets the *condition code,* two bits in the program status word (PSW). Many compare and arithmetic instructions set the condition code according to the results of the operation:

RESULTS OF OPERATION	CONDITION CODE SETTING
Equal or zero	0
Low or minus	1
High or plus	2
Arithmetic overflow	3 (arithmetic field is too small for the calculated answer)

The purpose of the condition code is to facilitate the computer logic. Certain operations set the condition code. Subsequently you can use other instructions that can test what condition was set. In this way, you can change the flow of the program logic.

As an example, a file of Accounts Receivable records must be read into the computer in sequence by Customer. The program *sequence-checks* the file by comparing the Customer number on the input record just read against the Customer number on the record that was previously read and processed. The possibilities are as follows:

NEW CUSTOMER NUMBER READ	CONDITION CODE SETING	DECISION
Equal	0	Same Customer as previous
Low	1	Out-of-sequence error
High	2	Next Customer

Similarly, a program may check an amount field to determine whether its contents are zero (0), negative (1), or positive (2).

FLOWCHART LOGIC

Programming is more than simply coding instructions for the computer to execute. Usually there are several steps: analysis, design, flowcharting, and coding.

ANALYSIS. The first step is to analyze the problem. This step may consist of interviewing people concerned with the problem, studying input data to be processed, and designing the output required. If other programs use the same input or require the output, then the new program must integrate with the present system.

DESIGN.   The data to be used may be at present on *source documents*. You may have to design an input record so that the data can be entered on a terminal. Next, you may have to design the printed report, depicting each print position to be used.

FLOWCHARTING.   The next step depicts the solution to the problem. One common approach is to draw a *flowchart,* a pictorial representation of the program's flow of logic, showing each step that the program coding is to take. If you can flowchart the program, you should be able to code it. A flowchart serves the following purposes:

- It ensures that the problem has been thoroughly analyzed.
- It aids in solving the problem and often reveals programming errors.
- It acts as documentation for future corrections and modifications.

Flowcharts can be an important element of program design and documentation. There are special symbols for operations such as processing, input/output, decisions, and terminals. After analyzing the problem, depict the flow of logic that the coded computer program is to follow, showing each step and action, in the sequence it will be executed. In this way you fully solve the problem at the detail level, and make adjustments as you proceed. When you code the instructions, you follow the flowchart logic. The flowchart therefore simplifies coding and minimizes errors.

Flowcharts should be neat and legible, drawn on one side of the page only, in *pencil* to facilitate revisions. They provide the identical logic as the coded program. In the case of small programs, such as the ones that accompany many of the chapters, a single flowchart is adequate. Large programs may require an additional summary flowchart depicting the program's general overall logic. Computer manufacturers provide a standard flowchart template. The common symbols are described next.

SYMBOL	IDENTIFICATION
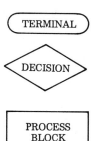	Start or termination of the program and of subroutines.
	Indicates that a compare or test is made with more than one possible result. This is the only symbol that permits more than one exit.
	Describes normal computer instructions such as MOVE or ADD. Notation within the block describes the operation(s). Several similar operations in a row, such as adding various fields, may all be included in one block.

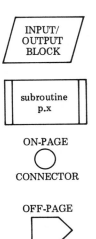

Depicts all input/output operations, such as READ A RECORD, or WRITE A LINE.

Indicates that the program links at this point to a subroutine and returns. Details of the subroutine logic are provided on another page, as p. x indicates.

Used if a continuous line cannot easily be drawn from one block to another. One on-page connector is an exit from the block, and one is an entry to the other block. Unique letters, such as 'A', in each connector relate them.

Signifies that the next block is on a different page. One off-page connector is an exit from the block, and one is an entry to the other block. Two items are entered in the connector: the page number on which the block is to be found, and an unique letter, such as 'A', to relate the connectors.

SAMPLE FLOWCHART   Figure 2-7 illustrates most of the flowchart symbols. The flowchart depicts a program that reads Customer Balance records. Each record is identified by a customer number, and contains also customer name and balance owing. There may be only one record for a customer. The objective is to print the balance owing for each valid customer. Note the following points:

1. The program compares the customer number on each input record against the customer number from the previously processed record. If the new one is higher (Y), the program prints customer number, name, and balance, and stores the new customer number in "previous" number for the next sequence-check. The program then reads the next record and loops to repeat the instructions. If the customer number is not higher, the program prints an error message and branches to read the next record.

2. Immediately following the read operation is the end-of-file condition. If there are no more records to be processed, the program closes the files and terminates processing (END-OF-JOB).

    Note: In developing flowcharts, the flow of logic is normally directed downward and to the right. Also, after the OPEN, the initial read does not show an end-of-file test. Technically, the test *always* occurs on a read, but the flowcharts in this book omit it for reasons of brevity.

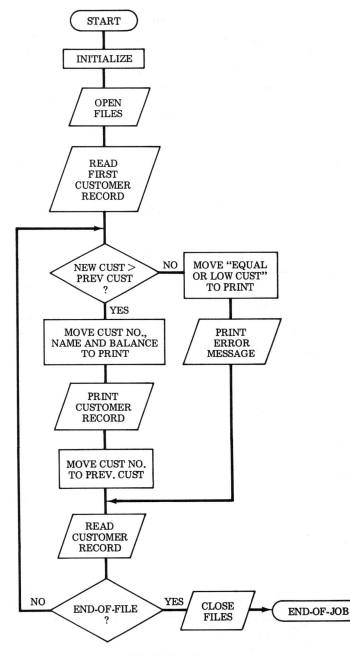

FIGURE 2-7

CODING.   The final step in programming involves coding the data areas and program instructions. Be sure to refrain from rushing into coding before you have thoroughly analyzed, designed, and flowcharted the problem. Perhaps the best approach is to define the data records first. In that way, when you later code the instructions, you can use as operands the names of the defined data fields. When coding instructions, refer to your flowchart and carefully follow its logic. As you ponder the problem in more depth, you may have to revise your logic. The rest of this text is concerned with this fourth step, coding.

A useful approach is to use a previous program as a guide. If you have a skeleton program already cataloged on disk and you are using a terminal system such as IBM CMS, you can copy the program, delete unwanted instructions, and add new instructions.

JOB CONTROL

All 370-series computers run under an operating system. In order to assemble or execute a program, you submit "job control" commands that tell the operating system what action to perform. A "job" may consist of one or more programs that are to execute with required data. The system recognizes the start of a job, such as "Payroll," by means of the first job control command, which contains an entry such as // JOB or // JOB jobname (DOS). Such entries that specify the job and the action to perform comprise the "job control language" (JCL).

Basically, job control for assembling and executing a program under most systems consists of three major steps: assembly, link edit, and execution. Following is a simplified example:

```
1.  // JOB jobname              Specify job name
2.  // EXEC ASSEMBLY            Request assembly
3.  [assembly source program]   Your source program
4.  /*                          End of source program
5.  // EXEC LNKEDT              Request link edit
6.  // EXEC [program-name]      Execute your linked program
7.  [data]                      Your input data
8.  /*                          End of input data
9.  /&                          End of your job
```

The following explains each job step:

1. You supply a job name to the system.
2. The system loads the Assembler program from disk into storage.
3. The Assembler reads your source program as input data, and converts its symbolic code into machine object code.
4. On encountering the end of the source program, the Assembler completes conversion to object code.

5. The system loads the Linkage Editor program from disk into storage. The Linkage Editor reads the assembled object program and includes any required cataloged input/output modules (and if necessary combines any separately assembled programs). The Linker writes the machine language module onto disk.

6. The linked object module now loads from disk into storage and begins execution.

7. The linked object module reads and processes your input data.

8. When your program reads the end-of-file indication, it prepares to terminate execution and returns control to the system.

9. The system terminates your job.

Note: You may assemble more than one program into one linked executable module. Therefore you would have one or more ASSEMBLY entries but only one LNKEDT entry. You can execute the linked program any number of times in a job because it resides during the session on disk. Each EXEC of the linked program causes it to read into storage, erasing the previous version.

The two main IBM operating systems are Disk Operating System (DOS) for medium size computers, and Operating System (OS) for large ones. Job control language for these two systems is quite different, and even within a system may vary considerably between installations. Appendix D gives example job control for some typical situations. Check the particular JCL requirements for your own installation.

PROBLEMS

2-1. An input file is called FILEIN and an output file is called FILEPR. Provide for your system: (a) the OPEN statement; (b) a properly defined area for input records; (c) the GET instruction; (d) a properly defined area for print records; (e) the write statement necessary to write and space two lines; (f) the CLOSE statement.

2-2. How does your system recognize the end of an input file?

2-3. A field tested in a program is found to be negative. What will be the condition code setting?

2-4. Given the Character, Hexadecimal or Binary, complete the representation.

	CHARACTER			HEX			BINARY					
Example	A	B	C	C1	C2	C3	1100	0001	1100	0010	1100	0011
(a)	3	7	0									
(b)	1	B	M									
(c)	S	a	m									
(d)	—	7	%									
(e)							1101	0111	1100	0001	1110	0011
(f)							0100	0000	1111	1001	1111	0000
(g)							0100	1101	0100	0000	0101	1101
(h)				C2	E4	C7						
(i)				E2	C1	D4						
(j)				5B	40	6B						

2-5. What is the purpose of the "flowchart?"

2-6. Draw a flowchart for the following problem. An input file contains sales data: salesman number and amount of sales for the week. For each record, calculate sales commission as follows:

AMOUNT OF SALES	COMMISSION RATE
up to $1,000.00	5.0%
$1,000.01 to $3,500.00	7.5%
over $3,500.00	8.5%

Multiply sales amount by the required commission rate and print sales, rate, and commission. At the end of the file terminate processing.

2-7. Code the job control for your installation for assembly, link-edit, and execution of an input program.

2-8. Code, assemble, and test a program that reads records and prints their contents.

You can define the print area as follows:

```
PRINT     DS     0CL133
          DC     CL20' '
RECOUT    DS     CL80
          DS     CL33' '
```

If you define the input record as RECDIN, then you can move the contents of each input record to the print area as follows:

```
MVC RECOUT,RECDIN
```

BASIC ASSEMBLER
CODING

3

PROGRAMMING FOR CHARACTER DATA

The chapter introduces character format in which data is normally read and printed. The first part describes the Assembler declaratives that define character fields: *areas* in storage to handle input and output records, and *constants* such as report headings. Because programs must manipulate data that is read or defined, the next sections cover the basic instructions to move and compare data. A sample program illustrates the use of these instructions and how they may be organized into a working program.

DECLARATIVES

Declaratives are instructions that the Assembler recognizes and assigns storage locations. They do not generate an executable instruction. Declaratives provide for the entry of data to the program in two ways:

1. The declarative *Define Storage (DS) defines areas* for the program to receive data that varies in content, such as an input area.
2. The declarative *Define Constant (DC) defines constants,* such as a title for a report heading, or the numeric value '1' to count the pages being printed, or an accumulator initially set to zero.

DEFINE STORAGE (DS). The DS statement reserves an area of storage, for example, to define areas for reading records and for printing. The general format of the DS statement on the coding sheet is:

NAME	OPERATION	OPERAND
(symbol)	DS	dTLn 'comments'

Optional: Symbol = the name assigned to the field. If the program needs to refer to the field by name, then assign a name in columns 1–8. The name refers to the first (leftmost) byte of the field. Chapter 1 gives the requirements of symbolic names.

Optional: d = duplication factor which tells the Assembler *how many* repetitions of the same area are required. If you omit the factor, the Assembler assumes one area. If 2 is specified, the Assembler creates two adjacent areas; the name (if any) refers to the first area.

Required: T = type of format, such as C for Character, or P for Packed.

Optional: Ln = length of the field in bytes (n), positive values only. For example, L3 designates a 3-byte field. If length and comments are omitted (such as DS C), the Assembler assumes a length of one byte. The maximum length of a character DS field is 65,535 bytes.

Optional: 'comments' = a description within apostrophes of the purpose of the field. If you omit the length (Ln), the Assembler assumes that the length is the number of bytes within the apostrophes. For example, DS C'LIZ' defines a 3-byte area, but containing no such value—the contents are still "garbage."

Figure 3-1 depicts various DS statements in character format. Note the headings on the Assembler listing:

```
   LOC   OBJECT CODE   STMT    SOURCE STATEMENT


Hex address of leftmost
  byte of defined field    5 *        ------------------------
                           6 *        DS    CHARACTER FORMAT
         |                 7 *        ------------------------
         ↓
   003600                  8 FIELDA   DS    1CL5            RESERVES 5 BYTES CALLED FIELDA

   003605                 10 FIELDB   DS    CL5             RESERVES 5 BYTES CALLED FIELDB

   00360A                 12          DS    CL10            RESERVES 10 BYTES

   003614                 14 INAREA   DS    CL80            RESERVES 80 BYTES FOR INPUT

   003664                 16          DS    80C             RESERVES 80 1-BYTE FIELDS

   0036B4                 18 FIELDS   DS    3CL5            RESERVES 3 5-BYTE FIELDS

   0036C3                 20 DATE     DS    CL8'DD/MM/YY'   RESERVES 8 BYTES. CONTENTS ARE
                          21 *                              DOCUMENTATION ONLY
```

FIGURE 3-1 Sample DS statements in character format.

SOURCE STATEMENT in the center lists the original source symbolic language code.

STMT, immediately to the left, gives the statement number of each source statement, as generated by the Assembler. FIELDA, for example, is statement-10. (Statement-11 is suppressed; it contains the directive SPACE that causes the Assembler to space one line.)

LOC at the far left is the contents of the location counter that lists the hexadecimal address location of each statement. FIELDA is a 5-byte field beginning in location X'003600'. FIELDB begins immediately following in X'003605'. The Assembler defines declaratives in the same sequence that they are coded, in locations directly one after the other.

OBJECT CODE lists the assembled machine code: object code instructions and the contents of DCs. A DS lists no object code because it merely reserves space.

ADDR1 and ADDR2 refer to instructions, not declaratives. Each declarative is explained next. Comments on the right of each statement describe the defined area.

Statement-8:	FIELDA is a 5-byte DS beginning in location X'003600'. The duplication factor 1 may be omitted, as shown in FIELDB.
Statement-10:	FIELDB at X'003605' immediately follows FIELDA.
Statement-12:	This DS is unnamed. Its address is X'360A' because FIELDB at X'3605' is five bytes: X'3605' + 5 = X'360A' (5 + 5 = 10 or A in hex).
Statement-14:	INAREA defines an 80-byte area to be used for input.
Statement-16:	Because there is no length (Ln), the Assembler assumes that each of the 80 fields is one byte.
Statement-18:	FIELDS defines three 5-byte fields. A reference to the name FIELDS is to the leftmost byte of the first 5-byte field.
Statement-20:	DATE illustrates the use of comments. The programmer expects to store the date in the field in the specified format.

There are three problems to resolve:

1. *Where in storage will a field reside?* The Assembler assigns a field's location and accounts for the length of every instruction, storage area, and constant. For this task it uses a *location counter* (see Chapter 1).

2. *How does the computer know where the field resides and how long its length is?* The Assembler translates the symbolic addresses into machine object addresses. If it has assigned, for example, FIELDA with the address X'3600' then any instruction's reference to FIELDA is to address X'3600'. For certain instructions, the Assembler stores the length of the field as part of the instruction.

3. *What are the contents of the field?* The contents of a DS field are unknown, because the Assembler merely reserves the defined area. At the start of program execution, a DS area may contain data from a previous program. Therefore, you may have to initialize DS fields with valid data. For example, if the print area is defined as a DS, clear it to blanks at the start of the program so that "garbage" is not printed along with valid data. The only purpose of DS is to define an area of storage with a specified length. The fact that the field's format is *defined* as character, packed, etc., is irrelevant, *because at execution-time the field may contain data in any format.* The defined format is merely a convenient reminder of what format you expect the field to contain. A major use of DS is to define input and output areas, covered next.

INPUT AREAS.   In order to define fields within a record, use a DS with a zero duplication factor, as DS 0CL80, and define the fields immediately following.

The set of DSs in Figure 3-2 fully defines the input area for a customer record. The DS defines RECDIN as an 80-byte record. However, because of the zero duplication factor in 0CL80, *the Assembler does not increment its location counter.* Consequently, the Assembler assigns the next field, CODEIN, with the *same location* as RECDIN, X'4201'. CODEIN, however, is a 2-byte field that increments the location counter. Although both RECDIN and CODEIN begin at X'4201', a reference to RECDIN is to an 80-byte field, whereas a reference to CODEIN is to a 2-byte field.

```
004201          27 RECDIN   DS   0CL80      80-BYTE INPUT AREA:
004201          28 CODEIN   DS   CL2        *   RECORD CODE
004203          29 ACCTIN   DS   CL3        *   ACCOUNT NUMBER
004206          30 NAMEIN   DS   CL13       *   NAME
004213          31 BALANIN  DS   CL7        *   BALANCE OWING
00421A          32          DS   CL55       *   REST OF RECORD (UNUSED)
```

FIGURE 3-2 Area defined for input record.

Each DS following RECDIN defines a field *within* the RECDIN area. In order to account for the full record length that reads into the program's storage area, the sum of their lengths should equal 80, the length of RECDIN. You may now refer to the entire 80-byte record or to any field defined within the record.

In the statement GET FILEIN,RECDIN, the GET macro reads an 80-byte record into an 80-byte area that the program defines as RECDIN. On input, column 1 of the record reads into the leftmost byte of RECDIN (location X'4201' on the assembled DS statement), column 2 reads into the next byte (X'4202'), and column 80 reads into the 80th byte (X'4250').

Note: A read operation enters all bytes, even if the input record contains blanks; all blanks enter storage as X'40' in your record area. Also, a read operation erases the previous contents of the input area.

OUTPUT AREAS.   Whereas a read operation erases the previous contents of the input area, a write operation leaves the contents of the output area unchanged. Therefore, if a DS defines the output area, ensure that the storage positions do not contain "garbage" from the previous program. At the beginning of the program, clear the output area to blanks (X'40'). An alternative solution is to use Define Constant (DC) to define the output area with an initial constant containing blanks. It is also often necessary to clear the print area after writing a line, so that it is blank for the next line to be printed.

Although the number of print positions varies with the printer used, a common requirement is to define a 133-byte print area as:

```
PRINT  DS  CL133        or
PRINT  DC  CL133' '
```

The 370-series computers use the leftmost byte of PRINT for a printer *forms control character*. This character controls forms movement, such as print and space one line, or skip to a new page. You may use the other 132 positions to store data to be printed. Chapter 2 gives the requirements for the print macro, PUTPR.

You may also define the print area with a zero duplication factor, as PRINT DS 0CL133, with a DS to define each field within the record. Alternatively, you may reference PRINT by *relative addressing*. (It is possible to reference any field in main storage by relative addressing, or to define it with a zero duplication factor and redefine the fields within it.) Since the leftmost byte (the position labeled PRINT) is reserved for the control character, you may refer to the first printable position as PRINT + 1, to the second as PRINT + 2, etc.:

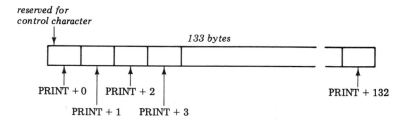

DEFINE CONSTANT (DC).   The DC statement, like DS, reserves storage of a defined length. In addition, DC defines a constant (or value) such as a heading to be printed on a report. A DC may define a constant in any format, such as Character, Binary, Packed, and Hexadecimal, and in various lengths. The general format for a DC statement is as follows:

NAME	*OPERATION*	*OPERAND*
(symbol)	DC	dTLn 'constant'

Optional: Symbol = the name that you may assign to the field.

Optional: d = duplication factor which tells the Assembler *how many* repetitions of the constant are required. The symbolic name (if any) refers to the first constant. If you omit the factor the Assembler assumes one constant.

Required: T = type of format, such as C for Character, P for Packed, X for Hexadecimal, Z for Zoned, etc.

Optional: Ln = length of the field in number (n) of bytes. If Ln is omitted the Assembler assumes the field length to be the number of bytes defined by the constant.

Required: 'constant' = the constant that is to be defined, contained within apostrophes. A DS 'constant' is for documentation; a DC 'constant' is stored.

The following are rules regarding *Character* constants:

1. Their length may be defined from one to 256 characters.
2. They may contain any character that may be keyed or printed, including blanks.
3. If the length (Ln) is not coded, the Assembler assumes that the field length is that of the defined constant. Thus, DC C'SAM' defines a 3-character constant.
4. If the length (Ln) is specified, then the following may occur:

   a. The defined length *equals* the length of the constant:

   ```
   FIELDA DC CL5'APRIL'
   ```

   The length of FIELDA is 5 bytes. The Assembler generates APRIL.

   b. The defined length is *less than* the length of the constant:

   ```
   FIELDB DC CL4'APRIL'
   ```

   The defined length, 4, overrides the length of the constant. The length of FIELDB will be *four* bytes. The Assembler *left-adjusts the constant and truncates rightmost characters* that exceed the defined length. APRI is generated.

   c. The defined length is *greater* than the length of the constant.

   ```
   FIELDC DC CL6'APRIL
   ```

The length of FIELDC will be *six* bytes. The Assembler left-adjusts the constant and *pads rightmost bytes with blanks.* APRIL followed by one blank is generated.

5. The apostrophe (') and the ampersand (&) have special meaning to the Assembler. If you define them within a constant, code them as two adjacent characters, although the Assembler counts and prints only one.

Figure 3-3 provides various character DCs with explanations. On the Assembler listing note the OBJECT CODE generated by each statement. LOC gives the hex address of the first byte of each constant. Under OBJECT CODE is the hex contents up to the first eight bytes (16 hex digits) of the constant. (The entire hex contents for constants exceeding eight bytes can be printed by means of the Assembler instruction PRINT DATA.)

The first pair of DCs defines fields containing blanks, or X'40' in object code.

- BLANK1 generates a 5-byte field containing five blanks. Its location is X'004301'. Under OBJECT CODE are the five bytes of blanks (X'40's).
- BLANK2 defines five 1-byte blank fields; its implicit length is therefore one.

The next section defines fields with zero values.

- ZERO1 generates a 5-byte field containing five zeros. Note that a character zero is X'F0.
- ZERO2 is a 5-byte field as well. But because only one zero is specified, the Assembler left-adjusts the zero and fills the remaining bytes with blanks, a common coding error.
- ZERO3 generates five 1-byte fields, each containing a zero.

The third section defines numeric values.

- FIVEA and FIVEB show two ways to define a 1-byte field containing the value 5 (X'F5').
- FIVEC generates 05, or X'F0F5'.

The fourth section defines alphabetic fields.

- AMT generates a field with a dollar sign (X'5B'), a comma (X'6B'), and a decimal point (X'4B').
- PADBLANK left-adjusts the constant and pads two blanks to the right.
- AMPERSND illustrates the use of the ampersand (&) and apostrophe ('), both of which must be defined twice. The generated constant in this case

```
LOC    OBJECT CODE        STMT  SOURCE STATEMENT                              CONSTANT GENERATED:
                                 -------------------------                    -------------------------
                           38 *  DC      CHARACTER FORMAT
                           39 *  -------------------------
                           40 *
                           41 *
                           42 *          DEFINE BLANKS:
004301 4040404040         43 BLANK1   DC  CL5' '                             '     ' ( 5 BLANKS )
004306 4040404040         44 BLANK2   DC  5CL1' '                            5 1-BYTE BLANKS
                           46 *          DEFINE ZEROS:
00430B F0F0F0F0F0         47 ZERO1    DC  C'00000'                           '00000'
004310 F04040404040       48 ZERO2    DC  CL5'0'                             '0'
004315 F0F0F0F0F0         49 ZERO3    DC  5C'0'                              '0','0','0','0','0'
                           51 *          DEFINE NUMBERS:
00431A F5                 52 FIVEA    DC  CL1'5'                             '5'
00431B F5                 53 FIVEB    DC  C'5'                               '5'
00431C F0F5               54 FIVEC    DC  C'05'                              '05'
                           56 *          DEFINE ALPHABETIC:
00431E 5BF16BF0F0F04BF0   57 AMT      DC  C'$1,000.00'                       '$1,000.00'
004327 C1C2C3C44040       58 PADBLANK DC  CL6'ABCD'                          'ABCD '
00432D 40D1D6C5405040C6   59 AMPERSND DC  C' JOE && FLO''S '                 ' JOE & FLO'S '
00433A C1C2C1C2           60 TRUNCATE DC  2CL2'ABCD'                         2 CONSTANTS = 'AB','AB'
00433E F0F7D1E4D3E8       61 JULY     DC  C'07',C'JULY'                      2 CONSTANTS = '07','JULY'
004344 404040C94DD540E3   62 TITLE    DC  C'INTERNATIONAL BUSINESS MAC+      'INTERNATIONAL BUSINESS MAC+
                                           HINES'                                  continuation
                           64 *          DEFINE ERRORS:
                           65 ERRORA   DC  CL3                               MISSING 'CONSTANT'
          *** ERROR ***
                           66 ERRORB   DC  ' '                               MISSING FORMAT
          *** ERROR ***
                           67 ERRORC   DC  CL'123'                           MISSING LENGTH N
          *** ERROR ***
                           68 ERRORD   DC  CL300' '                          LENGTH EXCEEDS 256 BYTES
          *** ERROR ***
```

DIAGNOSTICS AND STATISTICS

```
STMNT  ERROR NO.   MESSAGE
  65   IPK128      CONSTANT FIELD MISSING OR PRECEDED BY INVALID FIELD, ' '
  66   IPK123      INVALID TYPE SPECIFICATION, ' ',' '
  67   IPK129      INVALID DUPLICATION FACTOR OR MODIFIER, ''123''
  68   IPK140      INVALID LENGTH MODIFIER
```

FIGURE 3-3 Sample DC statements in character format.

is 13 bytes long, although the Assembler prints only the first eight bytes under OBJECT CODE.

- TRUNCATE defines two constants, each two bytes long. The Assembler truncates the constant ABCD on the right to two bytes (because we coded L2) and generates AB twice (see the hex object code).
- JULY shows one statement that defines two character constants, separated by a comma. A reference to the name JULY is to the first 2-byte field. (This feature, providing for definition of more than one constant with one DC, is not available in every level of Assembler.)

TITLE illustrates the continuation character, in this case a plus sign (+) in column 72. The constant continues on the next line in column 16. (Even though there is an Assembler directive TITLE, you can use TITLE for the name of a field.)

The last section defines some common coding errors. The comments on the right explain the cause of the error. The Assembler prints ERROR instead of the object code, and explains the cause at the end of the program listing. Any instruction in the program that references one of these invalid constants also causes an error message for that instruction.

INTERNAL REPRESENTATION. Let's examine the contents of data in storage. Assume the following hex contents of three fields:

F0F1F2F3E9D6D6C3D3C3

Before looking ahead for the solution, try to answer the following questions. (a) The length of each field is respectively four, three, and three bytes. What are the character contents of each field? (b) The address of the leftmost byte is X'80046'. What are the hex addresses of the second and third fields? Solution. (a) The character representation is 0123 ZOO CLC. (b) The two addresses are X'8004A' and X'8004D'.

- *Problems 3-1 and 3-2 should now be attempted.* •

CHARACTER INSTRUCTIONS

This section covers the movement and comparison of fields in character format. The content of these fields is made available to the program from an input record or declared as a constant value. There are two instruction formats that process data in main storage: Storage-to-Storage (SS) and Storage Immediate (SI). SS format processes data between two fields in main storage, whereas SI format processes between a one-byte constant built into the instruction and one main storage location.

STORAGE-TO-STORAGE FORMAT

Some instructions reference data in main storage only, others process data between main storage and the registers, and others process in registers only. Storage-to-storage (SS) format references only storage locations. In an instruction like MVC (Move Character), the operands are represented as S1,S2 meaning that both operand-1 (S1) and operand-2 (S2) reference main storage. Another representation in symbolic form is:

```
MVC D1(L,B1),D2(B2)
```

D1(L,B1) means that the operand-1 address consists of a base register (B1) and a displacement (D1).

L means that the length of operand-1 controls the number of bytes processed.

D2(B2) means that the operand-2 address consists of a base register (B2) and a displacement (D2).

This feature may be ignored for now; Chapter 6 describes it in detail.

MOVE CHARACTERS—MVC

Frequently a program must move the contents of one field to another. Fields in the input area must be moved to other areas in order to save them from erasure by the next record that the program reads. Also, constants, headings, and calculated values must be moved to the print area for printing. The following instructions move character fields, bytes, and half-bytes from one storage location to another: Move Character (MVC), Move Numerics (MVN), Move Zones (MVZ), Move Immediate (MVI), and Move With Offset (MVO). This chapter describes MVC and MVI. Although MVC may move data in any format, its use is normally confined to character fields.

NAME	OPERATION	OPERAND
(symbol)	MVC	S1,S2 or D1(L,B1),D2(B2)

MVC is a Storage-to-Storage (SS) instruction. Its rules are:

1. MVC may move from one to 256 bytes, usually character data, but technically any format.
2. Data beginning in the byte specified by operand-2 is moved one byte at a time to the field beginning with the byte specified by operand-1. The move does not affect the contents of the operand-2 field; the bytes

are *copied* into the operand-1 field. Thus, the instruction MVC FLDA,FLDB copies the contents of FLDB into FLDA.

3. Each operand specifies the *leftmost* byte of the field, and *movement is from left to right.*

4. *The length of the operand-1 field determines the number of bytes moved.* In the MVC instruction format there is a length code (L) for operand-1 only. The length of operand-2 is irrelevant to the operation. If the operand-1 field is five bytes long and operand-2 is six bytes, MVC moves only the first five bytes of operand-2 (from left to right one byte at a time) to the operand-1 field. If the operand-1 field is six bytes and operand-2 is five, MVC moves all five bytes of operand-2, plus one byte immediately to its right.

FIELD LENGTH. You may specify the number of bytes to be moved in one of two ways: *implicit or explicit length.* Assume the following DCs:

NAME	OPERATION	OPERAND
FIELD1	DC	C'JUNE'
FIELD2	DC	C'APRIL'

IMPLICIT LENGTH:

```
      MVC  FIELD1,FIELD2.
```

Operand-1, FIELD1, is implicitly defined above as a 4-byte constant. Since the Assembler recognizes that a reference to FIELD1 is to a 4-byte field, the MVC moves only the first four bytes of FIELD2, APRI. The contents of FIELD2 are unaffected.

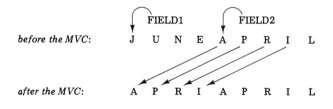

EXPLICIT LENGTH:

```
      MVC  FIELD1(3),FIELD2.
```

Assume the same DCs as before. Operand-1 has an explicit length (3) that overrides the defined length of FIELD1. Therefore, MVC moves only the first three bytes of FIELD2 (APR) into the first three bytes of FIELD1. The fourth byte of FIELD1 is unaltered:

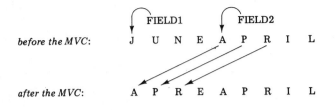

EXPLICIT LENGTH:

MVC FIELD1(5),FIELD2

moves 5 bytes. APRI is moved into FIELD1. The "L" is moved into the next byte to the right, the first byte of FIELD2, which in this example immediately follows FIELD1:

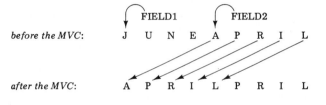

RELATIVE ADDRESSING. Any operand that references main storage may use relative addressing. If you have to refer to a byte that has no name, you may refer to its position relative to a byte that has a name. For example, suppose you want to move the third and fourth bytes of FIELD2 to the second and third bytes of FIELD1 using the following MVC instruction:

MVC FIELD1+1(2),FIELD2+2

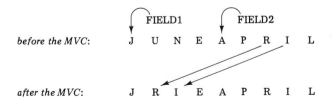

Note: In order to move two bytes, code an explicit length (2) in operand-1. A relative address of +1 refers to the second byte, and +2 refers to the third byte.

SYMBOL LENGTH ATTRIBUTE. The Assembler permits explicit lengths coded *absolutely,* as was described, and *symbolically:*

absolute explicit length:	MVC FIELD1(5),FIELD2
symbolic explicit length:	MVC FIELD1(L'FIELD2),FIELD2

The symbol length attribute uses L' followed by a symbolic name. In this example, we want to move five bytes. Since the length of FIELD2 is five, the Assembler understands the explicit length to be 5.

Figure 3-4 depicts unrelated MVC operations. Note the OBJECT CODE generated for each statement. The Assembler lists under ADDR1 and ADDR2 the addresses of operand-1 and operand-2 respectively. For example, statement-17 is MVC X,Y. The address of X, a 3-byte field, is 03002 and the address of Y, a 5-byte field, is 03005. The instruction may be read as: Move the first three bytes of Y, starting in location 03005, to the field called X, starting in location 03002. The object code instruction is six bytes long, beginning in location 003012. Chapter 6 gives the interpretation of this machine language. These examples illustrate some extreme cases, and although important to understand, most data movement is directly from one field to another defined with the same length.

> *Note instruction alignment:* All the MVCs begin on an even storage location, as shown under LOC (location): X'003012', X'003018', etc.

MOVE1: Operand-1, X, is shorter than operand-2, Y. The implicit length (3) of X governs the number of bytes moved.

MOVE2: Operand-1, Z, is longer than operand-2, X. The implicit length (8) of Z governs the number of bytes moved.

MOVE3: The explicit length (3) overrides Z's implicit length of 8; only 3 bytes are moved. With symbol length attribute, the statement could be: MVC Z(L'X),X.

MOVE4 and MOVE5 illustrate explicit length and relative addressing. In each case the explicit length overrides the defined implicit length.

MOVE6 shows how to copy a character a specified number of positions to the right. The leftmost byte of X contains 'A', which MVC copies four bytes to the right. It is possible to propagate any character in this fashion because MVC moves one character at a time, from left to right. This technique is useful for example to clear areas to blanks.

MOVE7 shifts data one byte to the left. It may be useful to check the operation by following the data movement one byte at a time.

MOVE8: We want to move three bytes, but have erroneously coded an explicit length of 3 in operand-2 instead of operand-1. The Assembler generates six bytes of hex zeros as the object code "instruction." These will

```
LOC     OBJECT CODE              ADDR1 ADDR2   STMT   SOURCE STATEMENT

                                                      6  *
                                                      7  ***    MVC  MOVE CHARACTERS
                                                      8  *

003002 C1C2C3                                        10 X    DC  C'ABC'        THESE FIELDS
003005 C4C5C6C7C8                                    11 Y    DC  C'DEFGH'      ARE ADJACENT
00300A C9D1D2D3D4D5D6D7                              12 Z    DC  C'IJKLMNOP'   IN STORAGE

                                                     14 *
                                                     15 *                      ACTION OF MOVE:            RESULT OF MOVE:

003012 D202 4000 4003  03002 03005                  17 MOVE1  MVC  X,Y         1ST 3 BYTES OF Y INTO     X= 'DEF'        +
                                                                               1ST 3 BYTES OF X
003018 D207 4008 4000  0300A 03002                  18 MOVE2  MVC  Z,X         ALL BYTES OF X &          Z= 'ABCDEFGH'   +
                                                                               Y INTO Z
00301E D202 4008 4000  0300A 03002                  19 MOVE3  MVC  Z(3),X      1ST 3 BYTES OF X INTO     Z= 'ABCLMNOP'   +
                                                                               1ST 3 BYTES OF Z
003024 D202 400A 4000  0300C 03002                  20 MOVE4  MVC  Z+2(L'X),X  3 BYTES OF X INTO         Z= 'IJABCNOP'   +
                                                                               BYTES 3-5 OF Z
00302A D201 400B 4002  0300D 03004                  21 MOVE5  MVC  Z+3(2),X+2  3RD BYTE OF X & 1ST       Z= 'IJKCDNOP'   +
                                                                               BYTE OF Y INTO Z
003030 D203 4001 4000  03003 03002                  22 MOVE6  MVC  X+1(4),X    X TO X+1, X+1 TO X+2, X+2 X= 'AAA'        +
                                                                               TO Y, & Y TO Y+1          Y= 'AAFGH'      +
003036 D202 4000 4001  03002 03003                  23 MOVE7  MVC  X,X+1       LEFT SHIFT. MOVES X+1 TO X, X= 'ECD'      +
                                                                               X+2 TO X+1, Y TO X+2
00303C 0000 0000 0000                               24 MOVE8  MVC  Z,X(3)      MVC DOES NOT PERMIT EXPLICIT LENGTH IN    +
                                                                               OPERAND-2

*** ERROR ***
```

FIGURE 3-4 Sample unrelated MVC operations.

cause a "program interrupt" if the program is executed. MOVE3 shows the instruction correctly written.

For illustrative purposes, this text uses examples with declaratives named as X, Y, and Z, but does not advocate such cryptic names in programs.

• *Problem 3-3 should now be attempted.* •

DUPLICATING CHARACTERS

This section describes how you can duplicate any character or group of characters through a field. Assume the following two declaratives defined below respectively at locations 5800 and 5801:

```
5800    ASTER    DC    C'*'
5801    FIELD    DC    CL3'
```

In order to duplicate the contents of ASTER through the following three bytes of FIELD, code the following instruction:

```
MVC FIELD,ASTER
```

An MVC moves one byte at a time from left to right. Initially, operand-1 references 5801 and operand-2 references 5800. The length of the move is three bytes, which is stored in machine code as one less, that is, 2. The MVC works as follows:

1. Copies the contents of ASTER at 5800 into the first byte of FIELD at 5801:

```
*   *   b   b
|   |
5800  5801
```

Since the length is not equal to zero, the operation deducts 1 from the length (it is now 1), and increments the operand-1 address to 5802 and the operand-2 address to 5801.

2. Copies the contents of 5801 into 5802:

```
*   *   *   b
|   |
5801  5802
```

Since the length is not equal to zero, the operation deducts 1 from the length (now 0), and increments the operand-1 address to 5803 and the operand-2 address to 5802.

3.   Copies the contents of 5802 into 5803:

```
            *   *   *   *
                    |  |
                5802  5803
```

Since the length is now zero, the operation terminates.

The MVC has now propagated the one byte ASTER through the 3-byte contents of FIELD. Now, suppose you want to repeat two characters ('/-') across a line that is to display on a video screen. The following provides the code:

```
STRING   DC    C'/-'
DISPLAY  DS    CL80
         . . .
         MVC   DISPLAY,STRING
```

The first step of the MVC moves the first '/' character to DISPLAY and the first '-' to DISPLAY+1. The operation continues copying these characters across the entire 80 bytes from DISPLAY to DISPLAY+2, DISPLAY+1 to DISPLAY+3, up to DISPLAY+77 to DISPLAY+79.

In this fashion, you can copy any character or string of characters through any number of bytes. One common application is the clearing of a print area to blank. The only requirement is that the character(s) to be copied must immediately precede the receiving field.

SAMPLE PROGRAM: PROCESS INVENTORY RECORDS

The program in Figure 3-5 provides more examples of declaratives and move operations. Input records for inventory parts consist of the following fields:

```
Column:
  1-5       Part number
  6-20      Part description
  21-24     Quantity-on-hand
```

Input data is the following:

```
Part#  Description        Quantity
  |       |                  |
  10436TERMINALS           0023
  10927MODEMS              0120
  24322REGULATORS          0152
  33569MICROPROCESSORS0022
```

```
LOC    OBJECT CODE      ADDR1 ADDR2  STMT   SOURCE STATEMENT

                                      3            PRINT  ON,NODATA,NOGEN

                                      5  *                   I N I T I A L I Z A T I O N
                                      6  *                   ---------------------------
000000                                8  PROG03   START
                                      9           INIT                        INITIALIZE
                                     15           OPEN   FILEIN,PRINTER       OPEN FILES

                                     25           PUTPR  PRINTER,PRHEAD,SK1   SKIP TO NEW PAGE
                                     32           PUTPR  PRINTER,PRHEAD,WSP2  PRINT HEADING
                                     39           GET    FILEIN,RECORDIN      READ 1ST RECORD

                                     46  *                   R E A D   &   P R I N T   R O U T I N E
                                     47  *                   -------------------------------------
00005A D204 33AF 32D0 003B1 002D2    49  A10LOOP  MVC    PARTPR,PARTIN        MOVE PART NO.,
000060 D20E 33B9 32D5 003BB 002D7    50           MVC    DESCPR,DESCIN        *  DESCRIPTION
000066 D203 33CD 32E4 003CF 002E6    51           MVC    QTYPR,QTYIN          *  QUANTITY
                                     52           PUTPR  PRINTER,PRLINE,WSP1  PRINT
                                     59           GET    FILEIN,RECORDIN      READ NEXT RECORD
000090 47F0 3058      0005A          65           B      A10LOOP             LOOP

                                     67  *                   E N D - O F - F I L E   R O U T I N E
                                     68  *                   -------------------------------------
                                     70  A90EOF   PUTPR  PRINTER,PRHEAD,SK1   SKIP PAGE
                                     77           CLOSE  FILEIN,PRINTER       CLOSE FILES
                                     86           EOJ    ,                    TERMINATE JOB

                                     90  *                   D E C L A R A T I V E S
                                     91  *                   -----------------------

                                     93  FILEIN   DEFIN  A90EOF              DEFINE INPUT FILE
                                    117  PRINTER  DEFPR                      DEFINE PRINTER

0002D2                              142  RECORDIN DS     0CL80               INPUT RECORD:
0002D2                              143  PARTIN   DS     CL05                *  PART #
0002D7                              144  DESCIN   DS     CL15                *  DESCRIPTION
0002E6                              145  QTYIN    DS     CL04                *  QUANTITY
0002EA                              146           DS     CL56                *  UNUSED

000322                              148  PRHEAD   DS     0CL133              HEADING LINE:
000322 4040404040404040             149           DC     CL10' '             *
00032C D3C9E2E340D6C640             150           DC     CL123'LIST OF PARTS FOR ACE ELECTRONICS'

0003A7                              152  PRLINE   DS     0CL133              PRINT AREA:
0003A7 4040404040404040             153           DC     CL10' '             *
0003B1                              154  PARTPR   DS     CL05                *  PART #
0003B6 4040404040                   155           DC     CL05' '             *
0003BB                              156  DESCPR   DS     CL15                *  DESCRIPTION
0003CA 4040404040                   157           DC     CL05' '             *
0003CF                              158  QTYPR    DS     CL04                *  QUANTITY
0003D3 4040404040404040             159           DC     CL89' '
```

FIGURE 3-5 (partial)

```
 LOC   OBJECT CODE      ADDR1 ADDR2  STMT    SOURCE STATEMENT

000430                                161      LTORG  ,                          GEN'D LITERALS
000430  5B5BC2D6D7C5D540              162             =C'$$BOPEN '
000438  5B5RC2C3D3D6E2C5              163             =C'$$CLOSE'
000440  00060178                      164             =A(PRINTER)
000444  00000322                      165             =A(PRHEAD)
000448  000000C0                      166             =A(FILEIN)
00044C  000002D2                      167             =A(RECORDIN)
000450  000003A7                      168             =A(PRLINE)
                                      .
                         00000       170      END     PROG03                    END OF ASSEMBLY
```

Output:-

```
┌─────────────────────────────────────────────────┐
│   LIST OF PARTS FOR ACE ELECTRONICS              │
│                                                  │
│   10436      TERMINALS           0023            │
│   10927      MODEMS              0120            │
│   24322      REGULATORS          0152            │
│   33569      MICROPROCESSORS     0022            │
│                                                  │
└─────────────────────────────────────────────────┘
```

FIGURE 3-5 Processing inventory records.

At the start, the program prints a heading to identify each printed field for the input records. The program moves the input fields to predefined fields in the output area for printing. In the print line, the fields are spaced apart for better readability, as follows:

```
          PART NO.      DESCRIPTION                  QTY
            XXXXX       X ------------- X            XXXX
              |         |                              |
        Column 10       20                            40
```

COMPARE LOGICAL CHARACTER—CLC

It is often necessary to determine if the contents of one field are equal to, greater than, or less than, the contents of another field. Examples of the need to compare character fields include:

1. Testing for valid codes;
2. Checking for valid dates on records;
3. Testing for ascending sequence of account numbers in an input file. In this test, sequence-checking, the new account number just read is compared to the previously processed account number.

The instructions to compare character fields are Compare Logical Characters (CLC), and Compare Logical Immediate (CLI). All compare instructions and certain others set the *condition code* described in Chapter 2. As a result of the operation, the condition code is set as high, low, or equal, and may be interrogated with a *conditional branch* instruction. CLC may compare data in any format, but you normally confine its use to comparing character fields.

NAME	OPERATION	OPERAND
(symbol)	CLC	S1,S2 or D1(L,B1),D2(B2)

The rules for CLC are:

1. CLC may compare fields from one to 256 bytes long.
2. CLC compares data beginning in the byte specified by operand-1 to the data beginning with the byte specified by operand-2. Comparison is left to right, one byte at a time. The condition code is set as follows:

COMPARISON	CONDITION CODE SETTING
Operand-1 equals operand-2	0 (equal)
Operand-1 is lower	1 (low)
Operand-1 is higher	2 (high)

3. CLC terrminates comparison as soon as an unequal condition is encountered, or if none, by the length of operand-1 (explicit or implicit).

Comparison is based on the binary contents of the bytes, and all possible bytes are valid. The lowest value is binary zeros (X'00'), and the highest is binary ones (X'FF'). A "character" field contains what is called "logical" data —unsigned, nonarithmetic data. CLC is not suitable to compare arithmetic data in packed or binary format. For compares that consider a plus or minus sign, use CP for packed data, and C, CH, or CR for binary. Another logical compare operation, CLCL (Compare Logical Long), has rather restricted use.

Carefully examine the examples of CLC instructions in Figure 3-6.

```
LOC     OBJECT CODE         ADDR1 ADDR2   STMT   SOURCE STATEMENT

                                          28  *        ------------------------------
                                          29  ***      CLC  COMPARE LOGICAL CHARACTER
                                          30  **       ------------------------------
003042  C1C2C3C4C5                        31  FIELD1   DC    C'ABCDE'          THESE FIELDS
003047  C6C7C8                            32  FIELD2   DC    C'FGH'            ARE ADJACENT
00304A  5C5C                              33  FIELD3   DC    C'**'            IN STORAGE

                                          35  *                              DATA COMPARED:    COND'N CODE:
                                          36  *                              -----------------  ------------
003042  D502 4045 4040  03047 03042       37  COMP1    CLC   FIELD2,FIELD1         'FGH'  >  'ABC'     HIGH
003052  D504 4040 4045  03042 03047       38  COMP2    CLC   FIELD1,FIELD2         'ABCDE' < 'FGH**'   LOW
003058  D502 4042 4045  03044 03047       39  COMP3    CLC   FIELD1+2(3),FIELD2    'CDE'  <  'FGH'     LOW
00305E  D504 4042 4045  03044 03047       40  COMP4    CLC   FIELD1+2,FIELD2       'CDEFG' < 'FGH**'   LOW
003064  D501 4048 4040  0304A 03042       41  COMP5    CLC   FIELD3,FIELD1         '**'  <  'AB'       LOW
00306A  0000 0000 0000                    42  COMP6    CLC   FIELD2,FIELD1+2(3)    CLC DOES NOT PERMIT EXPLICIT
                                                                                     LENGTH IN OPERAND-2

        *** ERROR ***
```

FIGURE 3-6 Sample unrelated CLC operations.

COMP1: The operand-1 field, FIELD2, is shorter. CLC compares the three bytes of FIELD2 against the first three bytes only of FIELD1. Because the data in FIELD2 is logically greater than that of FIELD1, the condition code is set to high.

COMP2: The operand-1 field is longer. CLC compares the five bytes of FIELD1 against the three bytes of FIELD2 plus the next rightmost two bytes of FIELD3 (two asterisks). Operand-1 is lower.

COMP3: Operand-1 uses relative addressing and explicit length. CLC compares bytes 3, 4 and 5 of FIELD1 against FIELD2.

COMP4: The instruction is similar to COMP3, with the explicit length omitted. The implicit length of operand-1 is therefore 5.

COMP5: An asterisk (X'5C') is lower than character 'A' (X'C1'), so the operation terminates as "low" after comparing only the first byte.

COMP6 illustrates erroneous use of explicit length in operand-2; omitting the length corrects the error.

You can minimize program bugs by ensuring that you compare fields that are defined the same length, and avoid where possible the use of relative addressing.

BRANCHING. CLC makes a comparison and sets the condition code. To test the condition code to determine what action to take (for example, was the result of the test high, low, or equal?) use the following conditional branch instructions:

CONDITION CODE	CONDITIONAL BRANCHES	
0 = Equal/zero	BE (Branch equal)	BNE (Branch not equal)
1 = Low/minus	BL (Branch low)	BNL (Branch not low)
2 = High/plus	BH (Branch high)	BNH (Branch not high)

Each of the preceding conditional branch instructions is called an "extended mnemonic," and is a unique use of the Branch on Condition (BC) instruction, explained in detail in Chapter 6.

With normal processing, the computer executes instructions in storage, one after another. Conditional branch instructions permit the program to 'branch' to different addresses in the program. You may therefore code your program to test, for example, for valid record codes. If a record does not contain the correct code in a specified column, you may branch to an error routine that prints a warning message.

Example: Compare and conditional branch.

NEW	DS	CL4	Contains the value of the account just read (assume '1347').
PREV	DS	CL4	Contains the value of the previous account read (assume '1208').
	CLC	NEW,PREV	Compare the contents of NEW to PREV.
	BH	R20HIGH	If NEW is higher, branch to R20HIGH (some address of a routine in the program).

Interpret the preceding instructions as follows: Compare the new account (containing 1347) to the previously read account (1208). NEW's contents being higher than PREV, the condition code is set to high (2). Next, BH tests if the high condition is set. Because the code is 'high', the program branches to R20HIGH. If the code was not 'high,' the computer would execute the next sequential instruction (NSI) following the BH.

Two other branch instructions are Unconditional Branch (B), and No-operation (NOP). The unconditional branch tests if any condition (high, low, equal) exists. Since there is always at least one condition, use B if a branch is always required. For example, after processing an input record, you may return to process the next record by means of an unconditional branch:

A10LOOP	.		
	.		Process the record
	.		
	GET	RECDIN	Read the next record
	B	A10LOOP	Branch to process record

NOP, which tests no condition, has specialized uses. You could use one or more NOP instructions where you later expect to insert different machine code.

COMPARE AND BRANCH.   The following examples illustrate the preceding discussion. Assume the declaratives X, Y, and Z contain data and are each defined as DS CL4:

Example 1:   If X is greater than or equal to Y, branch to J10HIEQ (an address elsewhere in the program).

CLC	X,Y	Compare contents of X to Y
BH	J10HIEQ	Branch if high
BE	J10HIEQ	Branch if equal

This example could also be coded more efficiently as:

CLC	X,Y	Compare contents of X to Y
BNL	J10HIEQ	Branch if X is not lower (high or equal)

Example 2: If X is greater than Z, branch to J20HI. Else, if Z does not equal Y, branch to J30NEQ.

```
CLC   X,Z        Compare X to Z
BH    J20HI      Branch if high
CLC   Z,Y        Compare Z to Y
BNE   J30NEQ     Branch if unequal
```

• *Problem 3-4 should now be attempted.* •

STORAGE IMMEDIATE FORMAT

Storage-to-Storage (SS) format references two fields in main storage, whereas the Storage-Immediate (SI) format references only one field. The other data used is a 1-byte constant, built into the instruction itself. The Assembler stores the immediate constant in the second byte of the object code instruction. The constant is therefore part of the object instruction.

MOVE IMMEDIATE (MVI) AND COMPARE LOGICAL IMMEDIATE (CLI). The immediate instructions Move Immediate (MVI) and Compare Logical Immediate (CLI) are efficient instructions to move or compare 1-byte fields.

NAME	*OPERATION*	*OPERAND*
(symbol)	MVI	S1,I2 or D1(B1),I2
(symbol)	CLI	S1,I2 or D1(B1),I2

The rules for MVI and CLI are similar to those for MVC and CLC, with the following exceptions:

1. Operand-1 references a single main storage location. The operand does not permit an explicit length code because the number of bytes is always one.
2. Operand-2 contains a 1-byte immediate constant. The immediate constant value may be character (C), hexadecimal (X), binary (B), or a decimal digit, but *not* zoned (Z) or packed (P).

Figure 3-7 depicts some typical uses of immediate operations.

```
003070 F0F0F0        46 SAVE    DC    C'000'              SAVE= |F0|F0|F0|
003073 F5            47 CODEIN  DC    C'5'

                     49 *       ---------------------------------
                     50 ***     MVI   MOVE IMMEDIATE
             MVI $   51 *       ---------------------------------
003074 925B 406E     52 MOVIMM1 MVI   SAVE,C'$'           SAVE= |5B|F0|F0|
003078 925B 406E 03070   53 MOVIMM2 MVI   SAVE,X'5B'          X'5B' IS IDENTICAL TO C'$'
00307C 0000 0000 03070   54 MOVIMM3 MVI   SAVE(1),C'?'        ERROR IF LENGTH IN OPERAND-1
       *** ERROR ***
003080 0000 0000     55 MOVIMM4 MVI   SAVE+1,=C'$'        ERROR: CANNOT USE LITERALS
       *** ERROR ***

                     57 *       ---------------------------------
                     58 ***     CLI   COMPARE LOGICAL IMMEDIATE
             CLI 5   59 *       ---------------------------------
003084 95F5 4071     60 COMIMM1 CLI   CODEIN,C'5'         SETS CONDITION CODE EQUAL.
003088 0000 0000 03073   61 COMIMM2 CLI   CODEIN(1),C'5'     ERROR IF LENGTH IN OPERAND-1
       *** ERROR ***
00308C 0000 0000     62 COMIMM3 CLI   CODEIN,P'5'         ERROR IF PACK OR ZONED IMMEDIATE
       *** ERROR ***


                        DIAGNOSTICS AND STATISTICS

STMNT ERROR NO.   MESSAGE

  54  IPK173      DISPLACEMENT VALUE IN OPERAND 1 NOT ABSOLUTE
  55  IPK131      ILLEGAL USE OF LITERAL
  61  IPK173      DISPLACEMENT VALUE IN OPERAND 1 NOT ABSOLUTE
  62  IPK116      INVALID SELF-DEFINING TERM, 'P'5''
```

FIGURE 3-7 Sample unrelated MVI and CLI operations.

MOVIMM1 moves a 1-byte dollar sign defined in character format.

MOVIMM2 shows a hexadecimal dollar defined. Both statements generate identical object code, although C'$' provides better clarity to users. Note the object code for MOVIMM1 begins at 003074 and contains 925B406E: The machine code for MVI is hex 92, and the dollar sign, X'5B', is in the next (second) byte.

COMIMM1 compares the contents of a 1-byte field, CODEIN, to an immediate operand. Because both contain the character value '5', the condition code is set to equal.

MOVIMM3, MOVIMM4, COMIMM2, and COMIMM3 illustrate common coding errors that the Assembler recognizes. MOVIMM4 incorrectly uses a "literal." Literals are covered in the next section.

LOGIC EXAMPLE

Assume that employee records contain (among other fields) the following data: employee number, employee name, monthly salary, male/female code, and department code. A program is to read each record from the file and display these fields if the following conditions are all true: (a) monthly salary is greater than \$2,000.00, (b) the employee is female (F), and (c) she is employed in department 27.

The following skeleton code shows the logic:

```
EMPREC      DS      0CL100                  Employee record:
EMPNO       DS      CL05                        Number
EMPNAME     DS      CL25                        Name
MFCODE      DS      CL01                        M/F code
EMPDPT      DS      CL02                        Department
MTHSAL      DS      CL07                        Monthly salary
            DS      CL60                        Rest of record
            ...
            GET     FILEIN,EMPREC           Read 1st record
C20         CLC     MTHSAL,=C'0200000'      Salary > 2,000.00?
            BNH     C30                         No - exit
            CLI     MFCODE,C'F'             Female?
            BNE     C30                         No - exit
            CLC     EMPDPT,=C'27'           Department 27?
            BNE     C30                         No - exit
            [display employee record]      Display
C30         GET     FILEIN,EMPREC           Read next record
            B       C20                     Loop
```

LITERALS

The use of literals is a shortcut way of writing a DC. The literal begins with an equal (=) sign followed by a character for the type of constant, and the constant contained within apostrophes ('). The same basic rules that apply to DCs apply as well to literals.

Example: Use of a literal in place of a DC.

```
use of a DC:        HEADING   DC    C'INVENTORY'
                              MVC   PRINT+20(9),HEADING
use of a literal:             MVC   PRINT+20(9),=C'INVENTORY'
```

Both operations accomplish the same results. However, the use of the literal, ='INVENTORY', saves you from writing the line of coding for the DC.

The Assembler recognizes that an operand beginning with an equal sign is a literal. The Assembler creates the object code constant, assigns an address, and stores the constant as part of the program in a "literal pool," without a name. Two or more literals defined identically within a program are usually set up as only one constant in the literal pool. Literals generated by IOCS (input/output control system) macros are also included in the pool.

> *Note:* A literal is different from an immediate operand. Immediate instructions, such as MVI and CLI, must have a 1-byte constant in operand-2. A literal, however, must be preceded by the equal sign, and generates a constant elsewhere in storage. For 1-byte nonarithmetic constants, use immediate instructions.

Example: Contrast of a literal and an immediate operand.

```
use of a literal:     MVC   DOLLARPR,=C'$'
use of immediate:     MVI   DOLLARPR,C'$'
```

Although both operations accomplish identical results, note: (a) MVC requires a length (1) in operand-1 if DOLLARPR is not defined with a length of one; (b) MVC uses a literal—the assembled address of operand-2 will contain the location of the constant ($); (c) MVI contains the $ as part of the assembled instruction; (d) MVI is more efficient coding here because it is only four bytes long. MVC requires six bytes for the instruction plus one for the constant defined by the literal =C'$'.

THE LITERAL POOL.   The Assembler organizes the literal pool into four sections, and within these sections stores the literals in order of their appearance in the program.

SECTION	CONTENTS
1	All literals whose length is a multiple of eight.
2	All remaining literals whose length is a multiple of four.
3	All remaining literals whose length is a multiple of two.
4	All odd-length literals.

The Assembler stores the literal pool at the end of the program and prints it immediately following the END statement. However, the Assembler directive LTORG can cause the Assembler to store literals anywhere in the program.

NAME	*OPERATION*	*OPERAND*
(symbol)	LTORG	Not used (omit)

Wherever you use LTORG, the Assembler stores and prints the literals up to that point, from either the start of the program or from the previous LTORG. Figure 3-8 depicts various uses of literals. Note that the sequence of the literals in the literal pool after LTORG is different from the sequence in which they were originally coded. (The next chapter covers the ZAP and AP instructions.)

EQUATE SYMBOL—EQU

The EQU directive is used to equate one symbolic address to another. The Assembler only acts on EQU, and does not generate executable code.

NAME	*OPERATION*	*OPERAND*
(symbol)	EQU	an expression

1. You may assign more than one symbolic name to a field, just as a person may have a full name and a nickname:

```
PRINT   DC    CL133' '      Define PRINT
P       EQU   PRINT         Equate P to PRINT
```

In this example, the Assembler assigns the identical attributes to P as it has to PRINT. You may now use either symbol to reference the same location, with a length of 133 bytes. Note, however, the Assembler rule: the symbol in the EQU operand field, PRINT, *must be defined before the EQU statement.*

```
LOC      OBJECT CODE        ADDR1 ADDR2   STMT   SOURCE STATEMENT

                                          69  *                        --------
                                          70  ***                      LITERALS
                                          71  *                        --------
003090   4040404040404040                 72  SAVLIT    DC    CL8' '
003098   00000C                           73  PAGECT    DC    PL3'0'
00309B   000C                             74  LINECT    DC    PL2'0'
00309D                                    75  VALUEPR   DS    CL6
0030A3                                    76  ASTERPR   DS    CL2

0030A5   00                               78            MVC   SAVLIT,=C'COMPUTER'      MOVE CONSTANT
0030A6   D207 408E 40C6  03090 030C8      79            ZAP   PAGECT,=P'0'             ZERO PAGECT
0030AC   F820 4096 40D6  03098 030D8      80            AP    LINECT,=P'1'             ADD ONE TO LINECT
0030B2   FA10 4099 40D7  0309B 030D9      81            MVC   VALUEPR,=X'40204B202060' MOVE HEX CONSTANT
0030B8   D205 409B 40CE  0309D 030D0      82            MVC   ASTERPR,=C'**'           MOVE ASTERISKS
0030BE   D201 40A1 40D4  030A3 030D6

0030C8                                    84            LTORG
0030C8   C3D6D4D7E4E3C5D9                 85                  =C'COMPUTER'      ⎫ Literal pool
0030D0   40204B202060                     86                  =X'40204B202060'  ⎬ generated by
0030D6   5C5C                             87                  =C'**'            ⎭ the Assembler
0030D8   0C                               88                  =P'0'
0030D9   1C                               89                  =P'1'
```

FIGURE 3-8 Sample use of literals.

2. You may give symbolic names to an immediate operand:

```
CODE   EQU   C'5'              Assign '5' to the name CODE.
       CLI   RECDNO,CODE       Compare RECDNO to C'5'.
```

You may use CODE in place of C'5' in an immediate operand. The Assembler recognizes that CODE is a reference to a value C'5', and substitutes C'5' wherever it encounters the operand CODE. This technique facilitates program modifications. You may have to change the value of the immediate operand. Rather than change many instructions in the program, merely change the operand in the EQU statement, and reassemble the program.

3. You can equate an address using the Assembler's location counter reference. An asterisk as an operand is a reference to the current value in the location counter:

```
LOC:  X'3012'   SAVE   DS    CL3
                KEEP   EQU   *+5
```

After the Assembler processes SAVE, its location counter contains X'3015'. The address of KEEP is equated to the "address" in the operand, *+5, meaning the contents of the location counter plus 5. KEEP is therefore assigned the address X'3015' plus 5, or X'301A'. KEEP will have a length attribute of one.

• *Problem 3-5 should now be attempted.* •

SET LOCATION COUNTER—ORG

The ORG directive is a command to the Assembler to alter or *reoriginate* the value of the location counter during assembly. You can use ORG to redefine data areas in the program, that is, one on top of the other.

NAME	OPERATION	OPERAND
(omit)	ORG	A symbol or not used

The *name* is normally used only in macro writing and is otherwise omitted. The operand, if any, is a symbolic address with or without relative addressing (i.e., A30, or A30+1000), or a reference to the location counter itself (as *+20). The Assembler sets the location counter to the value of the expression. The operand may not be an absolute address, such as 8192 or X'2000'.

Note: If the operand is omitted, the Assembler sets the location counter to the maximum value that it has been set up to this point.

Beware of ORG with no operand, because the Assembler may mistakenly use a comment for its operand. In the following, the Assembler will use the asterisk in column 41 as the ORG operand. Instead of setting the location counter to the previous high setting, it is set incorrectly to the current setting of the location counter:

```
column  10        16         41
         ORG                  *RESET LOCATION COUNTER
```

The solution is to insert a *comma* in column 16, which tells the Assembler explicitly that there is no operand:

```
         ORG      ,           *RESET LOCATION COUNTER
```

See Figure 3-10 for a program that uses ORG to redefine one input record on top of another input record.

SAMPLE PROGRAM: READ AND PRINT CUSTOMER RECORDS

Figure 3-9 depicts a flowchart for a simple program that reads customer records and prints selected fields, and Figure 3-10 provides the coding.

COLUMN	DESCRIPTION	PRINT POSITIONS
1	Record code	
6–10	Customer number	11–15
11–30	Customer name	18–37
41–46	Balance owing	40–46 (prints as xxxx.xx)

Procedure: 1. After opening the files, the initialization routine reads the first record. If the record is the date (record code 'D'), the program moves the date from the record to the heading and prints it. If not a date record, the program prints an error message and cancels.

2. Subsequently, the rest of the file must be customer records (record code '3'). If the code is invalid, a routine prints an error message. Technically, the flowchart could show an end-of-file test after reading the date and the first customer record.

3. To ensure that each customer record is in ascending sequence (one record per customer), the program compares the current customer (CUSTIN) to the previously processed customer number (PREV-CUST). If the new customer number is higher, the program stores

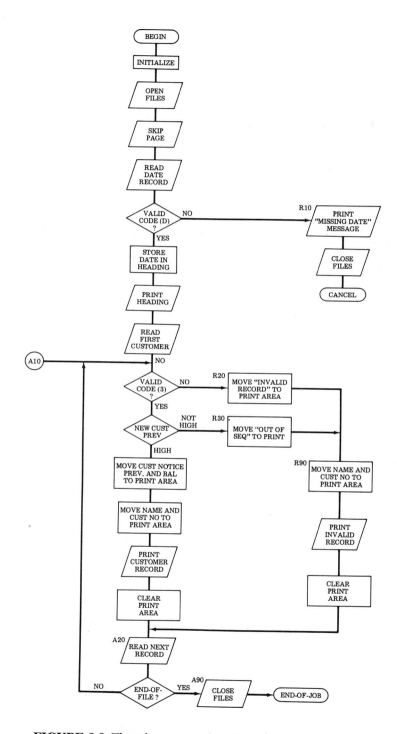

FIGURE 3-9 Flowchart to read and print customer records.

```
       LOC   OBJECT CODE    ADDR1 ADDR2  STMT   SOURCE STATEMENT

                                         4 *                 I N I T I A L I Z A T I O N
                                         5 *              -----------------------------
       000000                            6 PROG03  START
                                         7         INIT                              INITIALIZE
                                        13         OPEN    FILEIN,PRINTER
       000022 D284 3446 3445 00448 00447 22        MVC     CUSLINE,BLANK             CLEAR PRINT AREA

                                        24         PUTPR   PRINTER,HDGLINE,SK1       SKIP TO NEW PAGE
                                        31         GET     FILEIN,DRECDIN            READ DATE RECORD
       00004C 95C4 3370       00372     37         CLI     DCODEIN,DCODE             VALID DATE CODE?
       000050 4770 30F2       000F4     38         BNE     R10NODAT                  * NO - ERROR
       000054 D211 33F9 3377 003FB 00379 39        MVC     DATEPR,ALFDTIN            STORE DATE
                                        40         PUTPR   PRINTER,HDGLINE,WSP2      PRINT HEADING
                                        47         GET     FILEIN,CRECDIN           READ 1ST CUST

                                        54 ***               M A I N   P R O C E S S I N G
                                        55 *              -----------------------------
       00007E 95F3 3370       00372     56 A10LOOP CLI     CCODEIN,CCODE            VALID CUST REC CODE?
       000082 4770 3124       00126     57         BNE     R20INVCD                  * NO - ERRCR
       000086 D504 3375 3509 00377 0050B 58        CLC     CUSTIN,PREVCUST          CUST NO. IN SEQ?
       00008C 47D0 312E       00130     59         BNH     R30SEQER                  * NO - ERROR
       000090 D204 3509 3375 0050B 00377 60        MVC     PREVCUST,CUSTIN          SAVE NEW CUST#
                                        61 *                                        MOVE TO PRINT:
       000096 D201 3473 339C 00475 0039E 62        MVC     CENTSPR,BALIN+4          * CENTS POSITIONS
       00009C 924B 3472       00474     63         MVI     DECPR,C'.'               * DECIMAL POINT
       0000A0 D203 346E 3398 00470 0039A 64        MVC     DOLLPR,BALIN             * DOLLAR POSITIONS
       0000A6 D213 3458 337A 0045A 0037C 65        MVC     NAMEPR,NAMEIN            * NAME
       0000AC D204 3451 3375 00453 00377 66        MVC     CUSTPR,CUSTIN            * CUSTOMER NO.

                                        68         PUTPR   PRINTER,CUSLINE,WSP1     PRINT CUST RECORD
       0000C6 D284 3446 3445 00448 00447 75        MVC     CUSLINE,BLANK            CLEAR PRINT LINE
                                        76 A20READ GET     FILEIN,CRECDIN           READ NEXT
       0000DC 47F0 307C       0007E     82        B       A10LOOP                   LOOP

                                        84 ***          E N D - O F - F I L E   R O U T I N E
                                        85 *              --------------------------------------
                                        86 A90END  CLOSE   FILEIN,PRINTER
                                        95         EOJ

                                        99 ***               E R R O R   R O U T I N E S
                                       100 *              ------------------------------
       0000F4 D211 33F9 34CB 003FB 004CD 101 R10NODAT MVC  DATEPR,DATEMSG           ISSING DATE
                                       102         PUTPR   PRINTER,CUSLINE,WSP2
                                       109         CLOSE   FILEIN,PRINTER
                                       118         CANCEL  ,                        ABNORMAL TERMIN'N

       000126 D215 3478 34DD 0047A 004DF 123 R20INVCD MVC MESSAGPR,RECDMSG          INVALID RECORD CODE
       00012C 47F0 3134       00136     124        B       R90

       000130 D215 3478 34F3 0047A 004F5 126 R30SEQER MVC MESSAGPR,SEQMSG           OUT-OF-SEQUENCE

       000136 D213 3458 337A 0045A 0037C 128 R90    MVC   NAMEPR,NAMEIN            MOVE NAME &
       00013C D204 3451 3375 00453 00377 129        MVC   CUSTPR,CUSTIN            CUST NO. TO PRINT
                                       130        PUTPR   PRINTER,CUSLINE,WSP1     PRINT ERROR MESSAGE
       000156 D284 3446 3445 00448 00447 137        MVC   CUSLINE,BLANK
       00015C 47F0 30CA       000CC     138        B       A20READ                  CONTINUE

                                       141 ***               D E C L A R A T I V E S
                                       142 *              -----------------------
                                       144 FILEIN  DEFIN   A90END                   DEFINE INPUT FILE
                                       168 PRINTER DEFPR                            DEFINE PRINT FILE

       000372                          193 DRECDIN DS      0CL80                    DATE RECORD:
       000372                          194 DCODEIN DS      CL01                     * CODE (D)
       000373                          195 NUMDTIN DS      CL06                     * NUMERIC DATE
       000379                          196 ALFDTIN DS      CL18                     * ALPHA DATE
       00038B                          197         DS      CL55
```

FIGURE 3-10 (partial)

96

```
LOC    OBJECT CODE      ADDR1 ADDR2  STMT   SOURCE STATEMENT

0003C2                  00372        199         ORG     DRECDIN          RESET LOC'N CTR
000372                               200 CRECDIN DS      0CL80            CUSTOMER RECORD:
000372                               201 CCODEIN DS      CL01             01-01 CODE(3)
000373                               202         DS      CL04             02-05
000377                               203 CUSTIN  DS      CL05             06-10 CUST. NO.
00037C                               204 NAMEIN  DS      CL20             11-30 CUST NAME
000390                               205         DS      CL10             31-40
00039A                               206 BALIN   DS      CL06             41-46 BALANCE
0003A0                               207         DS      CL34             47-80

0003C2                               209 HDGLINE DS      0CL133           HEADING LINE:
0003C2 4040404040404040              210         DC      CL11' '          * ----------
0003CD C3E4E2E37B4040D5              211         DC      CL29'CUST#  NAME' *
0003EA C2C1D3C1D5C3C540              212         DC      CL17'BALANCE'     *
0003FB                               213 DATEPR  DS      CL18             *
00040D 4040404040404040              214         DC      CL58' '          *

000447 40                            216 BLANK   DC      C' '             BLANK TO CLEAR PRINT
000448                               217 CUSLINE DS      0CL133           CUST PRINT LINE:
000448 4040404040404040              218         DC      CL11' '          * -------------
000453                               219 CUSTPR  DS      CL05             *     CUST. NO.
000458 4040                          220         DC      CL02' '          *
00045A                               221 NAMEPR  DS      CL20             *     NAME
00046E 4040                          222         DC      CL02' '          *
000470                               223 DOLLPR  DS      CL04             *     $ POSITIONS
000474                               224 DECPR   DS      CL01             *     DECIMAL POINT
000475                               225 CENTSPR DS      CL02             *     CENTS POS'NS
000477 404040                        226         DC      CL03' '          *
00047A 4040404040404040              227 MESSAGPR DC     CL22' '          *     ERROR MESSAGE
000490 4040404040404040              228         DC      CL61' '          *

0004CD D5D640C4C1E3C540              230 DATEMSG DC      CL18'NO DATE RECORD'
0004DF C9D5E5C1D3C9C440              231 RECDMSG DC      CL22'INVALID RECORD CODE'
0004F5 D9C5C3D6D9C440D6              232 SEQMSG  DC      CL22'RECORD OUT OF SEQUENCE'

00050B 4040404040                    234 PREVCUST DC     CL5' '        .    PREV. CUST. NO.

                        000C4        236 DCODE   EQU     C'D'             DATE REC CODE
                        000F3        237 CCODE   EQU     C'3'             CUST REC CODE

000510                               239         LTORG
000510 5B5BC2D6D7C5D540              240                 =C'$$BOPEN '
000518 5B5BC2C3D3D6E2C5              241                 =C'$$BCLOSE'
000520 00000238                      242                 =A(PRINTER)
000524 000003C2                      243                 =A(HDGLINE)
000528 00000160                      244                 =A(FILEIN)
00052C 00000372                      245                 =A(DRECDIN)
000530 00000372                      246                 =A(CRECDIN)
000534 00000448                      247                 =A(CUSLINE)
                        00000        248         END     PROG03
```

Output:-

```
CUST#  NAME              .     BALANCE        01 JANUARY, 1995

12345  KE ANDERSON             1234.56
24680  D  BAKER                5432.10
33333  JW COUSTON              3333.33
34567  AB DONOVAN                     INVALID RECORD CODE
12312  KM EDWARDS                     RECORD OUT OF SEQUENCE
99999  WM FISHER               3456.32
```

FIGURE 3-10 Read and print customer records.

CUSTIN in PREVCUST for the next input test. An equal or low customer number causes an error message.

4. For valid customer records, the program moves customer name, number and balance owing to the print area, and inserts a decimal point in the balance field.

5. Immediately before PRCUST is a 1-byte constant called BLANK. After printing, the program copies the contents of BLANK through the 133 bytes of PRCUST. The blank character propagates through PRCUST, clearing the entire field. (See the earlier section, Duplicating characters, for an explanation.)

6. When the end-of-file is reached, the program branches to A90END, closes the files, and ends execution.

7. The program uses the ORG directive to redefine the input area for the two types of input records:

```
000372    DRECDIN    DS    0CL80    Define date record
000372    DCODEIN    DS    CL01     *
000373    NUMDTIN    DS    CL06     *
000379    ALFDTIN    DS    CL18     *
00038B               DS    CL55     *

          ORG    DRECDIN    Redefine
000372    CRECDIN    DS    0CL80    Define customer record
000372    CCODEIN    DS    CL01     *
000373               DS    CL04     *
000377               ...           *
```

Although relatively simple, the program is still organized into logical sections: Initialization, Main Processing, End-of-File, and Error routines. Also, program labels and data names are clear and meaningful, and along with the comments, the program is close to self-documenting.

DEBUGGING TIPS

Even a program that performs no arithmetic stands a good chance of containing errors. Check first the diagnostics immediately following the assembled program for any errors that the Assembler has located (these may cause execution errors as well). The most common error that the Assembler identifies is spelling mistakes: an operation is misspelled, such as MCV for MVC, or an operand is not spelled the way it is defined. Such errors may cause the Assembler to generate a "dummy" instruction of hex zeros that will cause an "Operation Exception" if executed. Failure to initialize with INIT (or the

USING directive introduced in a later chapter) will cause a large number of "Addressability" errors.

Violating the rules of declaratives is also common, such as defining a DS with a constant, which is treated as a comment, and defining a DC without a constant. Watch for defining a constant length (Ln) that does not agree with the defined constant, as CL3'DATE'. It is easy to code the wrong constant; for example, the constant DC CL5'0' generates '0bbbb' rather than '00000'.

Coding an explicit length in an MVI or CLI or in operand-2 of an MVC or CLC will also cause Assembler errors.

The program, when corrected and reassembled, may cause errors during execution. Be sure that the input definition agrees exactly with the actual input record format—any difference will cause incorrect results. Failure to clear the print area to blanks will cause "garbage" on the printed lines. A common error is caused by omitting the explicit length from an MVC used with relative addressing, as:

```
PRINT   DC    CL133'  '
        MVC   PRINT+95,=C'DATE'
```

The instruction moves 133 bytes, starting from the first byte of the literal 'DATE'—perhaps a good reason to minimize (or avoid?) use of relative addressing. The areas following PRINT will be clobbered, with often spectacular results that may not occur until later in the execution.

An error difficult to detect is caused by incorrect branching—reversing operands 1 and 2, or using, for example, BNH instead of BNL.

A disastrous error is caused by coding GET or PUT incorrectly, as, for example, GET RECDIN,FILEIN. The computer may end up executing outside of the program area, perhaps even executing garbage in the supervisor.

Be careful with the use of literals that are associated with character data. Assume the following definition:

```
AMOUNTIN   DS    CL7
```

Suppose you want to check if AMOUNTIN contains all blanks. The instruction CLC AMOUNTIN,=C' ' assumes the length of operand-1, seven bytes. The comparison is all seven bytes of AMOUNTIN to the one-byte literal plus the six bytes immediately following in the literal pool, whatever they may contain. To correct, change the literal to =7C' ' or =CL7' '.

Suppose you also want to check if AMOUNTIN contains all zeros. The instruction CLC AMOUNTIN,=C'0' causes the same error as the one-byte blank. Let's try a seven-byte literal, =CL7'0'. Watch out for this one! The Assembler generates a seven-byte literal with the 0 left-adjusted and six blanks filled to the right, as '0bbbbbb'. The correct literal is =7C'0' or C'0000000'.

Be especially careful when using an ORG directive. The following defines an input record and uses ORG to redefine the input area:

```
RECDIN    DS    0CL80
NAMEIN    DS    CL20
ADDR1IN   DS    CL30
ADDR2IN   DS    CL30
          ORG   RECDIN
NUMBIN    DS    CL10
```

The last instruction defines only the first ten bytes of RECDIN. Advance the Assembler location counter to the end of the 80-byte input area by means of either another DS or an ORG:

```
          DS    CL70
or        ORG   ,
or        ORG   *+70
or        ORG   RECDIN+80
```

Appendix B contains a list of program checks (interrupts) that can occur during program execution, along with possible causes of the errors.

PROBLEMS

3-1. DEFINE STORAGE. Define the following as DSs:
  (a) An 80-byte area called OUT to be used for output.
  (b) A 100-byte area that does not increment the Location Counter.
  (c) Five 10-byte areas defined with one statement.
  (d) An area called DATE, subdivided with three 2-byte fields called respectively DAY, MONTH, and YEAR.

3-2. DEFINE CONSTANT. Define the following as DCs:
  (a) A field called ASTER, one byte long, containing an asterisk.
  (b) A field of ten blanks, called BLANKS.
  (c) A constant containing SAM'S.
  (d) A constant of ten character zeros.
  (e) Three 5-byte constants all containing blanks, defined with one statement.

3-3. MOVE CHARACTER. Given the declaratives shown, code the following *unrelated* questions. Show the contents of both fields after completion of the operation.

```
A    DC    C'123'        These fields are defined in storage
B    DC    C'4567'       adjacent to each other.
C    DC    C'XY'
```

Example: Move the contents of C to the leftmost two bytes of A: MVC A(2),C.
  (a) Move the contents of C to the second and third bytes of B.
  (b) Move the rightmost byte of A to the third byte of B.

(c) Move A to the bytes starting at the third byte of B.

(d) Use one MVC to change all the contents of A, B, and C to character 1s.

(e) Use one MVC to shift both A and B one byte to the left, as follows:

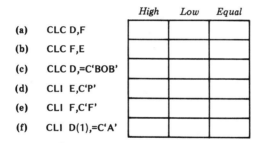

3-4. COMPARE AND BRANCH. Given the declaratives, code the following:

```
D    DC    C'ANN'
E    DC    C'MOE'
F    DC    C'SAL'
```

(a) If E is less than or equal to F, branch to G40.

(b) If D is greater than E but not less than F, branch to G50.

3-5. Show by an 'X' the Condition Code set by the following. D, E, and F refer to the DCs in Problem 3-4. Explain if invalid assemble or execute.

		High	*Low*	*Equal*
(a)	CLC D,F			
(b)	CLC F,E			
(c)	CLC D,=C'BOB'			
(d)	CLI E,C'P'			
(e)	CLI F,C'F'			
(f)	CLI D(1),=C'A'			

3-6. PROGRAM ASSIGNMENT.

Required: A program that reads Inventory records and prints selected data.

Input:

COLUMN	CONTENTS	COLUMN	CONTENTS
1	Record code ('4')	9–28	Description
2–3	Branch number	29–30	Month
4–8	Stock number	31–35	Quantity on hand
		36–42	Value (xxxxx.xx)

Output (including heading):

```
BRANCH  STOCK NO  DESCRIPTION  MONTH  QUANTITY    VALUE
  XX     XXXXX    X--------X    XX     XXXXX    XXXXX.XX
```

Procedure:

1. Check the record code ('4') to ensure that the program processes only valid records. Bypass invalid records and print a message 'INVALID RECORD'.

2. To ensure that the records are in proper order, sequence-check them on Stock number. If out of sequence, print an error message 'OUT OF SEQUENCE'.

3. Provide input data that tests for invalid record code and out-of-sequence condition.

4. Print the fields as shown, in any suitable print positions. As an optional extra, code the program to convert the numeric input month into alphabetic for printing (i.e., '01' should be 'JANUARY').

5. Analyze, code, and test the program. Be sure to use the programming standards for your installation.

4

DECIMAL DATA AND ARITHMETIC I

Chapter 3 covered the use of data in character format. Few programs are written using just this format, because generally we need to perform arithmetic—addition, multiplication, etc. The most common format for arithmetic is packed decimal. This chapter introduces three data formats: hexadecimal, zoned, and packed. The instructions, MVN and MVZ, although technically character operations, are covered here because they are mostly used with packed data. This chapter then covers the basic packed operations for packing, unpacking, addition, subtraction, and comparing.

HEXADECIMAL CONSTANTS

Two hexadecimal digits can represent any of the 256 different characters. They normally define constants that cannot easily be defined as character packed, zoned, or binary. A major use is in defining edit word constants (Chapter 5). The following rules apply to hexadecimal constants:

1. The constant may be defined in length from one byte (two hex digits) to 256 bytes (512 hex digits).
2. They may contain only the hex digits 0 through 9 and A through F.
3. A length (Ln) if defined specifies the number of bytes, *one byte for each pair of hex digits*. The Assembler right-adjusts hex constants. Therefore, if the defined length is less than the constant, the Assem-

bler truncates the constant on the left. If the defined length is longer, the Assembler pads hex zeros to the left.

See Figure 4-1 for example hex DCs. Compare the defined constant to the object code:

```
LOC   OBJECT   STMT    SOURCE STATEMENT

             6 *       ------------------------
             7 *       DC    HEXADECIMAL FORMAT
             8 *       ------------------------
003002 1A76  9 HEX1    DC    X'1A76'           |1A|76|
003004 76   10 HEX2    DC    XL1'1A76'         |76|              TRUNCATES
003005 001A76 11 HEX3  DC    XL3'1A76'         |00|1A|76|        PADS ZEROS
003008 012C 12 HEX4    DC    X'12C'            |01|2C|           PADS ZERO
00300A FFFFFF 13 HEX5  DC    3X'FF'            |FF|FF|FF|        3 CONSTANTS
```

FIGURE 4-1 Sample DC statements in hexadecimal format.

HEX1 defines a DC that requires two bytes of storage.

HEX2 has a length specified as one byte and a constant as two bytes. This is a possible coding error, because the Assembler truncated the constant on the left.

HEX3 has a length specified as three and a constant of two bytes. The Assembler pads zeros on the left.

HEX4 defines a constant with three hex digits—1½ bytes. The Assembler pads a hex zero to the left, resulting in a 2-byte constant.

HEX5 illustrates the duplication factor. Three constants each containing X'FF' are defined. The name HEX5 refers to the first constant with a length of one byte.

Do not confuse hex constants with constants of other formats. Note the difference between the following:

FORMAT	CONSTANT	BYTES	HEX REPRESENTATION
character	DC C'ABCD'	4	/C1/C2/C3/C4/
hexadecimal	DC X'ABCD'	2	/AB/CD/

MOVE NUMERIC (MVN) AND MOVE ZONES (MVZ)

NAME	OPERATION	OPERAND
(symbol)	MVN	S1,S2 or D1(L,B1),D2(B2)
(symbol)	MVZ	S1,S2 or D1(L,B1),D2(B2)

The main use of the MVN and MVZ instructions is to manipulate half-bytes for decimal arithmetic. The rules for both instructions are similar to those for MVC, with the following exceptions:

- MVN moves only the numeric portion of the half-byte, the rightmost four bits, numbered 4 to 7. From one to 256 numeric portions may be moved from the operand-2 field to the operand-1 field. The zone portion is undisturbed.

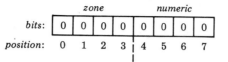

- MVZ moves only the zone half of the byte, the leftmost four bits, numbered 0 to 3. From one to 256 zones may be moved. The numeric portion is undisturbed.

Figure 4-2 provides examples of MVN and MVZ operations.

The first MVN moves the numeric portion of each byte of A (1, 2, and 3) to the numeric portion of each byte of B. The second MVN, illustrating relative addressing and explicit length, moves two numerics, starting from A to B+1.

The first MVZ moves zone portions (X'F's). The second MVZ moves one zone from B+1 to B+2.

```
LOC    OBJECT CODE       ADDR1 ADDR2   STMT      SOURCE STATEMENT

00300D F1F2F3                           18 A         DC    C'123'           A= |F1|F2|F3|
003010 45678C                           19 B         DC    X'45678C'        B= |45|67|8C|

                                        21 *         ------------------
                                        22 ***       MVN   MOVE NUMERICS
                                        23 *         ------------------
003013 00
003014 D102 400E 400B 03010 0300D       24           MVN   B,A              B= |41|62|83|
00301A D101 400F 400B 03011 0300D       25           MVN   B+1(2),A         B= |45|61|82|

                                        27 *         ------------------
                                        28 ***       MVZ   MOVE ZONES
                                        29 *         ------------------
003020 D302 400E 400B 03010 0300D       30           MVZ   B,A              B= |F5|F7|FC|
003026 D300 4010 400F 03012 03011       31           MVZ   B+2(1),B+1       B= |45|67|6C|
```

FIGURE 4-2 Sample unrelated MVN and MVZ operations.

• *Problem 4-1 should now be attempted.* •

ZONED DECIMAL DATA

Zoned decimal data is similar to character data, but is of limited use. Zoned is sometimes used, for example, to define a field containing data that will be later packed, such as a numeric field read from an input file. The following rules govern zoned declaratives:

1. The length may be defined from one to 16 bytes.

2. The constant may contain only the digits 0 through 9, a sign (+ or −), and a decimal point. The Assembler does not translate or store the decimal point—you code it only for documentation, where you intend the decimal to be.

3. You may define more than one zoned constant with one DC, separated by commas.

4. Except for the rightmost digit of the constant, the Assembler converts each zoned digit 0 through 9 to X'F0' through X'F9'. If the constant is positive, the Assembler generates a plus sign X'C', and if negative a minus sign, X'D'. For example, DC Z'123.45' becomes /F1/F2/F3/F4/C5/. The rightmost byte X'C5' contains the plus sign in the zone portion. The zone 'C' is equivalent to the plus sign (12-zone) on the punched card. The minus zone 'D' is equivalent to the punched card minus sign (11-zone).

5. Code the sign (+ or −) to the left of the constant, such as DC Z'−1.25'. To represent a positive value, code a + sign, or omit the sign altogether.

6. You may specify length (Ln) as for hexadecimal format. If the constant is shorter than the specified length, the Assembler right-adjusts the constant and pads leftmost zeros:

           DC ZL3'25'   /F0/F2/C5/

If the constant is longer than the specified length, the Assembler truncates the constant on the left:

           DC ZL2'1234'   /F3/C4/

Figure 4-3 illustrates zoned declaratives explained as follows:

ZONE0 defines a DS as five bytes long, to be used for zoned data.

ZONE1 is a DC with a decimal point in the constant. Note the generated object code on the left.

ZONE2 shows a DC with a minus sign coded to the left. The Assembler stores the sign in object code on the right as X'D'.

```
LOC    OBJECT CODE    STMT    SOURCE STATEMENT

                       35 *    -------------------
                       36 *      DC    ZONED FORMAT
                       37 *    -------------------
00302C                 38 ZONE0  DS    ZL5              5-BYTE ZONED AREA
003031 F1F2F3C5        39 ZONE1  DC    Z'123.5'         |F1|F2|F3|C5|           IGNORES DEC
003035 F5F0F0F0D0      40 ZONE2  DC    Z'-500.00'       |F5|F0|F0|F0|D0|        MINUS
00303A F0F1F2C3        41 ZONE3  DC    ZL4'123'         |F0|F1|F2|C3|           PADS ZEROS

00303E F2C3            43 ZONE4  DC    ZL2'123'         |F2|C3|                 TRUNCATES
003040 F0C0F0C0F0C0    44 ZONE5  DC    3ZL2'0'          |F0|C0|F0|C0|F0|C0|    3 CONSTANTS
003046 F1F2C3C4F6C7    45 ZONE6  DC    Z'123,4,67'      |F1|F2|C3|C4|F6|C7|    3 CONSTANTS
```

FIGURE 4-3 Sample zoned declaratives.

ZONE3 and ZONE4 use the length indication (Ln). In ZONE3, X'F0' is padded on the left, and in ZONE4 the constant is truncated.

ZONE5 defines three identical constants. A reference to ZONE5 is to the first 2-byte constant.

ZONE6 defines three constants, each separated by a comma. The comma is not stored. A reference to ZONE6 is to the first 3-byte constant.

Note the difference between the generated code for the following character and zoned DCs:

| *character*: | DC C'1,234.56' | /F1/6B/F2/F3/F4/4B/F5/F6 |
| *zoned*: | DC Z'1,234.56' | /C1/F2/F3/F4/F5/C6 |

2 constants generated by the comma

PACKED DECIMAL DATA

Ordinary decimal data is performed on fields in packed format. You may define these fields either initially as packed, or use the PACK instruction to translate character or zoned data into packed. Each packed byte contains two digits, one in each half-byte. The plus or minus sign is the rightmost half-byte of the field. For example, the packed value $+125$ requires two bytes, as

| 12 | 5C |

The binary representation of this field is

| 0001 | 0010 | 0101 | 1100 |

The standard plus sign (X'C' or binary 1100) is equivalent to the plus (12-zone) on a punched card. The standard minus sign (X'D' or binary 1101) is equivalent to the punched card minus (11-zone). All packed fields must conform to the following rules:

1. All digit positions (all half-bytes other than the rightmost sign) may contain only digits 0 through 9 (binary 0000 through 1001).

2. The rightmost half-byte must contain a sign. There are four valid plus signs and two valid minus signs:

BINARY	HEX	SIGN		BINARY	HEX	SIGN
1010	A	+		1101	D	− *standard minus sign*
1011	B	−		1110	E	+
1100	C	+ *standard plus sign*		1111	F	+

3. Packed fields may be a minimum of one byte long (one digit plus a sign) and a maximum of 16 bytes (31 digits plus a sign).

PACKED DECIMAL CONSTANTS.   Constants are defined as packed for use in decimal arithmetic. The rules for packed, which are similar to zoned, are as follows:

1. The length may be defined from one to 16 bytes.

2. A packed constant, like zoned, may contain only the digits 0 through 9, and optionally a decimal point (.) and a sign (+ or −). The Assembler does not store the decimal point, which is chiefly for program documentation.

3. One DC may define more than one packed constant, each separated by a comma.

4. You may also use length indication (Ln). The Assembler right-adjusts the constant to permit padding leftmost zeros or truncating on the left.

The Assembler converts the packed constant to object code as follows:

1. The rightmost half-byte (numeric portion) of the assembled constant contains the sign, X'C' for plus and X'D' for minus. For example, DC PL3'1234' is converted to packed as /01/23/4C/.

2. All other half-bytes contain a digit. Other than the rightmost byte which has a digit and a sign, all bytes contain two digits. A packed constant, therefore, always has an odd number of digits, one to 31.

Figure 4-4 depicts packed DCs, explained as follows:

PACK1 packs three digits into two bytes. The plus (+) sign is optional.

PACK2 defines a negative constant.

PACK3 packs four digits into three bytes. The Assembler inserts a zero digit in the leftmost half-byte. Note that a packed constant *defined* as an even number of digits results in an odd number of packed digits. Also, the decimal point acts as a comment, and is not stored.

PACK4 defines the length longer than the constant. The Assembler pads zeros on the left.

PACK5 defines the length shorter than the constant. The Assembler truncates the leftmost digit.

PACK6 defines three identical constants containing zeros.

PACK7 defines three constants, each separated by a comma, which is not stored. A reference to PACK7 is to the first 2-byte field.

PACK8 defines two constants, the first packed and the second character. A reference to PACK8 is to the first field, the 2-byte packed constant.

```
LOC       OBJECT CODE    STMT     SOURCE STATEMENT

                         49 *     --------------------
                         50 *        DC    PACKED FORMAT
                         51 *     --------------------
00304C    370C           52 PACK1    DC    P'+370'                |37|0C|          PLUS SIGN
00304E    500D           53 PACK2    DC    P'-500'                |50|0D|          MINUS SIGN
003050    01234C         54 PACK3    DC    P'12.34'               |01|23|4C|       IGNORES DEC
003053    0012345C       55 PACK4    DC    PL4'12345'             |00|12|34|5C|    PADS ZERO

003057    345C           57 PACK5    DC    PL2'12345'             |34|5C|          TRUNCATES
003059    000C000C000C   58 PACK6    DC    3PL2'0'                |00|0C|00|0C|00|0C|  3 CONSTANTS
00305F    125C215C387C   59 PACK7    DC    PL2'125,215,387'       |12|5C|21|5C|38|7C|  3 CONSTANTS
003065    007CD1E4D3E8   60 PACK8    DC    P'07',C'JULY'          |00|7C|D1|E4|D3|E8|  2 CONSTANTS
```

FIGURE 4-4 Sample DC statements in packed format.

PACKED OPERATIONS

The computer can perform arithmetic only on valid numeric fields (packed decimal and binary). Since input data from a terminal or card is in character format, it is necessary to convert into packed, using the PACK operation. In packed format, operations such as AP, SP, and ZAP can perform arithmetic, and CP can perform comparisons. The UNPK operation (and ED in the next chapter) converts the packed data into printable characters.

PACKING FIELDS—PACK. Data normally appears in packed format by (1) a constant defined as packed, or (2) an instruction, PACK, that converts character or zoned fields into packed. The standard steps to process decimal arithmetic are:

1. Read an input record. You may define input amount fields as character or zoned, but regardless of your definition, the content is read in character format.
2. Convert (PACK) character amount fields into packed.
3. Perform decimal arithmetic on packed fields.
4. Prepare the output area. Output on tape and disk may be any format. Output on a printer or video screen is usually in character format; the packed fields must be either unpacked or "edited" into the print area (the next chapter covers editing).
5. Write the output record.

Although PACK is normally used to convert character and zoned to packed, PACK executes regardless of the format. There is no checking for valid data, and PACK can easily generate "garbage" if applied to the wrong data field.

NAME	OPERATION	OPERAND
(symbol)	PACK	S1,S2 or D1(L1,B1),D2(L2,B2)

The rules for PACK are as follows:

1. The maximum length of each operand is 16 bytes. Either operand may specify an explicit length (L1 and L2).
2. Bytes referenced by operand-2 are packed one byte at a time from right to left into the operand-1 field. In the rightmost byte the half-bytes are reversed:

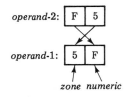

In the example, the zone portion of the rightmost byte of operand-2 (X'F') is placed in the numeric portion of the rightmost byte of operand-1. The numeric portion of operand-2 (X'5') is placed in the zone portion of operand-1. It becomes the rightmost, or units, digit.

3. Other than the rightmost byte, all other zones of operand-2 are ignored. PACK extracts numeric portions from operand-2 one at a time from right to left, and places them adjacent to one another in the operand-1 field. The following instruction packs the contents of ZONED into PACKED:

```
ZONED    DC    Z'12345'        /F1/F2/F3/F4/C5/
PACKED   DS    PL3
         PACK  PACKED,ZONED    12/34/5C/
```

Note that the zoned sign C becomes the packed sign. The zoned 5 becomes the rightmost digit, and each other numeric ZONED digit is extracted and placed in PACKED. PACKED now contains data on which you may perform arithmetic.

4. PACK terminates when all digits are transmitted. If operand-1 is too short to receive all the digits, the remaining leftmost digits of operand-2 are ignored. If operand-1 is longer than necessary to receive all the digits, its leftmost bytes are filled with zeros (X'0'). In any event, PACK fully erases the previous contents of the receiving field.

Figure 4-5 gives various unrelated PACK examples which should now be studied:

```
LOC    OBJECT CODE        ADDR1 ADDR2   STMT    SOURCE STATEMENT

                                        64 *       ------
                                        65 ***     PACK
                                        66 *       ------
00306B                                  67 G       DS     PL3
00306E F1F2F3F4C5                       68 H       DC     Z'12345'      H= |F1|F2|F3|F4|C5|
003073 F1F2F3                           69 J       DC     C'123'        J= |F1|F2|F3|
003076 F1F2F3F4F5C6                     70 K       DC     Z'123456'     K= |F1|F2|F3|F4|F5|C6|

00307C F224 4069 406C 0306B 0306E       72 PACKA   PACK   G,H           G= |12|34|5C|
003082 F222 4069 4071 0306B 03073       73 PACKB   PACK   G,J           G= |00|12|3F|
003088 F225 4069 4074 0306B 03076       74 PACKC   PACK   G,K           G= |23|45|6C|

00308E F244 406C 406C 0306E 0306E       76 PACKD   PACK   H,H           H= |00|00|12|34|5C|
003094 F221 4069 406D 0306B 0306F       77 PACKE   PACK   G,H+1(2)      G= |00|02|3F|
00309A F212 4077 406D 03079 0306F       78 PACKF   PACK   K+3(2),H+1(3) K= |F1|F2|F3|23|4F|C6|
```

FIGURE 4-5 Sample unrelated pack operations.

PACKA illustrates a conventional PACK operation. H, a 5-byte zoned field, requires 3 bytes when converted to packed format.

In **PACKB**, operand-1, G, is one byte longer than necessary for the PACK operation. PACK pads zeros in the leftmost byte.

PACKC depicts a common programming error. A 6-byte field, K, is packed into a 3-byte field, G. PACK proceeds from right to left, terminating before packing all the digits in G.

PACKD shows the effect of packing a field into itself. Although the operation works correctly, *this practice is not always desirable.* First, the field is defined as zoned, but now contains packed data. Second, the defined length is five bytes, but the field now contains only three bytes of significant data. It is generally preferable to pack into a field defined with the correct format and length.

PACKE and PACKF illustrate valid use of relative addressing and explicit lengths. In the case of PACKF, the second, third, and fourth bytes of H are packed into the fourth and fifth bytes of K—the other bytes are not affected by the operation. The example is illustrative, because there are few practical reasons to code in this way.

BLANK INPUT FIELDS. What if a numeric input field is blank? PACK will pack any kind of data, even blanks. Suppose that RATEIN is a 5-byte field that is to pack into RATEPK, a 3-byte field. If RATEIN is blank, then the result of packing RATEPK is X'000004'. Since the rightmost digit is supposed to be a valid sign, an attempt to perform arithmetic on RATEPK will cause a *data exception*.

One way to avert such an error is to assign zeros to a blank input field, as follows:

```
RATEIN   DS    ZL5                     Input field
RATEPK   DS    PL3                     Packed field
         ...
         CLC   RATEIN,=CL5' '          Blank field?
         BNE   D50                     No -- bypass
         MVC   RATEIN,=CL5'00000'      Yes - insert zeros
D50      PACK  RATEPK,RATEIN           Pack rate
```

A blank input field will now result in RATEPK containing X'00000F', a valid field of packed zeros.

UNPACKING FIELDS—UNPK. UNPK performs the reverse of PACK. Its main purpose is to convert packed data into zoned, in order, for example, to print the zoned field. However, UNPK may be used to manipulate data in any format; there is no checking for validity of data. Unpacking data that is not packed may result in "garbage."

NAME	OPERATION	OPERAND
(symbol)	UNPK	S1,S2 or D1(L1,B1),D2(L2,B2)

The rules for UNPK are as follows:

1. The maximum length for each field is 16 bytes. Either operand may specify an explicit length (L1 and L2).
2. Bytes referenced by operand-2 are unpacked one byte at a time from right to left into the operand-1 field.

3. As done also by PACK, the half-bytes of the rightmost byte of the operand-2 field are reversed in the operand-1 field.

4. UNPK successively places all other digits in operand-2 from right to left in the numeric portion of each byte in operand-1. The zone portions are filled with hex 'F'. The following unpacks PACKED into ZONED:

```
PACKED    DC   P'12345'              /12/34/5C/
ZONED     DS   PL5
          UNPK ZONED,PACKED          /F1/F2/F3/F4/C5/
```

Note that UNPK reverses the PACKED sign C and the digit '5' in the receiving field, ZONED. All other digits are placed in ZONED with a zone 'F'. The data in ZONED is now in a format that you can print, whereas PACKED contains bytes that are invalid for printing. (In practice, rather than use UNPK to translate packed data for printing, the normal practice is to use the ED operation covered in the next chapter.)

5. UNPK normally terminates when all digits are transmitted. If the operand-1 field is too short to receive all the digits, the remaining leftmost bytes of operand-2 are ignored. If the operand-1 field is longer than necessary to receive all the digits, its leftmost bytes are filled with character zeros (X'F0').

Consider the examples in Figure 4–6:

```
 LOC    OBJECT CODE      ADDR1 ADDR2   STMT     SOURCE STATEMENT

                                       82  *        --------------
                                       83  ***       UNPK   UNPACK
                                       84  *        --------------
0030A0  12345C                         85  L         DC     P'12345'          L=  |12|34|5C|
0030A3                                 86  M         DS     ZL5
0030A8  F9F9F9F9F9C9                   87  N         DC     Z'999999'         N=  |F9|F9|F9|F9|F9|C9|
0030AE                                 88  P         DS     CL3
0030B1  123456789C                     89  Q         DC     P'123456789'      Q=  |12|34|56|78|9C|

0030B6  F342 40A1 409E   030A3 030A0   91  UNPACK1   UNPK   M,L               M=  |F1|F2|F3|F4|C5|
0030BC  F352 40A6 409E   030A8 030A0   92  UNPACK2   UNPK   N,L               N=  |F0|F1|F2|F3|F4|C5|
0030C2  F322 40AC 409E   030AE 030A0   93  UNPACK3   UNPK   P,L               P=  |F3|F4|C5|
0030C8  F321 40AC 409F   030AE 030A1   94  UNPACK4   UNPK   P,L+1(2)          P=  |F3|F4|C5|

0030CE  F342 40A7 409E   030A9 030A0   96  UNPACK5   UNPK   N+1(5),L          N=  |F9|F1|F2|F3|F4|C5|
0030D4  F322 409E 409E   030A0 030A0   97  UNPACK6   UNPK   L,L               L=  |F3|F4|C5|
0030DA  F344 40AF 40AF   030B1 030B1   98  UNPACK7   UNPK   Q,Q               Q=  |FF|F7|F7|F8|C9|
```

FIGURE 4-6 Sample unrelated unpack operations.

UNPACK1 illustrates a 3-byte field unpacked into a 5-byte field, the correct size.

In **UNPACK2**, operand-1 is one byte longer than necessary. The unpack fills a character zero (X'Fo') to the left.

In **UNPACK3**, operand-1 is two bytes too short to receive all the unpacked data. Therefore, the two leftmost digits of the operand-2 field are not unpacked.

UNPACK4 and UNPACK5 depict the use of relative addressing and explicit length, fancy coding, but dangerous.

UNPACK6 and UNPACK7 unpack fields into themselves. The result is correct only if the field is one or two bytes long. The danger of this practice is seen by the results.

UNPACK6 attempts to unpack a 3-byte field called L into itself. Because L contains five digits which cannot fully unpack into a 3-byte field, the two leftmost digits (1 and 2) are erased.

UNPACK7 unpacks a 5-byte field called Q into itself, propagating an error. The error can be best understood if you consider the rule of UNPK: *one byte at a time is extracted and unpacked from right to left:*

— The zone and numeric portions of Q+4, C9, are reversed.

— Q+3 containing 78 is extracted. F8 is stored in Q+3 and F7 is stored in Q+2. Q now contains |12|34|F7|F8|9C|.

— Q+2, *now containing F7,* is extracted. F7 is stored in Q+1 and FF is stored in Q as follows: |FF|F7|F7|F8|C9|. The operation having filled all five bytes is now complete, but incorrect.

— The computer continues processing with no indication that an "error" occurred.

PACKED DECIMAL ARITHMETIC—ZAP, AP, AND SP. All decimal arithmetic is performed in main storage using valid packed data and the appropriate packed decimal instructions. This chapter introduces operations for simple arithmetic, and the next chapter covers multiply and divide.

NAME	OPERATION	OPERAND
(symbol)	ZAP	S1,S2 or D1(L1,B1),D2(L2,B2)
(symbol)	AP	S1,S2 or D1(L1,B1),D2(L2,B2)
(symbol)	SP	S1,S2 or D1(L1,B1),D2(L2,B2)

Use ZAP, Zero and Add Packed, to transfer packed data, just as you use MVC to transfer character data. However, if the receiving field is longer than the sending field, ZAP fills the leftmost bytes with zeros. You can use AP, Add Packed, and SP, Subtract Packed, for addition and subtraction of packed fields. The rules for ZAP, AP, and SP are as follows:

1. The maximum length of each field is 16 bytes. Either operand may contain an explicit length (L1 and L2), up to 16.

2. The operand-2 sending field must be a packed field with a valid sign (hex 'A' to hex 'F'). If the field is not valid, a program interrupt "data exception" will occur. On the 370, if the sign is invalid the operation may be suppressed rather than terminated.

3. For AP and SP the operand-1 receiving field must be a packed field with a valid sign. In the case of ZAP, the operand-1 field may be any format.

4. If the operand-1 field is shorter than the operand-2 field, a program interrupt overflow may occur. Normally an arithmetic field should be defined so that it can contain the largest answer that could ever occur, plus a byte for insurance.

5. The rules of algebra determine the resulting sign. A positive sum yields a plus (hex 'C') sign, and a negative sum yields a minus (hex 'D') sign. A zero result yields a positive (hex 'C') sign. X'C' and X'D' are the standard plus and minus signs, although X'A', X'B', X'E', and X'F' are valid.

Note: An arithmetic operation changes an X'F' sign to X'C'. If an input field contains the value '12345', its hex representation in main storage is X'F1F2F3F4F5'. If you pack the field, it becomes X'12345F', still with the F-sign. If you perform any arithmetic upon this packed field, its sign changes: X'C' if positive and X'D' if negative. This feature is algebraically correct, but confusing to the learner.

6. ZAP, AP, and SP set the condition code, so that you may test the results if necessary:

CODE	CONTENTS OF THE RESULT FIELD
0	Zero
1	Minus (less than zero)
2	Plus (greater than zero)
3	Overflow

The following conditional branches may then test for these conditions:

CONDITION CODE	CONDITIONAL BRANCHES	
0 = Zero	BZ (Branch Zero)	BNZ (Branch not Zero)
1 = Minus	BM (Branch Minus)	BNM (Branch not Minus)
2 = Plus	BP (Branch Plus)	BNP (Branch not Plus)
3 = Overflow	BO (Branch Overflow)	

Example testing of the condition code:

```
ACCUM    DC    PL2'0'
TOTAL    DC    PL3'0'
         AP    TOTAL,ACCUM        Add and set the condition code.
         BM    P10NEG             (Assume P10NEG is any valid address.)
```

Assume the contents of ACCUM and TOTAL are unknown. If the result of adding the contents of ACCUM to TOTAL is negative, the program branches to P10NEG. If the result is positive or zero, the program continues with the next instruction. Figure 4-7 provides various unrelated ZAP, AP, and SP examples:

```
LOC     OBJECT CODE       STMT    SOURCE STATEMENT

003002  123C               7 P1      DC    P'123'          P1= |12|3C|
003004  04567C             8 P2      DC    P'4567'         P2= |04|56|7C|
003007  0890123C           9 P3      DC    P'890123'       P3= |08|90|12|3C|
                          10 *       --------------------------
                          11 ***     ZAP   ZERO AND ADD PACKED
                          12 *       --------------------------
00300B  00
00300C  F821 4002 4000    13 ZAP1    ZAP   P2,P1           P2= |00|12|3C|
003012  F823 4002 4005    14 ZAP2    ZAP   P2,P3           ERROR - P2 IS TOO SHORT
003018  F822 4002 4005    15 ZAP3    ZAP   P2,P3(3)        ERROR - NO SIGN IN OPERAND-2
00301E  F822 4002 4006    16 ZAP4    ZAP   P2,P3+1(3)      P2= |90|12|3C|
003024  F811 4000 4000    17 ZAP5    ZAP   P1,P1           SETS CONDITION CODE HIGH/PLUS
00302A  F810 4000 40C4    18 ZAP6    ZAP   P1,=P'0'        P1= |00|0C|

                          20 *       ------------------
                          21 ***     AP    ADD PACKED
                          22 *       ------------------
003030  FA21 4002 4000    23 ADD1    AP    P2,P1           P2= |04|69|0C|
003036  FA12 4000 4002    24 ADD2    AP    P1,P2           ERROR - P1 IS TOO SHORT
00303C  FA21 4005 4000    25 ADD3    AP    P3(3),P1        ERROR - NO SIGN IN OPERAND-1
003042  FA11 4000 40BE    26 ADD4    AP    P1,=P'999'      P1= |12|2C| ERROR - OVERFLOW

                          28 *       -----------------------
                          29 ***     SP    SUBTRACT PACKED
                          30 *       -----------------------
003048  FB21 4002 4000    31 SUBTR1  SP    P2,P1           P2= |04|44|4C|
00304E  FB11 4000 4000    32 SUBTR2  SP    P1,P1           P1= |00|0C|
```

FIGURE 4-7 Sample unrelated ZAP, AP, and SP operations.

ZAP1, ADD1, and SUBTR1 illustrate conventional ZAP, AP, and SP operations. ZAP2 and ADD2 depict a coding error in which operand-1 is shorter than operand-2. The result at execute-time is an overflow condition.

ZAP3 and ADD3 also are coding errors not recognized by the Assembler. The explicit length P3(3) causes only the first three bytes to be processed. Since there is no sign in the explicitly defined field, the instruction will "bomb" with a data exception.

ZAP4 shows how you may correctly use explicit length and relative addressing.

ZAP5 tests the contents of a packed field. If you ZAP a field into itself the value is unchanged, but the condition code is set. Since P1 contains a positive value, the condition code is set to high/plus.

ZAP6 and SUBTR2 both clear a field to packed zeros. Subtracting a field from itself, as in SUBTR2, is more efficient, but requires valid packed data in operand-1. ZAP requires a constant defined for operand-2, in this case a literal =P'0'.

ADD4 depicts a common coding error caused by an operand-1 field that is too short:

Contents of P1	/12/3C/
Add '999'	/99/9C/
Total	/12/2C/

Because P1 is only two bytes and the total requires three, there is an overflow interrupt, and an answer of 122 instead of 1,122.

> • *Problem 4-2 should now be attempted.* •

COMPARISON OF PACKED DECIMAL FIELDS—CP. It is often necessary to test if a packed field is plus, minus, or zero, and to compare the result of one calculation to another. You compare packed decimal fields with CP, Compare Packed.

NAME	*OPERATION*	*OPERAND*
(symbol)	CP	S1,S2 or D1(L1,B1),D2(L2,B2)

The rules for CP are as follows:

1. Maximum field lengths are 16 bytes. Either operand may contain an explicit length (L1 and L2).

2. Both operands must contain valid packed data. Invalid data results in a program interrupt (data exception); the 370 suppresses the operation.

3. If the fields are not the same length, CP extends the shorter field (in the CPU, not in storage) with leftmost zeros (the value is not changed algebraically, and the test is still valid). There can be no overflow.

4. CP compares the contents of operand-1 *algebraically* to that of operand-2. That is, the positive value P'+001' is algebraically greater than P'−001'. (However, +0 is equal to −0.) CP sets the condition code, which you may then test with conditional branches, as for CLC.

COMPARISON	**CONDITION CODE**
Operand-1 equals operand-2	0 (equal)
Operand-1 is lower	1 (low)
Operand-1 is higher	2 (high)

Example: Contrast between CP and CLC. The following illustrates why you should use the correct operation for the data format, CLC for Character data and CP for Packed.

AMTCHAR	DC	C'123'	/F1/F2/F3/
AMTPACK	DS	PL2	↓ ↓ ↘
	PACK	AMTPACK,AMTCHAR	/12/3F/
	CP	AMTPACK,=P'123'	EQUAL
	CLC	AMTPACK,=P'123'	HIGH

AMTCHAR packed into AMTPACK gives the hex value /12/3F/. Both CP and CLC compare AMTPACK to a literal =P'123'. The literal generates a constant /12/3C/. For CP, /12/3F/ and /12/3C/ are algebraically equal (+123); the condition code is set to *equal*. For CLC, the two fields do not contain identical bits. Because F is greater than C, the condition code is set to *high*. Figure 4-8 depicts various CP operations:

```
LOC     OBJECT CODE      STMT    SOURCE STATEMENT

                         36 *    ---------------------
                         37 ***  CP     COMPARE PACKED
                         38 *    ---------------------
003054  012C             39 A    DC     P'12'         |01|2C|
003056  345C             40 B    DC     P'345'        |34|5C|
003058  05000C           41 C    DC     P'5000'       |05|00|0C|
00305B  025D             42 D    DC     P'-25'        |02|5D|
00305D  012A             43 E    DC     X'012A'       |01|2A|

                         45 *                         DATA COMPARED:   COND'N CODE:
                                                      -------------    -----------
00305F  00
003060  F911 4052 4054   46 COMP1  CP   A,B           '12+'  <  '345+'   LOW
003066  F921 4056 4052   47 COMP2  CP   C,A           '5000+' > '12+'    HIGH
00306C  F911 4052 4059   48 COMP3  CP   A,D           '12+'  >  '25-'    HIGH
003072  F911 4054 4057   49 COMP4  CP   B,C+1(2)      '345+' >  '000+'   HIGH

003078  F910 4052 40C4   51 COMP5  CP   A,=P'0'       '12+'  >  '0+'     HIGH
00307E  F911 4052 405B   52 COMP6  CP   A,E           '012+' =  '012+'   EQUAL
003084  F911 4056 4054   53 COMP7  CP   C(2),B        ERROR - NO SIGN IN OP-1
00308A  F911 4052 40C0   54 COMP8  CP   A,=C'12'      ERROR - NO SIGN IN OP-2
```

FIGURE 4-8 Sample compare packed operations.

COMP1 compares A to B. Because A's algebraic value is less, the condition code is set to low/minus.

COMP2 shows that CP correctly compares packed fields of unequal length.

COMP3 compares a positive amount in A against D's negative value. A's value is algebraically higher.

COMP4 uses relative addressing and explicit length to compare the two bytes of B against the second and third bytes of C.

COMP5 compares A to a literal containing packed zero.

COMP6 compares A against a hex constant, E, containing valid packed data. The sign in E is X'A', which, although a valid plus sign, is rarely used.

COMP7 and **COMP8** depict common programming errors made with packed data: the fields as *used* do not contain valid packed data. COMP7 should be coded with no explicit length, because C(2) means the first two bytes of C, containing no sign. In COMP8, the character literal does not define valid packed data. The literal should be defined as packed. Although these instructions assemble with no error message, at execute-time they will cause a program interrupt.

• *Problem 4-3 should now be attempted.* •

SUM OF DIGITS CALCULATION

Figure 4-9 provides an example of a routine that adds the sum of the digits from 1 to 10: $1 + 2 + 3 + \ldots + 10$. The example defines two fields: CTRPK is an accumulator that the routine increments by 1 for each loop (1, 2, 3, ..., 10) and SUMPK is the accumulator for the sum of the digits and increments by the value in CTRPK for each loop: 1, 3, 6, 10, ..., 55. You may find it worthwhile tracing the arithmetic and logic.

FORMATTING THE PRINT AREA

No problem was encountered in the previous chapter printing character data. Packed fields, however, contain nonprintable characters and must be unpacked for printing. A small problem arises when printing unpacked data. Assume you read an input field QTYIN containing the value 12345 (F1F2F3F4F5). Pack QTYIN into QTYPACK, add '50', and unpack QTYPACK into QTYOUT for printing:

```
QTYPACK   DC     PL3'0'
QTYOUT    DS     CL5
          PACK   QTYPACK,QTYIN      QTYPACK:   /12/34/5F/
          AP     QTYPACK,=P'50'     QTYPACK:   /12/39/5C/  ← sign
          UNPK   QTYOUT,QTYPACK     QTYOUT:    /F1/F2/F3/F9/C5
```

Note that AP changed the sign in QTYPACK from X'F' to X'C'. Now because the printer graphic for X'C5' is the letter E, QTYOUT will display

```
003002 000C                        6 CTRPK   DC   PL2'0'       COUNTER
003004 000C                        7 SUMPK   DC   PL2'0'       SUM DIGITS
                                   8 *
003006 FA10 4000 4052 03002 03054  9 LOOP    AP   CTRPK,=P'1'    1, 2, 3, 4, ..., 10
00300C FA11 4000 3004 03002 03002 10         AP   SUMPK,CTRPK    1, 3, 6, 10, ..., 55
003012 F911 4000 404E 03002 03050 11         CP   CTRPK,=P'10'   LOOPED 10 TIMES?
003018 4770 4004      03006       12         BNE  LOOP           NO - CONTINUE
                                  13 *        ...                YES - DONE
```

FIGURE 4-9 Sum of the digits.

or print as 1239E. In order to print the correct value 12395, you have to convert X'C5' to X'F5'. To accomplish this, move one of the other zone positions of QTYOUT into the units zone position. QTYOUT will now print correctly as 12345:

MVZ   QTYOUT+4(1),QTYOUT+3   /F1/F2/F3/F9/C5/

Another problem arises if the field is negative. Assume that QTYOUT contains /F1/F2/F3/F9/D5/. Inserting an F-zone to replace the D-zone changes the field's value from negative to positive. If you want the field to print, if positive as 12395, and if negative as 12395−, you may use the routine shown in Figure 4-10.

```
00301C F224 403F 403A 03041 0303C   17         PACK  QTYPK,QTYIN       PACK QTYIN
003022 FA21 403F 4050 03041 03052   18         AP    QTYPK,=P'50'      ADD 50 TO QTYPK
003028 47B0 402E      03030         19         BNM   D10               NOT MINUS?  BYPASS
                                    20  *                              MINUS:
00302C 9260 4047      03049         21         MVI   QTYOUT+5,'C'-'    * SET MINUS SIGN
003030 F342 4042 403F 03044 03041   22  D10    UNPK  QTYOUT,QTYPK      UNPACK QTYPK
003036 D300 4046 4045 03048 03047   23         MVZ   QTYOUT+4(1),QTYOUT+3  CORRECT SIGN POS'N
                                    24  *         .
                                    25  *         .
                                    26  *         .
00303C                              27  QTYIN  DS    ZL5               ZONED INPUT FIELD
003041                              28  QTYPK  DS    PL3               PACKED FIELD
003044                              29  QTYOUT DS    ZL5               ZONED OUTPUT FIELD
```

FIGURE 4-10 Formatting plus and minus unpacked amounts.

This procedure is quite cumbersome and inefficient. How about an instruction or routine that better facilitates printing the unit position digit and the minus sign? Indeed, there is an instruction, ED, described in the next chapter, which does just that, and much more.

PAGE OVERFLOW. The standard 11″ printer form provides for up to 60 lines of printing. Up to now we have not considered the possibility that the printer would reach the bottom of the form. Unless action is taken, the program will continue printing lines to the bottom of the page, over the horizontal perforation, and onto the top of the next page. Desirably, the program should know when printing has reached near to the bottom of the page, and the forms should eject to the top of the next page. Then the routine that printed the heading at the beginning of the program should be repeated, and normal printing of detail resumed.

The procedure to accommodate page overflow is for the program to count the lines that have been printed or spaced. The count is compared to some number, such as 40 or 50, that has been deemed the maximum number of print lines on a page. If the count exceeds this maximum, the program is directed to repeat the heading routine. The program at the end of this chapter provides for simple page overflow and should be carefully studied.

SUBROUTINES AND LINKAGE

A *subroutine* is a section of program coding that acts almost as an independent part of a program. Sometimes more than one part of the main program uses the subroutine. For example, you can treat the section of coding for page overflow as a separate part of the main program. It can be written as a subroutine used by different parts of the main program. Each time a line is printed, the program can check if the maximum number of lines per page has been reached. If so, the program branches, or links, to the subroutine. The subroutine executes the following:

- Skips to a new page.
- Prints the heading.
- Initializes the line counter.
- Adds one to the page count.
- Returns, or links, to the point of invocation in the main program.

The use of subroutines has several advantages: (a) It simplifies program writing. Commonly used routines, or complex routines, may be separated from the main program. The main program logic then is simplified. (b) A subroutine may be written once, then cataloged as a permanent part of the system, available for use by other programs. (c) It facilitates teams of programmers working on one program.

SUBROUTINE LINKAGE—BAL AND BR. Perform subroutine linkage by means of two instructions that use a register: BAL and BR.

NAME	OPERATION	OPERAND
(symbol)	BAL	R1,X2 or R1,D2(X2,B2)
(symbol)	BR	R1

BRANCH AND LINK—BAL. The rules for the BAL instruction are:

1. Operand-1 specifies a register to be used for subroutine linkage.
2. Operand-2 references an address, generally the subroutine.

3. On execution, BAL loads the address of the next instruction into the operand-1 register (the instruction address, bits 32–63 of the PSW). Then BAL branches unconditionally to the operand-2 storage address. For example, the instruction BAL 8,P10PAGE means: load the address of the next instruction in register-8, and branch to the address of P10PAGE.

BRANCH ON CONDITION REGISTER—BR. BR is an unconditional branch to an address in a register, and is commonly used to return from a subroutine. For example, the instruction BR 8 branches unconditionally to an address stored in register-8. BR is an "extended mnemonic," and is actually a BCR (Branch Condition Register) operation.

USE OF LINKAGE. You may allocate any available register for subroutine linkage, for now let's say registers 6–12 only. But be careful not to change the contents of the register between the time BAL loads the address and the time BR returns from the subroutine. In Figure 4-11, the main program has two linkages to the subroutine, statements 1 and 5. The program executes as follows:

STATEMENT	DESCRIPTION
1	BAL loads the address of the next instruction, statement 2, into register-8, and branches to P10PAGE, statement 9.
9–12	The subroutine, P10PAGE, is executed. At statement 12 the program branches to the address stored in register-8, statement 2.
2–4	Statements 2, 3, and 4 are executed.
5	BAL loads the address of the next instruction, statement 6, in register-8, and branches to P10PAGE, statement 9.
9–12	Statements 9, 10, and 11 are executed. At statement 12 the program branches to the address stored in register-8, statement 6.
6–8	Statements 6, 7, and 8 are executed. Statement 8 terminates program execution.

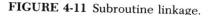

	Main program		*Subroutine*
1	BAL 8, P10PAGE	9	P10PAGE .
2	.	10	
3	.	11	.
4	.	12	BR 8
5	BAL 8, P10PAGE		
6	.		
7	.		
8	EOJ		

FIGURE 4-11 Subroutine linkage.

Ensure that the subroutine is a separate part of the program. The only way this subroutine should be normally entered is with BAL 8,P10PAGE. The normal exit in this example is back through register-8.

In this way, a subroutine can return to any number of addresses. The standard practice is to enter a subroutine at its top and to exit from its bottom. In the case of a serious error in the data, however, the program may have to exit earlier from a subroutine.

Some programmers prefer to use EQU to name registers, such as in the following manner:

```
LINKREG1    EQU       6
LINKREG2    EQU       7
```

LINKREG1 would be the register designated for the first level of subroutines, and LINKREG2 would be for the second (deeper) level of subroutines. For example, if P10PAGE is at the first level, then the instructions to link and to return would be:

```
BAL    LINKREG1,P10PAGE     Link to subroutine
 .
 .
 .
BR     LINKREG1             Return from subroutine
```

SUBROUTINE FLOWCHARTING. Both the subroutine coding and the subroutine flowchart are separated from the main program. The only new requirements are the flowchart symbols for linkage to and from the subroutine. The main program uses one symbol that represents the entire processing in the subroutine, as shown in Figure 4-12, one of several ways to represent subroutines.

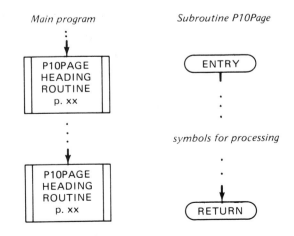

FIGURE 4-12 Subroutine symbols.

The symbol in the main program that represents the subroutine processing shows:

1. The name of the subroutine (P10PAGE),
2. A description of the subroutine (HEADING ROUTINE), and
3. The flowchart page number on which the subroutine detail is given.

For a complete example of main logic and subroutines, refer to the flowchart and program at the end of this chapter.

SAMPLE PROGRAM: BUDGET STATEMENT

The flowchart in Figure 4-13 depicts a program that reads company cost records containing Budget expense and Actual expense for the current period. The records are sequence-checked by general account number. The program calculates the variance: Budget less Actual expense. A negative variance means that the Actual expense exceeds the Budget. If this variance exceeds $-500.00, the program prints a message "OVER LIMIT." At the end of the run, the total variance is printed.

For reasons of brevity, the program omits many common procedures such as: checking for valid record code, printing total budget amount and actual expense, and providing for the current date on the report. Figure 4-14 gives the assembled and executed program. The input format is as follows:

COLUMN	CONTENTS
1	Record code
2–5	General account number
6–15	Expense description
16–21	Budget expense
22–27	Actual expense (plus or minus)
28–80	Unused

Note on sequence-checking: The program initializes PREVACC, the previously stored account number, with hexadecimal zeros (XL4'00'). This value represents two bytes of binary zeros, the lowest possible value on a computer. The blank character, X'40', for example is higher than X'00', and there is no single key on a keyboard that can enter X'00'. Under normal conditions, it would be virtually impossible for a data record to contain hex zeros in its account number field. As a consequence, the *first* input record is always higher than the contents of PREVACC. You could define PREVACC as CL4' ' or C'0000', but the first input account number could conceivably contain blanks or zeros. The program would then treat the account number as equal to PREVACC, resulting in an invalid error message.

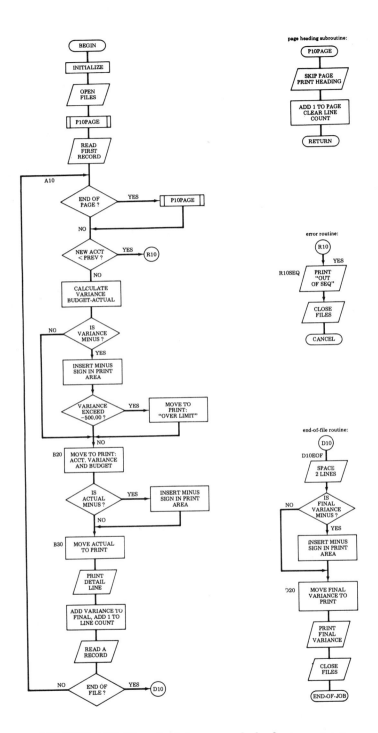

FIGURE 4-13 Flowchart for example budget program.

The program is organized by sections:

- The Initialization opens the files and clears the print area (this clearing could be omitted if the contents of the print area were fully defined with DC blanks).
- The Main Processing routine reads records, calculates, and prints the variance.
- The End-of-File routine prints the total variance and closes the files.
- The Page Heading routine prints headings and page number at the top of each page printed.
- The Error routine prints a message and terminates on an out-of-sequence record. Under OS, the ABEND macro would replace the CANCEL.

REPRESENTATION IN STORAGE

Figure 4-15 shows the hexadecimal contents of the declaratives defined in the preceding program from the first byte of RECDIN through PREVACC, as at the end of processing. The program listing shows RECDIN beginning at location (LOC) X'3D2'. In this particular execution, the program happened to load in storage beginning at X'867078'. Consequently, the actual location of RECDIN during execution would be:

Starting point of program:	X'867078'
Location (LOC) of RECDIN:	X'0003D2'
Actual storage location	X'86744A'

You can locate the contents of RECDIN in the "storage dump" beginning with the first hex characters on the top line. At the extreme left is the address of the leftmost byte of each line. This line "starts" at X'867440'. If you count across each pair of hex digits as one byte you'll find that X'86744A' is the actual storage location of RECDIN, just as was calculated above. The blank columns are only for readability. RECDIN contains the last input record:

```
867440  .  .  .  4040F3F7 F0F8F2D7  D6E2E3C1 C7C54040  .  .  .
                         |                   |
                    X'86744A'           X'867450'
```

CODEIN is the first byte X'F3' or 3, and ACCIN occupies the next four bytes, X'F7F0F8F2' or 7082. DESCRIN is the next 15 bytes containing POSTAGE. The rest of RECDIN continues on the second line.

Note that if X'867440' is the leftmost byte, then the address of the byte beginning the right half of the dump is X'867450'.

```
LOC     OBJECT CODE     ADDR1 ADDR2  STMT  SOURCE STATEMENT

                                       2         PRINT ON,NOGEN,NODATA

                                       4   *
                                       5   *       I N I T I A L I Z A T I O N
                                                   ---------------------------
000000                                 6   PROG04  START                           INITIALIZE
                                       7           INIT                            INITIALIZE
                                      13           OPEN  FILEIN,PRTR               CLEAR PRINT AREA
000022  D284 34A6 34A5  004A8 004A7   22           MVC   BUDLINE,BLANK             HEADING RTNE
000028  4560 314A        0014C        23           BAL   6,P10PAGE
                                      24           GET   FILEIN,RECDIN             1ST RECORD

                                      31   *
                                      32   *       M A I N   P R O C E S S I N G
                                                   -------------------------------
00003C  F911 35B4  35FE  005B6 00600  33   A10LOOP CP    LINEPK,=P'10'             END OF PAGE?
000042  4740 3048        0004A        34           BL    A20                       NO  - BYPASS
000046  4560 314A        0014C        35           BAL   6,P10PAGE                 YES - HEADING
00004A  D503 33D1  35D2  003D1 005D4  36   A20     CLC   ACCIN,PREVACC             NEW ACCOUNT < PREV ACCT?
000050  4740 318C        0018E        37           BL    R10SEQER                  YES - CANCEL JOB
000054  D203 35D2  35D1  005D4 003D1  38           MVC   PREVACC,ACCIN             MOVE NEW ACCT # TO PREV
00005A  F235 35B8  33E4  005B8 003E6  39           PACK  VARPK,BUDGETIN            PACK BUDGET &
000060  F235 35B0  33EA  005B0 003EC  40           PACK  ACTPK,ACTUALIN             ACTUAL AMOUNTS
000066  FB33 35B8  35B0  005B8 005B0  41           SP    VARPK,ACTPK               CALCULATE VARIANCE
00006C  47B0 3082        00084        42           BNM   A30                       VARIANCE NEGATIVE?
000070  9260 34EB        004ED        43           MVI   VAROUT+7,C'-'             YES - INSERT '-' SIGN

000074  F932 35B8  360A  005B8 0060C  45           CP    VARPK,=P'-500.00'         VARIANCE > 500.00 NEG
00007A  47B0 3082        00084        46           BNL   A30                       NO  - BYPASS
00007E  D209 34EF  3600  004F1 00602  47           MVC   MESSAGOT,=C'OVER LIMIT'   YES - PRINT WARNING

000084  D203 34BA  33D1  004BC 003D3  49   A30     MVC   ACCOT,ACCIN               MOVE ACCOUNT # &
00008A  D20E 34C0  33D5  004C2 003D7  50           MVC   DESCROT,DESCRIN           DESCR'N TO PRINT
000090  F363 34E4  35B8  004E4 005BA  51           UNPK  VAROUT,VARPK              UNPACK VARIANCE INTO PRINT
000096  D300 34EA  34E9  004EC 004EB  52           MVZ   VAROUT+6(1),VAROUT+5      CORRECT ZONE IN UNIT POS'N
00009C  D205 34D2  33E4  004D4 003E6  53           MVC   BUDGOUT,BUDGETIN          MOVE BUDGET TO PRINT AREA
0000A2  F833 35B0  35B2  005B0 005B2  54           ZAP   ACTPK,ACTPK              ACTUAL NEGATIVE?
0000A8  47B0 30AE        000B0        55           BNM   A40                       NO  - BYPASS
0000AC  9260 34E1        004E3        56           MVI   ACTOUT+6,C'-'             YES - INSERT '-' SIGN

0000B0  D205 34DB  33EA  004DD 003EC  58   A40     MVC   ACTOUT,ACTUALIN           MOVE ACTUAL EXPENSE
0000B6  D300 34E0  34E2  004E2 004E1  59           MVZ   ACTOUT+5(1),ACTOUT+4      CORRECT ZONE IN UNIT POS'N
                                      60           PUTPR PRTR,BUDLINE,WSP1         PRINT ACCOUNT
0000D0  FA10 35B4  360D  005B6 0060F  67           AP    LINEPK,=P'1'              ADD TO LINE COUNTER
0000D6  D284 34A6 34A5  004A8 004A7   68           MVC   BUDLINE,BLANK             CLEAR PRINT AREA
0000DC  FA43 35BC 35B8   005BE 005BA  69           AP    VFINPK,VARPK              ADD TO FINAL TOTAL VARIANCE
                                      70           GET   FILEIN,RECDIN             READ NEXT RECORD
0000F2  47F0 303A        0003C        76           B     A10LOOP

                                      78   *
                                      79   *       E N D - O F - F I L E
                                                   ---------------------
                                      80   D10EOF  PUTPR PRTR,BUDLINE,SP2
00010A  F844 35BC 35BC  005BE 005BE   87           ZAP   VFINPK,VFINPK             FINAL AMOUNT NEGATIVE?
000110  47B0 3116        00118        88           BNM   D20                       *   NO
000114  9260 3570        00572        89           MVI   TOTALPR+9,C'-'            *   YES - INSERT '-'
```

128

```
000118 F384 3567 35BC 00569 005BE   91 D20          UNPK  TOTALPR,VFINPK            MOVE TOTAL TO PRINT
00011E D300 356F 356E 00571 00570   92              MVZ   TOTALPR+8(1),TOTALPR+7    CORRECT ZONE IN UNIT POS'N
                                    93              PUTPR PRTR,TOTLINE,WSP1         PRINT FINAL TOTAL
                                   100              CLOSE FILEIN,PRTR
                                   109              EOJ                             NORMAL END-OF-JOB


LOC    OBJECT CODE      ADDR1 ADDR2   STMT   SOURCE STATEMENT                                      PAGE   2

                                   113  *          P A G E   H E A D I N G
                                   114  *          ---------------------
000160 F321 346E 35B6 00470 005B8  115 PIOPAGE     PUTPR PRTR,HDGLINE,SK1          SKIP NEXT PAGE
000166 D300 3470 346E 00472 00470  122         ,   UNPK  PAGEPR,PAGEPK             SET UP
                                   123         ,   MVZ   PAGEPR+2(1),PAGEPR        PAGE NO.
000180 FA10 35B6 360D 005B8 0060F  124             PUTPR PRTR,HDGLINE,WSP2         PRINT HEADING
000186 F810 35B4 360E 005B6 00610  131             AP    PAGEPK=P'1'              ADD TO PAGE NUMBER
00018C 07F6                        132             ZAP   LINEPK=P'0'              CLEAR LINE COUNTER
                                   133             BR    6                        RETURN

                                   135  *          E R R O R   R O U T I N E
                                   136  *          -------------------------
00018E D210 34EF 35C1 004F1 005C3  137 R10SEQER    MVC   MESSAGOT(17),MESSEQ       PRINT ERROR MESSAGE
                                   138             PUTPR PRTR,BUDLINE,WSP2
                                   145             CLOSE FILEIN,PRTR
                                   154             CANCEL ,                        ABNORMAL JOB TERM'N

                                   159  *          D E C L A R A T I V E S
                                   160  *          -----------------------
                                   162 FILEIN      DEFIN DIOEOF                    DEFINE INPUT FILE
                                   186 PRTR        DEFPR                           DEFINE PRINTER FILE
0003D2                             211 RECDIN      DS    0CL80                     INPUT AREA:
0003D2                             212 CODEIN      DS    CL01                      01-01 RECORD CODE
0003D3                             213 ACCIN       DS    CL04                      02-05 ACCOUNT NO.
0003D7                             214 DESCRIN     DS    CL15                      06-20 DESCRIPTION
0003E6                             215 BUDGETIN    DS    ZL06                      21-26 BUDGETTED EXPENSE
0003EC                             216 ACTUALIN    DS    ZL06                      27-32 ACTUAL EXPENSE
0003F2                             217             DS    CL48                      33-80 UNUSED
                                   219 HDGLINE     DS    0CL133                    HEADING LINE:
000422 40404040404040404040       220             DC    CL20' '                   *-------------
000436 C1C3C3E34040404040C5       221             DC    CL24'ACCT  DESCRIPTION'   *
00044E C2E4C4C7C5E34040           222             DC    CL34'BUDGET   ACTUAL   VARIANCE      PAGE'   *
000470                            223 PAGEPR      DS    CL03                       *
000473 40404040404040404040       224             DC    CL52' '                   *
```

FIGURE 4-14 (partial)

129

```
                                                                    BLANK FOR CLEARING PRINT
0004A7  40                                                          BUDGET PRINT LINE:
0004A8           226  BLANK     DC   C' '                           *-------------
0004A8           227  BUDLINE   DS   0CL133
0004BC           228            DS   CL20                           *  ACCOUNT NO.
0004C0           229  ACCOT     DS   CL04                           *
0004C2           230            DS   CL02                           *  DESCRIPTION
0004D1           231  DESCROT   DS   CL15                           *
0004D4           232            DS   CL03                           *  BUDGETTED EXPENSE
0004DA           233  BUDGOUT   DS   ZL06                           *
0004DD           234            DS   CL03                           *  ACTUAL EXPENSE
0004E3           235  ACTOUT    DS   ZL06                           *
0004E6           236            DS   CL03                           *  VARIANCE
0004ED           237  VAROUT    DS   ZL07                           *
0004F1           238            DS   CL04                           *  OVER BUDGET MESSAGE
0004FB           239  MESSAGOT  DS   CL10                           *
                 240            DS   CL50

00052D           242  TOTLINE   DS   0CL133                         TOTAL PRINT LINE:
00052D 404040404040404040    243            DC   CL26' '            *-------------
000547 C6C9D5C1D340E3D6      244            DC   CL34'FINAL TOTAL'  *
000569           245  TOTALPR   DS   ZL09                           *
000572 40404040404040404040  246            DC   CL64' '


LOC    OBJECT CODE    ADDR1 ADDR2   STMT  SOURCE STATEMENT                      PACKED CONSTANTS:

0005B2 0000000C               248  ACTPK     DC   PL4'0'                        *
0005B6 000C                   249  LINEPK    DC   PL2'0'                        *
0005B8 001C                   250  PAGEPK    DC   PL2'1'                        *
0005BA 0000000C               251  VARPK     DC   PL4'0'
0005BE 000000000C             252  VFINPK    DC   PL5'0'

0005C3 D9C5C3D6D9C440D6       254  MESSEQ    DC   C'RECORD OUT OF SEQ'          PREVIOUS ACCT NUMBER
0005D4 00000000               255  PREVACC   DC   XL4'00'

0005D8                        257            LTORG
0005D8 5B5BC2D6D7C5D540       258                 =C'$$BOPEN '
0005E0 5B5BC2C3D3D6E2C5       259                 =C'$$BCLOSE'
0005E8 000001C0               260                 =A(FILEIN)
0005EC 000003D2               261                 =A(RECDIN)
0005F0 00000298               262                 =A(PRTR)
0005F4 000004A8               263                 =A(BUDLINE)
0005F8 0000052D               264                 =A(TOTLINE)
0005FC 00000422               265                 =A(HDGLINE)
000600 010C                   266                 =P'10'
000602 D6E5C5D940D3C9D4       267                 =C'OVER LIMIT'
00060C 50000D                 268                 =P'-500.00'
00060F 1C                     269                 =P'1'
000610 0C                     270                 =P'0'
                      00000   271            END  PROG04
```

130

Output:-

```
ACCT  DESCRIPTION      BUDGET   ACTUAL   VARIANCE    PAGE 001

5301  LABOR            250000   268315   0018315-
5302  SUPERVISION      100000   100000   0000000
5315  HEAT, LIGHT      022000   029526   0007526-
5328  REPAIRS          000000   065315   0065315-    OVER LIMIT
6001  SALES SALARIES   123450   123450   0000000
6051  DELIVERY EXPEN   003333   005010   0001677-
6059  DEPRECIATION     015000   013356   0001644
6061  FREIGHT          008500   011520   0003020-
6075  ADVERTISING      005000   000000   0005000
6081  TRAVEL EXPENSE   010000   112016   0102016-    OVER LIMIT


ACCT  DESCRIPTION      BUDGET   ACTUAL   VARIANCE    PAGE 002

6084  INSURANCE        002500   002500   0000000
7011  OFFICE SUPPLIES  003500   001516   0001984
7029  BAD DEBTS        002500   068500   0066000-    OVER LIMIT
7082  POSTAGE          001000   001215   0000215-


      FINAL TOTAL                        000255456-
```

FIGURE 4-14 List of budget, actual expense, and variance.

```
                                 86744A
                                 RECDIN

867440                       4040 F3 F7  F0F8F2D7   D6E2E3C1 C7C54040 40404040 4040F0F0
867460    F1F0F0F0 F0F0F1F2 F1F54040 40404040   40404040 40404040 40404040 40404040
867480    40404040 --SAME--
8674A0    40404040 40404040 40404040 4040C1C3   C3E34040 C4C5E2C3 D9C9D7E3 C9D6D540
8674C0    40404040 4040C2E4 C4C7C5E3 404040C1   C3E3E4C1 D34040E5 C1D9C9C1 D5C3C540
8674E0    404040D7 C1C7C540 F0F0F240 40404040   40404040 40404040 40404040 40404040
867500    40404040 --SAME--
8675A0    40404040 40404040 40404040 40404040   40404040 40404040 40404040 404040C6
8675C0    C9D5C1D3 40E3D6E3 C1D3404U 40404040   40404040 40404040 40404040 40404040
8675E0    40F0F0F0 F2F5F5F4 F5F66040 40404040   40404040 40404040 40404040 40404040
867600    40404040 --SAME--
867620    40404040 40404040 40400001 215C004C   003C0000 215D0002 55456DD9 C5C3D6D9
867640    C440D6E4 E340D6C6 40E2C5D8 F7F0F8F2   5B5BC4D6
```

```
              86762A    86762E    867630    867632    867636
              ACTPK     LINEPK    PAGEPK    VARPK     VFINPK
```

FIGURE 4-15 Hexadecimal representation of storage.

Lines such as the one at X'867480' that show

```
              40404040  --SAME--
```

contain the same value in every byte, in this case X'40'.

The figure shows the contents of the defined declaratives HDGLINE, BUDLINE, ACTPK, LINEPK, PAGEPK, VARPK, VFINPK, MESSEQ, and PREVACC. As at the end of processing, ACTPK should contain 001215. Let's check that it's true:

Starting location of program:	X'867078'
Location (LOC) of ACTPK:	X'0005B2'
Actual location of ACTPK:	X'86762A'

Now find this value in the dump. Trace down the leftmost column until you reach X'867620'. Starting with this location for the first byte, count across until you reach X'86762A: you should be at the value 00001215C, the correct contents of ACTPK.

For practice, calculate the actual locations of the other declaratives, locate their contents in the dump, and check the hex values. Chapter 16 further develops storage dumps and the way that you can generate your own dumps.

DEBUGGING TIPS

Expect considerably more bugs in both the assembly and execution phases as your programs become larger and involve arithmetic data. Finding a bug for the first time is quite often time-consuming, but in time you can become proficient in tracing errors (especially if you have enough of them!).

New assembly errors that can occur involve, for example, coding packed DCs with characters other than 0–9, decimal point, and sign. Watch for coding hex constants: for example, DC XL3'FF' generates '0000FF', not 'FFFFFF'.

More likely, however, are errors during program execution. Packing a field that contains a blank (X'40') in its rightmost position generates a packed field with an invalid sign (X'04'); an attempt to perform arithmetic using this field will cause a data exception. A likely cause of the blank position is a blank input field, or an improperly defined input record. Another popular cause of data exceptions is adding to a field that has not been initialized as a DC, or is defined as Character or Hex, so that it contains invalid packed data.

Watch out also for using MVC and CLC on packed data (incorrect execution), or ZAP and CP on character data (data exceptions). Improper relative addressing and missing explicit lengths are always good for a few bugs.

ERROR DETECTION.   The system is designed to terminate a run on a "program check" interrupt, such as a data exception or an operation exception (Appendix B contains a complete list). The supervisor's error diagnostics vary considerably by operating system. See Chapter 16 for details.

PROBLEMS

4-1.   MVN and MVZ. Given the following declaratives, code the following un-related questions. Give results in hex and character.

```
HAM        DC        C'HAL'
EGGS       DC        C'2472'
TOAST      DC        X'C9E2C4E0'
```

(a)   Move the first 3 numeric half-bytes of TOAST to the numerics of HAM.

(b)   Move the zone half-bytes of TOAST to those of EGGS.

4-2.   Complete the hex representation for the following. Except for (a) and for (b), questions are unrelated.

								F3	F4	F5	F6	F7	F8
Example:	L	DC		C'345678'		L							
	M	DC		C'1234'		M							
	N	DC		Z'123'		N							
	P	DC		P'−123'		P							
	Q	DC		P'12.34'		Q							
(a)		PACK		P,N		P							
		UNPK		L,P		L							
(b)		PACK		Q,L		Q							
		UNPK		N,Q		N							
(c)		PACK		Q + 1(2),N + 1(2)		Q							
(d)		PACK		P,=CL2' '		P							
(e)		PACK		M,M		M							
(f)		UNPK		P,P		P							
(g)		ZAP		Q,P		Q							
(h)		ZAP		P,Q		P							
(i)		AP		Q,=P'5'		Q							
(j)		AP		Q,=X'5C'		Q							

4-3. Check the *condition code* set by the following. Symbolic names refer to Problem 4-2. Explain if invalid.

			HI	LO	EQ
(a)	CP	P,Q			
(b)	CP	Q,P			
(c)	CP	M,Q			
(d)	CLC	M,N			

4-4. PROGRAM ASSIGNMENT.

Required: A program that reads Accounts Receivable records, prints the detail, and accumulates totals.

Input: Data records similar to the format of the example program at the end of Chapter 3, with some additions:

COLUMN		COLUMN	
1	Record code (3)	31–32	Current month
4–5	Store number	41–46	Balance owing
6–10	Customer number	47–52	Customer limit
11–30	Customer name		

Procedure:

1. Check for valid record code (3).
2. Sequence-check the file according to Store-Customer number. Within a Store, the Customer numbers are in ascending sequence.
3. Check that the current month is the same for all records. If not, print a suitable message.
4. Compare Customer balances to their credit limits. If the balance exceeds the limit, print 'OVER LIMIT'.
5. Print all the data except record code from each record. At the end of each Store, print the total balance owing for all Customers for that Store (minor total). At the end of the run, print the total balance owing for all Stores (final total).
6. Provide test input data that will test all possible conditions in the program.
7. Analyze, code, and test the program. Be sure to use the programming standards for your installation.

5

DECIMAL ARITHMETIC II

This chapter continues with the additional decimal instructions commonly used in programming: edit, multiply, and divide. Editing involves sign and punctuation control to format packed fields for printing. The sections on multiply and divide provide practical techniques for handling various field lengths and decimal-point precision and more realistic programming examples and problems.

EDITING—ED

The purpose of ED is to make packed data suitable for printing. ED converts packed data into zoned format and provides for punctuation and sign. Once understood, ED greatly facilitates print formatting.

NAME	OPERATION	OPERAND
(symbol)	ED	S1,S2 or D1(L,B1),D2(B2)

Editing normally consists of two operations:

1. Define an edit word, or pattern, specifying where you want commas, decimal point, and sign to print. Use MVC to move this edit word to the print positions where the amount is to be printed.
2. Then use ED to modify the packed field according to the edit word definition. ED unpacks the amount field and provides the required editing for commas, decimal point, and minus sign.

137

The following simple example edits a 2-byte (3-digit) packed field called COUNT into a print field called COUNPR. (There is no provision for commas or decimal point.)

```
COUNT       DC    PL2'001'          3-digit packed field
COUNPR      DC    CL4' '            Print field for edited
                                    result
            MVC   COUNPR,=X'40202020'  Move editword to print
                                    field
            ED    COUNPR,COUNT      Edit the packed field
                                    into print field


COUNPR after MVC:  40202020
COUNPR after ED:   404040F1
```

THE EDIT WORD. The edit word consists of pairs of hex digits. Each pair represents one print position. The commonly used edit characters are:

HEX	NAME	PURPOSE
40	Fill character	Used for "zero suppression"—to fill or pad leftmost unwanted zeros with blanks. For example, ED can suppress 00025 so that it prints as 25. You may use any other character such as asterisk (5C) as a fill character, although X'40' is the commonly used EBCDIC blank.
20	Digit selector	One X'20' in the edit word represents each packed digit to be printed. Since a packed field always contains an odd number of digits, there must be an odd number of X'20s (including X'21s, if any). In the example earlier, COUNT contains three digits. Your edit word, therefore, contains three X'20s. ED selects one packed digit for each X'20'. It unpacks the digit in the X'20' position. However, if the digit is a leading (leftmost) zero, ED replaced the X'20' with the X'40' fill character.
6B	Comma (,)	Code X'6B' in the edit word wherever a comma is to be printed.
4B	Decimal point (.)	Code X'4B' in the edit word wherever a decimal point is to be printed.
60	Minus sign (−)	If the amount could be negative, code X'60' to print a minus sign to the right of the edited amount.
C3D9	Credit (CR)	To print CR instead of minus, use X'C3D9'.
21	Significance starter	A "significant" digit is 1 through 9 (nonzero). In the value 000.25, the '2' is the first significant digit in the field. The fill character X'40' "zero suppresses" the leftmost zeros by filling them with blanks: bbbb25. You may want to *force significance* so that a leftmost zero prints as bb0.25. For this purpose code X'21', the significance starter.

21 (cont)

Normally, you code only one X'21'. It acts the same as the digit selector, but in addition X'21' forces significance—all characters to its right are forced to print, whether they contain a significant digit or not.

BASIC RULES OF EDITING.

1. Move the required edit word into the print area.
2. The operands of the ED operation work as follows: Operand-1 references the leftmost byte of the edit word. This is normally the print area, the same position and length as specified by the MVC. Operand-2 references the packed field to be edited.
3. Editing proceeds from left to right. ED examines each character in the edit word to determine what action to take:

   - The leftmost hex byte is always assumed to be the fill character, which is normally X'40', but may be any other required character.

   - For each X'20', ED selects a packed digit. If the digit is nonzero, it is unpacked, replacing the X'20'. If zero, and significance has not been encountered, then ED replaces the X'20' with the fill character (usually X'40'). Significance is forced either by a significant digit or by the significance starter (X'21').

   - If the hex byte X'6B' (comma) or X'4B' (decimal), and significance has been encountered, they are preserved. If significance has not been encountered, ED replaces them with the fill character.

   - If the packed field is negative, then any CR or minus (X'60') is preserved. If positive, ED replaces them with the fill character. The condition code for minus, zero, and plus is set.

4. The length of operand-1 terminates the operation. The maximum length is 256 bytes. Only operand-1 may have an explicit length.

EXAMPLE EDIT OPERATION.

A 3-byte packed field, PACKAMT, is to be edited. The edit word must provide for decimal point, minus sign, and zero suppression of the three leftmost digits.

```
PACKAMT  DC   PL3'5'                 (contains /00/00/5C/)
EDWORD   DC   X'4020202144B202060'
```

The defined edit word, EDWORD, provides the necessary sign and punctuation control. Note that there is an X'20' or X'21' for each packed digit. The instructions to edit are:

```
MVC     P + 90(8),EDWORD          /40/20/20/21/4B/20/20/60/

ED      P + 90(8),PACKAMT         /40/40/40/40/4B/F0/F5/40/
```

P + 90	+ 92	+ 94	+ 96
+ 91	+ 93	+ 95	+ 97

MVC moved EDWORD into the required print positions. ED then edits PACKAMT into the same print positions. *The explicit length (8) in the ED operand refers to the length of the edit word* in the print area, not to the length of PACKAMT. Editing proceeds from left to right, starting at P+90:

P+90: X'40', assumed to be the fill character, is not changed: /40/20/20/21/4B/20/20/60

P+91: Because the position contains X'20', ED examines the first digit of PACKAMT. It contains zero, and therefore the fill character X'40' replaces the X'20': /40/40/20/21/4B/20/20/60

P+92: Because of the X'20' here, ED examines the second digit of PACKAMT. It also contains a zero, so the X'20' is changed to X'40': /40/40/40/21/4B/20/20/60

P+93: Because of the X'21' significance starter here, all characters to the right are to be printed. Also, ED examines the third digit of PACKAMT, a zero, and replaces the X'21' with X'40': /40/40/40/40/4B/20/20/60

P+94: X'4B' is a decimal point. Because X'21' has signalled to force printing, the X'4B' is not changed. (Had the X'21' not been encountered yet, the fill character would replace the X'4B'.): /40/40/40/40/4B/20/20/60

P+95: Because of the X'20', ED examines the fourth digit of PACKAMT, a zero. Because of the preceding X'21', ED unpacks the zero and replaces the X'20' with X'F0': /40/40/40/40/4B/F0/20/60

P+96: Because of the X'20', ED unpacks the fifth digit of PACKAMT, 5. X'F5' replaces the X'20': /40/40/40/40/4B/F0/F5/60

P+97: X'60' means that if the next half-byte of PACKAMT contains X'D' (a minus sign), the field is considered negative and the X'60' is not changed. Because PACKAMT is positive (X'C'), ED replaces the X'60' with the fill character, X'40': /40/40/40/40/4B/F0/F5/40

At this point the length (8) of operand-1 is exhausted, and the operation terminates. The edited amount will print as .05 (if EDWORD contained X'402021204B202060', the result would be 0.05). Figure 5-1 illustrates four example edit operations:

EDWD1 shows simple zero suppression. The packed amount in COUNTER is to print with leftmost zeros suppressed. The edit word, EDWD1, therefore consists of an X'40' fill character and an X'20' for each packed digit.

```
STMT    SOURCE STATEMENT

   6  *               ------------
   7  ***      ED     EDIT
   8  *               ------------
   9  *               ZERO SUPPRESSION:     HEX CONTENTS:
  10  *               ----------------      -------------
  11  P        DS     CL121
  12  COUNTER  DC     P'0015'               |00|01|5C|
  13  EDWD1    DC     X'402020202020'       |40|20|20|20|20|20|

  15           MVC    P+20(6),EDWD1         |40|20|20|20|20|20|
  16           ED     P+20(6),COUNTER       |40|40|40|40|F1|F5|

  18  *               COMMA, DECIMAL, MINUS SIGN:
  19  *               ---------------------------
  20  AMOUNT   DC     P'-2345.00'           |02|34|50|0D|
  21  EDWD2    DC     X'40202068202021482020 60'

  23           MVC    P+30(11),EDWD2        |40|20|20|6B|20|20|21|4B|20|20|60|
  24           ED     P+30(11),AMOUNT       |40|40|F2|6B|F3|F4|F5|4B|F0|F0|60|   +
                                                  2 ,  3  4  5  .  0  0  -
  25  *               CREDIT (CR) SIGN:
  26  *               ----------------
  27  TOTAL    DC     P'-0000.05'           |00|00|00|5D|
  28  EDWD3    DC     X'40202068202120482020C3D9'

  30           MVC    P+50(12),EDWD3        |40|20|20|6B|20|21|20|4B|20|20|C3|D9|
  31           ED     P+50(12),TOTAL        |40|40|40|40|40|40|F0|4B|F0|F5|C3|D9|  +
                                                     0  .  0  5  C  R
  32  *               ASTERISK AND DOLLAR SIGN:
  33  *               -------------------------
  34  ACCUM    DC     P'12.34'              |01|23|4C|
  35  EDWD4    DC     X'5B402020214B2020605C'

  37           MVC    P+70(10),EDWD4        |5B|40|20|20|21|4B|20|20|60|5C|
  38           ED     P+71(08),ACCUM        |5B|40|40|F1|F2|4B|F3|F4|40|5C|    +
                                              $       1  2  .  3  4     *
```

FIGURE 5-1 Sample edit operations.

EDWD2 edits and prints a 4-byte packed field. The edit word provides for zero suppression, comma, decimal point, and minus sign.

EDWD3 depicts use of the CR symbol commonly used in financial statements.

EDWD4 is explained in the next section.

DOLLAR SIGN AND ASTERISK.   The dollar sign (X'5B') and the asterisk (X'5C') when used in the edit word create certain problems. The normal purpose of the dollar sign ($) is to print Supplier and Employee checks and Customer bills, with the $ to the left of the amount. If X'5B' is coded on the left, ED improperly uses it as the fill character. Also, many installations print asterisks (*) to the right of the amount field to denote the level of total:

*	Minor total
* *	Intermediate total
* * *	Major total

If one or more X'5Cs are coded to the right of the edit word, ED leaves the asterisks undisturbed only if the amount is negative. If positive, ED replaces asterisks with the fill character, thus erasing them. One solution is to omit both X'5B' and X'5C' from the edit word and use separate operations to move $ and * to the print area. Another solution is the technique that EDWD4 uses in Figure 5-1, in which $ and * are defined as part of the edit word but do not participate in the ED operation. MVC moves the full edit word, starting in P+70. The ED operation begins in P+71, leaving the $ intact. Further, ED specifies editing only 8 bytes, although the MVC moved 10. The operation terminates just prior to the * at P+79, leaving it also intact.

Another instruction, EDMK, providing for floating dollar sign and asterisk is covered in a later chapter.

- *Problems 5-1, 5-2, and 5-3 should now be attempted.* •

MULTIPLY PACKED—MP

The purpose of MP is to multiply one packed field (the multiplicand) by another (the multiplier). Common examples are multiplying hours by rate-of-pay in payroll, and quantity by unit cost in inventory programs.

NAME	OPERATION	OPERAND
(symbol)	MP	S1,S2 or D1(L1,B1),D2(L2,B2)

The rules for MP are:

1. Either operand may contain an explicit length (L1 and L2).
2. The operand-1 field is the *multiplicand* and must contain valid packed data. The *product* is developed in this field, and replaces the multiplicand. The maximum length of operand-1 is 16 bytes, providing 31 digits. You should define the operand-1 field large enough to accommodate the largest possible product that the two operands can develop. Generally, the product length should equal at least the length in bytes of the multiplicand plus the multiplier.
3. Operand-2 references the *multiplier* in valid packed format. The maximum length is 8 bytes.
4. MP is governed by the normal rules of algebra: like signs yield a positive product, and unlike signs yield a negative product. A zero amount in either operand causes a zero product. MP does not set the condition code.

PRODUCT LENGTH. As a good programming practice, define the product length equal at least to the length *in bytes* of the multiplicand plus multiplier. From another point of view, prior to execution of the MP, for each byte in the multiplier, the product field must contain one byte of zeros to the left of the significant digits in the multiplicand. Consider the following:

```
MULTPLD   DC    PL4'1234560'        4-byte multiplicand
MULTPLR   DC    PL2'950'            2-byte multiplier
PRODUCT   DS    PL6                 6-byte product
          ZAP   PRODUCT,MULTPLD     /00/00/12/34/56/0C/
          MP    PRODUCT,MULTPLR     /01/17/28/32/00/0C/
```

Since MULTPLD is four bytes and MULTPLR is two, define PRODUCT as six bytes (PRODUCT may be defined longer). The example uses ZAP to move MULTPLD into PRODUCT. After the MP, PRODUCT contains a 6-byte product. If PRODUCT were shorter, the MP would cause a program interrupt.

DECIMAL PRECISION. Neither the Assembler nor the computer handles the decimal position. With all decimal arithmetic you must provide for the implied decimal point. The following is a useful rule:

The number of decimal positions in the product equals the number of decimals in the multiplicand plus multiplier.

For example, if the multiplicand has three decimals and the multiplier has two, then the product will have five decimal positions:

$$\begin{array}{r} \text{x x x . x x x} \\ \underline{\text{x x . x x}} \\ \text{x x x x x . x x x x x} \end{array}$$

Figure 5-2 illustrates multiply operations. The first example multiplies a 2-byte field, QTY, by a 2-byte field, PRICE. The product, AMT, is therefore defined as four bytes in length. Since PRICE contains two decimals and QTY none, there are two decimal positions generated in the product. This example requires a 2-decimal answer, and therefore no rounding is done.

The second example multiplies a 3-byte field, HRS, by a 2-byte field, RATE. The product, WAGE, is therefore five bytes long. Since HRS contains one decimal and RATE two, the product has three decimal positions. Because only two decimals are required, this example rounds the unwanted rightmost decimal digit. An SRP operation shifts the product one digit to the right, leaving two decimal positions, as explained in the next section.

SHIFTING AND ROUNDING

Basically, rounding consists of adding 5 to the first unwanted decimal position and dropping all the unwanted decimal positions. For a negative product,

```
                              6  *      --------------------------
                              7  ***    MP    MULTIPLY PACKED
                              8  *      --------------------------

                             10  *            MULTIPLY, GENERATE 2 DECIMALS, NO ROUNDING:
                             11  *            ---------------------------
003802  475C                 12  QTY    DC    P'475'         |47|5C|
003804  350C                 13  PRICE  DC    P'3.50'        |35|0C|
003806                       14  AMT    DS    PL4

00380A  F831 4004 4000 03806 03802  16  ZAP   AMT,QTY        |00|00|47|5C|
003810  FC31 4004 4002 03806 03804  17  MP    AMT,PRICE      |01|66|25|0C|  = 1662.50

                             19  *            MULTIPLY, GENERATE 3 DECIMALS, ROUND:
                             20  *            ---------------------------
003816  01205C               21  HRS    DC    P'120.5'       |01|20|5C|
003819  855C                 22  RATE   DC    P'8.55'        |85|5C|
00381B                       23  WAGE   DS    PL5

003820  F842 4019 4014 0381B 03816  25  ZAP   WAGE,HRS       |00|00|01|20|5C|
003826  FC41 4019 4017 0381B 03819  26  MP    WAGE,RATE      |00|10|30|27|5C|  MULTIPLY
00382C  F045 4019 003F 0381B 0003F  27  SRP   WAGE,63,5      |00|01|03|02|8C|  SHIFT/ROUND
```

FIGURE 5-2 Sample multiply packed operations.

subtract 5. The following two examples round a three-decimal value and a five-decimal value to two decimal places:

1. Round a three-decimal value:

Value	123.456
Add 5	5
Result	123.461

For a two-decimal result, drop the rightmost digit 1: 123.46.

2. Round a five-decimal value:

Value	123.45678
Add 500	500
Result	123.46178

For a two-decimal result, drop the rightmost three digits: 123.46.

In Assembler, there are (at least) two ways to perform rounding and shifting. The first way involves the SRP (Shift and Round Packed) instruction that was not available on the 360 system. The second way involves the AP and MVO (Move with Offset) instructions which is the way that 360 users typically handled rounding. The next two sections examine these methods.

SHIFT AND ROUND PACKED—SRP

The purpose of the SRP instruction is to shift packed data to the left or right. For right shifts, SRP can also provide rounding.

NAME	*OPERATION*	*OPERAND*
(symbol)	SRP	S1,S2 or D1(L,B1),D2(B2),I3

Although an SS-format instruction, SRP has three operands, coded for example as

SRP AMTPK,2,0

- Operand-1 denotes a packed field, AMTPK, to be shifted and optionally rounded.
- Operand-2 is a *displacement* that indicates the number of digits that are to shift. The maximum size of a packed field field, 31 digits, sets the limit to the shift.
- Operand-3 contains a value 0–9 to be used for rounding. For left shifts, you normally code 0 to indicate no rounding, and code 5 for right shifts with conventional rounding.

The operation sets the condition code to indicate zero, minus, and plus.

LEFT SHIFT. A *positive* value as a shift factor implies a left shift. Consider the following SRP instruction:

```
AMTPK       DC      P'0001234'      00 01 23 4C
            SRP     AMTPK,3,0       12 34 00 0C
```

Operand-2 of the SRP means shift left 3 digits (not bytes). The operation fills zeros in the rightmost vacated positions.

RIGHT SHIFT. A *negative* value as a shift factor implies a right shift. However, because the shift factor is technically a displacement, you cannot code the instruction for example as

SRP AMTPK,−2,5   (invalid shift factor)

You have to represent the negative number in a form that the Assembler will accept and that the computer will interpret as a negative shift—as a negative six-bit binary number. For example, the representation for +2 in binary is 000010. To express this value in binary as −2, you have to *convert* it to its "two's complement" form *by reversing the bit values and adding 1:*

	Binary	Hex	Decimal
Initial value	000010	02	2
Reverse bits	111101	3D	61
Add 1	111110	3E	62

Now you can code an SRP to shift and round two digits by either of the following examples:

```
AMTPK        DC    P'1234589'        12 34 58 9C

             SRP   AMTPK,X'3E',5     00 12 34 6C
       or    SRP   AMTPK,62,5        00 12 34 6C
```

The instruction adds the rounding factor 5 to the last digit that it shifts off, as follows:

Original value	12	34	58	9C
Shift first digit	01	23	45	8C
Add 5	01	23	46	3C
Shift second digit	00	12	34	6C

A shift and round is correct regardless of the sign of the packed field. For example, if the original value of AMTPK was negative, the result would be 00 12 34 6D.

Following are some examples of factors for right shifts:

Shift factor	Binary	Two's complement	Hex	Decimal
1	000001	111111	3F	63
2	000010	111110	3E	62
3	000011	111101	3D	61
.	.	.	.	.
.	.	.	.	.
.	.	.	.	.
31	011111	100001	21	33

You don't have to understand how a right shift works! Simply insert the correct decimal or hex value into operand-2. For example, a right shift of four digits would be

```
SRP AMTPK,60,5
```

Chapter 9 explains two's complement representation of binary numbers and Chapter 10 covers other technicalities of the SRP instruction.

MOVE WITH OFFSET—MVO

A convenient rounding technique in 360 Assembler programming is to add all the unwanted decimal positions to the product, regardless of the sign:

3-DECIMAL VALUE		5-DECIMAL VALUE	
123.456	Require a 2-decimal answer	123.45678—	Require a 2-decimal answer
6	Add 6	678—	Add minus 678
123.462	Answer is 123.46	123.46356—	Answer is 123.46—

The restriction is that you may adjust only an *odd-number* of unwanted decimal positions, because of the presence of the sign. For example, the value 123.4567 requires a 2-decimal answer. In storage, the value is /12/34/56/7C/. Assume that you would like to add the rightmost two digits, 67. This is impossible—you can add either one byte, /7C/, or two bytes, /56/7C/. Solve this problem by using MVO to shift the value one digit to the right as /01/23/45/6C/, and then add the 6C:/01/23/46/2C/, or 123.462. The next sections should further clarify this operation.

The MVO operation moves data an odd number of half-bytes to the right. Although MVO may be used on any format, its most common use is on packed data—to shift off unwanted decimal positions generated by MP and DP operations. For example, an MVO could shift a field containing 12/34/56/7C three digits to the right, yielding 00/01/23/4C.

NAME	OPERATION	OPERAND
(symbol)	MVO	S1,S2 or D1(L1,B1),D2(L2,B2)

The rules for MVO are:

1. The maximum length of each operand is 16 bytes. Either operand may specify an explicit length (L1 and L2).
2. MVO moves the operand-2 data to the operand-1 field and shifts to the right an odd number of half-bytes. (To shift an even number of half-bytes requires two MVOs.) The rightmost half-byte of operand-1 (if packed, the sign position) is not altered.
3. MVO fills leftmost shifted half-bytes with X'0'.
4. The length of operand-2 determines how many bytes MVO moves into the operand-1 field, and shifts to the rightmost half-byte of operand-1.

Refer now to the examples in Figure 5-3:

```
STMT    SOURCE STATEMENT

  68  *           --------------------
  69  ***    MVO   MOVE WITH OFFSET
  70  *           --------------------
  71  X      DC    P'123456789'    |12|34|56|78|9C|
  72  Y      DC    PL5'0'          |00|00|00|00|0C|

  74  MVO1   MVO   Y,X(4)          |01|23|45|67|8C|  SHIFT 1 DIGIT
  75  MVO2   MVO   Y,X(3)          |00|01|23|45|6C|  SHIFT 3 DIGITS
  76  MVO3   MVO   Y,X(2)          |00|00|01|23|4C|  SHIFT 5 DIGITS


  78  *           MULTIPLY, GENERATE 4 DECIMALS, ROUND TO 2 DECIMALS:
  79  *           -----------------------------
  80  HOUR   DC    P'20.5'         |20|5C|
  81  RATEPY DC    P'03.250'       |03|25|0C|
  82  PAY    DS    PL5

  84         ZAP   PAY,HOUR        |00|00|00|20|5C|
  85         MP    PAY,RATEPY      |00|06|66|25|0C|  MULTIPLY  66.6250
  86         MVO   PAY,PAY(4)      |00|00|66|62|5C|  SHIFT     66.625
  87         AP    PAY,PAY+4(1)    |00|00|66|63|0C|  ROUND     66.630
  88         MVO   PAY,PAY(4)      |00|00|06|66|3C|  SHIFT     66.63
```

FIGURE 5-3 Sample MVO operations.

- MVO1 moves the first four (leftmost) bytes of X into Y. The packed digits from X are right-shifted, one half-byte, to the rightmost half-byte of Y.
- MVO2 moves the first three bytes of X into Y and right-shifts 3 half-bytes, to the rightmost half-byte of Y.
- MVO3 moves the first two bytes of X into Y and right-shifts 5 half-bytes, to the rightmost half-byte of Y.

Figure 5-3 also illustrates a multiply operation that generates four decimal positions. Because only two positions are required, two MVOs are used to shift the unwanted two decimals to the right. The rounding operation, AP, is immediately after the first MVO. This is because you must round beginning with the first unwanted decimal position, in this case '5'. In the product, /00/06/66/25/0C/, the '5' is shifted one position so that it becomes the leftmost digit of the next byte, /00/00/66/62/5C/. Now round and shift off the unwanted '5'.

SAMPLE PROGRAM: LOAN REPAYMENT SCHEDULE

Figure 5-4 illustrates most of the instructions that Chapters 4 and 5 have covered to this point: PACK, ZAP, AP, SP, CP, ED, MP, and SRP. The program contains definitions of loan balance owing, monthly payment, and

```
                                    3                    PRINT ON,NODATA,NOGEN

                                    5 *                          M A I N   P R O C E S S I N G
                                    6 *                          ---------------------------
000000                             7 PROG5A    START
                                   8          INIT                          INITIALIZE
                                  14          OPEN   PRINTER                OPEN FILE

                                  23          PUTPR  PRINTER,PRHEAD,SK1     SKIP TO NEW PAGE
                                  30          PUTPR  PRINTER,PRHEAD,WSP2    PRINT HEADING

000046 F234 3367 3358  00369 0035A  38          PACK   PAYPK,PAYMENT
00004C F235 3363 3352  00365 00354  39          PACK   BALPK,BALANCE
000052 F233 336B 335D  0036D 0035F  40          PACK   RATEPK,RATE
000058 4560 306A             0006C  41          BAL    6,B10CALC            CALC SCHEDULE

                                  43          CLOSE  PRINTER
                                  51          EOJ    ,                      TERMINATE

                                  55 *                          L O A N   S C H E D U L E
                                  56 *                          -----------------------
00006C F873 3373 3363  00375 00365  57 B10CALC   ZAP    CALCPK,BALPK
000072 FC73 3373 336B  00375 0036D  58          MP     CALCPK,RATEPK        BAL X RATE
000078 F075 3373 003C  00375 0003C  59          SRP    CALCPK,60,5          SHIFT & ROUND
00007E F833 336F 3377  00371 00379  60          ZAP    INTPK,CALCPK+4(4)

000084 D203 32E7 337B  002E9 0037D  62          MVC    MONPR,EDMON          EDIT:
00008A DE03 32E7 3361  002E9 00363  63          ED     MONPR,MONPK            MONTH
000090 D20A 32EF 337F  002F1 00381  64          MVC    OLDBPR,EDAMT
000096 DE0A 32EF 3363  002F1 00365  65          ED     OLDBPR,BALPK           OLD BALANCE

00009C FB33 3363 3367  00365 00369  67          SP     BALPK,PAYPK          CALCULATE
0000A2 FA3  3363 336F  00365 00371  68          AP     BALPK,INTPK          * NEW BALANCE
0000A8 47B0 30B6             000B8  69          BNM    B20                  NEG BALANCE?
0000AC FA33 3367 3363  00369 00365  70          AP     PAYPK,BALPK          YES - ADD TO PAY'T
0000B2 FB33 3363 3363  00365 00365  71          SP     BALPK,BALPK          CLEAR BALANCE

0000B8 D20A 330D 337F  0030F 00381  73 B20        MVC    PAYPR,EDAMT          EDIT:
0000BE DE0A 330D 3367  0030F 00369  74          ED     PAYPR,PAYPK            PAYMENT
0000C4 D20A 32FE 337F  00300 00381  75          MVC    INTPR,EDAMT
0000CA DE0A 32FE 336F  00300 00371  76          ED     INTPR,INTPK            INTEREST
0000D0 D20A 331C 337F  0031E 00381  77          MVC    NEWBPR,EDAMT
0000D6 DE0A 331C 3363  0031E 00365  78          ED     NEWBPR,BALPK           NEW BALANCE

                                  80          PUTPR  PRINTER,PRLINE,WSP1   PRINT
0000F0 FA10 3361 33AA  00363 003AC  87          AP     MONPK,=P'1'          ADD TO MONTH
0000F6 F930 3363 33AB  00365 003AD  88          CP     BALPK,=P'0'          SCHEDULE ENDED?
0000FC 4780 3108             0010A  89          BE     B30                  YES - EXIT
000100 F933 336F 3367  00371 00369  90          CP     INTPK,PAYPK          INTEREST : PAY'T
000106 4740 306A             0006C  91          BL     B10CALC              * LOWER - CONTINUE
00010A 07F6                         92 B30        BR     6                    RETURN

                                  94 *                          D E C L A R A T I V E S
                                  95 *                          ----------------------

                                  97 PRINTER   DEFPR                        DEFINE PRINTER FILE

00024A                            122 PRHEAD    DS     0CL133               HEADING LINE:
00024A 4040404040404040          123          DC     CL25' '              *
000263 D4D6D5E3C8404040          124          DC     CL42'MONTH    OLD BAL.       INTEREST'
00028D D7C1E8D4C5D5E340          125          DC     CL66'PAYMENT      NEW BAL.'
```

FIGURE 5-4 (partial)

```
     LOC   OBJECT CODE    ADDR1 ADDR2  STMT    SOURCE STATEMENT                          PAGE    2

    0002CF                             127 PRLINE  DS    OCL133                 PRINT AREA:
    0002CF 4040404040404040            128         DC    CL26' '              *
    0002E9                             129 MONPR   DS    ZL04                 *   MONTH
    0002ED 40404040                    130         DC    CL04' '              *
    0002F1                             131 OLDBPR  DS    ZL11                 *   OLD BALANCE
    0002FC 40404040                    132         DC    CL04' '              *
    000300                             133 INTPR   DS    ZL11                 *   PAYMENT
    00030B 40404040                    134         DC    CL04' '              *
    00030F                             135 PAYPR   DS    ZL11                 *   INTEREST
    00031A 40404040                    136         DC    CL04' '              *
    00031E                             137 NEWBPR  DS    ZL11                 *   NEW BALANCE
    000329 4040404040404040            138         DC    CL43' '              *

    000354 F5F0F0F0F0C0                140 BALANCE DC    Z'5000.00'           ORIGINAL BAL.
    00035A F5F0F0F0F0C0                141 PAYMENT DC    Z'500.00'            REGULAR PAY'T
    00035F F0F1F2C5                    142 RATE    DC    Z'.0125'             INTEREST RATE

    000363 001C                        144 MONPK   DC    PL2'1'               PACKED FIELDS:
    000365                             145 BALPK   DS    PL4                  *
    000369                             146 PAYPK   DS    PL4                  *
    00036D                             147 RATEPK  DS    PL4                  *
    000371                             148 INTPK   DS    PL4                  *
    000375                             149 CALCPK  DS    PL8                  *

    00037D 40202020                    151 EDMON   DC    X'40202020'          EDIT WORDS:
    000381 4020206B2020214B            152 EDAMT   DC    X'4020206B2020214B202060'
    000390                             153         LTORG ,
    000390 5B5BC2D6D7C5D540            154                 =C'$$BOPEN '
    000398 5B5BC2C3D3D6E2C5            155                 =C'$$BCLOSE'
    0003A0 00000110                    156                 =A(PRINTER)
    0003A4 0000024A                    157                 =A(PRHEAD)
    0003A8 000002CF                    158                 =A(PRLINE)
    0003AC 1C                          159                 =P'1'
    0003AD 0C                          160                 =P'0'
           00000                       161         END   PROG5A
```

Output:-

```
     MONTH     OLD BAL.       INTEREST      PAYMENT      NEW BAL.

       1       5,000.00         62.50        500.00      4,562.50
       2       4,562.50         57.03        500.00      4,119.53
       3       4,119.53         51.49        500.00      3,671.02
       4       3,671.02         45.89        500.00      3,216.91
       5       3,216.91         40.21        500.00      2,757.12
       6       2,757.12         34.46        500.00      2,291.58
       7       2,291.58         28.64        500.00      1,820.22
       8       1,820.22         22.75        500.00      1,342.97
       9       1,342.97         16.79        500.00        859.76
      10         859.76         10.75        500.00        370.51
      11         370.51          4.63        375.14          .00
```

FIGURE 5-4 Loan repayment schedule.

monthly rate of interest, and generates a loan repayment schedule. The calculation for each month's interest is the following:

$$\text{interest} = \text{old balance} \times \text{rate of interest}$$

And the calculation for each month's new balance is:

new balance = old balance + month's interest − monthly payment

The schedule continues for each month until the balance of the loan is fully paid. Calculations and logic are straightforward, with two exceptions:

1. The interest rate may be so high or the monthly payment so low that the first calculation of interest exceeds the monthly payment. In such a case, the loan schedule would never end. On recognizing this situation, the program terminates the schedule after one month.

2. It is unlikely that the scheduled payment will be exact for the *last* month. For each calculation of new balance, the program checks if it is overpaid. For example, the last payment in the program contains the following results:

old balance	370.51
plus interest	4.63
	375.14
less payment	500.00
new balance	−124.86

The last payment should be smaller by the amount that the new balance would be overpaid. The solution is to add the new balance to the scheduled payment and clear the new balance to zero—see the last line of the program's output.

For brevity, the program uses defined data instead of input data for balance, payment, and interest rate. A more complete program would accept these values from a terminal and would produce any number of loan schedules.

• *Problems 5-4 and 5-5 should now be attempted.* •

DIVIDE PACKED—DP

The DP instruction divides one packed field (the dividend) by another (the divisor). Common examples include dividing inventory value by number of units to calculate unit cost, and computing ratios and percentages.

NAME	*OPERATION*	*OPERAND*
(symbol)	DP	S1,S2 or D1(L1,B1),D2(L2,B2)

The rules for DP are:

1. Either operand may contain an explicit length (L1 and L2).

2. Operand-1 is the *dividend*, and must contain valid packed data. The *quotient* and *remainder* are developed in this field. The maximum length is 16 bytes. Operand-1 should be defined large enough to accommodate the largest possible quotient, plus remainder.
3. Operand-2 is the *divisor* containing valid packed data. The maximum length is 8 bytes.
4. The length of the generated remainder is the length of the divisor.
5. DP is governed by the normal rules of algebra: like signs yield a positive quotient, and unlike signs yield a negative quotient. A zero divisor is invalid—it causes a program interrupt. DP does not set the condition code.

QUOTIENT LENGTH. Since you do not normally know the contents of arithmetic fields, provide for the worst possible case, in which the divisor contains the value 1 (zero divisors are not permitted). With a divisor of 1, the quotient will equal (and cannot exceed) the value of the dividend.

$$dividend \rightarrow \frac{1234567}{1} = 1234567 \quad (quotient = dividend)$$
$$\nwarrow quotient$$

As good programming practice, therefore, define the length of the quotient equal at least to the length of the dividend. Also, the length of the remainder always equals the length of the divisor. The remainder is generated in the operand-1 field to the right of the quotient. Both quotient and remainder contain a sign. Technically, the quotient length needs to be only long enough to contain the significant digits developed. If the quotient field is longer than necessary, DP inserts leftmost zeros. If the quotient field is too short to contain all the significant digits generated in the quotient, an overflow interrupt occurs. The following rule always provides adequate field lengths: *define the operand-1 field equal at least to the length of the dividend plus divisor.* The following provides an example:

DIVIDEND	DC	PL4'1234567'	/12/34/56/7C	4-byte dividend
DIVISOR	DC	PL1'3'	/3C/	1-byte divisor
ANSWER	DS	PL5		5-byte answer
	ZAP	ANSWER,DIVIDEND	/00/12/34/56/7C/	
	DP	ANSWER,DIVISOR	/04/11/52/2C/1C/	

quotient   remainder

Since DIVIDEND contains four bytes and DIVISOR one, ANSWER (to be used for the resulting quotient and remainder) should contain five bytes.

(ANSWER may be defined longer.) The example uses ZAP to move DIVI-
DEND into ANSWER. After the DP, the first four bytes of ANSWER contain
the quotient, with a sign. The fifth byte contains the signed remainder, one
byte long, the same length as the divisor.

DECIMAL PRECISION.   You must provide for an implied decimal point,
and can use the following rule as a useful guide:
   *The number of decimal positions in a quotient equals the number of
positions in the dividend minus the number in the divisor.*
   For example, if a dividend contains four decimal positions and the
divisor contains one, then the quotient has three decimal positions:

$$\frac{\text{xx . xxxx}}{\text{x . x}} = \text{xx . xxx}$$

   If a dividend does not contain sufficient decimal places for division, you
may generate the required additional positions by shifting the dividend to
the left, using an SRP to shift two digits (or use MP to multiply by 100). Thus,
12.34 = 12.3400 (the same algebraic value), provided that your program
always accounts for the new implied decimal point.
   It may facilitate programming to mentally "clear" the divisor of decimal positions first. For example, the following divisor can be "cleared" of its
decimal places with no added programming steps, by definition:

$$\frac{12.3400}{1.23} = \frac{1234.00}{123}$$

ROUNDING, OR HALF-ADJUSTING.   In the earlier example that divides
DIVISOR into DIVIDEND, the remainder in ANSWER was 1/3, not .1. The
remainder is not usually rounded or required. The quotient, however, is
rounded, similar to rounding a product. If you want additional precision for
rounding you may shift the dividend to the left. Note that after the left shift,
the length of the dividend is longer, so that the quotient will have to be
correspondingly longer. For example, assume a 3-byte dividend and a 2-byte
divisor. If you shift the dividend left 2 digits (one byte), the dividend is now
effectively 4 bytes, so that the quotient/remainder should be 6 bytes. You
may generate one more decimal position than you need, and round it off. The
following examples each divide 246.79 by 31:

Require a 1-decimal quotient (no left shift is required):

$$\frac{246.79}{31} = 7.96 \text{ (may be rounded to 8.0)}$$

Require a 2-decimal quotient—shift left one digit or multiply the dividend by 1.0:

$$\frac{246.79 \times 1.0}{31} = \frac{246.790}{31} = 7.960 \text{ (may be rounded to 7.96)}$$

Require a 3-decimal quotient—shift left two digits or multiply the dividend by 1.00:

$$\frac{246.79 \times 1.00}{31} = \frac{246.7900}{31} = 7.9609 \text{ (may be rounded to 7.961)}$$

The following example calculates speed by dividing distance by time. Distance contains one decimal place and time contains none. The result is to have one decimal place *after* rounding. If you were to divide directly with no left shift of distance, the speed would be in terms of one decimal place, with no provision for rounding. Consequently, the example shifts distance one digit to the left prior to dividing. This step converts the dividend from 1128.9 to 1128.90, and the divide generates a quotient of 53.75. The result after the round and shift is 53.8.

```
DIST      DC       P'1128.9'      11 28 9C
TIME      DC       P'021'         02 1C
SPEED     DS       PL6

ZAP       SPEED,DIST             00 00 00 11 28 9C
SRP       SPEED,1,0              00 00 01 12 89 0C
                                 -quotient:-|rmdr:
DP        SPEED,TIME             00 05 37 5C|01 5C
SRP       SPEED(4),63,5          00 00 53 8C|01 5C
```

Note: After the left shift, the size of the dividend is four bytes. Since the remainder is two bytes, the defined length of the quotient/remainder field is (at least) six bytes.

Each increase in precision provides a more accurate result. Required accuracy depends on the application and the user's needs, and should be determined before starting the program. The examples in Figure 5-5 divide distance (DIST) by gallons (GALS) to calculate miles-per-gallon. Both DIST and GALS contain one decimal position.

ANS1 contains the result of a direct divide of DIST by GALS. Since both fields contain one decimal place, the quotient, 15, has no decimal places.

ANS2 requires a result that has no decimal places after rounding. The example uses MP to shift the dividend to the left one digit (2356.5 becomes 2356.50). This is now the dividend that you must consider when defining the quotient-remainder area. Since the divisor (GALS) is three bytes, and the dividend is now four bytes, the answer area (ANS2) is defined as seven bytes.

ANS3 requires a one-decimal quotient. Therefore, to generate two decimal places, shift the dividend left two digits. Since the divisor is three bytes

```
LOC     OBJECT CODE    ADDR1 ADDR2   STMT   SOURCE STATEMENT

                                      55 *     ----------------------
                                      56 ***   DP   DIVIDE PACKED
                                      5' *     ----------------------
003876  23565C                        58 DIST  DC   P'2356.5'        |23|56|5C|
003879  01500C                        59 GALS  DC   P'150.0'         |01|50|0C|

                                      61 *     DIVIDE, NO DECIMAL, NO ROUNDING:
                                      62 *     ----------------------
00387C                                63 ANS1  DS   PL6

003882  F852 407A 4077 03876 03879    65       ZAP  ANS1,DIST        |00|00|00|23|56|5C|
                                      66 *                          --QUOT--|--RMDR--
003888  FD52 407A 4077 03876 03879    67       DP   ANS1,GALS        |00|01|5C|01|06|5C|

                                      69 *     DIVIDE, ROUND TO NO DECIMALS:
                                      70 *     ----------------------
00388E                                71 ANS2  DS   PL7

003895  00
003896  F862 408C 4074 0388E 03876    72       ZAP  ANS2,DIST        |00|00|00|00|23|56|5C|
00389C  FC61 408C 40F6 0388E 038F8    73       MP   ANS2,=P'10'      |00|00|00|02|35|65|0C|
                                      74 *                          -----QUOT----|--RMDR--
0038A2  FD62 408C 4077 0388E 03879    75       DP   ANS2(4),ANS2+3(1)|00|00|15|7C|00|15|0C|  DIVIDE 15.7
0038A8  FA30 408F 408C 03891 0388C    76       AP   ANS2(4),ANS2(3)  |00|00|16|4C|00|15|0C|  ROUND 16.4
0038AE  F132 408C 408C 0388E 0388E    77       MVO  ANS2(4),ANS2(3)  |00|00|01|6C|00|15|0C|  SHIFT 16

                                      79 *     DIVIDE, ROUND TO ONE DECIMAL:
                                      80 *     ----------------------
0038B4                                81 ANS3  DS   PL7

0038BB  00
0038BC  F862 40B2 4074 0388E 03876    82       ZAP  ANS3,DIST        |00|00|00|00|23|56|5C|
0038C2  F060 40B2 0002 0388E 00002    83       SRP  ANS3,2,0         |00|00|00|23|56|50|0C|
                                      84 *                          -----QUOT----|--RMDR--
0038C8  FD62 40B2 4077 0388E 03879    85       DP   ANS3,GALS        |00|01|57|1C|00|00|0C|  DIVIDE 15.71
0038CE  F035 40B2 003F 0388E 0003F    86       SRP  ANS3(4),63,5     |00|00|15|7C|00|00|0C|  SHIFT 15.7

                                      88 *     DIVIDE, ROUND TO TWO DECIMALS:
                                      89 *     ----------------------
0038D4                                90 ANS4  DS   0PL8      ZERO DUPLICATION FACTOR
0038D4                                91 QUOT  DS   PL5       QUOTIENT AREA
0038D9                                92 RMDR  DS   PL3       REMAINDER AREA

0038DC  F872 40D2 4074 0388D4 03876   94       ZAP  ANS4,DIST        |00|00|00|00|00|23|56|5C|
0038E2  F070 40D2 0003 0388D4 00003   95       SRP  ANS4,3,0         |00|00|00|02|35|65|00|0C|
                                      96 *                          -------QUOT-----|--RMDR--
0038E8  FD72 40D2 4077 0388D4 03879   97       DP   ANS4,GALS        |00|00|15|71|0C|00|00|0C|  15.710
0038EE  F045 40D2 003F 0388D4 0003F   98       SRP  QUOT,63,5        |00|00|01|57|1C|00|00|0C|  15.71
```

FIGURE 5-5 Sample divide packed operations.

155

and the dividend is now four, ANS3 is defined as seven bytes. After the DP, round and shift the second decimal place.

ANS4 requires a two-decimal quotient. Shifting the dividend left three digits generates three extra decimal positions. Since the divisor is three bytes and the dividend is now five, ANS4 is defined as eight bytes. This example also illustrates redefining the answer area. ANS4 is defined with a zero duplication factor (0PL8). It contains two subfields: QUOT defines the five-byte quotient area, and RMDR defines the three-byte remainder. You may reference by name the entire area ANS4, or the subfield QUOT.

> • *Problem 5-6 should now be attempted.* •

SAMPLE PROGRAM: INVENTORY CALCULATION

Figure 5-6 provides the flowchart for an inventory program. Input data consists of inventory records containing the following data:

COLUMN		
	1–2	Record code
	3–4	Branch number
	5–8	Stock item number
	9–24	Stock description
	25–28	Quantity on hand
	29–35	Cost on hand (two decimal places)

Input is in sequence by Stock item within Branch number. There may be only one record for each Stock item within a Branch. Equal or out-of-sequence conditions cause an error.

For each Stock item the program calculates unit cost ÷ cost / quantity, prints the result, and adds cost to the total for the Branch.

On a change of Branch number (a control break), the program prints the total cost for the Branch and adds it to a final total.

After reading the first input record on initialization, the program stores the input Branch in "previous Branch." The purpose is to avert a false control break at the beginning—that is, the printing of a Branch total of zeros before processing the first record. Note that if *both* Branch and Stock number were stored at the start in "previous," the first comparison would signal an equal condition (duplicate record) and print an error message.

On end-of-file, the program links to the Branch total routine to print the last stored Branch total and to the end-of-file routine to print final total cost.

Figure 5-7 provides the program listing. Carefully study the flowchart and listing and work through all conditions. For purposes of brevity, the program omits some features that it would normally include, such as printing the current date and page overflow.

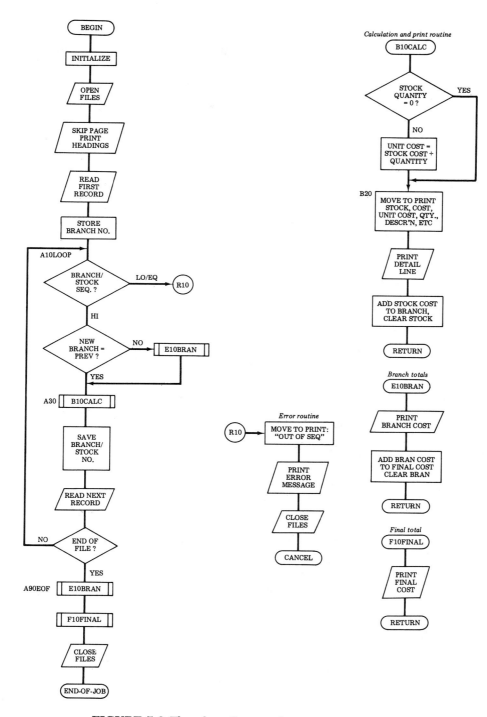

FIGURE 5-6 Flowchart for sample inventory program.

```
LOC     OBJECT CODE          ADDR1  ADDR2  STMT   SOURCE STATEMENT

                                             3            PRINT ON,NOGEN,NODATA

                                             5     *
                                             6     * *     I N I T I A L I Z A T I O N
                                                           -------------------------------
000000                                       7     PROG05  START                              INITIALIZE
                                             8             INIT                               INITIALIZE
                                            14             OPEN  FILEIN,PRTR

                                            24             PUTPR PRTR,HDG1LINE,SK1             SKIP TO NEW PAGE
                                            31             PUTPR PRTR,HDG1LINE,WSP2            PRINT HEADING-1
                                            38             PUTPR PRTR,HDG2LINE,WSP2            *     HEADING-2
                                            45             GET   FILEIN,RECDIN                 1ST RECORD
00006E  D201 36CE 3422       006D0  00424    51             MVC   PREVBR,BRANCHIN               INIT'ZE SEQ.

                                            53     *
                                            54     * *     M A I N   L O G I C

000074  D505 3422 36CE       00424  006D0    55     A10LOOP CLC   CTLIN,PREVCTL                 BR/STOCK NO. SEQUENCE?
00007A  47D0 31CA                   001CC    56             BNH   R10SEQ                        * EQ/LOW - ERROR

00007E  D501 3422 36CE       00424  006D0    58             CLC   BRANCHIN,PREVBR               NEW BRANCH = PREVIOUS?
000084  4780 308A                   0008C    59             BE    A30                           *  EQUAL - BYPASS
000088  4560 3152                   00154    60             BAL   6,E1OBRAN                     *  HIGH - TOTALS
00008C  4560 30C6                   000C8    61     A30     BAL   6,B1OCALC                     PROCESS RECORD
000090  D205 36CE 3422       006D0  00424    62             MVC   PREVCTL,CTLIN                 STORE BR/STOCK IN PREV
0000A6  47F0 3072                   00074    63             GET   FILEIN,RECDIN                 READ NEXT
                                            69             B     A10LOOP                       LOOP

                                            71     *
                                            72     * *     E N D   O F   F I L E

0000AA  4560 3152                   00154    73     A90EOF  BAL   6,E1OBRAN                     BRANCH TOTALS
0000AE  4560 3194                   00196    74             BAL   6,F1OFINAL                    FINAL TOTALS
                                            75             CLOSE FILEIN,PRTR
                                            84             EOJ

                                            88     *
                                            89     * *     C A L C U L A T E   N E W   U N I T   C O S T

0000C8  F236 3689 343C       0068B  0043E    90     B1OCALC PACK  COSTPK,COSTIN                 *
0000D4  F223 3691 3438       00693  0043A    91             PACK  QTYPK,QTYIN                   *
0000DA  F870 3694 3732       00696  00734    92             ZAP   UNCOSTPK,=P'0'                CLEAR UNIT-COST FIELD
0000E0  F822 3691 3691       00693  00693    93             ZAP   QTYPK,QTYPK                   STOCK QUANTITY = 0?
0000E6  4780 30FA                   000FC    94             BZ    B20                           *  YES - BYPASS DIVIDE
0000EA  F873 3694 3689       00696  0068B    95             ZAP   UNCOSTPK,COSTPK               |00|00|00|00|XX|XX|X.X|XX|XC|
0000F0  F070 3694 0001       00696  00001    96             SRP   UNCOSTPK,1,0                  |00|00|00|0X|XX|.XX|XX|XX|0C|
0000F6  FD72 3694 3691       00696  00693    97             DP    UNCOSTPK,QTYPK                |00|00|XX|.XX|XC|XX|XX|XC|
        F045 3694 003F       00696  0003F    98             SRP   UNCOSTPK(5),63,5              |00|00|CX|X.X|XC|XX|XX|XC|

0000FC  D20B 35BC 36D6       005BE  006D6   100     B20     MVC   COSTPR,EDCOST                 EDIT STOCK FIELDS
000102  DE0B 35BC 3689       005BE  0068B   101             ED    COSTPR,COSTPK                 * COST

000108  D206 35B4 36E2       005B6  006E4   103             MVC   UNCOSPR,EDUNIT                *
00010E  DE06 35B4 3696       005B6  00698   104             ED    UNCOSPR,UNCOSTPK+2            * * UNIT COST
```

158

```
                                                                          PAGE   2

LOC    OBJECT CODE         ADDR1 ADDR2   STMT   SOURCE STATEMENT

000114 D207 35A8 36E9      005AA 006EB    106          MVC   QTYPR,EDQTY              *
00011A DE07 35A8 3691      005AA 00693    107          ED    QTYPR,QTYPK              *      QUANTITY
000120 D20F 3598 3428      0059A 0042A    109          MVC   DESCRPR,DESCRIN          *
000126 D203 3592 3424      00594 00426    110          MVC   STOCKPR,STOCKIN          *
00012C D201 358C 3422      0058E 00424    111          MVC   BRANPR,BRANCHIN          *
                                          113          PUTPR PRTR,STKLINE,WSP1               PRINT STOCK RECORD
000146 D284 357B 357A      0057B 0057C    120          MVC   STKLINE,BLANK
00014C FA33 3685 3689      00687 0068B    121          AP    BRCOSTPK,COSTPK                 ADD COST TO BRANCH TOTAL
000152 07F6                               122          BR    6                               RETURN

                                          124   *      P R O C E S S   B R A N C H   T O T A L
                                          125   *      ------------------------------------
                                          126   E10BRAN PUTPR PRTR,TOTLINE,SP1
000168 D20B 3641 36D4      00643 006D6    133          MVC   BRTOTPR,EDCOST                  EDIT TOTAL BRANCH COST
00016E DE0B 3641 3685      00643 00687    134          ED    BRTOTPR,BRCOSTPK
                                          135          PUTPR PRTR,TOTLINE,WSP2                PRINT BRANCH TOTAL
000188 FA33 368D 3685      0068F 00687    143          AP    FINCOSPK,BRCOSTPK               ADD BRANCH COST TO FINAL
00018E F830 3685 3732      00687 00734    144          ZAP   BRCOSTPK,=P'0'                  CLEAR BRANCH COST
000194 07F6                               145          BR    6                               RETURN

                                          147   *      P R O C E S S   F I N A L   T O T A L
                                          148   *      ------------------------------------
000196 D20B 3641 36D4      00643 006D6    149   F10FINAL MVC  BRTOTPR,EDCOST                 EDIT FINAL TOTAL COST
00019C DE0B 3641 368D      00643 0068F    150          ED    BRTOTPR,FINCOSPK
0001A2 D20B 361E 36C2      00620 006C4    151          MVC   BITLPR,FINMSG
0001A8 925C 364E           00650         152          MVI   ASTERPR+1,C'*'
                                          153          PUTPR PRTR,TOTLINE,WSP1                PRINT FINAL TOTAL LINE
0001CA 07F6                               167          BR    6                               RETURN

                                          169   *      E R R O R   R O U T I N E S
                                          170   *      ------------------------------------
0001CC D21E 35C8 369C      005CA 0069E    171   R10SEQ  MVC   MSGPR,SEQERR                   OUT-OF-SEQUENCE BR/STOCK
0001D2 D203 3592 36D0      00594 006D2    172          MVC   STOCKPR,PREVSTK
0001D8 D201 358C 36CE      0058E 006D0    173          MVC   BRANPR,PREVBR
                                          174          PUTPR PRTR,STKLINE,WSP3                PRINT ERROR MESSAGE
                                          181          CLOSE FILEIN,PRTR
                                          190          CANCEL ,                              ABNORMAL TERMINATION
```

FIGURE 5-7 (partial)

159

```
                                  D E C L A R A T I V E S
                                  ------------------------

195 *
196 *
198 FILEIN   DEFIN A90EOF                  DEFINE INPUT FILE
222 PRTR     DEFPR                          DEFINE PRINTER FILE

247 RECDIN   DS  OCL80                      INPUT RECORD COLUMNS:
248 CODEIN   DS  CL02                       01-02  RECORD CODE
249 CTLIN    DS  OCL6                              BR/STOCK CTL FIELD:
250 BRANCHIN DS  CL02                       03-04  BRANCH
251 STOCKIN  DS  CL04                       05-08  STOCK NO.
252 DESCRIN  DS  CL16                       09-24  DESCRIPTION
253 QTYIN    DS  ZL04                       25-28  QUANTITY
254 COSTIN   DS  ZL07'00000.00'             29-35  COST
255          DS  CL45                       36-80  *

257 *                                       HEADING-1:
258 HDG1LINE DC  CL18' '
259          DC  CL15'INVENTORY UNIT-COST REPORT'

261 HDG2LINE DC  CL15' '                    HEADING-2:
262          DC  CL30'BRANCH STOCK'
263          DC  CL88'QUANTITY    UNITCOST    COST'


LOC    OBJECT CODE            ADDR1 ADDR2   STMT  SOURCE STATEMENT

00057C 40                                   265 BLANK    DC  C' '        BLANK FOR CLEARING PRINT AREA
00057D                                      266 STKLINE  DS  OCL133      STOCK PRINT LINE:
00057D 404040404040404040                   267          DC  CL17' '     *
00058E                                      268 BRANPR   DS  CL02        *     BRANCH NO.
000590 40404040                             269          DC  CL04' '     *
000594                                      270 STOCKPR  DS  CL04        *     STOCK NO.
000598 4040                                 271          DC  CL02' '     *
00059A                                      272 DESCRPR  DS  CL16        *     DESCRIPTION
0005AA                                      273 QTYPR    DS  ZL08        *     QUANTITY
0005B2 40404040                             274          DC  CL04' '     *
0005B6                                      275 UNCOSPR  DS  ZL07        *     UNIT COST
0005BD 40                                   276          DC  CL01' '     *
0005BE                                      277 COSTPR   DS  ZL12        *     COST
0005CA 404040404040404040                   278 MSGPR    DC  CL31' '     *
0005E9 404040404040404040                   279          DC  CL25' '

000602                                      281 TOTLINE  DS  OCL133      BRANCH & FINAL TOTAL LINE:
000602 404040404040404040                   282          DC  CL30' '     *
000620 C2D9C1D5C3C840E3                     283 BTITLPR  DC  CL12'BRANCH TOTAL'   *
00062C 404040404040404040                   284          DC  CL23' '
000643                                      285 BRTOTPR  DS  ZL12        *
00064F 5C                                   286 ASTERPR  DC  CL01'*'     *
000650 404040404040404040                   287          DC  CL55' '

000687 0000000C                             289 BRCOSTPK DC  PL4'0'      PACKED DECLARATIVES:
00068B 0000000C                             290 COSTPK   DC  PL4'0'      *
00068F 0000000C                             291 FINCOSPK DC  PL4'0'      *
```

(Statements 247–263 object code references:)
```
000422 40
000422
000424
000424
000426
000426
00042A
00043A
00043E
000445

000472 4040404040404040 40
000484 C940D540E540C540

0004F7 4040404040404040 40
000506 C2D9C1D5C3C840E2
000524 D8E4C1D5E3C9E3E8
```

160

```
000693 00000C            292 QTYPK    DC    PL3'0'                              *
000696 0000000000000000C 293 UNCOSTPK DC    PL8'0'                              *

00069E C5D8E4C1D361D3D6  295 SEQERR   DC    CL38'EQUAL/LOW SEQUENCE ON BRANCH/STOCK'
0006C4 40C6C9D5C1D340E3  296 FINMSG   DC    C' FINAL TOTAL'

0006D0                   298 PREVCTL  DS    0XL6                        CONTROL WORD:
0006D0 0000              299 PREVBR   DC    XL2'00'                     * BRANCH NO.
0006D2 00000000          300 PREVSTK  DC    XL4'00'                     * STOCK NO.
                         301 *                                          EDIT WORDS :
0006D6 4020206B2020214B  302 EDCOST   DC    X'4020206B2020214B2020C3D9',C'**'
0006E4 402020214B2020    303 EDUNIT   DC    X'402020214B2020'
0006EB 402020202020C3D9  304 EDQTY    DC    X'402020202020C3D9'

0006F8                   306          LTORG
0006F8 5B5BC2D6D7C5D540  307                 =C'$$BOPEN '
000700 5B5BC2C3D3D6E2C5  308                 =C'$$BCLOSE'
000708 5B5BC2D7C4E4D4D7  309                 =CL8'$$BPDUMP'
000710 0000042200006F2   310                 =A(RECDIN,EDQTY+7)
000718 000002E8          311                 =A(PRTR)
00071C 00000472          312                 =A(HDG1LINE)
000720 000004F7          313                 =A(HDG2LINE)
000724 00000210          314                 =A(FILEIN)
000728 00000422          315                 =A(RECDIN)
00072C 0000057D          316                 =A(STKLINE)
000730 00000602          317                 =A(TOTLINE)
000734 0C                318                 =P'0'
                         319          END   PROG05

00000
```

```
Output:-
        I N V E N T O R Y   U N I T - C O S T   R E P O R T

BRANCH  STOCK              QUANTITY    UNITCOST      COST

  01    1234  PLYWOOD 1/4       50         3.05      152.50
  01    2468  PLYWOOD 3/8      150         5.50      825.00

             BRANCH TOTAL                            977.50  *

  33    1234  PLYWOOD 1/4        5CR       3.05       15.25CR
  33    2468  PLYWOOD 3/8      155         5.48      850.00
  33    2470  PLYWOOD 1/2      155         5.48      850.00

             BRANCH TOTAL                          1,684.75  *

  40    1234  PLYWOOD 1/4       10         3.05       30.50
  40    2470  PLYWOOD 1/2        1          .00         .00
  40    2844  PLYWOOD 3/4        1         6.50        6.50

             BRANCH TOTAL                             37.00  *

              FINAL TOTAL                          2,699.25  **
```

FIGURE 5-7 Inventory update.

DEBUGGING TIPS

The ED instruction offers almost unlimited scope for new bugs. Before assembly, double-check the MVC/ED operations. Allow in the edit word X'20s and X'21s for each packed digit to be edited (there should be an odd number). Be sure that the print area field is the same size as the edit word.

The most common error with MP seems to be ignoring the rule that the product field must be at least the length of the multiplicand plus multiplier in bytes, regardless of the contents. If too short, then count on a much-deserved data exception.

DP suffers from the similar problem of field length: the quotient/remainder area must be at least as long as the dividend (after the left-shift, if any) plus divisor. Another popular error is attempting to divide by a zero value—check for a zero divisor first! Both errors cause decimal divide exceptions.

If the bug cannot be located, rerun the program with a request for a dump of storage, and trace the hex contents of the concerned storage areas. Almost always the error is in your program or data, rarely in the operating system, and never is it the computer.

As well as the technical misuse of instructions, there are the problems with programming logic—wrong compares, wrong branches, wrong calculations. Perhaps the worst error is misunderstanding the problem, and coding the incorrect solution. Analyze the program specifications carefully before coding the program.

PROBLEMS

5-1. Editing.

(a) What characters other than X'40' may be used as the fill character?

(b) An amount field containing zero is defined as TOTAL DC PL3'0'. Define an edit word to cause TOTAL to print as all blanks.

(c) Why must the edit word contain an odd number of X'20s and X'21s?

(d) Refer to the IBM Principles of Operation manual and define the purpose of the "field separator."

5-2. Complete the following edit words and edit operations as indicated.

> If zero amount, the edited field should print as:

```
(a)   AMT2     DS    PL4
      ED2      DC    X'                    .00 (Use comma, decimal point,
               MVC   PRINT+20                   minus sign)
               ED
```

(b)

AMT3	DS	PL5
ED3	DC	X'
	MVC	PRINT+40
	ED	

0.00 (Use commas, decimal point, minus sign)

(c)

AMT4	DS	PL4
ED4	DC	X'
	MVC	PRINT+60
	ED	

.00 (Use $, comma, decimal point, CR, and two asterisks)

5-3. Use MVO to shift the contents of the following DC. Indicate the results in hex. Questions are unrelated.

```
PKFIELD DC P'123456789'
```

(a) Shift right one digit.
(b) Shift right two digits.
(c) Shift right four digits.

5-4. *Rounding.* Why use two MVOs to shift an even number of digits right? If the field is to be rounded as well, why is the AP between the two MVOs and not before or after them?

5-5. *Multiply Packed.* Use a coding sheet to write the instructions as indicated. Show results in hex representation. Define the product area called PROD in each example.

```
A DC P'82.5'
B DC P'940.5'
C DC P'78.55'
D DC P'92.345'
```

(a) Multiply A × B, round and shift to 1 decimal position.
(b) Multiply B × C, round and shift to 2 decimal positions.
(c) Multiply B × D, round and shift to 2 decimal positions.
(d) Multiply C × D, round and shift to 2 decimal positions.
(e) Explain the error (if any): MP C,=P'2'.

5-6. *Divide Packed.* Use a coding sheet to write the required instructions. Show the hex results, and define the quotient-remainder area as RESULT.

```
A DC P'017'
B DC P'127.5'
C DC P'613.57'
D DC P'925.365'
```

(a) Divide B/A, round and shift to 1 decimal position.
(b) Divide C/B, round and shift to 2 decimal positions.
(c) Divide D/A, round and shift to 1 decimal position.
(d) Divide D/B, round and shift to 0 decimal positions.
(e) Explain the error (if any): DP D,=P'2'.

5-7. PROGRAM ASSIGNMENT.

Required: A program that reads Sales records containing selling price and cost, and calculates gross profit, percent gross profit, and sales commission.

Input: Sales records, containing in each column:

1–2	Record code (25)	11–13	Commission rate (e.g. .155 = 15.5%)
3–4	Store number	14–27	Category description
5–7	Salesman number	28–33	Selling price (xxxx.xx)
8–10	Category (type of sale, such as TV, furniture, appliance)	36–41	Cost price (xxxx.xx)

Procedure:

1. Check for valid record code (25) and that records are in sequence by Salesman (minor) within Store (major).

2. For each record, calculate and print:
   Gross Profit = Selling Price − Cost (Cost can exceed Selling Price).
   Percent Gross Profit = Gross Profit ÷ Cost.
   Commission = Gross Profit × Commission rate.

3. For each Salesman, print totals of Sales, Cost, Gross Profit, and Commission. Calculate Percent Gross Profit. For each Store and for final total, print and calculate as for Salesman.

4. Provide test data that checks all conditions, code, and test. Take a hex dump of storage and analyze the contents.

6

BASE REGISTERS AND INSTRUCTION FORMAT

Up to now we have used only instructions that access data in main storage —the storage-to-storage (SS) and storage immediate (SI) formats. The next step is to use the registers to perform binary arithmetic and to manipulate addresses. These operations enable the explicit use of registers in addressing for powerful programming capability, such as table look-up. For these purposes we must learn how to use registers for arithmetic and for addressing, and what is the *machine language object code format* for each instruction.

THE GENERAL-PURPOSE REGISTERS

The 16 general-purpose registers are separate from main storage. They are numbered from 0 through 15, and are referenced by number.

> *Note:* You can use EQU to assign a name to a register: e.g., LINKREG EQU 7 tells the Assembler to substitute the number 7 for each reference to the name LINKREG in the program. Thus, the instruction BAL LINKREG,H10HEAD becomes BAL 7,H10HEAD.

Each register contains 32 bits of data, numbered from left to right 0 through 31. The registers have two main purposes, binary arithmetic and addressing.

1. *Binary Arithmetic.* The general registers perform all binary arithmetic. For binary values, bit 0 is the sign bit, and bits 1–31 are data. Chapter 9 covers binary arithmetic in detail.

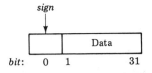

2. *Addressing.* The general registers perform all the addressing involved in referencing main storage. A register used for addressing purposes is called a base register. On most models, addressing uses only the rightmost 24 bits of the register (bits 8–31), giving a maximum address of $2^{24}-1$, or 16,777,215. The largest models use 31 bits for addressing. Certain instructions of "RX" format have the facility to modify or "index" an address; a register used for this purpose is called an *"index register."*

Unused	Address
bit: 0   7 8   31

Some of the registers have special functions, and the following restrictions apply:

REGISTER	RESTRICTIONS
0–1	You may use registers 0 and 1 freely for temporary calculations, but supervisor operations such as CALL and PUT destroy their contents. Also, because the supervisor uses register-0 as its own base register, the system does not permit you to use register-0 as a base register.
2	2 is available as a base register or for binary arithmetic, with one exception: the TRT instruction uses register-2 to store a generated value, thus limiting its use as a base register.
3–12	Registers 3–12 are always available for binary arithmetic or as base registers.
13	Control program routines including the input/output system use register-13. Use register-13 only when performing special linkage to a "subprogram," and otherwise do not use it.
14–15	Control program and subprogram routines also use these registers. Their use is restricted as for 0 and 1, for temporary calculations.

BASE REGISTER ADDRESSING

On earlier computers, instructions directly referenced main storage locations by their assigned number. The computer may have had an ADD instruction (coded as 21) to add the contents of location 01056 to 01232, coded as 21 01232 01056. Such a direct addressing system is simple, but limits the highest address, in this case to 99999. Modern large computers require considerably more storage because of (a) more complex input/output facilities, (b) complex operating systems, and (c) the capability of multiprogramming —the executing of two or more programs in storage concurrently.

For addressing main storage locations, the 370 uses the rightmost 24 bits of a register, providing a maximum address of 16,777,215. Every instruction operand that references a main storage location consists of more than just a direct reference to that location; the computer architecture compresses the addresses by splitting them into two parts, a base address and a displacement:

1. *Base Address.* This is an address of the beginning of an area of storage. Code the BALR instruction to load this address into a register, and code the USING directive to tell the Assembler that this register is to be the program's base register containing the address of the start of the program. The INIT macro has performed these functions up to now. You can allocate any registers (preferably 2 through 12) for the base address, and subsequently may not use that register for any other purpose in the program.

2. *Displacement.* The Assembler calculates the displacement for each instruction and declarative in the program, the number of bytes that the actual location is from the base address.

Each address referenced therefore consists of two parts: the contents of the base register combined with the displacement provides the effective address. Refer to Figure 6-1a. Assume that register-3 is the base register for a small program in main storage. Register-3 contains the value X'4200', which is the location of the first byte of the program in main storage. (Do not be concerned for now how X'4200' loads into register-3 or how the Assembler knows this value.)

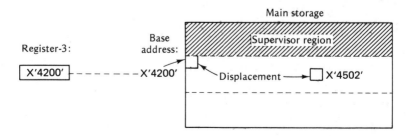

FIGURE 6-1a Base register addressing—one base register.

Every location within the program is relative to the first byte, X'4200'. For example, location X'4502' is X'302' bytes from the start, and therefore location X'4502' has a *displacement* of X'302' bytes. The computer then references location X'4502' by adding:

Base address	4200
Displacement	302
Effective address	4502

Any instruction referencing location X'4502' does so by means of the contents of the base register (X'4200') plus the displacement (X'302').

The Assembler calculates the displacement for every instruction and declarative in the program. For every instruction that references a main storage location, the Assembler forms an operand in object code comprised of the base register number and the displacement, and stores them as two bytes within the instruction:

B	D	D	D

bits: 0–3   4–15

Bits 0–3 provide four bits to reference a base register, as X'1' through X'F'. Bits 4–15 provide for a displacement from X'000' through X'FFF' (up to 4095 bytes). Thus, in Figure 6-1a an instruction referencing X'4502' would contain as its operand the hex value

3	302

To reference X'4502' the computer adds the contents of the base register-3, X'4200', with the displacement, X'302'. An MVC instruction containing this value for operand-1 would move data to the address X'4200' plus X'302'.

Example: Assume that a program defines PRINT+30 at location X'4502'. The Assembler would translate the instruction MVI PRINT+30,C'*' into hex object code as:

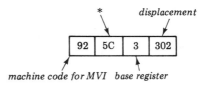

92	5C	3	302

machine code for MVI   base register

At execution-time, the computer processes the MVI instruction by combining the contents of base register-3 with the displacement, and moves the asterisk into the calculated effective address, X'4502'.

MORE THAN ONE BASE REGISTER. Since the maximum displacement is X'FFF', or 4095, the area covered by a base register and its displacement is X'000' through X'FFF', giving X'1000' or 4096 bytes. Each 4096 (4K) bytes of program being executed requires a base register. A program up to 12K bytes in size requires three base registers, as shown in Figure 6-1b.

The first 4K area in the example begins with base address X'4200', and any position defined within this area is subject to base register-3 and a displacement relative to the base address. The second 4K area begins at a location X'1000' higher, at X'5200'. In the example, the base register is register-4 (although it could have been some other available register), and any position defined within this area is subject to base register-4 and a displacement. Also, in the example, any position defined within the third 4K area beginning at X'6200' is subject to base register-5 and a displacement.

There are two advantages to base/displacement addressing:

1. Instruction length is reduced because each address requires only two rather than three bytes.

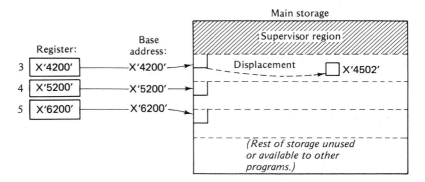

FIGURE 6-1b Base register addressing—three base registers.

2. Such a system facilitates *program relocatability.* The Assembler does not assign specific locations for each address. Instead, it determines where each address is relative to a base address. At execute-time the base address may be almost any location, loaded in a base register. Accordingly, the system may locate a program almost anywhere in main storage for execution. For example, the program may be executed beginning in X'4200' today, and next week in X'6840'. The purpose of relocatability is to facilitate *multiprogramming*—the executing of two or more programs in storage concurrently. (Although there are several programs in main storage, the computer can execute only one instruction at a time, and it "flip-flops" between programs, as available time permits.)

INSTRUCTION FORMAT

This section examines the instruction format in detail to make clear how the Assembler converts symbolic to machine language code and how it converts base registers and displacements. Each format has a specific purpose. RR format processes data between registers; RS and RX process data between registers and storage; SI and SS process data between storage positions, as follows:

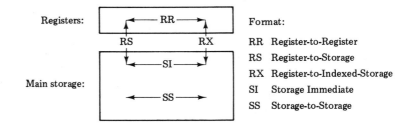

Figure 6-2 depicts the five formats. The column under Format contains the general symbolic coding format. For example, RR means that both operand-1 and operand-2 reference a register. SS means that both operands reference storage addresses. The other symbols, explained in the next section, are:

D = displacement
B = base register
X = index register
I = immediate operand

Format	Length in bytes	Explicit symbolic operands	Object code format					
RR	2	R1, R2	OP	R1R2				
RS	4	R1, R3, D2(B2)	OP	R1R3	B2D2	D2D2		
RX	4	R1, D2(X2, B2)	OP	R1X2	B2D2	D2D2		
SI	4	D1(B1), I2	OP	I I	B1D1	D1D1		
SS(1)	6	D1(L,B1), D2(B2)	OP	L L	B1D1	D1D1	B2D2	D2D2
SS(2)	6	D1(L1, B1), D2(L2, B2)	OP	L1L2	B1D1	D1D1	B2D2	D2D2
		Bits	0–7	8–15	16–23	24–31	32–39	40–47
		Byte	1	2	3	4	5	6

FIGURE 6-2 Instruction formats.

Under Object Code Format in Figure 6-2 is the hex representation of machine language—the format in which the Assembler converts from symbolic code and which the system loads into main storage for execution. The first byte, bits 0–7, is the operation code. For example, the CLC code is X'D5'. (The S-format—not covered—uses the first two bytes for the operation code.) IBM supplies a convenient and indispensable reference card, Form GX20-1850, containing all instruction codes, formats, and bit configurations.

The next sections explain the remaining bytes in the instruction format. The SI and SS formats, the most familiar at this point, are covered first.

SI, STORAGE IMMEDIATE FORMAT. SI instructions include MVI and CLI. Operand-1 in symbolic code references a storage location and operand-2 represents a 1-byte immediate constant. In object code, the second byte (two hex digits) contains the immediate constant, X'00' through X'FF' (this is the reason why immediate operands may be coded as only one byte). Byte-3 and byte-4 store the address as BD/DD.

The format for machine code is

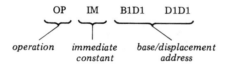

No length indication is permitted because immediate operations are defined as one byte. For example, MVI, machine code 92, moves an asterisk to PRINT: MVI PRINT+48,C'*'. The Assembler generates four bytes of object code and converts the asterisk X'5C' into the second byte as

| 92 | 5C | BD | DD |

(assume some base/displacement reference for PRINT+48).

SS, STORAGE-TO-STORAGE FORMAT. SS format instructions include MVC, ZAP, and CP. Both operands reference a storage address. There are two types, Character instructions of the form D1(L,B1),D2(B2) that provide a length only for operand-1, and Packed operations of the form D1(L1,B1),D2(L2,B2) that provide lengths for both operands.

1. *Character instructions* such as MVC and CLC permit a length up to 256 bytes of data. These use the length of operand-1 to govern the

number of bytes that are processed. Assume that MVC is used to move a field to the print area:

```
MVC PRINT+20(6),=C'RECORD'
```

Given register-3 as the base register and displacements of 426 for PRINT+20 and 62A for the literal, the generated object code is

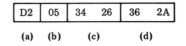

(a) D2 is the machine code for MVC.

(b) The length of operand-1 is explicitly coded as 6. However, *the Assembler deducts 1 from the length when converting to object code. At execute-time the computer increments the length by 1.* This process permits lengths of 256 rather than 255. If you code a length of 256 in an instruction, the Assembler deducts 1, giving 255 or X'FF'.

(c) The third and fourth bytes contain base/displacement for operand-1, BD/DD.
   The Assembler inserts base register-3 and the displacement 426 in these positions.

(d) The fifth and sixth bytes contain base register-3 and displacement 62A for operand-2.

At execute-time, the computer increments the length code 05 by 1, to 06. Also, it combines the contents of base register-3 with the displacement. If register-3 contains X'4200', then the effective addresses of the two operands are:

	OPERAND-1	OPERAND-2
Contents of base register	X'4200'	X'4200'
Displacement	X'0426'	X'062A'
Effective address	X'4626'	X'482A'

The instruction says, in effect, Move (D2) for six bytes (05 + 1) the contents beginning at location X'482A' to the field beginning at X'4626'.

2. *Packed operations* permit a length code for both operands, but limited to 16 bytes each. Assume that you use AP to add packed fields as:

```
AP PAGEPK,=P'1'
```

Given base register-3 and displacements of 624 for PAGEPK and 94E for the literal, the generated object code is

FA	10	36	24	39	4E
(a)	(b)	(c)		(d)	

(a) FA is the machine code for AP.

(b) The lengths of operand-1 and 2 are stored in the second byte. Assume that PAGEPK is defined as DC PL2'0'. For the AP instruction, the Assembler decrements the defined length 2 by 1, and stores 1 as the length. The literal =P'1' creates a 1-byte constant; the Assembler decrements and stores the length as 0. (For the maximum length, 16, the Assembler decrements the length to 15 and stores X'F'.)

(c) The third and fourth bytes contain base/displacement for operand-1. The Assembler inserts base register-3 and displacement 624 in these positions.

(d) The fifth and sixth bytes contain base/displacement for operand-2, the literal. The Assembler inserts base register-3 and displacement 94E in these positions.

At execute-time the computer increments the two length codes and combines the contents of the base register with the displacement. The effective addresses for the two operands are:

	OPERAND-1	OPERAND-2
Contents of base register	X'4200'	X'4200'
Displacement	X'0624'	X'094E'
Effective address	X'4824'	X'4B4E'

RR, REGISTER-TO-REGISTER FORMAT. RR format is used to process data between registers. The second byte in object code contains the reference to both registers. The four bits in a half-byte provide for decimal values 0 to 15, or X'0' to X'F'. (The Assembler converts references to registers 10 through 15 to A through F.) Because registers are fixed length 32 bits, no length indication is required or permitted—the length is implicitly known. For example, to add the contents of register-8 to register-6, simply code AR 6,8. The machine language code for AR (Add Register) is 1A. The Assembler converts the instruction to two bytes as

1A	68

Another instruction, AR 10,11 converts to

1A	AB

Exception: Branch on Condition, BCR, is specified as M1,R2. Operand-1 is a mask or a reference to the condition code in the PSW, not to a register. See the Technical Note at the end of this chapter.

RS, REGISTER-TO-STORAGE FORMAT.   Both RS and RX formats provide the facility to process data between registers and storage. RS also permits three operands. For example, you may code the Load Multiple operation (covered in Chapter 9) as LM 5,7,FIELDS (load registers 5, 6, and 7 with the three 4-byte fields in storage beginning at the address of FIELDS). The machine language code for LM is 98. The Assembler translates symbolic to four bytes of object code as

| 98 | 57 | BD | DD |

The two bytes referencing FIELDS in storage,

| BD | DD |

are filled by the Assembler. Given a base register to use, it inserts the register number (0 through F) in the specified half-byte. The Assembler calculates and stores the displacement in 1½ bytes.

Some RS instructions, such as shift, use only two operands. For these, you omit R3 as shown in Figure 6-2, and the Assembler inserts a zero in the machine language position. (Register-0 is not used as the third operand.)

RX, REGISTER-TO-INDEXED-STORAGE.   RX format also processes data between registers and storage, and is quite similar to RS format.

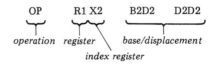

Operand-2 references a storage location with base and displacement. The operation determines the length of operand-2. For example, there are two operations that add binary data in storage to a register. A (Add Fullword) adds four bytes of storage to a register, and AH (Add Halfword) adds two bytes of storage.

As an example, assume the AH (Add Halfword) instruction, coded as AH 5,=H'7'. The literal, =H'7' defines a binary halfword (2-byte) constant. The operation adds the halfword value defined in storage to register-5. There is no length specification, because the operation AH indicates a 2-byte length for operand-2, and register length is always four bytes. The machine code for AH is X'4A', and assume that the base register is 3, containing X'4200'. If the literal =H'7' is stored at X'4704', then its displacement from the base address is X'504'. The Assembler completes the machine code as:

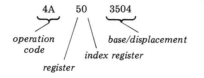

In this case, the Assembler sets the "index register" position to zero. In many cases, including this one, a reference to register-0 means no register reference. If the instruction is one that can specify an index register or an index register is explicitly coded, the Assembler inserts the register number into the machine code position. An index register is simply a specific use of one of the general registers, just as is a base register. Indexing is a feature that does not have too many uses, but an example is given in a later chapter under the LA (Load Address) instruction.

Exception: Branch on Condition, BC, is specified as M1,D2(X2,B2). Operand-1 is a mask, a reference to the condition code in the PSW. See the Technical Note at the end of this chapter.

• *Problems 6-1 through 6-5 should now be attempted.* •

CONTROL SECTIONS

For practical purposes, only eleven registers (2 through 12) are available as base registers. It would appear that the largest program you can assemble and execute is 11 × 4K, or 44K. But many programs require considerably more storage. You may write such large programs and, indeed, any program requiring more than 2 or 3 base registers in separate sections. These *control sections* (CSECTs) are assembled separately, each with its own set of base registers. They may then be combined (link-edited) into one object program. Up to this point, you have written programs comprised of one control section. By definition a control section is "a block of coding that can be relocated (independent of other coding) without altering the operating logic of the program." Neither the Assembler nor the Linkage Editor recognizes a "program"—they process one or more control sections.

Under an operating system where multiprogramming is common, there is often more than one program being executed in storage. On any given day these programs are located in storage depending on the sequence in which they are first required. Therefore, under such a system when you code a program you do not know where it will be located for execution. Under smaller systems where generally single programs are run, programs are normally loaded following the supervisor area, beginning in an available location that is evenly divisible by eight, a "doubleword" address.

The first or only control section of a program is identified by either the START or CSECT directive. Subsequent control sections, if any, are identified by CSECT. Because the programs to this point are still small, you may code them in one section using START. Chapter 19 covers program sectioning and CSECT.

NAME	OPERATION	OPERAND
(symbol)	START	a decimal or hex value, or blank
(symbol)	CSECT	blank

The START directive specifies the beginning of the first or only control section (CSECT may also be used for this purpose). The Assembler treats the name, if any, as the name of the control section. If you know where the program will be loaded, you may code an initial value (evenly divisible by eight) for the Assembler location counter. Under some operating systems such as OS and DOS/VS, you do not know where your program will reside for execution. If the value is omitted the location counter is set to zero. The following three examples illustrate various uses of START:

1. PROGA START X'4800'   The name of the control section is PROGA. The location counter is set to X'4800' or 18,432, where the program is assumed to be loaded.

2.   START 18432   The control section is unnamed. The location counter is set to 18,432 or X'4800'.

3. PROGB START   The name is PROGB. Because the operand is blank the location counter is set to zero. This coding practice is common, where it is generally not known in advance where the program will reside during execution.

The Assembler location counter assigns storage addresses to program statements. These are relative addresses that are printed under the LOC column in the assembled listing. The content of the location counter has no effect on program execution. Displacements are all relative to the contents of a base register. You may, for example, omit the operand in the START statement so that the location counter is set to zero. But at execute-time the program may be loaded at X'4200'. The first statement shown on the listing at X'0000' is actually at X'4200'. When debugging the program you have to reconcile the listing with the storage dump—for example, a statement listed under LOC at X'0048' is in storage at X'4200' + X'0048', or X'4248'.

ASSIGNING BASE REGISTERS

It is your responsibility to notify the Assembler which registers are available as base registers. For this purpose code the USING directive. Subject to the restrictions discussed earlier, you may assign any registers (generally 2 through 12)—*but the program should not use them for any other purpose.* The USING directive simply tells the Assembler which register(s) to use for base addressing and generates no executable code. Note that up to now the INIT macro has performed base register initialization—but it's now time for you to do your own!

NAME	OPERATION	OPERAND
blank	USING	S1,R1, . . . ,Rn

S1 in the operand field designates the address from which the Assembler calculates displacements. R2, . . ., Rn specifes the base registers (1 through 15) and their sequence. When coding the program you can only guess how much storage is required; assume about 25 coding sheets for each 4K of storage, excluding any large declaratives. Consider the following three examples:

1. USING *,3
   The asterisk in the operand references the current value in the Assembler location counter. The statement tells the Assembler that from this point on (for the next 4096 bytes) to use register-3 as the base register. In effect, the Assembler inserts a '3' as the base register into any machine address that references this region. The Assembler also calculates the displacement from this beginning address and inserts the displacement into the object code instruction.

2. ```
   USING A10,5
   A10  MVC   P+30(10),NAME
   ```
   At assembly-time the current value of the location counter is the address of A10. Here, register-5 becomes the assigned base register. The identical effect is achieved by USING *,5.

3. USING *,3,9,4
   Each 4096 bytes of storage referenced by the program requires one base register. In this case we expect to require between 8K and 12K of storage. Designate three base registers which the Assembler uses as required in the sequence coded. Suppose that the current value in the location counter is X'3802'. Then base register-3 is to apply to all locations from X'3802' through the next 4095 bytes. Since 4096 equals X'1000', when the location counter reaches X'4802', the Assembler assigns base register-9 for the next 4K region. At X'5802' and for the next region, register-4 becomes the base register.
   ```

LOADING THE BASE REGISTER

USING merely notifies the Assembler which base registers to use. *It is your responsibility to code the program to load the register with a base address.* For this purpose use the BALR instruction, Branch and Link Register.

NAME	OPERATION	OPERAND
(symbol)	BALR	R1,R2

BALR is an RR (register-to-register) format instruction. The rules are:

1. Both operands specify any general-purpose register.
2. The instruction loads bits 32–63 of the program status word into the operand-1 register. The rightmost 24 bits of the PSW contain the address of the next sequential instruction in the program. (The other 8 bits include the condition code and are not used for addressing.)

```
base register:    |   unused    |——— address ———|

position:         0.          7 8                31
```

3. If operand-2 specifies registers 1 through 15, the program branches to the address in that register (assuming an address is already there):

```
X'4000'   BALR   6,9     Load the address of the next instruction, X'4002', into
X'4002'   MVC    . . .   register-6, and branch to the address in register-9.
```

4. For certain instructions like BALR and BCTR, register-0 has special properties. When operand-2 specifies register-0, the computer assumes that there is *no register reference.* For BALR, if operand-2 is register-0, no branch is taken. The program continues with the next sequential instruction:

```
X'5800'   BALR   3,0     Load the address of the next instruction, X'5802', into
X'5802'   MVC    . . .   register-3, and execute the next instruction, the MVC
                         in X'5802'.
```

This is the most common use of BALR. (0 in operand-2 means no register.)

Figure 6-3 shows how BALR and USING are combined at the beginning of a program to initialize and assign a base register. This is a skeleton program for illustrative purposes—there would normally be instructions following the MVC. Carefully distinguish in the example between assembly and execute operations.

```
   LOC   OBJECT CODE    ADDR1 ADDR2  STMT   SOURCE STATEMENT

003800                                 4            START X'3800'        INIT LOC'N COUNTER
003800 0530                            5  BEGIN     BALR  3,0            LOAD BASE REGISTER
                              03802     6            USING *,3           ASSIGN BASE REG 3

003802 D20E 3029 3006 0382B 03808      8            MVC   HDGPR,HEADING
                                       9  *         .
                                      10  *         .
                                      11  *         .
003808 C9D5E5D6C9C3C540               12  HEADING   DC    CL15'INVOICE LISTING'
003817                               13  PRINT     DS    0CL133
003817 4040404040404040              14            DC    CL20' '
00382B                               15  HDGPR     DS    CL15
00383A 4040404040404040              16            DC    CL98' '


                              03800    18            END   BEGIN
```

FIGURE 6.3 Base register initialization.

AT ASSEMBLY-TIME. The START directive initializes the Assembler location counter to X'3800' where we expect the program to load at execute-time. Therefore, under LOC the program listing shows the initial value 003800, and the location counter is incremented to show where each assembled statement is located. This is the only effect of START—it has nothing to do with initializing base registers or telling the system where to load the program. Under DOS/VS and OS, START or CSECT usually contain a blank or zero operand.

BALR is the first executable instruction. BALR is RR format with machine code 05. The Assembler generates the two bytes of object code 0530, and increments the location counter to 3802. USING next tells the Assembler from this point (X'3802') to use register-3 as the base register. USING generates no object code. The next instruction, MVC, is assigned to X'3802'. The generated MVC instruction is

D2	0E	30	29	30	06
(a)	(b)	(c)		(d)	

(a)   D2 is the machine language code for MVC.

(b)   The length of operand-1 is explicitly coded as 15. The Assembler deducts 1 from this length and inserts 14 (X'0E') in the second byte of the object code. *The machine length code is therefore always one less than the actual length.* At execute-time, the computer in effect "adds" one to this length. For any operand that references main storage, the object code length is one less than its length in the source program.

(c) Operand-1, X'3029', references HDGPR. The Assembler inserts 3 for base register-3 in the first half-byte of object code. Note that the Assembler defines HDGPR at location X'382B'. Since the displacement of HDGPR from the USING directive at X'3802' is X'0029' bytes, the Assembler inserts a displacement value of 029 into the rightmost three half-bytes of the object code.

(d) Operand-2, X'3006', references HEADING. The Assembler inserts 3 for the base register into the first half-byte of object code. The Assembler calculates the displacement of HEADING as six bytes from USING, and inserts 006 into the object code.

AT EXECUTE-TIME.   After assembly and link-edit, the program is ready to execute. Assume that it is loaded beginning at X'3800'. The contents of storage would appear in hexadecimal as follows:

```
3800 3802       3808                    3817
  |    |          |                       |
 0530D20E30293006C9D5E5D6C9C3C540 ... 404040 ...
  |    |          |                       |
 BALR MVC       HEADING                 PRINT
```

The first instruction, BALR, loads into register-3 the instruction address in the PSW containing the address of the next instruction, X'3802'. When executing the MVC, the computer calculates the effective addresses for its two operands as follows:

	OPERAND-1	OPERAND-2
Contents of base register-3	X'3802'	X'3802'
Displacement	X'0029'	X'0006'
Effective address	X'382B'	X'3808'

These are the effective addresses for the locations of PRHDG and HEADING respectively. On execution, the computer also adds 1 to the length (14 + 1 = 15), and moves 15 bytes beginning at X'3808' to the location beginning at X'382B'.

> *Note: You must reserve a base register and ensure that it is loaded with the correct value. The Assembler cannot check that the base register is correctly initialized. It is possible to get an error-free assembly, but one that at execute-time references the wrong locations!* One way to cause such an execute error is to code the USING before the BALR. The Assembler sets the location counter to X'3800' instead of X'3802', and calculates displacements from X'3800'. But at execute-time BALR may load the base register with a value such as X'3802', causing all displacements to be incorrect by two bytes.

OS INITIALIZATION

Both DOS and OS require the BALR/USING initialization instructions, used identically. But OS is a more complex system, and its supervisor treats all users' programs like "subprograms." There is additional code to supply a linkage between the supervisor and your OS program, as Figure 6-4 illustrates.

```
 1    PROGNAME  START
 2              SAVE   (14,12)        STORE SUPERVISOR'S REGISTERS
 3              BALR   ...
 4              USING  ...
 5              ST     13,SAVEAREA+4  STORE REGISTER 13
 6              LA     13,SAVEAREA    LOAD ADDRESS OF SAVEAREA
 7              OPEN   ...
                   .
                   .
                   .
 8              CLOSE  ...
 9              L      13,SAVEAREA+4  RE-LOAD REGISTER 13
10              RETURN (14,12)        RE-LOAD REGS, RETURN TO SPVR
                   .
11    SAVEAREA  DS     18F            SAVE AREA, 18 FULLWORDS
12              END    PROGNAME
```

FIGURE 6-4 OS initialization and return linkage.

Statement 1 is the usual START, under OS omitting the operand or coding it as 0. At execute-time the system tells you where the program has loaded by means of a "Location Factor." If the Load or Entry Point is X'50000' (the starting address) and the program listing indicates that a field called AMOUNT is at location (LOC) X'68A', then its actual location during the particular execution is X'50000' plus X'68A', or X'5068A'.

Statement 2 is a special SAVE macro that immediately saves the contents of the registers for the supervisor. The program will change the register contents for its own purposes, but will restore the original values before returning to the supervisor.

Statements 3 and 4 are conventional BALR and USING instructions, coded after the SAVE.

Statement 5 stores the contents of register-13 in a special register save area, called SAVEAREA in statement 11. Statement 6 loads into register-13 the address of the SAVEAREA. Register-13 is important to such linkage between two programs, and should not be used for any other purpose. There is continual traffic between the user program and the supervisor, for all I/O operations and program checks.

Statements 9 and 10 are coded following the CLOSE at the end of all processing, and are equivalent to the DOS EOJ macro. The L (Load) instruction reloads the registers that were saved at the start, and the RETURN macro returns control to the supervisor.

Statement 11 defines SAVEAREA as 18 "fullwords" (each four bytes long), for storing the contents of the 16 registers and two other values.

Later chapters cover in detail these register operations, and the linkage is explained in the chapter "Subprograms and Overlays." When using this linkage, be sure to code it exactly as illustrated, using the same instructions and registers, in the same sequence. The Assembler does not check for accuracy, and any variation could be disastrous at execution-time.

•   *Problems 6-6 through 6-10 should now be attempted.*   •

THE ASSEMBLY PROCESS

Most Assemblers adopt a similar approach to assembling a program. Typically, an Assembler requires two passes through a source program, although the second pass involves a modified version of the program.

An Assembler has to deal with and integrate such diverse features as location counter, base registers, symbolic instructions, explicit base/displacement, literals, declaratives, directives, macro instructions, I/O files, and linkage to other programs.

To deal with these features, the Assembler has two basic types of *tables*. One type of table provides for Assembler words that are input to the translation process. The other type of table that the Assembler must construct is for your own words in your source program.

The Assembler's own tables include one for symbolic instructions (such as BALR and MVC). Associated with each table entry is its machine code and general format. Another table is for directives and declaratives (such as DC, EQU, START, and USING). Associated with each entry is an address of a routine to which the Assembler links to process the directive. If a word in the operation code of your program is not in either table nor is it a macro, the Assembler tags it as an error.

The tables that the Assembler constructs are for symbolic names and for literals used in your program.

Because the Assembler cannot handle all the many forward and backward references in a source program, it requires a second pass. For example, consider the following instruction:

```
MVC CODE,=CL3' '
```

The reference to CODE appears before its definition. As a consequence, the Assembler cannot complete the object code for the MVC instruction until it knows the length and relative location of CODE. As pass-1 progresses through the source program, the Assembler determines the length and relative location of each statement that generates machine code and constructs a *symbol table* in a format such as:

Name	Location	Length
CODE	0126	03

Pass-1 generates a modified source program file that now includes the location counter setting and statement number. This phase terminates on encountering the END directive. Pass-2 reads through the modified file and completes the object code. It converts symbolic op-codes to machine code, operands to base register/displacement, and DC constants to hexadecimal. A DS does not convert at all, and accordingly its contents will be whatever happens to be in storage at the time of execution.

Pass-2 generates an optional source listing file and an object file. The source listing file, as you have seen, contains your original source statements plus a statement number and a representation of the generated object code. The object file consists of four types of entries:

1. External Symbol Dictionary (ESD) entries identify each control section, external reference, and entry point in your program.
2. Text (TXT) entries provide the executable object code instructions and the constants.
3. Relocation Dictionary (RLD) entries furnish all A-type and external V-type address constants. These may be either DC statements or literals and appear for example as =A(TAXTABLE).
4. An END entry that supplies the address of the first instruction that is to execute when the program is run.

LINKAGE EDITOR. The next step (if requested) is link editing in which the *Linkage Editor program* examines the ESD entries to determine what I/O modules to include and, if there is more than one program to link together, to complete any linkage addresses between the programs. The linker then writes the executable module onto disk under its assigned name.

THE LOADER. For execution, there is a special *loader program* whose purpose is to read the executable module from disk (where the linker stored it) and load it into an available area in storage.

The loader is also concerned with address constants in the *relocation dictionary*. The Assembler deals with relative locations only from a starting point. As a consequence, when it defines an address constant, its address is only a displacement such as X'360'. But the program loads for execution at a specific location in storage, such as X'20400'. A reference to the constant during execution should be X'20400' plus X'360', or X'20760'.

The loader secures a load point address (also known as *entry point address* and *relocation factor*) from the operating system, loads the program into storage beginning at the load point and adds this relocation factor to each address constant in the relocation dictionary. It then transfers control to the address in the END entry and your program (at last) begins execution.

Figure 6-5 provides a chart of the flow of assembly, link, and execution of a program.

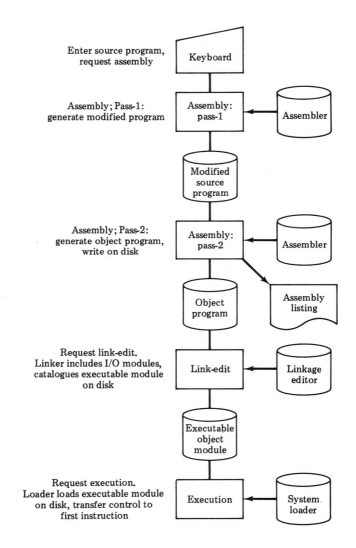

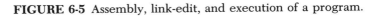

FIGURE 6-5 Assembly, link-edit, and execution of a program.

TECHNICAL NOTE ABOUT BCR AND BC

Up to this point, for comparisons programs have used the *extended mnemonic* instructions such as B, BE, BH, and BL. Technically, these are special variations on the BC (branch on condition) instruction which has the general format

```
BC M1,D2(X2,B2)
```

M1 is a *mask*, a reference to the condition code in the program status word (PSW). You could, for example, code an unconditional branch (B) instruction or a conditional branch (BH) instruction either of two ways:

	extended mnemonic	branch on condition (BC)
unconditional branch	B addr	BC 15,addr
conditional branch	BH addr	BC 2,addr

The BCR (Branch on Condition Register) instruction has the general format

```
BCR M1,R2
```

A common extended mnemonic for BCR is the BR instruction that causes an unconditional branch to an address in a register. You could code the instruction using either BR or BCR as follows:

	extended mnemonic	branch on condition register (BCR)
unconditional branch	BR reg	BCR 15,reg

The two bits in the condition code represent the following:

CONDITION CODE BITS	VALUE	INDICATION
00	0	Equal/Zero
01	1	Low/Minus
10	2	High/Plus
11	3	Overflow

Figure 6-6 provides the four-bit mask for the nine common branch conditions. You can test for *Equal/Zero* with either BE addr or BC 8,addr. The Assembler translates the 8 to binary 1000 in the object code mask position. Note that bits are numbered from left to right, beginning with zero for the leftmost bit, as 0, 1, 2, 3. On execution, the computer checks the mask —binary 1000 asks if bit 0 is on, meaning: does the condition code value equal zero?

The 4-bit Mask

Condition	Eq/zero 0	Low/min 1	High/plus 2	Overflow 3	Branch on condition	Extended mnemonic	
0 = Equal/zero	1	0	0	0	BC 8,addr	BE addr	BZ addr
1 = Low/minus	0	1	0	0	BC 4,addr	BL addr	BM addr
2 = High/plus	0	0	1	0	BC 2,addr	BH addr	BP addr
3 = Overflow	0	0	0	1	BC 1,addr	BO addr	
No branch	0	0	0	0	BC 0,addr	NOP addr	
1,2,3 = Not equal	0	1	1	1	BC 7,addr	BNE addr	BNZ addr
0,2,3 = Not low	1	0	1	1	BC 11,addr	BNL addr	BNM addr
0,1,3 = Not high	1	1	0	1	BC 13,addr	BNH addr	BNP addr
0,1,2,3 = Any	1	1	1	1	BC 15,addr	B addr	

FIGURE 6-6 Branch on condition mask.

For *Not Equal,* you could code either BNE addr or BC 7,addr. The Assembler translates the 7 to binary 0111 in the mask. On execution, the computer checks the mask:

> If bit number 1 is on, does the condition code value equal 1?
> If bit number 2 is on, does the condition code value equal 2?
> If bit number 3 is on, does the condition code value equal 3?

If any one of these conditions exists, then the condition is not equal. The Assembler provides the extended mnemonics to save you coding and memorizing the mask. But whichever way you code, for example BNE addr or BC 7,addr, the Assembler generates the identical object code.

In the interests of clarity and reducing program bugs, this text recommends using the *extended mnemonics*. An understanding of the mask and the condition is useful, however, to aid in deciphering machine language code.

DEBUGGING TIPS

Except for the special OS initialization, the only new instructions introduced in this chapter are BALR and USING. Typical errors involved with their use are:

- Omission of either BALR or USING. Omitting BALR causes an unpredictable error at execute-time, and omitting USING prevents the Assembler from generating machine code for instructions that require an implicit base register (addressability errors).

- Failure to assign and load enough base registers for a large program (Assembler addressability errors). A fairly common error is to load the second and third base registers with incorrect values.
- Using the base register for some other purpose in the program, thereby destroying the base address reference.
- Reversing BALR/USING, as USING/BALR. BALR will load the base register with a value of two bytes more than the Assembler expects when calculating displacements. The following code is sometimes used to initialize and adjust the base register to the correct value:

```
USING  *,3
BALR  3,0
BCTR  3,0      Decrement register-3 by 1
BCTR  3,0      Decrement register-3 by 1
```

PROBLEMS

6-1. What are the two main purposes of the general registers?

6-2. What are the two main advantages of base/displacement addressing?

6-3. Why is explicit length indication permitted only for SS format?

6-4. Give the machine language code generated for the following. Assume base register-2 contains X'4800'.

    (a) BALR 9,10

    (b) LM   3,15,SAVE   Assume SAVE is at location 4920.

    (c) CLI CODE,C'X'   Assume CODE is at location 4A26.

    (d) CLC NEW,OLD   NEW is 3 bytes at 521A and OLD is 3 bytes at 5308.

    (e) ZAP LINECT,=P'0'   LINECT is 2 bytes at 522B and =P'0' is at 5444.

6-5. Explain how the instruction format limits: (a) the number of registers to 16; (b) character lengths to 256; (c) packed lengths to 16; (d) maximum displacement to 4095 bytes.

6-6. Does the operand in START X'5000' affect where the program loads for execution? Explain.

6-7. Code a USING directive for a program requiring 19,000 bytes.

6-8. Distinguish between BALR and USING. What is the purpose of each? Explain what happens at assembly and at execute-time by:

```
X'5800'   BALR   3,0      Load base register-3
          USING  *,4      Assign base register-4
```

6-9. Revise any previous program for base register initialization. Replace the INIT macro (or whatever macro you used for initialization). If under OS, code the linkage carefully.

6-10. The first base register is loaded using BALR, and additional ones with L, LA, or LM. Assign and load registers 6, 7, and 8 as base registers, and define any required declaratives. (*Hint:* Look ahead in the book.)

    (a) Use one LM instruction to load registers 7 and 8.

    (b) Use LA instructions to load registers 7 and 8.

6-11. Give the extended mnemonics for the following: (a) BC 8,C90; (b) BC 2,D90; (c) BC 11,E90; (d) BC 15,F90.

6-12. Code the following in machine language (assuming base register-3 contains X'5200' and B30 is at X'5C38'): (a) B B30; (b) BNL B30; (c) BAL 5,B30; (d) BR 5.

6-13. What would BC 9,addr mean?

6-14. Explain the *effect* of the following pair of related instructions—what happens?

```
BALR      8,0
BR        8
```

7

INPUT AND OUTPUT

Input/output on the 370-series computers is significantly complex and for this reason its discussion has been delayed until now. This chapter covers only a fraction of the technical material available. (See especially the IBM Supervisor manuals.)

Earlier computers transmitted data directly between storage and I/O devices. Such computers used to read records directly into storage in a specified area and wrote out of an area. During the I/O operation, all other processing was suspended until transmission was completed. Such a system considerably delays processing, especially when many devices are attached. I/O processing has been improved by:

- At the software (programming) level, *buffers* are used (covered in a later section).
- The I/O devices now generally are faster.
- CPU processing and data transmission are designed to *overlap*. For example, while a print operation transmits data to the printer, the CPU continues executing instructions. This advantage is achieved by the use of a hardware feature, *channels,* covered in the chapter on Operating Systems.
- Many more I/O devices are available, requiring more powerful I/O capability.

INPUT/OUTPUT CONTROL SYSTEM

A 370 program always executes in one of two states—the *problem* and the *supervisor state.* At any given time, the computer is either in the problem state executing a user's "problem" program, or in the supervisor state, executing the supervisor program. The supervisor program handles the transition between jobs and all interrupts, which include program and machine checks and all input/output operations. The problem program cannot actually issue I/O operations—these are *privileged instructions* that only the supervisor can execute. The PSW indication is in bit 15 : 0 means supervisor and 1 means the problem program is being executed. Privileged instructions execute only when the program is in the supervisor state (PSW bit 15 = 0). For all I/O, the problem program interrupts and transfers control to the supervisor.

For its I/O operations, the supervisor uses the privileged instructions: Start I/O, Test I/O, Halt I/O, and Test Channel. You can (but usually do not) code I/O operations for the channel program by linking to the supervisor with SVC (supervisor call) and CCW (channel command word). This detailed level requires that you synchronize I/O operations with the program and provide for channel scheduling and interrupts. Few programmers code at this level. Instead, there is available a generalized input/output control system, IOCS (called data management services under OS). You can simplify I/O programming considerably by coding IOCS macro instructions. There are two main forms of IOCS: *physical IOCS (PIOCS) and logical IOCS (LIOCS)*.

PHYSICAL IOCS.   The PIOCS level is still close to the actual machine operation, and coding is similar to that already discussed. You code the channel program using the macros EXCP (execute channel program), WAIT, and CCB (command control block). This level initiates execution of channel commands, and handles I/O interrupts and channel scheduling, but you must still synchronize I/O operations with your program. Chapter 20 provides more information on physical IOCS.

LOGICAL IOCS.   The LIOCS level uses the capabilities of physical IOCS, but provides many more features. On input, LIOCS locates the required record and delivers it to the program as a *logical record*. On output, LIOCS delivers the logical record to the channel program. LIOCS handles end-of-file conditions and many more functions not yet discussed, including:

- Switching (*flip-flopping*) between I/O areas (*buffers*) if more than one buffer is designated.
- *Blocking* and *unblocking* tape and disk records.
- Checking and writing tape and disk *labels*.

To obtain a record using logical IOCS simply code the GET macro, and to write a record code the PUT macro (sometimes READ and WRITE in special cases). IOCS saves you from coding the complex but repetitive input/output routines. The rest of this chapter covers programming using logical IOCS. You have already used logical IOCS for OPEN, CLOSE, and GET. This chapter explains these and other macros in detail.

BUFFERS. Under a conventional unbuffered input/output system, you read a record, then process it, then read another record:

Read-1	Process-1	Read-2	Process-2	etc . . .

time ➤

Better efficiency can be achieved by overlapping reading with processing. Read a record, *then while processing this record, read the next record:*

Read-1	Process-1	Process-2	Process-3	
	Read-2	Read-3	Read-4	etc . . .

time ➤

As can be seen, reading and processing are overlapped. The input records are read into areas in your program called *buffers* or *I/O areas.* You can extend this facility by increasing the number of buffers (up to 2 for DOS and 256 for OS). Similarly, writing can be overlapped with processing. Under DOS the programmer must designate the buffer areas, but OS automatically supplies them.

There are two types of IOCS macros: *file definition macros* and *imperative macros.*

FILE DEFINITION MACROS. Up to this point, program examples have used two special shortcut macros to define files: DEFIN and DEFPR. However, the proper IBM macros require more elaborate definitions. The file definition macros define, for example, the symbolic name of the file, the length of the records, the buffers, and the actual device to be used. The Assembler is then able to construct a table of applicable channel commands. Under DOS, the DTFnn macro (define the file) defines a file. For example, DTFSD means define a sequential disk file, and DTFPR means define a printer file. OS uses a data control block, DCB, to define a "data set." Both are more fully described later in this chapter and in the chapters on magnetic tape and disk.

REGISTER USAGE. IOCS makes full use of the linkage registers 0, 1, 13, 14, and 15:

0 and 1: Logical IOCS macros, supervisor macros, and other IBM macros use these registers to pass addresses.

13: Logical IOCS and other supervisor routines use register-13 to address an area used to save the contents of your registers and to restore them on return to your program.

14 and 15: Logical IOCS uses these registers for linkage. A GET or PUT automatically loads the address of the following instruction into register-14 to facilitate return from the I/O operation, and automatically loads register-15 with the address of the actual I/O routine (and uses it when executing that routine as a base register). For debugging from a storage dump, you can check the contents of register-14 to see the address of the last I/O operation that executed.

IMPERATIVE MACROS

Imperative macros initiate an input/output operation and include OPEN, CLOSE, GET, and PUT. These macros relate to the generalized DTF or DCB channel commands and link to the supervisor to issue the data transmission.

THE OPEN MACRO. OPEN makes a file available to a program. Control is passed to the supervisor which checks that the file exists and that the device is ready. (IOCS does considerably more when opening disk and tape.) One OPEN may open from one to 16 files. For example, assume the following macro statements:

```
DOS Coding:

        FILEIN      DTFCD ...        Define input file
        PRINTER     DTFPR ...        Define output file
                    OPEN  FILEIN,PRINTER

OS Coding:

        FILEIN      DCB   ...        Define input file
        PRINTER     DCB   ...        Define output file
                    OPEN  (FILEIN,(INPUT),PRINTER,(OUTPUT))
```

THE CLOSE MACRO. CLOSE deactivates all files previously opened that you no longer require. (IOCS performs many additional features when closing a tape or disk file.) You may close a file any time, and should close all files before terminating program execution. Also, once you close a file you may further process it only by reopening it.

```
DOS:  CLOSE  FILEIN,PRINTER
OS:   CLOSE  (FILEIN,,PRINTER)
```

In a multiprogramming system, be sure to close a file promptly once it is fully processed. The device and file are then available to other programs in the system.

Many systems provide for automatic *self-relocating programs*. If your system does not have this capability, then to facilitate self-relocatability under DOS, code the macros as OPENR and CLOSER. The IBM DOS Supervisor manual provides full details.

THE GET MACRO. GET makes available the next record from a sequential input file. The input record erases the previous contents of the input area.

OPERATION	OPERAND
GET	filename, workarea
or GET	(1),(0)

The file name is that of the DTF or DCB for the file. IOCS delivers the record to the workarea specified in operand-2. For instance:

```
FILEIN    DTFCD OR DCB ...      Define the input file
RECDIN    DS    CL80            Define the input area
          GET   FILEIN,RECDIN   Read a record into RECDIN
```

In the above example, the filename is FILEIN and the workarea is RECDIN. You may also load the DTF or DCB address and the workarea address into registers 1 and 0, as follows:

```
LA    1,FILEIN        Load address of FILEIN
LA    0,RECDIN        Load address of RECDIN
GET   (1),(0)         Read a record into RECDIN
```

Figure 7-1a depicts the relationship of the GET statement with two buffers. The first GET issued in the program reads record-1 into the first buffer, I/O area1. Record-1 is transferred to RECDIN, available for processing. Then while the program processes the record in RECDIN, IOCS reads record-2 into the second buffer, I/O area2:

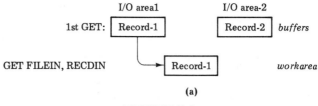

(a)

FIGURE 7-1a

In Figure 7-1b the second GET issued in the program transfers record-2 to RECDIN, and while the program processes RECDIN, IOCS reads record-3 into the first buffer:

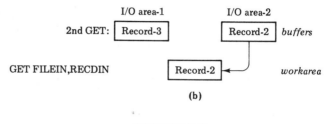

(b)

FIGURE 7-1b

You must inform IOCS where to branch when it encounters the end-of-file (the /* trailer record). Designate the address where the system is to branch in the DCB or DTF statement. IOCS reads the /* record directly into a buffer. When a GET attempts to transfer the /* record to your workarea, the system instead will automatically direct the program to your end-of-file address.

THE PUT MACRO.   PUT writes your record from your output (work) area. The rules for coding PUT are similar to those for GET.

OPERATION	OPERAND
PUT	filename, workarea
or PUT	(1),(0)

For example:

```
PRINTER  DTFPR or DCB ...          Define the print file
PRINT    DC          CL133' '      The print workarea
         PUT         PRINTER,PRINT Write a record
```

The PUT macro causes the contents of the workarea PRINT to write onto the device called PRINTER. *Note: The contents of the workarea and the buffers are not erased.* If you move data into the print area, be sure to clear the area after writing.

Before printing, insert a special forms control character into the first byte of the print workarea. (An alternative method is to use the CNTRL macro—see the IBM Supervisor Macro manuals.) The character informs the channel what action to take, such as print, space, eject. Punching cards may also require a special control character before the punch area. The common forms control characters in hex are:

	NO WRITE	WRITE
Space 1 line	0B	09
Space 2 lines	13	11
Space 3 lines	1B	19
Skip to new page	8B	89

Note also: X'01' is Write, space 0 lines.

For example, write and space two lines:

```
PRINT    DS    0CL133          Print area:
CTLPR    DS    XL1             * control char.
         DC    CL132' '        * rest of print

         MVI   CTLPR,X'11'     Insert control char.
         PUT   PRINTER,PRINT   Print & space 2 lines
```

If you use X'13' as the control character, the printer spaces two lines, *without printing, regardless of the contents of PRINT.* "Skip to a new page" is actually "skip to channel 1." Earlier model printers are equipped with a carriage control tape punched with a hole in channel 1. The hole usually aligns with the printer forms at the top of the page as shown in Figure 7-2. Punches and control channels are available for channels 1 through 12 to permit skipping to various lines on the page. Most tapes are punched with channel 1, but not necessarily with the other channels.

More recent printers do not use carriage control tapes, but establish channel locations by means of job control entries. As a result, any program can set its own top-of-page with no need for operator intervention.

ASA CONTROL CHARACTER. An alternative forms control character that is more universal for different computers is the American Standards Association set, which is less efficient on the 370. Following are the more common characters:

blank   Space 1 line, then print
  0   Space 2 lines, then print
  —   Space 3 lines, then print
  +   Print without spacing
  1   Skip to the next page, then print

Note that execution involves spacing *before* printing, whereas the IBM code spaces *after* printing. As an example, the following instruction initializes an ASA control character for spacing two lines before printing:

```
MVI    CTLPR,C'0'       Insert control char.
PUT    PRTR,PRINT       Space 2 and print
```

In order to space without printing, clear PRINT to blanks; the PUT operation then "prints" a blank line.

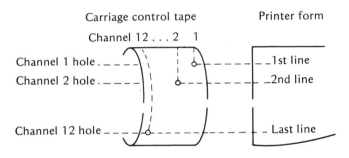

FIGURE 7-2 Carriage control tape.

EXAMPLE PROGRAMS.   The next two example programs in Figures 7-3 and 7-4 both illustrate the same program, using DOS and OS imperative and file definition macros. The programs simply read and write input records. They load register-3 as the base register and open the files; this initialization need be performed only once, at the start of the program execution.

At AP10PAGE the program skips to a new page to print the heading. Note that CTLCHAR is defined as the first byte of the print area. In the loop routine A10LOOP, a record is read into RECDIN. This field is moved to the print area and printed. The line counter is incremented and checked for page overflow as in previous programs.

When all the input records have been read, IOCS recognizes the end-of-file (/* trailer record under DOS), and directs the program to the end-file address, A90END, where the files are closed and execution terminates.

Both file definition macros, DTF and DCB, are *keyword macros*. That is, the entries are recognized by specific names, and may be coded in any sequence. The keyword is followed by an equal sign (=) and a *parameter*, such as EOFADDR=A90END. One entry is coded per line, followed immediately by a comma to separate the entries. Enter a continuation character in column 72 to indicate that the macro continues on the next line, in column 16. (It is possible to code several entries per line, but this practice makes the listing difficult to read and to change.) The last entry has no comma or continuation character. Some entries may be omitted; in these cases the Assembler assumes an entry—such assumptions are called *default values*. Precise entries and defaults vary by version of operating system, so that it is necessary to refer to the appropriate IBM Supervisor manual.

THE DOS DTF FILE DEFINITION MACRO

Figure 7-3 provides the requirements for a program written under DOS. The specifications for DTFCD and DTFPR follow:

DTFCD—DEFINE THE CARD FILE. DTFCD is suitable for defining an input file on cards or on a terminal under CMS. The name in Figure 7-3 given to the input file is FILEIN (any unique name may be given). The entries are:

BLKSIZE=80 tells IOCS that the size of each block of data to be read is 80 bytes, or 80 columns. If this entry is omitted, the Assembler assumes a default of 80 (depending on the device).

DEVADDR=SYSIPT gives the entry SYSIPT, the primary system input device. Depending on the system, you may designate SYSRDR (the system reader device), or a "programmer logical unit," SYSnn appropriate to the computer installation.

DEVICE=1442 designates the reader device to be used by the file. If the operand is omitted, the Assembler assumes a 2540 reader.

EOFADDR=A90END indicates the address of your end-of-file routine, and may be any unique program name. IOCS recognizes the /* trailer record and links to your end-of-file address. Never branch to this address from any other point.

IOAREA1=IOARIN1 is a required entry that specifies the name of the first buffer (or I/O area). Another instruction defines this buffer elsewhere in the program as IOARIN1 DC CL80. Any unique name could be used. IOCS reads input records into this area.

IOAREA2=IOARIN2 gives the name of the second buffer (or I/O area). It is

```
LOC    OBJECT CODE        STMT   SOURCE STATEMENT

                            2          PRINT ON,NOGEN,NODATA

                            4  ***        I N I T I A L I Z A T I O N
000000                      5  PROG7A  START
000000 0530                 6          BALR  3,0                INITIALIZE BASE REGISTER
                            7          USING *,3
                            8          OPEN  FILEIN,PRINTER     ACTIVATE FILES
                           17          GET   FILEIN,RECDIN      READ 1ST RECORD
000026 4570 307E           23          BAL   7,P10PAGE          HEADING ROUTINE

                           25  ***        M A I N   P R O C E S S I N G
00002A F911 3385 33AE      26  A10LOOP CP    LINECT,=P'50'      END OF PAGE ?
000030 47D0 3036           27          BNH   A20
000034 4570 307E           28          BAL   7,P10PAGE          PAGE HEADING
000038 D24F 3314 3170      29  A20     MVC   RECDPR,RECDIN      MOVE RECORD TO PRINT AREA
00003E 9209 3300           30          MVI   CTLCHAR,X'09'      SET CONTROL CHARACTER
                           31          PUT   PRINTER,PRINT      PRINT, SPACE 1 LINE
000052 FA10 3385 33B0      37          AP    LINECT,=P'1'       ADD TO LINE COUNT
                           38          GET   FILEIN,RECDIN      READ NEXT
000068 47F0 3028           44          B     A10LOOP            LOOP

                           46  ***        E N D - O F - F I L E
                           47  A90END  CLOSE FILEIN,PRINTER     DE-ACTIVATE FILES
                           56          EOJ                      NORMAL END-OF-JOB

                           59  ***        P A G E   O V E R F L O W
000080 928B 3300           60  P10PAGE MVI   CTLCHAR,X'8B'      MOVE FORMS CTL CHAR
                           61          PUT   PRINTER,PRINT      SKIP TO NEW PAGE
000094 F810 3385 33B1      67          ZAP   LINECT,=P'0'       CLEAR LINE COUNT
00009A 07F7                68          BR    7                  RETURN


LOC    OBJECT CODE        STMT   SOURCE STATEMENT

                           70  ***        D E C L A R A T I V E S
                           72  FILEIN  DTFCD BLKSIZE=80,         DEFINE THE INPUT FILE
                                             DEVADDR=SYSIPT,
                                             DEVICE=1442,
                                             EOFADDR=A90END,     EOF ADDRESS
                                             IOAREA1=IOARIN1,
                                             IOAREA2=IOARIN2,
                                             RECFORM=FIXUNB,
                                             TYPEFLE=INPUT,
                                             WORKA=YES

0000D2 404040404040404040  94  IOARIN1 DC    CL80' '            INPUT BUFFER 1
000122 404040404040404040  95  IOARIN2 DC    CL80' '            INPUT BUFFER 2

000172                     97  RECDIN  DS    CL80               INPUT WORKAREA
```

```
 99 PRINTER DTFPR BLKSIZE=133,                    DEFINE PRINTER FILE      +
                  CTLCHR=YES,                                              +
                  DEVADDR=SYSLST,                                          +
                  DEVICE=3203,                                             +
                  IOAREA1=IOARPR1,                                         +
                  IOAREA2=IOARPR2,                                         +
                  RECFORM=FIXUNB,                                          +
                  WORKA=YES

0001F8 40404040404040404040  121 IOARPR1  DC   CL133' '       PRINT BUFFER 1
00027D 40404040404040404040  122 IOARPR2  DC   CL133' '       PRINT BUFFER 2

000302                       124 PRINT    DS   0CL133         PRINT AREA :
000302                       125 CTLCHAR  DS   XL01      *    CONTROL CHAR POSITION
000303 404040404040404040    126          DC   CL19' '
000316                       127 RECDPR   DS   CL80      **   RECORD PRINT AREA
000366 40404040404040404040  128          DC   CL33' '   **

000387 000C                  130 LINECT   DC   PL2'0'         LINE COUNTER

000390                       132          LTORG
000390 5B5BC2D6D7C5D540      133               =C'$$BOPEN '
000398 5B5BC2C3D3D6E2C5      134               =C'$$BCLOSE'
0003A0 000000A0              135               =A(FILEIN)
0003A4 00000172              136               =A(RECDIN)
0003A8 000001C8              137               =A(PRINTER)
0003AC 00000302              138               =A(PRINT)
0003B0 050C                  139               =P'50'
0003B2 1C                    140               =P'1'
0003B3 0C                    141               =P'0'
                             142          END  PROG7A
```

FIGURE 7-3 DOS input/output macros.

defined elsewhere in the program as IOARIN2 DC CL80. A second buffer is optional, but provides more efficient processing.

RECFORM=FIXUNB means that the format of records to be read is "fixed length, unblocked." All card or terminal records are in this format normally, but tape and disk records may be variable in length, and "blocked" —several records per block. If this entry is omitted, the Assember assumes FIXUNB.

TYPEFLE=INPUT means that the type of file is input. The operand for punched output is OUTPUT, and for a combined punch-feed-read device is CMBND. If the entry is omitted, the Assembler assumes INPUT. Watch out for the spelling of TYPEFLE!

WORKA=YES tells IOCS to process records in a "workarea" rather than directly in a buffer. IOCS is to transfer records from the buffers to your workarea, as specified in the macro GET FILEIN, RECDIN. RECDIN is defined elsewhere as DS CL80. The WORKA entry may be omitted, but if so, you must specify another entry as IOREG=(r), and process the input records directly in the buffers. This practice may be done with DTFCD, but is illustrated later under DTFDI.

Other entries may also be coded; however, IOCS varies by operating system, and many programs have unique needs. The supervisor manual for each system gives more specific details.

DTFPR—DEFINE THE PRINTER FILE.   The name in Figure 7-3 given to the printer is PRINTER. Note that there is no entry for TYPEFLE because DTFPR is understood to be an output file. The entry EOFADDR is omitted because it is only for input files. DTFPR also permits entries other than the ones shown in the example.

BLKSIZE=133 tells IOCS that the size of the block of output data is 133 bytes. The first (leftmost) byte is reserved for the forms control character, so that only 132 bytes are printed. The maximum block length depends on the particular printer device.

CTLCHR=YES means that the program is using the 370 forms control character set. Alternatively, coding CTLCHR=ASA stipulates the American Standards Association set, but watch out—ASA codes are different from IBM codes.

DEVADDR=SYSLST defines SYSLST, the primary system printing device to be used by this file. Depending on the system, you may also designate a programmer logical unit, as SYSnnn appropriate to the computer installation.

DEVICE=3203 designates the printer device for the file, such as 1443, 3203, etc., whatever printer is installed in the installation.

IOAREA1=IOARPR1 specifies the name of the first buffer (I/O area). Another statement defines this buffer elsewhere in the program as follows: IOARPR1 DC CL133. Any unique name could be used. The entry is required.

IOAREA2=IOARPR2 gives the name of the second (optional) buffer. It is defined elsewhere as IOARPR2 DC CL133. The use of more than one buffer provides more efficient processing.

RECFORM=FIXUNB means that the output format is "fixed length, unblocked."

WORKA=YES tells IOCS to process records in a "workarea" rather than in buffers. IOCS is to transfer records from our workarea to the buffers, in the example by means of the macro PUT PRINTER,PRINT. PRINT is defined elsewhere as DS CL121, and is the workarea for defining output records.

IOCS MODULES. For each file, the Linkage Editor includes an IOCS logic module immediately following the program. Use of a macro such as PUT PRINTER,PRINT links to the DTFPR, which in turn links to the printer logic module following the program.

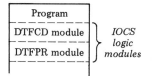

The size and location of these modules are available on the Linkage Editor Map (use the control statement ACTION MAP). An example of the Linkage Editor Map and names of the IOCS logic modules are given in Chapter 19.

The IOCS modules are preassembled and cataloged in libraries on disk, and the Linkage Editor includes the appropriate modules with all programs that require input/output.

THE OS DCB FILE DEFINITION MACRO

DCB, data control block, is equivalent to the DOS DTF macro, and is used to define a "data set." Because OS has considerable device independence capability, a recommended approach is to define all data sets as disk in order to facilitate this feature. Many of the entries required for DTFs are omitted for DCBs. Under OS, you may specify additional I/O attributes at execute-time by means of the DD, Data Definition, job control entries. This feature permits some programming changes concerned with I/O without reassembling the program.

```
***                 I N I T I A L I Z A T I O N
*
PROG7B   START 0
*
         SAVE  (14,12)                  SAVE REGS FOR SUPERVISOR
*
         BALR  3,0                       INITIALIZE BASE REGISTER
         USING *,3
*
         ST    13,SAVEAREA+4             SAVE ADDRESSES FOR RETURN
         LA    13,SAVEAREA               *    TO SUPERVISOR
*
         BAL   6,P10PAGE                 PAGE HEADING
         OPEN  (FILEIN,(INPUT),FILEOT,(OUTPUT))
         GET   FILEIN,INAREA            READ 1ST RECORD
*
***              M A I N   P R O C E S S I N G
*
A10LOOP  CP    LINECT,=P'50'            END OF PAGE ?
         BNH   A20                       NO - BYPASS
         BAL   6,P10PAGE
A20      MVC   RECPR,INAREA             MOVE RECORD TO PRINT AREA
         MVI   CTLCHPR,X'09'            MOVE CONTROL CHARACTER
         PUT   FILEOT,PRINT            PRINT, SPACE 1 LINE
         AP    LINECT,=P'1'             ADD TO LINE COUNT
         GET   FILEIN,INAREA           READ NEXT
         B     A10LOOP                   LOOP
*
***              E N D - O F - F I L E
*
A90END   CLOSE (FILEIN,,FILEOT)
         L     13,SAVEAREA+4            END-OF-JOB,  RETURN
         RETURN (14,12)                 *    TO SUPERVISOR
*
***              P A G E   O V E R F L O W
*
P10PAGE  MVI   CTLCHPR,X'8B'           FORMS CONTROL CHARACTER
         PUT   FILEOT,PRINT            SKIP TO NEW PAGE
         ZAP   LINECT,=P'0'             CLEAR LINE COUNT
         BR    6
*
***              D E C L A R A T I V E S
*
FILEIN   DCB   BLKSIZE=80,              DEFINE INPUT FILE           +
               DDNAME=SYSIN,                                        +
               DEVD=DA,                                             +
               DSORG=PS,                                            +
               EODAD=A90END,                                        +
               MACRF=(GM)
INAREA   DS    CL80                     INPUT WORKAREA
*
FILEOT   DCB   BLKSIZE=133,             DEFINE OUTPUT FILE          +
               DDNAME=SYSPRINT,                                     +
               DEVD=DA,                                             +
               DSORG=PS,                                            +
               MACRF=(PM),                                          +
               RECFM=FM
*
PRINT    DS    0CL133                   PRINT AREA :
CTLCHPR  DS    XL1                      *    CONTROL CHAR
         DC    CL19' '                  *
RECPR    DS    CL80                     *    RECORD PRINT AREA
         DC    CL33' '                  *
*
SAVEAREA DS    18F                      REGISTER SAVE AREA
LINECT   DC    PL2'0'                   LINE COUNTER
         LTORG
         END   PROG7B
```

FIGURE 7-4 OS input/output macros.

The Assembler completes as much of the "data control block" as possible from the DCB entries. Prior to execution, the system checks for missing entries, and accesses them from the DD command. In this way, entries in the DCB have priority over those in the DD command. If there is information not provided, the system may make a default assumption, or if not possible, the program will possibly "bomb" when attempting an I/O operation.

Figure 7-4 illustrates the OS DCB macro and initialization, using the same example as the previous one for DOS, reading and writing records.

DCB FOR INPUT. In the example, the name of the data set is FILEIN. Some of the DCB entries may be made on the DD job control entries.

BLKSIZE=80 means that the size of each data block is 80 bytes.

DDNAME=SYSIN tells data management that the "data definition name" is the logical address SYSIN (or whichever unit applies).

DEVD=DA means that the device for the data set is "direct access," or disk. The use of this entry instead of RD for reader facilitates device independence, so that, for example, records may be "spooled" onto disk for later processing.

DSORG=PS means that the data set organization is "physical sequential" (that is, the data is organized as sequential, rather than as direct access or indexed sequential—two disk processing methods). This entry may appear only in the DCB macro, and not in the DD job statement.

EODAD=A90END tells data management that the end-of-data address is A90END (or any other program label designated as the end routine). Data management (like IOCS) directs the program to this address on encountering the end-of-file indication on the input data set (/* on cards or terminal).

MACRF=(GM) means that the "macro format" to be used in the program is "Get and Move" to a workarea (the coding is to be GET FILEIN,workarea).

You may provide other definitions at execute-time with the DD (data definition) job control command, such as assigning the actual I/O device to be used (printer, tape, disk, etc.). Also, you do not define the buffers with the DCB. The DD command specifies the number of buffers; if omitted, OS assumes two buffers by default.

DCB FOR OUTPUT. In Figure 7-4, the name of the DCB printer data set is FILEOT, and provides one possible coding:

BLKSIZE, DEVD, AND DSORG are similar to the definitions for the input data set.

DDNAME=SYSPRINT means that the system printer is the device for this data set.

MACRF=(PM) means that the macro format is "Put and Move" from a workarea (the coding is to be PUT FILEOT,workarea).

RECFM=FM. The F means "fixed, unblocked." The M is for "machine code," the format for the regular 370 print control characters. For ASA characters, use A. The requirements for other installations may be quite different. Some systems block print records onto disk prior to printing, and the entry may be FBM or FBSM.

LOCATE MODE

It is possible to process input/output records directly in the buffers. The advantage (not very great) is that the workarea need not be defined. GET and PUT are coded without specifying a workarea in operand-2, as

```
GET FILEIN and PUT FILEOUT
```

The DTF and DCB requirements differ. For the DTF, the entry IOREG replaces WORKA, as IOREG=(reg) specifying an available general register. IOCS is to load the register with the address of the buffer that contains the next record to be processed. The DCB entry to denote processing in a buffer ("locate mode") is MACRF=(GL) for input and MACRF=(PL) for output. The system uses register-1 for the address of the buffer that contains the record to be processed.

The example in Figure 7-5a shows the first GET executed. IOCS reads record-1 into buffer-1 and loads the address of buffer-1 into "register-r." Then, while the program processes the record in buffer-1, IOCS reads record-2 into buffer-2:

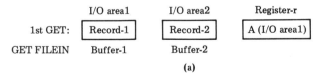

(a)

FIGURE 7-5a

The example cites "register-r" to mean the specified register in the DTF or register-1 for the DCB.

Figure 7-5b shows the second GET executed. IOCS loads the address of buffer-2 (which contains record-2) into register-r. Then, while the program processes record-2, IOCS reads record-3 into buffer-1:

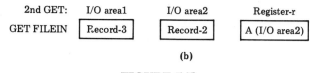

(b)

FIGURE 7-5b

Processing continues "flip-flopping" between the two buffers (or more under OS). GET reads a record into one of the buffers, but which one? After the GET, the register will contain the address of the first byte of the buffer in which the next input record is located. For the programmer, the simplest action is to move the contents of the buffer to a workarea for processing. You can use the address in the register explicitly in an MVC operation immediately following the GET. The symbolic format for MVC is

```
MVC D1(L,B1),D2(B2)
```

You can use explicit base/displacement addressing in either operand. In this case, since register-r contains the address of the buffer, you can code the following:

```
GET    FILEIN        Read file—load register with buffer address
MVC    INAREA,0(r)   Move buffer to INAREA
```

The MVC instruction works as follows: Using the address in register-r (base register-r, no displacement), move from the specified storage location to INAREA (an 80-byte move, based on the length of INAREA). The GET operation is basically the same for DOS and OS, although OS requires the use of register-1 only. The PUT statements and file definitions differ.

DOS CODING FOR LOCATE MODE. Figure 7-6 compares the changes required to process in a buffer with the conventional use of a workarea. The example arbitrarily selects register-4 for the input register and register-5 for the output register, with the IOREG entry replacing the WORKA entry. Any available register (2 through 12) will work, but not the base register(s). For printing, the OPEN statement establishes in register-5 (in this case) the address of the first available print buffer. Before the PUT, move the contents of the PRINT area to the buffer: operand-1 of the MVC, coded as 0(121,5) uses base register-5, displacement zero and length 121 explicitly to move the contents of PRINT to the designated storage locations. The following PUT statement initializes register-5 with the address of the next available buffer.

MACRO	USING WORKAREA	USING LOCATE MODE
Read	GET FILEIN,RECDIN	GET FILEIN MVC RECDIN,0(4)
Write	PUT PRTR,PRINT	MVC 0(121,5),PRINT PUT PRTR
Input file definition	DTFCD . . . WORKA = YES	DTFCD . . . IOREG = (4)
Output file definition	DTFPR . . . WORKA = YES	DTFPR . . . IOREG = (5)

FIGURE 7-6 DOS locate mode.

OS CODING FOR LOCATE MODE. Under OS, the DCB entry for processing in a buffer for the input data set is MACRF=(GL) for Get Locate, and the entry for the output data set is MACRF=(PL) for Put Locate. Figure 7-7 compares the conventional use of a workarea with Locate Mode. Since the DCB contains the entry for (PL), you must code the PUT with no operand-2. PUT inserts into register-1 the address of the first byte of the buffer that is to receive the next output record. Code PUT to locate the output buffer, and then you can use register-1 explicitly to move data into the buffer. But watch out—under OS the PUT macro is coded *before* the MVC.

MACRO	USING WORKAREA	USING LOCATE MODE
Read	GET FILEIN,INAREA	GET FILEIN MVC INAREA,0(1)
Write	PUT FILEOT,OUTAREA	PUT FILEOT MVC 0(133,1),OUTAREA
Input file definition	DCB . . . MACRF = (GM)	DCB . . . MACRF = (GL)
Output file definition	DCB . . . MACRF = (PM)	DCB . . . MACRF = (PL)

FIGURE 7-7 OS locate mode.

What have we accomplished? Using standard workareas, IOCS would perform these functions automatically. Processing fully in a buffer without moving to a workarea requires extensive use of explicit base/displacement processing, a topic covered in detail in Chapter 10. Chapter 19, under DSECT, does provide a sophisticated method of processing within a buffer, and giving names to the various fields in that area. Meanwhile, feel free to continue using workareas, the approach most commonly used in handling input/output.

DEVICE INDEPENDENCE UNDER DOS

With the DOS macros DTFCD and DTFPR you can normally read and write data only on a terminal, card reader, punch, and printer. Some situations, however, require more I/O flexibility. For example, assume a multiprogramming system that is executing two programs. The first program fully uses the only printer, but the second program also needs the printer. You may ask the system to direct the second program's output onto magnetic tape, which can later be used to print the output when the printer is available. You can enhance the flexibility of *device independence* (assigning tape output for a printer, for example) with the use of the macro DTFDI (define the file device independent) in place of DTFCD and DTFPR. OS and larger DOS/VS versions, designed for device independence, do not require such a special macro.

The module that DTFDI generates is larger than those for DTFCD and DTFPR, but is more versatile. Among restrictions, records must be fixed length, unblocked, and with no workarea specified. Figure 7-8 illustrates DTFDI macros for input and for output.

```
FILEIN     DTFDI  DEVADDR=SYSIPT,        DEFINE INPUT FILE          +
                  EOFADDR=Z10END,                                   +
                  RECSIZE=80,                                       +
                  IOAREA1=BUFFIN1,                                  +
                  IOAREA2=BUFFIN2,                                  +
                  IOREG=(4)

BUFFIN1    DC     CL80' '               INPUT  BUFFER  1
BUFFIN2    DC     CL80' '               INPUT  BUFFER  2
```

```
PRTR       DTFDI  DEVADDR=SYSLST,        DEFINE PRINT FILE          +
                  RECSIZE=121,                                      +
                  IOAREA1=BUFFOUT1,                                 +
                  IOAREA2=BUFFOUT2,                                 +
                  IOREG=(5)

BUFFOUT1   DC     CL121' '              OUTPUT BUFFER  1
BUFFOUT2   DC     CL121' '              OUTPUT BUFFER  2
```

FIGURE 7-8 DOS DTFDI macros.

DTFDI FOR INPUT. The name in Figure 7-8 given to the input file is FILEIN. Entries EOFADDR, IOAREA1, and IOAREA2 are coded the same as for DTFCD.

DEVADDR uses only the primary system input device names SYSIPT and SYSRDR.

IOREG=(4) tells IOCS to load register-4 with the address of the buffer that contains the current input record. Any available register, 2 through 12; may be assigned. With IOREG, code GET filename (with no workarea indicated).

RECSIZE=80 designates the length of the input area as 80 bytes, the maximum length allowed.

Note the use of RECSIZE instead of BLKSIZE. Do not code DEVICE (because it is device independent), RECFORM (always fixed, blocked), TYPEFLE (files can be input or output), or WORKA (processing is in a buffer, not a workarea).

DTFDI FOR OUTPUT. The name given to the output file in Figure 7-8 is PRTR. Note that you do not code CTLCHR, DEVICE, RECFORM, or TYPEFLE. Entries DEVADDR, IOAREA1, and IOAREA2 are the same as for DTFPR.

IOREG=(5) tells IOCS to load register-5 with the address of the buffer that is next to be used for output. Initially, the OPEN macro loads register-5, and subsequently the PUT macro as executed. Any available register, 2 through 12, may be assigned. With IOREG, code PUT filename (with no workarea indicated).

RECSIZE=(121) defines the length of the output record. The first byte is reserved for the control character. The maximum length is normally 121 for SYSLST (printer) and 81 for SYSPCH (system punch).

ABNORMAL TERMINATION

Both DOS and OS have macros that are used to terminate a program abnormally when a serious error condition is encountered. Both provide a hexadecimal dump of the registers and the program storage area. The DOS macro is DUMP and the OS macro is ABEND.

NAME	OPERATION	OPERAND
	DUMP ABEND	Ignored, use for comments completion-code, DUMP

THE DOS DUMP MACRO. DUMP terminates program execution and provides a storage dump. Generally, PDUMP is more convenient to use when testing a program because it continues processing the program. The

CANCEL macro also terminates processing, and flushes all input records through to the /& Job End job control entry. If you precede program execution with a // OPTION DUMP job command, the supervisor automatically produces a storage dump after the CANCEL. (// OPTION PARTDUMP on larger systems.)

THE OS ABEND MACRO. To provide for a serious error condition where you want an "abnormal end" of the program, code the ABEND macro. The operand includes a "completion-code," any decimal value up to 4095, as ABEND 25, DUMP. There could be several ABENDs in the program, but the completion code 25 identifies which ABEND when it prints at termination. The DUMP operand invokes the ABDUMP macro (abnormal DUMP) which prints a hexadecimal dump of the registers and relevant parts of main storage.

TERMINAL I/O

Under DOS, DTFCN (define console) provides the file definition for a terminal with keyboard input and either screen or printer output. For input/output, you can define the usual GET and PUT macros. Another macro, PUTR (PUT with Reply) allows a program to display a message which stays on the screen until the operator replies. PUTR is useful for prompting a user to enter data, and requires DTFCN entries DEVADDR=SYSLOG, INPSIZE= len, and TYPEFLE=CMBND.

The following provides parameters for DTFCN:

DEVADDR   Code SYSLOG (normally) or SYSnnn.

BLKSIZE   The length of the I/O area.

INPSIZE   The length of the input part of the I/O area for the PUTR macro.

IOAREA1   The name of the buffer. For PUTR, the first part is reserved for the output message and the second part for the input reply.

RECFORM   The entry is FIXUNB or UNDEF (undefined).

RECSIZE   Use this parameter if RECFORM=UNDEF. For output, set the length in any register 2–12, and code this entry as (reg). For input, IOCS loads the actual length into the specified register.

TYPEFLE   INPUT allows both input and output; OUTPUT allows output only; use CMBND for the PUTR macro.

WORKA   Code WORKA=YES if GET or PUT designate a workarea.

Other DOS file definition macros include the following:

DTFDR   3886 optical character reader.

DTFDU   Diskette.

DTFMR   Magnetic ink character reader.

DTFOR   Optical scan reader.

DEBUGGING TIPS

Coding errors based on input/output are many and serious. The Assembler can identify the most obvious spelling errors, but others include:

- Under DOS, failure to open a file.
- Use of an invalid forms control character. An invalid IBM machine code causes a terminating "I/O error," and an invalid ASA code causes a default to space and print.
- Conflicting record lengths defined in the file definition macro, in work-areas, in DOS buffers, and in OS DD entries. This type of error is easy to make but difficult to trace. If the input workarea or buffer is too small, a GET operation will destroy the data immediately following. When at some later point the program tries to execute the "garbage," the results will be unpredictable.
- Incomplete file definition macro entries, allowing the Assembler to default to unexpected values (such as ASA forms control character).
- Confusion in use of Locate Mode with file definition, imperative macro, or register.

PROBLEMS

7-1.   What is the difference between "supervisor" and "problem" state?

7-2.   What is a "privileged" instruction?

7-3.   What is the advantage (if any) of buffers?

7-4.   What is a "file definition" macro and an "imperative" macro?

7-5.   Give the MVI and the PUT statements to print and space 3 lines, using file PRTR and workarea PRINT.

7-6.   Provide the file definition macro for an input device called READER, end-of-file address P35END, device 2540, and a workarea. If using DOS, define two buffers.

7-7.   Provide the file definition macro for a printer called PRTR, device 1403, and a workarea of 133 bytes. If using DOS, define two buffers.

7-8.   Redefine the file in Problem 7-6 for Locate Mode. Provide the GET statement.

7-9.   Redefine the file in Problem 7-7 for Locate Mode. Provide a PUT and MVI for print space 2.

7-10.   Recode any previous program. Assign base registers and use full IOCS. Replace any special macros such as INIT with BALR/USING, PUTPR with PUT, and DEFCD and DEFPR with suitable file definition macros.

8

STRATEGY, STYLE, AND STANDARDS

Up to now, most of the emphasis in this book has been with the technical aspects of Assembler programming. In this chapter we take a break and examine program organization, style, and standards. Much of this material is relevant to any programming language.

PROGRAMMING OBJECTIVES

The goal of a computer system is to produce information. We reach this goal by means of three objectives: accuracy, efficiency, and clarity.

1. *Accuracy.* A program must produce 100 percent accurate results, since the recipient of the report may base decisions on the information. For example, if a report detailing delinquent customer payments is incorrect, the company may start badgering customers who are fully paid up.

2. *Efficiency.* In these days of large main storage, "virtual" storage, and fast execute-time, efficiency is no longer such a consideration as once it was. There may even be justification for some inefficiency, where the added cost of programming time exceeds the expected cost of CPU time, or when there is an urgent need for information. However, in the interests of less execute-time and storage space, an efficient program is always a reasonable objective.

3.   *Clarity.* Since many installations devote considerable time to program corrections and revisions, it is vital to design programs that are clear and maintainable. In the past, there have been many programmers with great technical skill who coded incredibly complex routines, and used the most sophisticated instructions where simple ones would work equally well. Today's emphasis is on code that is simple, clear, and well-organized.

This chapter first examines an approach to program organization, Programming Style, and finally Standardization and Documentation.

PROGRAMMING STYLE

Good programming practice today is in the style of "structured programming." Now, Assembler language does not lend itself well to all the structured programming requirements, which are better facilitated by high-level languages like PL/I and COBOL. But you can adhere to some of its main features:

- Organization of the program into a "main logic" section with various subsidiary routines (subroutines). The main logic handles input and testing for record code or sequence to determine the action to take. It then uses BAL to perform the required subroutine.
- Each subroutine has a specific identifiable purpose and contains only logic related to its purpose. In a Payroll program, for example, one subroutine calculates income tax, another calculates pension deduction, etc.
- The main logic and the subroutines are each contained within one page of printed code (or the number of lines on a visual display terminal). By this limitation, the mind can grasp (hopefully!) the entire processing logic of the routine. Routines that continue for pages become incomprehensible. (One exception could be for a routine that performs many repetitious Move/Edit operations.)
- Each subroutine has one entry-point, at its start, and one exit-point, at its end. The program accordingly organizes itself into clear, logical sections, with no confusing branches back and forth between routines.
- Within a subroutine, branch statements should go forward as much as possible. The only statements that branch backwards are those that loop (e.g., branch back to process the next input record). The following example illustrates an unnecessary branch backwards caused by an illogical approach. If the customer's balance owing exceeds the credit limit, the program moves a warning message to the print area:

```
              UNNECESSARY BRANCH                      PROPER CODING
        CP    CUSTBAL,CREDLIM            CP    CUSTBAL,CREDLIM
        BH    D30                        BNH   D20
 D20 .                                   MVC   MESSOUT,=C'OVER
                                               LIMIT'
    .                               D20 .
    .                                   .
 D30 MVC  MESSOUT,=C'OVER LIMIT'        .
      B   D20
```

Fully structured programming as used in PL/I and COBOL entirely eliminates the GO TO statement (in Assembler, B, BH, BNE, etc.) because of their powerful "macro statements," DO WHILE and PERFORM.

The example program at the end of this chapter illustrates a Payroll program that is organized according to the foregoing conventions. The objective of such programming style is to gain better clarity and to facilitate program maintenance. Because a large part of programming effort is in correcting and revising programs, there is an urgent need for clear, concise, and well-organized programs.

Good programming style is only one way to provide better clarity. Others are:

- The use of meaningful names that describe the fields being defined, such as TOTALTAX instead of AMOUNTA, or worst of all, cryptic one-letter names such as A and X.

- A systematic labelling convention that provides easy locating of branch points and clearly identifies the section in which it belongs. In the example program at the end of this chapter, the Main Logic routine has labels that all begin with 'A': A10READ, A20, A30; the Wage Calculation subroutine labels are 'B'; and Employee Total subroutine labels begin with 'D'; etc.

- Assigning certain registers always with specific purposes, such as 3, 4, and 5 for base registers; 6 and 7 for subroutine linkage; etc. Such conventions help minimize errors in register usage.

HIERARCHY CHARTS

When a program consists of a variety of subroutines, it is often useful to design a hierarchy chart to indicate the dependency of subroutines. Figure 8-1 provides a hierarchy chart for the program at the end of this chapter. Note the similarity to an organization chart. Each box represents a logical unit of related code, with the name at the top of the box and a description of its purpose inside.

The top box contains the program's main logic which directly links to

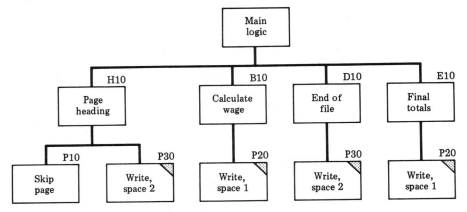

FIGURE 8-1 Hierarchy chart.

the subroutines in the line below: page heading, wage calculation, end-of-file, and final totals. Each of these subroutines also links to subroutines indicated in boxes in the next line below. According to the chart, the main logic does not link directly to the bottom level, nor does for example B10 link to P30.

Note a convention where two (or more) routines link to the same subroutine. Both B10 and E10 link to P20, and both D10 and H10 link to P30. The convention for common subroutines is to indicate this fact with a black triangle in the top right corner of the box.

A standard convention would be to assign a specific register for each level, for example register-6 for level 1 and register-7 for level 2. If the program contains a subroutine that is referenced from both levels, you could set it at the third level and link to it by say register-8. You could also use EQU to assign names to these registers such as LINKREG1, LINKREG2, and LINKREG3.

PROGRAM DOCUMENTATION

An important element of program maintenance is adequate documentation. There is certainly no universal standard of documentation. Some installations keep a program listing only, well-documented with comments, sometimes stored on disk and available to users through visual display terminals. Others keep a record of each program in files or binders for quick reference, along with other related material, such as flowcharts and test runs. This text does not advocate any particular method of documentation. Programmers quickly develop bad habits in areas that are nonproductive and uninteresting (such as documentation). Learners should at least begin developing good habits and apply them to their installation's standards.

THE PROGRAM DOCUMENTATION FILE. The following is an example of one possible documentation file, by section.

1. *Title Page.* The first page could contain program number, program name, the names of the programmers who wrote it, and the date completed. It might also specify who authorized the program originally, and the date. This section could also contain the dates of any revisions, who requested them, and who made them.

2. *Contents Page.* If the size of the program warrants it, a contents page may be useful.

3. *Program Objective.* This section consists of one or two paragraphs providing the objective(s) of the program, in effect what the program is to accomplish.

4. *Operator's Guide.* Many installations have a preprinted operator's guide that the programmer completes to facilitate running of the program. The guide contains inputs and their sequence, output devices, printer forms, control totals, and error messages, listing of job control, and approximate run time. A copy of this guide is often usefully included in the program documentation file.

5. *Layouts for Input and Output Records and the Printed Report.* The report layout shows the print position of every field in the headings, detail line, total lines, and error messages.

6. *Flowcharts.* The current program flowchart or hierarchy chart should be filed. A large program could also have an overall summary flowchart.

7. *The Program Listing.* The current program listing is included, with the date clearly identified.

8. *Example Test Data.* A program using tape or disk input generally is tested using "live" data. If input is from a terminal or cards, it is not difficult to arrange and list sample data for testing the program. On the listing of the data, each input field should be clearly indicated, along with any intentional errors. The list of input data should show *expected results* (the totals that you expect the run to produce), and a random sample of calculations (such as hour × rate in the documented program following).

9. *Program Report Output.* This section gives a sample of the program's printed output, either from "live" data or from test data, with sample calculations and totals to prove the accuracy of the test.

10. *Previous Listing.* The previous program listing should be preserved in case revisions turn out to be wrong, or the revision is cancelled and you have to reverse the changes.

The next section illustrates an Assembler program fully documented according to the preceding discussion. The example is somewhat overdocumented to make it clearer to readers not familiar with Assembler language. The only topic in the program not yet covered is table look-up.

DOCUMENTED PROGRAM

TITLE PAGE

Program Number: PROG08
Program Name: Weekly Wage Calculation
Programmer: Oliver Twit
Completion Date: January 28, 19xx
Authorization: J. P. Megabuck
                   Payroll Department
                   January 27, 19xx
Language: Assembler
Status: Tested and fully working.
Revisions:

WEEKLY WAGE CALCULATION PROGRAM PROG08

CONTENTS

	Page
Program Objective	1
Operator Guide	2
Program Description	3
Input Record Layout	4
Printer Forms Layout	5
Program Flowchart	6
Program Listing	8
Listing of Test Input Data	12
Test Output	13

PROGRAM OBJECTIVE   1

To calculate employees' wages for the current pay period, and to produce the weekly wage report.

PROGRAM:	PROG08, Weekly Wage Calculation
INPUT FILE:	Employee weekly time records (code 04) for the current pay period.
SEQUENCE:	Employee number
RUN TIME:	10 minutes
FREQUENCY OF RUN:	Weekly
OUTPUT:	Printer:

        Employee Weekly Wage Report
        Forms: 8½ × 14 management report form
                 2-part
                 standard carriage control tape

RECIPIENT OF REPORT: Payroll Department, both parts

CONTROL TOTALS: The program produces total hours and wages by employee number (indicated by *) and for final total (indicated by **). Final total hours on the report must agree with the precalculated hours in the Payroll Control Register before continuing with the next payroll job. Total wages from the report is to be entered in the Control Register.

ERROR MESSAGES:	CAUSE:
'INVALID RECORD CODE'	A record does not contain '04' in columns 1-2.
'RECORD OUT OF SEQUENCE'	An employee number read is lower than the preceding record.
'JOB NO. NOT IN TABLE'	A job number on an input record is not in the table of jobs in the program.

Action: The program prints the error message and continues processing with the next input record. Invalid records should be corrected and the job rerun.

The program is organized into the following sections:

SECTION A: MAIN LOGIC (READ & CHECK VALIDITY & SEQUENCE)

Checks each record for valid code. Sequence-checks on Employee number:

Equal   — Process the record (Section B).

Low   — Sequence error (Section R).

High   — Control break; tests for first record of file:

               First record — **Bypasses control break (goes to Section B).**

               Not first   — Performs Employee totals (Section D).

On end-of-file, links to address A50END (see DTFCD in program). This routine performs Employee Totals, Section D, then Final Totals, Section E, and terminates processing.

SECTION B: PROCESS EMPLOYEE RECORD

Uses Job number from the input record to locate related rate-of-pay in a stored table. (A Job not found in the table is an error.) For example, Job number is '02' and located rate-of-pay is $6.15. The program multiplies Hours worked (21.5) by rate to calculate Wage:

$$21.5 \times \$6.15 = \$132.225 \text{ (rounded to } \$132.23)$$

Accumulates total Employee hours and wages, and prints Employee detail line (see print layout). Returns to read the next record (Section B).

SECTION D: EMPLOYEE TOTALS

Prints total Employee hours and wages (one *), accumulates final total hours and wages, and clears Employee totals.

SECTION E: FINAL TOTALS

Prints total hours and wages (two **'s).

SECTION H: PAGE OVERFLOW & HEADINGS

Prints page heading at the start of the run and on reaching the end of each page.

SECTION P: PRINT SUBROUTINE

Performs all printing and adding to line counter.

SECTION R: ERROR ROUTINES

The Operator's Guide describes the three error routines.

REGISTERS USED: Register: Purpose:

                      3   Base register for addressing

                      7   Subroutine linkage

                      9   Table look-up for Job number

SWITCHES USED: None.

MULTIPLE-CARD LAYOUT FORM

Company

Application _Weekly Wage Report_   by _P. R. Ogram_   Date _July 7, 19xx_   Job No. _PROG08_   Sheet No.

4

INPUT RECORD FORMAT

Code (04)	Emp. no.	Employee name	Job no.	Hours

219

PROGRAM TITLE **PROG2R** _Weekly Wage Calculation_

PROGRAMMER OR DOCUMENTALIST: _Oliver Twit_

CHART TITLE

PRINT CHART

DATE _Jan. 28, 19xx_

	NAME				
HEADING 1:			WEEKLY WAGE REPORT		PAGE XXX
HEADING 2:	EMPLOYEE NAME	JOB	RATE	HOURS	WAGE
DETAIL:	XXXXX X———	XX	X.XX	XX.X—	XXX.XX CR
EMPLOYEE TOTAL:				X,XXX.X—*	XX,XXX.XX CR**
FINAL TOTAL:				X,XXX.X—**	XX,XXX.XX CR***
ERRORS:	XXXXX X		INVALID RECORD CODE		
	XXXXX X		JOB NO. NOT IN TABLE		
	XXXXX X		RECORD OUT OF SEQUENCE		

REPORT FORMAT

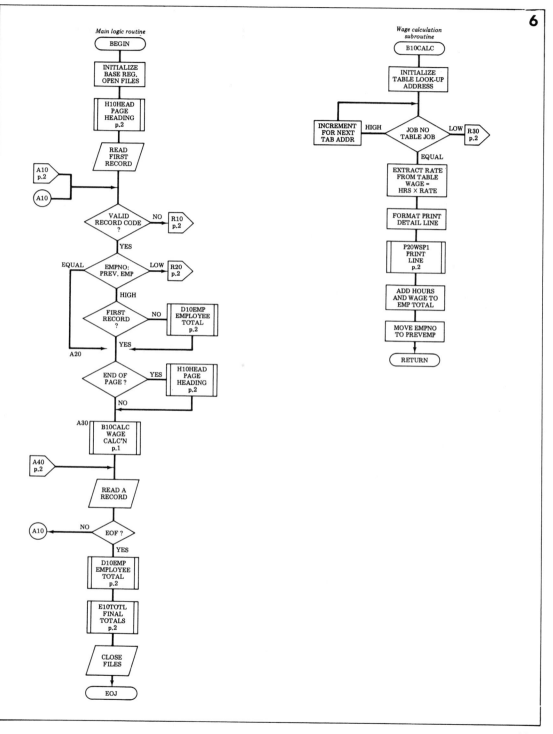

Main logic routine

BEGIN

INITIALIZE
BASE REG.
OPEN FILES

H10HEAD
PAGE
HEADING
p.2

READ
FIRST
RECORD

A10
p.2

A10

VALID
RECORD CODE
? →NO→ R10
p.2

YES

EQUAL ← EMPNO:
PREV. EMP →LOW→ R20
p.2

HIGH

FIRST
RECORD
? →NO→ D10EMP
EMPLOYEE
TOTAL
p.2

YES

A20

END OF
PAGE ? →YES→ H10HEAD
PAGE
HEADING
p.2

NO

A30 B10CALC
WAGE
CALC'N
p.1

A40
p.2

READ A
RECORD

A10 ←NO← EOF ?

YES

D10EMP
EMPLOYEE
TOTAL
p.2

E10TOTL
FINAL
TOTALS
p.2

CLOSE
FILES

EOJ

*Wage calculation
subroutine*

B10CALC

INITIALIZE
TABLE LOOK-UP
ADDRESS

INCREMENT
FOR NEXT
TAB ADDR ←HIGH← JOB NO
TABLE JOB →LOW→ R30
p.2

EQUAL

EXTRACT RATE
FROM TABLE
WAGE =
HRS × RATE

FORMAT PRINT
DETAIL LINE

P20WSP1
PRINT
LINE
p.2

ADD HOURS
AND WAGE TO
EMP TOTAL

MOVE EMPNO
TO PREVEMP

RETURN

Employee total subroutine

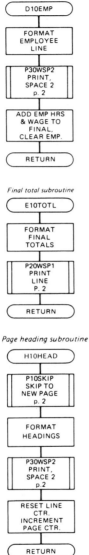

```
   ( D10EMP )
        │
┌───────────────┐
│    FORMAT     │
│   EMPLOYEE    │
│     LINE      │
└───────────────┘
        │
╞═══════════════╡
│   P30WSP2     │
│    PRINT,     │
│   SPACE 2     │
│     p. 2      │
╞═══════════════╡
        │
┌───────────────┐
│  ADD EMP HRS  │
│   & WAGE TO   │
│    FINAL,     │
│   CLEAR EMP.  │
└───────────────┘
        │
   ( RETURN )
```

Final total subroutine

```
   ( E10TOTL )
        │
┌───────────────┐
│    FORMAT     │
│    FINAL      │
│    TOTALS     │
└───────────────┘
        │
╞═══════════════╡
│   P20WSP1     │
│    PRINT      │
│    LINE       │
│     P. 2      │
╞═══════════════╡
        │
   ( RETURN )
```

Page heading subroutine

```
   ( H10HEAD )
        │
╞═══════════════╡
│   P10SKIP     │
│   SKIP TO     │
│   NEW PAGE    │
│     p. 2      │
╞═══════════════╡
        │
┌───────────────┐
│    FORMAT     │
│   HEADINGS    │
└───────────────┘
        │
╞═══════════════╡
│   P30WSP2     │
│    PRINT,     │
│   SPACE 2     │
│     p.2       │
╞═══════════════╡
        │
┌───────────────┐
│  RESET LINE   │
│     CTR.      │
│  INCREMENT    │
│  PAGE CTR.    │
└───────────────┘
        │
   ( RETURN )
```

Print subroutine

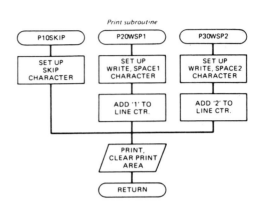

Error message routines

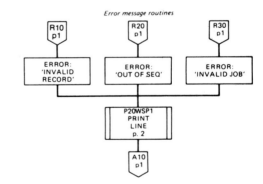

```
 4 *            I N I T I A L I Z A T I O N

 6 PROG08     START   0
 7            BALR    3,0                  INITIALIZE
 8            USING   *,3                  BASE REG

10            OPEN    FILEIN,PRTR
19            BAL     7,H10HEAD            PRINT HEADING
20            GET     FILEIN,INAREA        READ 1ST RECORD
26            MVC     PREVEMP,EMPNOIN      INIT'ZE SEQ

28 ***         M A I N   L O G I C

30 A10LOOP    CLC     CODEIN,=C'04'        VALID RECORD CODE?
31            BNE     R10CODE                NO - ERROR

33            CLC     EMPNOIN,PREVEMP      EMPLOYEE SEQUENCE?
34            BE      A20                    EQU - PROCESS
35            BL      R20SEQ                 LOW - ERROR
36 *                                        HI  - NEW EMPLOYEE
37            BAL     7,D10EMP             PRINT EMPL TOTALS

39 A20        CP      LINECTR,ENDPAGE      END OF PAGE?
40            BL      A30                    NO
41            BAL     7,H10HEAD              YES - PRINT HEADINGS

43 A30        BAL     7,B10CALC            PERFORM CALCULATIONS
44 A40READ    GET     FILEIN,INAREA        READ NEXT
50            B       A10LOOP              LOOP

52 ***         E N D - O F - F I L E

54 A90END     BAL     7,D10EMP             EMPLOYEE TOTALS
55            BAL     7,E10TOTL            FINAL TOTALS
56            CLOSE   FILEIN,PRTR
65            EOJ                          TERMINATE

69 **          C A L C U L A T E   W A G E

71 B10CALC    LA      9,JOBTAB             INIT. SEARCH FOR JOB RATE
72 B20        CLC     JOBIN,0(9)           COMP JOB NO. TO TABLE ENTRY
73            BL      R30JOB                 LOW - NOT IN TABLE
74            BE      B30                    EQU - FOUND
75            AH      9,=H'4'                HI  - INCREM. NEXT ADDRESS
76            B       B20

78 B30        ZAP     RATEPK,2(2,9)        EXTRACT RATE FROM TABLE
79            PACK    HRSPK,HRSIN
80            ZAP     WAGEPK,HRSPK         CALCULATE WAGE =
81            MP      WAGEPK,RATEPK          HOURS X RATE
82            SRP     WAGEPK,63,5            SHIFT & ROUND 1 DIGIT

84            MVC     WAGEPR,EDAMT3        EDIT:
85            ED      WAGEPR,WAGEPK+1        WAGE
86            MVC     HOURSPR,EDHRS2
87            ED      HOURSPR,HRSPK          HOURS
88            MVC     RATEPR,EDRATE2
89            ED      RATEPR,RATEPK          RATE
90            MVC     JOBPR,JOBIN

92            CLC     EMPNOIN,PREVEMP      IF NEW EMPLOYEE NO.
93            BNE     B40                  OR
94            CP      LINECTR,TOPAGE       IF TOP OF PAGE
95            BNE     B50                    MOVE
96 B40        MVC     NAMEPR,NAMEIN          NAME &
97            MVC     EMPNOPR,EMPNOIN        EMPLOYEE NO. TO PRINT
```

```
 99 B50      MVC    PRINT,DETALINE
100          BAL    8,P20WSP1              PRINT & SPACE 1
101          MVC    DETALINE,BLANK         CLEAR PRINT AREA
102          AP     EMPHRPK,HRSPK          ADD TOTAL HOURS & WAGES
103          AP     EMPWGPK,WAGEPK           FOR EMPLOYEE
104          MVC    PREVEMP,EMPNOIN
105          BR     7                      RETURN

107 **       P R I N T   E M P L O Y E E   T O T A L S

109 D10EMP   MVC    TOTWAGPR,EDAMT4        EDIT EMPLOYEE TOTALS:
110          ED     TOTWAGPR,EMPWGPK         WAGES
111          MVC    TOTHRSPR,EDHRS3
112          ED     TOTHRSPR,EMPHRPK        HOURS
113          MVC    PRINT,TOTALINE
114          BAL    8,P30WSP2              PRINT & SPACE 2

116          AP     TOTHRPK,EMPHRPK        ADD TO FINAL TOTAL HOURS
117          AP     TOTWGPK,EMPWGPK          & WAGES
118          ZAP    EMPHRPK,=P'0'          CLEAR EMPLOYEE HOURS
119          ZAP    EMPWGPK,=P'0'            & WAGES
120          BR     7                      RETURN

122 **       P R I N T   F I N A L   T O T A L S

124 E10TOTL  MVC    ASTERPR2(2),=C'**'
125          MVC    TOTWAGPR,EDAMT4        EDIT FINAL TOTAL:
126          ED     TOTWAGPR,TOTWGPK         WAGES
127          MVC    ASTERPR1(2),=C'**'
128          MVC    TOTHRSPR,EDHRS3
129          ED     TOTHRSPR,TOTHRPK        HOURS
130          MVC    PRINT,TOTALINE
131          BAL    8,P20WSP1              PRINT & SPACE 1
132          BR     7

134 **       P A G E   H E A D I N G

136 H10HEAD  BAL    8,P10SKIP              SKIP TO NEXT PAGE
137 '        MVC    PAGEPR,EDPAGE          SET UP HEADING LINE 1
138          ED     PAGEPR,PAGECTR
139          MVC    PRINT,HEADING1
140          BAL    8,P30WSP2              PRINT & SPACE 2

142          MVC    PRINT,HEADING2
143          BAL    8,P30WSP2              PRINT & SPACE 2
144          ZAP    LINECTR,TOPAGE         INITIALIZE LINE COUNT
145          AP     PAGECTR,=P'1'          INCREMENT PAGE NO.
146          BR     7                      RETURN

148 **       C O M M O N   P R I N T   R O U T I N E

150 P10SKIP  MVI    CTLCHPR,SKIP           SKIP CHARACTER
151          B      P90
152 P20WSP1  MVI    CTLCHPR,WSP1           WRITE/SPACE CHARACTER
153          AP     LINECTR,=P'1'          ADD TO LINE COUNTER
154          B      P90
155 P30WSP2  MVI    CTLCHPR,WSP2           WRITE/DOUBLE-SPACE CHAR
156          AP     LINECTR,=P'2'          ADD TO LINE COUNTER
157 P90      PUT    PRTR,PRINT             PRINT
163          BR     8                      RETURN

165 SKIP     EQU    X'8B'
166 WSP1     EQU    X'09'
167 WSP2     EQU    X'11'
```

```
169 **          E R R O R   R O U T I N E S

171 R10CODE   MVC    DETALINE+60(L'ERRCODE),ERRCODE
172           B      R50

174 R20SEQ    MVC    DETALINE+60(L'ERRSEQ),ERRSEQ
175           B      R50

177 R30JOB    MVC    DETALINE+60(L'ERRJOB),ERRJOB

179 R50       MVC    EMPNOPR,EMPNOIN
180           MVC    NAMEPR,NAMEIN
181           MVC    PRINT,DETALINE
182           BAL    8,P20WSP1              PRINT ERROR MESSAGE
183           MVC    DETALINE,BLANK
184           B      A40READ

186 *          D E C L A R A T I V E S

188 FILEIN    DTFCD  BLKSIZE=80,            DEFINE INPUT FILE          +
                     DEVADDR=SYSIPT,                                   +
                     DEVICE=1442,                                      +
                     EOFADDR=A90END,                                   +
                     IOAREA1=INBUFF1,                                  +
                     IOAREA2=INBUFF2,                                  +
                     TYPEFLE=INPUT,                                    +
                     WORKA=YES

210 INBUFF1   DC     CL80' '               INPUT BUFFER-1
211 INBUFF2   DC     CL80' '               INPUT BUFFER-2

213 INAREA    DS     0CL80                 INPUT AREA
214 CODEIN    DS     CL02            *       RECORD CODE
215 EMPNOIN   DS     CL05            *       EMPLOYEE NO.
216 NAMEIN    DS     CL15            *       EMPLOYEE NAME
217 JOBIN     DS     CL02            *       JOB NO.
218 HRSIN     DS     ZL03            *       HOURS WORKED (XX.X)
219           DS     CL53            *       UNUSED

221 PRTR      DTFPR  BLKSIZE=133,          DEFINE PRINTER FILE        +
                     CTLCHR=YES,                                       +
                     DEVADDR=SYSLST,                                   +
                     DEVICE=3203,                                      +
                     IOAREA1=PRBUFF1,                                  +
                     IOAREA2=PRBUFF2,                                  +
                     WORKA=YES

243 PRBUFF1   DC     CL133' '              PRINTER BUFFER-1
244 PRBUFF2   DC     CL133' '              PRINTER BUFFER-2

246 PRINT     DS     0CL133                COMMON PRINT AREA:
247 CTLCHPR   DS     XL1                   PRINT CTL CHARACTER
248           DC     CL132' '        *

250 HEADING1  DS     0CL133                1ST HEADING LINE:
251           DC     CL23' '
252           DC     CL48'W E E K L Y   W A G E   R E P O R T'
253           DC     CL05'PAGE'
254 PAGEPR    DS     ZL04
255           DC     CL53' '
```

```
257 HEADING2 DS    0CL133                      2ND HEADING LINE:
258          DC    CL13' '
259          DC    CL26'EMPLOYEE  NAME'
260          DC    CL94'JOB    RATE  HOURS           WAGE'

262 BLANK    DC    C' '                        BLANK TO CLEAR PRINT AREA
263 DETALINE DS    0CL133                      EMPLOYEE DETAIL PRINT LINE:
264          DC    CL15' '
265 EMPNOPR  DS    CL05
266          DC    CL03' '
267 NAMEPR   DS    CL15
268          DC    CL02' '
269 JOBPR    DS    CL02
270          DC    CL02' '
271 RATEPR   DS    ZL05
272          DC    CL02' '
273 HOURSPR  DS    ZL06
274          DC    CL06' '
275 WAGEPR   DS    ZL09
276          DC    CL61' '

278 TOTALINE DS    0CL133                      TOTAL WAGE PRINT LINE:
279          DC    CL48' '
280 TOTHRSPR DS    ZL9
281 ASTERPR1 DC    CL3'*'
282 TOTWAGPR DS    ZL12
283 ASTERPR2 DC    CL61'*'

285 ERRCODE  DC    C'INVALID RECORD CODE'
286 ERRJOB   DC    C'JOB NO. NOT IN TABLE'
287 ERRSEQ   DC    C'RECORD OUT OF SEQUENCE'
288 PREVEMP  DC    XL5'00'
289 *                                          PACKED DECLARATIVES:
290 HRSPK    DC    PL2'0'                       |XX|.XC|
291 RATEPK   DC    PL2'0'                       |X.X|XC|
292 WAGEPK   DC    PL4'0'
293 EMPHRPK  DC    PL3'0'
294 EMPWGPK  DC    PL4'0'
295 TOTHRPK  DC    PL3'0'
296 TOTWGPK  DC    PL4'0'
297 LINECTR  DC    PL2'0'
298 PAGECTR  DC    PL2'1'
299 TOPAGE   DC    P'5'
300 ENDPAGE  DC    P'40'

302 EDPAGE   DC    X'40202020'                 EDIT WORDS:
303 EDHRS2   DC    X'4020214B2060'
304 EDRATE2  DC    X'40204B2020'
305 EDAMT3   DC    X'402020214B2020C3D9'
306 EDHRS3   DC    X'40206B2020214B2060'
307 EDAMT4   DC    X'4020206B2020214B2020C3D9'

309 JOBTAB   DC    C'01',P'7.25'               TABLE OF JOB NOS.
310          DC    C'02',P'6.15'               *        & RATES
311          DC    C'04',P'7.45'               *
312          DC    C'05',P'8.55'               *
313          DC    C'06',P'7.50'               *
314          DC    C'08',P'9.25'               *
315          DC    C'10',P'8.95'               *
316          DC    X'FFFF',P'0.00'             * END OF TABLE
317          LTORG

330          END   PROG08
```

RUN #1   VALID TEST INPUT DATA

```
04 11111 ANDERSON          04 105
04 11111 ANDERSON          01 215
04 11111 ANDERSON          01 315
04 11111 ANDERSON          01 105
04 11111 ANDERSON          04 105
04 22222 BROWN             02 400
04 22222 BROWN             02 500
04 22233 CARPENTER         01 999      neg. hrs
04 22233 CARPENTER         04 010
04 22233 CARPENTER         02 250
04 22235 DIXON             02 400
04 22240 EMMETT            01 150
04 22240 EMMETT            01 150
04 22240 EMMETT            04 050
04 22301 FLANDERS          01 255
04 22301 FLANDERS          01 255
04 22301 FLANDERS          01 050
04 22355 GAROWSKI          04 015
04 22355 GAROWSKI          04 015
04 22355 GAROWSKI          04 015
04 22360 HENDERSON         02 080
04 22360 HENDERSON         02 080
04 22360 HENDERSON         02 080
04 22360 HENDERSON         02 080
04 22360 HENDERSON         02 080
                   Total hours   473.9
```

Expected results:

Employee 22233:
Job 01   7.25 x
Hours   99.9
        724.28 *

Job 04   7.45-x
Hours   01.0
          7.45-*

Job 02   6.15 x
Hours   25.0
        153.75 *

Total   724.28
wages   7.45-
        153.75
        870.58 *

- - - - - - - - - - - - - - - -

Employee 22360:
Job 02   6.15 x
Hours   8.0
         49.20 *

Total   49.20 x
wages   5
        246.00 *

RUN #2   INVALID TEST INPUT DATA

```
04 11111 ANDERSON          04 105
04 11111 ANDERSON          01 215
04 11111 ANDERSON          01 315
04 11111 ANDERSON          01 105
04 11111 ANDERSON          04 105
04 22222 BROWN             02 400
03 22222 BROWN             02 500        INVALID CODE
04 22222 BROWN             02 500
04 22222 BROWN             03 200        INVALID JOB
04 11111 ANDERSON          04 105        OUT-OF-SEQUENCE
04 22222 BROWN             02 400
Code Emp.# Name            Job Hours
```

```
OUTPUT RUN #1       W E E K L Y  W A G E  R E P C R T              PAGE    1

          EMPLOYEE   NAME           JOB   RATE  HOURS         WAGE

           11111    ANDERSON         04   7.45   10.5          78.23
                                     01   7.25   21.5         155.88
                                     01   7.25   31.5         228.38
                                     01   7.25   10.5          76.13
                                     04   7.45   10.5          78.23
                                                84.5 *        616.85 *


           22222    BROWN            02   6.15   40.0         246.00
                                     02   6.15   50.0         307.50
                                                90.0 *        553.50 *


           22233    CARPENTER        01   7.25   99.9         724.28  } Agrees with
                                     04   7.45    1.0-          7.45CR } expected
                                     02   6.15   25.0         153.75  } results for
                                               123.9 *        870.58 *} Emp. 22233


           22235    DIXON            02   6.15   40.0         246.00
                                                40.0 *        246.00 *


           22240    EMMETT           01   7.25   15.0         108.75
                                     01   7.25   15.0         108.75
                                     04   7.45    5.0          37.25
                                                35.0 *        254.75 *


           22301    FLANDERS         01   7.25   25.5         184.88
                                     01   7.25   25.5         184.88
                                     01   7.25    5.0          36.25
                                                56.0 *        406.01 *


           22355    GARCWSKI         04   7.45    1.5          11.18
                                     04   7.45    1.5          11.18
                                     04   7.45    1.5          11.18
                                                 4.5 *         33.54 *


           22360    HENDERSON        02   6.15    8.0          49.20
- - - - - - - - - - - - - - - - - - - - - - - - - - - - - - - - - - - - - - -
                    W E E K L Y  W A G E  R E P O R T              PAGE    2

          EMPLOYEE   NAME           JOB   RATE  HOURS         WAGE

           22360    HENDERSON        02   6.15    8.0          49.20  } Agrees with
                                     02   6.15    8.0          49.20  } expected
                                     02   6.15    8.0          49.20  } results for
                                     02   6.15    8.0          49.20  } Emp. 22360
                                                40.0 *        246.00 *

   Agrees with "Total Hrs" in expected   (473.9) **   (3,227.23) ** Total
                         results →                                   checked


OUTPUT RUN #2       W E E K L Y  W A G E  R E P C R T              PAGE    1

          EMPLOYEE   NAME           JOB   RATE  HOURS         WAGE

           11111    ANDERSON         04   7.45   10.5          78.23
                                     01   7.25   21.5         155.88
                                     01   7.25   31.5         228.38
                                     01   7.25   10.5          76.13
                                     04   7.45   10.5          78.23
                                                84.5 *        616.85 *


           22222    BROWN            02   6.15   40.0         246.00
           22222    BROWN                             INVALID RECORD CODE
                                     C2   6.15   50.0         307.50
           22222    BROWN                             JOB NO. NCT IN TABLE
           11111    ANDERSON                          RECORD OUT OF SEGUENCE
                                     C2   6.15   40.0         246.00
                                               130.0 *        799.50 *


                                               214.5 **     1,416.35 **
```

DEBUGGING TIPS

"Preventive programming" can minimize the bugs in the program. A recommended approach is to organize the program into logical segments—a main logic routine to handle input processing, and various subroutines, each containing related processing. With such an approach, you are more likely to keep a firm grip on the logic, and can more readily locate execution bugs.

When using subroutines, be especially careful in the use of registers. If all subroutines are at the same "level," then the main logic could link to every subroutine using the same register, as:

```
BAL 9,subroutine
```

Sometimes, however, it is necessary to link from one subroutine to another. In large programs, the linkage can become complex and confusing. Double-check the linkage, and ensure that the return register is the correct one.

PROBLEMS

8-1. Three programming objectives are accuracy, efficiency, and clarity. Discuss the significance of each objective.

8-2. Devise a hierarchy chart for your most recent program.

8-3. Consider the following code. Is there a bug? If so, explain.

```
BALR  3,0
USING *,3
   .
   .
BAL   3,P10PAGE          P10PAGE ·
                                  ·
                                BR 3
```

8-4. Consider the following code. If there is a bug, explain.

```
BALR  3,0
USING *,3
   .
   .
BAL   5,P10PAGE          P10PAGE ·
                                  ·
                                BR 3
```

8-5. What are the features of "structured programming" that can be applied to Assembler programs?

8-6. What are the purposes (if any) of program documentation?

8-7. Revise a previous program, organizing it into a main logic routine and various subroutines, each containing related processing, in a logical sequence.

BINARY OPERATIONS

9

REGISTERS AND BINARY PROGRAMMING

Chapter 6 introduced registers for their use in base addressing. The registers may also perform binary arithmetic and manipulate data in binary format. Indeed, binary arithmetic is done only in the general registers, and conversely the registers perform arithmetic only in binary format. This chapter covers basic binary and register operations: first, defining binary data and then the instructions for binary arithmetic. Binary data may enter the program from sources such as:

- Defined in storage as a constant, as binary (B-type), fullword (F-type), and halfword (H-type).
- Generated in a register by such operations as CVB, LA, BAL, EDMK.
- Received from external input such as disk or tape where the data was written in binary format.

Although processing binary data in registers is extremely fast, there may be additional steps converting data from character input to packed and to binary, and then into printable format: binary to packed to edited character. Binary format does have useful applications, however, especially in manipulating addresses for table searching, as covered in the next chapter.

BINARY DATA REPRESENTATION

Binary numbers, whether defined in storage by constants of types B, F, and H, or used in the general registers, have the following features:

1. For reference, bits are numbered from left to right, with the leftmost bit numbered zero:

    Binary value: 00000000
    Position: 01234567 etc.

2. The sign is the leftmost bit, position zero: a 0-bit indicates a positive value, and a 1-bit indicates negative. A zero value is always positive.

3. The rules of binary addition are:

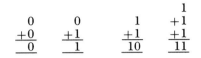

$$
\begin{array}{cccc}
 & & & 1 \\
0 & 0 & 1 & +1 \\
+0 & +1 & +1 & +1 \\
\hline
0 & 1 & 10 & 11
\end{array}
$$

For simplicity, the following examples of decimal and binary addition assume 5-bit fields, with the leftmost bit the sign:

DEC	BINARY	DEC	BINARY	DEC	BINARY
4	0 0100	7	0 0111	7	0 0111
+2	0 0010	+2	0 0010	+7	0 0111
6	0 0110	9	0 1001	14	0 1110

4. Negative numbers are expressed in what is called *two's complement* form. To obtain a negative binary number, reverse all the bits of its positive value (a 0-bit becomes 1, and a 1-bit becomes 0), then add 1. The same procedure converts negative values to positive values. For example, what is the binary representation of −7, assuming a 5-bit field?:

    Decimal value 7   = 0 0111
    Reverse bits   = 1 1000
    Add 1   = 1 1001   (two's complement representation of −7)
                          ↑
                      sign bit

5. For subtraction, convert the field being subtracted to its two's complement, and then add:

    Decimal value   7   0 0111   0 0111
    Subtract   −5 = −0 0101 = 1 1011   (add two's complement of 5)
    Result   2   0 0010   (binary value 2)

Note that there is a *carry into and out of* the sign position. Where there is both a carry into and out of the sign bit, the result is correct, not an overflow.

6. *Invalid overflows* occur on the following conditions:

a. Overflow caused by carry into the sign position:

Decimal value	9	0 1001	
Add	+9 =	0 1001	
Result	18	1 0010	(negative value, minus 14)

There is a carry into the sign position, and none out of it. The sum is an incorrect negative value. To determine the value of 1 0010, reverse the bits (0 1101), then add 1 (0 1110). Since this value is +14, then 1 0010 has a value of −14, but was supposed to be +18.

b. Overflow caused by carry out of the sign position:

Decimal value	−9	1 0111	
Add	+(−9) =	1 0111	
Result	−18	0 1110	(positive value, plus 14)

There is no carry into the sign position but one out of it. The sum is an incorrect positive value, +14 instead of −18.

- *Problem 9-1 should now be done.* •

BINARY CONSTANTS

Both DS and DC declaratives may define a binary field. There are three types: B (ordinary binary), F (fullword fixed-point), and H (halfword fixed-point). The following sections describe DCs; DS statements are written similarly except that the constant is optional and acts as a comment.

BINARY CONSTANT—B. Type B constants contain binary ones and zeros. A common use is for immediate operands for instructions such as NI, OI, XI, and TM, covered in a later chapter. Although the format has some specialized uses, its use is limited by the fact that the binary instruction set is designed to work better with F and H formats.

NAME	*OPERATION*	*OPERAND*
(symbol)	DC	dBLn'constant'

Optional: d = duplication factor.

Required: B specifying binary constant.

Optional: Ln = length of the field in bytes, maximum 256.

Required: constant, containing ones and zeros. If the length of the defined constant is different from the specified length (Ln), the Assembler pads or truncates the constant on the left.

Example B-format declaratives:

			LENGTH IN BYTES	ASSEMBLED AS		DECIMAL VALUE
BIN1	DC	B'00010011'	1	00010011		19
BIN2	DC	BL1'110'	1	00000110		6
BIN3	DC	BL2'100010011'	2	00000001	00010011	275

You may also code B-format as an immediate operand, such as: CLI CODE,B'10110010'

BINARY (FIXED-POINT) CONSTANTS—F AND H. Fixed-point constants (F and H formats) are commonly used in register arithmetic.

NAME	OPERATION	OPERAND
(symbol)	DC	dF'constant' (Fullword)
(symbol)	DC	dH'constant' (Halfword)

Optional: d = duplication factor.

Required: Type: F = Fullword (4 bytes) and H = Halfword (2 bytes). For F-type, the Assembler generates a binary constant in a 4-byte field, aligned on a *fullword boundary* (a storage address evenly divisible by four). For H-types, the Assembler generates a 2-byte constant aligned on a *halfword boundary* (a storage address evenly divisible by two). These are the normal required formats for binary arithmetic.

Required: constant, containing a *decimal number* which the Assembler converts to a binary number. If the length of the constant is greater than its explicit or implicit length, the Assembler truncates it on the left.

With bit 0 (the leftmost bit) as the sign, maximum and minimum binary fixed-point values are:

	BITS	MAXIMUM	MINIMUM
Halfword	16	$2^{15} - 1 = 32,767$	$-2^{15} = -32,768$
Fullword	32	$2^{31} - 1 = 2,147,483,647$	$-2^{31} = -2,147,483,648$

Figure 9-1 depicts Fullword and Halfword declaratives.

BINVAL1 is a DS that simply causes the location counter to align on a fullword boundary. (Check the hex address for the statement.)

BINVAL2 defines a 2-byte field aligned on a halfword boundary.

BINVAL3 defines two adjacent fullwords; a reference to the name BINVAL3 is to the first fullword.

```
                    23  *      -------------------------------------------
                    24  *          DS & DC FULLWORD & HALFWORD DECLARES
                    25  *      -------------------------------------------
003834              26  BINVAL1    DS    0F            ALIGNS ON FULLWORD ADDR.
003834              27  BINVAL2    DS    H             HALFWORD AREA
003838              28  BINVAL3    DS    2F            2 FULLWORD AREAS
003840 0019         29  BINVAL4    DC    H'25'         HALFWORD WITH POS. VALUE
003842 0000
003844 FFFFFFFB     30  BINVAL5    DC    F'-5'         FULLWORD WITH NEG. VALUE
003848 8001         31  BINVAL6    DC    H'32769'      EXCEEDS MAXIMUM OF 32767
       *** ERROR ***
```

DIAGNOSTICS AND STATISTICS

```
STMNT  ERROR NO.   MESSAGE

  31   IPK189   DATA ITEM TOO LARGE IN CONSTANT 1
```

FIGURE 9-1 Defining Fullword and Halfword constants.

BINVAL4 is a halfword that defines the decimal value 25. The Assembler converts 25 to a binary value 00011001, shown in object code on the left as X'19'.

BINVAL5 defines a fullword containing −5. Note the two's complement of 5 in object code. Try converting binary +5 (00000101): flip the bits (11111010), add '1' (11111011), which equals X'FB'.

BINVAL6 depicts an error in coding: the halfword defines a value exceeding 32,767. The Assembler generates an error message and truncates the leftmost bits changing the value of the field. In terms of dollars and cents, the maximum halfword value is $327.67, a trivial amount in many computer problems, and is easily exceeded.

In storage, these declaratives would appear as follows:

```
BINVAL1
BINVAL2          BINVAL3                        BINVAL4      BINVAL5       BINVAL6
  |                |                              |            |             |
| | |xx|xx| | | | | | | | | | |00|19|xx|xx|FF|FF|FF|FB|80|01|
  |                |                              |            |             |
3834  3836  3838  383A  383C  383E  3840  3842  3844  3846  3848
```

Both BINVAL1 and BINVAL2 align on the same halfword address. Since BINVAL3 is a fullword, the Assembler aligns it on a fullword boundary, X'3838'; consequently, bytes X'3836 and X'3837 are unused ("slack" bytes). Similarly, BINVAL5 begins at X'3844' and leaves slack bytes at X'3842' and X'3843'.

There may be occasions when it is necessary to define a binary H or F field without the Assembler's automatic halfword or fullword alignment. One case occurs when an input or output record for tape or disk contains a binary field. Consider the following disk input record:

```
LOC
8420   RECORDIN   DS   0CL29
8420   ACCTIN     DS   CL5
8428   AMTIN      DS   F          (F-format causes alignment here)
842C   NAMEIN     DS   CL20
```

In the example, the Assembler location counter for ACCTIN is at X'8420'. Since ACCTIN is a 5-byte field, the next field (AMTIN) would normally begin at 8425. But AMTIN is defined as DS F, so the Assembler aligns its address on a fullword boundary following: 8428. There are now three "slack" bytes between the two fields, causing the record to be defined with 32 bytes instead of the expected 29. Unfortunately, an *input operation* would read the 29-byte record byte-for-byte beginning at RECORDIN. The first three bytes of the binary amount will be in the slack bytes, and the program will reference incorrect data in AMTIN and NAMEIN.

A simple remedy is to code the binary fullword as FL4 rather than F as follows:

```
8425   AMTIN DS FL4 (No alignment)
```

If a fullword or halfword declarative contains a *length* (Ln), the Assembler does not align the field.

ADDRESS CONSTANTS—A.   It is often necessary to use DC to define the address of a declarative or of an instruction. For example, BALR initializes the first base register. Address constants may be used to initialize additional base registers. Of the four types of address constants, this chapter discusses only the common A-format.

NAME	OPERATION	OPERAND
(symbol)	DC	A (address-1,address-2, . . .,address-n)

The rules for A-type constants are:

1. The address constant is enclosed within brackets. You may define more than one address, each separated by a comma. The constant may be either an absolute value (rarely used) or a symbolic name.

2. The Assembler generates a fullword constant, aligned on a fullword boundary (provided no length indication is coded). The constant is

```
                                 4  *      -----------------------------
                                 5  *      DC    ADDRESS CONSTANTS
                                 6  *      -----------------------------
003800 0530                      7  BEGIN  BALR  3,0                 INIT'IZE BASE REG 3
                        03802     8         USING *,3,4,5,6           ASSIGN BASE REGS
003802 9846 3026        03828     9  A10    LM    4,6,ADDRESS5        LOAD REGS 4, 5, 6
                                 10  *       .
                                 11  *       .
003806 C1C4C4D9C5E2E240          12  DECLAR DC    C'ADDRESS CONSTANTS'
00380E C3D6D5E2E3C1D5E3
003816 E2
003817 00
003818 00004F20                  13  ADDRESS1 DC  A(20000)           ADDR OF 20000
00381C 00003806                  14  ADDRESS2 DC  A(DECLAR)          ADDR OF DECLAR
003820 00003802                  15  ADDRESS3 DC  A(A10)             ADDR OF A10
003824 00004802                  16  ADDRESS4 DC  A(A10+4096)        ADDR OF A10+X'1000'
003828 0000480200005802          17  ADDRESS5 DC  A(A10+4096,A10+2*4096,A10+3*4096)
003830 00006802
                                 18  ***             A10+X'1000', A10+X'2000', A10+X'3000'
```

FIGURE 9-2 Defining address constants.

right-adjusted in the field. The maximum value is $2^{31}-1$ (the highest fullword value).

Figure 9-2 gives a number of examples. (At A10, the LM instruction loads the three addresses into registers 4, 5, and 6. A later section describes this way to initialize base registers.)

ADDRESS1 depicts an address constant with an absolute value. Absolute addresses are rarely defined, since you do not normally know where the Assembler assigns addresses or where the program resides for execution.

ADDRESS2 defines the address of DECLAR. The object code hex value generated by the statement (X'3806'), is the same as the hex address of DECLAR.

ADDRESS3 defines the address of A10. Compare the object code address constant with that of the actual address of A10.

ADDRESS4 illustrates a relative address, A10+4096. The Assembler converts the decimal value 4096 to X'1000'. Therefore, the object code address is X'3802' + X'1000', or X'4802'.

ADDRESS5 illustrates three address constants, separated by commas. Note the use of Assembler arithmetic: 2*4096 = 8192.

Note on Alignment: On the 360, instructions such as CVB and CVD required doubleword alignment; L, A, C, M, and D required fullword alignment; and those like LH, AH, and CH required halfword alignment. The purpose, especially on larger models, was to ensure faster processing of binary operations. On the 370 and subsequent models, such alignment is not necessary—operand-2 of these instructions need not reference an aligned storage location during execution.

However, if the instructions are aligned, they will require fewer machine cycles and will execute faster. This text therefore recommends providing for alignment. On the 370, only channel command words and operands of certain privileged instructions must align on integral boundaries.

The following sections contain binary instructions for such operations as convert binary, multiply, and divide. Table 9-1 provides a summary of these instructions by their formats.

OPERATION	RR	RX (fullword)	RX (halfword)	RS
Convert		CVB, CVD		
Load	LR	L	LH	LM
Load complement	LCR			
Load negative	LNR			
Load positive	LPR			
Load and test	LTR			
Store		ST	STH	STM
Add	AR	A	AH	
Subtract	SR	S	SH	
Compare	CR	C	CH	
Multiply	MR	M	MH	
Divide	DR	D		
Shift				SLA, SLDA, SRA, SRDA

TABLE 9-1 Binary instructions.

CONVERSION OF DECIMAL AND BINARY DATA— CVB AND CVD

CVB, convert to binary, converts packed decimal data in storage into binary in a register. The packed data must be contained in a *doubleword* field (8 bytes), aligned on a doubleword boundary (evenly divisible by eight). For this purpose, the definition DS D is often conveniently used. (A D-type DC normally defines *floating-point* values, but a DS may store data in any format.) Similarly, CVD (convert to decimal) converts binary data in a register into packed decimal in storage, also defined as a doubleword.

NAME	OPERATION	OPERAND
(symbol)	CVB	R1,X2 or R1,D2(X2,B2)
(symbol)	CVD	R1,X2 or R1,D2(X2,B2)

For both operations, operand-1 specifies a general register, and operand-2 references a storage location defined as a doubleword, aligned, containing packed data. Note a significant difference. CVB converts data from operand-2 (storage) to operand-1 (a register); CVD converts data from operand-1 (a register) to operand-2 (storage). You can use CVB to convert packed to binary in a register, perform binary arithmetic, use CVD to convert back to packed, and then edit for printing.

In Figure 9-3, the packed field, AMTPK, is moved to a doubleword field, DBLWD1. CVB converts the packed contents of DBLWD1 into binary format in register-6. CVD converts the binary contents of register-6 into packed format in a doubleword, DBLWD2.

```
                       37  *      ---------------------------
                       38  *      CVB      CONVERT TO BINARY
                       39  *      ---------------------------
00384E  F871  305E     40         ZAP      DBLWD1,AMTPK         MOVE TO DOUBLE WORD
003854  4F60  305E     41         CVB      6,DBLWD1            CONVERT DBLWD1 TO BINARY

                       43  *      ---------------------------------
                       44  *      CVD      CONVERT TO PACKED DECIMAL
                       45  *      ---------------------------------
003858  4F60  3066     46         CVD      6,DBLWD2            CONVERT BINARY TO PACKED
                       47  *        .
                       48  *        .
                       49  *        .
00385C  125C           50  AMTPK   DC       P'125'
003860                 51  DBLWD1  DS       D                   ALIGNED DOUBLEWORD
003868                 52  DBLWD2  DS       D                   ALIGNED DOUBLEWORD
```

FIGURE 9-3 Conversion of packed and binary data: CVB, CVD.

LOADING REGISTERS—L, LH, LR, LM, LA

To load binary fullwords and halfwords in registers, use load operations. The most common load instructions are L (Load Fullword), LH (Load Halfword), LR (Load Register), LM (Load Multiple), and LA (Load Address). These instructions do not set the condition code. The next section gives a number of less-used Load operations: LCR, LNR, LPR, and LTR.

NAME	*OPERATION*	*OPERAND*
	L	R1,X2 or R1,D2(X2,B2)
	LH	R1,X2 or R1,D2(X2,B2)
(symbol)	LR	R1,R2
	LM	R1,R3,S2 or R1,R3,D2(B2)
	LA	R1,X2 or R1,D2(X2,B2)

LOAD FULLWORD—L. The L instruction loads a binary fullword value into a register. The rules are:

1. Operand-1 specifies any general register.
2. Operand-2 references a fullword in storage, aligned on a fullword boundary. Typically you use a declarative or literal with F-format.
3. The contents of the fullword are loaded into the register, replacing the previous contents.

Figure 9-4 illustrates four L operations, under LOADFULL. The first loads a fullword literal into register-2. (The Assembler aligns H and F literals the same as declaratives.) The second example loads the fullword FULWRD1 into register-8. The third example depicts a coding error: operand-2 is a halfword literal rather than a fullword. (The Assembler does not generate an error message, even if the literal is not a fullword. The error occurs at execute-time, when the computer loads the halfword plus the following two bytes.) The fourth example loads a literal address constant into register-5.

LOAD HALFWORD—LH. The LH construction loads a binary halfword into a register. LH is similar to L, with the following differences:

1. Operand-2 specifies a halfword aligned on a halfword storage boundary. LH loads its contents into the operand-1 register.
2. LH expands the halfword to a fullword by propagating the sign-bit through the 16 leftmost positions, in the register. If the halfword is negative, LH fills 1-bits to the left, maintaining the correct two's complement value.

Figure 9-4 depicts LH under LOADHALF. The first example loads a halfword literal into register-9. The second example loads a halfword constant into register-0. The third example illustrates a coding error: operand-2 is a fullword rather than a halfword. Again the Assembler does not generate an error message. At execute-time LH loads only the leftmost two bytes of the fullword into register-8, causing an error that may be difficult to locate.

LOAD REGISTER—LR. Basically, you use LR to move data from one register to another one. Both operands reference a register. LR loads the contents of the register specified by operand-2 into the operand-1 register. Figure 9-4 illustrates the LR operation under LOADREG. First an L instruction loads a fullword into register-8. Then LR loads the contents of register-8 into register-7.

LOAD MULTIPLE—LM. LM can load data from main storage into more than one register in one operation. LM is an RS-format instruction, with three operands. The rules are:

1. Operands 1 and 2 each specify a register that represents a *span* of registers. That is, 8,10 means registers 8 through 10, or 8, 9, and 10.
2. Operand-3 references a fullword address in storage, the first of a number of adjacent fullword values—one for each register that LM is to load successively into the designated registers.

Figure 9-4 illustrates LM under LOADMULT. The first example loads registers 6, 7, and 8 with FULWRD1, FULWRD2, and FULWRD3 respectively. The second example shows how the registers may "wrap around." Because registers 15 through 1 are referenced, LM loads registers 15, 0, and 1 with the fullwords.

LM has two common uses. One is to restore registers that were saved when the program links to a subprogram (covered in Chapter 19). The other use is in base register initialization. We have used BALR to initialize the first base register. LM may load subsequent registers with base addresses, although LM is restricted to sequential register loading. Figure 9-2 gave an example of the use of LM to load base registers 4, 5, and 6. But watch out —after the BALR only base register-3 is initialized, and the LM will execute correctly *only* if the constant ADDRESS5 is defined within the first 4K of the program.

LOAD ADDRESS—LA. Load Address is a convenient RX instruction to load base registers and to initialize an address in a register for table look-up. The rules are:

1. Operand-1 specifies any available general register.
2. Operand-2 contains a storage address of the form D2(X2,B2).
3. LA loads the operand-2 address into bits 8–31 of the operand-1 register and clears bits 0–7 to zero. The 24 bits used give a maximum address of $2^{24} - 1$.

The following illustrates several uses of LA:

LA 9,A10   Assume A10 is subject to base register-3 containing X'4200' with a displacement of X'0660'. The object code instruction is

41	90	36	60
(a)	(b) (c)		(d)

(a) The machine language code for LA is X'41'.
(b) The operand-1 register is 9.
(c) There is no index register signified.
(d) The base register is 3 and displacement is 660.

```
                    55  *         --------------------
                    56  *         L         LOAD FULLWORD            DECIMAL
                    57  *         --------------------       REG:      VALUE
003870  5820  31A6  58  LOADFULL  L    2,=F'123456'          2:      123456
003874  5880  309A  59            L    8,FULWRD1             8:      6936
003878  5810  31AE  60            L    1,=H'287'             ERROR: OP-2 SHOULD BE FULLWORD
00387C  5850  31AA  61            L    5,=A(TABLE)           5: ADDRESS OF TABLE


                    63  *         --------------------
                    64  *         LH        LOAD HALFWORD
                    65  *         --------------------
003880  4890  31B0  66  LOADHALF  LH   9,=H'500'             9:        0500
003884  4800  3098  67            LH   0,HALFWRD1            0:        0595
003888  4880  309A  68            LH   8,FULWRD1             ERROR: OP-2 SHOULD BE HALFWORD


                    70  *         --------------------
                    71  *         LR        LOAD REGISTER
                    72  *         --------------------
00388C  5880  309E  73  LOADREG   L    8,FULWRD2             8:        4174
003890  1878        74            LR   7,8                   7:        4174


                    76  *         --------------------
                    77  *         LM        LOAD MULTIPLE
                    78  *         --------------------
                    79  LOADMULT  LM   6,8,FULWRD1           6:        6936    7:        4174
003892  9868  309A                                          8:        5637
                    80            LM   15,1,FULWRD1          15:       6936    0:        4174
003896  98F1  309A                                          1:        5637

00389A  0253        82  HALFWRD1  DC   H'595'
00389C  00001B18    83  FULWRD1   DC   F'6936'
0038A0  0000104E    84  FULWRD2   DC   F'4174'
0038A4  00001605    85  FULWRD3   DC   F'5637'
0038A8              86  TABLE     DS   50CL5
0039A8              87            LTORG
0039A8  0001E240    88            =F'123456'
0039AC  000038A8    89            =A(TABLE)
0039B0  011F        90            =H'287'
0039B2  01F4        91            =H'500'
```

FIGURE 9-4 Load register operations: L, LH, LR, LM.

The instruction adds the contents of the base register (X'4200') plus the displacement (X'0660'). The sum X'004860', the address of A10, is loaded into register-9.

LA 9,5(0,0) This example illustrates explicit use of base/displacement. (The next chapter covers this practice more fully.) The object code instruction is

| 41 | 90 | 00 | 05 |

—assume no base register, no index register, but load the displacement X'005' into register-9. In effect, the value 5 loads into register-9. *Note:* The 5 is a *displacement*, not a register, and consequently its maximum value is 4095.

LA 9,5   The Assembler treats operand-2 as if it were coded like the previous example; that is, 9,5(0,0). This is a convenient way to load a value into a register, up to a maximum displacement of 4095.

LA 9,1(0,9)   The generated object code is

41	90	90	01

—load the contents of "base" register-9 plus a displacement of 001 into register-9. In effect, the contents of register-9 are incremented by 1. This method of adding to a register, although efficient, works only for increments up to 4095 (the maximum displacement), and only if the value in the register is positive and does not exceed 24 bits (because LA clears bits 0–7 to zero).

Figure 9-5 illustrates an efficient way to load additional base registers by means of the index register feature. The program is assumed to load at X'4800'. BALR loads register-3 with X'4802'. Suppose you now want to load registers 4, 5, and 6 with each base address successively containing X'5802', X'6802' and X'7802'. First load 2048 or X'0800' into register-6, and then load register-4 with the following value:

Contents of base register-3	X'4802'
Contents of index register-6	X'0800'
Displacement	X'0800'
Total generated address	X'5802'

						REG-3	REG-4	REG-5	REG-6
004800			2		START X'4800'				
			3	*		-----	-----	-----	-----
			4	*					
004800	0530		5		BALR 3,0	4802			
004802			6		USING *,3,4,5,6				
004802	4160	0800	7		LA 6,2048	4802			0800
004806	4146	3800	8		LA 4,2048(6,3)	4802	5802		0800
00480A	4156	4800	9		LA 5,2048(6,4)	4802	5802	6802	0800
00480E	4166	5800	10		LA 6,2048(6,5)	4802	5802	6802	7802

FIGURE 9-5 Initialization of four base registers with LA.

(In hex, 800 + 800 = 1000.) Check the generated object code for each LA operation. Registers 5 and 6 are loaded accordingly.

Note: LA is a "logical" instruction (like MVC and CLC) that treats data as unsigned.

OTHER LOAD OPERATIONS—LCR, LNR, LPR, LTR. You may find occasional use for these load register (RR) instructions. Each sets the condition code.

LOAD COMPLEMENT—LCR. LCR loads the contents of the operand-2 register (R2) into the operand-1 register (R1), and reverses the sign.

> L C R 5 , 8 Load the contents of register-8 into register-5, reverse the sign, and set the condition code.

LOAD NEGATIVE—LNR. LNR loads the contents of R2 into R1 and sets the value to negative. The condition code is set to 0 (zero) or 1 (nonzero minus).

> L N R 5 , 5 Load the contents of register-5 into register-5, force a negative sign, and set the condition code.

LOAD POSITIVE—LPR. LPR loads the contents of R2 into R1 and sets the value to positive. The condition code is set to 0 (zero) or 2 (nonzero plus).

> L P R 9 , 7 Load the contents of register-7 into register-9, force a positive sign, and set the condition code.

LOAD AND TEST—LTR. LTR loads the contents of R2 into R1, just as LR, but in addition sets the condition code for zero, minus, and plus.

> L T R 4 , 4 Load the contents of register-4 into register-4 and set the condition code. This example sets the condition code only, a useful technique to test a register's contents for sign.

STORE REGISTER OPERATIONS—ST, STH, STM

The purpose of the store operations is to store or "save" the contents of registers. A large program may require the use of many registers for base addressing, binary calculations, subroutines, and input/output operations. It is necessary then to save the contents of registers, use them for other purposes, and then use L or LM to reload them.

NAME	OPERATION	OPERAND
	ST	R1,X2 or R1,D2(X2,B2)
(symbol)	STH	R1,X2 or R1,D2(X2,B2)
	STM	R1,S2 or R1,R3,D2(B2)

The Store operations, ST, STH, and STM, are effectively the reverse of L, LH, and LM, respectively. They store the contents of registers in storage, on fullword or halfword boundaries. Note that like CVD, these store instructions move the contents of operand-1 (a register) to operand-2 (storage).

STORE—ST. ST stores the contents of the operand-1 register (R1) into the fullword in storage referenced by operand-2. The fullword should be aligned on a fullword boundary.

STORE HALFWORD—STH. STH stores the rightmost 16 bits of R1 into the operand-2 halfword, aligned in storage.

STORE MULTIPLE—STM. For STM, R1 and R3 specify a span of registers to be stored. STM stores the fullword contents of R1 and the fullword contents of each register up to and including R3 consecutively starting with the operand-2 address. If R1 references a higher register than R3 (such as 14,3) then the registers stored are 14, 15, 0, 1, 2, and 3.

Figure 9-6 illustrates the Store operations. LM initializes registers 4, 5, and 6 with fullword values. In STORE1, the Store (ST) instruction stores the contents of register-5 in the fullword SAVEFULL. In STORE2, STH stores the rightmost 16-bit contents of register-6 in the halfword SAVEHALF.

```
003984  00000675     96 FULLA      DC    F'1653'
003988  00000138     97            DC    F'312'
00398C  00002103     98            DC    F'8451'
0039C0               99 SAVEFULL   DS    F
0039C4              100 SAVEHALF   DS    H
0039C8              101 THREEFW    DS    3F
                    102 FIVEFW     DS    5F
0039D4
0039E8  9846 31B2   103            LM    4,6,FULLA      REGS 4,5,6 : 1653, 312, 8451

                    105 *          ---------------------
                    106 *          ST    STORE FULLWORD
                    107 *          ---------------------
0039EC  5050 31BE   108 STORE1     ST    5,SAVEFULL     SAVEFULL : 312

                    110 *          ---------------------
                    111 *          STH   STORE HALFWORD
                    112 *          ---------------------
0039F0  4060 31C2   113 STORE2     STH   6,SAVEHALF     SAVEHALF : 8451

                    115 *          ---------------------
                    116 *          STM   STORE MULTIPLE
                    117 *          ---------------------
0039F4  9046 31C6   118 STORE3     STM   4,6,THREEFW    THREEFW  : 1653, 312, 8451
                    119            STM   15,3,FIVEFW    FIVEFW RECEIVES CONTENTS OF
0039F8  90F3 31D2                                       *    REGISTERS 15,0,1,2,3
```

FIGURE 9-6 Store register operations: ST, STH, STM.

In STORE3, the first STM stores the contents of registers 4, 5, and 6 in three fullwords labelled THREEFW. The second STM stores the contents of registers 15, 0, 1, 2, and 3 in five fullwords labelled FIVEFW.

USE OF STM AND LM FOR SAVING REGISTERS.   STM is useful for saving the contents of a number of registers, and LM is useful for reloading them. The following example links to a subroutine named R10SUB and uses STM to save registers 6 through 12 in SAVEADD. Assume that the subroutine then uses registers 6 through 12 for its own purposes. On exit, the subroutine uses LM to reload the saved registers.

```
           BAL    6,R10SUB          Link to subroutine
           .
           .
           .
R10SUB     STM    6,12,SAVEADD      Save registers 6-12
           .
           .
           .
           LM     6,12,SAVEADD      Reload registers 6-12
           BR     6                 Return to caller
SAVEADD    DC     7A(0)             Area for saving registers
```

•   *Problems 9-2 and 9-3 should now be attempted*   •

BINARY ARITHMETIC—A, S, AH, SH, AR, SR

The following instructions perform binary addition and subtraction in registers. These operations all treat the leftmost sign bit as a plus or minus sign, not data.

NAME	OPERATION	OPERAND
(symbol)	A	R1,X2 or R1,D2(X2,B2)
	S	R1,X2 or R1,D2(X2,B2)
	AH	R1,X2 or R1,D2(X2,B2)
	SH	R1,X2 or R1,D2(X2,B2)
	AR	R1,R2
	SR	R1,R2

For valid results, all data must be in binary format. These instructions all set the condition code (to zero, minus, or plus), which the usual BC operation may interrogate.

ADD AND SUBTRACT—A AND S. These instructions add or subtract a fullword in storage from a register. Operand-1 references a register. Operand-2 references a storage location aligned on a fullword boundary, containing data in binary format. All 31 data bits of the fullword are algebraically added to or subtracted from the contents of the register.

ADD AND SUBTRACT HALFWORD—AH AND SH. These instructions add or subtract a halfword in storage from a register. Operand-1 references a register, and operand-2 references a storage location aligned on a halfword boundary, containing binary data. Before the add or subtract, the halfword is expanded to a fullword by filling the sign-bit through the 16 leftmost bit positions. All 31 data bits are then algebraically added or subtracted, as A and S. Remember that a halfword has a maximum of 32,767.

ADD AND SUBTRACT REGISTER—AR AND SR. These instructions add or subtract the contents of one register from another register. Both operands reference a register. All 32 bits of operand-2 are algebraically added or subtracted from operand-1.

Figure 9-7 illustrates the preceding. Each example is unrelated to the others. Note that because of the rules of halfword and fullword alignment for RX instructions, define binary fields in H and F format, not B. In ADDFULL, a fullword containing 125 (in decimal notation) is loaded into register-5. A fullword containing 70 is added, and a fullword literal containing 50 is subtracted. Although notation is in decimal format for ease of reading, the fields and registers actually contain binary values.

In ADDHALF, a fullword is loaded into register-8, a halfword is added, and a halfword is subtracted. In ADDREG, two packed fields are defined as doublewords. DS 0D forces alignment on a doubleword boundary. The packed values are converted to binary in registers 0 and 1. (These registers should be used only for temporary calculations.) AR adds the contents of register-1 to register-0. Then SR clears register-1, and CVD converts the contents of register-0 to packed format.

BINARY COMPARISON—C, CH, CR

The C, CH, and CR instructions compare binary data, just as CLC compares character data, and CP compares packed data. Each of these operations

```
                            7  *        -----------------------
                            8  *    A       ADD FULLWORD          DECIMAL
                            9  *    S       SUBTRACT FULLWORD     VALUE:
                           10  *        -----------------------  -----
003002 5850 402A           11 ADDFULL  L   5,FWD1                REG-5:   125
003006 5A50 402E           12          A   5,FWD2                REG-5:   195
00300A 5B50 4046           13          S   5,=F'50'             REG-5:   145

                           15  *        -----------------------
                           16  *    AH      ADD HALFWORD
                           17  *    SH      SUBTRACT HALFWORD
                           18  *        -----------------------
00300E 5880 402A           19 ADDHALF  L   8,FWD1                REG-8:   125
003012 4A80 404A           20          AH  8,=H'50'             REG-8:   175
003016 4B80 404C           21          SH  8,=H'25'             REG-8:   150

                           23  *        -----------------------
                           24  *    AR      ADD REGISTER
                           25  *    SR      SUBTRACT REGISTER
                           26  *        -----------------------
00301A 4F10 4036           27 ADDREG   CVB 1,DBPK1               REG-1:   250
00301E 4F00 403E           28          CVB 0,DBPK2               REG-0:   075
003022 1A01                29          AR  0,1                   REG-0:   325
003024 1B11                30          SR  1,1                   REG-1:   000
003026 4E00 4036           31          CVD 0,DBPK1              CONVERT 325 TO PACKED

00302A 0000
00302C 0000007D            33 FWD1     DC  F'125'               BINARY FULLWORD
003030 00000046            34 FWD2     DC  F'70'                BINARY FULLWORD
003038                     35          DS  0D                   FORCE DOUBLEWORD ALIGN.
003038 000000000000250C    36 DBPK1    DC  PL8'250'             PACKED VALUE
003040 000000000000075C    37 DBPK2    DC  PL8'075'             PACKED VALUE
003048                     38          LTORG
003048 00000032            39          =F'50'
00304C 0032                40          =H'50'
00304E 0019                41          =H'25'
```

FIGURE 9-7 Binary addition and subtraction.

algebraically compares the contents of operand-1 to operand-2, and sets the condition code (to equal, low, or high).

NAME	OPERATION	OPERAND
	C	R1,X2 or R1,D2(X2,B2)
(symbol)	CH	R1,X2 or R1,D2(X2,B2)
	CR	R1,R2

COMPARE—C. The C instruction compares the contents of a register to a fullword in storage. Operand-1 references a register. Operand-2 references a fullword aligned on a fullword boundary, containing binary data.

COMPARE HALFWORD—CH. The CH instruction compares the contents of a register to a halfword in storage. Operand-2 references a halfword, aligned on a halfword boundary containing binary data. Before the compare,

CH expands the halfword to a full word by filling of the sign-bit value through the leftmost 16 bits.

COMPARE REGISTER—CR. The CR instruction compares the contents of one register to another register. Both operands specify a register. CR compares the contents of operand-1 to that of operand-2.

Figure 9-8 illustrates the binary compare operations. Note how each instruction sets the condition code. COMP1 loads a fullword FWD3 into register-6. C then compares register-6 to the contents of FWD4 in storage. COMP2 loads a halfword HWD1 into register-7 and compares its contents to HWD2, another halfword in storage. COMP3 loads FWD3 into register-8 and a fullword literal into register-9. Then CR compares registers 8 and 9.

```
                          46  *       --------------------------
                          47  *       C      COMPARE FULLWORD      DATA        COND'N
                          48  *       -------------------- COMPARED:          CODE:
003050  5860 406A         49 COMP1    L      6,FWD3              --------       ----
003054  5960 406E         50          C      6,FWD4         1250 < 2575        LOW

                          52  *       --------------------------
                          53  *       CH     COMPARE HALFWORD
                          54  *       --------------------------
003058  4870 4072         55 COMP2    LH     7,HWD1
00305C  4970 4074         56          CH     7,HWD2          365  >  215       HIGH

                          58  *       --------------------------
                          59  *       CR     COMPARE REGISTERS
                          60  *       --------------------------
003060  5880 406A         61 COMP3    L      8,FWD3
003064  5890 4076         62          L      9,=F'975'
003068  1989              63          CR     8,9            1250 >  975        HIGH

00306A  0000
00306C  000004E2          65 FWD3     DC     F'1250'
003070  00000A0F          66 FWD4     DC     F'2575'
003074  016D              67 HWD1     DC     H'365'
003076  00D7              68 HWD2     DC     H'215'
003078                    69          LTORG
003078  000003CF          70          =F'975'
```

FIGURE 9-8 Binary compare operations: C, CH, CR.

EXAMPLE USE OF BINARY ARITHMETIC

An example in Chapter 4 used packed data to add the sum of digits from 1 to 10: $1 + 2 + 3 + \ldots + 10$. Figure 9-9 in this chapter provides a similar example to illustrate binary operations. The routine uses three registers:

5: The value 1 to act as an increment.

6: A counter that increments by 1 for each loop.

7:    An accumulator for the sum of digits (the routine adds register-6, the counter, to this register).

If there were only two registers available, the routine could add the literal =H'1' to register-6, as

<pre>   LOOP AH 6,=H'1'</pre>

Note: RR-format instructions such as AR, however, are more efficient than RX-format instructions such as AH that have to reference storage.

```
00384A 4850 30F2      038F4    36        LH    5,=H'1'        INIT'ZE INCREMENT
00384E 1B66                     37        SR    6,6            CLEAR CTR
003850 1B77                     38        SR    7,7            CLEAR SUM

003852 1A65                     40 LOOP   AR    6,5            CTR: 1, 2, 3, 4, ...
003854 1A76                     41        AR    7,6            SUM: 1, 3, 6, 10, ...
003856 4960 30F4      038F6    42        CH    6,=H'10'       LOOPED 10 TIMES?
00385A 4770 3050      03852    43        BNE   LOOP           NO - CONTINUE
                                44 *      ...                  YES - END
```

FIGURE 9-9 Sum of the digits in binary.

MULTIPLICATION—M, MH, MR

M, MH, and MR multiply fields in binary format. They do not set the condition code.

NAME	OPERATION	OPERAND
	M	R1,X2 or R1,D2(X2,B2)
(symbol)	MH	R1,X2 or R1,D2(X2,B2)
	MR	R1,R2

Certain binary operations require a pair of registers to express values greater than $2^{31} - 1$. A double register permits values up to $2^{63} - 1$. The registers are an *even-odd numbered pair,* such as 4 and 5, or 8 and 9, with the sign bit in the leftmost bit of the even register.

Both M and MR require an even-odd pair of registers. You load the multiplicand into the odd-numbered register. The product is developed in the pair of registers, with one sign bit and 63 data bits. For *most* multiplication operations, the product never exceeds $2^{31} - 1$ or 2,147,483,647.

Therefore, only one register (the odd one) is sufficient to contain the product. In this case, the leftmost bit of the odd register contains the correct sign, the same as that of the even register. Provided you are sure the product cannot exceed $2^{31}-1$, you may treat the value in the odd register as the correct signed product.

	EVEN REGISTER	*ODD REGISTER*
Before the M or MR:	(Garbage)	Multiplicand
After the multiply:	(Product)	Product

Note: When you compute averages and ratios, a value such as 21,474.83647 may be easily exceeded. Ensure that such a value is not exceeded regardless of the decimal position. (See double-precision in a later section.)

MULTIPLY FULLWORD—M. The M instruction multiplies the contents of a register by a fullword in storage. Operand-1 specifies the even register of an even-odd pair. The odd register contains the multiplicand. Operand-2 references a fullword in storage, aligned, containing the multiplier in binary format. The product is developed in the even-odd pair, and erases the multiplicand. Note: The even register need not be initially cleared to zero (M ignores its contents).

MULTIPLY HALFWORD—MH. The MH instruction multiplies the contents of a register by a halfword in storage. MH is similar to M, with the following exceptions:

1. Operand-1, the multiplicand, specifies any register, not necessarily an even one. The multiplicand is assumed to be 31 data bits.
2. Operand-2 references the multiplier—a halfword of binary data aligned on a halfword boundary in storage.
3. On execution, MH expands the halfword to a fullword by filling the sign-bit value through the 16 leftmost bits. The 32-bit product is developed in the operand-1 register only, and erases the multiplicand.

MULTIPLY REGISTER—MR. The MR instruction multiplies the contents of one register by another register. MR is similar to M except that operand-2 references a register containing the multiplier. You may load the multiplier in the even register, although the product erases it.

Figure 9-10 provides examples of multiply operations. In MULT1, the even-odd pair of registers is 4 and 5. The fullword MULTCAND is loaded into register-5. The Load instructions are for data in binary format, and CVB

```
                                74  *                                      REG:        REG:
                                75  *           ----------------------
                                76  *       M       MULTIPLY FULLWORD
                                77  *           ----------------------
        00307C  5850  409E      78  MULT1   L       5,MULTCAND                        5:  03333
        003080  5C40  40A2      79          M       4,MULTPLER         4:  00000      5:  66660

                                81  *           ----------------------
                                82  *       MH      MULTIPLY HALFWORD
                                83  *           ----------------------
        003084  5870  409E      84  MULT2   L       7,MULTCAND         7:  03333
        003088  4C70  40A6      85          MH      7,MULTHALF         7:  09999

                                87  *           ----------------------
                                88  *       MR      MULTIPLY REGISTER
                                89  *           ----------------------
        00308C  5830  40A2      90  MULT3   L       3,MULTPLER         3:  00020
        003090  5890  409E      91          L       9,MULTCAND                        9:  03333
        003094  1C83            92          MR      8,3                8:  00000      9:  66660

        003096  5880  40A2      94  MULT4   L       8,MULTPLER         8:  00020
        00309A  5890  409E      95          L       9,MULTCAND                        9:  03333
        00309E  1C88            96          MR      8,8                8:  00000      9:  66660

        0030A0  00000D05        98  MULTCAND  DC    F'3333'
        0030A4  00000014        99  MULTPLER  DC    F'20'
        0030A8  0003           100  MULTHALF  DC    H'3'
```

FIGURE 9-10 Binary multiplication: M, MH, MR.

in packed format. To multiply, specify the even register (4) in operand-1. Operand-2 specifies the fullword multiplier in storage. The product is generated in registers 4 and 5.

MULT2, because MH is used, needs only one register. A fullword is loaded into register-7, and then MH multiplies register-7 by a halfword in storage. The product is generated in register-7.

In MULT3, the even-odd pair of registers is 8 and 9. Registers 3 and 9 are loaded with fullwords which are to be multiplied. For MR, specify the multiplicand in the even register (8) as operand-1. The multiplier in register-3 is operand-2. The product is developed in registers 8 and 9.

In MULT4, the MR operation uses only two registers. Registers 8 and 9 are the even-odd pair. The multiplicand is loaded into register-9, and the multiplier in register-8. In spite of its appearance, MR 8,8 does not mean multiply the contents of register-8 and register-8. Operand-1 refers to the multiplicand in the odd register (9) of an even-odd pair (8 and 9). Operand-2 refers to the multiplier that happens to be in register-8. It is erased by the multiplication.

Warning: In these examples, the product does not exceed the capacity of a single register, which is $2^{31}-1$ or 2,147,483,647. If there is a possibility of such a large product, then you must provide additional programming. The technique is given later in this chapter in Conversion of Double Precision Binary to Decimal Format.

REGISTER SHIFT INSTRUCTIONS

You can shift binary data in a register either left or right a specified number of bit positions. This feature, for example, can clear unwanted bit positions from a field, or multiply or divide a field by a power of two. The following operations shift the bit contents of registers, other than the leftmost sign bit which is unaffected. Bits shifted out of the register are lost. The condition code is set.

NAME	*OPERATION*	*OPERAND*
(symbol)	SRA	R1,S2 or R1,D2(B2)
	SLA	R1,S2 or R1,D2(B2)
	SRDA	R1,S2 or R1,D2(B2)
	SLDA	R1,S2 or R1,D2(B2)

SHIFT RIGHT ALGEBRAIC—SRA. The rules for SRA are:

1. Operand-1 specifies a register whose 31-bit contents other than the sign bit are to be shifted to the right. The leftmost sign bit is not moved.

2. Operand-2 denotes the number of bits to be shifted. Normally you code the shift factor as a decimal number less than 32.

3. Bits shifted off to the right are lost. The sign bit replaces leftmost shifted bits. There is no overflow or program interrupt.

You may use SRA to divide the contents of a register by a power of 2. For example, shifting right one bit is equivalent to dividing by 2^1, or 2; shifting right two bits is equivalent to dividing by 2^2, or 4, etc. Consider a 4-bit register containing initially (a) 1000, and (b) 1111:

	(a) **CONTENTS**	(b) **CONTENTS**
Initial value:	1000 (8)	1111 (15)
Shift right 1:	0100 (4)	0111 (7)
Shift right 2:	0010 (2)	0011 (3)
Shift right 3:	0001 (1)	0001 (1)

SHIFT LEFT ALGEBRAIC—SLA. SLA is similar to SRA with the following differences:

1. SLA shifts up to 31 bit positions to the left. The leftmost sign bit is unaffected.

2. SLA replaces rightmost shifted bit positions with 0-bits. For example, shift left three bits: 00001011 becomes 01011000.

3. A leftmost bit shifted out that is *different* from the sign bit may cause an overflow and interrupt.

You may use SLA to multiply the contents of a register by a power of 2. For example, shifting left three bits is equivalent to multiplying by 2^3, or 8.

SHIFT RIGHT DOUBLE ALGEBRAIC—SRDA. SRDA is similar to SRA except that the contents of *two* registers shift as a single unit. SRDA is commonly used with binary divide operations.

1. Operand-1 specifies the even-numbered register of an even-odd pair of registers. The pair is treated as a single doubleword.
2. Up to 63 bits may be shifted. The sign bit in the even register, considered the sign for the pair, replaces leftmost shifted bits in both registers. The sign bit in the odd registers is treated as *data*, therefore yielding 63 bits of data.

SHIFT LEFT DOUBLE ALGEBRAIC—SLDA. SLDA is similar to SLA except that, like SRDA, operand-1 specifies the even-numbered register of an even-odd pair. The sign bit of the pair is that of the even register. The sign bit of the odd register is treated as a data-bit, giving a 63-bit doubleword.

For each shift operation, if operand-2 contains *zero*, the instruction executes without shifting. This use of shift is a convenient way to set the condition code. If you want to *vary* the number of bits shifted throughout the program, you may use the base-displacement facility of operand-2, D(B). For example, register-3 contains the value 12. Given the instruction

```
        SRA 9,0(3)
```

the contents of register-9 shift right according to the contents of register-3, that is 12 bits.

Figure 9-11 illustrates shift operations. Check the hex representation for the fullword constants, and the effect of the shift. Note that it is the *bits* that shift. For example, if a binary value containing 0001 (X'1') is left-shifted two bits, the result is 0100 (X'4').

In SHIFT1, SRA shifts the contents of register-9 two bits to the right. This shift is equivalent to dividing by four. The second example specifies zero in operand-2. No shift occurs, but, since the value is positive, the condition code is set to high/plus.

In SHIFT2, SLA shifts the contents of register-7 two bits to the left. This shift is equivalent to multiplying by four. The second example explicitly uses a base register. The value 3 is loaded into register-8. Then register-8 is referenced explicitly in operand-2 of the SLA to cause a left shift of 3 bits.

In SHIFT3, SRDA shifts the contents of the even-odd registers 6 and

```
                        123  *                              HEX CONTENTS:
                        124  *          ------------------------------
                        125  *          SRA   SHIFT RIGHT ALGEBRAIC
                        126  *          ------------------------------
0039FC 5890 322A        127  SHIFT1     L     9,FULLWD2      00004327
003A00 8A90 0002        128             SRA   9,2            000010C9

003A04 8A90 0000        130             SRA   9,0            NO SHIFT. SET COND'N CODE
                                                                         TO HIGH/PLUS
                        132  *          ------------------------------
                        133  *          SLA   SHIFT LEFT   ALGEBRAIC
                        134  *          ------------------------------
003A08 5870 3256        135  SHIFT2     L     7,=F'17191'    00004327
003A0C 8B70 0002        136             SLA   7,2            00010C9C

003A10 4180 0003        138             LA    8,3            LOAD 3 IN REG 8
003A14 8B70 8000        139             SLA   7,0(8)         SHIFT REG-7 LEFT 3 BITS

                        141  *          -------------------------------------
                        142  *          SRDA  SHIFT RIGHT DOUBLE ALGEBRAIC
                        143  *          -------------------------------------
003A18 9867 3226        144  SHIFT3     LM    6,7,FULLWD1    0000013F/00004327
003A1C 8E60 0004        145             SRDA  6,4            00000013/F0000432

                        147  *          -------------------------------------
                        148  *          SLDA  SHIFT LEFT   DOUBLE ALGEBRAIC
                        149  *          -------------------------------------
003A20 9889 3226        150  SHIFT4     LM    8,9,FULLWD1    0000013F/00004327
003A24 8F80 0012        151             SLDA  8,18           04FC0001/0C9C0000

003A28 0000013F        153  FULLWD1     DC    F'319'         0000013F
003A2C 00004327        154  FULLWD2     DC    F'17191'       00004327
```

FIGURE 9-11 Binary algebraic shift operations.

7 four bits to the right. In SHIFT4, SLDA shifts the contents of the even-odd registers 8 and 9 eighteen bits to the left.

Earlier, Figure 9-9 added the sum of digits from 1 to 10. You can also calculate the sum using the formula

$$\text{sum of digits} = (n^2 + n)/2$$

where n is any value. For example, if n is 10, then the sum of the digits from 1 to 10 is

$$(10^2 + 10)/2 = 110/2 = 55$$

Let's use binary multiplication and shift instructions to perform the calculation. Assume that the value n is 10 and is in register-12:

```
                                                   reg-9:
            LR    9,12      Init'ze n               10
            MR    8,12      Square n               100
            AR    9,12      Add n                  110
            SRA   9,1       Divide by 2             55
```

If the value n is a fullword is storage, you could use the L instruction to load it into an available register, and use ST to store the result in a fullword in storage.

- *Problems 9-4, 9-5, and 9-6 should now be attempted.* •

BINARY DIVISION—D, DR

The D and DR instructions divide fields in binary format. (Unexpectedly, there is no Divide Halfword operation.)

NAME	OPERATION	OPERAND
(symbol)	D	R1,X2 or R1,D2(X2,B2)
	DR	R1,R2

DIVIDE AND DIVIDE REGISTER. Both D and DR, like M and MR, require the use of a doubleword of 63 bits plus a sign in an even-odd pair of registers. D and DR treat the pair of registers, all 63 bits, as a dividend field. Possibly, for example, an M or MR operation generated a two-register product, and it is now necessary to divide this product by some value. Often, however, the programmer loads the dividend into a register, and only one register is required to contain the fullword dividend. In this case, the dividend is in the odd register, but *the even register must be initialized so that it contains the same sign as the dividend.* You may force similar signs by the following practice:

- Load the dividend into the even register.
- Using SRDA, shift the dividend 32 bits out of the even into the odd register. The even register now is cleared of "garbage" from any previous operation, and initialized with the correct sign.

EVEN REGISTER, INITIALIZED	ODD REGISTER, DIVIDEND SIGN
Binary zeros	Positive
Binary ones	Negative

The rules for D and DR are:

1. Operand-1 specifies the even register of an even-odd pair of registers containing the dividend.
2. Operand-2 references the 32-bit divisor. For D, the divisor is a fullword aligned in storage. For DR, the divisor is a register.
3. After execution, the remainder is in the even register and the quotient is in the odd register. Both contain 31 data bits and a leftmost sign bit.

A quotient that exceeds 31 bits plus the sign causes an overflow and program interrupt. Dividing by zero will cause this condition.

4. The sign of the quotient is determined by normal algebraic rules. The remainder's sign is the same as the dividend. The condition code is not set, but you can ZAP the quotient into itself to set it.

	EVEN REGISTER	*ODD REGISTER*
Before the D or DR:	Dividend	Dividend
After the divide:	Remainder	Quotient

Figure 9-12 illustrates the D and DR operations. For D, the even-odd pair is registers 0 and 1. The binary fullword DIVD is loaded into register-0. Then the contents of register-0 are shifted into register-1, leaving register-0 correctly initialized. The fullword divisor DIVSR divides into the even-odd pair. Register-1 now contains the quotient, 326, and register-0 contains the remainder, 5. Remember that registers 0, 1, 14, and 15 are always available, but input/output and linkage to subprograms change their contents.

```
LOC     OBJECT CODE    ADDR1 ADDR2   STMT    SOURCE STATEMENT

                                      48 *        --------------
                                      49 *        D      DIVIDE              REG-0:     REG-1:
                                      50 *        --------------             ------     ------
00385E  5800 3076            03878    51          L      0,DIVD              4569
003862  8E00 0020            00020    52          SRDA   0,32                0000       4569
003866  5D00 307A            0387C    53          D      0,DIVSR             0005       0326

                                      55 *        ----------------------
                                      56 *        DR     DIVIDE REGISTER     REG-10 :   REG-11:
                                      57 *        ----------------------     ------     ------
00386A  58C0 307A            0387C    58          L      12,DIVSR
00386E  58A0 3076            03878    59          L      10,DIVD             4569
003872  8EA0 0020            00020    60          SRDA   10,32               0000       4569
003876  1DAC                          61          DR     10,12               0005       0326

003878  000011D9                      63 DIVD     DC     F'4569'             FULLWORD DIVIDEND
00387C  0000000E                      64 DIVSR    DC     F'14'               FULLWORD DIVISOR
```

FIGURE 9-12 Binary division operations: D and DR.

For DR, the even-odd pair is registers 10 and 11. The divisor and dividend are loaded respectively into registers 12 and 10. The contents of register-10 are shifted into register-11, leaving register-10 correctly initialized. DR then divides register-12 into the even-odd pair. Register-11 now contains the quotient, 326, and register-10 contains the remainder.

SCALING AND ROUNDING. Assembler performs arithmetic on integers only. The problem of scaling, that is, providing for the decimal point, is

```
LOC      OBJECT CODE    ADDR1 ADDR2  STMT   SOURCE STATEMENT

                                       68 DISTPK    DC    P'2356.5'
003880   23565C                        69 GALSPK    DC    P'150.0'
003883   01500C                        70 DISTDW    DS    D
003888                                 71 GALSDW    DS    D
003890                                 72 ANSWPK    DS    D
003898

                                                          REG CONTENTS AS DEC FORMAT:

0038A0   F872 3086 307E  03888 03880   74 DIVIDE    ZAP   DISTDW,DISTPK
0038A6   F872 3086 3081  03890 03883   75           ZAP   GALSDW,GALSPK

                                       77 *         DIVIDE, NO ROUNDING:
                                       78 *         --------------------
0038AC   4F90 308E       03890         79 DIVID10   CVB   9,GALSDW          9: 0000001500
0038B0   4F60 3086       03888         80           CVB   6,DISTDW          6: 0000023565
0038B4   8E60 0020       00020         81           SRDA  6,32              6: 0000000000   7: 0000023565
0038B8   1D69                          82           DR    6,9               6: 0000001065   7: 0000000015
0038BA   4E70 3096       03898         83           CVD   7,ANSWPK          ANSWER = PACKED 15

                                       85 *         DIVIDE & ROUND TO TWO DECIMALS :
                                       86 *         --------------------------------
0038BE   4F90 308E       03890         87 DIVID30   CVB   9,GALSDW          9: 0000001500
0038C2   4F60 3086       03888         88           CVB   6,DISTDW          6: 0000023565
0038C6   8E60 0020       00020         89           SRDA  6,32              6: 0000000000   7: 0000023565
0038CA   4C70 30F6       038F8         90           MH    7,=H'1000'        6: 0000000000   7: 0023565000
0038CE   1D69                          91           DR    6,9               6: 0000000000   7: 0000001571
0038D0   1267                          92           LTR   6,7               LOAD QUOTIENT INTO REG-6,
0038D2   4740 30DC       038DE         93           BM    DIVID32           *    TEST CONDITION CODE
0038D6   4A60 30F8       038FA         94           AH    6,=H'5'           6: 0000015715   7: 0000001571
0038DA   47F0 30E0       038E2         95           B     DIVID34

0038DE   4B60 30F8       038F8         97 DIVID32   SH    6,=H'5'
0038E2   8E60 0020       00020         98 DIVID34   SRDA  6,32              6: 0000000000   7: 0000015715
0038E6   5D60 30EE       038F0         99           D     6,=F'10'          6: 0000000000   7: 0000001571
0038EA   4E70 3096       03898        100           CVD   7,ANSWPK          ANSWER = PACKED 15.71
```

FIGURE 9-13 Binary division with decimal point scaling.

similar to that for DP. You must mentally account for the implicit decimal point. *It simplifies programming to think of binary as decimal values.*

Refer to Figure 9-13, which is similar to a DP example in Figure 5-5 which divides distance (DISTPK) by gallons (GALSPK) to calculate miles-per-gallon (ANSWER). Both DISTPK and GALSPK are transferred to aligned doublewords to permit CVB to convert them to binary.

The first example, DIVID10, is a direct divide operation with no scaling for decimal point. A CVB instruction converts gallons into binary in register-9 and a second CVB converts distance into binary in register-6. Registers 6 and 7 are to contain the dividend, distance. In order to initialize register-6 with the correct 0- or 1-bit sign, an SRDA instruction shifts all 32 bits of distance from register-6 into register-7. Since distance in this example is positive, register-6 now contains all 0-bits. A DR instruction next performs the division, and CVD converts the quotient to packed in main storage.

The second example, DIVID30, requires generating a two-decimal quotient after rounding. Since both distance and gallons contain one decimal position, the example has to generate three additional decimal positions.

To generate three decimal places, multiply by 1000. (Note that shift operations, such as SLA, multiply by powers of 2, not 10.) LTR is used to set the condition code: if positive add 5; if negative subtract 5. LTR as well loaded the quotient from register-7 into register-6, erasing the remainder. This move is done because the quotient is to be divided again, by 10. Before dividing, shift the quotient out of register-6 back into register-7, thereby clearing and initializing register-6 to the correct sign. The division by 10 adjusts for the required number of decimal positions.

The following facts should be clearly understood: LTR cleared the remainder from register-6 because of the subsequent divide by 10. If the remainder were left in register-6 the second divide would have treated the contents of registers 6 and 7 as one extremely large 63-bit value. The contents of the registers and fullwords are in binary format. However, coding in decimal format is a convenient way to *represent* the binary values.

CONVERSION OF DOUBLE PRECISION BINARY TO DECIMAL FORMAT

A binary multiplication may develop a product that exceeds the capacity of one register (2,147,483,647). The result is a double precision, or a two register, product. This situation requires additional programming in order to convert the result to decimal format. Consider a situation in which registers 4 and 5 contain only four bits, 0011 and 0111 respectively. The sign is the leftmost bit of register-4. The decimal value of this quantity in the pair of registers is $32 + 16 + 0 + 4 + 2 + 1 = 55$. Converting register-4 to decimal yields the decimal value 3, instead of $32 + 16 = 48$. To correct this value 3, you may multiply it by a constant value 16, or $3 \times 16 = 48$. The constant 16 is used because the "register" contains four bits, and the maximum value is $2^4 = 16$. (Determine the constant required if the registers contain 5, 6, or 32 bits.) With register-4 correctly converted to decimal value 48, you may now process register-5. Conversion of register-5 to decimal results in the value 7, which when added to 48 yields the correct answer 55.

Consider another example of a negative value, minus 59. Its bit representation in two's complement is:

REGISTER	EVEN	ODD
Binary value:	0011	1011 (plus 59)
Reverse bits:	1100	0100
Add 1:	1100	0101 (minus 59)

The even register contains the minus sign, a 1-bit, in the leftmost bit. CVD would convert the contents of the even register to -4. (Depict 4 in binary, reverse the bits, and add 1 to check that the two's complement of -4 is 1100.) Multiplying -4 by 16 gives -64. The odd register containing 0101 when converted to decimal yields $+5$. And $-64 + 5$ gives the correct answer, -59.

But a problem arises if the odd register contains a 1 in its leftmost bit, because CVD treats the value as negative. Assume the value in the double-register is $+40$, or 0010 1000. Converting the even register to decimal yields $+2$. Multiplying $+2$ by 16 gives $+32$. CVD converts the odd register to -8, and the sum of $+32$ and -8, which is 24, is incorrect.

You can use LTR to test the leftmost sign bit in the odd register. If there is a 0-bit, the nonminus condition code is set; the conversion may proceed as already described. If, however, the odd register sign is a 1-bit, the condition code is minus. The following procedure produces the correct answer for the same example of 0010 1000:

- The odd register is "minus." Add 1 to the even register, giving 0011 1000.
- Converting the even register to decimal gives $+3$. Multiplying $+3$ by 16 yields $+48$.
- Converting the odd register to decimal gives -8. 48 plus -8 gives the correct answer, 40.

This additional step of testing if the odd register is "minus" and adding 1 to the even register provides the correct answer in all cases. Note that the incorrect answer was 24 instead of 40, a difference of 16. But the addition of 1 was equivalent to incrementing the double precision value by 2^4, or 16. Figure 9-14 gives the programming for this procedure, in which multiplication of binary values produces a two register product.

```
 8           DS     OD
 9 DATA1     DC     PL8'0123456'
10 DATA2     DC     PL8'-456789'
11 DBLWD     DS     D
12 PRODPK    DC     PL16'0'
13 CONSTANT  DC     P'4294967296'
14 *                                REG-6 HEX  REG-7 HEX     DECIMAL    +
                                    ---------  ---------     -------
15 E10DOUBL  CVB    6,DATA1         0001E240
16           CVB    7,DATA2         0001E240   FF8907AB
17           MR     6,6             FFFFFFF2   DEB1E0C0
18           LTR    7,7
19           BNM    E20
20           AH     6,=H'1'         FFFFFFF3   DEB1E0C0

22 E20       CVD    6,PRODPK+8      PRODPK:                        013-
23           MP     PRODPK,CONSTANT PRODPK:             55,834,574,848-
24           CVD    7,DBLWD         DBLWD :                558,767,936-
25           AP     PRODPK,DBLWD    PRODPK:             56,393,342,784-
```

FIGURE 9-14 Conversion of double precision binary to packed.

The two fields, DATA1 and DATA2, are converted into binary format in registers of 6 and 7. When the registers are multiplied, the product exceeds the capacity of register-7. Since register-7 contains a "minus value," 1 is added to register-6. Register-6 is converted to decimal format into PRODPK. The constant used to multiply is no longer 2^4, but 2^{32} or 4,294,967,296. Register-7 is next converted to decimal format in DBLWD, and PRODPK is added to it. The final product is correct: 56,393,342,784 −.

SAMPLE PARTIAL PROGRAM: FINANCE CHARGE REBATES

For some types of loans, finance charges are precomputed; that is, the amount of interest for the term of the loan is precalculated and added to the amount of the loan. For example, $500.00 is borrowed for a term of 6 months with precomputed finance charge of $30.00. The sum of $530.00 is repayable in 6 equal instalments of $88.33. A borrower who repays the full amount of the balance remaining before the end of the term is entitled to a partial rebate on the precomputed finance charge. The rebate can be calculated by the "sum of digits" formula.

t = original term in months F = precomputed finance charge
r = remaining term in months R = rebate

$$R = \frac{\dfrac{r^2+r}{2}}{\dfrac{t^2+t}{2}} \times F = \frac{r^2+r}{t^2+t} \times F$$

Example calculation of rebate:

$$t = 6, r = 5, F = \$30.00$$

$$\frac{5^2+5}{6^2+6} \times \$30.00 = \frac{30}{42} \times \$30.00 = \$21.42$$

Figure 9-15 gives the programming that calculates the rebate. The program also checks for minimum finance charge of $10.00. That is, finance charge less rebate must equal at least $10.00. *Example:* $30.00 − $21.42 = $8.58. Since $8.58 is less than $10.00, the rebate is $30.00 − $10.00 = $20.00.

MOVE LONG AND COMPARE LONG—MVCL AND CLCL

Move Long (MVCL) moves data areas that exceed 256 bytes; one major use is to clear large areas of storage. Compare Long (CLCL) compares data areas that exceed 256 bytes; one major use is to compare if the contents of a record has been changed.

NAME	OPERATION	OPERAND
(symbol)	MVCL	R1,R2
(symbol)	CLCL	R1,R2

Both MVCL and CLCL require the use of four registers. Operand-1 and operand-2 both reference the even-numbered register of an even-odd pair, for example 6/7and 10/11:

operand-1:		operand-2:	
¦address-1 ¦	¦length-1 ¦	¦address-2 ¦	¦pad length-2 ¦
even	odd	even	odd

Operand-1: The even register (bits 8–31) references the address of the receiving field for MVCL or the comparing field for CLCL. The odd register (bits 8–31) provides the length of this field.

Operand-2: The even register (bits 8–31) references the address of the sending field for MVCL or the compared field for CLCL. The odd register (bits 8–31) provides the length of this field, as well as an optional "padding" character (bits 0–7).

Since 24 bits are available for the operations, you may move or compare fields of virtually any length.

```
003806 0000
003808 00000006      8 ORIGTERM DC    F'06'
00380C 00000005      9 REMGTERM DC    F'05'
003810 00000BB8     10 FINCHGE  DC    F'03000'         030.00
003814              11 REBATE   DS    F                XXX.XX
                    12 *                               REG:  DECIMAL FORMAT:
                    13 * CALCULATE R SQUARED + R :
003818 5890 300A    14 CALCREB  L     9,REMGTERM       9: 05
00381C 1879         15          LR    7,9
00381E 1C69         16          MR    6,9              7: 25
003820 1A79         17          AR    7,9              7: 30

                    19 * MULTIPLY BY FINANCE CHARGE :
003822 5880 300E    20          L     8,FINCHGE        8: 030.00
003826 1C68         21          MR    6,8              7: 900.00
003828 5C60 3176    22          M     6,=F'100'        7: 900.0000    SHIFT LEFT

                    24 * CALCULATE T SQUARED + T :
00382C 5890 3006    25          L     9,ORIGTERM       9: 06
003830 1859         26          LR    5,9              5: 06
003832 1C49         27          MR    4,9              5: 36
003834 1A59         28          AR    5,9              5: 42

                    30 * DIVIDE TO CALCULATE REBATE:
003836 1D65         31          DR    6,5              7: 21.4285
003838 4A70 3182    32          AH    7,=H'50'         7: 21.4335     ROUND
00383C 1866         33          SR    6,6                             CLEAR REMAINDER
00383E 5D60 3176    34          D     6,=F'100'        7: 21.43       SHIFT RIGHT

                    36 * CHECK FOR $10.00 MINIMUM CHARGE :
003842 1898         37          LR    9,8              9: 30.00
003844 1B87         38          SR    8,7              8: 08.57
003846 5980 317A    39          C     8,=F'1000'
00384A 47B0 3052    40          BNL   B10NOTLO
00384E 5B90 317A    41          S     9,=F'1000'       9: 20.00
003852 1879         42          LR    7,9              7: 20.00

003854 5070 3012    44 B10NOTLO ST    7,REBATE         7: 20.00
```

FIGURE 9-15 Calculation of finance charge rebate.

MOVE LONG—MVCL.   Assume that an MVCL instruction is to move a 512-byte record using the register pairs 6/7 and 10/11:

```
RCVADR  DS    CL512           Receiving field
SNDADR  DS    CL512           Sending field

        LA    6,RCVADR        Address of receiving field
        L     7,=F'512'       Length of receiving field
        LA    10,SNDADR       Address of sending field
        L     11,=F'512'      Length of sending field (or LR 11,7)
        MVCL  6,10            Move sending to receiving
```

MVCL moves from the address specified by register-10 to the address specified by register-6, from left to right. For each byte moved, the instruction deducts 1 from the length in registers 7 and 11, and adds 1 to the addresses in registers 6 and 10. For example, assume that the actual location of RCVADR is X'10000' and that the location of SNDADR is X'20000'. On completion of the move of 512 bytes (X'200'), the four registers contain:

REGISTER:	CONTENTS:
6	10200
7	zero
10	20200
11	zero (bits 8–31)

One additional feature is the use of the padding character if the receiving length is greater than that of the sending field. You may insert any character in bits 0–7 of the register that contains the length of the sending field. Typical padding characters are X'40' and X'00'. For example, if the receiving field is 512 bytes and the sending field is 500 bytes, MVCL fills the padding character in the rightmost 12 bytes of the receiving field.

MVCL does not permit overlapping of the receiving and sending fields —the two designated fields should be distinctly separate. If the fields do overlap, the operation sets condition code 3 (overflow) which you may test using BO.

You may want to use MVCL where the field lengths are unknown at the time of assembly, one example being variable-length records.

COMPARE LONG—CLCL.   Assume that a CLCL instruction is to compare two 512-byte records using the register pairs 4/5 and 8/9:

```
COMP1   DS    CL512            Comparing field
COMP2   DS    CL512            Compared field

        LA    4,COMP1          Address of comparing field
        L     5,=F'512'        Length of comparing field
        LA    8,COMP2          Address of compared field
        LR    9,5              Length of compared field
        CLCL  4,8              Compare
        BNE   address          Branch if not equal
```

CLCL compares logically from left to right beginning with the address in the two even registers. As long as the compared bytes are equal, the operation deducts 1 from the lengths in the two odd registers, and adds 1 to the addresses in the two even registers. Unequal compared bytes cause the operation to terminate with the addresses of the unequal bytes in the even registers, and the appropriate condition code set for high or low.

If the two compared fields are of unequal length, you may insert any padding character in bits 0–7 of the register that contains the length of operand-2 (in the example, register-9). Typical padding characters are X'40' and X'00'. The operation uses the padding character for the remaining right-most bytes of the shorter field.

DEBUGGING TIPS

The instructions introduced in this chapter provide an additional dimension of error possibilities:

- Operand-2 of CVD and CVB must be a doubleword.
- For many operations, the selection of the correct instruction is critical. Consider the following similar-looking instructions that assemble with no error but may produce unexpected results:

```
LR    7,4    Loads contents of register-4 into register-7.
L     7,4    Loads contents of storage locations 4, 5, 6, 7 into register-7.
LH    7,4    Loads contents of storage locations 4 and 5 into register-7.
LA    7,4    Loads the displacement value 4 into register-7.
```

- For binary multiplication (M and MR), operand-1 must designate an even register of an even-odd pair. The multiplicand is in the odd register, and the operation develops the product in the even-odd pair.
- For binary division (D and DR), operand-1 must designate an even register of an even-odd pair containing the dividend. The operation develops the remainder in the even register and the quotient in the odd register.
- Binary division causes more problems than multiplication because the even register should be initialized with the same sign as the odd one.
- Binary calculations may unexpectedly generate a large value that exceeds the capacity of one register.

PROBLEMS

9-1. Add the following as 5-bit binary numbers:

$$
\begin{array}{ccccc}
6 & 9 & 8 & 7 & -9 \\
+5 & +4 & -5 & +(-4) & -8 \\
\hline
11 & 13 & 3 & 3 & -17
\end{array}
$$

9-2. Explain halfword, fullword, and doubleword alignment, and the significance of alignment on the 360 and the 370.

9-3. Given the following declaratives, explain concisely what each of the following unrelated operations does. Check for possible coding errors.

```
BINA   DC   F'285'
BINB   DC   F'394'
```

```
                        BINC  DS  D
(a) L      6,BINA      (e) LA   6,BINA      (i) MVC   BINA,BINB
(b) CVB    6,=P'500'   (f) LM   6,7,BINA    (j) CVD   6,BINC
(c) LR     9,5         (g) LH   8,=H'25'    (k) ST    12,BINB
(d) LA     12,5000     (h) ZAP  12,=P'5'    (l) LH    8,BINA
```

9-4. Use the same declaratives as in the previous problem to explain the following unrelated problems. Check for coding errors.

```
(a) SH    8,=H'9'      (e) C    9,BINB      (i) MH    8,=H'9'
(b) S     8,BINA       (f) SH   8,BINB      (j) MR    8,9
(c) SR    8,9          (g) S    8,=F'9'     (k) SRA   8,9
(d) CR    8,9          (h) M    8,BINA      (l) SLDA  8,9
```

9-5. Revise Problem 5-5 (Multiply Packed) to perform binary multiplication. Use the same constants and store the final product in decimal format in PROD.

9-6. Explain the effect of the following related operations. BINA refers to 9-3.

```
(a) SR   4,4           (b) ACCUM  DS PL3        (c) L    5,BINA
    L    5,=F'15'          LA 6,ACCUM               SLA  5,2
    MR   4,5              AP 0(3,6),0(3,6)         ST   5,BINA
```

9-7. Follow the same requirements as for Problems 9-3 and 9-4:

```
(a) D  8,BINA          (b) DR  8,9          (c)  DR  8,8
```

9-8. Revise Problem 5-6 (Divide Packed) to perform binary division. Use the same constants and store the final quotient in binary format in QUOT.

9-9. Code the following routine. There are two binary values: BINAM contains a value to be raised to a power n, called EXPON. Perform repetitious binary multiplying of BINAM n times to compute $BINAM^n$. Program for a double precision result, and print the final answer. Both BINAM and EXPON may be defined as DC H with constant values.

10

EXPLICIT USE OF BASE REGISTERS

Many previous examples contain instructions in which the length explicitly overrides the implicit length of the field, such as:

```
MVC  P+30(2),=C'**'
```

In a similar fashion *a base register may explicitly override the assigned base register.* This chapter uses base registers explicitly to permit the use of such operations as EDMK and COMRG, and to modify an address for table look-up. You may use a base register explicitly in any operand that references storage, with a reference to a base register (B1 or B2). Since a base register contains the address of an area of storage, you may override the program's normal base register with another register containing an address of some other area.

EXPLICIT BASE/DISPLACEMENT ADDRESSING FOR MVC

Figure 10-1 depicts the explicit use of register-8 to override the implicit base register-4. The figure shows three different ways to move a field named ASTERS to the print area. Assume that the BALR instruction has initialized register-4 with X'8002'. Note also that although this example illustrates explicit base addressing with MVC, you may use this feature with any instruction that references main storage.

ASSGN1 shows a conventional move operation, with both operands subject implicitly to base register-4. The assembled object code for operand-1 (PRINT+60), is 4056, or base register-4, displacement X'056'. The effective address is therefore:

Contents of base register-4	X'8002'
Displacement	X'0056'
Effective address	X'8058'

ASSGN2 explicitly uses a base register. The address of PRINT+60 (X'3058') is loaded into register-8. MVC explicitly uses the contents of register-8. Since the format for MVC is D1(L,B1),D2(B2), you can code the first operand explicitly with zero displacement, a length of 2, and base register-8, or 0(2,8). The assembled object code for operand-1 is 8000, or base register-8, displacement zero. The effective address is therefore:

Base register-8	X'8058'
Displacement	X'0000'
Effective address	X'8058'

ASSGN3 illustrates the use of both explicit base addressing and displacement. LA loads the address of PRINT into register-8. Since the MVC is to reference PRINT+60, you need a displacement of 60, coded in operand-1 as 60(2,8). The assembled object code for operand-1 is 803C, or base register-8 plus displacement 03C. The effective address is therefore:

Base register-8	X'801C'
Displacement	X'003C'
Effective address	X'8058'

Although these examples use only MVC, you can use explicit base addressing for any operand that references main storage.

EXPLICIT BASE ADDRESSING FOR PACKED INSTRUCTIONS

Instructions such as MVC and CLC provide an explicit length only for operand-1. The packed instructions however permit lengths for *both* operands, as

```
D1(L1,B1),D2(L2,B2)
```

```
LOC    OBJECT CODE      ADDR1 ADDR2  STMT     SOURCE STATEMENT

008000                                  3 PROG10    START X'8000'
008000 0540                             4          BALR  4,0
                              08002     5          USING *,4


                                        7 *        -----------------------
                                        8 *        IMPLICIT BASE REGISTER:
                                        9 *        -----------------------
008002 D201 4056 409F 08058 080A1      10 ASSGN1   MVC   PRINT+60(2),ASTERS


                                       12 *        -----------------------
                                       13 *        EXPLICIT BASE REGISTER:
                                       14 *        -----------------------
008008 4180 4056            08058      15 ASSGN2   LA    8,PRINT+60
00800C D201 8000 409F 00000 080A1      16          MVC   0(2,8),ASTERS


                                       18 *        ----------------------------
                                       19 *        EXPLICIT BASE/DISPLACEMENT:
                                       20 *        ----------------------------
008012 4180 401A            0801C      21 ASSGN3   LA    8,PRINT
008016 D201 803C 409F 0003C 080A1      22          MVC   60(2,8),ASTERS
                                       23 *        .
                                       24 *        .
                                       25 *        .
00801C 4040404040404040               26 PRINT    DC    CL133' '
0080A1 5C5C                           27 ASTERS   DC    C'**'

                              08000    29          END   PROG10
```

FIGURE 10-1 Base register assignment and explicit use of a base register.

Consider a program that is to convert kilograms into pounds. The conversion is: 1 kg = 2.2 pounds. The following are the required declaratives:

```
KGS         DS     PL3'12.53'
CONVRN      DC     PL2'2.2'
POUNDS      DS     PL5
```

As a first example, let's initialize three registers with the address of each declarative, and use explicit base addressing to perform the conversion:

```
LA    6,KGS          Address of KGS
LA    7,CONVRN       Address of conversion
LA    8,POUNDS       Address of pounds
ZAP   0(5,8),0(3,6)  Move KGS to POUNDS
MP    0(5,8),0(2,7)  Mult by CONVRN:  27.566
SRP   0(5,8),63,5    Shift and round:  27.57
```

Since the three declaratives are defined consecutively beginning with KGS, you could also code the program using one base register and an explicit displacement to reference each declarative, as follows:

```
LA      6,KGS               Address of KGS
ZAP     5(5,6),0(3,6)       Move KGS to POUNDS
MP      5(5,6),3(2,6)       Mult by CONVRN:   27.566
SRP     5(5,6),63,5         Shift and round:  27.57
```

As another example, assume that a program has stored a last name and one or two initials in the following fields:

```
SURNAMPR    DS      CL20        Surname such as BROWN
INITPR      DS      CL2         Initials such as JL
```

The program is to move the initials with a comma and periods immediately to the right of the surname, as follows:

BROWN, J.L.

The routine in Figure 10-2 provides the logic. The first step is to scan the surname from left to right for a blank which denotes the end of the name. At this point, the routine inserts a comma, and then moves the first initial two positions to the right followed by a period, as BROWN, J. If the second initial is nonblank, the routine moves the initial and another period immediately to the right, as BROWN, J.L.

The TRT instruction discussed later in this chapter could replace the instructions that scan the surname for a blank.

OPERATIONS EXPLICITLY USING BASE REGISTERS

Some instructions require explicit use of base registers. These include the Assembler instructions EDMK and the IBM macros COMRG and TIME. The following sections examine these operations in detail.

EDIT AND MARK—EDMK. On printed checks and customer bills, it is usually desirable to print a dollar sign to the immediate left of the first significant digit of the amount. This feature is a form of check protection to prevent anyone from forging a leading digit. If a field provides for seven digits, and only five are significant, the resulting edited field could appear as $bbb123.45. You may use EDMK to print the amount as $123.45.

```
003002                                      7 SURNAMPR DS    CL30              SURNAME
003020 40                                   8          DC    CL01' '           BLANK
003021                                      9 INITPR   DS    CL02              INITIALS

003023 00
003024 4160 3000              03002        11          LA    6,SURNAMPR        ADDRESS OF NAME
003028 9540 6000     00000               12 M10       CLI   0(6),C' '         SCAN NAME
00302C 4780 3036              03038        13          BE    M20                   FOR BLANK
003030 4A60 30B6              030B8        14          AH    6,=H'1'
003034 47F0 3026              03028        15          B     M10
                             03038        16 M20       EQU   *
003038 926B 6000     00000               17          MVI   0(6),C','         INSERT COMMA
00303C D200 6002 301F 00002 03021        18          MVC   2(1,6),INITPR     INSERT 1ST INITIAL
003042 924B 6003     00003               19          MVI   3(6),C'.'         INSERT 1ST PERIOD
003046 9540 3020              03022        20          CLI   INITPR+1,C' '     2ND INITIAL BLANK?
00304A 4780 3056              03058        21          BE    M30               YES - EXIT
00304E D200 6004 3020 00004 03022        22          MVC   4(1,6),INITPR+1   NO  - INSERT 2ND
003054 924B 6005     00005               23          MVI   5(6),C'.'         INITIAL & PERIOD
                             03058        24 M30       EQU   *
```

FIGURE 10-2 Adjusting name and initials.

NAME	*OPERATION*	*OPERAND*
(symbol)	EDMK	S1,S2 or D1(L1,B1),D2(B2)

EDMK is identical to ED except that it inserts into *register-1 the address of the first significant digit* in the edited field. You may then decrement register-1 by one since the dollar sign must be printed one position to the left. Then use register-1 as an explicit base register to move a dollar sign into the required print position.

Note: If the significance start character (X'21') forces a zero digit to be printed, EDMK does not store the address in register-1. Therefore, you should ensure against this possibility by initially loading into register-1 the address of the significance starter plus one. After the EDMK operation, deduct one from register-1; if the significance starter forced the first printed digit, then register-1 will contain the address of the significance starter, where the dollar sign should appear.

The example in Figure 10-3 moves the editword into AMTPR. The address of the X'21' is therefore at AMTPR+3. The next instruction loads the address of AMTPR+4 into register-1. After execution of the EDMK instruction, register-1 contains the address of the first significant digit at AMTPR+3. Decrementing register-1 results in the address of AMTPR+2 where an MVI instruction inserts a dollar sign. The final edited value is $3.52.

```
                                        -------------------------
                                        EDMK  EDIT & MARK
                                        -------------------------
003058 4110 307C                0307E  32      LA    1,AMTPR+4    LOAD ADDRESS OF SIGNIFICANT
                                29 *                               START CHARACTER +1
                                30 *                               *
                                31 *
                                33      MVC   AMTPR,EDWORD   |40|20|20|21|4B|20|20|
00305C D206 3078 306E 0307A 03070  34  EDMK  AMTPR,AMOUNT1  |40|40|40|F3|4B|F5|F2|
003062 DF06 3078 3075 0307A 03077  35  SH    1,=H'1'        |40|40|40|4B|4B|F5|F2|
003068 4B10 30B6            030B8  36  MVI   0(1),C'$'      DECREMENT REG1 (OR BCTR 1,0)
00306C 925B 1000           00000                           |40|40|5B|F3|4B|F5|F2|
                                37 *                         $   3  .  5   2
                                38 *
                                39 *
003070 402020214B2020      40 EDWORD  DC   X'402020214B2020'
003077 00352C              41 AMOUNT1 DC   P'003.52'        WILL EDIT AS $3.52
00307A                     42 AMTPR   DS   ZL7
```

FIGURE 10-3 Sample edit and mark operation.

THE COMRG AND TIME MACROS. The communication region is a storage area in the supervisor. The first eight bytes contain the date as initialized each day by the computer operator. The format for the date, including the slashes, is: dd/mm/yy or mm/dd/yy. The address of the communication region varies by operating system and version, but under DOS you can use COMRG to ask the supervisor for the address. *The supervisor places the address of the communications region in register-1.* You then can use register-1 explicitly to address the communications region:

```
DATE        DS      CL8'DD/MM/YY'   Area to store date
            COMRG                   Locate address of comm'n region
            MVC     DATE,0(1)       Move date from comm'n region
```

The OS macro is called TIME. It returns the date in packed format in register-1, as /00/YY/DD/DC/. The day (D) is Julian, the day of the year. C is a sign digit. Also, the time is stored in register-0.

```
FULLWD      DS      F               Fullword area
DATE        DS      CL7             Area for date 00YYDDD
            TIME    DEC             OS TIME macro, packs date in reg-
                                    ister-1
            ST      1,FULLWD        Store packed date in FULLWD
            UNPK    DATE,FULLWD     Unpack date in DATE
```

Note: The communications region contains other fields that may be of interest to the advanced programmer. See the IBM Supervisor manual for your installation. The 370 also contains a different area called "input/output communications area."

SHIFT AND ROUND PACKED—SRP. The SRP instruction permits rounding, and shifting of packed digits either left or right. SRP can therefore replace MVO and AP in decimal multiply and divide, and replace MP where used to shift the dividend to the left.

NAME	*OPERATION*	*OPERAND*
(symbol)	SRP	S1,S2 or D1(L,B1),D2(B2),I3

Although SS-format, SRP has three operands. Operand-1 denotes the field containing packed data to be shifted and optionally rounded. Operand-2 is a base/displacement reference that indicates the number of digits to be shifted. The maximum shift is 31 digits. Operand-3 provides the value 0–9 to be used for rounding: a left shift will normally have a 0 to indicate no rounding, and a right shift usually rounds with 5. SRP sets the condition code for zero, minus, and plus.

LEFT SHIFT. A *positive* value as the shift factor indicates a left shift. For example, +2 means shift left two digits (digits, not bytes). You may load the shift factor in a register, and then code SRP to reference the register explicitly, as shown by Figure 10-4. More conveniently, code the shift factor as an explicit displacement using base register-0 (that is, no base register), as shown by SHIFL2B and SHIFL2C.

You may use any one of these three examples to shift two digits left. Because shifting off a significant digit (1–9) left sets the decimal overflow condition but does not cause termination, you can use Branch Overflow to test if a significant digit was lost.

```
                                    47  *                                    HEX REPRESENTATION:
003081 001234567C                   48  AMOUNT  DC    PL5'1234567'              00 12 34 56 7C

                                    50  *             SHIFT LEFT 2 DIGITS:      RESULT IN AMOUNT:
                                    51  *             -------------------       -----------------
003086 48E0 30B8            030BA   52  SHIFL2A LH    14,=H'2'
00308A F040 307F E000 03081 00000   53          SRP   AMOUNT,0(14),0            12 34 56 70 0C

003090 F040 307F 0002 03081 00002   55  SHIFL2B SRP   AMOUNT,2(0),0            12 34 56 70 0C

003096 F040 307F 0002 03081 00002   57  SHIFL2C SRP   AMOUNT,2,0               12 34 56 70 0C

                                    59  *             SHIFT RIGHT 2 DIGITS (AND ROUND):
                                    60  *             --------------------------------
00309C 48E0 30BA            030BC   61  SHIFR2A LH    14,=H'-2'
0030A0 F045 307F E000 03081 00000   62          SRP   AMOUNT,0(14),5           00 00 12 34 6C

0030A6 F045 307F 003E 03081 0003E   64  SHIFR2B SRP   AMOUNT,X'3E',5           00 00 12 34 6C

0030AC F045 307F 003E 03081 0003E   66  SHIFR2C SRP   AMOUNT,62,5              00 00 12 34 6C
```

FIGURE 10-4 Use of SRP—shift and round packed.

RIGHT SHIFT. A *negative* shift factor indicates a right shift. As shown by the example in SHIFR2A, you may load the negative factor into a register and code SRP to reference the register explicitly. Although it is more convenient to code a shift factor as a displacement rather than load a base register, you cannot code such a right shift as SRP AMOUNT,−2,5. The reason is that the Assembler does not accept negative "displacements" [that is, −2(0) for D2(B2)]. You can solve the problem by representing −2 as a hexadecimal value. Now, SRP can shift up to a maximum of 31 decimal digits, which six bits can represent (five data bits plus a "sign" bit: 011111 = 31). The value 2 as six binary digits is 00 0010, and −2 in two's complement notation is 11 1110. The hex representation of this binary number is X'3E', which, as SHIFR2B in Figure 10-4 shows, you can use directly as a shift factor. Similarly, you may a shift factor as a decimal number; SHIFR2B uses decimal 62, which is equivalent to X'3E'.

You can use any one of these three examples to shift two digits right and round. Note that right shifts include: 1 = X'3F' or 63, 3 = X'3D' or 61, and 4 = X'3C' or 60, up to a shift of 31 decimal digits.

TABLES

Many programs require the use of tables (or arrays) in storage for the following purposes: (1) To provide additional information, such as the tax rate for an income tax table; and (2) To provide storage by categories as data is processed, such as accumulating sales according to inventory number.

A simple example of a table is one that stores the numeric and the alphabetic month. The numeric month from an input record is used to locate the alphabetic month in the table, used to print on the report heading. In tabular form, the table appears as:

```
01JANUARY
02FEBRUARY
.
.
.
12DECEMBER
```

TERMINOLOGY.   In the preceding example, the numeric month on the input record used to search through the table is called the *search argument.* Each entry in the table in storage consists of a *table argument* (the numeric month against which the search argument is compared), and a *function* (the alphabetic month, which is the item for which you are searching). The function may contain more than one field. Each table argument in the table is the same length and format, and each function is the same length and format. The search argument is the same length and format (such as character or packed) as the table argument. Further, the table arguments normally are defined in an ascending sequence.

TYPES OF TABLES.   There are two common types of tables used in business programming. The preceding table of months consists of discrete entries in which the table argument must exactly equal the search argument. Another example of this type could be an inventory table containing stock numbers as arguments and stock prices as functions. Also, a second field in the function could be used to accumulate total stock issues by stock number. The stock numbers in the table are *sequential* but not necessarily *consecutive,* because not all stock numbers are used. If the search argument does not equal one of the table arguments, then a possible error condition exists. The table could appear as:

STOCK NUMBER (TABLE ARGUMENT)	PRICE (FUNCTION)
121	5.25
135	3.10
137	4.00 etc . . .

The second common type of table consists of table arguments that provide ranges or segments, such as the sequential steps of taxable income in an income tax table. In this case, the search argument will fall *within* one of the segments. The function is the tax rate for the segment. The table could appear in the following simplified form:

TAXABLE INCOME (TABLE ARGUMENT)	TAX RATE (FUNCTION)
6,000.00	8.0 %
8,000.00	10.0 %
10,000.00 etc . . .	12.0 % etc . . .

In the table, all taxable income up to $6,000 is taxed at 8.0%, and taxable income from $6,000.01 through $8,000 is at 10%.

You may define and store tables one of two ways:

1. The table arguments and functions are defined by DCs as constants. This method is useful when the arguments and functions do not change very often.

2. The area for the table is defined, but the contents of the table, the argument and function, are read sequentially as data at the start of the program and stored in the table. This method is useful when the arguments or functions are subject to frequent change. This method permits changes to the table without reassembling the program.

TABLE LOOK-UP.   A table search requires repetitive processing. You may initialize a search by loading the address of the table into a register, which the program uses explicitly as a base register. The search argument is compared against the first table argument. To compare against successive table arguments, the address in the register is incremented by the length of the argument/function entries in the table. When you compare the search argument to a table argument, there are three possibilities:

1. *The Search Argument Is Equal.* In this case the required function has been found, and the search is terminated.

2. *The Search Argument Is High.* Continue the search by examining the next entry in the table.

3. *The Search Argument Is Low.* The action depends on the type of table. If the table contains *segments* such as a tax table, then the required function has been found; the tax rate is in this step. If, however, the

table contains *discrete entries* (such as nonconsecutive inventory stock numbers), then the required table argument does not exist. This latter condition is a common situation that must be checked for in this type of table.

TERMINATION OF THE LOOP. Be sure that the search can be terminated. If no provision is made to end the loop, then the program may compare a very high search argument against all the entries in the table and against the area following the table. Several means may force termination:

1. Assign the last table argument with *the highest possible value,* such as packed nines for packed fields, and hex Fs for character or hex fields. Because the search argument cannot exceed this value, there will always occur a branch on equal (found), or low (found or nonexistent argument depending on the type of table). Figure 10-5 gives an example.

2. If you know the *number of entries* in the table, code the program to count each time it compares to an entry. When the count exceeds the number of entries, the search is terminated. Figure 10-7 gives an example.

3. If you know the *address of the last table argument,* compare the address being modified against this address. If the modified address exceeds the address of the last argument, then the table argument does not exist. Figure 10-8 gives an example.

4. If you know the *value of the highest table argument,* compare the value of the search argument to this value. If the value of the search argument exceeds the known value, then the table argument does not exist, and the search does not have to be performed.

TABLE LOOK-UP WITH HIGH ARGUMENT. Figure 10-5 provides the coding for the table look-up of the numeric and alphabetic month discussed earlier, explained as follows:

- The table consists of a 2-character numeric month and a 9-character alphabetic month. (The longest month, September, is nine characters.) The last table argument contains hex Fs.
- Initialization: The address of the table, MONTAB (at location X'300C'), is loaded into register-8, to be used explicitly as a base register. (*Note:* LA loads the address of the table, not its contents.)
- At C10LOOP, operand-2 of the CLC has the form D2(B2), and the coding 0(8) references base register-8 and zero displacement, giving the address X'300C'. The CLC compares the 2-character search argument, MONIN, against the first two bytes of the table, 01 at X'300C'.

- If the condition is equal, the month is found, and the program branches to C20EQUAL.
- If the condition is low, the month is not in the table, and the program branches to an error routine. This error could occur if the search argument invalidly contained a value either less than 01 or greater than 12. All search arguments will be lower than hex Fs at the end of the table, so a low condition is always an error.
- If the condition is high, it is necessary to examine the next table argument. Therefore, increment base register-8 by 11, the length of each entry. The base register now contains X'3017, where table argument 02 resides. The program then branches back to C10LOOP which compares the search argument against table argument 02.
- At C20EQUAL, the found function, the alphabetic month, is moved to the print area. Operand-1 indicates a move of nine bytes. Operand-2 references base register-8 which contains the address of the found table argument. The displacement is two bytes because the function is two bytes from the first position of the table argument (the address in register-8).

```
LOC    OBJECT CODE        ADDR1 ADDR2  STMT   SOURCE STATEMENT

00300C F0F1D1C1D5E4C1D9               10 MONTAB  DC    C'01JANUARY  '      TABLE OF NUMERIC &
003017 F0F2C6C5C2D9E4C1               11         DC    C'02FEBRUARY '      *    ALPHA MONTHS
003022 F0F3D4C1D9C3C840               12         DC    C'03MARCH    '      *
00302D F0F4C1D7D9C9D340               13         DC    C'04APRIL    '      *
003038 F0F5D4C1E8404040               14         DC    C'05MAY      '      *
003043 F0F6D1E4D5C54040               15         DC    C'06JUNE     '      *
00304E F0F7D1E4D3E84040               16         DC    C'07JULY     '      *
003059 F0F8C1E4C7E4E2E3               17         DC    C'08AUGUST   '      *
003064 F0F9E2C5D7E3C5D4               18         DC    C'09SEPTEMBER'      *
00306F F1F0D6C3E3D6C2C5               19         DC    C'10OCTOBER  '      *
00307A F1F1D5D6E5C5D4C2               20         DC    C'11NOVEMBER '      *
003085 F1F2C4C5C3C5D4C2               21         DC    C'12DECEMBER '      *
003090 FFFF                           22         DC    X'FFFF'            *    END OF TABLE

003092                                24 MONIN   DS    CL2                SEARCH ARGUMENT
003094 4040404040404040               25 MONOUT  DC    CL9' '             PRINT AREA
                                      26 *       .
                                      27 *       .
00309D 00
00309E 4180 400A           0300C     28         LA    8,MONTAB           INIT ADDR OF TABLE

0030A2 D501 4090 8000 03092 00000     30 C10LOOP CLC   MONIN,0(8)         INPUT MON: TABLE MON?
0030A8 4780 40B6           030B8      31         BE    C20EQUAL           *   EQUAL - FOUND
0030AC 4740 50AE           040B0      32         BL    R10INV             *   LOW  - NOT IN TAB

0030B0 4A80 42E6           032E8      33         AH    8,=H'11'           INCR FOR NEXT ENTRY
0030B4 47F0 40A0           030A2      34         B     C10LOOP            *   IN THE TABLE

0030B8 D208 4092 8002 03094 00002     36 C20EQUAL MVC  MONOUT,2(8)        MOVE ALPHA MON TO PRINT
```

FIGURE 10-5 Table look-up on character data.

TABLE LOOK-UP ON PACKED DATA. A table may also contain arguments defined in packed format. Figure 10-6 provides the Assembler instructions for calculating the discount to customers based on quantity sold. For example, there is no discount on quantity ordered up to 20 units, 5% discount for orders between 21 and 50 units, 10% discount for orders between 51 and 100 units, and so forth. The maximum discount is 15% for quantities over 250, as indicated by nines in the last table argument.

In the comparison of quantity ordered to table quantity, an equal/low condition in this example means that the discount rate has been found, and the routine extracts the rate from the table. Further instructions would involve calculating discount amount by multiplying sales amount by discount rate.

```
0030BE  00020C000C                              40 DSCTAB    DC   P'00020',P'.000'
0030C3  00050C050C                              41           DC   P'00050',P'.050'
0030C8  00100C100C                              42           DC   P'00100',P'.100'
0030CD  00250C125C                              43           DC   P'00250',P'.125'
0030D2  99999C150C                              44           DC   P'99999',P'.150'

0030D7                                          46 QTYIN     DS   PL3          QTY SOLD
0030DA                                          47 DSCRATE   DS   PL2          DISCOUNT RATE

0030DC  4180 40BC                     030BE     49           LA   8,DSCTAB     INIT ADDR OF TABLE
0030E0  F922 40D5 8000 030D7 00000    50 D10          CP   QTYIN,0(3,8)  QTY SOLD : TABLE
0030E6  47D0 40F0           030F2     51           BNH  D20          * LOW/EQ - EXIT
0030EA  4A80 42E8           032EA     52           AH   8,=H'5'      * HIGH CONTINUE
0030EE  47F0 40DE           030E0     53           B    D10

0030F2  F811 40D8 8003 030DA 00003    55 D20          ZAP  DSCRATE,3(2,8) EXTRACT DISC RATE
```

FIGURE 10-6 Table look-up on packed data.

TABLE LOOK-UP USING A COUNT: BCT, BCTR, BXLE, BXH. This section examines two ways of performing a table search using the techniques for loop termination described earlier. The following instructions may be used to decrement a count and to test termination of a loop. The condition code is not changed.

NAME	*OPERATION*	*OPERAND*
(symbol)	BCT	R1,X2 or R1,D2(X2,B2)
	BCTR	R1,R2
	BXLE	R1,S2 or R1,R3,D2(B2)
	BXH	R1,S2 or R1,R3,D2(B2)

BRANCH ON COUNT—BCT AND BCTR. Before using these instructions, you normally load a count in a register, such as the number of entries in the table. The routine may then use Branch on Count in the loop to decrement the count by 1 and to check if the count has been reduced to zero. The rules are:

1. Operand-1 specifies any register, which contains a count.
2. Operand-2 references an address in storage if BCT, or a register containing an address if BCTR. On execution, the computer decrements the contents of the operand-1 register by 1. If the contents are not zero, the program branches to the operand-2 address. If the contents are zero, the operation continues with the next sequential instruction. Since the operation performs no other checking, you must ensure that the count is initialized with a positive, nonzero amount.
3. For BCTR, if operand-2 specifies register-0, 1 is decremented from the operand-1 register, but no test is made and no branch taken. This use of BCTR is a convenient way of decrementing by 1 the value in any register.

In the following three examples, assume that register-7 contains a positive value:

Example 1:   BCT   7,K50   decrement register-7 by 1, and if nonzero branch to address K50.

Example 2:   LA   9,K50

             BCTR   7,9   decrement register-7 by 1, and if nonzero, branch to the address in register-9 (K50).

Example 3:   BCTR   11,0   decrement register-11 by 1 and continue with the next instruction.

Figure 10-7 depicts a table search using two registers and BCT. The search argument is a 3-character field called JOBNO. The table, called JOBTABLE, contains 60 5-byte entries, a 3-character job number as the table argument, and a 2-byte packed rate as the function. The function when found is to be stored in a field called RATE. The example loads the number of entries in the table, 60, into a register. BCT is used to decrement this count. If the loop is performed 60 times, the count is reduced to zero, and the required argument is known to be not in the table. An advantage of this approach is that job numbers need not be in ascending sequence, so that the most commonly referenced job numbers could be first in the table.

If you have another register available, you could also improve the efficiency of the loop by replacing the BCT instruction with BCTR. RR-format instructions such as BCTR execute faster than other formats. Add one instruction at the start to initialize the address of K10LOOP:

```
              LA  10,K10LOOP
```

```
LOC    OBJECT CODE     STMT    SOURCE STATEMENT

0030F8                 60 JOBNO    DS    CL3             JOB NUMBER (SEARCH ARG'T)
0030FB                 61 RATE     DS    PL2             RATE FOR FOUND FUNC'N

0030FD FOFOF6585C      63 JOBTABLE DC    C'006',P'5.85'  *  JOB# 3 BYTES,
003102 FOF1F2715C      64          DC    C'012',P'7.15'  *    RATE 2 BYTES
003107 FOF1F5830C      65          DC    C'015',P'8.30'  *
00310C                 66          DS    57CL5           *  REST OF TABLE
                       67 *        .
                       68 *        .
                       69 *        .

003229 00
00322A 4160 40FB       71          LA    6,JOBTABLE      LOAD ADDR OF JOB TABLE
00322E 4190 003C       72          LA    9,60            LOAD NO. OF ENTRIES

003232 D502 40F6 6000  74 K10LOOP  CLC   JOBNO,0(6)      INPUT JOB# : TABLE JOB# ?
003238 4780 4246       75          BE    K20EQUAL        *  EQUAL - FOUND
00323C 4160 6005       76          LA    6,5(0,6)        INCREMENT FOR NEXT ENTRY
003240 4690 4230       77          BCT   9,K10LOOP       DECR REG 9. NOT ZERO, LOOP
003244 47F0 50AE       78          B     R10INV          *  ZERO, NOT IN TABLE.

003248 F811 40F9 6003  80 K20EQUAL ZAP   RATE,3(2,6)     STORE RATE FROM TABLE
```

FIGURE 10-7 Table look-up using a count and BCT operation.

and replace the BCT with BCTR as follows:

BCTR 9,10

In fact, if the LA immediately precedes K10LOOP, you could replace it with a BALR instruction:

BALR 10,0

that loads the address of the next instruction (K10LOOP) into register-10 and continues with the next instruction. Figure 10-8 shows the revised version, more efficient but perhaps less clear than the previous example.

```
00324E 4160 40FB       85          LA    6,JOBTABLE      LOAD ADDR OF JOB TABLE
003252 4190 003C       86          LA    9,60            LOAD NO. OF ENTRIES
003256 05A0            87          BALR  10,0            INIT'ZE ADDR OF LOOP

003258 D502 40F6 6000  89 K10LOOP2 CLC   JOBNO,0(6)      INPUT JOB# : TABLE JOB# ?
00325E 4780 426A       90          BE    K20EQU2         *  EQUAL - FOUND
003262 4160 6005       91          LA    6,5(0,6)        INCREMENT FOR NEXT ENTRY
003266 069A            92          BCTR  9,10            DECR REG 9. NOT ZERO, LOOP
003268 47F0 50AE       93          B     R10INV          *  ZERO, NOT IN TABLE.

00326C F811 40F9 6003  95 K20EQU2  ZAP   RATE,3(2,6)     STORE RATE FROM TABLE
```

FIGURE 10-8 Table look-up using a count and BCTR operation.

BRANCH ON INDEX LOW OR EQUAL—BXLE. This instruction requires the use of three registers, two of which are an even-odd pair. BXLE does not directly reference the odd-numbered register. Before executing the

BXLE be sure that all three registers are properly initialized. BXLE is an RS format instruction with three operands. The rules are:

1. Operand-1 specifies a register containing generally a count or an address.

2. Operand-2 normally denotes the even-numbered register of an even-odd pair such as 10 and 11. The even-numbered register contains a value used to increment or decrement the operand-1 register. All 31 bits are added in normal binary addition. The odd-numbered register, which is not directly referenced, contains the limit or address against which operand-1 is compared.

3. Operand-3 references a storage address, the branch point for low/equal conditions.

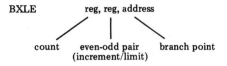

On execution, BXLE adds the operand-2 even register constant to the operand-1 register. Operand-1 is then compared to the unreferenced odd register. If the operand-1 contents are low or equal, the program branches to the address in operand-3. If the contents are high, the program continues with the next sequential instruction.

Note: If the register in operand-2 is odd rather than even, the comparison is made to the operand-2 odd register rather than to the next register. Therefore, the operand-2 register is both the increment (decrement), and the limit.

```
66  *       ------------------------------------
67  *       BXLE  BRANCH CN INDEX LOW OR EQUAL
68  *       ------------------------------------
69          LA    6,JOBTABLE          LOAD ADDRESS OF JOB TABLE
70          LA    8,5                 LOAD LENGTH OF EACH ENTRY
71          LA    9,JOBTABLE+59*5     LOAD ADDRESS OF LAST ENTRY

73  L10LOOP CLC   JOBNC,0(6)          INPUT JOB# : TABLE JOB# ?
74          BE    L20ECUAL            *    EQUAL - FOUND
75          BXLE  6,8,L10LOOP         INCR REG 6 BY 5, CCMP REG 6 : 9
76  *                                 *    LO/EQ? - BRANCH TO L10LOOP
77          B     R1CINV             *    HIGH? - NOT IN TABLE

79  L20EQUAL ZAP  RATE,3(2,6)         STORE RATE FROM TABLE
```

FIGURE 10-9 Table look-up using BXLE.

Figure 10-9 illustrates a table search using three registers and the BXLE instruction. The table, JOBTABLE, is the same one defined in Figure 10-7. This example loads the length of each entry (5) and the address of the last entry into the even-odd registers, 8 and 9. BXLE increments the address of base register-6 by the constant 5 in register-8. If the base register exceeds the address of the last entry, the program has stepped through the table without locating the required argument.

BRANCH ON INDEX HIGH—BXH. BXH is similar to BXLE except that whereas BXLE branches if not high (low or equal), BXH branches if high. BXH is used to search through tables from the high argument through the low argument, that is, a "reverse scan."

The preceding examples give some of the common methods of terminating a table search. The commonest and simplest method is to define the last table argument with a high value, such as hex Fs for character and nines for packed format. The methods using BCT and BXLE are efficient if enough registers are available. As a rule, use whatever method is efficient and clearly understood.

OTHER TABLE HANDLING ROUTINES

You may want to process a table for reasons other than a search for a function. For example, you may need to accumulate the contents of a table to determine the total and its mean average. Following are two other techniques used in table processing. Assume the definitions of two tables both containing valid packed data:

```
TABLE1      DC      50PL5'0'
TABLE2      DC      50PL6'0'
```

The following routine adds the contents of TABLE1 to TABLE2 entry-for-entry:

```
        LA      10,TABLE1           Initialize address
        LA      11,TABLE2              of tables
        LA      12,50               Init for 50 entries
LOOP1   AP      0(6,11),0(5,10)     Add entries
        AH      10,=H'5'            Increment for
        AH      11,=H'6'               next entries
        BCT     12,LOOP1            Loop 50 times
```

Now let's code a loop to clear TABLE1 to zeros:

```
        LA      10,TABLE1           Initialize address
        LA      12,50               Init for 50 entries
LOOP2   SP      0(5,10),0(5,10)     Clear an entry
        AH      10,=H'5'            Set for next entry
        BCT     12,LOOP2            Loop 50 times
```

Another common practice is to print the entire contents of a table by initializing its address and extracting each entry one at a time.

• *Problems 10-1, 10-2, and 10-3 should now be attempted.* •

DIRECT TABLE ADDRESSING

Table arguments are normally arranged sequentially, but are not necessarily consecutive. Consider a table composed of discrete arguments, such as job numbers or inventory stock numbers. If the table is *both* sequential and consecutive, such as 10, 11, 12, . . . , then you do not require table arguments or a table look-up. To locate the required function, you can by *direct table addressing* calculate its *relative position* in the table. For example, the function for stock item 0010 would be the tenth entry in the table. Direct table addressing is an extremely efficient way of locating functions, because no repetitive looping and comparing are required.

Refer to the table of numeric and alphabetic months in Figure 10-5. The table contains arguments of numeric months from 01 through 12 that are both sequential and consecutive. Figure 10-10 omits the arguments and finds the function by direct table addressing. Assume that the search argument, MONIN, contains 04 for April. The month is tested and found valid. It is converted into a register and decremented by 1, giving 3.

The following are the program steps:

```
Numeric value for April        04
Deduct 1                       -1
                               --
                               03
Multiply by length of entries  x9
                               --
Relative location of April     27, or X'001B'
Add address of table               X'4000'
                                   ----
Actual location of April           X'401B'
```

Note: Ensure that the search argument is valid. For example, if the search argument is incorrectly entered as 14, then the program will calculate an address that is outside the bounds of the table.

CALCULATION OF THE DIRECT ADDRESS.   Assume the following:

A(F)   = the address of the required function

A(T)   = the address of the table

SA   = the value of the search argument

L   = the length of each function

N   = the value of the table argument representing the first, or lowest, function in the table. SA $\geq$ N.

The function is located by the formula:

$$A(F) = A(T) + [(SA-N)\times L]$$

In the example program in Figure 10-10, A(T) = X'4000', L = 9, and N = 01 (for January). Given search arguments of respectively 01, 02, and 12, the calculation of A(F) is as follows:

SA: Calculation of A(F):
01   X'4000' + [(01−1) × 9] = X'4000' (January)
02   X'4000' + [(02−1) × 9] = X'4009' (February)
12   X'4000' + [(12−1) × 9] = X'4063' (December)

Check the logic of the formula and the calculations of A(F) against the table in Figure 10-10.

```
004000 D1C1C5E4C1D9E840   88 MONTABLE DC    C'JANUARY  '   TABLE OF 12 9-CHARACTER
004009 C6C5C2D9E4C1D9E8   89          DC    C'FEBRUARY '   *    ALPHABETIC MONTHS
004012 D4C1D9C3C8404040   90          DC    C'MARCH    '   *
00401B C1D7D9C9D3404040   91          DC    C'APRIL    '   *
004024 D4C1E8404040404C40 92          DC    C'MAY      '   *
00402D D1E4D5C540404040   93          DC    C'JUNE     '   *
004036 D1E4D3E840404040   94          DC    C'JULY     '   *
00403F C1E4C7E4E2E34040   95          DC    C'AUGUST   '   *
004048 E2C5D7E3C5D4C2C5   96          DC    C'SEPTEMBER'   *
004051 D6C3E3D6C2C5D940   97          DC    C'OCTOBER  '   *
00405A D5D6E5C5D4C2C5D9   98          DC    C'NOVEMBER '   *
004063 C4C5C3C5D4C2C5D9   99          DC    C'DECEMBER '   *

00406C 00004000          101 ADDRTAB  DC    A(MONTABLE)    ADDRESS OF TABLE
004070                    102 DBLEWORD DS    D              DOUBLE WORD FOR SEARCH ARG
                          103 *        .
                          104 *        .
004078 F271 506E 4C90     105          PACK  DBLEWORD,MONIN  PACK MONTH IN DOUBLE WORD
00407E F970 506E 50AA     106          CP    DBLEWORD,=P'1'  IS MONTH < 1 ?
0C40E4 4740 50A4          107          BL    R50LOW           YES - ERROR

004088 F971 506E 50A6     109          CP    DBLEWORD,=P'12' IS MONTH > 12 ?
C0408E 4720 50A4          110          BH    R60HIGH          YES - ERROR

004092 4F7C 506E          112          CVB   7,DBLEWORD     CONVERT MONTH TO BINARY
C04096 0670               113          BCTR  7,0            DECREMENT MONTH BY 1
0040C8 4C70 50A8          114          MH    7,=H'9'        MULTIPLY MONTH BY LENGTH
00409C 5A70 506A          115          A     7,ADCRTAB      ADD TABLE ADDRESS
0C40A0 D2C8 40F6 7C00     116          MVC   PRINT+100(9),0(7)  MOVE ALPHABETIC MONTH
```

FIGURE 10-10 Direct table addressing.

SORTING DATA IN STORAGE

Computer manufacturers supply package "utility" programs for such operations as sorting. These programs are used to sort disk and tape *records* according to some user-specified sequence. Records are read by the sort program into main storage, sorted into the new sequence, and written on another disk or tape. More records are read, sorted, and eventually merged with the previously sorted records on disk or tape. Finally, the entire file is processed and the file is fully sorted.

Occasionally a program must be written to sort *data*. This problem should not be confused with the sorting of *records* on disk or tape. To sort data you must write your own routine. Data to be sorted typically is in the form of a table. The table is arranged in sequence of the argument; often it is to be rearranged in sequence of the function.

This section includes two program examples that both sort the same data. The first routine is simpler whereas the second routine is more efficient. Both programs sort a table of five five-character descriptions, and on completion produce a hex dump of the table. (The programs use the DOS PDUMP macro; an OS user would use SNAP as described in Chapter 16.)

You could improve these sorts by generalizing them for entries of any length and any number of entries. One way would be to use the EX instruction to permit modifying the lengths for the MVC and CLC.

EXAMPLE I—SIMPLE SORT. The program in Figure 10-11 compares successively entry-1 to entry-2, entry-2 to entry-3, entry-3 to entry-4, and entry-4 to entry-5, exchanging entries where the first is higher than the second. The routine repeats this process until the entries are all in ascending sequence.

```
entry-1
        )
entry-2        |
        )      |
entry-3        |  exchange if first > second
        )      |
entry-4        |
        )
entry-5
```

How the routine knows when the entries are in sequence is by means of an indicator named XCHANGE in this example. Each initialization of the table sets XCHANGED to 0, and whenever the routine exchanges entries it sets XCHANGED to 1. On completion of a pass through the table, the

```
STMT    SOURCE STATEMENT

    3               PRINT ON,NOGEN,NODATA

    5 SORT1         START
    6               BALR   10,0                    INITIALIZE
    7               USING  *,10
    8               BAL    4,S10SORT
    9               PDUMP  TABLE,SAVENT+5
   15               EOJ                            TERMINATE

   19 S10SORT       MVI    XCHANGED,C'0'           CLEAR INDICATOR
   20               LA     6,TABLE                 INIT ADDRESS OF TABLE
   21 S20           EQU    *
   22               C      6,=A(TABLE+4*LEN)       END OF TABLE?
   23               BE     S40                       YES - CHECK IF DONE
   24               CLC    0(LEN,6),LEN(6)         COMPARE ADJACENT ENTRIES
   25               BNH    S30                       EQUAL/LOW- BYPASS
   26               MVC    SAVENT,0(6)               HIGH - EXCHANGE
   27               MVC    0(LEN,6),LEN(6)                   ENTRIES
   28               MVC    LEN(LEN,6),SAVENT
   29               MVI    XCHANGED,C'1'             SET INDICATOR
   30 S30           EQU    *
   31               LA     6,LEN(0,6)              INCREMENT ADDRESS
   32               B      S20                     REPEAT
   33 S40           EQU    *
   34               CLI    XCHANGED,C'1'           ANY EXCHANGED?
   35               BE     S10SORT                   YES - REPEAT
   36               BR     4                         NO -- RETURN

   38 *                    ---------------------
   39 *                    D E C L A R A T I V E S
   40 *                    ---------------------
   41 LEN           EQU    5                       ENTRY LENGTH
   42 TABLE         DC     C'SORT '
   43               DC     C'TABLE'
   44               DC     C'STACK'
   45               DC     C'LIST '
   46               DC     C'DUMP '
   47 SAVENT        DS     CL5                     TEMP'Y SAVE
   48 XCHANGED      DC     C'0'                    EXCHANGE INDICATOR

   50               LTORG
   51                      =CL8'$$BPDUMP'
   52                      =A(TABLE,SAVENT+5)
   53                      =A(TABLE+4*LEN)
   54               END    SORT1
```

Dump of sorted table:-

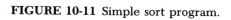

```
7CE0C0                                          C4E4D4C7  40 03C9E2 E340 E2D6 C9E340 E2 E3C1C3D2
7CE0E0    E3C1C2C3 C5 C3C9E2 E340 F0F0
               SAVENT              Start of TABLE
```

FIGURE 10-11 Simple sort program.

program tests if any entries were exchanged (does XCHANGED contain 1?). If there were any entries switched, the routine reinitializes the table address, sets XCHANGED to 0, and performs another pass through the table. If no entries were switched, the routine recognizes that the table is now in sequence, and dumps the table contents.

The advantage of this sort, other than its simplicity, is that it exits quickly if entries are already in or near sequence.

Some tables may have entries with equal values. If so, be sure that your routine exchanges only if the first entry is *higher* than the second. If you exchange on not low (high/equal), equal entries will exchange. Since XCHANGED will be set to 1, the sort will run endlessly.

EXAMPLE II—STRAIGHT INSERTION.   Let's now examine a more sophisticated and efficient technique known as *straight insertion*. In simple terms, here's how it operates. Assume an array containing the values D, C, B, and A, in that sequence. Select and save entry-2, C. Compare it to entry-1, D. Since C is lower, move D to entry-2 and move the saved C to entry-1:

```
Entry-1    D    C    (first two entries
     -2    C    D    now in sequence)
     -3    B
     -4    A
```

Now select and save entry-3, B. Compare it to entry-2, D; since B is lower, move D to entry-3. Next compare the saved B to entry-1; since B is lower, move C to entry-2. Move the saved B to entry-1:

```
Entry-1    C    B    (first three
     -2    D    C    entries now
     -3    B    D    in sequence)
     -4    A
```

Now select and save entry-4, A. Compare it to entry-3, D; since A is lower, move D to entry-4. Next compare the saved A to entry-2, C; since A is lower, move C to entry-3. Compare the saved A to entry-1, B; since A is lower, move B to entry-2. Finally, move the saved A to entry-1:

```
Entry-1    B    A    (all four
     -2    C    B    entries
     -3    D    C    now in
     -4    A    D    sequence)
```

In effect, the straight insertion technique steps through the table only once, but always *backfills* preceding entries.

```
    3              PRINT  ON,NOGEN,NODATA

    5 SORT2        START
    6              BALR   10,0                      INITIALIZE
    7              USING  *,10
    8              BAL    4,S10SORT
    9              PDUMP  TABLE,SAVENT+5
   15              EOJ                              TERMINATE

   19 S10SCRT  LA     L,LEN(0)                      SET LENGTH OF ENTRY
   20          LA     J,TABLE                       INIT ADDRESS OF TABLE
   21 S20      EQU    *
   22          LR     I,J                           MOVE J TO I
   23          AR     J,L                           INCR J TO NEXT
   24          MVC    SAVENT,0(J)                   SAVE ENTRY(J)
   25 S30      ECU    *
   26          CLC    SAVENT,0(I)                   SAVE : ENTRY(I)?
   27          BNL    S4C                             NOT LOW -- BYPASS
   28          MVC    LEN(LEN,I),0(I)                 LCW -- MOVE ENTRY(I) TO NEXT
   29          SR     I,L                           DECREMENT I
   30          C      I,=A(TABLE-LEN)               BEFORE START TABLE?
   31          BNE    S30                             NO -- REPEAT
   32 S40      EQU    *
   33          MVC    LEN(LEN,I),SAVENT               YES - STCRE SAVE IN ENTRY
   34          C      J,=A(TABLE+LEN*4)             AT END OF TABLE?
   35          BNE    S20                             NC -- REPEAT
   36          BR     4                             RETURN

   38 *               ----------------------
   39 *               D E C L A R A T I V E S
   40 *               ----------------------
   41 J        EQU    6                            ADDR OF FORWARD REG
   42 I        EQU    7                            ADRR OF BACKWARD REG
   43 L        EQU    8                            REG WITH LENGTH
   44 LEN      EQU    5                            ENTRY LENGTH
   45 TABLE    DC     C'SORT TABLESTACKLIST DUMP '
   46 SAVENT   DS     CL5                          TEMP'Y SAVE

   48          LTORG
   49                 =CL8'$$BPDUMP'
   50                 =A(TABLE,SAVENT+5)
   51                 =A(TABLE-LEN)
   52                 =A(TABLE+LEN*4)
   53          END    SCRT2
```

Dump of sorted table:-

```
7CEOCO           07F4 C4E4 D4D740 D3 C9E2E340   E2D6D9E3 40 E2E3C1 C302 E3C1 C2D3C5 C4
7CEOEO   E4C4D74C 4CCCCCO0
```

Start of TABLE   SAVENT

FIGURE 10-12 Sort with straight insertion.

The program in Figure 10-12 depicts the use of straight insertion to sort the table of five 5-byte entries. In this example, the program *equates* the name J to register-6, I to register-7, and LEN to the length (5) of each entry. At the end of the sort, the program dumps the contents of the table.

There are many other sort routines available. However, many tables are not unduly large, and the instructions execute at electronic (not I/O) speed. Further, a sort written in Assembler rather than a high-level language is most likely to be extremely fast. For more on this topic, see Donald E. Knuth, *The Art of Computer Programming*, Vol. 3 (Addison Wesley). Also, the magazines *Byte* and *Creative Computing* often present new sort and search techniques.

BINARY SEARCH

For long tables that do not lend themselves to direct addressing, it is often more efficient to use a *binary search* rather than a regular sequential table look-up. The search uses an approach of successive halving. It starts at the midpoint of the table—if the search argument is higher than the mid entry, compare to the midpoint of the upper half of the table; if lower than the mid entry, compare to the midpoint of the lower half. The search continues in this fashion until the argument is found or determined as not in the table. The following routine uses the same table of job numbers as in Figure 10-7.

Note that COUNT initially contains a value of one more than the number of arguments in JOBTABLE (i.e., if JOBTABLE has 50 arguments, then COUNT contains 51). The routine initializes register-6 with 1 for the low entry-point, and loads COUNT in register-10 for the initial high entry-point. It uses these two values to calculate the midpoint (initially [1 + 51] ÷ 2 would give entry 26 as the middle). Since the length of each entry is five bytes, the routine multiplies this midpoint value by 5 to calculate a displacement, and adds the starting address of JOBTABLE (actually JOBTABLE-5) for the direct address of the midpoint. Use JOBTABLE as defined in Figure 10-7 with five arguments, and work through the binary search routine in Figure 10-13 to locate each of the five arguments.

SAMPLE PROGRAM: CALCULATE STOCK VALUE

The flowchart in Figure 10-14 and the program in Figure 10-15 illustrate the use of many features in the last two chapters. Basically, the program begins by loading entries from input records into a table. The input records contain record code (ST), stock number (four bytes), price (five bytes), and description (seven bytes). These fields load one after another into a table with the following definition:

COSTABLE   DC   10X'FFFFFFFF00000C40404040404040'

The table provides for up to ten entries for stock number, price, and description. Stock number moves into the first four bytes replacing the X'FFs, price packs into the next three bytes replacing X'00000C', and description moves into the next seven bytes replacing the X'40s.

Once the program has completed loading the stock table records, it then processes inventory stock records containing the following data:

Column	1–2	Record code (12)
	3–4	Branch number
	5–8	Stock number
	11–13	Quantity

The objective is to calculate the cost of inventory stock on hand for each Stock item in the file.

The program reads each input record and checks sequence on Branch/Stock number:

```
COUNT      DS    F                         NUMBER OF ENTRIES IN TABLE + 1
SEARCH     DS    CL3                       SEARCH ARGUMENT

           LA    6,1                       LOAD INITIAL LOW ENTRY
           L     10,COUNT                  LOAD INITIAL HIGH ENTRY
           LA    8,0                       CLEAR MID-POINT

C10LOOP    LR    9,6                       LOAD LOW ENTRY IN CALC'N REGISTER
           AR    9,10                      ADD HIGH ENTRY TO CALC'N REGISTER
           SRA   9,1                       MID = 1/2 SUM
           CR    8,9                       COMPARE NEW MID TO PREV. MID
           BE    R10ERR                    ERROR IF EQUAL - ENTRY NOT IN TABLE

           LR    8,9                       MID NEW MID INTO PREVIOUS
           LA    5,JOBTABLE-5              LOAD ADDR OF TAB MINUS ENTRY LENGTH
           MH    9,=H'5'                   DISPLACEMENT = MID X ENTRY LENGTH
           AR    5,9                       ADD DISPLACEMENT TO ADDRESS
           CLC   SEARCH,0(5)               COMPARE SEARCH TO TABLE
           BE    D10FOUND               *     EQUAL - FOUND
           BL    C20LOW                 *     LOW

           LR    6,8                    *     HIGH - LOAD MID INTO LOW
           B     C10LOOP

C20LOW     LR    10,8                   *     LOW  - LOAD MID INTO HIGH
           B     C10LOOP

D10FOUND   ...                           ROUTINE FOR FOUND CONDITION
R10ERR     ...                           ROUTINE FOR NOT FOUND

REGISTER USAGE:
           5     FOR CALCULATION OF THE TABLE ADDRESS.
           6     LOW ENTRY NUMBER FOR THE TABLE.  INITIALIZED TO 1.
           8     MID-POINT NUMBER FOR THE TABLE.
           9     FOR CALCULATION OF THE TABLE DISPLACEMENT.
           10    HIGH ENTRY NO. FOR TABLE.  INITIALIZED WITH NO. OF ENTRIES + 1
```

FIGURE 10-13 Binary search.

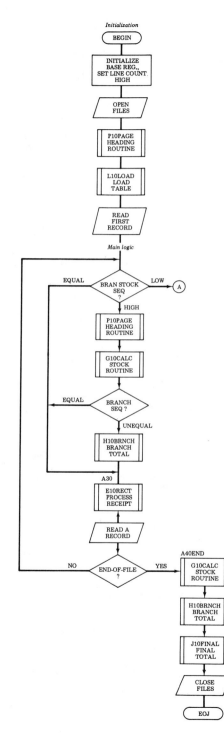

Initialization

BEGIN

INITIALIZE BASE REG., SET LINE COUNT HIGH

OPEN FILES

P10PAGE HEADING ROUTINE

L10LOAD LOAD TABLE

READ FIRST RECORD

Main logic

BRAN STOCK SEQ ?
  EQUAL
  LOW → A
  HIGH

P10PAGE HEADING ROUTINE

G10CALC STOCK ROUTINE

BRANCH SEQ ?
  EQUAL
  UNEQUAL

H10BRNCH BRANCH TOTAL

A30

E10RECT PROCESS RECEIPT

READ A RECORD

END-OF-FILE ?
  NO
  YES

A40END

G10CALC STOCK ROUTINE

H10BRNCH BRANCH TOTAL

J10FINAL FINAL TOTAL

CLOSE FILES

EOJ

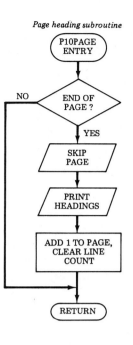

Page heading subroutine

P10PAGE ENTRY

END OF PAGE ?
  NO
  YES

SKIP PAGE

PRINT HEADINGS

ADD 1 TO PAGE, CLEAR LINE COUNT

RETURN

Table load subroutine

L10LOAD

(detail not shown)

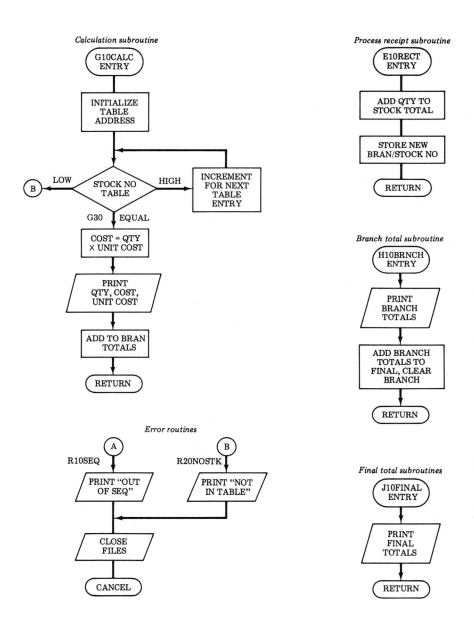

FIGURE 10-14 Flowchart to calculate stock values.

```
  4 *                    I N I T I A L I Z A T I O N
  5 *                    ---------------------------
  6 PROG10    START
  7           BALR    3,0                      INITIALIZE
  8           USING   *,3,4                    *  BASE REGS
  9           LA      4,2048                   *  3 & 4
 10           LA      4,2048(3,4)
 11           OPEN    FILEIN,PRTR
 20           LH      10,=H'55'                SET LINE COUNT PAST MAXIMUM
 21           BAL     9,P10PAGE                PRINT HEADING FOR PAGE 1
 22           BAL     9,L10LOAD                LOAD TABLE

 24           GET     FILEIN,STRECIN           READ 1ST STOCK RECORD
 30           MVC     PREVCTL,CTLIN            INIT'ZE SEQ

 32 *                    M A I N   L O G I C
 33 *                    -------------------
 34 A10LOOP   CLC     CTLIN,PREVCTL            NEW BRANCH/STOCK : PREVIOUS?
 35           BE      A30                      *    EQUAL - PROCESS RECEIPT
 36           BL      R10SEQ                   *    LOW   - OUT-OF-SEQUENCE
 37 *                                          *    HIGH  - NEW STOCK NO.
 38           BAL     9,P10PAGE                CHECK FOR PAGE OVERFLOW
 39           BAL     9,G10CALC                CALC. & PRINT UNIT COST

 41           CLC     BRANCHIN,PREVBR          NEW BRANCH = PREV BRANCH?
 42           BE      A30                      *    YES - PROCESS RECORD
 43           BAL     9,H10BRNCH               *    NO  - PRINT BRANCH TOTAL
 44 A30       BAL     9,E10RECT                PROCESS RECEIPT RECORD
 45           GET     FILEIN,STRECIN           READ NEXT RECORD
 51           B       A10LOOP                  LOOP

 53 *                    E N D - O F - F I L E
 54 *                    ---------------------
 55 A90END    BAL     9,G10CALC                EOF - CALC & PRINT UNIT COST
 56           BAL     9,H10BRNCH               *      PRINT BRANCH TOTAL
 57           BAL     9,J10FINAL               *      PRINT FINAL TOTAL
 58           CLOSE   FILEIN,PRTR
 67           EOJ                              TERMINATE

 71 *                    P R O C E S S    R E C E I P T    R O U T I N E
 72 *                    -----------------------------------------------
 73 E10RECT   PACK    QTYPK,QTYRECIN
 74           AP      QTYPKDW,QTYPK            ADD QUANTITY RECEIVED TO STOCK
 75           MVC     PREVCTL,CTLIN            STORE BRANCH-STOCK IN PREV
 76           BR      9

 78 *                    C O S T   C A L C U L A T I O N    R O U T I N E
 79 *                    -----------------------------------------------
 80 G10CALC   LA      2,COSTABLE               INITIALIZE TABLE SEARCH
 81 G20       CLC     PREVSTK,0(2)             INPUT STOCK# : TABLE STOCK#?
 82           BE      G30                      *    EQUAL - FOUND
 83           BL      R20NOSTK                 *    LOW   - NOT IN TABLE
 84           AH      2,=H'14'                 *    HIGH  - TEST NEXT ENTRY
 85           B       G20
```

FIGURE 10-15 (partial).

```
 87 G30       ZAP     COSTPKDW,4(3,2)          EXTRACT UNIT COST FROM TABLE
 88           CVB     1,COSTPKDW              CONVERT UNIT COST,
 89           CVB     0,QTYPKDW               *         QUANTITY  TO BINARY
 90           MR      0,0                     MULT UNIT COST BY QUANTITY
 91           CVD     1,COSTPKDW              CONVERT COST TO PACKED
 92           MVC     COSTPR,EDCOS            EDIT:
 93           ED      COSTPR,COSTPKDW+4       *     STOCK COST
 94           MVC     UNCOSPR,EDUNIT
 95           ED      UNCOSPR,4(2)            *     UNIT COST (FROM TABLE)
 96           MVC     QTYPR,EDQTY
 97           ED      QTYPR,QTYPKDW+5         *     QUANTITY

 99           MVC     DESCRIPR,7(2)           MOVE DESCRIPTION (FROM TABLE)
100           MVC     STOCKPR,PREVSTK         *     STOCK NO.
101           MVC     BRANPR,PREVBR           *     BRANCH NO.
102           BAL     11,M10WSP1              PRINT STOCK INFORMATION
103           AP      BRCOSTPK,COSTPKDW+4(4)  ADD COST TO BRANCH TOTAL
104           ZAP     QTYPKDW,=P'0'           CLEAR STOCK QUANTITY
105           BR      9

107 *                 B R A N C H   T O T A L   R O U T I N E
108 *                 -----------------------------------------
109 H10BRNCH  BAL     11,M50SPC1
110           MVC     COSTPR(L'EDCOS+1),EDCOS
111           ED      COSTPR,BRCOSTPK
112           MVC     DESCRIPR(12),=C'BRANCH TOTAL'
113           BAL     11,M20WSP2              PRINT BRANCH TOTAL
114           AP      FINCOSPK,BRCOSTPK       ADD BRANCH COST TO FINAL
115           ZAP     BRCOSTPK,=P'0'          CLEAR BRANCH COST
116           BR      9

118 *                 F I N A L   T O T A L   R O U T I N E
119 *                 -----------------------------------------
120 J10FINAL  LA      1,PRINT+69              ADDRESS OF SIGNIF. START + 1
121           MVC     COSTPR(L'EDCOS+2),EDCOS EDIT FINAL TOTAL COST
122           EDMK    COSTPR,FINCOSPK         *     WITH FLOATING $ SIGN
123           SH      1,=H'1'                 *     DECREMENT REGISTER-1
124           MVI     0(1),C'$'               *     INSERT $ SIGN
125           MVC     DESCRIPR(12),=C'FINAL TOTAL'
126           BAL     11,M10WSP1              PRINT FINAL TOTAL
127           BR      9

129 *                 T A B L E   L O A D   R O U T I N E
130 *                 -----------------------------------------
131 L10LOAD   LA      2,COSTABLE              INIT TABLE ADDRESS
132           LA      11,10                   MAX. NO. ENTRIES

134 L20       GET     FILEIN,TABRECIN         GET TABLE RECORD
140           CLC     TABCODIN,=C'ST'         TABLE CODE?
141           BNE     R50CODE                 * NO - ERROR
142           CLC     TABSTKIN,PREVSTK        STOCK# IN SEQ?
143           BNH     R30TSEQ                 * NO - ERROR

145           BCT     11,L30                  TOO MANY ENTRIES?
146           B       R40OVER                 * YES - ERROR
147 L30       MVC     0(4,2),TABSTKIN         STORE STOCK#
148           PACK    4(3,2),TABPRCIN         PACK PRICE
149           MVC     7(7,2),TABDESIN         STORE DESCR'N
150           AH      2,=H'14'                SET NEXT TABLE ENTRY
151           MVC     PREVSTK,TABSTKIN        SET SEQ TEST
152           CLC     TABSTKIN,=C'9999'       LAST ENTRY?
153           BNE     L20                     * NO - CONTINUE
154           BR      9                       * YES - RETURN
```

FIGURE 10-15 (partial).

```
156 *                    P R I N T   R O U T I N E
157 *                    ------------------------
158 M00SKIP   MVI   CTLPR,X'8B'              SKIP TO PAGE
159           SR    10,10                    CLEAR LINE COUNT
160           B     M90PRINT
161 M10WSP1   MVI   CTLPR,X'09'              WRITE, SPACE 1
162           AH    10,=H'1'                 ADD 1 TO LINE COUNT
163           B     M90PRINT
164 M20WSP2   MVI   CTLPR,X'11'              WRITE, SPACE 2
165           AH    10,=H'2'                 ADD 2 TO LINE COUNT
166           B     M90PRINT
167 M50SPC1   MVI   CTLPR,X'0B'              SPACE, NO WRITE
168           AH    10,=H'1'                 ADD 1 TO LINE COUNT
169 M90PRINT  PUT   PRTR,PRINT
175           MVC   PRINT,BLANK
176           BR    11

178 *                    P A G E   H E A D I N G
179 *                    ---------------------
180 P10PAGE   CH    10,=H'55'                END OF PAGE?
181           BL    P20                      *    NO - BYPASS PAGE OVERFLOW
182           BAL   11,M00SKIP               SKIP TO A NEW PAGE
183           MVC   PRINT,PRHEAD1
184           BAL   11,M20WSP2               PRINT REPORT HEADING-1
185           MVC   PAGEPR,EDPAGE            SET UP
186           ED    PAGEPR,PAGEPK            *    PAGE NO.
187           MVC   PRINT,PRHEAD2
188           BAL   11,M20WSP2               PRINT REPORT HEADING-2
189           AP    PAGEPK,=P'1'             INCREMENT PAGE COUNT
190 P20       BR    9

192 *                    E R R O R   R O U T I N E S
193 *                    -------------------------
194 R10SEQ    MVC   MSGPR(L'ERRSEQ),ERRSEQ   OUT OF SEQUENCE BRANCH-STOCK
195           B     R90

197 R20NOSTK  MVC   MSGPR(L'ERRSTK),ERRSTK   STOCK ITEM NOT IN TABLE
198           B     R90

200 R30TSEQ   MVC   MSGPR(L'TABSEQ),TABSEQ   TABLE OUT OF SEQ
201           B     R90

203 R40OVER   MVC   MSGPR(L'TABOVER),TABOVER TOO MANY TABLE ENTRIES
204           B     R90
205 R50CODE   MVC   MSGPR(L'ERRCDE),ERRCDE   INVALID RECORD CODE

207 R90       MVC   STOCKPR,PREVSTK
208           MVC   BRANPR,PREVBR
209           BAL   11,M20WSP2               PRINT ERROR MESSAGE
210           CLOSE FILEIN,PRTR
219           CANCEL ALL                     FORCE ABNORMAL END-OF-JOB
```

FIGURE 10-15 (partial).

```
224 *               D E C L A R A T I V E S
225 *               ------------------------
226 FILEIN    DTFCD BLKSIZE=80,               DEFINE INPUT FILE              +
                    DEVADDR=SYSIPT,                                          +
                    DEVICE=1442,                                             +
                    EOFADDR=A90END,                                          +
                    IOAREA1=INBUFF1,                                         +
                    IOAREA2=INBUFF2,                                         +
                    TYPEFLE=INPUT,                                           +
                    WORKA=YES
247 INBUFF1   DC    CL80' '                   INPUT BUFFER-1
248 INBUFF2   DC    CL80' '                   INPUT BUFFER-2

250 TABRECIN  DS    0CL80                     TABLE RECORD:
251 TABCODIN  DS    CL02                      *   RECORD CODE (ST)
252 TABSTKIN  DS    CL04                      *   STOCK #
253 TABPRCIN  DS    ZL05                      *   PRICE
254 TABDESIN  DS    CL07                      *   DESCRIPTION
255           DS    CL62                      *

257           ORG   TABRECIN
258 STRECIN   DS    0CL80                     STOCK RECORD:
259 CODEIN    DS    CL02                      01-02 RECORD CODE (12)
260 CTLIN     DS    0CL6                      BR/STOCK CONTROL WORD
261 BRANCHIN  DS    CL02                      03-04 BRANCH
262 STOCKIN   DS    CL04                      05-08 STOCK NO.
263           DS    CL02                      09-10 UNUSED
264 QTYRECIN  DS    ZL03                      11-13 QUANTITY
265           DS    CL67                      14-80 UNUSED

267 PRTR      DTFPR BLKSIZE=133,              DEFINE PRINTER FILE           +
                    CTLCHR=YES,                                             +
                    DEVADDR=SYSLST,                                         +
                    DEVICE=3203,                                            +
                    IOAREA1=PRBUFF1,                                        +
                    IOAREA2=PRBUFF2,                                        +
                    WORKA=YES
288 PRBUFF1   DC    CL133' '                  PRINTER BUFFER-1
289 PRBUFF2   DC    CL133' '                  PRINTER BUFFER-2

291 PRHEAD1   DS    0CL133                    HEADING-1 AREA:
292           DC    CL29' '                   *
293           DC    CL104'I N V E N T O R Y   U N I T   C O S T   R E P O R T'

295 PRHEAD2   DS    0CL133                    HEADING-2 AREA
296           DC    CL15' '                   *
297           DC    CL29'BRANCH STOCK'        *
298           DC    CL42'QUANTITY UNITCOST      COST'
299           DC    CL09'    PAGE'            *
300 PAGEPR    DS    CL04                      *
301           DC    CL34' '                   *
```

FIGURE 10-15 (partial).

```
303 BLANK      DC    C' '                     BLANK FOR CLEARING PRINT AREA
304 PRINT      DS    0CL133                   REPORT PRINT AREA
305 CTLPR      DS    XL01                     *
30ι            DC    CL16' '                  *
307 BRANPR     DS    CL02                     *    BRANCH NO.
308            DC    CL03' '                  *
309 STOCKPR    DS    CL04                     *    STOCK NO.
310            DC    CL02' '                  *
311 DESCRIPR   DS    CL07                     *    DESCRIPTION
312            DC    CL09' '                  *
313 QTYPR      DS    ZL08                     *    QUANTITY
314            DC    CL01' '                  *
315 UNCOSPR    DS    ZL07                     *    UNIT COST
316            DC    CL01' '                  *
317 COSTPR     DS    ZL12                     *    COST
318 MSGPR      DC    CL60' '                  *

320            DS    0D                       PACKED - ALIGNED DOUBLEWORD:
321 COSTPKDW   DC    PL8'0'                   *
322 QTYPKDW    DC    PL8'0'                   *

324 QTYPK      DC    PL2'0'                   NORMAL PACKED DECLARES:
325 BRCOSTPK   DC    PL4'0'                   *
326 FINCOSPK   DC    PL4'0'                   *
327 PAGEPK     DC    PL2'1'                   *

329 ERRCDE     DC    C'INVALID RECORD CODE'
330 ERRSEQ     DC    C'RECORD OUT OF SEQUENCE ON BRANCH/STOCK'
331 ERRSTK     DC    C'STOCK ITEM NOT IN TABLE'
332 TABSEQ     DC    C'TABLE ENTRY OUT OF SEQUENCE'
333 TABOVER    DC    C'TOO MANY TABLE ENTRIES'

335 PREVCTL    DS    0XL6                     PREVIOUS CONTROL WORD
336 PREVBR     DC    XL2'00'                  *    BRANCH NO.
337 PREVSTK    DC    XL4'00'                  *    STOCK NO.
338 EDCOS      DC    X'4020206B2020214B2020C3D9',C'**'
339 EDUNIT     DC    X'402020214B2020'
340 EDQTY      DC    X'402020202020C3D9'
341 EDPAGE     DC    X'40202020'

343 COSTABLE   DC    10X'FFFFFFFF00000C40404040404040'
344            LTORG
362            END   PROG10
```

Output:-

```
             I N V E N T O R Y   U N I T   C O S T   R E P O R T

BRANCH STOCK                 QUANTITY UNITCOST      COST          PAGE   1

   03   1234  GIDGETS           125     1.00       125.00
   03   2844  FIDGETS           172    20.00     3,440.00

              BRANCH TOTAL                        3,565.00  *

   05   2470  MIDGETS            35   100.17     3,505.95
   05   2844  FIDGETS            20    20.00       400.00

              BRANCH TOTAL                        3,905.95  *

              FINAL  TOTAL                       $7,470.95  **
```

FIGURE 10-15 Program to calculate stock values.

LOW   Error routine for out-of-sequence input.

EQUAL   Add the quantity on the record to the accumulated quantity for that stock number.

HIGH   Use the Stock number for the previously stored stock to search the table containing Stock number, unit cost, and description. If the item is found, the routine calculates cost = quantity × unit cost. If the item number is not found, the program prints an error message.

The program prints totals of cost by Stock number (minor), Branch number (intermediate), and final total (major). It is organized as follows:

INITIALIZATION SECTION   initializes the base register, opens the reader and print files, and sets the line counter to a high value to force an initial page overflow.

MAIN LOGIC SECTION   reads input records and sequence-checks by Branch/ Stock number. At the end of file, A40END, the program prints Stock, Branch, and Final totals.

PROCESS RECEIPTS SUBROUTINE, E10RECT,   adds the quantity received to Stock quantity.

COST CALCULATION SUBROUTINE, G10CALC,   is performed for a new Stock number and for end-of-file. The routine includes a table look-up, binary multiplication, and printing of the Stock detail line. It also adds Stock cost to Branch cost.

BRANCH TOTAL SUBROUTINE, H10BRNCH,   is performed on a change of Branch and at the end-of-file. It prints Branch cost and adds to Final cost.

FINAL TOTAL SUBROUTINE, J10FINAL,   performed at the end-of-file, prints total Final cost.

TABLE LOAD SUBROUTINE, L10LOAD,   is performed only once, at initialization. The routine sets the address of COSTABLE and then performs a loop:

- Reads a table record.
- If a Stock Table code (ST), performs the following:
    (1) Checks that the Stock number is in ascending sequence.
    (2) Checks that the table is not about to be overloaded—that is, the table is large enough to contain the new entry.
    (3) Moves Stock number, packs price, and moves description into the table.
    (4) Increments for the address of the next table entry.

The routine exits normally on either of two conditions: the record code is not 'ST' or the input Stock number is 9999. Note that for loading tables, it is a good idea to allow for expansion—define the table large enough to accept more entries than you would normally ever expect.

PAGE HEADING SUBROUTINE, P10PAGE, is performed at the start of the program and whenever the end of a page is reached.

ERROR ROUTINES process out-of-sequence records, Stock items not in the table, and too many table entries loaded.

REGISTER USAGE:

0,1 Calculation of binary cost

1 EDMK

2 Table look-up on the Stock Cost Table

3 Base register for program addressing

9 Subroutine linkage

10 Line count for page overflow

11 Count for entries loaded in table

Input data consists of the following records:

stock table:	Code	Stock	Price	Description
	ST	1234	00100	GIDGETS
	ST	2468	01525	WIDGETS
	ST	2470	10017	MIDGETS
	ST	2844	02000	FIDGETS
	ST	9999		

stock records:	Code	Br.	Stock	Qty.
	12	03	1234	125
	12	03	2844	076
	12	03	2844	096
	12	05	2470	035
	12	05	2844	020

DEBUGGING TIPS

A common error that programmers make when using explicit base/displacement addressing is in confusing the formats for character and packed decimal instructions. For example:

FORMAT	EXAMPLES	EXPLICIT NOTATION
Character	MVC, CLC, ED	D1(L,B1),D2(B2)
Packed decimal	ZAP, AP, PACK	D1(L1,B1),D2(L2,B2)

If you mistakenly code a length in operand-2 for an MVC, as

```
MVC  RATE,0(3,5)  (error)
```

the Assembler signals an error message. However, if you *omit* the length in operand-2 for a ZAP for example, as

```
ZAP  RATEPK,0(5)  (error)
```

the Assembler *assumes* that you intended the operand to be 0(5,0). That is, a length of five bytes and base register 0. Actually, the zero means no base register, and the instruction will fail on a Data Exception or possibly Protection Exception. Among the many common errors that programmers tend to make when using tables are the following:

- There are arguments missing from the table, or the functions are incorrect. Argument/function also may not be consistently the same length.
- The increment value for stepping through the table is incorrect.
- There is no way to ensure termination of the search, so that a CLC, for example, may continue frantically checking right through main storage.
- The branch instruction that returns to perform the next compare goes instead to the preceding instruction that initializes the search:

```
W30SRCH  LA    9,TABLE
         CLC
           .  .  .
         B     W30SRCH
```

  The program loops endlessly—an error more popular with programmers than with operators.
- Sophisticated routines such as direct addressing, binary search, and sorting can generate spectacular errors. Most programmers code these so carefully they execute perfectly the first time (but everything else blows up!).

At this point you are far enough advanced and your programs so complex that your best debugging aids are carefulness, detective skills, hex storage dumps, and access to an experienced systems programmer.

PROBLEMS

10-1. Given the contents of registers: 7 = X'3000', 8 = X'4500', and 9 = X'4000', what is the result in register-6 for LA 6,7(8,9)?

10-2. What is the effect of the following AP?

```
TOTAL       DS  PL5
AMOUNT      DS  PL4
            LA  8,TOTAL
            LA  9,AMOUNT
            AP  0(5,8),0(4,9)
```

10-3. Provide the code to extract today's date from your computer system. Assume any necessary declaratives.

10-4. What are the various ways an Assembler program may use to force termination of a table look-up? What may be the result if some provision is not made to force termination if the argument is (a) packed; or (b) character?

10-5. Assume that register-4 is initialized to zero in each case. Given declaratives BIN1 and BIN2, explain the code and determine the contents of register-4 in each case.

```
                        (a)                      (b)
BIN1 DC F'20'     L     6,BIN1         LA    5,100
BIN2 DC F'200' A15 A    4,=F'2'        LM    8,9,BIN1
                  BCT   6,A15      B15 A     4,=F'3'
                                       BXLE  5,8,B15
```

10-6. What does the following accomplish?

```
      (a)                  (b)                      (c)
LA    6,W30          LA    8,25         LA    8,25
LA    5,10      P20  BCT   8,P20        BALR  9,0
BCTR  5,6                               BCTR  8,9
```

10-7. Define the table required to calculate the current federal income tax. Use a field called TAXINC for taxable income to locate the required rate. Calculate TAX based on this rate.

10-8. *Direct table addressing.* Assume a payroll table, with consecutive job numbers from 031 through 055. Each job number has an associated rate-of-pay (xx.xx) as the function. The following declaratives are given:

```
JOBNO   DS  CL3
HOURS   DS  P'00.0'
WAGES   DS  P'0000.00'
```

Code the declaratives for the payroll rate table, called JOBTAB. Write the routine to use JOBNO to locate the correct rate in the table. Multiply HOURS by the rate, round the result to two decimals, and store it in WAGES.

10-9. Customer Billing for Electric Consumption.

Required: A program that reads customer billing records containing previous and present electric reading, and calculates consumption and the billing amount.

Input: Customer billing records containing:

	BILLING MASTER	CONSUMPTION RECORD
Record code	1–2 (31)	1–2 (32)
Region	3–4	3–4
Customer number	5–9	5–9
Customer name and address	10–69	

Previous reading: Day/month/year		10–15 (dd/mm/yy)
Meter reading		16–20
Present reading: Day/month/year		21–26 (dd/mm/yy)
Meter reading		27–31

Procedure:

- Check for valid record code, and sequence-check the file according to region-customer number. Within a region, customer numbers are in ascending sequence. Each customer has one billing master record (31) followed by one consumption record (32).

- Calculate electric consumption in kilowatt-hours = present reading − previous reading and calculate the billing amount based on the electric billing schedule for your community. Note that the meter can "turn over" on reaching 99999, like an automobile odometer. Consider the following two examples:

	PRESENT READING	PREVIOUS READING	CONSUMPTION
Example-1:	22840	21320	01520+
Example-2:	00840	99320	98480−

In Example-2, the meter has turned over. The "negative" consumption can be corrected by adding 100,000:
− 98480 plus 100,000 equals 1,520.

- Print the detail for each customer, and print total consumption and billing amount for each region and for the final total.
- Use subroutines extensively.

11

LOGICAL OPERATIONS AND BIT MANIPULATION

Certain logical operations, such as CLC, CLI, MVC, and LA treat data as "logical." The operations assume that the fields contain no sign, and act nonalgebraically on each byte as a string of eight bits. Similarly, certain binary operations process binary data as logical by treating all 32 bits of the binary fullword as unsigned data. The first section discusses the logical operations that add, subtract, compare, and shift. These instructions are useful if arithmetic fields are of such magnitude that they require *double precision*, a 63-bit field plus a sign bit. Such a field requires two registers: the left one contains the sign and the leftmost 31 data bits; the right register contains the rightmost 32 data bits.

Of greater use are the other logical operations: Test Under Mask, Translate, and Translate and Test. Although technically a branch operation, Execute is also included. These instructions provide a repertoire of powerful techniques to manipulate bits, to translate bits to other codes, and to handle variable length records. Logical operations are also used to translate binary (fixed-point) to floating point format.

LOGICAL OPERATIONS

ADD AND SUBTRACT LOGICAL—AL, ALR, SL, SLR. These instructions treat binary fields as unsigned logical data.

NAME	*OPERATION*	*OPERAND*
(symbol)	AL	R1,X2 or R1,D2(X2,B2)
	ALR	R1,R2
	SL	R1,X2 or R1,D2(X2,B2)
	SLR	R1,R2

AL, ALR, SL, and SLR are similar to A, AR, S, and SR, with the following differences: (1) Since the field is treated as logical data there is no sign; all 32 bits are added or subtracted; (2) There may be a carry out of the leftmost bit (bit 0). For subtract, if the carry out of bit 0 differs from bit 1, an overflow occurs; (3) The condition code is set as follows:

CODE	ADD	SUBTRACT
0	Zero sum	Zero difference
1	Nonzero sum	Minus
2	Zero sum, with carry	Plus
3	Nonzero sum, carry	Overflow

DOUBLE PRECISION ADDITION.   Double precision binary fields contain a sign bit and 63 data bits. Because a register can handle only 32 bits, you must give such fields special programming consideration.

Assume two 64-bit fields, called DBL1 and DBL2, are to be added, and the result stored in DBL1. Figure 11-1 gives the coding. It is necessary to split each field into two 32-bit fields. DBL1 is loaded into register-6 (the leftmost 32 bits) and register-7 (the rightmost 32 bits). The sign is the left bit of register-6. The rightmost 32 bits of DBL2 are added to register-7. You have to use a logical add because register-7 has no sign bit. If an overflow occurs, a bit has been lost; adding '1' to register-6 remedies this situation. Then the leftmost 32 bits of DBL2 are added to register-6. The example shows two 5-bit registers for ease of understanding. Check the binary values for each step.

```
 6  *                            REG-6: REG-7:
 7  DBL1     DS    D             00101 11010   ASSUME 10-BIT FIELC 186
 8  DBL2     DS    D             00011 10110   ASSUME 10-BIT FIELD 118

10           L     6,DBL1        00101         LOAD LEFTMCST  32 EITS
11           L     7,DBL1+4      00101 11010   LOAD RIGHTMOST 32 BITS
12           AL    7,DBL2+4      00101 10000   ADD   RIGHTMOST 32 BITS
13           BC    12,NCFLOW     BRANCH IF COND CODE 0 GR 1
14  *                           NO BRANCH IF CARRY SUM OR
15  *                           NON-ZERO SUM.
16           AH    6,=H'1'       00110 10000   ADD 1 TO LEFTMCST FIELD
17  NOFLOW   A     6,DBL2        01001 10000   ADD LEFTMOST 32 BITS
18           ST    6,DBL1        STORE LEFTMOST  32 BITS
19           ST    7,DBL1+4      STORE RIGHTMOST 32 BITS
```

FIGURE 11-1 Addition of double precision binary fields.

NAME	*OPERATION*	*OPERAND*
(symbol)	CL	R1,X2 or R1,D2(X2,B2)
	CLR	R1,R2

COMPARE LOGICAL—CL, CLR. The CL and CLR instructions are similar to C and CR. However, CL and CLR compare logically all 32 bits from left to right regardless of sign. Consequently, if the leftmost bit of operand-1 is 1 and the leftmost bit of operand-2 is 0, the comparison is high. (C and CR would compare as low.) An unequal compare terminates the operation. The usual condition code is set: Equal (0), Low (1), High (2).

SHIFT LOGICAL—SRL, SLL, SRDL, SLDL. These instructions shift bits right or left logically regardless of sign, and treat the entire 32 or 64 bits as a single unsigned field. Operand-1 of SRDL and SLDL references the even register of an even-odd pair.

NAME	*OPERATION*	*OPERAND*
(symbol)	SRL	R1,S2 or R1,D2(B2)
	SLL	R1,S2 or R1,D2(B2)
	SRDL	R1,S2 or R1,D2(B2)
	SLDL	R1,S2 or R1,D2(B2)

The rules for SRL, SLL, SRDL, and SLDL are similar to those for SRA, SLA, SRDA, and SLDA except that: (1) All 32 or 64 bits shift; (2) Zero bits replace bits shifted off the left or right; (3) The condition code is *not* set and no overflow occurs.

BINARY DATA PACKING AND UNPACKING. The following routine illustrates shifting of logical data in registers. Frequently a file consists of thousands or hundreds of thousands of records stored on tape or disk. One way to conserve storage is to "pack" fields in binary format. Assume an electric utility with part of each Customer record in character format.

	NUMBER OF CHARACTERS	NUMBER OF BITS FOR BINARY REPRESENTATION
District	3	10
Account	5	17
Rate Code	1	1
Service Code	1	2
	10 bytes	30 bits or 4 bytes

You can store the contents of District in 3 characters or alternatively in a 10-bit binary field, which can store a value up to 1023. Similarly, Account, with a maximum value of 99999, can be stored in a 17-bit binary field. Rate Code requires only a 1-bit field: 0 for domestic or 1 for commercial rate. Service Code can contain 4 possibilities requiring two bits:

	CODE	BITS		CODE	BITS
None	0	00	Meter rental	2	10
Budget	1	01	Both	3	11

Whereas character format requires 10 bytes to store the data, binary format requires only 30 bits or one fullword of 4 bytes. If there are 400,000 records kept on a disk or tape file, then the saving is $400,000 \times 6 = 2,400,000$ bytes of disk or tape storage (not main storage). You have to condense or compress these fields into one binary fullword prior to writing the data on disk or tape. Figure 11-2 illustrates coding that performs this condensing. Because there are no signs, you can use logical shift operations. The "packed" binary format is to be:

	BITS		BITS
Unused	0–1	Rate	29–29
District	2–11	Service	30–31
Account	12–28		

```
145  *                        ASSUMED VALUES-  CHAR:  BINARY:
146  DISTRICT  DC    CL3'838'              838   1101000110
147  ACCOUNT   DC    CL5'17683'          17683   00100010100010011
148  RATE      DC    CL1'1'                  1   1
149  SERVICE   DC    CL1'2'                  2   10
150  DOUBWORD  DS    D
151  FULLWORD  DS    F
152  *                             REG:         BINARY FORMAT:
153  BINPACK   PACK  DOUBWORD,DISTRICT
154            CVB   6,DOUBWORD        6:  --    --22ZEROS--      --1101000110
156            PACK  DOUBWORD,ACCOUNT
157            CVB   7,DOUBWORD        7:  -- 15ZEROS --   00100010100010011
158            SLL   7,15              7:  00100010100010011--   15ZEROS   --
159            SLDL  6,17              6:  00000110100011000100010100010011
161            PACK  DOUBWORD,RATE
162            CVB   7,DOUBWORD        7:  ----    --31ZEROS--           ---1
163            SLL   7,31              7:  1---    --31ZEROS--           ----
164            SLDL  6,1               6:  00001101000110001000101000100111
166            PACK  DOUBWORD,SERVICE
167            CVB   7,DOUBWORD        7:  ----    --30ZEROS--           --10
168            SLL   7,30              7:  10 -    --30ZEROS--           ---
169            SLDL  6,2               6:  0011010001100010001010001001110
170            ST    6,FULLWORD
```

FIGURE 11-2 Binary data packing.

• *Problem 11-1 should now be attempted.* •

BOOLEAN LOGIC

Boolean logic was devised by George Boole (1815–1864). Practical applications have been in switches for telephone circuits and in the design of electronic computers. Boolean logic uses only digits 0 and 1 and has two arithmetic functions—addition and multiplication:

		ADDITION					MULTIPLICATION	
0	0	1	1		0	0	1	1
+0	+1	+0	+1		×0	×1	×0	×1
0	1	1	1		0	0	0	1

Assembler language uses Boolean logic for the logical functions AND, OR, and Exclusive OR (XOR) to perform bit manipulation. For each of the three logical functions there are four instructions, in RR, RX, SI, and SS format.

AND:	*OR:*	*XOR:*	*Instruction Format:*
NR	OR	XR	RR
N	O	X	RX or R1,D2(X2,B2)
NI	OI	XI	SI or D1(B1),I2
NC	OC	XC	SS or D1(L,B1),D2,(B2)

For all twelve instructions, operand-1 is called the *target* field and operand-2 is the *mask*. The operations compare the bits in the mask against those in the target, one at a time from left to right. The target bits are modified to 0 or 1 according to the bit contents and the logical operation. The condition code is set as follows:

0 if all target bits are set to 0.   Test with BZ or BNZ.
1 if any target bit is set to 1.   Test with BM or BNM.

The following shows two 4-bit fields, called MASK and TARGET. The three unrelated cases illustrate AND, OR, and XOR. Each case sets the condition code to 1.

Field:	*AND*	*OR*	*XOR*
MASK	0011	0011	0011
TARGET	0101	0101	0101
Result	0001	0111	0110

AND. The logical function AND is equivalent to Boolean multiplication. If both the mask AND and the target bit are 1, then the target bit is set to 1.

All other cases set the target bit to zero. In Figure 11-3, NR ANDs the contents of register-8 (the mask) with that of register-9 (the target). N ANDs the contents of MASK in storage (a fullword aligned) with the target in register-8. NI, an immediate operation, ANDs the single immediate byte with the first byte of TARGET. NC ANDs the first two bytes of MASK and TARGET.

OR.   The logical function OR is equivalent to Boolean addition. If either or both the mask or the target bit is 1, then the target bit is set to 1. Where both bits are zero, the target bit is set to zero. Figure 11-3 illustrates the four OR operations.

```
23              DS      OF                          FORCE FULLWORD ALIGNMENT
24  MASK        DC      B'00110111001010011111000011001101'
25  TARGET      DC      B'01010101110010011000011110011110'
26  *           --------------------
27  *           AND - NR, N, NI, NC
28  *           --------------------
29  AND         L       8,MASK                      LOAD MASK VALUE
30              L       9,TARGET                    LOAD TARGET VALUE
31              NR      9,8                         'AND' TARGET WITH MASK

33              L       8,TARGET                    LOAD TARGET VALUE
34              N       8,MASK                      'AND' TARGET WITH MASK

36              NI      TARGET,B'01010101'          'AND' FIRST BYTE OF TARGET

38              NC      TARGET(2),MASK              'AND' FIRST 2 BYTES OF TARGET

40  *           --------------------
41  *           OR  - OR, C, OI, OC
42  *           --------------------
43  OR          L       8,MASK                      LOAD MASK VALUE
44              L       9,TARGET                    LOAD TARGET VALUE
45              OR      9,8                         'OR'  TARGET WITH MASK

47              L       8,TARGET                    LOAD TARGET VALUE
48              C       8,MASK                      'OR'  TARGET WITH MASK

50              OI      TARGET,B'01010101'          'OR'  FIRST BYTE OF TARGET

52              OC      TARGET(2),MASK              'OR'  FIRST 2 BYTES OF TARGET

54  *           --------------------------------
55  *           EXCLUSIVE OR - XR, X, XI, XC
56  *           --------------------------------
57  XOR         L       8,MASK                      LOAD MASK VALUE
58              L       9,TARGET                    LOAD TARGET VALUE
59              XR      9,8                         'XOR' TARGET WITH MASK

61              L       8,TARGET                    LOAD TARGET VALUE
62              X       8,MASK                      'XOR' TARGET WITH MASK

64              XI      TARGET,B'01010101'          'XOR' FIRST BYTE OF TARGET

66              XC      TARGET(2),MASK              'XOR' FIRST 2 BYTES OF TARGET
```

FIGURE 11-3 Boolean operations: AND, OR, Exclusive OR.

EXCLUSIVE OR (XOR). If either the mask *or* the target bit (but not both) is 1, then XOR sets the target bit to 1. Where both are zero or 1, the target is set to zero. Figure 11-3 illustrates the four XOR operations.

COMMON USES FOR BOOLEAN OPERATIONS. Figure 11-4 shows several applications of Boolean operations. In CLEAR, the Exclusive OR clears an area to hex zeros. Since both mask and target contain the same bits, Exclusive OR sets all bits to zero. The example clears a binary field to X'00s, all binary zeros. Some programmers use XC to clear the print area, as XC PRINT, PRINT, although X'40' is the normal blank character.

```
70 FULLWD     DS    F                           BINARY FULLWORD
71 PAGENO     DC    PL2'1'                       PAGE COUNTER

73 *                CLEAR A FIELD TO HEX ZEROS:
                    ---------------------------                    +
74 CLEAR      XC    FULLWD,FULLWD                CLEAR BINARY VALUE

76 *                CORRECT SIGN FOR PRINTING:
                    --------------------------                     +
77 SIGN       UNPK  PRINT+91(3),PAGENO           UNPACK PAGE COUNTER
78            OI    PRINT+93,X'F0'               FORCE F-SIGN WITH OR OPERATOR

80 *                EXCHANGE 2 REGISTERS:        7: 1010    8: 1001
                    ---------------------                          +
81 REVERSE    XR    7,8                          7: 0011    8: 1001
82            XR    8,7                          7: 0011    8: 1010
83            XR    7,8                          7: 1001    8: 1010

85 *                CHANGE NOP TO BRANCH
                    --------------------                           +
86 SWITCH     NOP   CHANGE                       INSTRUCTION DEFINED AS NO-OP
87 *          .
88 *          .
89            OI    SWITCH+1,X'F0'               CHANGE SWITCH MASK TO
90 *          .                                  X'F' (B)
91 *          .
92            B     SWITCH
93 CHANGE     NI    SWITCH+1,X'0F'               CHANGE SWITCH MASK TO
94 *          .                                  X'0' (NOP)
95 *          .

97 *                TEST BITS ON FOR CUSTOMER CODE:
                    -------------------------------                +
98 CODES      MVC   TEST,CODE                    MOVE CODE TO TEST
99            NI    TEST,B'11100000'             'AND' FIRST 3 BITS
100 *         BNZ   ...                          BRANCH IF ANY BIT IS ON
101 *         .
102 *         .
103 CODE      DS    BL1
104 TEST      DS    BL1

106 *               TEST CHARACTERS FOR F-ZONE
                    --------------------------                     +
107 ZONES     MVC   STORE,FIELD                  MOVE CHARACTER FIELD TO STORE
108           NC    STORE,=X'F0F0F0F0F0'         'AND' WITH X'F0'S
109           CLC   STORE,=X'F0F0F0F0F0'         IF UNEQUAL, SOME BYTE HAS
110 *         BNE   ...                          NO F-ZONE
111 *         .
112 *         .
113 FIELD     DS    CL5
114 STORE     DS    CL5
```

FIGURE 11-4 Sample use of Boolean operators.

SIGN corrects the sign in an unpacked field. Earlier you saw that a packed field such as /23/4C/ when unpacked becomes /F2/F3/C4/. This amount prints incorrectly as 23D. The solution used MVZ to insert an "F"-sign in place of the C-sign, /F2/F3/F4/. This example unpacks a page counter, PAGENO, in the print area. OI forces all four sign bits to be turned on, thereby adjusting the sign to X'F'. For example, C4 ORed with F0 gives F4.

REVERSE shows how XR may interchange two registers without the use of an intermediary register. The 4-bit areas illustrate how the example works.

SWITCH illustrates switching. You may manipulate the mask in the Branch on Condition (BC) instruction to change the program flow. BC 15 (unconditional branch) is commonly written as B. BC 0 is a no-operation condition which performs no branch at all; the extended mnemonic is NOP. The mask is in bits 8–11 of the object code. The example switches the mask from X'0' to X'F' (NOP becomes B) and vice versa. Clever, but not good programming practice.

CODES uses bits that represent yes or no conditions for customers. In the example, a utility company customer has an 8-bit code designed as follows:

Bit 0—Electric account	Bit 4—Electric heating
Bit 1—Gas account	Bit 5—30 days delinquent
Bit 2—Budget account	Bit 6—Rented meter
Bit 3—Industrial	Bit 7—Not used

A 1-bit means the condition exists, and more than one bit may be validly on. The example tests if the customer has *any* of the conditions: electric, gas, budget. The NI operation tests bits 0, 1, and 2; any equal bits set the condition code to 1.

ZONES tests for F-zones in a character field. This is a useful check for validity of input data, such as date, account number, and amounts (except the units portion of minus amounts, such as F1F2F3F4D5).

The TM instruction in the next section may more effectively test bits.

OTHER OPERATIONS—TM, IC, STC, EX, TR, TRT

TEST UNDER MASK—TM. The previous section used bits as switches or indicators. An efficient instruction to test bit conditions is TM, Test Under Mask.

NAME	OPERATION	OPERAND
(symbol)	TM	S1,I2 or D1(B1),I2

TM is an immediate instruction (like MVI) with two operands: Operand-1 refers to one byte in storage, containing the bits to be tested; operand-2 is the 8-bit mask in immediate format. One-bits in the mask indicate which bits to test in operand-1. TM compares the 1-bits in the mask against the selected bits in operand-1, bit for bit. For example, if the immediate operand is B'01001100', then TM tests only bits 1, 4, and 5 of operand-1. Operand-1 is unchanged. The condition code is set as follows:

SELECTED BITS IN OPERAND-1	CONDITION CODE	TEST USING
All selected bits are 0	0	BZ Branch Zeros or BNZ not Zeros
Bits are mixed—some are 1, some are 0	1	BM Branch Mixed or BNM Branch not Mixed
All selected bits are 1	3	BO Branch Ones or BNO Branch not Ones

TM tests only the bit position of the mask that contains a 1 and ignores zero mask positions. (Boolean operators, however, process all bit positions regardless of 0 or 1.) The extended mnemonics for testing the condition code are the same—BZ, BM, and BO, but for TM are described differently. Branch Minus is called Branch Mixed and Branch Overflow becomes Branch Ones.

In the example CODES in the previous section, an 8-bit code represented yes or no conditions for utility customers. The next three examples in Figure 11-5 test this code for BZ, BM, and BO.

```
 6  *          ---------------------
 7  *      TM   TEST UNDER MASK
 8  *          ---------------------
 9 CODE   DC   B'11100100'


11 TESTZERO TM   CODE,B'00010010'      ALL SELECTED BITS ARE ZERO
12 *        BZ   ...                   BRANCH ON ZEROS

14 TESTMIX  TM   CODE,B'10001100'      ALL SELECTED BITS ARE MIXED
15 *        BM   ...                   BRANCH ON MIXED

17 TESTONES TM   CODE,B'11100000'      ALL SELECTED BITS ARE ONES
18 *        BO   ...                   BRANCH ON ONES
```

FIGURE 11-5 Sample uses of test under mask—TM.

To determine if a customer has an industrial account with a rented meter, test bits 3 and 6 of CODE. In the example TESTZERO, the selected bits in CODE are both 0. Because the condition code is set to 0, BZ causes a branch. To determine if a customer has an electric account, electric heating, and is 30 days delinquent in paying his bill, test bits 0, 4, and 5 of CODE. In the example TESTMIX, the selected bits are: bit 0 is on, bit 4 is off, bit 5 is on. Because the bits are mixed off and on, the condition code is set to 1. BM causes a branch. To determine if a customer has electric, gas, and budget, test bits 0, 1, and 2. In the example TESTONES, the selected bits in CODE all contain 1. The condition code is set to 3, and BO causes a branch.

INSERT CHARACTER AND STORE CHARACTER—IC AND STC.   IC moves a single byte (8 bits) from storage into a register, and STC moves a byte from a register into storage.

NAME	OPERATION	OPERAND
(symbol)	IC	R1,X2 or R1,D2(X2,B2)
	STC	R1,X2 or R1,D2(X2,B2)

For both instructions, operand-1 references the rightmost 8 bits of a register (bits 24–31). Operand-2 references one byte of storage. IC, like LH, transfers data from operand-2 (storage) to operand-1 (register). STC, like STH, transfers data from operand-1 (register) to operand-2 (storage). However, the IC and STC operations do not affect the other bits (0–23) of the register. Further, operand-2 can specify any storage position, odd or even.

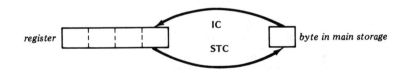

EXTENDED IC AND STC EXAMPLE.   Figure 11-6 illustrates both IC and STC and introduces variable length fields. This example reads a record from an input device. The record, called NAMEADDR, consists of two fields, name and address, both of which may be any length. The length of each field is defined by a 1-byte binary number preceding the field, as shown:

	name			address	
0A	ADAM	SMITH	0C	423	JONES ST
hex	*character*		*hex*	*character*	

The name is 10 characters long. Therefore X'0A' is stored as a length indicator before the name. Because the address is 12 characters long, X'0C' is stored before the address. The entire record consists of 1 + 10 + 1 + 12 = 24 bytes. Other records would vary in length accordingly. The maximum record length is assumed to be 42 bytes. The purpose is to move the name and the address separately to the print area. IC extracts the length indicator, and STC inserts the length indicator (minus 1) into the second byte, the length, of the MVC instruction. (At execute-time, the computer adds 1 to the instruction length.) Carefully check each instruction. The next section uses the EX instruction for the same example.

print area: ADAM SMITH   423 JONES ST

PRINT+20   PRINT+50

```
118 *       ----------------------
119 *       IC     INSERT CHARACTER
120 *       STC    STORE CHARACTER
121 *       ----------------------
122         XR     1,1                  CLEAR REG 1
123         LA     9,NAMADDR            ADDRESS OF 1ST LENGTH INDICATOR
124         IC     1,0(0,9)             LENGTH OF NAME IN REG 1
125         LR     8,1                  LOAD REG 1 INTO REG 8
126         BCTR   1,0                  DECREMENT REG 1 BY 1

128         STC    1,M10MOVE+1          STORE DECREMENTED LENGTH
129         LA     9,1(0,9)             INCREMENT FOR NAME FIELD
130 M10MOVE MVC    PRINT+20(0),0(9)     MOVE NAME TO PRINT
131         AR     9,8                  ADDRESS OF NAME + LENGTH FOR  +
                                        2ND LENGTH INDICATOR
132         IC     1,0(0,9)             LENGTH OF ADDRESS IN REG 1
133         BCTR   1,0                  DECREMENT REG 1 BY 1
134         STC    1,M20MOVE+1          STORE DECREMENTED LENGTH
135         LA     9,1(0,9)             INCREMENT FOR ADDRESS FIELD
136 M20MOVE MVC    PRINT+50(0),0(9)     MOVE ADDRESS TO PRINT
137 *       .
138 *       .
139 NAMADDR DS     CL42                 VARIABLE NAME & ADDRESS
140 PRINT   DC     CL121' '             PRINT AREA
```

FIGURE 11-6 Moving variable name and address fields using IC and STC.

• *Problems 11-2, 11-3 and 11-4 should now be done.* •

EXECUTE—EX. Although generally the declarative section is separate from instructions, under certain unique circumstances an instruction may be coded within the declaratives, or at least outside of the normal execute flow. This is called a *"subject instruction"* and may be executed by means of the EX (Execute) operation.

NAME	*OPERATION*	*OPERAND*
(symbol)	EX	R1,X2 or R1,D2(X2,B2)

The ability of EX to modify the second byte of the subject instruction gives you the power, depending on the instruction format, to change a register reference, an immediate operand, or an operand length. The second byte (in machine object code) that is subject to change is underlined:

```
FORMAT                OPERANDS
RR          R1,R2
RS          R1,R3,D2(B2)
RX          R1,D2(X2,B2)
SI          D1(B1),I2
SS  (1)     D1(L,B1),D2(B2)        (one length)
SS  (2)     D1(L1,B1),D2(L2,B2)    (two lengths)
```

The rules for EX are: (1) Operand-1 designates a register containing some value used to modify the second byte of the subject instruction; (2) operand-2 refers to the subject instruction, defined elsewhere in storage, to be executed by EX. Any instruction except another EX may be subject to EX; (3) EX ORs bits 8–15 (byte 2) of the subject instruction with bits 24–31 (the rightmost byte) of the operand-1 register. The subject instruction, however, is not actually changed in storage. Exception: If register-0 is specified, no modification is done. After executing the subject instruction, the program either returns to the next sequential instruction following the EX or, if the subject instruction is a branch, to where the branch is directed.

Figure 11-7 depicts each of the five instruction formats, RR, RS, RX, SI, and SS, subject to EX. (In practice, the contents of the operand-1 register would generally be a result of a calculation.) In each case the second byte of the subject instruction (ADDREG, STOREGS, etc.) is defined as zero because the byte is to be ORed. These examples are intended to illustrate how EX works, but not how you would necessarily use it in practice.

RR FORMAT.   EXRR inserts X'14' into register-5 and ORs byte 2 of ADDREG with X'14'. This process causes the second byte of ADDREG to reference temporarily registers 1 and 4. ADDREG executes out-of-line as: add the contents of register-4 to register-1.

RS FORMAT.   EXRS ORs the second byte of STOREGS with X'DF'. This process causes byte 2 of STOREGS to reference registers 13 and 15. STOREGS executes out-of-line as: store the contents of registers 13, 14, and 15 in SAVEREGS.

RX FORMAT.   EXRX ORs the second byte of STORCH with X'20'. This process causes byte 2 of STORCH to reference base register-2 and index register-0. STORCH executes as: store the rightmost 8 bits of register-2 in SAVEBYTE.

```
                        6  *        --------------
                        7  *        EX   EXECUTE
                        8  *        --------------
003802 435C 43EE        9  EXRR     IC   5,=X'14'     INSERT X'14' IN REG 5
00380C 4450 40C0       10           EX   5,ADDREG     ADD CONTENTS OF REG 4 TO REG 1

00380A 436C 43EF       12  EXRS     IC   6,=X'DF'     INSERT X'DF' IN REG 6
00380E 4460 40C2       13           EX   6,STOREGS    STORE CONTENTS OF REGS 13,14,15

003812 4370 43F0       15  EXRX     IC   7,=X'20'     INSERT X'20' IN REG 7
003816 447C 40C6       16           EX   7,STORCH     STORE RIGHTMOST BYTE OF REG 2

00381A 438C 43F1       18  EXSI     IC   8,=X'5B'     INSERT X'5B' IN REG 8
00381E 4480 40CA       19           EX   8,MOVIMM     MOVE $ TO PRINT AREA

003822 4390 43F2       21  EXSSL    IC   9,=X'02'     INSERT X'02' IN REG 9
003826 4490 40CE       22           EX   9,MOVECHAR   MOVE *** TO PRINT AREA

00382A 43A0 43F3       24  EXSSLL   IC   10,=X'32'    INSERT X'32' IN REG 10
00382E 44AC 40D4       25           EX   10,ADDPK     ADD FLD2 TO FLD1
                       26  *        .
                       27  *        .

003834                 29  SAVEREGS DS   3F           3 FULLWORDS
003840                 30  SAVEBYTE DS   C            ONE BYTE
003841 4C404040404040... 31 PRINT   DC   CL121' '     PRINT AREA
0038EA                 32  FLD1     DS   PL4
0038BE                 33  FLD2     DS   PL3

                       35  *        SUBJECT INSTRUCTIONS FOR EX:

0038C1 00
0038C2 1A00            36  ADDREG   AR   0,0                ADD REGISTERS        RR
0038C4 9000 4032       37  STOREGS  STM  0,0,SAVEREGS       STORE REGISTERS      RS
0038C8 4200 403E       38  STORCH   STC  0,SAVEBYTE         STORE CHARACTER      RX
0038CC 9200 4053       39  MOVIMM   MVI  PRINT+20,X'00'     MOVE IMMEDIATE       SI
0038D0 D200 405D 43F4  40  MOVECHAR MVC  PRINT+30(0),=C'***' MOVE ASTERISKS      SS
0038D6 FA00 4088 408C  41  ADDPK    AP   FLD1(0),FLD2(0)    ADD PACKED FIELDS    SS
```

FIGURE 11-7 Sample operations using EX.

SI FORMAT.   EXSI ORs the second byte of MOVIMM with X'5B'($). This process causes byte 2 of MOVIMM to "contain" X'5B'. (Remember that the subject instruction is not physically changed.) MOVIMM then moves X'5B' to P+20, and the instruction can thus move any immediate value.

SS FORMAT.   EXSSL and EXSSLL both modify operand lengths. Remember that when executing an SS instruction, the computer adds 1 to the operand length. EXSSL uses MOVECHAR to move a specified number of asterisks (up to three) to the print area, and could be used to print one, two, or three asterisks to denote the total level. EXSSLL executes an AP operation in which byte-2 contains both length codes.

EXTENDED EX EXAMPLE.   Figure 11-6 illustrated variable length move operations. Figure 11-8 in this section uses EX to code the same example. Carefully compare the two examples to see how EX is used. A later section uses the same example to illustrate the TRT instruction.

```
22              XR      1,1                     CLEAR REG 1
23              LA      9,NAMADDR               ADDRESS OF 1ST LENGTH INDICATOR
24              IC      1,0(0,9)                LENGTH OF NAME IN REG 1
25              LR      8,1                     SAVE LENGTH IN REG 8

27              BCTR    1,0                     DECREMENT REG 1 BY 1
28              LA      9,1(0,9)                INCREMENT FOR NAME FIELD
29              EX      1,M30MOVE               EXECUTE M30MOVE INSTRUCTION
30              AR      9,8                     ADDRESS OF NAME + LENGTH FOR    +
                                                2ND LENGTH INDICATOR
31              IC      1,0(0,9)                LENGTH OF ADDRESS IN REG 1
32              BCTR    1,0                     DECREMENT REG 1 BY 1
33              LA      9,1(0,9)                INCREMENT FOR ADDRESS FIELD
34              EX      1,M40MOVE               EXECUTE M40MOVE INSTRUCTION
35 *            .
36 *            .
37 *            .
38 NAMADDR      DS      CL42                    VARIABLE NAME & ADDRESS
39 PRINT        DC      CL121' '                PRINT AREA

41 M30MOVE      MVC     PRINT+20(0),0(9)        MOVE NAME TO PRINT
42 M40MOVE      MVC     PRINT+50(0),0(9)        MOVE ADDRESS TO PRINT
```

FIGURE 11-8 Moving variable name and address fields using EX.

CENTER A VARIABLE STRING. Let's say that a program is to move any number of dashes (–) up to 80, and is to center these dashes on a screen or page. Thus, 80 dashes would fill the entire screen, but 20 dashes would fill positions 30–49.

Assume that register-5 contains the actual number of dashes to display, and that the receiving field is named LINE. Before checking the example in Figure 11-9, see if you can solve the problem.

As an example, assume that register-5 contains a length of 20. The example in Figure 11-9 would calculate the starting location in LINE as follows:

```
Initial value          80
Subtract 20            60
Divide by 2            30
Add address of LINE    A(LINE+30)
```

The routine moves the 20 dashes beginning at LINE+30. Note that if the line is 80, the starting location in LINE is (as it should be) LINE+0. You could also make the routine more general; for example, by means of base/displacement addressing, operand-2 of M10MOVE could contain a reference to the address of any defined string. If the routine loads the address into register-10, the MVC instruction would appear as the following:

```
M10MOVE MVC 0(0,9),0(10)
```

TRANSLATE—TR. At times data introduced into a program is not in the required EBCDIC code. (EBCDIC is the standard 8-bit code on the 370-

```
003802 4890 444A          03C4C    8              LH    9,=H'80'       CALC SCREEN POS'N
003806 1B95                         9              SR    9,5            * 80 - LENGTH
003808 8A90 0001          00001    10              SRA   9,1            * DIVIDE BY 2
00380C 5A90 4446          03C48    11              A     9,=A(LINE)     * ADD ADDRESS
003810 0650                        12              BCTR  5,0            DECR LENGTH
003812 4450 4014          03816    13              EX    5,M10MOVE      MOVE N DASHES
                                   14  *           .
                                   15  *           .
                                   16  *           .
003816 D200 9000 43F6 00000 03BF8  17  M10MOVE  MVC   0(0,9),=80C'-'   EXEC'D MOVE
00381C 4040404040404040             18  LINE     DC    CL80' '
```

FIGURE 11-9 Centering a variable string.

series computers.) Or, it may be necessary to translate certain EBCDIC characters into some other characters. Examples of the need to translate code include:

- Some systems use ASCII mode (American Standard Code for Information Interchange). If delivered as input to the 370 (by magnetic tape or teleprocessing), ASCII must be translated to EBCDIC.

- Input records may contain invalid characters in numeric fields that the program is to pack for arithmetic. For example, a 3-byte field that contains asterisks, X'5C5C5C', when packed becomes X'CCC5'. Because the field does not contain valid packed data, an operation such as AP or SP would cause a Data Exception.

- Responses from a terminal keyboard may require only alphabetic letters, or numeric characters with optional decimal point and minus sign.

- It may be necessary to translate lowercase characters entered from a keyboard into uppercase, or uppercase letters to lowercase to display on a screen or on a letter-quality printer.

The instruction that translates code from one format to another is Translate, TR. The rules for TR are: (1) Operand-1 references the address of the *argument*—the byte or bytes to be translated. TR may translate a field or record up to 256 bytes long (such as a record coded in ASCII). (2) Operand-2 references a *table of functions*, which contains the required new code (such as the correct EBCDIC code). The definition of the table is the key to the use of TR (and TRT in a later section).

NAME	*OPERATION*	*OPERAND*
(symbol)	TR	S1,S2 or D1(L,B1),D2(B2)

TR starts with the leftmost byte of the argument. A byte can contain any value X'00' − X'FF', and TR adds this value to the address of the table, giving a range of addresses from table+X'00' through table+X'FF'. The contents of the table address is the *function* that TR uses to replace the argument byte. The operation continues then with the next argument, proceeding from left to right one byte at a time until completing the argument length.

Figure 11-10 translates hex numbers to alphabetic characters. Assume that the number one (X'01') is to be translated to the first character 'A' (X'C1'), 10 or X'OA' to the tenth character 'J', 19 or X'13' to the 19th character 'S', etc. The only valid expected values are 0 through 26 (X'1A'). The table is defined as TABLE, with a blank followed by the letters A through Z. Assume that the argument, ARGUMENT, contains X'0104010D'. The example works as follows:

```
                                   22 *      ------------------
                                   23 *      TR    TRANSLATE
                                   24 *      ------------------
00386C                             25 ARGUMENT DS   CL4                        ASSUME X'0104010D'
003870 40C1C2C3C4C5C6C7            26 TABLE    DC   C' ABCDEFGHIJKLMNOPQRSTUVWXYZ'

00388B 00
00388C DC03 406A 406E 0386C 03870  28       TR    ARGUMENT,TABLE      TRANSLATE ARGUMENT
```

FIGURE 11-10 Translation of argument using TR.

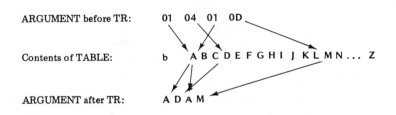

TR adds the first byte of ARGUMENT containing X'01' to the address of TABLE. At TABLE+1 is the letter 'A' (X'C1'). 'A' replaces X'01' in ARGUMENT.

TR adds the second byte of ARGUMENT containing X'04' to the address of TABLE. At TABLE+4 is the letter 'D' which replaces X'04' in ARGUMENT.

TR adds the third byte of ARGUMENT containing X'01' to TABLE. The letter 'A' replaces X'01' in ARGUMENT.

TR adds the fourth and last byte of ARGUMENT containing X'0D' to TABLE. At TABLE+13 is the letter 'M' which replaces the X'0D'. ARGUMENT is now correctly translated to 'ADAM'.

Question: Why does TABLE begin with a blank byte rather than the letter 'A'? *Warning:* An argument may be invalid with respect to the table of functions. For example, assume that ARGUMENT contains X'28', or decimal value 40. TR will access the address TABLE+40, which yields a "function" that is outside the bounds of the table. Preediting the argument for validity prior to the TR is recommended. For many types of translations where almost any argument is valid, it is necessary to define a table with all possible 256 EBCDIC codes, as illustrated in the next section.

EXTENDED TR EXAMPLE.   A character field that is to be packed should contain only numbers 0–9 and sign. Figure 11-11 depicts an example which translates bytes in an input amount field that are invalid. When read in character format, these bytes should contain only the values:

−0 through −9, represented by X'D0' through X'D9'
and
+0 through +9, represented by X'F0' through X'F9'

```
55 *                                           POSITION:
56 TABLE2   DC      208X'F0'                    000-2C7    208 BYTES INVALID
57          DC      X'D0D1D2D3D4D5D6D7D8D9'     208-217     10 BYTES -0 THRU -9
58          DC      22X'F0'                     218-239     22 BYTES INVALID
59          DC      X'F0F1F2F3F4F5F6F7F8F9'     240-249     10 BYTES +0 THRU +9
60          DC      6X'F0'                      250-255      6 BYTES INVALID

62 INAREA   DS      CL80                        INPUT AREA
63 AMTPK    DS      PL4                         PACK AREA

65          TR      INAREA+10(6),TABLE2         TRANSLATE INPUT AREA
66          PACK    AMTPK,INAREA+10(6)          PACK VALIDATED FIELD
```

FIGURE 11-11 Translate invalid bytes for packing using TR.

These valid values are to stay the same, whereas all other hex values are to translate arbitrarily to X'F0'. A table of functions could therefore define all possible EBCDIC codes that "translate" valid argument bytes to the same value, and translate invalid bytes to X'F0'. Note the positioning of the table functions:

TABLE FUNCTIONS			HEX VALUE	DEC. VAL.	TRANSLATES TO
First	208	Invalid hex arguments	X'00'–X'CF'	0–207	X'F0'
Next	10	Valid characters −0 through −9	X'D0'–X'D9'	208–217	not changed
Next	22	Invalid	X'DA'–X'EF'	218–239	X'F0'
Next	10	Valid characters +0 through +9	X'F0'–X'F9'	240–249	not changed
Last	6	Invalid	X'FA'–X'FF'	250–255	X'F0'

The example shows how invalid bytes in INAREA, assumed to be an amount field, are translated to X'F0'. Devise some examples of valid and invalid data to check the operation. Another approach translates a field to check if all bytes are numeric. The following translates all numeric (0–9) bytes to asterisks, and checks if the TR changed every one to an asterisk. (Checking if the rightmost byte could contain a minus sign will require special treatment.)

```
TEST      DS      CL6               Test field
TABLE     DC      240X'00'          Translate table
          DC      10C'*'            *
          DC      6X'00'            *

          MVC     TEST,INAREA       Move numeric amount
          TR      TEST,TABLE        Translate numerics to *
          CLC     TEST,=6C'*'       All asterisks?
          BNE     error             No - perform error routine
```

If it is necessary to know *which* record positions contain an invalid character and to print a warning message, you can use the TRT instruction covered next.

TRANSLATE AND TEST—TRT. It is sometimes necessary to *scan* a record in order to detect an invalid character (as in the previous example under TR), or to detect a unique character, such as a "delimiter" that terminates a variable length record. Translate and test, TRT, conveniently serves this purpose.

NAME	*OPERATION*	*OPERAND*
(symbol)	TRT	S1,S2 or D1(L,B1),D2(B2)

TRT is similar to TR in that: (1) Operand-1 references the address of the argument, up to 256 bytes in length; (2) operand-2 references a table of functions containing the required new code; (3) the operation begins with the first byte of the argument, and processes one byte at a time. TRT adds the value of each argument byte to the address of the table to find each function in the table.

TRT differs from TR in that: (1) If the value of the table function is *zero*, TRT continues with the next argument byte; (2) if the value of the function is *nonzero*, TRT inserts into register-1 the address of the argument in bits 8–31 (bits 0–7 are unchanged), and inserts into register-2 the contents of the function in bits 24–31 (bits 0–23 are unchanged); (3) *the argument byte is unchanged*—there is no translation. In effect, TRT is a *scan* operation; (4) TRT terminates on finding a nonzero function or on reaching the end of the argument; (5) the condition code is set as follows:

CODE	CAUSED BY	TEST WITH
0	All functions found were zero	BZ, BNZ
1	A nonzero function found, but not yet at the end of the argument	BM, BNM
2	A nonzero function found at the end of the argument	BP, BNP

The three examples in Figure 11-12 illustrate the condition codes set by TRT. Each example assumes the same argument, ARG. For SCAN1, each byte (pair of hex digits) of ARG is scanned. For instance, X'02' is directed to TABLEA+2, etc. All function bytes are found to be zero. Therefore, the condition code is set to zero and registers 1 and 2 remain unchanged, as shown in comments to the right.

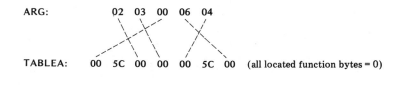

```
70  *    --------------------------
71  *    TRT    TRANSLATE & TEST
72  *    --------------------------
73  ARG      DC     X'0203000604'
74  *                                        REG-1:       REG-2:    CODE:

75  SCAN1    TRT    ARG,TABLEA               UNCHANGED    UNCHANGED   0
76  TABLEA   DC     X'005C0000005C00'

78  SCAN2    TRT    ARG,TABLEB               A(ARG+3)     X'5C'       1
79  TABLEB   DC     X'004B0000004B5C'

81  SCAN3    TRT    ARG,TABLEC               A(ARG+4)     X'5B'       2
82  TABLEC   DC     X'004B00005B5C00'
```

FIGURE 11-12 Sample translate and test TRT operations.

For SCAN2, X'02', X'03', and X'00' in ARG direct the operation to zero functions in TABLEB. X'06' in ARG, however, directs the operation to TABLEB+6, which contains X'5C'. Therefore TRT does the following: (1) Inserts the address of ARG+3 in register-1; (2) inserts the table function X'5C' in register-2; and (3) sets the condition code to 1.

For SCAN3, the first four bytes of ARG locate zero functions in TABLEC. The last byte, X'04', however, directs the operation to TABLEC+4, which contains X'5B'. TRT does the following: (1) Inserts the address of ARG+4 in register-1; (2) inserts the table function X'5B' in register-2; and (3) because the last byte of ARG was processed, sets the condition code to 2.

SCANNING FOR A BLANK.   Way back at the beginning of Chapter 10, Figure 10-2 described a routine that inserted a comma, initials, and periods to the right of surnames, as BROWN, J.L. The program used base/displacement addressing to step through the surname scanning for a blank. In the example in Figure 11-13, a TRT instruction replaces the earlier technique.

The scan table contains all hex zeros except for one in the blank (hex '40') position. TRT scans the surname for a blank. If a blank is found, the routine uses the address in register-1 to insert the commas, initials, and periods. If a blank is not found, the routine exits—presumably the surname fills all available characters in its field. To avert this situation, the surname could have blanks appended to the right.

```
LOC     OBJECT CODE      ADDR1 ADDR2  STMT    SOURCE STATEMENT


003892  0000000000000000              33  TABLNK  DC    64X'00'              SCAN TABLE:
0038D2  40                            34          DC    X'40'               *    BLANK POS'N
0038D3  0000000000000000              35          DC    191X'00'            *

003992                                37  SURNAMPR DS   CL20                SURNAME
0039A6  40404040                      38          DC    CL04' '             *
0039AA                                39  INITPR  DS    CL02                INITIALS

0039AC  DD13 4190 4090   03992 03892  41          TRT   SURNAMPR,TABLNK     SCAN FOR BLANK
0039B2  4780 41D4        039D6        42          BZ    S20                 NOT FOUND - EXIT
0039B6  926B 1000        00000        43          MVI   0(1),C','           INSERT COMMA,
0039BA  D200 1002 41A8   00002 039AA  44          MVC   2(1,1),INITPR         INITIAL,
0039C0  924B 1003        00003        45          MVI   3(1),C'.'           & PERIOD

0039C4  9540 41A9        039AB        47          CLI   INITPR+1,C' '       2ND INITIAL?
0039C8  4780 41D4        039D6        48          BE    S20                 *   NO - EXIT
0039CC  D200 1004 41A9   00004 039AB  49          MVC   4(1,1),INITPR+1     INSERT INITIAL
0039D2  924B 1005        00005        50          MVI   5(1),C'.'           & PERIOD
                         039D6        51  S20     EQU   *
```

FIGURE 11-13 Scanning for a blank.

CHECK FOR POSITIVE AND NEGATIVE NUMBERS.   Let's now see how to use TRT successfully to scan an input field for valid positive numbers in all positions and valid negative numbers only in the units position.

In the example in Figure 11-14, the input field is VALUEIN. The table named POSTAB defines the valid positive numbers X'F0' through X'F9' and NEGTAB defines the valid negative numbers X'D0' through X'D9'.

The first TRT scans VALUEIN for positive numbers. If all numbers are positive, the routine performs no further checking. If there is an invalid number before the units positive, branch to an error routine. If the unit's position contains a nonpositive character, the second TRT checks the position for a valid negative number.

```
  LOC   OBJECT CODE        STMT    SOURCE STATEMENT

                            56 *                                         POSITION:
0039D6  0000000000000000    57 POSTAB   DC    240X'00'                   000-239   240 BYTES INVALID
003AC6  F0F1F2F3F4F5F6F7     58          DC    X'F0F1F2F3F4F5F6F7F8F9'    240-249    10 BYTES +0 THRU +9
003AD0  000000000000        59          DC    6X'00'                     250-255     6 BYTES INVALID

                            61 *                                         POSITION:
003AD6  0000000000000000    62 NEGTAB   DC    208X'00'                   000-207   208 BYTES INVALID
003BA6  D0D1D2D3D4D5D6D7     63          DC    X'D0D1D2D3D4D5D6D7D8D9'    208-217    10 BYTES -0 THRU -9
003BB0  0000000000000000    64          DC    38X'00'                    218-255    38 BYTES INVALID

003BD6                      66 VALUEIN  DS    ZL7

003BDD  00
003BDE  DD06 43D4 41D4      68          TRT   VALUEIN,POSTAB         TEST FOR POS CHARS.
003BE4  4780 43F4           69          BZ    G200K                 * ALL CHARS ARE 0-9
003BE8  4740 43F4           70          BM    R95INV                * INVALID BEFORE LAST
                            71 *                                    * LAST CHAR NOT POS
003BEC  DD00 43DA 42D4      72          TRT   VALUEIN+6(1),NEGTAB   TEST LAST FOR NEG
003BF2  4770 43F4           73          BNZ   R95INV                * INVALID LAST CHAR
                            74 *                                    * LAST IS NEG.
                            75 G200K    EQU   *                     PROCESS VALID FIELD
                            76 *         ...
                            77 R95INV   EQU   *                     ERROR ROUTINE
```

FIGURE 11-14 Checking for positive and negative numbers.

SCANNING VARIABLE-LENGTH FIELDS. The next example for variable length fields is similar to those for IC, STC, and EX in Figures 11-6 and 11-8. This example has no length indicator preceding the name and address. Instead, a delimiter character, in this case an *, indicates the end of the variable length field:

ADAM SMITH*423 JONES ST*

In Figure 11-15 TRT scans the record to find the delimiter, and then uses the address of the delimiter to calculate the length of the name and the address, and to determine the address of the next field. The program uses two TRT and two EX operations to move the name and address to the print area. The table, TABSCAN, contains only a nonzero function for the X'5C'(*) position, and zero functions for all other codes. The example assumes, perhaps unwisely, that a delimiter always follows both name and address. TRT instruction in statement 95 assumes a maximum length of 21.

Further examples of EX, TRT, and variable length records are in the next chapter.

MASKED BYTE OPERATIONS—ICM, STCM, AND CLM

The three Assembler instructions ICM, STCM, and CLM provide for handling one to four selected bytes. ICM inserts up to four bytes from storage

```
                              86  *                              POSITION:
003AS1  OCCOOCOCCC000000      87  TABSCAN  CC   92X'00'          000-091     92 ZERO FUNCTICNS
0C3AED  5C                    88           DC   X'5C'            092-092      1 ASTERISK *
UC3AEE  000C0C000C000000      89           DC   163X'00'         093-255    163 ZERO FUNCTICNS

003B91                        91  NAMADD   DS   CL42             VARIABLE NAME & ADDRESS

UG3BBB  0G
003BBC  1B11                  93           SR   1.1              CLEAR REG 1
003BBE  4190  438F            94           LA   9.NAMADD         LOAD ADDRESS OF VARIABLE RECORD
0C3BC2  DD14  9000  428F      95           TRT  0(21.9).TABSCAN  SCAN FOR NAME DELIMITER
                              96  *         EZ   ...             *    NOT FOUND. ERROR

003BCE  1B71                  98           LR   7.1              SAVE ADDRESS OF DELIMITER
003BCA  1B19                  99           SR   1.9              CALCULATE LENGTH OF NAME
003BCC  0610                 100           BCTR 1.0              DECREMENT LENGTH BY 1
003BCE  4410  43E2           101           EX   1.M50MOVE        EXECUTE M50MOVE INSTRUCTION
003BD2  4190  7001           102           LA   9.1(0.7)         INCREMENT FOR ADDRESS FIELD

003BD6  DD14  9000  428F     104           TRT  0(21.9).TABSCAN  SCAN FOR ADDRESS DELIMITER
                             105  *         BZ   ...             *    NOT FOUND. ERROR
003BDC  1B19                 106           SR   1.9              CALCULATE LENGTH OF ADDRESS
003BDE  0610                 107           BCTR 1.0              DECREMENT LENGTH BY 1
003BE0  4410  43E8           108           EX   1.M60MOVE        EXECUTE M60MOVE INSTRUCTION
                             1C9  *         .
                             110  *         .

                             112  *              SUBJECT INSTRUCTIONS FOR EX:
003BE4  D20C  4053  9000     113  M50MOVE  MVC   PRINT+20(0).0(9)         MOVE NAME TO PRINT
0C3BEA  D20C  4071  9000     114  M60MOVE  MVC   PRINT+50(0).0(9)         MOVE ADDRESS TO PRINT
```

FIGURE 11-15 Moving variable name and address fields using TRT.

into a register, STCM stores up to four bytes from a register into storage, and CLM makes a logical comparison of bytes between a register and storage.

NAME	OPERATION	OPERAND
(symbol)	ICM STCM CLM	R1,S2 or R1,M3,D2(B2)

OPERAND-1 designates any one of the 16 general registers.

OPERAND-2 supplies the name of a data field in storage. There is no required alignment, and although you may define the field in any format, the instruction can reference only the first four bytes. The number of 1-bits in the mask determines the length in bytes of operand-2.

OPERAND-3 defines a *mask* that can be any value 0 through 15 (hex 0 — F). Each 1-bit specifies a byte position in the register from left to right. Thus, a mask of 10 (bits 1010) indicates the first and third bytes of the register.

INSERT CHARACTERS UNDER MASK—ICM. The ICM instruction begins with the leftmost byte of storage and inserts up to four bytes into the designated register according to the mask. In the following examples, each ICM is *unrelated:*

```
FLDA       DC     X'31323334'          mask:    register-7:

           SR     7,7                           00 00 00 00
           ICM    7,1,FLDA             0001     00 00 00 31
           ICM    7,3,FLDA             0011     00 00 31 32
           ICM    7,9,FLDA            1001     31 00 00 32
           ICM    7,15,FLDA           1111     31 32 33 34
```

If the mask is 0, the operation acts like a NOP, except that the condition code is set to 0. Otherwise, ICM sets the condition code according to the leftmost bit of the storage field—a value of 0 sets the code to 2 (positive) and 1 sets the code to 1 (negative). Note that the mask in the last ICM example, 15, acts like an LTR with no alignment requirement.

STORE CHARACTERS UNDER MASK—STCM.   The STCM instruction is the reverse of ICM. The instruction begins with the leftmost byte of the register and stores into storage up to four bytes, according to the mask. In the following unrelated examples, assume that register-8 contains X'41424344':

```
FLDB       DC     X'00000000'          mask:      FLDB:

           STCM   8,1,FLDB             0001     00 00 00 41
           STCM   8,5,FLDB             0101     00 41 00 42
           STCM   8,11,FLDB           1011     41 00 42 43
```

STCM does not set the condition code.

COMPARE LOGICAL UNDER MASK—CLM.   The CLM instruction performs a logical (not algebraic) comparison left to right of bytes in a register with bytes in storage, according to the mask. The condition code settings are:

```
    0        compared bytes are equal or mask is 0.
    1        compared bytes in the register are low.
    2        compared bytes in the register are high.
```

In the following example, assume that register-9 contains X'51525354':

```
FLDC       DC     X'51524040'          bits:  condition code:

           CLM    9,14,FLDC           1110     high (02)
```

The example compares the three leftmost bytes of register-9 (X'515253') to the three leftmost bytes of FLDC (X'515240'), from left to right. The third byte of register-9 is higher.

BINARY OPERATIONS—SUMMARY

Most arithmetic can be performed adequately with packed data and decimal arithmetic. Since input data from a terminal or cards is normally in character format, an additional step is required to translate into packed format. To convert the packed data to binary requires yet another step. However, the following reasons often determine the need for binary format:

- Explicit use of base registers for address modification.
- Faster processing *if* there are many repetitive arithmetic operations.
- Certain operations can only be accomplished with binary operations.
- Data may be stored efficiently in binary format on disk and tape, and read into storage in this format.

DEBUGGING TIPS

1. Keep in mind that logical operations treat the leftmost bit of a field as data.
2. Double-check your use of the Boolean operations AND, OR, and XOR. For example, if two matched bits are both 1, OR converts the destination bit to 1, whereas XOR converts it to 0.
3. Design a table for TR and TRT with care. A byte offset in the wrong table position can cause infrequent, subtle errors. One common error is forgetting that the first table position is numbered zero. Another error is failure to account for all 256 possible positions.
4. Note also that TRT delivers values to both registers 1 (the address of the located byte) and 2 (the byte value).

PROBLEMS

11-1. Figure 11-2 "packs" four fields into one binary fullword. Assume that the fullword has been read from tape into storage field FULLWORD DS FL4. Write the coding to "unpack" the fullword into four individual character fields called DIST, ACCOUNT, RATE, SERVICE.

11-2. STC stores the rightmost 8 bits of a register into a field called BYTE. Use Boolean operations to (a) force the leftmost 4 bits of BYTE to be zeros;

(b) force the leftmost 4 bits of BYTE to be ones; (c) reverse all 8 bits, zeros to ones and vice versa.

11-3. Figure 11-5 shows how to test bit values. Code the instruction to test if the customer has both gas and industrial account.

11-4. Figure 11-6 demonstrates variable length name and address. Change NAMADDR to 63 bytes, allowing for a *third* variable field, city. Revise the coding to move this field to P+80. Also, recode the routine as a *loop* so that there is one set of instructions executed three times, one for each field. HINT: Change operand-1 of the MVC to explicit register format. Expand the code to include a read and print, then test the program.

11-5. Recode Figure 11-8 using one EX for the same changes required in Problem 11-4.

11-6. Design a table for TR to translate upper case letters (A–Z) to lower case (a–z). Leave unchanged characters 0–9, comma, and period. Convert all other characters to X'40'.

11-7. ASCII code is given in the table in Appendix F. Design two tables of functions to translate (a) ASCII to EBCDIC and (b)EBCDIC to ASCII.

11-8. In Figure 11-11, TR translates invalid bytes in an input field to character zero. Change the example so that the program prints the column where the invalid code occurred. A record may contain more than one invalid column.

11-9. Translate hex into character format. Each 4 bits (hex digit) of register-9 is to print as a single character (as is done by dumping the contents of storage). Hex zero should print as character zero, X'9' as character 9, X'A' as character A, etc. Since register-9 contains 32 bits, eight characters are required, printing from P+11 to P+18. Suggestion: Shift the 4 leftmost bits of register-9 into register-8. Store these in a 1-byte field and use TR to translate from hex to character. Repeat the loop eight times. The table can be defined as quite short.

11-10. Recode Figure 11-15 using one TRT for the same changes required in Problem 11-4.

12

MAGNETIC TAPE

This chapter and the next cover two common input-output devices that store data—magnetic tape and disk storage. Tape stores data as *records*, and a series of related records comprises a file. The reel is "loaded" onto a tape drive in much the same manner as a conventional tape recorder.

The computer writes data on tape and disk over the old data, much as a tape recorder records a new sound over the previous. The data may be reread and rewritten, almost indefinitely. Tape and disks are used for both input and output. Normally a tape reel designated as input to a program is only read, and not written on until its contents are obsolete, and a reel designated as output is written on, to be read later. The data on the reel is saved for a predetermined time as an "audit trail" or "backup" if jobs must be rerun. Recent developments in disk storage devices have permitted storing large files on disks. Disk storage gives the advantage of processing records both sequentially and directly. Most installations now use disk to store large files, but use tape for backup files and temporary storage for data that is to be printed on a report.

USES OF MAGNETIC TAPE

Magnetic tape is not only a means of rapid input-output. It also acts as a medium to store large quantities of condensed, easily filed data. Tape is used to store master and transaction files. It also acts as intermediary storage, for example as output from a program, storing data to be used in a subsequent program. Many department store chains and utility companies maintain customer records on magnetic tape. Their records are many in number, long in length, and are stored sequentially. Among the features of magnetic tape are the following:

- Tape input-output is extremely fast.
- Tape files require little storage space.
- Tape records when sorted (by an IBM tape library program) are virtually assured of being in the correct sequence.
- Tape stores data not only in character format but also in packed and binary, permitting condensed records.
- Tape may be reused almost indefinitely.
- Tape permits records of virtually any length.
- Tape is an inexpensive, convenient way to mail large volumes of data.

MAGNETIC TAPE CHARACTERISTICS

This chapter limits discussion to IBM magnetic tape units, although tape units of other manufacturers have similar features. The tape consists of a thin ferromagnetic coating on flexible plastic, 1/2-inch wide. A full reel is 2400 feet long, with shorter lengths available such as 1200 and 600 feet.

TAPE DENSITY.   Tape density is expressed in bytes-per-inch (bpi), such as 800, 1600, and 6250 bpi. A 2400-foot reel (28,800") contains a maximum storage of about 23 million bytes with 800 bpi, and 46 million bytes with 1600 bpi tape.

TAPE SPEED.   Tape read/write speed varies considerably by tape drive model. At 125 inches per second (ips), a tape drive could read a 2400-foot reel, with little time for processing, in about 230 seconds. For example, IBM 3420 Magnetic Tape units are available in the following models, with tape densities of 800, 1600, and 6250 bpi.

IBM 3420	MODEL 3	MODEL 4	MODEL 5	MODEL 6	MODEL 7	MODEL 8
Tape speed (ips)	75	75	125	125	200	200
Data rate (KB/sec):						
At 800 bpi	60		100		160	
At 1600 bpi	120	120	200	200	320	320
At 6250 bpi		470		780		1250

CODE STRUCTURE. A tape device records data using a 9-bit code similar to the byte in storage: eight bits for data and one bit for odd parity, arranged vertically on the tape. (A 7-bit code is also accepted to provide compatibility with earlier tape models.)

TAPE MARKERS. Near both ends of the reel is an aluminum strip called a tape marker that is sensed by a photoelectric device on the tape drive. These strips are on the side of the tape that does not record data:

THE LOAD POINT MARKER is a strip about ten feet from the start of the reel to provide space for the initial threading of the tape. Reading or writing begins after this point.

THE END-OF-TAPE MARKER is a strip about 14 feet from the end of the reel. When tape is being written, the marker warns the system that the end of the tape is near. Four feet provides space to finish writing data after the marker, and ten feet permits threading of the tape.

TAPE READ/WRITE. The operator loads the reel to be processed onto the tape drive and initializes the tape at the load point marker. The drive contains an empty reel to take up the processed tape. The tape passes a read/write head. For *input* each byte is read, then reread, to ensure the read was performed correctly. For *output* an erase operation prior to the write clears old data from the tape. The write operation magnetizes small areas within the tracks. A byte written is reread to check its validity. These validity checks are entirely automatic. When the tape has been completely processed, there are two alternatives:

1. Most often the tape is rewound onto the original reel. The operator may then unload it from the tape drive or leave it for further processing.
2. The tape may be reprocessed by reading it *backwards.* Although the tape runs backwards, data from each record reads into storage in the normal sequence. IBM library tape sort programs and occasionally programmers use this feature.

TAPE FORMATS. A *block* of data written on tape consists of one or more records. The minimum block length is about 18 bytes. The maximum is subject to available storage in programs using the tape file and the operating system used. IOCS reads a tape block into, and writes from, an input-output area (or buffer) in storage. Blocks consisting of one record only are *unblocked.* Blocks having more than one record are *blocked.* The *blocking* *factor* specifies the number of records in a block. The program that initially writes (or creates) the tape file defines the record length and block length. All other programs that read the file must designate the same record and block lengths. After each block, the tape drive automatically generates a space of about 0.6 inch. On tape with density of 6250 bytes per inch, the space is about 0.3 inch. This space, called an *interblock gap (IBG)*, has two functions:

1. The IBG clearly defines the beginning and end of a block of data. A tape read starts with the first byte of data in a block. The IBG terminates the read operation.

2. The IBG allows space for the tape drive to slow down after a read or write, and to restart with the next read/write (stop/start time).

FIXED AND VARIABLE LENGTHS.   Records and blocks may be *fixed* in length (each has the same length throughout the entire file), or *variable* (the length of each record and the blocking factor are not predetermined). There are five distinct tape formats:

1. *Fixed, unblocked*—one record of fixed length per block.
2. *Fixed, blocked*—more than one fixed length record per block.
3. *Variable, unblocked*—one variable length record per block.
4. *Variable, blocked*—more than one variable length record per block.
5. *Undefined*—not all operating systems support this format; see the IBM Supervisor manuals for details.

Figure 12-1 depicts the first two formats. A later section describes variable length records.

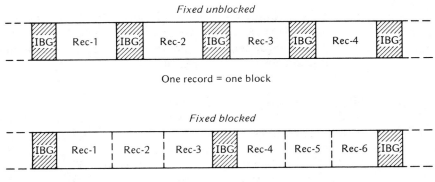

Fixed unblocked

One record = one block

Fixed blocked

Three records = one block

FIGURE 12-1 Tape formats for fixed unblocked and blocked records.

• *Problems 12-1, 12-2, and 12-3 should now be done.* •

DOS TAPE PROGRAMMING EXAMPLE: CREATING A TAPE FILE

The DOS file definition macro that defines a magnetic tape file is DTFMT (OS uses DCB). You specify one DTFMT entry with a unique name for each tape input or output file that the program processes. The entries are similar to the DTFCD, DTFPR, and DTFDI macros covered earlier. You use the same imperative macros: OPEN, CLOSE, GET, and PUT. As explained later, IOCS (Data Management) handles all label processing, blocking and deblocking.

Figure 12-2 illustrates reading input records and writing them on tape. The records are read into RECDIN and required fields are transferred to the tape workarea called TAPEWORK. This workarea is then "PUT" to a tape output file called FILEOTP. IOCS blocks four records before physically writing the block onto tape. Therefore, for every four input records, IOCS writes one tape block containing the four records onto tape. The DTFMT entries are described next:

BLKSIZE=360 means that each block to be written from the IOAREA is 360 bytes long (4 records × 90 bytes).

DEVADDR=SYS025 denotes the logical address of the tape device that will write the file. The operator assigns one of the system's tape drives with this (or some other) logical device name, as required by the installation.

FILABL=STD indicates that the tape file contains "standard labels," as discussed in a later section.

IOAREA1 AND IOAREA2 are the two IOCS buffers, similar to those for card and printer files. You define the two IOAREAs as the same length as BLKSIZE, 360 bytes. Some programmers omit defining a second buffer in order to reduce program size, especially if the blocked record area is large.

RECFORM=FIXBLK specifies that output records are to be fixed in length, and blocked (tape records may also be variable length or unblocked).

RECSIZE=90 means that each fixed-length record is 90 bytes in length, the same as the workarea.

TYPEFLE=OUTPUT stipulates that the type of file is output: the file is for writing tape, not reading.

WORKA=YES means that the program is to process output records in a workarea. In this program, tapework is the workarea, and is the same length as RECSIZE, 90 bytes. (Alternatively, you may code IOREG, just

```
  1              PRINT ON,NODATA,NOGEN

  3 *                          I N I T I A L I Z A T I O N

  5 PROG12A    START X'0050'                    X'50' FOR LBLTYP
  6            BALR  3,0                         INITIALIZE BASE REGISTER
  7            USING *,3
  8            OPEN  FILEIN,FILEOTP              ACTIVATE FILES
 17            GET   FILEIN,RECDIN              READ 1ST RECORD

 24 ***                        M A I N   P R O C E S S I N G

 26 A10LOOP    MVC   ACCTTPO,ACCTIN             MOVE INPUT FIELDS
 27            MVC   NAMETPO,NAMEIN             *   TO WORK AREA
 28            MVC   ADDRTPO,ADDRIN             *
 29            PACK  BALNTPO,BALNIN             *
 30            MVC   DATETPO,DATEIN             *
 31            PUT   FILEOTP,TAPEWORK           WRITE TAPE WORKAREA
 37            GET   FILEIN,RECDIN              READ NEXT
 43            B     A10LOOP

 45 *                          E N D - O F - F I L E

 47 A90EOF     CLOSE FILEIN,FILEOTP             DE-ACTIVATE FILES
 56            EOJ                              NORMAL END-OF-JOB
```

```
 60 *                          D E C L A R A T I V E S

 62 FILEIN     DTFCD DEVADDR=SYSIPT,            INPUT FILE                        +
                     IOAREA1=IOARIN1,                                            +
                     IOAREA2=IOARIN2,                                            +
                     BLKSIZE=80,                                                 +
                     DEVICE=2501,                                                +
                     EOFADDR=A90EOF,                                             +
                     TYPEFLE=INPUT,                                              +
                     WORKA=YES

104 IOARIN1    DC    CL80' '                    INPUT BUFFER 1
105 IOARIN2    DC    CL80' '                    INPUT BUFFER 2

107 RECDIN     DS    0CL80                      INPUT AREA:
108 CODEIN     DS    CL2                        01-02   RECORD CODE
109 ACCTIN     DS    CL6                        03-08   ACCOUNT NO.
110 NAMEIN     DS    CL20                       09-28   NAME
111 ADDRIN     DS    CL40                       29-68   ADDRESS
112 BALNIN     DS    ZL6'0000.00'               69-74   BALANCE
113 DATEIN     DS    CL6'DDMMYY'                75-80   DATE

115 FILEOTP    DTFMT BLKSIZE=360,               TAPE FILE                        +
                     DEVADDR=SYS025,                                             +
                     FILABL=STD,                                                 +
                     IOAREA1=IOARTPO1,                                           +
                     IOAREA2=IOARTPO2,                                           +
                     RECFORM=FIXBLK,                                             +
                     RECSIZE=90,                                                 +
                     TYPEFLE=OUTPUT,                                             +
                     WORKA=YES

152 IOARTPO1   DS    CL360                      TAPE BUFFER-1
153 IOARTPO2   DS    CL360                      TAPE BUFFER-2
```

FIGURE 12-2 (partial).

```
155 TAPEWORK DS    0CL90          TAPE WORK AREA:
156 ACCTTPO  DS    CL6            01-06  ACCOUNT NO.
157 NAMETPO  DS    CL20      .    07-26  NAME
158 ADDRTPO  DS    CL40           27-66  ADDRESS
159 BALNTPO  DS    PL4            67-70  BALANCE
160 DATETPO  DS    CL6            71-76  DATE
161          DC    CL14' '        77-90  RESERVED

163          LTORG
164                =C'$$BOPEN '
165                =C'$$BCLOSE'
166                =A(FILEIN)
167                =A(RECDIN)
168                =A(FILEOTP)
169                =A(TAPEWORK)
170          END   PROG12A
```

FIGURE 12-2 Writing a tape file under DOS.

as for card and printer files, and use the macro PUT FILEOTP with no workarea coded.)

The DTFMT entry for magnetic tape input requires an entry EOFADDR=address to denote the name of the routine where IOCS branches when it reaches the end of the tape file. The next chapter illustrates tape input. Further information on DTFMT is in the IBM Supervisor manuals.

OS CODING FOR MAGNETIC TAPE

For OS, there are several additional entries that the DCB requires for magnetic tape. The entry DEN specifies tape density: DEN=2 is for 800 bytes per inch and DEN=3 is 1600, and must agree with the actual tape drive setting. LRECL (logical record length) designates the length of each record, if fixed-length. RECFM indicates the "record format": F (Fixed), FB (Fixed Blocked), V (Variable), and VB (Variable Blocked).

The program in Figure 12-3 is a revision of the preceding DOS example that reads records and writes them on tape. The DD (Data Definition) job commands appear first. Note that the example illustrates a common practice: BLKSIZE, RECFM, and DEN are coded in the tape DD entry instead of the DCB, enabling a user to change the entries without reassembling the program.

The OS Data Management system relates the name in the DD job command. Not shown, but would be

```
//GO.TAPEOT DD . . .
```

to the same name in the program's DCB statement,

```
DDNAME=TAPEOT
```

```
//GO.TAPEOT   DD DSNAME=TRFILE,DISP=(NEW,PASS),UNIT=3420,        +
              DCB=(BLKSIZE=360,RECFM=FB,DEN=3)         ←——— DD for tape
                                                             data set output
//GO.SYSIN    DD *                                ←——————— DD for input file


*                 I N I T I A L I Z A T I O N
*
PROG12B  START
         SAVE   (14,12)
         BALR   3,0
         USING  *,3
         ST     13,SAVEAREA+4
         LA     13,SAVEAREA
         OPEN   (FILEIN,(INPUT),FILEOTP,(OUTPUT))
         GET    FILEIN,RECRDIN            READ 1ST RECORD
*
***               M A I N   P R O C E S S I N G
*
A10LOOP  MVC    ACCTTPO,ACCTIN           MOVE INPUT FIELDS TO TAPE
         MVC    NAMETPO,NAMEIN           *    WORK AREA
         MVC    ADDRTPO,ADDRIN           *
         PACK   BALNTPO,BALNIN           *
         MVC    DATETPO,DATEIN           *
         PUT    FILEOTP,TAPEWORK         WRITE WORK AREA ONTO TAPE
         GET    FILEIN,RECRDIN           READ NEXT RECORD
         B      A10LOOP
*
*                 E N D - O F - F I L E
*
A90EOF   CLOSE  (FILEIN,,FILEOTP)
         L      13,SAVEAREA+4
         RETURN (14,12)
*
*                 D E C L A R A T I V E S
*
FILEIN   DCB    DDNAME=SYSIN,            DCB FOR INPUT DATA SET     +
                DEVD=DA,                                            +
                DSORG=PS,                                           +
                EODAD=A90EOF,                                       +
                MACRF=(GM)

RECRDIN  DS     0CL80                    INPUT RECORD AREA:
CODEIN   DS     CL02                     01-02  RECORD CODE
ACCTIN   DS     CL06                     03-08  ACCOUNT NO.
NAMEIN   DS     CL20                     09-28  NAME
ADDRIN   DS     CL40                     29-68  ADDRESS
BALNIN   DS     ZL06'0000.00'            69-74  BALANCE
DATEIN   DS     CL06'DDMMYY'             75-80  DATE

FILEOTP  DCB    DDNAME=TAPEOT,           DCB FOR TAPE DATA SET      +
                DSORG=PS,                                           +
                LRECL=90,                                           +
                MACRF=(PM)

TAPEWORK DS     0CL90                    TAPE WORK AREA:
ACCTTPO  DS     CL06                     01-06  ACCOUNT NO.
NAMETPO  DS     CL20                     07-26  NAME
ADDRTPO  DS     CL40                     27-66  ADDRESS
BALNTPO  DS     PL04                     67-70  BALANCE(PACKED)
DATETPO  DS     CL06                     71-76  DATE
         DC     CL14' '                  77-90  RESERVED FOR EXPANSION

SAVEAREA DS     18F                      REGISTER SAVE AREA
         LTORG
         END    PROG12B
```

FIGURE 12-3 Writing a tape file under OS.

Tape and disk records may also be processed directly in the buffers, using Locate Mode. The DCB requires MACRF=(GL) for input and (PL) for output.

Another DCB entry, EROPT, provides for specifying the action if an input operation encounters problems. The options are:

=ACC Accept the possibly erroneous data block.
=SKP Skip the data block entirely and continue with the next one.
=ABE Abend—abnormal end of program execution, the normal default if the entry is omitted.

ACC and SKP can use a SYNAD entry for printing an error message and continue processing. If the error routine is called R20ERROR, the DCB coding could be:

```
EROPT=SKP,
SYNAD=R20ERROR
```

Use of ACC and SKP may cause invalid results, so it may be preferable to use ABE (or allow it to default) for important production jobs. Be sure to examine the OS Supervisor manuals for other DCB options.

TAPE FILE ORGANIZATION Tape files ("data sets" under OS) are typically stored in ascending sequence by control field, such as Customer number. For compatibility with disks, a reel of tape is called a *volume*. The simplest case is a *one-volume file*, in which one file is entirely and exclusively stored on one reel (volume). This storage is common where the file is medium-sized.

An extremely large file (such as department store accounts receivable) uses a *multivolume file* which requires more than one volume for the file. Many small files can be stored in a *multifile volume*, one after the other on one volume, although you may have to rewrite the entire tape even if updating only one file.

IOCS and job control handle the complexities of such file organization, requiring no special programming effort.

STANDARD LABELS. Under the various operating systems, tapes require unique identification. Each reel and each file on a reel contains certain descriptive *standard labels* supported by IOCS for the following reasons:

- To uniquely identify the reel and the file for each program.
- To provide compatibility with disk storage devices (to facilitate device independence).
- To provide compatibility with other IBM systems and those of other manufacturers.

Most installations use standard labels. Nonstandard labels and unlabeled tapes are permitted but are not covered in this text. There are two kinds of standard labels: *volume* and *file labels*. Figure 12-4 illustrates standard tape labels for the cases: one file on a volume, a multivolume file, and a multifile volume. The figure denotes IBGs by striped lines. TM, meaning tape mark, is discussed in a later section, IOCS.

VOLUME LABELS.   The volume label is the first record after the load point marker and describes the volume (reel). The first three bytes contain the identification VOL. Although some systems support more than one volume label, this text describes only the common situation of one label.

On receipt of a new tape reel, an operator uses an IBM utility program to write the volume label and a temporary file label ("header"). In all programs that process the reel, IOCS expects the volume label to be the first record. It checks the tape serial number against the number supplied by the

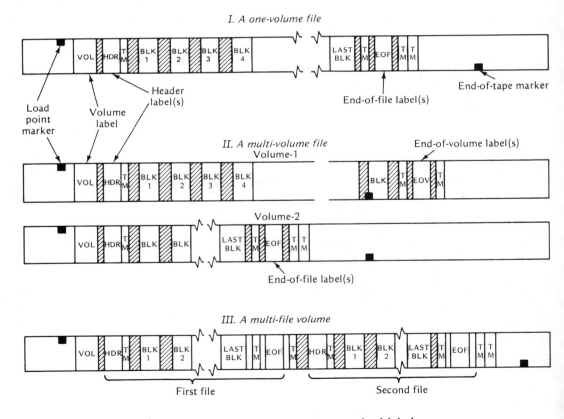

FIGURE 12-4 Magnetic tape standard labels.

special tape job control command TLBL or under OS, DD (Data Definition). The following describes each field of the 80-byte standard volume label:

POSITIONS	NAME	DESCRIPTION
01–03	Label Identifier	Contains VOL to identify the label.
04–04	Volume Label Number	Some systems permit more than one volume label; this field contains the numeric sequence of the volume label.
05–10	Volume Serial Number	The permanent unique number usually assigned when the reel is received. (The number also becomes the File Serial number in the Header label.)
11–11	Volume Security	A special security code, supported by OS.
12–41		Not used, reserved.
42–51	Owner Name and Address Code	May be used under OS to identify the owner of the reel.
52–80		Reserved for future expansion.

STANDARD FILE LABELS.   A tape volume contains a file of data, part of a file, or more than one file. Each file is uniquely identified to ensure, for example, that the correct file is being processed and that the tape being used to write on is obsolete. To provide such identification there are two file labels for each file for each reel: a *header label* and a *trailer label*.

1. HEADER LABEL. There is a header label at the start of the file. If the file requires more than one reel (multivolume file) then each reel contains a header label, numbered consecutively from one. If there is more than one file on a volume (multifile volume) then a header label begins each file.

    The header label contains HDR in the first three bytes, the file identification (such as ACCTS RECEIVABLE), the date the file may be deleted, etc. IOCS expects a header label to be the first record of the file, immediately following the volume label. IOCS checks the file identification, date, etc., against information supplied by the tape job control command, TLBL or DD.

    OS upports two header labels, HDR1 and HDR2, plus two trailer labels. The second label is also 80 bytes and immediately follows the first. It contains such data as record format (fixed, variable, or undefined), the block length, record length, and density in which the tape is written.

2. TRAILER LABEL. There is a trailer label at the end of each file (EOF). For a multivolume file, there is also a trailer at the end of each volume

(EOV). (OS requires a second trailer label.) If the trailer label is the end of the *file* (the file may require more than one volume), then the first three bytes of the label contain EOF. If the file requires more than one volume, then the first three bytes of the trailer label at the end of each volume contain EOV. The trailer label is otherwise identical to the header label with one exception: a block count field. IOCS counts the blocks as they are written and writes the total in the trailer label. Remember that IOCS fully performs label processing for standard labels.

The following describes each field of the 80-byte standard file label, for both the header and the trailer.

POSITIONS	NAME	DESCRIPTION
01–03	Label Identifier	Contains HDR if Header label, EOF if end of a data file, or EOV if end of volume (reel).
04–04	File Label Number	Some systems permit more than one file label; this field specifies the sequence of the file label. OS supports two labels each for HDR, EOF, and EOV.
05–21	File Identifier	Unique name to describe the file, such as INVENTORY MASTER.
22–27	File Serial Number	Same as the volume serial number of the first or only volume of the file. For a multivolume file, all file serial numbers are the same as the first one.
28–31	Volume Sequence Number	For multivolume files, this gives the sequence of volume numbers. The first or only volume contains 0001, the second 0002, etc.
32–35	File Sequence Number	For a multifile volume, this gives the sequence of the file. The first file on a volume contains 0001, the second 0002, etc.
36–39	Generation Number	Each time the file is rewritten, IOCS increments the generation number by 1 to identify the edition of the file.
40–41	Version Number of Generation	Specifies the version of the generation of the file.

42–47	Creation Date	Provides the year and the day when the file was written. For example, January 17, 1994 is stored as b94017.
		POSITION
		  1 Not used
		  2–3 Year
		  4–6 Day of year

48–53	Expiration Date	The year and day when the file may be erased and rewritten. Same format as creation date.
54–54	File Security	A special security code used by OS.
55–60	Block Count	Used in trailer labels to store the number of blocks since the previous header label.
61–73	System Code	Identifies the programming system.
74–80		Reserved.

IOCS FOR MAGNETIC TAPE

Assuming standard labels, IOCS (Data Management) performs the following functions for output and for input.

OUTPUT.   If the file is being written, processing is as follows:

1. *Processing the Volume Label.* Through the OPEN macro, IOCS checks that the first record is a volume label (VOL). It compares the volume serial number against the serial number (if any) on the tape job control command (TLBL or DD).

2. *Processing the Header Label.* After the volume label, IOCS reads the header label. It checks the expiration date in the header label against the date in the communications region. If the expire date has passed, IOCS backspaces the tape and writes a new header (HDR1) over the old header, using data from the tape job command. (Under OS, a second header (HDR2) is written next.) If this is a multivolume file, IOCS records the volume sequence number for this volume. Then IOCS writes a *tape mark*, a special block that it recognizes.

3. *Writing Records.* The PUT macro uses either a workarea or an IOREG. If the records are unblocked (one record per block), processing is similar to printing. If records are to be blocked, however, IOCS performs the required blocking. For example, assume two IOAREAs (buffers), three records per block, and a workarea. You format the record to be printed in the workarea. The first PUT executed writes the workarea record into the first record of IOAREA1:

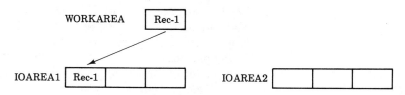

There is *no physical writing of tape* at this time. The second PUT writes the workarea record in the second record of IOAREA1, and the third PUT writes in the third record:

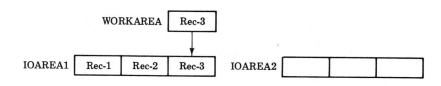

Now that the buffer is full, IOCS physically writes the contents of IOAREA1 onto tape, and while this is happening, *internal processing continues*. The fourth PUT writes the workarea in the first record of IOAREA2, the fifth in the second record of IOAREA2, and the sixth in the third record. At this time, IOCS physically writes IOAREA2 onto tape. The seventh PUT resumes writing the workarea in the first record of IOAREA1. Records blocked in three therefore require three PUT commands before IOCS physically writes a block.

4. *End-of-Volume.* If the system detects the reflective marker near the end of the reel, IOCS writes an EOV trailer label similar to the header label. The EOV label includes a block count of all blocks written. Next, IOCS writes a tape mark. Since the reflective marker is on the opposite side of the tape, data may be recorded right through its area. If an alternate tape drive is assigned, IOCS OPENs the alternate volume, processes its labels, and resumes writing of the file. It rewinds the old reel if required.

5. *End-of-File.* When all data is processed, you CLOSE the tape file. IOCS writes the last block of data (if any). The last block may contain fewer records than the blocking factor specifies. IOCS then writes a tape mark and an EOF trailer label with a block count. Finally, IOCS writes two tape marks and deactivates the file from further processing.

INPUT. The processing for reading a tape file is as follows:

1. *Processing the Volume Label.* IOCS reads the volume label and compares its serial number against the serial number (if any) on the job control entry.

2. *Processing the Header Label.* IOCS next reads the header label and checks that the file identification agrees with that on the TLBL or DD job control command to ensure that it is reading the correct file. For input, IOCS does not check the expiration date or write a new header. Also, if this is a multivolume file, the volume sequence numbers must be in consecutive, ascending sequence.

3. *Reading Records.* The GET macro reads records, specifying either a workarea or IOREG. If the tape records are unblocked, each GET reads one record (a block) from tape into storage. If records are blocked, IOCS performs the required deblocking as follows:

Assume again two IOAREAs, three records per block, and a workarea. The first GET executed reads a tape block containing records 1, 2, and 3, into IOAREA1, filling it with three records. IOCS then transfers the first record to the workarea, and reads the second tape block, containing records 4, 5, and 6, into IOAREA2:

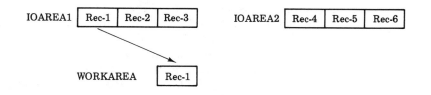

4. *End-of-Volume.* If IOCS encounters the end-of-volume label before the end of file (meaning that the file is continued on another reel), IOCS checks that the block count is correct. The reel is rewound, an alternate tape drive is opened, labels are checked, and reading of the next reel resumes.

5. *End-of-File.* Each GET operation causes IOCS to transfer a record to the workarea. Once every record has been transferred and processed and you attempt to perform another GET, IOCS recognizes an end-of-file condition. It then checks the block count, rewinds the reel (normally), and transfers control to your end-of-file address designated in the DTFMT or DCB macro. You should now CLOSE the tape file. In order to attempt further reading of the rewound tape file, you must perform another OPEN.

   • *Problems 12-4 through 12-7 should now be done.* •

VARIABLE-LENGTH RECORDS

Tape and disk files provide for variable-length records, both unblocked and blocked. The use of variable-length reduces the amount of unused tape or disk storage, but a disadvantage is in additional programming steps. A record may be variable-length because it contains one or more variable-length fields or a variable number of fixed-length fields:

1. *Variable-Length Fields.* Some fields, such as name and address, may vary considerably in length. In the normal fixed-length format you define the length as that of the longest possible content. It is possible to store only the significant characters of the field. For example, an address such as 123 W. 35TH ST. requires only 15 characters, whereas an address such as 1234 SOUTH HOLLINGSWORTH DRIVE requires 30 characters.

2. *Variable Number of Fields.* Certain applications require some data fields for one customer and not for another. For example, a utility

company sells both electricity and gas, and customers may adopt paying by budget. For any given customer, the *basic* subrecord could be customer number, name, address, and balance owing. Optionally, the customer may have an *electric* subrecord (containing rate and history of consumptions), a *gas* subrecord (containing rate and history of consumptions), and a *budget* subrecord (containing payment record). Customers may have any combination of these subrecords, but their record need not provide space for all possibilities. If the customer buys only electricity and does not pay by budget, then only the basic subrecord and electric subrecord are stored.

VARIABLE UNBLOCKED AND BLOCKED RECORDS. IOCS processes variable-length records similar to its processing of fixed-length records. However, both IOCS and the programmer must know the length of each *record* that is being read or written. Therefore, immediately preceding each record you define a 4-byte *record control word* containing the length of the record. For example, if the record is 310 bytes long, then the record control word contains 314 (310 plus 4 bytes required by the record control word itself). Further, IOCS must know the length of each *block*. Therefore, immediately preceding each block is a 4-byte *block control word* containing the length of the block. Your program calculates and stores the record length; IOCS calculates and stores the block length.

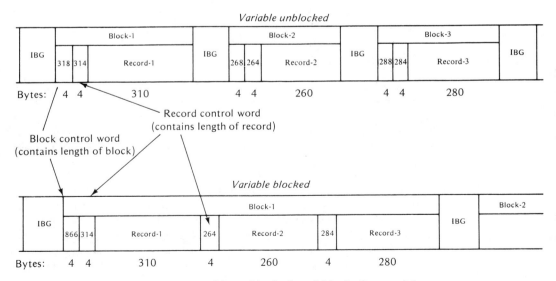

FIGURE 12-5 Variable unblocked and blocked record formats.

Figure 12-5 illustrates both variable unblocked and blocked records. For *variable unblocked* note the following: (1) The first record (Rec-1) is 310 bytes long and the record control word contains '314'. The block control word contains '318', which is the length of the entire block. (IOCS generates a block control word even for unblocked records.) (2) The second record (Rec-2) is 260 bytes long. The record control word contains '264', and the block control word contains '268'.

For *variable blocked* the example shows three records stored in the first block. A record control word precedes each record, and a block control word (containing '866') precedes the block. IOCS calculates the length in the block control word as:

Length of record-1:	310 + 4	=	314 bytes
Length of record-2:	260 + 4	=	264
Length of record-3:	280 + 4	=	284
			862 bytes
Add length of block control word:			4
Total length of block:			866 bytes

You designate a maximum block length in the DTF entry BLKSIZE, and IOCS fits as many records into this block as possible. For example, the block length may have been defined as (maximum) 900. If it had been defined as 800, only the first two records would have fit in this block and IOCS would begin the next block with the third record. Although records are blocked, the block length and the number of records per block will vary depending on the lengths of the records.

VARIABLE TAPE PROGRAMMING. Although IOCS performs most of the processing required for variable-length records, you must provide the record length. The additional programming steps are concerned with record and block length:

1. *Record Length.* As with fixed-length records, a program may process variable records in a workarea or in the I/O areas (buffers). You define the workarea as the *length of the largest possible record,* including the 4-byte record control word. When creating the record, calculate and store the record length in the record control word field. This field must be four bytes in binary format, aligned on a halfword boundary (DOS uses only the first two bytes).

2. *Block Length.* Define the I/O area as the *length of the largest desired block,* including the 4-byte block control word. On output, IOCS stores as many complete records in the block as will fit. IOCS performs all blocking and calculating of the block length. On input, IOCS deblocks the records similar to its deblocking of fixed-length records.

```
STMT    SOURCE STATEMENT                              DOS/VSE ASSEMBLER 18.14

  1              PRINT ON,NODATA,NOGEN

  3 *                  I N I T I A L I Z A T I O N

  5 PROG12C    START X'0050'                      X'50' FOR LBLTYP
  6            BALR  3,0
  7            USING *,3
  8            OPEN  FILEITP,FILEOPR
 17            GET   FILEITP,TAPEWORK             READ 1ST TAPE RECORD

 24 ***                M A I N   P R O C E S S I N G

 26 A10LOOP    BAL   5,B10SCAN                    SCAN
 27            GET   FILEITP,TAPEWORK             READ TAPE RECORD
 33            B     A10LOOP

 35 *                  E N D - O F - F I L E

 37 A90EOF     CLOSE FILEITP,FILEOPR              TERMINATE
 46            EOJ

 50 *                  P R O C E S S   V A R I A B L E   R E C O R D

 52 B10SCAN    LA    6,IDENTPIN                   ESTAB. ADDR OF INPUT IDENT
 53            LR    7,6                          ESTABLISH ADDRESS OF
 54            AH    7,RECLEN                         END OF RECORD
 55            SH    7,=H'9'
 56            MVC   PRINT+10(5),ACCTTPIN         MOVE ACCOUNT NO. TO PRINT

 58 B20        TRT   0(73,6),SCANTAB              SCAN FOR DELIMITER
 59            BZ    B30                          *  NO DELIMITER FOUND
 60            LR    4,1                          SAVE ADDR OF DELIMITER
 61            SR    1,6                          CALC. LENGTH OF FIELD
 62            BCTR  1,0                          DECREMENT LENGTH BY 1
 63            EX    1,M10MOVE                     MOVE VAR LENGTH FIELD
 64            MVI   CTLCHPR,WSP1
 65            PUT   FILEOPR,PRINT                PRINT, SPACE 1
 71            MVC   PRINT,BLANKPR                CLEAR PRINT AREA
 72            LA    6,1(0,4)                     INCREMENT FOR NEXT FIELD
 73            CR    6,7                          PAST END OF RECORD?
 74            BL    B20                          *  NO  - SCAN NEXT
 75 *                                             *  YES - END
 76 B30        MVI   CTLCHPR,WSP2
 77            PUT   FILEOPR,PRINT                PRINT 3RD LINE
 83            BR    5                            RETURN

 85 M10MOVE    MVC   PRINT+20(0),0(6)             MOVE VAR FIELD TO PRINT
```

FIGURE 12-6 (partial).

```
 87 *                         D E C L A R A T I V E S

 89 SCANTAB   DC      78X'00'                    TRT TABLE:
 90           DC      X'4E'                      *   DELIMITER POSITION
 91           DC      177X'00'                   *   REST OF TABLE

 93 FILEITP   DTFMT   BLKSIZE=300,               TAPE FILE                    +
                      DEVADDR=SYS025,                                         +
                      EOFADDR=A90EOF,                                         +
                      FILABL=STD,                                            +
                      IOAREA1=IOARTPI1,                                       +
                      IOAREA2=IOARTPI2,                                       +
                      RECFORM=VARBLK,                                         +
                      TYPEFLE=INPUT,                                          +
                      WORKA=YES

134           DS      0H                         ALIGN ON EVEN BOUNDARY
135 IOARTPI1  DS      CL300                      BUFFER-1 TAPE FILE
136 IOARTPI2  DS      CL300                      BUFFER-2 TAPE FILE

138 *                                            TAPE AREA:
139           DS      0H                         *   ALIGN ON EVEN BOUNDARY
140 TAPEWORK  DS      0CL82                      *   TOTAL MAX. RECORD + LENGTH
141 RECLEN    DS      H                          *   2-BYTE RECORD LENGTH
142           DC      H'0'                       *   2 BYTES UNUSED IN DOS
143 ACCTTPIN  DS      CL5                        *   ACCOUNT NUMBER
144 IDENTPIN  DS      CL73                       *   AREA FOR VAR. NAME|ADDR

146 FILEOPR   DTFPR   BLKSIZE=133,               PRINTER FILE                 +
                      CTLCHR=YES,                                             +
                      DEVADDR=SYSLST,                                         +
                      DEVICE=3203,                                           +
                      IOAREA1=IOARPR1,                                        +
                      IOAREA2=IOARPR2,                                        +
                      WORKA=YES
167 IOARPR1   DC      CL133' '                   BUFFER-1 PRINT FILE
168 IOARPR2   DC      CL133' '                   BUFFER-2 PRINT FILE

170 WSP1      EQU     X'09'                      CTL CHAR: PRINT, SPACE 1
171 WSP2      EQU     X'13'                      *         PRINT, SPACE 2

173 BLANKPR   DC      C' '
174 PRINT     DS      0CL133                     PRINT AREA
175 CTLCHPR   DS      XL1                        *
176           DC      CL132' '                   *
177           LTORG
178                   =C'$$BOPEN '
179                   =C'$$BCLOSE'
180                   =A(FILEITP)
181                   =A(TAPEWORK)
182                   =A(FILEOPR)
183                   =A(PRINT)
184                   =H'9'
185           END     PROG12C
```

FIGURE 12-6 Printing variable length records.

EXAMPLE: READ AND PRINT VARIABLE LENGTH RECORDS. Assume a file of tape records that contains variable-length name and address, with fields defined as:

1–4 Record length
5–9 Account number
10–82 Variable name and address

The name is immediately followed by a delimiter, in this case a '+' (X'4E'), to denote the end of the name. A '+' delimiter also terminates the next field, the house address, and another terminates the city:

```
JP PROGRAMMER+1327 NORTH 37TH STREET+KINGSTOWN+
```

Figure 12-6 illustrates a simple program that reads and prints the variable-length records. Devise several records and trace the logic of this routine carefully, step by step. Note that DTFMT specifies RECFORM=VARBLK (record form = variable blocked). The program reads each record and uses TRT and a loop to scan each of the three variable-length fields for the record delimiter. The length of the field is calculated, and EX moves each field to the print area. The program also checks for the absence of a delimiter. Output would appear as follows:

```
JP PROGRAMMER
1327 NORTH 37TH STREET
KINGSTOWN
```

Note: RECSIZE is omitted, because IOCS needs to know only the maximum block length. For OS, the DCB entry for variable, blocked record format is RECFM=VB.

DEBUGGING TIPS

1. Supply the correct job control entries for a magnetic tape file. For input, be sure to provide the correct file identification. Also, the name in the job control entry must agree with the name in the DTFMT or DCB statement.

2. Be sure to allow ample time for expiration dates when you create files.

3. Be especially careful of blocking factors. The block size must be a multiple of record size, and all programs that read the file must provide for the same lengths.

4. For variable-length records, be sure to align the tape workareas and buffers on an even boundary. When creating the file, you must calculate and store the record length, whereas IOCS calculates the block length. Your designated maximum block size must equal or exceed the size of any record.

PROBLEMS

12-1. Name seven advantages that magnetic tape provided over the old punched card system. What are some disadvantages?

12-2. Explain the following: (a) tape density; (b) tape markers; (c) IBG; (d) blocking factor; (e) fixed and variable-length.

12-3. Give an advantage and a disadvantage of increasing the blocking factor.

12-4. What is the purpose of (a) volume label; (b) header label; (c) trailer label?

12-5. Distinguish between (a) EOV and EOF on the trailer label; (b) a multifile volume and a multivolume file; (c) volume sequence number and file sequence number.

12-6. Revise the program in Figure 12-2 or 12-3 for the following: 6 records per block and locate mode. Change the file identification to your own name. Assemble and test the program.

12-7. Revise any previous program so that the input data is on magnetic tape. Provide for fixed, blocked records.

12-8. Assume a variable tape file, with six records whose lengths respectively are 326, 414, 502, 384, 293, and 504. Maximum block length is 1200 bytes. Depict the records showing all block and record lengths.

12-9. Write a program that creates a Supplier Master File.

- Input fields are: Supplier number (7 bytes); Amount payable (7 digits to be stored in packed format); Name (20 bytes); Street (24 bytes); City (24 bytes); Date of last purchase (ddmmyy).
- Name, street, and city are to be stored as variable-length fields, with hex 'FF' as a delimiter after each field.
- Next, write a program that updates the file with two tape files: (1) purchase entries (supplier number, amount, date); and (2) miscellaneous changes to name and address records.

13
DIRECT ACCESS STORAGE

Every installation has its own unique file organization and processing requirements. Also, its budget constraint limits the size of main storage and the type and number of devices. For one installation, the optimum configuration is a simple small diskette system, whereas for another it is a combination of magnetic tapes, direct access storage devices, and teleprocessing terminals. Direct Access Storage devices (DASD) have a significant advantage not provided by other devices: *DASD permits the organization and processing of files not only in sequence (as for tape), but also directly (randomly).* On tape, to access a particular record, you must process every preceding record; under DASD, however, you may directly access any record on a file.

This capability of direct accessing is particularly useful for *"on-line" processing*. For example, a department store keeps its accounts receivable on a DASD. When customers present their credit cards for a purchase, the cashier submits the customer credit number through a terminal to the computer center. A computer program uses this credit number to directly access the customer number in the file, determines the customer's credit rating, and signals the rating to the cashier. The cashier is informed almost immediately whether the customer can have more credit, or has exceeded the limit, or possibly that the credit card was reported lost.

DASDs are also commonly used for storing on-line the installation's operating system, the various support programs, and cataloged macros and subroutines. The DASD then, like tape, acts as both an input-output device and external storage. There are many types of direct access storage devices, of which the more common ones include:

- Drives with removable disk packs: 2314, 3330, and 3340.
- Drives with nonremovable storage: 3344, 3350, 3375, and 3380.

Each type of device has unique physical differences. However, the programming for each device is similar. Each record stored on a device has a specific location with a unique address and has a control field ("key") for identification.

DASD CHARACTERISTICS

Although there are DASDs that are drum storage, this text will discuss only DASDs that contain *disks* for recording data. These disks, made of metal coated with magnetic oxide, are similar to phonograph record surfaces. But a record has tracks that spiral inward, whereas the DASD tracks are concentric—each track makes a unique circle, as shown in Figure 13-1.

The track contains the data, generally recorded bit-by-bit, with records and blocks stored just as on magnetic tape. Similarly, data may be written and rewritten on the same track for permanent or temporary records. Although innermost tracks are shorter in circumference, all tracks contain the same number of bytes. On a 3350, for example, the disk surface has 555 *primary tracks* plus 5 *alternate tracks* used if any of the primary tracks become defective. The number of tracks on a disk surface and their capacity varies by device.

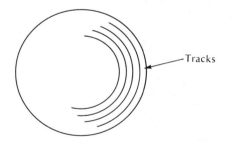

FIGURE 13-1 Disk tracks.

A *disk pack* consists of a number of rotating disks on a vertical shaft. Except for the top and bottom disk in some cases, the surfaces are recorded on both sides. Figure 13-2 shows the access arms that move horizontally to position at any track. Each arm has two read/write heads—one for the upper surface and one for the lower. Only one head at a time reads and writes. To read a record, for example, on the outermost track, all the access arms position there. The record to be read is on one of the surfaces—only the head for that surface is activated to read the record. As the disk rotates, the read occurs when the data record reaches the head.

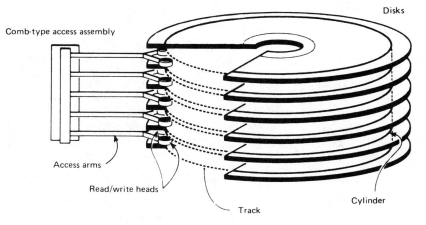

FIGURE 13-2 Disk storage device mechanism.

Figure 13-3 lists the number of tracks and their capacity. The 3380, for example, has 15 tracks per cylinder, giving a total of 1.26 billion bytes of storage (certain of this space is required for nondata records and gaps).

TIMING. There is some delay from the time a read/write instruction is executed until the data is actually received. As shown in Figure 13-3, the time varies considerably by device, but includes:

ACCESS MOTION. The more often and farther that the access arm moves, the more time is taken. The section Cylinder Concept explains how data is organized to minimize this seek time.

ROTATIONAL DELAY. As the disk rotates, time is required for the data to reach the read/write head. The average rotational delay ("latency") is half a rotation.

DATA TRANSFER RATE. The device's rotation speed and density of data affect the time to transfer data between the device and main storage.

IBM and other equipment manufacturers (OEMs) supply two types of DASDs. The earliest type and still widely in use is count-key-data (CKD) architecture that stores records according to count, key, and data areas. Examples are 3330, 3340, and 3350. The newer type is fixed block architecture (FBA) that stores data in fixed-length blocks of 512 bytes, and is designed to work especially with virtual storage systems. Examples are 3310 and 3370.

Device	CAPACITY				SPEED		
	Bytes per track	Tracks per cylinder	Number of cylinders	Total bytes	Ave. seek time (ms)	Ave. rot'l delay (ms)	Data rate KB/sec.
3340-1	8368	12	348	35,000,000 ⎤			
3340-2	8368	12	696	70,000,000 ⎬ 25		10.1	885
3344	8368	12	4 × 696	280,000,000 ⎦			
3330-1	13030	19	404	100,000,000 ⎫ 30		8.4	806
3330-11	13030	19	808	200,000,000 ⎭			
3350	19069	30	555	317,500,000	25	8.4	1200
3375	35616	12	2 × 959	819,738,000	19	10.1	1859
3380	47476	15	2 × 885	1,260,500,000	16	8.3	3000

FIGURE 13-3 IBM direct access devices.

COUNT-KEY-DATA ARCHITECTURE—CKD

CYLINDER CONCEPT. Under CKD architecture, data is organized to minimize arm movement. The DASD does not store data on a surface starting with the outermost track through to the inner tracks of the same surface. Such a storage method would require considerable access arm movement back and forth across surfaces. Rather, *the DASD stores data downwards beginning with the outermost track of the top surface through to the outermost track of the bottom surface.* This series of vertical tracks is called a *cylinder,* and the outermost one is cylinder-0.

The tracks for a cylinder are numbered beginning with 0, so that cylinder-0, track-0 is the outermost track of the top surface, and cylinder-0, track-1 is the next one below it. When all cylinder-0 is filled with data, the DASD stores next on cylinder-1 (the next inner series of tracks), beginning at cylinder-1, track-0. (The cylinder concept may be clearer if you imagine a series of different size tin cans, with no top or bottom lids, one inside the other. Each can is a "cylinder," with data stored in grooves around the sides.)

When the DASD reads sequentially, it positions the heads at cylinder-0. Head-0 begins reading from cylinder-0, track-0. When all track-0 records are read, the device selects head-1 to read from track-1—no access motion is required. The device then continues reading down through to the last track on cylinder-0. Next, the access arm moves (for the first time) to cylinder-1, where it processes successively from track-0 through to the last track of cylinder-1.

TRACK FORMAT. Every track contains certain information about its address and condition. Between the different records on the track are gaps;

these vary by device and their location on the track. The basic format for a track is:

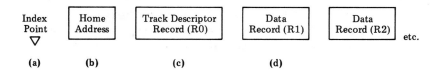

Index Point (a) Home Address (b) Track Descriptor Record (R0) (c) Data Record (R1) (d) Data Record (R2) etc.

(a) *The Index Point* tells the read/write device that this point is the physical beginning of the track—data is recorded following the Index Point.

(b) *The Home Address* tells the system the address of the track (the cylinder and head, or surface, number) and whether the track is a primary or alternate track, or defective.

(c) *The Track Descriptor Record (R0)* immediately follows the Home Address. The system stores information about the track in this record. There are two separate fields: a *Count Area* and a *Data Area*. The Count Area contains '0' for record number and '8' for data length. It is otherwise similar to the Count Area described next for Data Record under item (D). The Data Area contains eight bytes of information used by the system. The Track Descriptor Record is not normally accessible to the programmer.

(d) *Data Record Formats (R1 through Rn)*. Following the Track Descriptor (R0) record is one or more user data records, each consisting of the following:

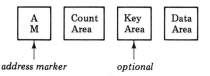

A M — address marker   Count Area   Key Area — optional   Data Area

Address Marker. The I/O control unit stores a two-byte Address Marker prior to each block of data. When reading records, the control unit uses the Address Marker to locate the beginning of data.

Count Area. This is a field that the system also stores and uses. Included are:

An Identifier field gives the cylinder/head number (similar to that in the Home Address), and the sequential record number (0–255) in binary, representing R0 through R255. (The Track Descriptor Record, R0, contains zero for record number.)

The Key Length field is explained in the next section, Key area.

The Data Length is a binary value 0 through 65,535 that specifies the number of bytes in the Data Area field (the length of your block of data).

For the end-of-file, the system generates a last ("dummy") record containing a length of zero in this field. When the system reads the file, this zero length indicates that there are no more records.

Key Area. Under DASD, the *key* is the control field for the records in the file, such as customer or inventory number. The key, if stored in this separate Key Area, can facilitate locating of records. The key area is *optional.* If omitted, then the file is called *formatted without keys (Count-Data-Format)* and the key length in the Count Area contains zero. If the file is *formatted with keys (Count-Key-Data-Format)*, then the Key Length contains the length of the Key area.

Data Area. You store data blocks in this area in any format—unblocked or blocked, fixed length or variable, just as on magnetic tape.

Under normal circumstances, a programmer is not concerned with the Home Address and Track Descriptor record, nor with the Address Marker, Count Area, and Key Area portions of the Data Record field. The system completely handles the processing of these fields. It is simply necessary to specify appropriate entries in the DTF or DCB and job control statements. You can then read and write sequential disk records much like tape.

The system stores as many records on the track as possible. Usually, records are stored completely (intact) on a track. A *record overflow* feature permits records to overlap from one track to the next.

FIXED BLOCK ARCHITECTURE—FBA

Another type of IBM DASD uses what is called *fixed-block architecture,* or FBA. The recording surfaces on the disks contain equal-length blocks of 512 bytes. For FBA, you need not be concerned with bytes per track or tracks per cylinder, only with the blocks on a device.

Device	Bytes per block	Blocks per track	No. of cylinders	Tracks per cylinder	Total bytes
3310	512	32	358	11	64,520,192
3370	512	62	2 × 750	12	571,392,000

FIGURE 13-4 Fixed-block architecture DASDs.

Figure 13-4 provides the details for two DASD models using fixed-block architecture, the 3310 and 3370.

FILE ORGANIZATION

There are several ways to organize a DASD file. Because the choice of method is a systems, not a programming, problem, this text gives a limited description of organization methods. The four main methods of DASD file organization are:

1. *Sequential Organization.* In this method, also used by terminals, cards, and magnetic tape, each record follows another successively according to a predetermined key (control field). A Sequential File would be appropriate where no on-line processing is required, and if most records are processed when the file is read. The DOS organization method is Sequential Access Method (SAM), and uses the macro DTFSD (Define The File Sequential Disk). The advantage is that sequential provides simplest design and programming, and minimizes DASD storage space. Disadvantage: it is difficult to locate a unique record and to insert a new record without rewriting the file.

2. *Direct (Random) Organization.* This method stores records based on a relationship between the key (control field) and the track address where the DASD record is stored. The program performs a calculation on the key number to locate the address of the record. The DOS method is Direct Access Method (DAM), and uses DTFDA (Direct Access). The advantage is that Direct Access provides fast and efficient use of DASD storage for directly accessing any record. Disadvantages are: (1) The file keys must lend themselves to such a calculation. (2) A calculation for more than one key may generate the same track address ("synonyms"). (3) The file may be arranged in a sequence other than sequential, and require special programming to produce sequential reports. (4) You must provide special programming to locate the record.

3. *Indexed Sequential Organization.* Records are stored *sequentially,* permitting normal sequential processing. In addition, this method has *indexes* related to the file; you may use these indexes to locate records *directly.* The DOS method is Indexed Sequential Access Method (ISAM), and uses DTFIS (Indexed Sequential). The advantage is that Indexed Sequential permits both sequential and direct processing of files with little special programming effort. Disadvantage: IS may use more DASD storage and process more slowly.

4. *Virtual Storage Access Method.* VSAM is available under DOS/VS and OS/VS systems, and permits both sequential and direct processing.

This text covers programming for Sequential, Indexed Sequential, and VSAM organization.

•   *Problems 13-1 through 13-5 should now be attempted.*   •

DOS PROGRAMMING EXAMPLE: CREATING A SEQUENTIAL DISK FILE

Programming for sequential disk is similar to that for magnetic tape. The program in Figure 13-5 creates a sequential disk file. The input is the tape file created in Chapter 12, Figure 12-2. A later section describes the disk job control entries, DLBL and EXTENT (bottom of the figure). Entries for the DTFSD macro are similar to those for DTFMT.

Note that there is no FILABL entry because DASD labels must be standard.

BLKSIZE=368   means that the blocksize for output is 360 bytes (4 × 90) plus 8 bytes for IOCS to construct a count field. The IOAREAs are also 368 bytes. You provide for these extra 8 bytes only for output; for input the entry is 360.

DEVICE=3340   means that for this program, records are written on a 3340 DASD.

VERIFY=YES   tells the system to reread each output record to check its validity. If the reread record is not identical to the record that was supposed to be written, the sytem rewrites the record, and performs another reread. Although this operation involves a disk read and more time, it helps ensure the accuracy of the written record.

```
STMT    SOURCE STATEMENT                              DOS/VSE ASSEMBLER 18.18

   2            PRINT ON,NOGEN,NODATA


   4 *                  I N I T I A L I Z A T I O N
   5 PROG13A   START X'0050'                    X'50' FOR LBLTYP
   6           BALR  3,0
   7           USING *,3
   8           OPEN  TAPE,SDISK
  17           GET   TAPE                        READ 1ST TAPE RECORD

  23 *                  M A I N   P R O C E S S I N G
  24 A10LOOP   MVC   TAPEIN,0(5)                 MOVE FROM TAPE BUFFER
  25           MVC   ACCTDKO,ACCTIN              MOVE TAPE FIELDS TO DISK
  26           MVC   NAMEDKO,NAMEIN              *     WORK AREA
  27           MVC   ADDRDKO,ADDRIN              *
  28           ZAP   BALNDKO,BALNIN              *
  29           MVC   DATEDKO,DATEIN              *
  30           PUT   SDISK,DISKWORK             WRITE WORK AREA ONTO DISK
  36           GET   TAPE                        READ NEXT TAPE RECORD
  41           B     A10LOOP

  43 *                  E N D - O F - F I L E
  44 A90END    CLOSE TAPE,SDISK
  53           EOJ
```

FIGURE 13-5 (partial).

```
 57 *               D E C L A R A T I V E S
 58 TAPE      DTFMT BLKSIZE=360,                TAPE FILE                        +
                    DEVADDR=SYS025,                                              +
                    EOFADDR=A90END,                                             +
                    ERROPT=IGNORE,                                              +
                    FILABL=STD,                                                 +
                    IOAREA1=IOARTPI1,                                           +
                    IOREG=(5),                                                  +
                    RECFORM=FIXBLK,                                             +
                    RECSIZE=090,                                                +
                    TYPEFLE=INPUT
 96 IOARTPI1 DS     CL360                       INPUT TAPE BUFFER-1

 98 TAPEIN   DS     0CL90                       TAPE INPUT AREA:
 99 ACCTIN   DS     CL6                         *   ACCOUNT NO.
100 NAMEIN   DS     CL20                        *   NAME
101 ADDRIN   DS     CL40                        *   ADDRESS
102 BALNIN   DS     PL4                         *   BALANCE
103 DATEIN   DS     CL6'DDMMYY'                 *   DATE
104          DS     CL14                        *   UNUSED

106 SDISK    DTFSD BLKSIZE=368,                 DISK FILE                        +
                    DEVADDR=SYS015,                                             +
                    DEVICE=3340,                                                +
                    IOAREA1=IOARDK,                                             +
                    RECFORM=FIXBLK,                                             +
                    RECSIZE=90,                                                 +
                    TYPEFLE=OUTPUT,                                             +
                    VERIFY=YES,                                                 +
                    WORKA=YES
171 IOARDK   DS     CL368                       DISK BUFFER-1

173 DISKWORK DS     0CL90                       DISK WORK AREA:
174 ACCTDKO  DS     CL6                         *   ACCOUNT NO.
175 NAMEDKO  DS     CL20                        *   NAME
176 ADDRDKO  DS     CL40                        *   ADDRESS
177 BALNDKO  DS     PL4                         *   BALANCE
178 DATEDKO  DS     CL6                         *   DATE
179          DC     CL14' '                     *   RESERVED
180          LTORG
181                 =C'$$BOPEN '
182                 =C'$$BCLOSE'
183                 =A(TAPE)
184                 =A(SDISK)
185                 =A(DISKWORK)
186          END    PROG13A


// LBLTYP TAPE
// EXEC LNKEDT

// TLBL   TAPE,'CUST REC TP',0,100236
// ASSGN  SYS015,X'381'
// DLBL   SDISK,'CUSTOMER RECORDS SD',0,SD
// EXTENT SYS015,222222,1,0,0700,10
```

FIGURE 13-5 Sequential disk processing under DOS.

This example creates a sequential disk (SD) file. In the next chapter, this file becomes input to create ("load") an Indexed Sequential (IS) file. You can also update an SD file directly by rewriting a record over a previous one.

Note: If you omit the entry for DEVADDR, the system uses the SYSnnn address from the job control entry.

OS PROGRAM EXAMPLE

The example OS coding in Figure 13-6 is a revision of the previous DOS example that reads tape records and copies them onto disk. The DD job control entries contain some of the DCB entries: for tape input, BLKSIZE, RECFM, and DEN, and for disk output, BLKSIZE and RECFM.

The OS Data Management system relates the name DISKOT in the DD job command to the same name in the program's DCB statement, DDNAME=DISKOT.

DISK LABELS

Disks, like magnetic tape, use labels to identify a volume and a file. This text describes the standard IBM labels that IOCS supports. The system reserves cylinder-0, track-0 for labels, as Figure 13-7 depicts. The following describes the contents of track-0:

RECORD-0   The track descriptor, R(0).

RECORD-1 AND 2   Certain devices, if the disk is SYSRES (containing the operating system), reserve R(1) and R(2) for the IPL (Initial Program Load) routine. For all other cases, R(1) and R(2) contain zeros.

RECORD-3   The VOL1 label. (There may actually be more than one volume label, from R(3) through R(10), supported by OS.)

RECORD-4 THROUGH THE END OF THE TRACK   This is the standard location for the *Volume Table of Contents (VTOC).* The VTOC contains the file label(s) for the files on the DASD.

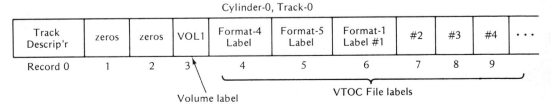

FIGURE 13-7 Disk volume layout.

```
//GO.TAPEIN  DD DSNAME=TRFILE,DISP=(OLD,PASS),UNIT=3420,              +
              DCB=(BLKSIZE=360,RECFM=FB,DEN=3)

//GO.DISKOT  DD DSNAME=&TEMPDSK,DISP=(NEW,PASS),UNIT=3350,SPACE=(TRK,10),  +
              DCB=(BLKSIZE=360,RECFM=FB)


***            I N I T I A L I Z A T I O N
*
PROG13B  START  0
         SAVE   (14,12)
         BALR   3,0
         USING  *,3
         ST     13,SAVEAREA+4
         LA     13,SAVEAREA
         OPEN   (TAPE,(INPUT),SDISK,(OUTPUT))
         GET    TAPE                       READ 1ST TAPE RECORD
*
***            M A I N   P R O C E S S I N G
*
A10LOOP  MVC    TAPEIN,0(1)                MOVE FROM TAPE BUFFER
         MVC    ACCTDKO,ACCTIN             MOVE TAPE FIELDS TO DISK
         MVC    NAMEDKO,NAMEIN             *     WORK AREA
         MVC    ADDRDKO,ADDRIN             *
         ZAP    BALNDKO,BALNIN             *
         MVC    DATEDKO,DATEIN             *
         PUT    SDISK,DISKWORK             WRITE WORK AREA ONTO DISK
         GET    TAPE                       READ NEXT TAPE RECORD
         B      A10LOOP
*
***            E N D - O F - F I L E
*
A90END   CLOSE  (TAPE,,SDISK)
         L      13,SAVEAREA+4
         RETURN (14,12)
*
***            D E C L A R A T I V E S
*
TAPE     DCB    DDNAME=TAPEIN,             TAPE INPUT DATA SET         +
                DSORG=PS,                                             +
                EODAD=A90END,                                         +
                LRECL=90,                                             +
                MACRF=(GL)

TAPEIN   DS     0CL90                      TAPE INPUT AREA:
ACCTIN   DS     CL06                       *  ACCOUNT NO.
NAMEIN   DS     CL20                       *  NAME
ADDRIN   DS     CL40                       *  ADDRESS
BALNIN   DS     PL04                       *  BALANCE
DATEIN   DS     CL06'DDMMYY'               *  DATE
         DS     CL14                       *  UNUSED

SDISK    DCB    DDNAME=DISKOT,             DISK OUTPUT DATA SET        +
                DSORG=PS,                                             +
                LRECL=90,                                             +
                MACRF=(PM)

DISKWORK DS     0CL90                      DISK WORK AREA:
ACCTDKO  DS     CL06                       *  ACCOUNT NO.
NAMEDKO  DS     CL20                       *  NAME
ADDRDKO  DS     CL40                       *  ADDRESS
BALNDKO  DS     PL04                       *  BALANCE(PACKED)
DATEDKO  DS     CL06                       *  DATE
         DC     CL14' '                    *  RESERVED FOR EXPANSION

SAVEAREA DS     18F                        REGISTER SAVE AREA
         LTORG

         END    PROG13B
```

FIGURE 13-6 Sequential disk processing under OS.

VOLUME LABELS. The standard volume label uniquely identifies the DASD volume. A 4-byte key area immediately precedes the 80-byte volume data area. The volume label is the fourth record (R3) on cylinder-0. The 80 bytes are arranged similarly to a tape volume label with one exception: positions 12–21 are the "Data File Directory," containing the starting address of the VTOC.

FILE LABELS. File labels identify and describe a file (data set) on a volume. The file label is 140 bytes long, consisting of a 44-byte key area and a 96-byte file data area. Each file on a volume requires a file label for identification. In Figure 13-7 all file labels for a volume are stored together in the Volume Table of Contents (VTOC). Although you may place the VTOC in any cylinder, its standard location is cylinder-0, track-0. There are four types of file labels:

1. The *Format-1 label* is equivalent to a magnetic tape file label. The Format-1 label differs, however, in that it defines the actual cylinder-track addresses of the start and end of the file—the "extent." Further, a file may be stored intact in an extent or in several extents on the same volume. Format-1 permits up to three extents on a volume. (Format-3 is used if the file is scattered over more than three extents.)

2. The *Format-2 label* is used for indexed sequential files.

3. The *Format-3 label* is stored if a file occupies more than three extents.

4. The *Format-4 label* is the first record in the VTOC, and defines the VTOC for the system.

The *Format-1 File Label* contains the following:

POSITIONS	NAME	DESCRIPTION
01–44	File Identification	A unique identification consisting of File-ID. Generation number. Version Number, separated by periods as indicated (you may use simply File-ID).
45–45	Format Identifier	'1' for Format-1.
46–51	File Serial Number	The Volume Serial number from the volume label.
52–53	Volume Sequence Number	The file may require more than one volume—this is the sequence number.
54–56	Creation Date	ydd (Binary) y = year (0–99), dd = day (1–366)
57–59	Expiration Date	Same Format as creation date
60–60	Extent Count No.	Number of extents for this file on this volume.

POSITIONS	NAME	DESCRIPTION
61–61	Bytes Used in Last Block of Directory	Used by OS only.
62–62		Reserved.
63–75	System Code	Contains the name of the operating system.
76–82		Reserved.
83–84	File Type	Contains a code to identify if SD, DA, or IS type of organization.
85–85	Record Format	Used by OS only.
86–86	Option Codes	IS only—to indicate if file contains Master index and type of overflow areas.
87–88	Block Length	IS only—the length of each block.
89–90	Record Length	IS only—the length of each record.
91–91	Key Length	IS only—the length of the key area for data records.
92–93	Key Location	IS only—the leftmost position of the key field within the record.
94–94	Data Set Indicators	SD only—indicates if this is the last volume.
95–98		OS only.
99–103	Last Record Pointer	OS only.
104–105		Reserved.
106–106	Extent Type	
107–107	Extent Sequence No.	Descriptors for the first or only extent for the file
108–111	Extent Lower Limit	
112–115	Extent Upper Limit	
116–125		Descriptors for the second extent, if any.
126–135		Descriptors for the third extent, if any.
136–140	Pointer	Address of the next label. For IS, the format-2 label; for SD and DA, the format-3 label if any.

Note: In the above example, IS means Indexed Sequential and OS means Operating System.

• *Problems 13-6 through 13-9 should now be attempted.* •

DASD CAPACITY

Knowing the length of records and the blocking factor, you can calculate the number of records on a track and on a cylinder. Knowing the number of records, you can also calculate the number of cylinders for the entire file. Based on the values in Figure 13-4, the formula for the number of blocks of data per track is the following:

$$\text{blocks per track} = \frac{\text{track capacity}}{\text{overhead} + C + KL + DL}$$

In the formula, C is a constant overhead value for keyed records, KL means key length, and DL is data (block) length. These values vary by disk device, as shown in Figure 13-8. The two following examples illustrate the above formula.

Device	Maximum capacity (bytes)	One data block	Key overhead	Track capacity
3330	13,030	135 + C + KL + DL	C = 0 when KL = 0 C = 56 when KL ≠ 0	13,165
3340	8,368	167 + C + KL + DL	C = 0 when KL = 0 C = 75 when KL ≠ 0	8,535
3350	19,069	185 + C + KL + DL	C = 0 when KL = 0 C = 82 when KL ≠ 0	19,254

FIGURE 13-8 Track capacity table.

Example 1. Device is a 3350, records are 242 bytes, five records per block (block size = 1210), and formatted without keys:

$$\text{Blocks per track} = \frac{19,254}{185 + (5 \times 242)} = \frac{19,254}{1395} = 13.8$$

$$\text{Records per track} = \text{blocks per track} \times \text{blocking factor}$$

$$= 5 \times 13 = 65$$

Example 2. Same as Example 1, but formatted with keys (key length is 12):

$$\text{Blocks per track} = \frac{19,254}{185 + 82 + 12 + 1210} = \frac{19,254}{1489} = 12.93$$

$$\text{Records per track} = 5 \times 12 = 60$$

Note that a DASD can store only a full block, not a fraction. Therefore, even if you calculate 13.8 or 12.9 blocks per track, the DASD stores only 13 or 12 blocks respectively.

To determine the number of records on a cylinder, refer to Figure 13-3 which discloses that a 3350 has 30 tracks per cylinder. Based on Example 1 above where the number of records per track is 65, a cylinder on the 3350 could contain $65 \times 30 = 1950$ records.

Using these figures, you can now calculate how much disk storage a file of, say, 100,000 of these records would require. Based on the preceding figures of 1950 records per cylinder, the file would require $100,000/1950 = 51.28$ cylinders.

DEBUGGING TIPS

1. Supply the correct job control entries for a disk file. For input, be sure to submit the correct file identification. Also, the name in the job entry must agree with the DTF or DCB statement. Under DOS, the EXTENT job entry must specify the correct location on the DASD.
2. Be sure to allow ample time for expiration dates when you create files.
3. Be especially careful of blocking factors. The block size must be a multiple of record size, and all programs that process the file must provide the same length.

PROBLEMS

13-1. What is the advantage of disk storage compared with magnetic tape?

13-2. Based on Figure 13-3, how many bytes can be stored on a cylinder for each device listed?

13-3. Why does a CKD disk store data vertically by cylinder rather than by tracks across a surface?

13-4. What is the purpose of (a) Home Address? (b) Track Descriptor Record? (c) Key Area?

13-5. What is the difference between a CKD and an FBA disk?

13-6. Distinguish the differences among Sequential, Direct, and Indexed Sequential organization methods.

13-7. Revise the file definition macro entries and I/O areas in Figure 13-5 or 13-6 for the following. Input records are 90 bytes long and six records per block. Output records are three records per block, to be loaded on a 3350 as SYS017. Assemble and test.

13-8. What is the purpose, location, and contents of the VTOC?

13-9. What is the DASD equivalent to the magnetic tape header label—what is its location and how does it differ?

13-10. Revise the job control for Figure 13-5 or 13-6 for the following. The filename is DISKOUT, the file-ID is ACCTS.RECEIVABLE, retention is 30 days, to be run on SYS017, serial number 123456, using a 3330 on cylinder-15 track-0 for 15 tracks.

13-11. Assume disk device 3350, record length 300 bytes, and six records per block. Based on the data in Figure 13-12, calculate the number of records that a track can store for the following: (a) records formatted without keys, and (b) records formatted with keys, key length = 10.

14

INDEXED SEQUENTIAL
FILE ORGANIZATION

Indexed Sequential file organization uses Indexed Sequential Access Method (ISAM) and is available in many variations on the microcomputers, minicomputers, and large mainframes of many manufacturers. Two systems on which ISAM is not available are DOS/VS and OS/VS which use instead Virtual Storage Access Method (VSAM).

THE PRIME DATA AREA

ISAM writes ("loads") your records on tracks in the *"prime data area."* These records are written *with keys,* in key sequence, and may be unblocked or blocked. Preceding your data records in the track is the Home Address (HA). See Figure 14-1: Under the Prime Data Area, for cylinder-0/track-1, the first key is 0001 and the highest is 0021. The last record on the ISAM file is on track-n (the number of surfaces varies by device) and contains the highest key on the cylinder, 0825.

THE TRACK INDEX

When creating a file, ISAM establishes a *"track index"* in track-0 of each cylinder used. The track index contains an entry for the highest key for each track on the cylinder. See Figure 14-1: For the track index for cylinder-0, the first entry is the Home Address. Next is the "Cylinder Overflow Control Record" (COCR), covered later. Next is an entry "key 0021, cylinder-0/track-1," which means that the highest key on cylinder-0/track-1 is 0021. The last entry is key 0825 on cylinder-0/track-n. This entry is followed by "dummy entry" to indicate the end of the index. The dummy entry contains the highest possible value in the key, X'Fs. Therefore, never use X'Fs as your own key. (Figure 14-1 is intentionally simplified. There are actually two entries for each track: a *normal entry* (shown) and an *overflow entry* (not shown).)

THE CYLINDER INDEX

ISAM creates a *"cylinder index"* for a file on a separate cylinder (or on a separate volume). The cylinder index contains an entry for the highest key for each cylinder—the home address. In Figure 14-1, the first entry is "key 0825, cylinder-0," meaning that the highest key on cylinder-0 is 0825. The

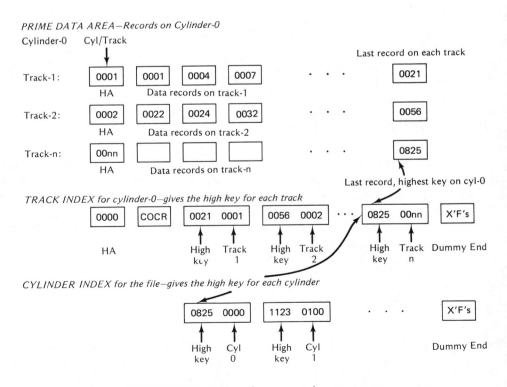

FIGURE 14-1 Indexed sequential organization.

cylinder index is also terminated by a dummy record containing X'Fs in the key. You tell ISAM where to store the cylinder index. At execute-time, ISAM can load the cylinder index into main storage for faster reference during the run, thereby reducing disk access and processing time.

A program may access an ISAM file either sequentially or directly. Sequential processing involves the use of the GET and PUT macros, coded for example as

```
GET  filename,workarea
```

Direct processing involves the use of the READ and WRITE macros; to access a record directly, code

```
READ  filename,key
```

ISAM then uses your key to locate the specified record. Assume that your required key is 0024 and your program is accessing directly:

1. ISAM searches the cylinder index to locate the cylinder where the required record is stored. The first entry in the index is high key 0825, cylinder-0. Since your key 0024 is lower than high key 0825, your record must be on cylinder-0.

2. Having located the cylinder, ISAM next accesses cylinder-0/track-0 for the track index in order to locate the track where your record is stored. The first index entry is high key 0021, track-1. Since your key 0024 is greater, your record is not on track-1. The second index entry is key 0056, track-2. Since your key is lower, your record (if it exists at all) must be on cylinder-0/track-2.

3. Having located the correct cylinder/track, ISAM now accesses track-2, reads record 0024 into a buffer in storage, and (finally!) transfers the record to your program's input area.

THE MASTER INDEX

If a cylinder index occupies more than four tracks, it may be more efficient to have an optional higher level of index, called a "master index." The master index immediately precedes the cylinder index and contains one entry for each track of the cylinder index—the highest key and the track. The system can first search the master index to locate the track where the required cylinder index is stored.

OVERFLOW AREAS

When updating a file you may often have to insert new records, such as new employees and customers. Under sequential processing you have to rewrite the entire file, inserting the new records. But ISAM permits inserting new records without rewriting the entire file. ISAM writes the new records as unblocked in an *overflow area,* and stores an overflow entry in the track index to point to the overflow record. There are two types of overflow areas; either or both may be used:

1. *Cylinder Overflow Area.* An EXENT job entry defines the number of tracks in each cylinder for ISAM to insert added records. The cylinder overflow area is in the prime area and stores all overflow records for that cylinder. The cylinder overflow control record (COCR) in Figure 14-1 stores the address of the last overflow record in the track and the number of unused bytes in the overflow area.

2. *Independent Overflow Area.* You may define the number and location of cylinders used exclusively for new added records. Your job control EXTENT statement at execute-time tells ISAM where to store records in the independent overflow area.

3. *Use of Both Areas.* If you specify both types of overflow areas, ISAM places all new records first in the cylinder overflow area. When any cylinder is full, ISAM places excess overflow records for that cylinder in the independent overflow area.

ISAM handles all overflow records and the linkage from the prime area to the overflow area. As the overflow areas become full, more processing time is required to access records. You may periodically use a special utility program to "reorganize" the file. The program rewrites the file, and merges the overflow records in with the prime area records.

There are four approaches to programming ISAM:

1. *Load or Extend an ISAM File.* The initial creation of an ISAM file is called *"loading."* Once the file is loaded, it is possible to include higher-key records at the end of the file—*"extending."*

2. *Adding Records to an ISAM File.* New records have keys that do not exist on the file. Special programming is required to insert or *"add"* these records within the file.

3. *Random Retrieval of an ISAM File.* New data requires that the file be updated at regular intervals. You can read the new data (such as sales records), use the key to randomly locate the ISAM master record, and rewrite the updated ISAM master.

4. *Sequential Processing of an ISAM File.* If there are many records to update and the new detail records are in sequence, then you can sequentially read and rewrite the ISAM master.

PROCESSING DOS INDEXED SEQUENTIAL FILES

The following illustrates required imperative macros and the DTFIS file definition macro for indexed sequential file organization under DOS. The DOS Supervisor and I/O Macros manual supplies additional useful information.

LOAD OR EXTEND AN ISAM FILE UNDER DOS. Figure 14-2 creates an ISAM file. The input is sequential disk (SD) records created in Figure 13-5. This program writes these records onto an indexed sequential (IS) file called DISKIS. The new instructions are macros SETFL, WRITE, ENDFL, and DTFIS. The job control entries also vary for ISAM: (1) The DLBL job entry for "codes" contains ISC meaning indexed sequential create (Load), and (2) there is an EXTENT entry both for the cylinder index and for the data area. In addition, ISAM requires that you check the *status condition* caused by each macro (covered later).

ISAM MACROS FOR LOAD AND EXTEND. For Load and Extend, code the usual OPEN and CLOSE to activate and deactivate the files. The new macros are:

SETFL	filename
WRITE	filename, NEWKEY
ENDFL	filename

SETFL (Set File Load Mode). When you load or extend a file, SETFL initializes the ISAM file by preformatting the last track of each track index. The operand references the DTFIS name of the ISAM file to be loaded.

WRITE. The WRITE macro loads a record onto the ISAM file. The filename is your DTFIS name. Operand-2 is the word NEWKEY. You store the key and data area in a workarea (called ISAMOUT in Figure 14-2). DTFIS knows this area through the entry WORKL=ISAMOUT. For the WRITE statement, ISAM checks that the new key is in ascending sequence. Then ISAM transfers the key and data area to an I/O area (this is IOARISAM in the program, known to DTFIS by IOAREAL=IOARISAM). Here ISAM constructs the count area:

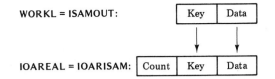

WORKL = ISAMOUT:

IOAREAL = IOARISAM:

ENDFL (End File Load Mode). After all records are written, ENDFL performs the following: (1) writes the last block of data (if any); (2) writes an end-of-file record; and (3) writes any required index entries.

THE DTFIS MACRO. The maximum length for an ISAM filename is seven. In Figure 14-2, the DTFIS entries for the file to be loaded are:

CYLOFL=1 gives the number of tracks on each cylinder to be reserved for each cylinder overflow area (if any). The maximum depends on the device.

DEVICE=3340 is the DASD unit containing the prime data area or overflow area for the file.

DSKXTNT=2 designates the number of extents that the file uses. The number consists of one for each data extent and one for each index area and independent overflow area extent. This program has one extent for the prime data area and one for the cylinder index.

IOAREAL=IOARISAM provides the name, IOARISAM, of the ISAM load I/O area. The symbolic name IOARISAM references the DS output area. For loading unblocked records, the IOAREAL field length is calculated as:

$$\text{Count Area (8)} + \text{Key Length (6)} + \text{Record Length (90)} = 104$$

IOROUT=LOAD tells the Assembler that the program is to load an ISAM file.

KEYLEN=6 provides the length of your key area.

NRECDS=1 gives the number of records per block for this file (unblocked).

RECFORM=FIXUNB means that the records are to be fixed-length and unblocked.

RECSIZE=90 is the length of each record's data area.

VERIFY=YES tells the system to check the parity of each record as it is written.

WORKL=ISAMOUT gives the name, ISAMOUT, of your load workarea (the DS for the workarea is defined elsewhere in the program). For unblocked records, this length is calculated as:

$$\text{Key Length (6)} + \text{Data Area (90)} = 96$$

STATUS CONDITION. ISAM macros may generate certain error conditions, which the system allows you to test. After each I/O macro operation, ISAM places the *"status"* in a 1-byte field called *filename*C. For example, if your DTFIS name is DISKIS, then ISAM calls the status byte DISKISC.

Following is a list of the eight bits in *filename*C that the system may set when a program loads an ISAM file:

BIT	LOAD STATUS ERROR CONDITION
0	Any uncorrectable DASD error except wrong length record.
1	Wrong length record detected during output.
2	The prime data area is full.
3	The cylinder index is full, discovered by SETFL.
4	The master index is full, discovered by SETFL.
5	Duplicate record—the current key is the same as the one previously loaded.
6	Sequence check—the current key is lower than the one previously loaded.
7	The prime data area is full and there is no space for ENDFL to store the end-of-file record.

In Figure 14-2, TM operations test DISKIS after the macros SETFL, WRITE, and ENDFL. After SETFL, for example, the TM instruction tests if bits 0, 3, and 4 are on. If any of the conditions exist, the program branches to an error routine (not coded). There, special programming action may isolate the error, print an error message, and possibly terminate the job.

RANDOM RETRIEVAL OF AN ISAM FILE. Figure 14-3 randomly retrieves an ISAM file. The DLBL job command has one difference: the entry for "codes" contains ISE, used to indicate any load extension, add, or retrieve. The program reads modification records in random sequence, with changes to the ISAM master file. The ISAM master is the one loaded in the previous example. For each modification record, the program uses the account number (key) to locate the correct ISAM record. The program then rewrites the updated record on the ISAM file.

ISAM MACROS FOR RANDOM RETRIEVAL. The new macros for random retrieval are:

READ	filename, KEY
WAITF	filename
WRITE	filename, KEY

READ. The READ macro causes ISAM to access a required record from the file. Operand-1 contains the DTFIS filename, and operand-2 contains the word KEY. You must store your key in the field referenced by the DTFIS entry KEYARG. In this program KEYARG=KEYNO. For each modifica-

```
   1              PRINT ON,NODATA,NOGEN

   3 *                      I N I T I A L I Z A T I O N
   4 PROG13C  START X'0050'                       X'50' FOR LBLTYP NSD
   5              BALR  3,0
   6              USING *,3
   7              OPEN  DISKSD,DISKIS
  16              SETFL DISKIS                     SET ISAM LIMITS
  22              TM    DISKISC,B'10011000'        ANY SETFL ERRORS?
  23              BO    R10ERR                        YES - ERROR ROUTINE
  24              GET   DISKSD,SDISKIN             GET 1ST SEQ'L DISK RECORD

  31 *                      M A I N   P R O C E S S I N G
  32 A10LOOP  MVC   KEYNO,ACCTIN               SET UP KEY NUMBER
  33              MVC   RECORD,SDISKIN            SET UP ISAM DISK RECORD
  34              WRITE DISKIS,NEWKEY             WRITE ISAM RECORD
  39              TM    DISKISC,B'11111110'        ANY WRITE ERRORS?
  40              BO    R10ERR                        YES - ERROR ROUTINE
  41              GET   DISKSD,SDISKIN             GET NEXT SEQ'L DISK RECORD
  47              B     A10LOOP                   NO  - CONTINUE

  49 *                      E N D - O F - F I L E
  50 A90END   ENDFL DISKIS                     END ISAM FILE LIMITS
  62              TM    DISKISC,B'11000001'        ANY ENDFL ERRORS?
  63              BO    R10ERR                        YES - ERROR ROUTINE
  64              CLOSE DISKSD,DISKIS             NORMAL TERMINATION
  73              EOJ

  77 *                      D A S D   E R R O R   R O U T I N E S
  78 R10ERR   EQU   *                         DASD ERROR
  79 *              .                          RECOVERY ROUTINES
  80 *              .
  81              CLOSE DISKSD,DISKIS             ABNORMAL TERMINATION
  90              EOJ

  94 *                      D E C L A R A T I V E S
  95 DISKSD   DTFSD BLKSIZE=360,               SEQUENTIAL DISK INPUT        +
                    DEVADDR=SYS015,                                         +
                    EOFADDR=A90END,                                         +
                    DEVICE=3340,                                            +
                    IOAREA1=IOARSD1,                                        +
                    RECFORM=FIXBLK,                                         +
                    RECSIZE=90,                                             +
                    TYPEFLE=INPUT,                                          +
                    WORKA=YES
 155 IOARSD1  DS    CL360                     SEQ'L DISK BUFFER-1

 157 SDISKIN  DS    0CL90                     SEQ'L DISK INPUT AREA
 158 ACCTIN   DS    CL6                       *    KEY
 159          DS    CL84                      *    REST OF RECORD
```

FIGURE 14-2 (partial).

```
161 DISKIS    DTFIS  CYLOFL=1,                INDEXED SEQ'L DISK LOAD      +
                     DEVICE=3340,                                          +
                     DSKXTNT=2,                                            +
                     IOAREAL=IOARISAM,                                     +
                     IOROUT=LOAD,                                          +
                     KEYLEN=6,                                             +
                     NRECDS=1,                                             +
                     RECFORM=FIXUNB,                                       +
                     RECSIZE=90,                                           +
                     VERIFY=YES,                                           +
                     WORKL=ISAMOUT
211 IOARISAM  DS     CL104                    ISAM OUTPUT AREA

213 ISAMOUT   DS     0CL96                    ISAM WORKAREA
214 KEYNO     DS     CL6                      *    KEY LOCATION
215 RECORD    DS     CL90                     *    DATA AREA

217           LTORG
218                  =C'$$BOPEN '
219                  =C'$$BSETFL'
220                  =C'$$BENDFL'
221                  =C'$$BCLOSE'
222                  =A(DISKIS)
223                  =A(DISKSD)
224                  =A(SDISKIN)
225           END    PROG13C
```

FIGURE 14-2 Creating (loading) a DOS ISAM file.

tion record read, the program transfers the account key number to KEYNO.

WAITF. The WAITF macro allows a READ or WRITE operation to be completed before another is attempted. In a random retrieval you are reading and rewriting the same records, and you must ensure that the operation is finished. You may code WAITF anywhere following a READ/WRITE, and preceding the next READ/WRITE.

WRITE. The WRITE macro rewrites an ISAM record. Operand-1 is the DTFIS filename, and operand-2 is the word KEY. KEY refers to your entry in KEYARG.

THE DTFIS MACRO. DTFIS differences for random retrieval include:

IOAREAR=IOARISAM gives the name, IOARISAM, to the ISAM retrieve I/O area. The symbolic name IOARISAM references the DS area for retrieving unblocked records. The IOAREAR field length is calculated as:

Key length (6) + "Sequence Link field" (10) + Record length (90) = 106

TYPEFLE=RANDOM means that you are to retrieve records randomly, by key. Other entries are SEQNTL for sequential processing, and RANSEQ for both random and sequential.

WORKR=ISAMOUT is the name of your retrieval work area.

```
  1               PRINT ON,NODATA,NOGEN


  3 PROG13D       START X'0050'                    X'50' FOR LBLTYP NSD
  4               BALR  3,0
  5               USING *,3
  6               OPEN  FILEIN,DISKIS
 15               GET   FILEIN,RECDIN              READ 1ST INPUT RECORD

 22 *                   M A I N   P R O C E S S I N G
 23 A10LOOP  MVC   KEYNO,ACCTIN               SET UP KEY NUMBER
 24               READ  DISKIS,KEY                 READ ISAM RANDOMLY
 29               TM    DISKISC,B'11010101'        ANY READ ERROR?
 30               BO    R10ERR                         YES - ERROR ROUTINE
 31               WAITF DISKIS                      COMPLETE READ OPERATION
 36               MVC   ACCTDKO,ACCTIN             MOVE FIELDS
 37               MVC   NAMEDKO,NAMEIN             *  TO DISK
 38               MVC   ADDRDKO,ADDRIN             *   WORKAREA
 39               PACK  BALNDKO,BALNIN             *
 40               MVC   DATEDKO,DATEIN             *

 42               WRITE DISKIS,KEY                 WRITE NEW ISAM RECORD
 47               TM    DISKISC,B'11000000'        ANY WRITE ERROR?
 48               BO    R10ERR                      * YES - ERROR ROUTINE
 49               GET   FILEIN,RECDIN              READ NEXT INPUT RECORD
 55               B     A10LOOP                     *  NO  - CONTINUE

 57 *                   E N D - O F - F I L E
 58 A90END   CLOSE FILEIN,DISKIS               TERMINATION
 67               EOJ

 71 *                   D A S D   E R R O R   R O U T I N E S
 72 R10ERR   EQU   *                           DASD ERROR
 73 *                                           RECOVERY ROUTINES
 74               B     A90END

 76 *                   D E C L A R A T I V E S
 77 FILEIN   DTFCD DEVADDR=SYSIPT,             INPUT FILE                        +
                   IOAREA1=IOARIN1,                                             +
                   IOAREA2=IOARIN2,                                             +
                   BLKSIZE=80,                                                  +
                   DEVICE=1442,                                                 +
                   EOFADDR=A90END,                                             +
                   TYPEFLE=INPUT,                                              +
                   WORKA=YES
 98 IOARIN1  DS    CL80                        INPUT BUFFER 1
 99 IOARIN2  DS    CL80                        INPUT BUFFER 2

101 RECDIN   DS    0CL80                       INPUT AREA:
102 CODEIN   DS    CL2                         *  RECORD CODE '01'
103 ACCTIN   DS    CL6                         *  ACCOUNT NO.
104 NAMEIN   DS    CL20                        *  NAME
105 ADDRIN   DS    CL40                        *  ADDRESS
106 BALNIN   DS    ZL6'0000.00'                *  BALANCE
107 DATEIN   DS    CL6'DDMMYY'                 *  DATE
```

FIGURE 14-3 (partial).

```
STMT    SOURCE STATEMENT                              DOS/VSE ASSEMBLER 18.26

109 DISKIS    DTFIS CYLOFL=1,            ISAM RANDOM RETRIEVAL              +
                    DEVICE=3340,                                           +
                    DSKXTNT=2,                                             +
                    IOAREAR=IOARISAM,                                      +
                    IOROUT=RETRVE,                                         +
                    KEYARG=KEYNO,                                          +
                    KEYLEN=6,                                              +
                    NRECDS=1,                                              +
                    RECFORM=FIXUNB,                                        +
                    RECSIZE=90,                                            +
                    TYPEFLE=RANDOM,                                        +
                    VERIFY=YES,                                            +
                    WORKR=ISAMOUT
191 IOARISAM  DS    CL106                KEY LEN + 10 + REC LENGTH

193 ISAMOUT   DS    0CL96                ISAM WORKAREA:
194 KEYNO     DS    CL6                  KEY AREA
195 RECORD    DS    0CL90                DATA AREA
196 ACCTDKO   DS    CL6                  *  ACCOUNT NO.
197 NAMEDKO   DS    CL20                 *  NAME
198 ADDRDKO   DS    CL40                 *  ADDRESS
199 BALNDKO   DS    PL4                  *  BALANCE
200 DATEDKO   DS    CL6                  *  DATE
201           DC    CL14' '              *  RESERVED

203           LTORG
204                 =C'$$BOPEN '
205                 =C'$$BCLOSE'
206                 =A(FILEIN)
207                 =A(RECDIN)
208                 =A(DISKIS)
209           END   PROG13D
```

FIGURE 14-3 Random retrieval of a DOS ISAM file.

STATUS CONDITION.   The status condition byte for Add and Retrieve is different from Load. The following is a list of the bits:

BIT	ADD AND RETRIEVE CONDITION
0	Any uncorrectable DASD error except wrong length record.
1	Wrong length record detected during an I/O operation.
2	End-of-file during sequential retrieval *(not an error!)*.
3	The record to be retrieved is not in the data file.
4	The ID specified to the SETL in SEQNTL is outside the prime data limits.
5	An attempt to add a record to the file for which the key already exists.
6	The cylinder overflow area is full.
7	A retrieval function is trying to process an overflow record.

Figure 14-3 tests for various conditions after the ISAM macros. Once again, the program would normally isolate the error, print a message, and perhaps terminate the job.

SEQUENTIAL READING OF AN ISAM FILE. Sequential reading of a DOS ISAM file involves use of the macros SETL, GET, and ESETL. SETL (Set Low) establishes the starting point for the first record to be processed. SETL options include:

```
SETL  filename,BOF     Set start at first record of the file.
SETL  filename,KEY     Set start at the record with the key in the field defined
                       by the DTFIS KEYARG entry.
SETL  filename,GKEY    Set start at first record within a required group. The
                       KEYARG field could contain, for example, "A340000"
                       to indicate all records with keys beginning with A34.
```

The ESETL macro terminates sequential mode, and is coded as ESETL,filename. DTFIS entries include:

```
IOROUT=RETRVE
TYPEFLE=SEQNTL or RANSEQ
KEYLOC=n               (to indicate the first byte of the key in a record, if
                       processing begins with a specified key or group of
                       keys, and records are blocked)
```

PROCESSING OS INDEXED SEQUENTIAL FILES

Processing ISAM files under OS is similar to, but not identical to, DOS processing. (Fortunately, DOS coding for VSAM has been designed to be more compatible with OS.) Under OS, ISAM provides for a "delete code"— if the first byte of a record contains X'FF', ISAM will automatically delete the record where required. The following provides some features of OS ISAM processing.

LOAD AN ISAM FILE UNDER OS. The OS imperative macros concerned with creating an indexed sequential file are the conventional OPEN, PUT, and CLOSE. DCB entries are:

```
DDNAME   = name of the data set
DSORG    = IS for indexed sequential
MACRF    = (PM) or (PL)
BLKSIZE  = length of each block
CYLOFL   = number of overflow tracks per cylinder
KEYLEN   = length of the key area
LRECL    = length of each record
NTM      = number of tracks for master index, if any
OPTCD    = options required. For example, MYLRU:
           M establishes a master index (or omit M)
           Y & R control use of cylinder overflow and independent areas
```

L is delete code to cause bypassing records with X'FF' in first byte
U (for fixed length only) establishes track index in main storage

RECFM   =   record format for fixed/variable and unblocked/blocked: F, FB, V, VB

SEQUENTIAL RETRIEVAL AND UPDATE.

SEQUENTIAL RETRIEVAL AND UPDATE. Under OS, sequential retrieval and update involves the OPEN, SETL, GET, PUTX, ESETL, and CLOSE macros. Once the data set has been created with standard labels, many DCB entries are no longer required. DDNAME and DSORG=IS are still used, and the following are applicable:

MACRF=(entry)	(GM) or (GL) for input only. (PM) or (PL) for output only. (GM,SK,PU) if read and rewrite in place: S = use of SETL, K = Key or Key class used, PU = use of PUTX macro.
EODAD=eofaddress	For input, if reading to end-of-file.
SYNAD=address	Optional error checking.

THE SETL MACRO. SETL (Set Low address) establishes the first sequential record to be processed, used because a programmer may want to start anywhere in a data set. The general format for the SETL macro is the following:

```
SETL dcb-name,start-position,address
```

The "start-position" operand has a number of options:

B	=	Begin with first record in the data set. (Omit operand-3 for B or BD.)
K	=	Begin with the record with the key in the operand-3 address.
KC	=	Begin with the first record of the "Key class" in operand-3. If the first record is "deleted," begin with the next nondeleted record. A Key class is any group of keys beginning with a common value, such as all keys 287XXXX.
I	=	Begin with the record at the actual device address in operand-3.

BD, KD, KDH, KCD, and ID cause retrieval of only the data portion of a record.

Following are some examples of SETL to set the first record in an ISAM file called DISKIS, using a six-character key:

	SETL	DISKIS,B	Begin with the first record of the data set
	SETL	DISKIS,K,KEYADD1	Begin with key 012644 in data set
	SETL	DISKIS,KC,KEYADD2	Begin with first record that begins with key 012
KEYADD1	DC	C'012644'	6-character key
KEYADD2	DC	C'012',XL3'00'	3-character key followed by 3 bytes of hex zeros

The ESETL macro, used as ESETL dcb-name, terminates sequential retrieval. If there is more than one SETL, ESETL must precede each additional one.

In Figure 14-4, the program sequentially reads an ISAM file. The objective is to insert a delete code (X'FF') in any record that is more than five years old. The standard date from the TIME macro is packed 00yyddd+, and the date in the records in positions 26–28 is in the same format. The PUTX macro rewrites any such old record, with the delete byte.

There are many other features and macros associated with OS. Check especially the IBM OS Data Management Services Guide and Data Management Macro Instructions manuals.

```
PROG13     START
           SAVE    (14,12)
           BALR    3,0
           USING   *,3
           ST      13,SAVEAREA+4
           LA      13,SAVEAREA

           OPEN    (ISFILE)
           SETL    ISFILE,B               START 1ST RECORD OF DATA SET
           TIME
           ST      1,TODAY
           SP      TODAY,=P'5000'         CALC DATE 5 YEARS AGO
           GET     ISFILE                 GET 1ST RECORD

A10LOOP    CP      26(3,1),TODAY          5 YEARS OR OLDER?
           BNL     A20                    *    NO  - BYPASS
           MVI     0(1),X'FF'             *    YES - SET DELETE CODE
           PUTX    ISFILE                 *    RE-WRITE RECORD
A20        GET     ISFILE                 GET NEXT
           B       A10LOOP                LOOP

A90END     ESETL   ISFILE                 END-OF-FILE
           CLOSE   (ISFILE)
           L       13,SAVEAREA+4
           RETURN  (14,12)

SAVEAREA   DS      18F
TODAY      DS      F                      TODAY'S DATE: 00YYDDD+
IOAREA     DS      CL100                  DISK IO AREA

ISFILE     DCB     DDNAME=INDEXDD,DSORG=IS,EODAD=A90END,MACRF=(GL,S,PU)

           LTORG
           END     PROG13
```

FIGURE 14-4 Sequential retrieval of an OS ISAM file.

PROBLEMS

14-1. For ISAM, what is the purpose of (a) master index? (b) cylinder index? (c) track index?

14-2. What are the different ways to process an ISAM file? What is the difference between extending and adding records?

14-3. Revise Figure 14-2 for the input as revised in Problem 13-7, and for the new ISAM output: three records per block and both a cylinder and independent overflow area. You will have to review the IBM Supervisor manual for this. Assemble and test.

14-4. Revise, assemble, and test Figure 14-3 according to the changes in the previous problem.

15

VIRTUAL STORAGE ACCESS METHOD–VSAM

Virtual Storage Access Method (VSAM) is a relatively recent file organization method for users of IBM OS/VS and DOS/VS. VSAM facilitates both sequential and indexed processing and supplies as well a number of useful utility programs. OS/VS and DOS/VS are the only systems that support VSAM, but do not support ISAM.

The term file is somewhat ambiguous since it may reference an I/O device or the records that the device processes. To distinguish a collection of records, IBM OS literature uses the term data set.

VSAM provides three types of data sets:

1. *Key Sequenced data set (KSDS).* KSDS maintains records in sequence of key, such as employee or part number, and is equivalent to indexed sequential.

2. *Entry Sequenced data set (ESDS).* ESDS maintains records in the sequence that they were initially entered, and is equivalent to sequential organization.

3. *Relative Record data set (RRDS)* maintains records in order of relative record number and is equivalent to direct file organization.

Both OS/VS and DOS/VS handle VSAM the same way and use similar support programs and macros. OS however has a number of extended features.

Thorough coverage of Assembler VSAM would require an entire textbook. However, this chapter supplies enough information to enable you to code programs that create, retrieve, and update a VSAM data set. For complete details, see the IBM Access Methods Services manual and the IBM DOS/VS or OS/VS Supervisor and I/O Macros manual.

CONTROL INTERVAL

For all three types of data sets, VSAM stores records in groups (one or more) of control intervals. You may select the control interval size, but if you allow VSAM to do so, it optimizes the size based on the record length and the type of disk device being used. The maximum size of a control interval is 32,768 bytes.

At the end of each control interval is control information that describes the data records:

```
| rec-1 | rec-2 | rec-3 |  . . .  |control information|
```

A control interval contains one or more data records, and a specified number of control intervals comprises a control area. VSAM addresses a data record by relative byte address (RBA)—its displacement from the start of the data set. Consequently, the first record of a data set is at RBA zero, and if records are 500 bytes long, the second record is at RBA 500.

The following list compares the three types of VSAM organizations:

FEATURE	KEY SEQUENCED	ENTRY SEQUENCED	RELATIVE RECORD
Record sequence	By key	In sequence in which entered	In sequence of relative record number
Record length	Fixed or variable	Fixed or variable	Fixed only
Access of records	By key via index or RBA	By RBA	By relative record number
Change of address	Can change record RBA	Cannot change record RBA	Cannot change relative record number
New records	Distributed free space for records	Space at end of data set	Empty slots in data set
Recovery of space	Reclaims space if record is deleted	No delete, but can overwrite an old record	Can reuse deleted space

ENTRY SEQUENCED DATA SETS

An Entry Sequenced data set (ESDS) acts like sequential file organization but has the advantages of being under control of VSAM, some use of direct processing, and password facilities. Basically, the data set is in the sequence in which it is created, and you normally (but not necessarily) process from the start to the end of the data set. Sequential processing of an ESDS by RBA is known as *addressed access,* which is the method you use to create the data set. You may also process ESDS records directly by RBA. Since ESDS is not concerned with keys, the data set may legally contain duplicate records.

Assume an ESDS containing records with keys 001, 003, 004, and 006. The data set would appear as follows:

I 001 I 003 I 004 I 006 I

You may want to use ESDS for tables that are to load into programs, for small files that are always in ascending sequence, and for files extracted from a KSDS that are to be sorted.

RELATIVE RECORD DATA SETS

A Relative Record data set (RRDS) acts like direct file organization but also has the advantages of being under control of VSAM, and has keyed access and password facilities. Basically, records in the data set are located according to their keys. For example, a record with key 001 is in the first location, a record with key 003 is in the third location, and so forth. If there is no record with key 002, then that location is empty, and you can subsequently insert the record.

Assume an RRDS containing records with keys 001, 003, 004, and 006. The data set would appear as follows:

I 001 I . . . I 003 I 004 I . . . I 006 I

Since RRDS stores and retrieves records according to key, each key in the data set must be unique.

You may want to use RRDS where you have a small to medium sized file and keys are reasonably consecutive so that there are not large numbers of spaces. One example would be a data set with keys that are regions or states, and contents are product sales or population and demographic data.

You could also store keys after performing a computation on them. As a simple example, imagine a data set with keys 101, 103, 104, and 106. Rather than store them with those keys, you could subtract 100 from the key value and store the records as keys 001, 003, 004, and 006.

KEY SEQUENCED DATA SETS

A Key Sequenced data set (KSDS) is considerably more complex than either ESDS or RRDS, but is accordingly more useful and versatile. You always create ("load") a KSDS in ascending sequence by key, and may process a

KSDS directly by key or sequentially. Since KSDS stores and retrieves records according to key, each key in the data set must be unique.

Figure 15-1 portrays a simplified view of a Key Sequenced data set. In Figure 15-1, the control intervals that contain the data records are depicted vertically, and for this example three control intervals comprise a control area. A sequence set contains an entry for each control interval in a control area. Entries within a sequence set consist of the highest key for each control interval and the address of the control interval; the address acts as a pointer to the begining of the control interval. The highest keys for the first control area are respectively 22, 32, and 40. VSAM stores each high key along with an address pointer in the sequence set for the first control area.

At a higher level, an *index set* (various levels depending on the size of the data set) contains high keys and address pointers for the sequence sets. In Figure 15-1, the highest key for the first control area is 40. VSAM stores this value in the index set along with an address pointer for the first sequence.

When a program wants to directly access a record in the data set, VSAM locates the record by means of, first, the index set and then second, the

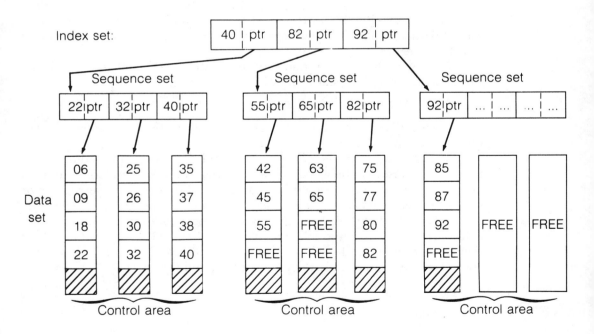

FIGURE 15-1 Key sequenced organization.

sequence set. For example, a program requests access to record with key 63. VSAM first checks the index set as follows:

RECORD KEY	INDEX SET	
63	40	Record key high, not in first control area.
63	82	Record key low, in second control area.

VSAM has determined that key 63 is in the second control area. It next examines the sequence set for the second control area to locate the correct control interval. Following are the steps:

RECORD KEY	SEQUENCE SET	
63	55	Record key high, not in first control interval.
63	65	Record key low, in second control interval.

VSAM has now determined that key 63 is in the second control interval of the second control area. The address pointer in the sequence set directs VSAM to the correct control interval. VSAM then reads the keys of the data set and locates key 63 as the first record which it delivers to the program.

FREE SPACE. You normally allow a certain amount of free space in a data set for VSAM to insert new records. When creating a Key Sequenced data set, you can tell VSAM to allocate free space in two ways:

1. Leave space at the end of each control interval, or
2. Leave some control intervals vacant.

If a program deletes or shortens a record, VSAM reclaims the space by shifting to the left all following records in the control interval. If the program adds or lengthens a record, VSAM inserts the record in its correct space and moves to the right all following records in the control interval. VSAM updates RBAs and indexes accordingly.

A control interval may not contain enough space for an inserted record. In such a case, VSAM causes a control interval split by removing about half the records to a vacant control interval in the same control area. Although records are now no longer *physically* in key order, for VSAM they are *logically* in sequence. The updated sequence set controls the order for subsequent retrieval of records.

If there is no vacant control interval in a control area, VSAM causes a control area split, using free space outside the control area. Under normal conditions, such a split seldom occurs. To a large degree, a VSAM data set is self-organizing, and requires reorganization less often than an ISAM file.

ACCESS METHOD SERVICES (AMS)

Before physically writing (or "loading") records in a VSAM data set, you must first catalog its structure. IBM supplies a utility package, *Access Method Services (AMS)* that enables you to furnish VSAM with such details about the data set as its name, organization type, record length, key location, and password (if any). Since VSAM subsequently knows the physical characteristics of the data set, your program need not supply as much detailed information as would a program accessing an ISAM file.

The following describes the more important features of AMS. Full details are in the IBM OS/VS and DOS/VS Access Methods Services manual. You catalog a VSAM structure using an AMS program named IDCAMS, as follows:

```
OS:     //STEP EXEC PGM=IDCAMS
DOS:    // EXEC IDCAMS,SIZE=AUTO
```

Immediately following the above command are various entries that DEFINE the data set. The first group under CLUSTER provides required and optional entries that describe all the information that VSAM must maintain for the data set. The second group, DATA, creates an entry in the catalog for a data component, that is the set of all control area and intervals for the storage of records. The third group, INDEX, creates an entry in the catalog for a KSDS index component for the handling of the KSDS indexes.

Figure 15-2 provides the more common DEFINE CLUSTER entries. Note that to indicate continuation, a hyphen (-) follows every entry except the last.

DEFINE CLUSTER (abbreviated DEF CL) provides various parameters all contained within parentheses.

NAME is a required parameter that supplies the name of the data set. You can code the name up to 44 characters with a period after each eight or fewer characters, as EMPLOYEE.RECORDS.P030. The name corresponds to job control, as follows

```
OS:     //FILEVS DD DSNAME=EMPLOYEE.RECORDS.P030 . . .
DOS:    // DLBL FILEVS,'EMPLOYEE.RECORDS.P030',0,VSAM
```

The name FILEVS in this example is whatever name you assign to the file definition (ACB) in your program, such as

```
filename ACB DDNAME=FILEVS . . .
```

BLOCKS. You may want to load the data set on an FBA device (such as 3310 or 3370) or on a CKD device (such as 3340 or 3350). For FBA devices, allocate the number of 512-byte blocks for the data set. For CKD devices, the entries CYLINDERS (or CYL) or TRACKS allocate space. The entry RECORD allocates space for either FBA or CKD. In all cases, indicate a primary allocation for a generous expected amount of space, and an optional secondary allocation for expansion if required.

Choose one entry to designate the type of data set: INDEXED designates Key Sequenced, NONINDEXED is Entry Sequenced, and NUMBERED is Relative Record.

KEYS for indexed only defines the length (from 1 to 255) and position of the key in each record. For example, KEYS (6 0) indicates that the key is 6 bytes long beginning in position 0 (the first byte).

```
Cluster Level:

DEFINE    CLUSTER
          ( NAME(data-set-name) -
          {CYLINDERS(primary[ secondary])|
           BLOCKS(primary[ secondary])|            (choose
           RECORDS( primary[ secondary])|          one)
           TRACKS(primary[ secondary])} -
          [INDEXED|NONINDEXED|NUMBERED] -          (choose one)
          [KEYS(length offset)] -
          [RECORDSIZE(average maximum)] -
          [VOLUMES(vol-ser[ vol-ser ...])]
          )

Data Component Level:

          [DATA
          ([CONTROLINTERVALSIZE(size)] -
          [NAME(data-name)] -
          [VOLUMES(vol-ser[ vol-ser ...])]
          )]

Index Component Level:

          [INDEX
          ([NAME(index-name)] -
          [VOLUMES(vol-ser[ vol-ser ...])]
          )]

Note: Symbol:      Meaning:
       []          An optional entry, may be omitted.
       {}          Select one of the following options.
       ()          You must code these parentheses.
       |           "or".
```

FIGURE 15-2 Entries for defining a VSAM data set.

RECORDSIZE (OR RECSZ) provides the average and maximum lengths in bytes of data records. For fixed-length records and for RRDS, the two entries are identical. For example, code (120 120) for 120-byte records.

VOLUMES (OR VOL) identifies the volume serial number(s) of the DASD volume(s) where the data set is to reside. You may specify VOLUMES at any of the three levels; for example, the DATA and INDEX components may reside on different volumes.

DEFINE CLUSTER supplies a number of additional specialized options which you can read in the IBM AMS manual.

ACCESSING AND PROCESSING

VSAM furnishes two types of *accessing,* keyed and addressed, and three types of *processing,* sequential, direct, and skip sequential. The following chart shows the legal accessing and processing by type of organization:

TYPE	KEYED ACCESS	ADDRESSED ACCESS
KSDS	Sequential	Sequential
	Direct	Direct
	Skip sequential	
ESDS		Sequential
		Direct
RRDS	Sequential	
	Direct	
	Skip sequential	

In simple terms, *keyed accessing* is concerned with the key (for KSDS) and relative record number (for RRDS). For example, if you read a KSDS sequentially, VSAM delivers the records in sequence by key (although they may be in a different sequence physically).

Addressed accessing is concerned with the RBA. For example, you can access a record in an ESDS using the RBA by which it was stored.

For either type of accessing method, you can process records sequentially or directly (and by skip sequential for keyed access). Thus, you always use addressed accessing for ESDS and keyed accessing for RRDS, and may process either type sequentially or directly. KSDS on the other hand permits both keyed access (the normal), and addressed access, with both sequential and direct processing.

VSAM MACRO INSTRUCTIONS

VSAM uses a number of familiar macros as well as a few new ones to enable you to retrieve, add, change, and delete records. In the following list of macros marked with an asterisk (*), see the IBM DOS/VS or OS/VS Supervisor and I/O Macros manual for details.

To relate a program and the data:

A C B	(Access Method Control Block)
E X L S T	(Exit List)

To connect and disconnect a program and a data set:

O P E N	(Open a data set)
C L O S E	(Close a data set)
T C L O S E *	(Temporary Close)

To define requests for accessing data:

R P L	(Request Parameter List)

To request access to a file:

G E T	(Get a record)
P U T	(Write or rewrite a record)
P O I N T *	(Position VSAM at a record)
E R A S E	(Erase a record previously retrieved with a GET)
E N D R E Q *	(End request)

To manipulate the information that relates a program to the data:

G E N C B *	(Generate control block)
M O D C B *	(Modify control block)
S H O W C B	(Show control block)
T E S T C B *	(Test control block)

A program that accesses a VSAM data set requires the usual OPEN to connect the data set and CLOSE to disconnect it, the GET macro to read records, and PUT to write or rewrite records. An important difference in the use of macros under VSAM is the RPL (Request for Parameter List) macro. As shown in the following relationship, a GET or PUT specifies an RPL macro name rather than a file name. The RPL in turn specifies an ACB (Access Control Block) macro, which in its turn relates to the job control entry for the data set:

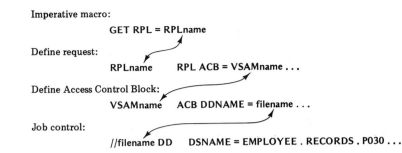

The ACB macro is equivalent to the OS DCB or DOS DTF file definition macros. As well, the OPEN macro supplies information about the type of file organization, record length, and key. Each execution of OPEN, CLOSE, GET, PUT, and ERASE causes VSAM to check its validity, and to insert a code into register-15 which you can check. A return code of X'00' means that the operation was successful. You can use the SHOWCB macro to determine the exact cause of the error.

THE ACB MACRO—ACCESS METHOD CONTROL BLOCK

The ACB macro identifies a data set that is to be processed. Its main purpose is to indicate the proposed type of processing (sequential or direct) and the use of exit routines, if any. The DEFINE CLUSTER command of AMS has already stored much of the information about the data set in the VSAM catalog. When a program opens the data set via the ACB, VSAM delivers this information to virtual storage.

Entries for an ACB macro may be in any sequence and you may code only those that you need. Following is the general format which you code like a DCB or DTF, with a comma following each entry and a continuation character in column 72. All operands are optional:

```
name  ACB    AM=VSAM,                              +
             DDNAME=filename,                      +
             EXLST=address,                        +
             MACRF=([ADR][,KEY]                    
                    [,DIR][,SEQ][,SKP]             
                    [,IN][,OUT]                    
                    [,NRM|AIX]),                   +
             STRNO=number
```

name   The name indicates the symbolic address for the ACB when assembled. If you omit the DDname operand from the ACB definition, this name should match the filename in your DLBL or DD job statement.

AM=VSAM   Code this parameter if your installation also uses VTAM; otherwise, the Assembler assumes VSAM.

DDNAME   This entry provides the name of your data set that the program is to process. This name matches the filename in your DLBL or DD job statement.

EXLST   The address references a list of your addresses of routines that provide exits. Use the EXLST macro to generate the list, and enter its name as the address. A common use is to code an entry for an end-of-file exit for sequential reading. If you have no exit routines, omit the operand.

MACRF   The options define the type of processing that you plan. In the following, an underlined entry is a default:

> ADR | *KEY*   Use ADR for addressed access (KS and ES) and KEY for keyed access (KS and RR).
>
> DIR | *SEQ* | SKP   DIR provides direct processing, SEQ provides sequential processing, and SKP means skip sequential (for KS and RR).
>
> *IN* | OUT   IN retrieves records and OUT permits retrieval, insertion, add-to-end, or update for keyed access, and retrieval, update, or add-to-end for addressed access.
>
> *NRM* | AIX   The DDNAME operand supplies the name of the data set (or path). NRM means normal processing of the data set, whereas AIX means that this is an alternate index.
>
> Other MACRF options are RST | NRS for resetting catalog information, and NUB | UBF for user buffers.

STRNO   The entry supplies the total number of RPLs (Request Parameter Lists) that your program will use at the same time (the default is 1).

ACB also has provision for parameters that define the number and size of buffers; however, the macro has standard defaults.

In the program example in Figure 15-3, the ACB macro VSMFILOT has only two entries and allows the rest to default. Access is keyed (KEY), processing is sequential (SEQ), and the file is output (OUT). There is no exit list, STRNO defaults to 1, and MACRF defaults to NRM (normal path).

The Assembler does not generate an I/O module for an ACB, nor does the Linkage Editor include one. Instead, the system dynamically generates the module at execute-time.

THE RPL MACRO—REQUEST PARAMETER LIST

The request macros GET, PUT, ERASE, and POINT require a reference to an RPL macro. For example, the program in Figure 15-3 issues the following GET macro:

```
GET  RPL=RECPL
```

The operand supplies the name of the RPL macro that contains the information needed to access a record. If your program is to access a data set in different ways, you can code an RPL macro for each type of access; each RPL keeps track of its location in the data set.

The standard format for RPL is the following. The name for the RPL macro is the one that you code in the GET or PUT operand. Every entry is optional:

```
RPLname     RPL    AM=VSAM,                    +
                   ACB=address,                +
                   AREA=address,               +
                   AREALEN=length,             +
                   ARG=address,                +
                   KEYLEN=length,              +
                   OPTCD=(options),            +
                   RECLEN=length
```

AM The entry VSAM specifies that this is a VSAM (not VTAM) control block.

ACB The entry gives the name of the associated ACB that defines the data set.

AREA The address references an I/O workarea in which a record is available for output or is to be entered on input.

AREALEN The entry supplies the length of the record area.

ARG The address supplies the search argument—a key, including a relative record number or an RBA.

KEYLEN The length is that of the key if processing by generic key. (For normal keyed access, the catalog supplies the key length.)

OPTCD Processing options are SEQ, SKP, and DIR; request options are UPD (update) and NUP (no update). For example, a direct update would be (DIR,UPD).

RECLEN For writing a record, your program supplies the length to VSAM, and for retrieval VSAM supplies the length to your program. If records are variable length, you can use the SHOWCB and TESTCB macros to examine the field (see the IBM Supervisor manual).

THE OPEN MACRO

The OPEN macro ensures that your program has authority to access the specified data set, and generates VSAM control blocks.

```
[name] OPEN address[,address  .  .  . ]
```

The operand designates the address of one or more ACBs, which you may code either as a macro name or as a register notation (registers 2–12). For example:

```
OPEN VSFILE     or      LA    6,VSFILE
                        OPEN  (6)
```

You can code up to 16 filenames in one OPEN, and can include both ACB names and DCB or DTF names. Note however that to facilitate debugging, avoid mixing them in the same OPEN. OPEN sets a return code in register-15 to indicate success (zero) or failure (nonzero) which your program can test:

X'00'   Opened all ACBs successfully.
X'04'   Opened all ACBs successfully but issued a warning message for one or more.
X'08'   Failed to open one or more ACBs.

On a failed OPEN or CLOSE, you can also check the diagnostics following program execution for a message such as OPEN ERROR X'6E', and check Appendix K of the IBM Supervisor manual for an explanation of the code.

THE CLOSE MACRO

The CLOSE macro completes any I/O operations that are still outstanding, writes any remaining output buffers, and updates catalog entries for the data set.

```
[name] CLOSE address[,address . . . ]
```

You can code up to 16 names in one CLOSE, and can include both ACB names and DCB or DTF names. CLOSE sets a return code in register-15 to indicate success or failure which your program can test:

X'00'   Closed all ACBs successfully.
X'04'   Failed to close one or more ACBs successfully.
X'08'   Insufficient virtual storage space for close routine or could not locate modules.

THE REQUEST MACROS—GET, PUT, AND ERASE

The VSAM request macros are GET, PUT, ERASE, POINT, and ENDREQ. For each of these, VSAM sets register-15 with a return code to indicate success or failure of the operation, as follows:

X'00'   Successful operation.

X'04'   Request not accepted because of an active request from another task on the same RPL. End-of-file also causes this return code.

X'08'   A logical error; examine the specific error code in the RPL.

X'0C'   Uncorrectable I/O error; examine the specific error code in the RPL.

THE GET MACRO.   GET retrieves a record from a data set. The operand specifies the address of an RPL that defines the data set being processed. The entry may either (1) cite the address by name, or (2) use register notation, any register 2–12, in parentheses. You may use register-1; its use is more efficient but GET does not preserve its address.

```
(1) GET  RPL=RPLname          (2) LA   reg,RPLname
                                  GET  RPL=(reg)
```

The RPL macro provides the address of your workarea where GET is to deliver an input record. Register-13 must contain the address of a savearea defined as 18 fullwords.

Under sequential input, GET delivers the next record in the data set. The OPTCD entry in the RPL macro would appear for example as

```
OPTCD=(KEY,SEQ)
```

or

```
OPTCD=(ADR,SEQ)
```

You have to provide for end-of-file by means of an EXLST operand in the associated ACB macro; see Figure 15-2 for an example.

For nonsequential accessing, GET delivers the record that the key or relative record number specifies in the search argument field. The OPTCD entry in the RPL macro would appear for example as

```
OPTCD=(KEY,SKP)
```

or

```
OPTCD=(KEY,DIR)
```

or by an RBA in the search argument field, as

```
OPTCD=(ADR,DIR)
```

You also use GET in order to update or delete a record.

THE PUT MACRO.   PUT writes or rewrites a record in a data set. The operand of PUT specifies the address of an RPL that defines the data set being processed. The entry may either (1) cite the address by name, or (2) use register notation, any register 2-12, in parentheses. You may use register-1; its use is more efficient but PUT does not preserve its address.

(1) PUT RPL=RPLname   (2) LA   reg,RPLname
                                   PUT   RPL=(reg)

The RPL macro provides the address of your workarea containing the record that PUT is to add or update in the data set. Register-13 must contain the address of a savearea defined as 18 fullwords.

In order to create ("load") or extend a data set, use sequential output. The OPTCD entry in the RPL macro would appear for example as

OPTCD=(SEQ or SKP)

SKP means "skip sequential" and enables you to start writing at any specific record.

For writing a KSDS or RRDS, if OPTCD contains any of the following, PUT stores a new record in key sequence or relative record sequence:

OPTCD=(KEY,SKP,NUP)   Skip, no update
OPTCD=(KEY,DIR,NUP)   Direct, no update
OPTCD=(KEY,SEQ,NUP)   Sequential, no update

Note that VSAM does not allow you to change a *key* in a KSDS (delete the record and write a new one). To *change* a record, first GET it using

OPTCD=UPD

change its contents (but not the key), and PUT it also using

OPTCD=UPD

To write a record in ESDS, use

OPTCD=(ADR, . . .)

THE ERASE MACRO.   The purpose of the ERASE macro is to delete a record from a KSDS or an RRDS. To locate an unwanted record, you must previously issue a GET with an RPL specifying

OPTCD=(UPD. . .)

[name] ERASE RPL=address or =(register)

For ESDS, a common practice is to define a delete byte in the record. To "delete" a record, insert a special character such as X'FF'; all programs that process the data set should bypass all records containing the delete byte. You can occasionally rewrite the data set, dropping all deletes.

THE EXLST MACRO

If your ACB macro indicates an EXLST operand, then code a related EXLST macro. EXLST provides an optional list of addresses for user-exit routines that handle end-of-file and error analysis. All operands in the macro are optional:

```
[name]  EXLST  AM=VSAM,                        +
               EODAD=address,                   +
               LERAD=address,                   +
               SYNAD=address
```

When VSAM detects the coded condition, the program enters your exit routine. Register-13 must contain the address of your register savearea. For example, if you are reading sequentially, then supply an end-of-data address (EODAD) in the EXLST macro—see the ACB for VSMFILIN in Figure 15-3.

The following explains the operands for EXLST:

VSAM   Indicates a VSAM control block.

EODAD   Supplies the address of your end-of-data routine. You may also read sequentially backwards and VSAM enters your routine when reading past the first record. The request return code for this condition is X'04'.

LERAD   Indicates the address of the routine that analyzes logical errors that occurred during GET, PUT, POINT, and ERASE. The request return code for this condition is X'08'.

SYNAD   Provides the address of your routine that analyzes physical I/O errors on GET, PUT, POINT, ERASE, and CLOSE. The request return code for this condition is X'0C'.

Other operands are EXCPAD and JRNAD.

THE SHOWCB MACRO

The original program in Figure 15-3 contained an error that caused it to fail on a PUT operation. The use of the SHOWCB macro in the error routine for PUT (R30PUT) helped determine the actual cause of the error.

The purpose of SHOWCB is to display fields in an ACB, EXLST, or RPL. Code SHOWCB following a VSAM macro where you want to identify errors that VSAM has detected. The SHOWCB in the PUT error routine in Figure 15-3 is the following:

```
        SHOWCB   RPL=RPLISTOT,AREA=FDBKWD,FIELDS=(FDBK),LENGTH=4
                 . . .
FDBKWD  DC       F'0'
```

AREA   Designates the name of a fullword where VSAM is to place an error code.

FIELDS   Tells SHOWCB the type of display; the keyword FDBK (feedback) causes a display of error codes for request macros.

LENGTH Provides the length of the area in bytes.

On a failed request, VSAM stores the error code in the rightmost byte of the fullword area. Some common error codes are the following:

08	Attempt to store a record with a duplicate key.
0C	Out of sequence or duplicate record for KSDS or RRDS.
10	No record located on retrieval.
1C	No space available to store a record.

Your program can test for the type of error and display a message. For nonfatal errors, it could continue processing, and for fatal errors, it could terminate.

The original error in Figure 15-3 was caused by the fact that the RPL macro RPLISTOT did not contain an entry for RECLEN; the program terminated on the first PUT error, with register-15 containing X'08' (a "logical error"). Insertion of the SHOWCB macro in the next run revealed the cause of the error in FDBKWD: 00006C. Appendix K of the IBM Supervisor manual explains the error (in part) as:

"The RECLEN value specified in the RPL macro was

- larger than the allowed maximum
- equal to zero . . ."

Coding a RECLEN operand in the RPL macro solved the problem, and the program then executed through to normal termination. One added point: Technically, after each SHOWCB you should test register-15 for a successful or failed operation.

PROGRAM EXAMPLE—LOADING A KEY SEQUENCED DATA SET

The program in Figure 15-3 reads records from the system reader and sequentially creates a Key Sequenced data set. A DEFINE CLUSTER command has allocated space for this data set as INDEXED (KSDS), with five blocks, a 4-byte key starting in position 0, and an 80-byte record size. The program loads the entire data set and closes it on completion. For illustrative (but not practical) purposes, it then reopens the data set and reads and prints each record.

The PUT macro that writes records into the data set is:

```
PUT RPL=RPLISTOT
```

RPLISTOT defines the name of the ACB macro (VSMFILOT), the address of the output record, and its length. Although the example simply duplicates the records into the data set, in practice you would probably define various fields, and store numeric values as packed or binary.

```
IDCAMS   SYSTEM SERVICES

    DELETE (VSAMFIL.ABEL) CLUSTER PURGE CATALOG(ACOMCAT)

IDC0550I ENTRY (C) VSAMFIL.ABEL DELETED

IDC055CI ENTRY (D) VSAMFIL.DATA DELETED

IDC055CI ENTRY (I) VSAMFIL.INDEX DELETED

IDC0001I FUNCTION COMPLETED. HIGHEST CONDITION CODE WAS 0


    DEFINE CLUSTER (NAME(VSAMFIL.ABEL) -
                    BLOCKS(5) -
                    VOLUME(SYSWK1) -
                    INDEXED -
                    KEYS(4 0) -
                    RECORDSIZE(80 80) ) -
               DATA (NAME(VSAMFIL.DATA) ) -
               INDEX (NAME(VSAMFIL.INDEX) )

IDC0001I FUNCTION COMPLETED. HIGHEST CONDITION CODE WAS 0


IDC0002I IDCAMS PROCESSING COMPLETE. MAXIMUM CONDITION CODE WAS 0


// OPTION LINK,PARTDUMP,NOXREF,LOG
   ACTION NOMAP
// EXEC ASSEMBLY,SIZE=128K



  3            PRINT NOGEN,NODATA
  4 *                MAIN  PROCESSING
  5 *                -----------------------------
  6 PROGVSM  START
  7            BALR  12,0                 INITIALIZE
  8            USING *,12                 BASE REG &
  9            LA    13,VSAMSAVE          VSAM SAVEAREA
 10            OPEN  FILEIN,VSMFILOT
 15            LTR   15,15                SUCCESSFUL OPEN?
 20            BNZ   R100PEN              NO - TERMINATE
 21            GET   FILEIN,VSMREC        READ 1ST RECORD

 28            BAL   6,B10LOAD            CREATE FILE

 30 A80EOF   CLOSE FILEIN,VSMFILOT
 39            LA    13,VSAMSAVE
 40            OPEN  FILEPRT,VSMFILIN
 49            LTR   15,15                SUCCESSFUL OPEN?
 50            BNZ   R100PEN              NO -- TERMINATE
 51            BAL   6,C10PRINT           READ & PRINT VSAM FILE

 53 A90EOF   CLOSE FILEPRT,VSMFILOT
 62            EOJ                        NORMAL TERMINATION

 66 *                LOAD  VSAM  FILE
 67 *                -----------------------------
 68 B10LOAD   PUT   RPL=RPLISTOT         WRITE VSAM RECORD
 75            LTR   15,15                SUCCESSFUL WRITE?
 76            BNZ   R30PUT               NO --ERROR
 77            GET   FILEIN,VSMREC        READ NEXT
 83            B     B10LOAD
```

FIGURE 15-3 (partial).

```
 85 *                 R E A D   &   P R I N T   V S A M   F I L E
 86 *                 --------------------------------------
 87 C1CPRINT GET      RPL=RPLISTIN
 94          LTR      15,15                    SUCCESSFUL READ?
 95          BNZ      R40GET                   NO - TERMINATE
 96          MVC      PRREC,VSMREC
 97          PUT      FILEPRT,PRINT            PRINT RECORD
103          B        C1OPRINT


105 *                 E R R O R   R O U T I N E S
106 *                 ---------------------------
107 R1OCPEN  MVI      ERRCCE,C'C'              OPEN ERROR
108          B        R9ODUMP
109 R30PUT   MVI      ERRCCE,C'P'              PUT ERROR
110          ST       15,SAVE15
111          SHOWCB   RPL=RPLISTOT,AREA=FDBKWD,FIELDS=(FDBK),LENGTH=4
163          CLOSE    FILEIN,VSMFILOT
172          B        R9ODUMP
173 R4CGET   MVI      ERRCCE,C'G'              GET ERROR
174          ST       15,SAVE15
175          SHOWCB   RPL=RPLISTIN,AREA=FDBKWD,FIELDS=(FDBK),LENGTH=4
227          CLOSE    FILEPRT,VSMFILOT
236 R9OCUMP  EQU      *
237          PDUMP    ERRCDE,PRINT+133
243          EOJ                               ABNORMAL TERMINATION


247 *                 ---------------------------
248 *                 D E C L A R A T I V E S
249 *                 ---------------------------

251 FILEIN   DEFIN    A80EOF                   DEFINE INPUT FILE
275 FILEPRT  DEFPR                             DEFINE PRINTER FILE

300 VSMFILOT ACB      CCNAME=VSAMFIL,          DEFINE VSAM O/P FILE         +
                      MACRF=(KEY,SEQ,OUT)

333 RPLISTOT RPL      ACB=VSMFILOT,            RPL FOR VSMFILOT             +
                      AREA=VSMREC,                                          +
                      AREALEN=80,                                          +
                      RECLEN=80,                                           +
                      OPTCD=(KEY,SEQ,NUP)

363 VSMFILIN ACB      CDNAME=VSAMFIL,          DEFINE VSAM I/P FILE         +
                      MACRF=(KEY,SEQ,IN),                                   +
                      EXLST=EOFDCB

396 EOFDCB   EXLST    EOCAD=A90EOF             EOF EXIT FOR VSAM I/P

408 RPLISTIN RPL      ACB=VSMFILIN,            RPL FOR VSMFILIN             +
                      AREA=VSMREC,                                          +
                      AREALEN=80,                                          +
                      OPTCD=(KEY,SEQ,NUP)

438 VSAMSAVE DS       18F                      VSAM SAVEAREA
439 ERRCDE   DC       X'00'                    ERRCR CODE
44C SAVE15   DS       F
441 FDBKWD   DC       F'0'
442 VSMREC   DS       OCL80                    INPUT/OUTPUT RECORD
443 RECKEY   DS       CL04                     *
444          DS       CL76                     *

446 PRINT    DS       OCL133                   PRINT RECORD
447          DC       X'09'                    *
448 PRREC    DC       CL80' '                  *
```

FIGURE 15-3 (partial).

```
449         DC    CL52' '                        *
450         LTORG
451               =C'$$BOPEN '
452               =C'$$BCLOSE'
453               =CL8'IKQVTMS'
454               =CL8'$$BPDUMP'
455               =A(ERRCODE,PRINT+133)
456               =A(FILEIN)
457               =A(VSMREC)
458               =A(RPLISTCT)
459               =A(RPLISTIN)
460               =A(FILEPRT)
461               =A(PRINT)
462         END   PROGVSM
```

```
// EXEC LNKEDT
// DLBL VSAMFIL,'VSAMFIL.ABEL',,VSAM
// EXTENT SYS008,SYSWK1
// ASSGN SYS008,X'381'
// EXEC ,SIZE=128K
C034AES PROCESSORS            ⎫
C047MICROTEL INDUSTRIES       ⎬   (Output from printing contents
0065ACE ELECTRONICS           ⎭       of loaded data set)
```

FIGURE 15-3 Loading of a key sequenced data set.

The ACB macro defines VSMFILOT for keyed accessing, sequential processing, and output. The DDNAME, VSAMFIL, in this example relates to the name for the data set in the DLBL job control entry (DD under OS).

For reading the data set, the GET macro is

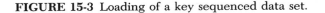

```
GET RPL=RPLISTIN
```

RPLISTIN defines the name of the ACB macro (VSMFILIN), the address in which GET is to read an input record, and the record length.

The ACB macro defines VSMFILIN for keyed access, sequential processing, and input. The DDNAME, VSAMFIL, relates to the name for the data set in the DLBL job control entry. Note that there is an ACB and RPL macro for both input and output, but both ACB macros specify the same DDNAME: VSAMFIL.

Error routines are for failures on OPEN, GET, and PUT. These rather primitive routines supply an error code and the contents of the declaratives; in practice, you may want to enlarge these routines. If you fail to provide error routines, your program may crash with no clear cause.

LOADING AN ESDS. To convert the program from KSDS to ESDS, change DEFINE CLUSTER from INDEXED to NONINDEXED and delete the KEYS and INDEX entries. Change the ACB MACRF from KEY to ADR and change the RPL OPTCD from KEY to ADR—that's all!

KEYED DIRECT RETRIEVAL

Key Sequenced data sets provide for both sequential and direct processing by key. For direct processing, you must supply VSAM with the key of the record to be accessed. If you use a key to access a record directly, it must be the same length as the keys in the data set (as indicated in the KEYS operand of DEFINE CLUSTER), and the key must actually exist in the data set. For example, if you request a record with key 0028, and there is no such record, VSAM returns an error code in register-15.

Assume the same data set as in Figure 15-3 and that a program is to access records directly. A user enters record key numbers via a terminal and the program is to display the record on the screen. In this partial example, the RPL macro specifies the name (ARG) of the key to be in a 4-byte field named KEYFLD. Following are the specific coding requirements for the ACB, RPL, and GET macros:

```
VSMFILE   ACB   DDNAME=name,                    +
                MACRF=(KEY,DIR,IN)

RPLIST    RPL   ACB=VSMFILE,                     +
                AREA=DCBREC,                     +
                AREALEN=80,                      +
                ARG=KEYFLD,                      +
                OPTCD=(KEY,DIR,NUP)

KEYFLD    DS    CL4
DCBREC    DS    CL80
          ...
          [Accept a key number from the terminal]
          MVC   KEYFLD,keyno
          GET   RPL=RPLIST
          LTR   15,15
          BNZ   error
          [Display the record on the screen]
```

For *updating* a KSDS record, change the MACRF from IN to OUT and change the OPTCD from NUP to UPD. GET the record, make the required changes to it (but not the key!), and PUT the record using the same RPL.

VSAM SORT

IDCAMS supplies a handly utility for sorting records in a VSAM data set. You can sort records into either ascending or descending sequence. You must first use DEFINE CLUSTER to allocate a vacant data set (NONINDEXED) for SORT to write the sorted data set. A typical SORT specification follows:

```
// EXEC SORT,SIZE=256K
   SORT FIELDS=(1,4,CH,A,9,4,PD,D)
   RECORD TYPE=F,LENGTH=(150)
   INPFIL VSAM
   OUTFIL ESDS
   END
/*
```

sort causes the SORT program to load into storage and begin execution.

sort fields defines the fields to be sorted, indicated by major control to minor, from left to right. In this example, the major sort field begins in position 1 (the first position), is four bytes long, is in character (CH) format, and is to be sorted in ascending (A) sequence. The minor sort field begins in position 9, is four bytes long, is in packed (PD) format, and is to be sorted in descending (D) sequence. The example could be a sort of departments in ascending sequence, and within each department are employee salaries in descending sequence.

record type indicates fixed (F) length and record length (150 bytes).

inpfil informs SORT that the input file is VSAM; SORT can determine the type of data set from the VSAM catalog.

outfil defines the type of output file, in this case Entry Sequenced. This entry should match the DEFINE CLUSTER for this data set: NONINDEXED.

Job control statements for SORTIN and SORTOUT provide the names of the data sets. Since job control varies by operating system and by installation requirements, check with your installation before attempting the SORT utility.

VSAM UTILITY PRINT

IDCAMS furnishes a convenient utility program named PRINT that can print the contents of a VSAM, SAM or ISAM data set. The following provides the steps:

```
OS: //STEP EXEC PGM=IDCAMS or
DOS: // EXEC IDCAMS,SIZE=256K
      PRINT INFILE(filename) CHARACTER or HEX or DUMP
   /*
```

The options for PRINT indicate the format of the printout, in character, hexadecimal, or both (DUMP prints hex on the left and character format on the right).

INFILE(filename) matches the name in the OS DD or DOS DLBL job statement, with any valid filename as long as the two are identical. The DD or DLBL statement notifies VSAM which data set is to print.

PRINT lists KSDS and ISAM data sets in key sequence, and lists ESDS, RRDS, and SAM data sets in physical sequence. You can also print beginning and ending at a specific record.

DEBUGGING TIPS

The most common errors in processing VSAM data sets occur because of the need to match definitions in the program, job control, and the cataloged VSAM data set.

1. The data-set-name in job control (such as CUSTOMER.INQUIRY) must agree with the NAME(data-set-name) entry in DEFINE CLUSTER. This name is the only one by which VSAM recognizes the data set. VSAM relates the ACB DDNAME in the program to the job control name, and the job control name to the data-set-name.

2. If a data set is cataloged as KSDS, ESDS, or RRDS, the program must access it accordingly.

3. For KSDS, the length and starting position of the key in a record must agree with the KEYS entry in DEFINE CLUSTER, and for direct input with the defined ARG in the OPTCD.

4. Ensure that every program that references the data set defines the fields with identical formats and lengths in the same positions; the actual field names need not be identical. Technically, you may define as character any input field in a record that the program does not reference. The simplest practice is to catalog all record definitions in the Assembler source library and COPY the definition into the program during assembly.

5. Load register-13 with the address of a 72-byte savearea for VSAM's use.

6. After each OPEN, CLOSE, GET, PUT, and SHOWCB, test register-15 for success or failure, and use SHOWCB (and TESTCB) as debugging aids.

7. During testing, you may have changed the contents of a VSAM data set and now want to reload (recreate) the original data set. Except for updating with new keys, VSAM does not permit overwriting records in a data set. You have to use IDCAMS to DELETE and reDEFINE the data set as follows:

```
DELETE(data-set-name) CLUSTER PURGE CATALOG(disk-name)
DEFINE CLUSTER(NAME(data-set-name) -
   etc. . .)
```

PROBLEMS

15-1. What are the three types of VSAM data sets and how do they differ?

15-2. Explain control interval, control interval split, and RBA.

15-3. Assume a KSDS that contains records with keys in two control areas as follows:

control area 1:	260,	273,	285
	290,	312,	315
control area 2:	320,	375,	380
	412,	490,	495

What are the contents of (a) the two sequence sets, and (b) the index set?

15-4. What is the program that catalogs the structure of a VSAM data set and what are its three component levels?

15-5. Code the DEFINE CLUSTER for the data-set-name CUSTOMER.FILE, assuming 20 blocks, ESDS, and 100-byte records.

15-6. Code the job control (OS DD and DOS DLBL) for the above data set with file name CUSTVS.

15-7. Code the ACB macro named CUSVSIN for the above data set for addressed sequential input and an EXLST macro named EOFCUS for end-of-file.

15-8. Code the RPL macro named RPLCUSIN for the above ACB, with an input area named CUSVSREC.

15-9. Code the GET macro to read the above data set.

PART

V

SPECIAL TOPICS

16

DEBUGGING

Each chapter to this point presents debugging tips suitable to the material that it introduced. One of the most common errors in an early assembly is a result of spelling an instruction or operand incorrectly. The Assembler generates hex zeros for machine code which when executed cause an Operation Exception. Most program bugs however are not so easily recognized.

One of the more charming features of an Assembler program is that *every instruction can be wrong*—either *syntactically* (failure to follow its rules) or *logically* (failure to follow the objective of the program). Typical syntactical errors are coding an instruction incorrectly and failing to code a required explicit length. Typical logical errors are branching to an incorrect address and making a wrong computation.

This chapter covers syntactical errors that can occur during program execution by general category, such as character data, packed data, addressing, and input-output, and then explores reading of storage dumps. For handling logical errors, your best bet is to provide input data that thoroughly tests the program logic.

CHARACTER DATA

A common error that occurs with handling character data is from the use of the MVC instruction. Since MVC can move up to 256 bytes of any type of data, the error may appear during execution of a subsequent instruction. For example:

```
PRINT     DS      CL133
          ...
          MVC     PRINT+115,=C'MEGABYTE CORP'
```

Because operand-1 of the MVC has no explicit length, the Assembler assumes a length from the declarative of 133. Assume that the literal pool contains the following:

```
=C'MEGABYTE CORP'
=C'AKRON OHIO'
...
```

MVC moves 133 bytes: the 13-byte literal plus the 120 bytes following in the literal pool. The data moves beginning at PRINT+115, as follows:

```
        MEGABYTE CORPAKRON OHIO ...
        !                  !
    PRINT+115          PRINT+132
```

In effect, the MVC fills the print record with 18 bytes and moves an additional 115 bytes into the area following. The system generates no error message based on the MVC. An unpredictable error occurs when you subsequently attempt to process one of the damaged fields, but the precise type of error depends on the data that is erased. For example, erasure of packed data may cause a Data Exception, and erasure of the first part of the literal pool may cause an input-output error. This type of error is often difficult to locate because another instruction is the indirect cause of the error. A check of a storage dump (if any) can help shed light on the cause of the error.

Suggestion: Avoid relative addressing, or double-check that such operands contain an explicit length. Another example of errors in the use of literals is coding =CL5'0' when you mean =CL5'00000' and =C' ' when you mean =5CL' '.

See also Appendix B for program check interrupts: 1 (Operation Exception), 2 (Privileged Exception), 5 (Addressing Exception), and 6 (Specification Exception).

PACKED DECIMAL DATA

DATA EXCEPTION. A Data Exception is particularly common because there are so many clever ways to cause it. Here's a common cause:

```
LINECTR    DS     PL3
           ...
           AP     LINECTR,=P'1'
```

As you may have noticed, LINECTR does not contain an initial value. Since its contents are unpredictable, the AP will likely cause a Data Exception. Another common error is a blank input field. For example:

```
RATEIN     DS     ZL5
RATEPK     DS     PL3
MULTPR     DS     PL6
           ...
           PACK   RATEPK,RATEIN
           ZAP    MULTPR,RATEPK
```

If RATEIN is blank, its contents are 4040404040. After the PACK, RATEPK contains 000004. The ZAP instruction will cause a Data Exception because its second operand must contain valid packed data. Although you may have no control over the initial contents of input fields, you could replace blanks with zeros. In fact, you may prefer to use TR to *translate* any invalid character to zero.

Some programmers manage to cause a Data Exception on packed fields even when the data is valid:

```
HOURSPK    DC     PL3'120.00'
RATEPK     DC     PL3'12.35'
WAGEPK     DS     PL5
           ...
           ZAP    WAGEPK,RATEPK       |00|00|01|23|5C|
           MP     WAGEPK,HOURSPK      |01|48|20|00|0C|
```

A quick calculation discloses that a 5-byte product should be adequate for the product, but the MP fails on a Data Exception. The reason? Violation of a rule of MP: the product field must contain a byte of zeros to its left for each byte in the multiplier. Consequently, WAGEPK must be at least six bytes long.

DIVIDE BY ZERO.   Attempting to divide by zero is another popular error that causes a Decimal-Divide Exception. The error is easy to locate because most programs contain few DP operations.

DECIMAL OVERFLOW.   An arithmetic operation can easily lose leftmost significant digits. Assume the following definition:

```
LINEPK DC PL1'0'
```

Once LINEPK reaches the value 9 (hex 9C), the next instruction that adds 1 has now no space for the carried 1, and a Decimal Overflow occurs. Note that if you examine the contents of LINEPK in a storage dump, it contains hex 0C.

See Appendix B for program check interrupts 7 (Data Exception), A (Decimal-Overflow Exception), and B (Decimal-Divide Exception).

BINARY DATA

Because *all* data is in binary format, you cannot get program checks on referencing binary data. But you can perform binary arithmetic operations that generate invalid results and cause program checks. One way is to generate a value that exceeds the capacity of a register, a Fixed-Point-Overflow Exception.

See Appendix B for program check interrupts 8 (Fixed-Point-Overflow Exception), and 9 (Fixed-Point-Divide Exception).

ENDLESS LOOPING

There are a number of ways to incur an endless loop. One way is simply to branch back to an address and have no exit:

```
B50     .
        .
        .
   B     B50
```

You can avoid this type of error by branching only forward. There are exceptions. For example, a table search and a table sort typically require looping backwards; be especially careful of coding these routines.

You can also cause an endless loop in a table search by branching back to the instruction that initializes the address of the table, or by failing to increment the register that addresses the table.

A difficult error to trace is one that involves BAL and BR. If you BAL to a subroutine via register-9, then you must return via register-9, with the original address still intact. A BR that returns via the wrong register may cause an endless loop. (It may also cause an unpredictable error, depending on the contents of the referenced register.)

ADDRESSING

For base registers, you cannot use register-0 at all, and avoid the use of registers 1, 13, 14, and 15 because I/O operations and subprogram linkage change their contents. Also, the TRT instruction uses register-2. Assume that a program 10K in size is to initialize three base registers. It doesn't matter which of registers 3 through 12 you use as long as you reserve them for that exclusive purpose. The following uses registers 10, 11, and 12:

```
BALR    10,0
USING   *,10,11,12
LA      12,2048
LA      11,2048(10,12)
LA      12,2048(11,12)
```

BALR and USING must specify the same register. The second register must contain an address that is 4096 (X'1000') more than the first, and the third register must contain an address that is 4096 more than the second. Any minor change can make the above coding incorrect and cause curious results during program execution.

If your program loads one of these base registers for another purpose, its base address is lost. A subsequent attempt using that base register will reference the wrong storage location, with unpredictable results. This type of error is *very* difficult to trace.

INPUT/OUTPUT

One of the more common errors concerned with input/output is in printing: failure to initialize the print control character, or initializing it with an incorrect value (this error could occur using PUT but not PUTPR). For example, the control character for skipping to a new page is X'8B'; many programmers have misread the code as X'88'. Regardless of the cause, the system generates a message such as

```
INVALID INPUT/OUTPUT
```

When you get such a diagnostic, first check your PUT routines. In fact, you may minimize output bugs by coding a *common* print routine, as the program in Chapter 8 illustrates.

An I/O error may also occur because of an incorrect definition of a file or an improper reference to it. For example, the Assembler does not recognize the error in the transposed operands in GET RECDIN,FILEIN. Subsequently, when the first GET executes, the program links to the RECDIN area expecting to find the file definition instructions.

If you cannot locate the guilty macro that caused an I/O error, check the contents of register-14, provided that there was a storage dump. Examine the second line of registers beginning with GR 0-F (general registers 0–15). Assume the following:

```
GR 8-F   . . .   x------x 00051268   x------x
                 |          |          |
               reg-13    reg-14     reg-15
```

When your program performs an I/O operation, it exits and links to the supervisor program. But before leaving, it loads into register-14 the address of the instruction following the GET or PUT. This action enables the supervisor to return to your program after the I/O is completed. If the program crashes on the I/O operation, the supervisor issues a diagnostic and (if directed) dumps the contents of the registers and storage. An examination of register-14 indicates the address of the instruction immediately following the GET or PUT, in this case X'00051268'. You may have to calculate the location of the macro in the program listing by subtracting the program's load point (also known as entry point). You can determine the load point either from the contents of the base register or by an OS diagnostic that indicates EPA (Entry Point Address). Let's assume that the load point is X'051210':

Address in register-14	X'051268'
Load point of program	X'051210'
Location in listing	X'000058'

In this case, the instruction at LOC X'58' should immediately follow the GET or PUT that caused the error.

A common way of causing an I/O error is to erase a file definition (DTF or DCB) or the literal pool. The literal pool contains such vital information as addresses for handling the I/O macros. In either case, an attempt to perform an I/O operation may cause a mysterious execution error that confuses both the system and yourself!

There are three common ways to erase a file definition (DTF or DCB) and literal pool. First, if an input workarea or buffer area is defined smaller than the actual record length, an input operation fills the area plus the bytes immediately following. If this damaged area contains a file definition or literal pool, a subsequent I/O operation could fail.

Second, an instruction such as

```
MVC PRINT+100,HEADING
```

(missing explicit length) could erase data following PRINT, such as a file definition or literal pool.

Third, a program could build a table, as follows:

```
NAMETAB   DS      10CL20      Table of names
          LTORG               Literal pool
```

In this case, the program could store names successively in the table. There is provision for only ten names; if the program stores an eleventh name, it will erase the first 20 bytes of the literal pool. Why not define the literal pool before the table?

```
                 LTORG
       NAMETAB   DS        10CL20
```

Storing eleven names no longer erases the literal pool; instead, it now erases input/output modules that the Link Editor has coupled to the end of the program. Once again, program execution will terminate on an unpredictable error. The solution is to increase the size of the table *and* to check the number of entries that are stored.

UNCATALOGED I/O MODULES

Another type of error for which you should be alert is related to the coding of a DTF or DCB. One symptom of this error (although other errors may also cause it) is that the supervisor displays a diagnostic message such as

```
PROGRAM CHECK INTERRUPT HEX LOCATION 000008 CONDITION CODE x
OPERATION EXCEPTION
```

A system programmer must catalog all the *expected* I/O modules, such as a module for handling a terminal. Under DOS, the macro is DTFCN (console). If you code this macro in a program and the module is not cataloged, or it is cataloged in a different version from the one that you have coded, the Assembler has no way of knowing that it does not exist. It simply leaves an address in the External Symbol Dictionary for the Linkage Editor to complete. When the Linker fails to locate the module, it inserts a diagnostic in the Link Edit Map:

```
       UNRESOLVED EXTERNAL REFERENCES EXTRN xxxxxxx
       001 UNRESOLVED ADDRESS CONSTANTS
```

Take note of EXTRN addresses that the Link Editor cannot locate. But if your system defaults to ACTION NOMAP, you won't get the message (code ACTION MAP). To remedy the error, have the systems programmer catalog the I/O module, or define a file definition macro that is already cataloged.

Often, an examination of a diagnostic message, the assembled program listing, and the Link Edit Map does not disclose the cause of an error, and the only resort is to study a storage dump, as the next section explains.

STORAGE DUMPS

One of the main debugging tools of experienced programmers is the storage dump. Indeed, a dump is often the easiest and only way to locate a bug. You can force a dump on an execution error by coding your job control as follows:

```
DOS:    // OPTION LINK,DUMP          (or PARTDUMP if parti-
                                      tioned)

OS:     //GO.SYSUDUMP DD SYSOUT=A    (include after the source
                                      program with other //GO
                                      entries)
```

The computer cannot process an invalid instruction, an invalid address, or invalid packed data. In such cases, the supervisor interrupts program execution and prints the location of the failing instruction and the type of error. Unless you provide for error recovery with the DOS STXIT or OS SPIE macros, the supervisor produces the dump, terminates execution, and begins execution of the next job. The diagnostic messages vary by operating system.

DUMPS UNDER DOS.   On a processing error, the DOS supervisor prints an error message such as the following:

```
PROGRAM CHECK—INTERRUPTION-HEX LOCATION—051340-
          CONDITION CODE 3—DATA EXCEPTION
```

"Hex location" is the address of the instruction in error, in this case X'051340'. The condition code is seldom useful, but knowing the type of program check, in this case a Data Exception, is very useful.

If your program's START directive specifies the program's actual "load point" (starting location for execution), then you simply have to check the program listing for the failed instruction. Assume the following instruction at X'51340':

```
51340    ZAP AMTPK,AMTIN  (instruction causing the error)
```

Assume also that the defined fields are the following:

```
AMTIN    DS  ZL6           (in input record)
AMTPK    DS  PL4           (with packed declaratives)
```

You may realize immediately that AMTIN is supposed to be an input field containing zoned data, whereas ZAP requires that operand-2 reference packed data. The instruction code presumably should be PACK.

If the START directive does not supply the program's load point (that is, START has a blank or zero operand), then you have to calculate the storage address. If the supervisor has printed a dump of the registers and storage, then check the address in the base register. Since the INIT macro in this text initializes base register-3, then it contains the starting address, and the first line of the dump beginning with GR 0-F (general registers 0–15) would appear as follows:

```
GR  0-F  x------x  x------x   x------x  40051212  . . .
            I          I          I         I
         reg-0      reg-1      reg-2     reg-3
```

In this case, register-3 contains the address X'051212' (ignore the 40 to the left—other than the most recent supercomputers, addresses are six digits). Deduct two from this address: X'051212' − 2 = X'051210', the true load point for this program. Subtract this load point from the hex location in the supervisor diagnostic:

Location of interrupt	X'051340'
Load point of program	X'051210'
Location of error in list	X'000130'

Now check X'130' in the printout of the assembled program which could appear as follows:

```
130 ZAP AMTPK,AMTIN
```

The ZAP instruction is the one in error, as shown earlier. In the next section DUMP EXAMPLE you will see how to get the load point from a Link Edit Map as well.

DUMPS UNDER OS. OS provides a mass of diagnostic messages, telling you more than you may ever want to know. Provided that you have inserted a SYSUDUMP job control entry, the system will supply the Entry (or Load Point) of your program, the address of the failed instruction, and a hex dump of the registers and storage area. If your program encounters a program check interrupt, examine the printout following the program listing and output (if any). The first diagnostics could appear as follows:

```
JOB jobname STEP GO
COMPLETION CODE SYSTEM 0C7  (7 is the code for Data Exception)
PSW AT ENTRY TO ABEND FFB5000D C0051346  (051346 is instruc-
                                          tion address)
```

"Completion Code" indicates the type of program check. In this case, code '7' is Data Exception—see Appendix B for all codes. The PSW (program status word) indicates the "instruction address" in the rightmost six hex digits, in this case 051346, and is the address following the failed instruction. Since you don't know where an OS program will load for execution, the START or CSECT directives contain a zero operand. You can determine the entry point in the diagnostics under the CDE section. The first statement there could appear as follows:

```
. . . NM MAIN (or NM GO) USE 01 EPA 051210
```

The Entry Point Address (EPA) is therefore 051210, the "relocation factor." You can now determine the failed instruction in the program listing:

Address in the PSW	X'51346'
Entry Point Address	X'51210'
Location of instruction following the error	X'00136'

An examination of the program listing discloses the following:

```
LOC:          Instruction:
130           ZAP AMTPK,AMTIN
136           . . .
```

The instruction preceding 136 is the ZAP at 130. The data exception indicates invalid packed data, once again the contents of AMTIN as discussed in the previous section.

ERROR RECOVERY.   Program checks cause a program to terminate; however, when testing you usually want to push the program through to detect as many errors as possible. The special macros that provide for error recovery are STXIT under DOS and SPIE under OS.

DUMP EXAMPLE

The program in Figure 16-1 reads stock records and calculates unit cost (cost/quantity). The output consists of a heading, the first detail line, an error diagnostic caused by a program check, and finally a storage dump.

The diagnostics disclose that a data exception occurred at hex location 7CE166. You can use this address to locate the actual instruction that caused the data exception. (The contents of the PSW on line 3 shows the address following the failed instruction.) You have to know the program's load point which you can derive from the dump:

- Lines 1 and 2 display the hex contents of the 16 general-purpose registers GR 0-F or 0–15, each containing eight hex digits.
- Line 3 displays the contents of the floating-point registers (FP REG).
- Lines 4 and 5 display the 16 control registers (CR) that the operating system uses for its own purposes.

Following is the hexadecimal dump of storage, reduced in size here for brevity. To the extreme left is the address of the leftmost byte on the line, always at an address evenly divisible by hex 10 (decimal 16). The first line contains:

```
7CE060 006B81E3 . . .
```

7CE060 is the address of the first pair of hex digits, 07. Each line displays 32 (hex 20) bytes, collected in groups of four bytes for readability. The left half of the first line provides the contents of locations 7CE060 through 7CE06F; the right half provides the contents of 7CE070 through 7CE07F.

LCC OBJECT CODE   ADDR1 ADDR2 STMT SOURCE STATEMENT

```
C0CC00                                  3  PRDUMP  START
C0C000  0530                            4          BALR  3,0
                                        5          USING *,3
                              00C02     6          OPEN  FILEIN,PRTR
                                       15          PUTPR PRTR,HDGLINE,SK1    SKIP TO NEW PAGE
                                       22          PUTPR PRTR,HDGLINE,WSP2   PRINT HEADING
                                       29          GET   FILEIN,RECDIN       1ST RECORD
00004E  456C 307A          0CC7C       36  A1CLOOP BAL   6,B1OCALC           PROCESS RECORD
                                       37          GET   FILEIN,RECDIN       READ NEXT
0C0C62  47FC 304C    CCC4E             43          B     A1OLOOP             LOOP
                                       45  A9OEOF  CLOSE FILEIN,PRTR         TERMINATE
                                       54          EOJ
                                       58  *
                                       59  *          C A L C U L A T E   U N I T   C O S T
C00C7C  F236 3464 332C  0C466 00322    60  B1OCALC PACK  COSTPK,COSTIN       *
C0C082  F223 3468 331C  0046A 0031E    61          PACK  QTYPK,QTYIN         *
C0C088  F822 3468 3468  0046A 0046A    62          ZAP   CTYPK,QTYPK         QUANTITY = 0?
00008E  4780 30A8       000AA          63          BZ    B20                 *  YES - BYPASS
C0C092  F873 3468 3464  0046D 00466    64          ZAP   UNCOSTPK,COSTPK     CALCULATE
C00098  FC7C 3468 0CC1  0046D 0CC01    65          SRP   UNCOSTPK,1,0        *  UNIT COST
CCC0A0  FC72 3468 3468  0046D 0046A    66          DP    UNCOSTPK,QTYPK      *
CCC0A4  FC45 3468 3468  0046D 0003F    67          SRP   UNCOSTPK(5),63,5    *
0000AA  D20B 3420 347B  CC422 0047D    69  B20     MVC   COSTPR,EDCOST       EDIT STOCK FIELDS
C0C080  DE0B 3420 3464  00422 00466    70          ED    COSTPR,COSTPK       *  COST
000086  D20E 3418 3487  CC41A 00489    71          MVC   UNCOSPR,EDUNIT      *
C000BC  DE06 3418 3460  0041A 0046F    72          ED    UNCOSPR,UNCOSTPK+2  *  UNIT COST
C000C2  D207 340C 348E  0040E 00490    73          MVC   QTYPR,EDQTY         *
C0C0C8  DEC7 340C 3468  0040E 0046A    74          EC    QTYPR,QTYPK         *  QUANTITY
C000CE  D20F 33FC 3CC   03FE 0030E     75          MVC   DESCRPR,CESCRIN     *
C000D4  D2C3 33F6 3308  003F8 0030A    76          MVC   STOCKPR,STOCKIN     *
C0C0EE  FA73 3473 3464  00475 0046E    78          PUTPR PRTR,STKLINE,WSP1   PRINT STOCK RECORD
                                       85          AP    FINCSTPK,COSTPK     ADD COST TO TOTAL
C000F4  07F6                           86          BR    6                   RETURN
                                       88  *
                                       89  *          D E C L A R A T I V E S
                                       90  FILEIN  DEFIN A90EOF              DEFINE INPUT FILE
                                      114  PRTR    DEFPR                     DEFINE PRINTER
                                      139  RECDIN  DS    0CL80               INPUT RECORD:
C00030A                               140  STOCKIN DS    CL04                 STOCK NO.
C00030E                               141  DESCRIN DS    CL16                 DESCRIPTION
C0C31E                                142  CTYIN   DS    ZL04                 QUANTITY
000322                                143  COSTIN  DS    ZL07                 COST
000329                                144          DS    CL51                 *
```

FIGURE 16-1 (partial).

```
LCC  OBJECT CODE      ADDR1 ADDR2  STMT  SOURCE STATEMENT

00035C 404040404040404040                146  HDGLINE   DC    CL22' '              HEADING:
000372 E2E3C6C3D24C4040                   147            DC    CL23'STOCK'
000389 D8E4C1D5E3C9E3E8                   148            DC    CL88'CUANTITY    UNITCOST      COST'
0003E1                                    149            DS    OCL133               STOCK PRINT LINE:
0003E1 4C4C4C4C4C4C4C4040                 150  STKLINE   DC    CL23' '          *---------------------
0003F8                                    151            DS    CL04                 *         STOCK NO.
0003F8 4040                               152  STCCKPR   DC    CL02' '          *
CCC3FE                                    153            DS    CL16                 *         DESCRIPTION
00040E                                    154  DESCRPR   DS    ZL08                 *         QUANTITY
000416 40404040                           155  QTYPR     DS    CL04' '          *
00041A                                    156            DS    ZL07                 *         UNIT COST
000421 4C                                 157  UNCCSPR   DS    CL01' '          *
000422                                    158            DS    ZL12                 *         COST
00042E 4C40404040404040404040             159  COSTPR    DS    CL56' '          *

000466 CCCCCCOC                           162  CCSTPK    DC    PL4'0'               PACKED FIELDS:
00046A C0000C                             163  QTYPK     DC    PL3'0'           *
00046D CCCCCCCCCCCCCCCC                    164  UACCSTPK  DC    PL8'0'           *
000475                                    165  FINCSTPK  DS    PL8              *
                                          166  *                                  EDIT WORCS :
CCC04D 4C2C206B2020214B                   167  EDCCST    DC    X'40202068202021482020C3D9'
000489 4C2C2021482020                     168  EDUNIT    DC    X'40202021482020'
000490 40202020212DC3D9                   169  EDQTY     DC    X'40202020212DC3D9'
000498                                    170            LTORG
000498 5B5BC2D6C7C5D54C                   171            =C'$$BOPEN '
CC04A0 5B5BC2C3D3D6E2C5                   172            =C'$$BCLOSE'
CCC4A8 CCCC01D0                           173            =A(PRTR)
0004AC C0C0035C                           174            =A(HDGLINE)
0004B0 0C0000F8                           175            =A(FILEIN)
0004B4 CCCCC30A                           176            =A(RECDIN)
CCC4B8 CCC003E1                           177            =A(STKLINE)
                       COCCO              178            END   PRDUMP

       Link edit map:-

02/05/83 PHASE   XFR-AD  LOCCRE  HICORE  CSK-AC  LABEL    LOADED  REL-FR  OFFSET  INPUT

         PHASE*** 7CE078 7CE078 7CE63D 00225179         PRDUMP   7CE078  000C00  SYSLNK
                                                        IJCFZIB1 7CE538  0004C0  IJCFZIB1
                                                        IJDFYZIW 7CE5D8  C00560  IJDFYZIW

       Output:-                          STCCK           CUANTITY  UNITCOST     COST

                                  1234   PLYWOOC 1/4     50        3.05         152.50

OSO3I PROGRAM CHECK INTERRUPTION - HEX LCCATICN 7CE166 - CONDITION CODE 3 - CATA EXCEPTION
OSCCI JOE ABEL   CANCELED
OSO7I PRCBLEM PROGRAM  PSW  036D30CCC07CE16C
```

FIGURE 16-1 (partial)

426

```
                              register 3
GR 0-F   C07CE459 007CE248 007DDFFF 407CE07A   0084CFFF 007DE000 907CE0CA 907D1726
         807CF712 0A16180C C000C0C0 182F07F1   CC7CE078 D7C8C1E2 A07CE166 007CE5D8
FP REG   3F6CD755 C20C624D C06B81E3 2AE20B46   C00000C0 0C000000 41500000 00000000
CR 0-F   8C400C61 000C000C FFFFFFFF CCC0C0CC   C0000000 00000000 00000000 00000000
         00000000 0CCCC0CC 0CC0CCC0 0CCC0C00   CC0000C0 C0000000 8F000000 C0000200

7CE060   C06B81E3 2AE20B46 C0C0CCC0 CCCCC000   41500CC0 CC0C0C00 C5300700 41103496   * . T S                          *
7CE080   45C03012 C07CE170 007CE248 0A02928B   335A5810 34A65800 34AA58F1 001045EF   *            S               1   *
7CE0A0   CCCC9211 335A581C 34A658C0 34AA58F1   001045EF 000C5810 34AE5800 34B258F1   *                 1             1*
7CE0C0   C01045EF CC08456C 307A5810 34AE580C   34B258F1 CC1045EF 000847F0 304C0700   *         -           1      0   *
7CE0E0   4110349E 45003076 007CE170 007CE248   0A020ACE F2363464 3320F223 3468331C   *                 S      2     2  *
7CE100   F8223468 3468478C 30A8F873 346B3464   F070346B 0001FC72 346B3468 F045346B   *8       8 . 0 .      . 0 .*
7CE120   003F020B 3420347B DE0B3420 3464D206   34183487 DE063418 346D0207 340C348E   * K           K            K     *
7CE140   DEC7340C 3468D20F 33FC330C D20333F6   33089209 33DF5810 34A65800 34B658F1   *     K     K  6                1*
7CE160   CC1045EF 000CFA73 34733464 07F60C00   0C0080C0 0C000001 007CE190 007CE198   *               6                *
7CE180   CC7CE538 02E40202 027CE1A2 007CECEC   C27CE1F2 2C000050 47000000 D24FD000   *  V  U               2      K    *
7CE1A0   E000F1F2 F3F4D7C3 E8E6D6C6 C440F161   F4404040 4040F0F0 F5F0F0F0 F1F5F2F5   * 1234PLYWOOD 1/4      0050001525*
7CE1C0   F0404040 4C4C4C4C 40404040 4040404C   4C404040 40404040 40404040 40404040   *0                               *
7CE1E0   4C404040 404C404C 40404040 404C4040   4040F2F4 F6F8D7D3 E8E6D6D6 C440F361   *                2468PLYWOOD 3/*
7CE200   F84C4040 4040F0F1 F5F0F0F0 F8F2F5FC   F0404040 40404040 40404040 40404040   *8      01500082500              *
7CE220   4C4C4040 --SAME--                                                           *                                *
7CE240   4040C0C0 CCCC0CC0 00008C00 0CC00003   C07CE270 007CE278 007CE5D8 08B60909   *                  S   S   VQ   *
7CE260   C97CE2FE 0C0C0000 07004700 CC000000   C97CE279 2CCCCC84 09404040 404C4040   *  S                S             *
7CE280   4C4C4040 4C4C4040 4C404040 404040F1   F2F3F440 40D7C3E8 E6D6D6C4 40F161F4   *              1234   PLYWOOD 1/4*
7CE2A0   40404040 404C404C 40F5F040 4C4C4040   4C404040 F34BF0F5 40404040 40F1F5F2   *         50            3.05     152*
7CE2C0   4BF5F040 404C4040 40404040 40404040   4C404040 4C404040 40404040 404C4040   *.50                             *
7CE2E0   404C4040 404C404C 40404040 404C4040   40404040 40404040 40404040 40114040   *                                *
7CE300   4C       4C4C4040 4C4C4040 4040404C   4C4040E2 E3D6C3D2 40404040 40404040   *                    STOCK       *
7CE320   40       40404040 4040D8E4 C1D5E3C9   E3E84040 4040E4D5 C9E3C3D6 E2E34040   *            QUANTITY    UNITCOST *
7CE340   4C       C3D6E2E3 4C404040 40404040   40404040 40404040 40404040 40404040   *    COST                          *
7CE360   4C       --SAME--                                                           *                                *
7CE380   4040F1F2 F3F4D7D3 E8E6D6D6 C440F161   F4404040 4040F0F0 F5F0F0F0 F1F5F2F5   * 1234PLYWOOD 1/4      0050001525*
7CE3A0   FC404040 4C4C4C4C 404C4040 4040404C   40404040 40404040 4C4C4040 404C4040   *0                               *
7CE3C0   4C404040 4C4C4C4C 40404040 4040404C   40404040 11404040 40404040 40404040   *                                *
7CE3E0   40404040 4C40404C 4040E2E3 D6C3D24C   4C404040 4C4C4040 40404040 40404040   *            STOCK               *
7CE400   40D8E4C1 D5E3C9E3 E8404040 40E4D5C9   E3C3D6E2 E3404040 404040C3 D6E2E340   * QUANTITY    UNITCOST      COST *
7CE420   4C4C4040 --SAME--                                                           *                                *
7CE440   40404040 40404040 4C4C4040 4040404C   40404040 40404040 40094040 40404040   *                                *
7CE460   40404040 40404040 40404040 40404040   F1F2F3F4 4040D7D3 E8E6D6D6 C440F161   *              1234   PLYWOOD 1/*
7CE480   F4404040 404C404C 4040F5F0 40404040   4C404040 40F34BF0 F5404040 4040F1F5   *         50          3.05      15*
7CE4A0   F24BF5F0 4040404C 404C4040 4C4C4040   40404040 40404040 40404040 40404040   *                                *
7CE4C0   40404040 404C4040 404C4040 40404040   40404040 40404040 40404040 40400015   *                                *
7CE4E0   250F0005 0C0C00C0 305C0000 0C00000C   C00000C0 0C402C20 6B202021 4B2020C3   *        *           .  .   C*
7CE500   C                 402C2020            5B5BC2C6 C7C5D540 5B5BC2C3 D3D6E2C5   *R    .          CR$$BOPEN $$BCLOSE*
7CE520   C                 C07CE170            007CE459 C07CE3DC 0A320000 0A320000   * S    TM       T    U    T       *
7CE540   4                 C9D1C3C6            71309140 10154710 F0289640 10150AC0   * 00       IJCFZIB1          0     *
7CE560   S                 0AC7C2C0            50E0F098 58E01020 C2021021 101950E0   *      0    K         0      K     *

Annotations: 7CE382 RECDIN;  7CE4E2 QTYPK;  7CE4E5 UNCOSTPK;  7CE4ED FINCSTPK;  7CE4DE COSTPK
```

FIGURE 16-1 Program interrupt and dump.

The extreme right displays the *character* contents of the dump, where printable. This information is a guide only to fast identification of character constants and input/output records.

The example program uses register-3 as its base register, and you can use its contents to determine where a program is loaded. According to the dump, the first line contains the contents of the general registers, as follows:

```
GR  0-F  007CE459   007CE248   007DDFFF   407CE07A  . . .
           |          |          |          |
         reg-0      reg-1      reg-2      reg-3
```

Ignore the hex 40 to the left in register-3 because addresses are six hex digits. Also, because the initial BALR at statement 4 loads the starting address plus 2, subtract 2 from this address: 7CE07A − 2 = 7CE078, the program's true load point. An OS program supplies the load point as EPA, Entry Point Address, as explained earlier. (Chapter 6 explains BALR and base register addressing in detail.) Now you can locate the failed instruction in the listing as follows:

Address of failed instruction	7CE166
Load point of program	7CE078
Location in listing	0000EE

A check of location (LOC) 0000EE on the left of the program printout reveals that the instruction is

```
AP FINCSTPK,COSTPK
```

Either operand of an AP may cause a data exception. Let's check the contents of the operands in the dump. To determine the locations of the fields in storage, add the load point address with the displacement values under ADDR1 and ADDR2 on the listing:

	FINCSTPK	COSTPK
Load point	7CE078	7CE078
ADDR of operand	475	466
Storage location	7CE4ED	7CE4DE

Now trace these two addresses in the dump in Figure 16-1. The contents of FINCSTPK begins at 7CE4ED. Trace down the leftmost column of the dump until you reach an address that is close. Five lines up from the bottom is address 7CE4E0. Count each pair of hex digits as one, and count across 13 pairs (or count 4's, as 4, 8, C). FINCSTPK is an 8-byte field beginning at 7CE4ED.

As you can see, FINCSTPK does not contain valid packed data. A check back in the program listing shows that FINCSTPK is defined as a DS instead of a DC. That explains the Data Exception, and the correction is easy to make. Actually, since the program doesn't even print final totals, a solution is to delete both the DS and the AP instruction.

But before quitting so soon, it may be a wise idea to ensure that the contents of COSTPK are valid. Trace the storage address of 7CE4DE in the dump. You'll have to step up one line beginning at 7CE4C0, then advance to the center of the line, which is 7CE4D0. Now count across 14 pairs of hex digits until you reach 7CE4DE. The beginning of COSTPK contains 0015, and continues on the next line with 250F. As you can see, COSTPK contains a valid packed value.

The program contains another error that the test data did not detect. A later section on Partial Dumps explains how to dump a selected area of storage to help locate the error.

LINK EDIT MAP.   The previous program also produced a Link Edit Map following the assembled listing. The system may generate a map depending on the system defaults or your request of ACTION MAP. As shown in Figure 16-1, the map contains the following:

xfr-ad   The address where the loader program is to transfer for the start of program execution. The address in the base register is normally two bytes higher than this address.

locore   The lowest address of the program.

hicore   The highest address of the program (you can calculate a program's size by the difference between HICORE and LOCORE).

label   The names of external addresses in the program, in this example PRDUMP (the name of the program), and the two I/O modules for system reader and printer that the Linker has included.

loaded   The storage location of each module.

rel-fr   The "relocation factor" which you can use to add to the START value to locate addresses, in this case 7CE078.

offset   The number of bytes from the lowest address. For example, PRDUMP is offset zero bytes and IJCFZIB1 is offset X'4C0' bytes from the lowest address.

input   The source where the Linker located the module.

PARTIAL DUMPS OF STORAGE—PDUMP AND SNAP

Both DOS and OS have provision for intentional dumps of storage during program execution. The DOS macro is PDUMP and the OS macro is SNAP. Both enable you to view the contents of any storage area. When your program encounters a dump macro, it transfers control to the supervisor, which produces a hexadecimal printout of the contents of the registers and the specified storage area. At termination of the dump, control returns to the statement immediately following the dump macro. In effect, it produces a *snapshot* of storage.

Often a program executes through to completion but produces the wrong results. If a check of the program listing and input data cannot reveal the cause of the error, a common practice is to insert the dump macro (one or more) in the executable part of your program where you want to see the changed contents of one or more declaratives, I/O areas, or buffers. Once you have located and corrected the error(s), be sure to take the dump macros out.

DOS PDUMP MACRO.   The PDUMP macro has the following format:

NAME	OPERATION	OPERAND
(name)	PDUMP	address1, address2 or (reg), (reg)

Address1 and address2 specify the start and end positions of an area to be dumped, as RECDIN,TOTALPAY+10. You may also supply the addresses in registers and code them for example as (6), (9). In either event, PDUMP executes only if the second address is higher and generates the hexadecimal contents of the registers and the defined storage area. The operation changes the contents of registers 0 and 1; the other registers still contain the contents that your own program generated.

DOS supports two other dump macros: DUMP and JDUMP, both of which have blank operands. DUMP terminates the job step and produces a hexadecimal dump of the registers, the supervisor, and the entire partition in which the program was executing. JDUMP terminates the entire job and produces a similar dump. Since a dump of the supervisor can be enormous and of little value to a production programmer, normally only a systems programmer is concerned with these macros.

Refer now to the program in Figure 16-2. Statement 54 contains the instruction:

```
PDUMP RECDIN,EDCOST
```

to display the contents of storage from RECDIN through EDCOST. The program is the same as the one in Figure 16-1, with the DS and AP instructions now deleted. The program still contains an error which the PDUMP can help to locate. The program was run with only two input records:

```
Stock Description     Qty    Cost
|1234|Plywood 1/4"   |0050|0015250|
|1234|Plywood 1/4"   |0000|0026730|
```

You can detect the problem in the output. The first detail line provides a correct calculation of unit cost, but the second line appears to be incorrect. Although quantity is zero, unit cost prints as 3.05, but should be zero. Let's check the dump for the contents of cost, quantity, and unit cost.

Lines 1 and 2 display the hex contents of the 16 general registers, GR 0-F or 0 through 15, each containing eight hex digits.

Note that register-3 (the fourth one on the first line) contains 407CE07A. Since the program loaded register-3 with the base address for the program, you can tell where in storage the program has loaded for execution. Since an address consists of only the rightmost 24 bits (six hex digits) of a register, you can ignore the X'40' to the left, and the address is 7CE07A. The first instruction is BALR 3,0 that loads the storage address of the following instruction into register-3. (Chapter 6 explains BALR and base addressing in detail.) Since BALR is two bytes long, then the address of the program's load point is two bytes less than the address in register-3:

Base address in register-3	7CE07A
Less two bytes for BALR	2
Load point of program	7CE078

You can see then that the supervisor has loaded the executable program into storage beginning at 7CE078. In this example, the declaratives that PDUMP displays begin at 7CE380.

The third and fourth lines contain respectively the contents of the floating-point registers (FP REG) and the 16 control registers (CR 0-F). Neither contains useful information for this example.

Following the printout of the registers is the contents of storage that PDUMP specified, in the same format as the previous dump in Figure 16-1. At the extreme left is the hex address of the first byte of the line, always at an address evenly divisible by X'10' (decimal 16). Each line (except for the first and last) lists 64 hex digits (32 bytes) with a space between each eight hex digits for readability. To the right is the character representation for each byte, if the character is printable. For example, X'F0' displays as a zero, but X'00' appears as a blank.

Note the line beginning at 7CE440: all the locations on that line contain the same character, X'40'. PDUMP minimizes printing and displays —SAME—.

Now let's locate COSTPK in the dump. According to the Assembler printout, COSTPK is at relative location (LOC) 00046E:

Load point of the program	7CE078
Relative location of COSTPK	46E
Actual location of COSTPK	7CE4E6

Scan down the leftmost column of the dump and stop at 7CE4E0 (the last line). The line begins with:

```
7CE4E0   40404040   40400026   730F0000  . . .
         |                     |
         7CE4E0                7CE4E6
```

Count across until reaching 7CE4E6. COSTPK beginning at this address is a four-byte field containing 0026730F. You can derive the contents of QTYPK and UNCOSTPK by the same method.

Note that UNCOSTPK is defined as eight bytes but now contains two packed fields: a quotient (000000305C) and a remainder (00000C). Although the quotient is incorrect, the divide operation presumably did not calculate it incorrectly; the error must be in the program logic.

As you probably noticed, the unit cost 305 is the same as that for the previously printed stock item. The second stock item differs from the first item in that it contains a zero quantity. A check of program logic following B10CALC shows a test for zero QTYPK and a branch to B20. Consequently, if QTYPK is zero, the routine does not calculate unit cost. But since there is no value stored in unit cost, the field still contains the previously calculated unit cost. A solution is to initialize UNCOSTPK to zero immediately before the instruction at statement 68 that tests for zero quantity.

Smaller DOS systems always load programs at a predictable location. You could therefore set the START directive to this value and relate addresses on the assembled listing directly to addresses in the dump.

THE OS SNAP MACRO.   The OS SNAP macro requires that you define a related output file. The general format for SNAP and its associated DCB are the following:

```
[name]   SNAP DCB=dcbname,ID=n,PDATA=(PSW,REGS),STORAGE=(from,to)

dcbname DCB  DSORG=PS,DDNAME=ddname,RECFM=VBA,MACRF=(W),        +
             LRECL=125,BLKSIZE=1632
```

Place the SNAP macro (one or more) in the executing part of your program where you want the dump to occur, and insert the DCB macro in your declarative section. The following describes SNAP parameters:

DCB Provides the name of a DCB macro that handles output for the SNAP.

```
LCC    OBJECT CODE        ACCR1  ADCR2   STMT  SOURCE STATEMENT

C00000                                     3   PRDUMP  START                      INITIALIZE
C00000 0530                                4           BALR  3,0
                                           5           USING *,3
                           00002           6           OPEN  FILEIN,PRTR
                                          15           PUTPR PRTR,HDGLINE,SKI     SKIP TO NEW PAGE
                                          22           PUTPR PRTR,HDGLINE,WSP2    PRINT HEADING
                                          29           GET   FILEIN,RECDIN        1ST RECORD

C0004E 4560 3084                  00086   36   A1CLOOP BAL   6,BIOCALC            PROCESS RECORD
                                          37           GET   FILEIN,RECDIN        READ NEXT
C0C062 47FC 304C           CCC4E         43           B     A1OLOOP              LOOP

                                          45   A9CEOF  CLOSE FILEIN,PRTR          TERMINATE
                                          54           PDUMP RECDIN,EDCOST        *** PDUMP MACRC ***
                                          60           ECJ

                                               *                   C A L C U L A T E   U N I T   C O S T
                                          64   *                   -------------------------------------
                                          65   *

C00086 F236 346C 3328      0046E 0032A   66   BIOCALC PACK  COSTPK,COSTIN         *
C0008C F223 3470 3324      0C472 00326   67           PACK  QTYPK,QTYIN          *
C00092 F822 3470 3470      0C472 00472   68           ZAP   QTYPK,QTYPK          QUANTITY = 0?
C0C098 4780 3082           CCC84         69           BZ    B20                   *   YES - BYPASS
C0009C F873 3473 346C      00475 0046E   70           ZAP   UNCOSTPK,COSTPK       CALCULATE
C0C0A2 F070 3473 0001      0C475 00C01   71           SRP   UNCOSTPK,1,0          *   UNIT COST
C0C0A8 FD72 3473 3470      CC475 00472   72           DP    UNCOSTPK,QTYPK        *
C0C0AE F045 3473 0C3F      CC475 C0C3F   73           SRP   UNCOSTPK(5),63,5      *

C0C0B4 D208 3428 3478      0C42A 0047D   75   B20     MVC   COSTPR,EDCOST         EDIT STOCK FIELDS
C0C0BA DE0B 3428 346C      CC42A 0046E   76           ED    CCSTPR,COSTPK         *   COST

C0C0C0 D206 3420 3487      CC422 0C485   78           MVC   UNCOSPR,ECUNIT        *   UNIT COST
C0C0C6 DE06 3420 3475      CC422 00477   79           ED    UNCOSPR,UNCOSTPK+2    *

C0C0CC D2C7 3414 348E      CC416 CC49C   81           MVC   QTYPR,EDQTY           *
C0C0D2 DE07 3414 3470      CC416 00472   82           ED    QTYPR,QTYPK           *   QUANTITY

C0C0D8 D20F 3404 3314      00406 00316   84           MVC   DESCRPR,DESCRIN       *
C0C0DE D203 33FE 331C      C04C0 00312   85           MVC   STCCKPR,STOCKIN       *

                                          87           PUTPR PRTR,STKLINE,WSP1    PRINT STOCK RECORD
C000F8 07F6                               94           BR    6                    RETURN

                                               *                   D E C L A R A T I V E S
                                          96   *                   -----------------------
                                          97   *
                                          98   FILEIN  DEFIN A90EOF               DEFINE INPUT FILE
                                         122   PRTR    DEFPR                      DEFINE PRINTER
```

FIGURE 16-2 (partial).

433

```
LOC   OBJECT CODE        ADDR1 ADDR2  STMT   SOURCE STATEMENT

                                      147    RECDIN     DS    0CL80        INPUT RECORD:
000312                                148    STOCKIN    DS    CL04         STOCK NO.
000312                                149    DESCRIN    DS    CL16         DESCRIPTION
000316                                150    QTYIN      DS    ZL04         QUANTITY
000326                                151    COSTIN     DS    ZL07         COST
00032A                                152             DS    CL51         *
0CC331

                                      154    HDGLINE    DC    CL22' '      HEADING:
000364  4C4C4C4C40404C4C              155             DC    CL23'STOCK'
C0037A  E2E3C6C3C2404040              156             DC    CL88'QUANTITY  UNITCOST  COST'
CCC391  D8E4C1D5E3C9E3E8              157             DS    0CL133
0C03E9  4C4040404040404C              158  *STKLINE    DC    CL23' '      STOCK PRINT LINE:
0CC400                                159             DS    CL04         * ----------  STOCK NO.
CCC4C0  4C4C                          160    STOCKPF    DC    CL02' '      *
000404                                161    DESCRPR    DS    CL16         * DESCRIPTION
000406                                162    QTYPR      DS    ZL08         * QUANTITY
000416                                163             DC    CL04' '      *
00041E  4C4C4040                      164    UNCOSPR    DS    ZL07         * UNIT COST
000422  40                            165             DC    CL01' '      *
00042A                                166    CCSTPR     DS    ZL12         *
000436  404040404040404C4C4C          167             DC    CL56' '      * COST
                                      168
                                                                          PACKED FIELDS:
00046E  CCCCCCCC                      170    COSTPK     DC    PL4'0'       *
000472  CCCCCC                        171    QTYPK      DC    PL3'0'       *
000475                                172    UNCOSTPK   DS    PL8          *
                                      173  *                              EDIT WORDS :
0C047D  4C2C206B202021148            174    EDCOST     DC    X'4020206B2020214B20202C3D9'
0CC489  4C20202148202C               175    EDUNIT     DC    X'40202021482020'
0CC490  402020202120C3D9             176    EDQTY      DC    X'40202020212OC3D9'
0CC458                                177             LTORG
0C0498  585BC2D6D7C5D540              178             =C'$$BOPEN '
0C04A0  585BC2C3D3D6E2C5              179             =C'$$BCLOSE'
0C04A8  585BC2D7C4E4D4D7              180             =CL8'$$BPDUMP'
0004B0  CCC0312000000047D            181             =A(RECDIN,EDCOST)
0004B8  CCC001D8                      182             =A(PRTR)
0CC4BC  CCC00364                      183             =A(HDGLINE)
0CC4C0  CCCCC100                      184             =A(FILEIN)
0004C4  CCC00312                      185             =A(RECDIN)
0004C8  000003E9                      186             =A(STKLINE)
                                      187             PRDUMP
                          00C00                       END
```

Output:-

```
STOCK             QUANTITY   UNITCOST   COST

1234  PLYWOOD 1/4     50       3.05     152.50
1234  PLYWOOD 1/4      0       3.05     267.30
```

FIGURE 16-2 (partial).

434

```
                                  02/C5/87  21.22.49    CPUID=FF01039143410000                                   PAGE   1
                         register 3
GR 0-F   007CE528 007CE520 007DDFFF 407CE07A   CC84DFFF 007DE000 907CE0CA 907C1726
         807CF712 0A1618CC COCOCOCO 182F07F1   OC7CE078 D7C8C1E2 007CE0E0 007CE548
FP REG   3F6CD755 C20C624C C06B81E3 2AE20B46   C0000000 00000000 41500000 00000000
CR 0-F   80400C61 CCCCOCCC FFFFFFFF C000000C   CC00CCC0 CC000000 00000000 00000000
         CCCC0000 000C0000 0000COCO 0CCCC00C   CC00CCC0 CC000000 8F000000 00000200

7CE380                     4040F1F2 F3F4D7D3   E8E6D6D6 C440F161 F4404040 4040F0F0   *        1234PLYWOOD 1/4      00*
7CE3A0   F0F0F0F0 F2F6F7F3 F040         404C   40404040 4C4C4040 40404040 40404040   *000026730                       *
7CE3C0   4C4C4040 404C404C 4040 7CE38A  4C40   40404040 404C4040 40404040 114C4040   *                                *
7CE3E0   4C4C4040 404C4C4C 404C RECDIN  4040   4040E2E3 C6C3C240 40404040 40404040   *                  STOCK         *
7CE400   40404040 4C4C4C4C 40D8E4C1 D5E3C9E3   E8404040 40E4D5C9 E3C3D6E2 E3404040   *          QUANTITY     UNITCOST *
7CE420   4C4040C3 D6E2E340 40404040 404C4040   40404040 4C4C4C40 4C404040 40404040   *   CCST                         *
7CE440   4C4C404C --SAME--                                                           *                                *
7CE460   4C094040 404C4040 404C4040 4C4C4C40   40404040 40404040 F1F2F3F4 40400703   *                         1234 PL*
7CE480   E8E6D6D6 C440F161 F4404040 404C4C4C   4C4040F0 4C4C4040 40404040 40F34BF0   *YWOCD 1/4         0         3.0*
7CE4A0   F5404040 404CF2F6 F74BF3F0 404C4C40   40404040 40404040 40404040 40404040   *5      267.30                   *
7CE4C0   4C404C4C --SAME--                                                           *                                *
7CE4E0   40404040 40400026 730FCCC0 0CDC0000   305C00C0 0C402020                     *                    *           *
                      |          |      |
                  7CE4E6         |   7CE4ED
                  COSTPK         |   UNCOSTPK
                              7CE4EA
                               QTYPK

         ———— Hexadecimal representation ————                                        —— Character representation ——
```

FIGURE 16-2 Partial dump of storage.

ID=n   Optionally specifies a number between 0 and 127 that SNAP uses for identification on output. Your program for example may have any number of SNAP macros executing.

PDATA   Optionally directs SNAP to generate the contents of the PSW and registers.

STORAGE   Optionally identifies the two storage addresses where the dump is to begin and end. The second address must be higher.

For the DCB, the dcbname must agree with that for the SNAP DCB entry. DDNAME relates to a job control entry that specifies the system listing device:

```
//ddname DD SYSOUT=A
```

You must OPEN the SNAP file prior to executing the first SNAP and CLOSE the file on termination. The dump is in the same format as a regular dump and a PDUMP. Note that any dump changes the contents of registers 0 and 1.

Figure 16-3 provides a skeleton of SNAP logic. Further information is available in the IBM OS Supervisor and Macros instructions manual.

```
progname CSECT
         ...
         OPEN      (OSSNAP,(OUTPUT))
         ...
         SNAP      DCB=OSSNAP,ID=3,PDATA=(PSW,REGS),          +
                   STORAGE=(SNBEG,SNEND)
         ...
         CLOSE     (OSSNAP)
         ...
***                D E C L A R A T I V E S

OSSNAP   DCB       DSORG=PS,DDNAME=SNAPIT,RECFM=VBA,MACRF=(W),  +
                   LRECL=125,BLKSIZE=1632
         ...
SNBEG    EQU       *
         .
         .         (Declaratives to be dumped)
         .
SNEND    EQU       *
         ...
         END       progname
/*
//SNAPIT   DD SYSOUT=A
```

FIGURE 16-3 Skeleton use of the OS SNAP macro.

STXIT—SET EXIT

Without some kind of recovery, a program check such as a Data Exception or Decimal Overflow causes the supervisor to interrupt the processing of your program, display an error diagnostic, and terminate the program. One way to force your program to resume processing after a supervisor message is to code a special recovery macro, STXIT under DOS and SPIE under OS.

The STXIT macro has three operands:

```
[name] STXIT exit,address,savearea
```

Operand-1 provides the type of exit, coded as PC, OC, IT, or AB. PC (the common entry) is for program checks, OC is for an operator (external) check, IT is for an interval timer check, and AB is for an abnormal task termination.

Operand-2 provides the storage address where you want the supervisor to branch after its message. The routine could print a message or issue a PDUMP of the declarative area.

Operand-3 references a savearea of 18 fullwords in which the supervisor stores the old interrupt status information and the contents of registers 0–15, in that order.

```
PROG16      START
            BALR  12,0
            USING *,12
            STXIT PC,X10PC,SAVEPC      Set error recovery
            OPEN  files
              .                        *
              .                        Processing
              .                        *
            CLOSE files
            EOJ

X10PC       PDUMP STDECL,ENDECL        Dump Declaratives
            EXIT  PC

*           D E C L A R A T I V E S

filename    DTFxx ..                   Define files

STDECL      EQU   *
SAVEPC      DC    18F'0'               *
              .                        Declaratives
              .                        *
ENDECL      EQU   *
            END   PROG16
```

FIGURE 16-4 Use of the DOS STXIT macro.

Use the EXIT macro to return from your own recovery routine. The operand for EXIT matches the type of interrupt:

```
[name] EXIT PC or OC or IT
```

As an example, refer to the skeleton program in Figure 16-4. STXIT provides for recovery from a program check. Assume that an AP instruction has caused a Data Exception. The supervisor displays an error diagnostic and then branches to X10PC where the routine dumps the declarative area (there is usually no advantage dumping the contents of file definition macros). The EXIT macro causes a return to the address immediately following the AP.

Although your calculations will be incorrect, your program will push through more instructions and provide more thorough testing. More details are available in the IBM DOS Supervisor and I/O Macros manual. See the IBM OS manual for details on the SPIE macro.

PROBLEMS

16-1. Character data. Identify and correct the following unrelated bugs.

```
         HOURSIN    DS      CL5

(a)                 CLC     HOURSIN,=C' '        HOURSIN blank?
(b)                 MVC     HOURSIN,=C'0'        Move zeros to HOURSIN
(c)                 CLI     HOURSIN,C'0'         HOURSIN = zero?
(d)                 MVC     HOURSIN+3,=C'  '     Move 2 blanks
```

16-2. Packed data. Identify and correct the following unrelated bugs.

```
         HOURIN     DS      ZL5
         HOURPK     DS      PL3'25'
         HOURTOT    DS      PL5
         PAGENO     DC      PL1'1'

(a)                 AP      HOURTOT,HOURPK
(b)                 AP      PAGENO,=P'9'
(c)                 CP      HOURIN,=P'0'
(d)                 CLC     HOURPK,=P'0'
(e)                 DP      HOURPK,=P'0'
```

16-3. Branch and link. Identify and correct the following bug.

```
                    BAL    5,H10HDG
                    BAL    6,C10CALC
                    ...
        C10CALC     .
                    .
                    BR     5
        H10HDG      .
                    .
                    BR     5
```

16-4. Input/output. Identify and correct the following unrelated bugs.

```
        PRTR        DTF or DCB (assume correct definition)
        PRINT       DS     CL133

  (a)               OPEN   PRINT

  (b)               MVI    PRINT,X'40'
                    PUT    PRTR,PRINT
```

16-5. Explicit base addressing. Identify and correct the following unrelated bugs. Assume the same declaratives as Problem 16-2 and assume that HOURIN contains valid numeric data.

```
  (a)               LA     6,HOURIN
                    PACK   HOURPK,0(6)

  (b)               LA     7,HOURIN
                    LA     8,HOURPK
                    PACK   0(3,7),0(5,8)
```

16-6. A dump displays a Data Exception at address X'36894' and the contents of the base register as X'4003684A'.

(a) Assuming the directive START 0, what would be the location on the assembled listing of the instruction that failed?

(b) Assume that the failed instruction is AP TOTAL,VALUE. The assembled listing shows the address of the operands as follows:

```
        LOC    Name     Op'n    Operand
        7A     TOTAL    DS      PL5
        7F     VALUE    DS      PL3
```

What are the locations of the two fields in the dump?

(c)   The dump displays the following for line 368C0:

```
368C0        F0F10000 00000000 00040426 7C404040 ...
```

Locate the two fields in the dump and determine the two errors in the data.

17

FLOATING POINT OPERATIONS

The preceding chapters discussed arithmetic data in two formats: packed decimal and binary, or fixed point. There are two disadvantages that may derive from performing arithmetic in these formats: (1) The maximum and minimum values may be inadequate for the calculation being performed; and (2) the programmer is fully responsible for maintaining decimal and binary point precision. Assembler floating point format has its own unique set of instructions designed to overcome these disadvantages. Its most common use is for calculations such as in aerodynamics, weather forecasting, and electronics design that require extremely high or low values. Most programs requiring floating point arithmetic are written in high-level languages such as FORTRAN and PL/I. These languages replace much of the tedious detail that Assembler programming requires. Studying the Assembler floating point instructions gives better understanding of the high-level languages and results in better programming performance. However, be warned that the problem in Assembler of translating between binary and floating point is challenging.

FLOATING POINT FORMATS

BASE 10 FLOATING POINT. Floating point can be best explained in terms of decimal (base 10) values. Any decimal value can be expressed by the formula

$$N = 10^e \times f$$

where:

N = the decimal value
e = exponent, or power, to which the base 10 is raised
f = fraction

Consider the following decimal values:

Decimal value N	$= 10^e \times f$				
123.45	$= 10^3$	$\times$ .12345	$=$	1000	$\times$ .12345
1.2345	$= 10^1$	$\times$ .12345	$=$	10	$\times$ .12345
0.12345	$= 10^0$	$\times$ .12345	$=$	1	$\times$ .12345
0.0012345	$= 10^{-2}$	$\times$ .12345	$=$	0.01	$\times$ .12345

A floating point value omits the base (10) and stores only the exponent (e) and the fraction (f). As a fullword, the floating point value could be stored as

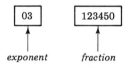

meaning $10^3 \times 0.123450$.

CONVERTING BASE 10 TO BASE 16.   The 370-series computers store floating point values in base 16. The following technique converts decimal values into hexadecimal. Assume a decimal value of 123.45:

1. Use the decimal-to-hexadecimal conversion table in Appendix A to convert the integer portion 123 to base 16 = 7B.0000.

2. Convert the fraction portion as:

				7B.0000
	0.45			
	$\times$ 16	Multiply by 16		
$=$	7.20	Extract the 7	$=$	.7000
	0.20			
	$\times$ 16	Multiply by 16		
$=$	3.20	Extract the 3	$=$	.0300
	0.20			
	$\times$ 16	Multiply by 16		
$=$	3.20	Extract the 3	$=$	.0030
	0.20			
	$\times$ 16	Multiply by 16		
$=$	3.20	Extract the 3	$=$	.0003
	Hexadecimal value			7B.7333

Float numbers are stored as 6 digits in single precision, or 14 digits in double precision. The value is stored in single precision as 7B.7333, but is expressed more accurately with double precision as 7B.733333333333—there is no exact hex representation for 123.45.

BASE 16 FLOATING POINT. The previous example converted 123.45 to X'7B.7333'. This hex number can be represented by:

$$N_{16} = 16^e \times f_{16}$$
$$7B.7333 = 16^0 \times 7B.7333$$
$$= 16^1 \times 7.B7333$$
$$= 16^2 \times .7B7333$$

You may therefore store this floating point number without the base (16) as

meaning $16^2 \times$ X'.7B7333'.

Floating point, like binary data, may be defined in storage or loaded in registers. Either way, floating point values are represented in three formats:

FORMAT	PRECISION	LENGTH
Short	Single	Fullword
Long	Double	Doubleword
Extended Long	Extended	Two doublewords (larger systems)

The float number consists of a *sign, characteristic (exponent),* and *fraction:*

single-precision	s	char	fraction		
bits	0	1 − 7	8	−	31

double-precision		char	fraction		
bits	0	1 − 7	8	−	63

SIGN. The sign, in bit position zero, applies to the *fraction.* A 0-bit means plus, and a 1-bit means minus fraction.

CHARACTERISTIC. In a value such as 16^3, 16 is the fraction, and 3 is the exponent, and means $16 \times 16 \times 16$, or 4096. The computer stores the exponent (characteristic) in *excess-64 notation* by adding 64 (X'40') to the stored exponent, as follows:

DECIMAL REPRESENTATION	HEXADECIMAL REPRESENTATION
Exponent + 64 = Characteristic	Exponent + 40 = Characteristic
03 + 64 = 67	03 + 40 = 43
00 + 64 = 64	00 + 40 = 40
−03 + 64 = 61	−03 + 40 = 3D

The exponent is incremented by 64 (X'40'), and stored in hex format in bit positions 1–7. The lowest exponent is X'−40'; it is stored as X'−40' + X'40' = X'00'. The highest exponent is X'3F'; it is stored as X'3F' + X'40' = X'7F'. This maximum exponent is stored with all 7 bits on. Although the characteristic has no sign stored, there is an implicit sign. For example, the exponent −2 is stored as X'−02' + X'40' = X'3E'. Under base 16, such an exponent means 16^{-2}.

FRACTION.   The fraction may be represented as single precision (short), double precision (long), or as extended long. Single precision processes faster and requires less storage; double precision provides greater accuracy. Single precision stores the fraction in hex in bits 8–31, and double precision in bits 8–63. (Bit zero is the sign.) Negative fractions are stored the same as positive fractions (unlike binary that uses two's complement for negatives). The *radix point* (in base-10 the decimal point) *is immediately to the left of the fraction.*

Following are examples of floating point values:

Example: *Positive exponent, positive fraction.* The decimal value 128.0 equals X'80', or $16^2 \times$ X'.8'. It is stored in short form as:

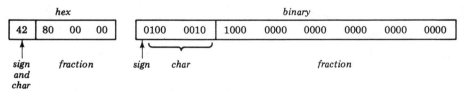

Based on $16^2 \times$ X'.8', the characteristic is calculated as 02 + 40 = X'42'. Because the fraction is positive, the sign bit becomes 0. The fraction with the radix point to the left is represented as X'.8'. You may now compute its value using the exponent 2 and the fraction as $16^2 \times$ X'.8' = 256 × 0.5 = 128.

Example: *Positive exponent, negative fraction.* The decimal value −2816.0 equals X'−B00', or $16^3 \times$ X'−.B'. It is stored in short form as:

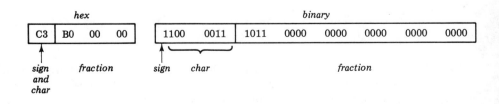

The characteristic is calculated as $03 + 40 = $ X'43'. Because the fraction is negative, the characteristic is stored as X'C3'. The fraction becomes X'$-$.B0'. You may now compute its value using exponent 3 and the fraction as $16^3 \times$ X'$-$.B0' $= 16^3 \times -11/16 = 16^2 \times -11 = -2816$.

Example: *Negative exponent, positive fraction.* Assume a floating point value stored in short form as:

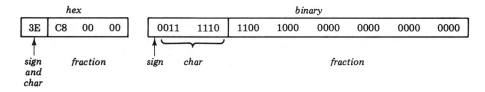

The characteristic is calculated as X'3E' $-$ X'40' $= -02$. You may now compute the value as

$$16^{-2} \times \text{X'.68'} = \frac{1}{16^2} \times \left(\frac{12}{16} + \frac{8}{16^2}\right) = \text{approximately } 0.0030517.$$

NORMALIZATION.   Precision is maintained more accurately by means of *"normalization."* The normalization procedure left-adjusts the floating point fraction until the leftmost hex digit is nonzero, and decrements the characteristic by 1 for each fraction digit shifted. For example, consider the floating point value:

$$\boxed{43 \mid 00 \mid 88 \mid 00} = 16^3 \times \left(\frac{8}{16^3} + \frac{8}{16^4}\right) = 8 + \frac{8}{16} = 8.5$$

Normalize by shifting the fraction left two digits and decrement the characteristic by 2:

$$\boxed{41 \mid 88 \mid 00 \mid 00} = 16^1 \times \left(\frac{8}{16} + \frac{8}{16^2}\right) = 8 + \frac{8}{16} = 8.5$$

Certain float operations involve prenormalizing (before the operation) and postnormalizing (after the operation). This practice is discussed along with the instructions.

• *Problems 17-1 through 17-4 should now be attempted.* •

DECLARATIVES

You define floating point data in decimal format, which the Assembler converts to float. You may define data as single precision (E-format), double precision (D format), or on some systems extended long (L format). (D format was used earlier as a DS to facilitate the CVB and CVD operations.) Also, you may define float constants with or without an *exponent modifier En.*

NAME	OPERATION	OPERAND
(symbol)	DC	dTLn'constant'

OPTIONAL: d = duplication factor to signify the number of repetitions of the constant. If it is omitted, the Assembler assumes one constant.

REQUIRED: T = type. E defines single precision (32 bits of which 24 are the fraction). D is double precision (64 bits of which 56 are the fraction). L defines extended long as two doublewords.

OPTIONAL: Ln = length in bytes. This factor is normally omitted because the Assembler aligns E on a fullword and D on a doubleword boundary —the required format for floating point RX instructions. If Ln is specified, this alignment is not done.

REQUIRED: 'constant'. Define the constant as a decimal value, with a preceding minus sign if necessary. You may also code a decimal point; if omitted, it is assumed to be to the right. The Assembler uses the decimal point in the conversion to float. You may further modify the value with an optional exponent En. For example, 3.1416 may be coded as .31416E1 (meaning 0.31416×10^1) or as 3141.6E−3 (meaning 3141.6×10^{-3}). The Assembler rounds and normalizes the constant if necessary. For an *unnormalized* constant, you may use a *scale modifier,* written as Sn. The *n* tells the Assembler how many hex digits to right-shift the fraction so that there are hex zeros to the left.

Figure 17-1 illustrates various definitions of floating point declaratives. Note the alignment and the generated object code in each case. The first group defines single precision or short form.

FLOATE1 simply defines a 4-byte DS aligned on a fullword boundary.

FLOATE2 AND FLOATE3 define the same constant as positive and as negative.

FLOATE4 has a duplication factor of 3, causing definition of three identical constants.

FLOATE5 illustrates a multiple declaration: one statement defines three different constants. The third constant, 0, defines "true zero"—a zero fraction and characteristic.

```
                        6  *      -------------------------
                        7  *      DC    E SINGLE-PRECISION
                        8  *      -------------------------
003804                  9  FLOATE1  DS   E                    DEFINE FULLWORD AREA
003808  427B7333       10  FLOATE2  DC   E'123.45'            POSITIVE VALUE
00380C  C27B7333       11  FLOATE3  DC   E'-123.45'           NEGATIVE VALUE
003810  413243FE413243FE 12 FLOATE4 DC   3E'3.1416'           3 CONSTANTS
003818  413243FE
00381C  4164FDF4BD9D4952 13 FLOATE5 DC   E'6.312,-.00015,0'   MULTIPLE DECLARATION
003824  00000000
003828  427B7333       14  FLOATE6  DC   E'123.45E0'          123.45 X 1    = 123.45
00382C  427B7333       15  FLOATE7  DC   E'1.2345E2'          1.2345 X 100  = 123.45
003830  427B7333       16  FLOATE8  DC   E'12345E-2'          12345  X .01  = 123.45
003834  450007B7       17  FLOATE9  DC   ES3'123.45'          UNNORMALIZED, USE OF SCALE
                                                                          MODIFIER
                       19  *      -------------------------
                       20  *      DC    D DOUBLE-PRECISION
                       21  *      -------------------------
003838                 22  FLOATD1  DS   OD                   ALIGN ON DOUBLEWORD BOUNDARY
003838  427B733333333333 23 FLOATD2 DC   D'123.45'            POSITIVE DOUBLE-PRECISION
003840  475912BC00000000 24 FLOATD3 DC   D'93.4E6'            93,400,000
003848  450007B733333333 25 FLOATD4 DC   DS3'123.45'          UNNORMALIZED, USE OF SCALE
                                                                          MODIFIER
```

FIGURE 17-1 Floating point declaratives in single and double precision.

FLOATE6, FLOATE7, AND FLOATE8 depict the exponent modifier. Each case generates the same float constant.

FLOATE9 uses a scale modifier, S3, to prevent normalization. The S3 causes the assembler to shift the fraction three positions to the right. The generated constant, 450007B7, is interpreted as

$$16^5 \times \left(\frac{7}{16^4} + \frac{11}{16^5} + \frac{7}{16^6} \right)$$

Note that compared to FLOATE6, this constant has lost some precision. The second group defines double precision or long form.

FLOATD1 is a DS with a zero duplication factor to force alignment on a doubleword boundary.

FLOATD2 and FLOATD3 define double precision constants. FLOATD2 gives more precision than the same constant defined as short form in FLOATE2.

FLOATD4 uses a scale modifier and defines the same constant as FLOATE9.

• *Problems 17-5 and 17-6 should now be attempted.* •

FLOATING POINT REGISTERS

From context it should be clear where "register" in this chapter means floating point and where it means general register. The four floating point registers (FPRs) numbered 0, 2, 4, and 6, are each a doubleword in length (8 bytes or 64 bits). The only valid references to FPRs are 0, 2, 4, and 6. The type of instruction determines that it is a floating point and not a general register. For example, AR references two general registers, whereas ADR references two floating point registers. A float operation may specify the use of the entire 64-bit register (double precision) or the leftmost 32 bits (single precision).

FLOATING POINT INSTRUCTIONS

The floating point instruction set, although less extensive, is similar to that for binary. The instructions are in RR and RX format, where R references an FPR and X references a storage address subject to the usual base and index register. These instructions permit data manipulation between registers and between registers and storage. Operations include load, store, add, subtract, compare, halve, multiply, and divide. The operations are named to describe their purpose. Consider the following three LOAD operations:

```
operation:      LE       LER      LTER
                ||       |||      ||||
position:       12       123      1 23
```

POSITION-1 signifies the type of operation, such as L for load, A for add. Exceptions are LC, LN, LP, LT, and ST which require two letters.

POSITION-2 defines the length of the operation. E as in LE means single precision, and D as in LD means double precision. U as in AUR implies single precision unnormalized, and W as in AWR implies double precision unnormalized.

POSITION-3 for RX format is blank. For RR, the letter R indicates a register, such as LER and LTER.

LOAD INSTRUCTIONS. The Load instructions load floating point values from storage into a register or between registers, similar to binary L and LR. The most common load instructions are:

NAME	OPERATION	OPERAND
(symbol)	LE	R1,X2 or R1,D2(X2,B2)
	LD	R1,X2 or R1,D2(X2,B2)
	LER	R1,R2
	LDR	R1,R2

The rules are:

1. The operations load the floating point number referenced by the operand-2 address (storage or register) into the operand-1 register without normalization.

2. For LE, operand-2 is an aligned fullword in storage; for LD, operand-2 is an aligned doubleword.

3. LE and LER, being single precision, process only the leftmost 32 bits of the register; the right half is not affected.

4. These load instructions do not set the condition code.

Refer to Figure 17-2. In LOADE1, LE loads a short form constant called FLOATEP1 into register-2. In LOADE2, LER loads the contents of register-2 into register-4. Only the leftmost 32 bits of both operands engage in these operations—the rightmost 32 bits are undisturbed. In LOADD1, LD loads a long form constant called FLOATDP1 into register-0. In LOADD2, LDR loads the contents of register-0 into register-6. All 64 bits of both operands engage in these operations.

```
                      29 *    -----------------------------------
                      30 *      LE & LER   LOAD SINGLE-PRECISION
                      31 *    -----------------------------------
003850 7820 3066      32 LOADE1  LE   2,FLOATEP1        REG-2: 434D28F6
003854 3842           33 LOADE2  LER  4,2              REG-4: 434D28F6

                      35 *    -----------------------------------
                      36 *      LD & LDR   LOAD DOUBLE PRECISION
                      37 *    -----------------------------------
003856 6800 305E      38 LOADD1  LD   0,FLOATDP1        REG-0: C27B74BC 6A7EF9DB
00385A 2860           39 LOADD2  LDR  6,0              REG-6: C27B74BC 6A7EF9DB

00385C 00000000
003860 C27B74BC6A7EF9DB  41 FLOATDP1 DC  D'-123.456'
003868 434D28F6          42 FLOATEP1 DC  E'1234.56'
```

FIGURE 17-2 Floating point load operations: LE, LER, LD, LDR.

SPECIAL LOAD INSTRUCTIONS. You may use certain load operations, for example, to reverse the sign or to set the condition code. (The binary correlates are LCR, LNR, LPR, and LTR.)

NAME	OPERATION	OPERAND		NAME	OPERATION	OPERAND
(symbol)	LCER	R1,R2		(symbol)	LPER	R1,R2
	LCDR	R1,R2			LPDR	R1,R2
	LNER	R1,R2			LTER	R1,R2
	LNDR	R1,R2			LTDR	R1,R2

These instructions are similar to the previous load operations. In addition, each sets the condition code: 0—zero fraction, 1—less than zero (except LPER and LPDR), 2—greater than zero (except LNER and LNDR).

LOAD COMPLEMENT—LCER AND LCDR load the operand-2 register into operand-1 and reverse the sign bit: 0 becomes 1 and 1 becomes 0.

LOAD NEGATIVE—LNER AND LNDR load the operand-2 register into operand-1 and set the sign bit to 1, for minus.

LOAD POSITIVE—LPER AND LPDR load the operand-2 register into operand-1 and set the sign bit to 0, for positive.

LOAD AND TEST—LTER AND LTDR load the operand-2 register into operand-1. These work the same as LER and LDR but in addition set the condition code.

STORE INSTRUCTIONS. STE and STD store the contents of a floating point register into a storage address. (The binary correlates are STH and ST.) The rules are: (1) STE and STD store the contents of the operand-1 register in the operand-2 storage address without normalization; (2) STE stores the leftmost 32 bits of the register; the storage address must be an aligned fullword; (3) STD stores the entire 64 bits into an aligned doubleword address.

NAME	OPERATION	OPERAND
(symbol)	STE	R1,X2 or R1,D2(X2,B2)
	STD	R1,X2 or R1,D2(X2,B2)

In Figure 17-3, LD loads a long form value into register-0. STE stores the leftmost 32 bits of register-0 in the fullword area, STORSING. STD stores the entire 64 bits of register-0 in the doubleword area, STORDOUB.

```
                       46  *      -------------------------------------
                       47  *      STE & STD   STORE FLOATING-POINT
                       48  *      -------------------------------------
00386C 6800 3076       49        LD    0,FLTD1        REG-0:    44392800 00000000
003870 7000 3086       50        STE   0,STORSING     STORSING: 44392800
003874 6000 307E       51        STD   0,STORDOUB     STORDOUB: 44392800 00000000

003878 4439280000000000 53 FLTD1  DC    D'146.32E2'    DOUBLEWORD CONSTANT
003880                  54 STORDOUB DS   D              DOUBLEWORD AREA
003888                  55 STORSING DS   E              FULLWORD   AREA
```

FIGURE 17-3 Floating point store operations: STE and STD.

ADDITION AND SUBTRACTION. There are instructions for both normalized and unnormalized addition and subtraction. Subtraction inverts the sign of operand-2 and then adds the operands. The first step in add and subtract ensures that the characteristics of both operands are equal. If unequal, the field with the smaller characteristic is adjusted by shifting its fraction to the right and incrementing the characteristic by 1 until the characteristics are equal.

Example: *simple addition of short form:*

$$
\begin{array}{l}
41\ 290000 \qquad 41\ 290000 \\
+\underline{40\ 120000} = +\underline{41\ 012000} \qquad \textit{shift right and add} \\
41\ 2A2000
\end{array}
$$

Example: *fraction overflow.* If the fraction overflows because of addition, then the operation shifts the fraction right one hex digit, and increments the characteristic by 1. (If the characteristic overflows a program interrupt occurs.)

$$
\begin{array}{ll}
41\ 940000 & \\
\underline{41\ 760000} & \\
41\ 11A0000 & \textit{fraction overflows} \\
42\ 11A000 & \textit{shift fraction right, add 1 to characteristic}
\end{array}
$$

Example: *guard digit and normalization.* Normalized addition and subtraction normalize the result after the operation (postnormalization). Also, single precision add and subtract maintain improved precision by means of a *guard digit*. When the fraction is shifted right, this guard digit saves the last digit shifted. The digit is restored during postnormalization.

$$
\begin{array}{lll}
& 42\ 0B2584 \quad 42\ 0B2584 & \textit{guard digit} \\
& \underline{40\ 114256} = \underline{42\ 001142(5)} & \textit{shift right 2 digits} \\
\text{Add:} & 42\ 0B36C6(5) & \\
\text{Normalize:} & 41\ B36C65 & \textit{shift left 1 digit}
\end{array}
$$

ADD AND SUBTRACT NORMALIZED. The normalized add and subtract instructions are:

NAME	OPERATION	OPERAND
(symbol)	AE	R1,X2 or R1,D2(X2,B2)
	AD	R1,X2 or R1,D2(X2,B2)
	AER	R1,R2
	ADR	R1,R2

NAME	OPERATION	OPERAND
(symbol)	SE	R1,X2 or R1,D2(X2,B2)
	SD	R1,X2 or R1,D2(X2,B2)
	SER	R1,R2
	SDR	R1,R2

Each operation sets the condition code as follows: 0—zero fraction in the result, 1—fraction less than zero, 2—fraction greater than zero, 3—exponent overflow in the result.

ADD NORMALIZED. AE, AD, AER, and ADR add the contents of operand-2 to operand-1, and normalize the result. The short form operations—AE and AER—process only the leftmost 32 bits of the register; the rightmost 32 bits are unaffected.

SUBTRACT NORMALIZED. SE, SD, SER, and SDR subtract the contents of operand-2 from operand-1 and normalize the result. The short form operations—SE and SER—process only the leftmost 32 bits of a register; the rightmost 32 bits are unaffected.

In Figure 17-4 ADDFLTE depicts single precision add. A doubleword is loaded into register-2, and AE adds the left half of a doubleword to register-2. A third doubleword is loaded into register-4, and AER adds the left half of register-2 to register-4. The right half contents of the registers are undisturbed.

ADDFLTD is similar to ADDFLTE except that it uses double precision. All 64 bits engage in the operations and the results (shown in comments) are more precise.

SUBFLTE is similar to ADDFLTE except that it performs single precision subtraction. SUBFLTD is similar to SUBFLTE, but uses double precision subtraction with more precise answers.

```
                          59 *        -------------------------------------------------
                          60 *        AE & AER   ADD SINGLE-PRECISION NORMALIZED
                          61 *        -------------------------------------------------
0038BC 6820 30C6          62 ADDFLTE  LD    2,AMTFLT1            REG-2: 427B7333 33333333
003890 7A20 30CE          63         AE    2,AMTFLT2            REG-2: 429AB603 33333333
003894 6840 30D6          64         LD    4,AMTFLT3            REG-4: 435C0999 9999999A
003898 3A42               65         AER   4,2                 REG-4: 4365B4F9 9999999A

                          67 *        -------------------------------------------------
                          68 *        AD & ADR   ADD DOUBLE-PRECISION NORMALIZED
                          69 *        -------------------------------------------------
00389A 6820 30C6          70 ADDFLTD  LD    2,AMTFLT1            REG-2: 427B7333 33333333
00389E 6A20 30CE          71         AD    2,AMTFLT2            REG-2: 429AB604 189374BC
0038A2 6840 30D6          72         LD    4,AMTFLT3            REG-4: 435C0999 9999999A
0038A6 2A42               73         ADR   4,2                 REG-4: 4365B4F9 DB22D0E5

                          75 *        -------------------------------------------------
                          76 *        SE & SER   SUBTRACT SINGLE-PRECISION NORMALIZED
                          77 *        -------------------------------------------------
0038A8 6820 30C6          78 SUBFLTE  LD    2,AMTFLT1            REG-2: 427B7333 33333333
0038AC 7B20 30CE          79         SE    2,AMTFLT2            REG-2: 425C3063 33333333
0038B0 6840 30D6          80         LD    4,AMTFLT3            REG-4: 435C0999 9999999A
0038B4 3B42               81         SER   4,2                 REG-4: 43564692 9999999A

                          83 *        -------------------------------------------------
                          84 *        SD & SDR   SUBTRACT DOUBLE-PRECISION NORMALIZED
                          85 *        -------------------------------------------------
0038B6 6820 30C6          86 SUBFLTD  LD    2,AMTFLT1            REG-2: 427B7333 33333333
0038BA 6B20 30CE          87         SD    2,AMTFLT2            REG-2: 425C3062 4DD2F1AA
0038BE 6840 30D6          88         LD    4,AMTFLT3            REG-4: 435C0999 9999999A
0038C2 2B42               89         SDR   4,2                 REG-4: 43564693 74BC6A7F

0038C4 00000000
0038C8 427B733333333333   91 AMTFLT1  DC    D'123.45'            DOUBLEWORD
0038D0 421F42D0E5604189   92 AMTFLT2  DC    D'31.261'            DOUBLEWORD
0038D8 435C09999999999A   93 AMTFLT3  DC    D'1472.6'            DOUBLEWORD
```

FIGURE 17-4 Floating point normalized add and subtract.

ADD AND SUBTRACT UNNORMALIZED. You may want to control precision by preventing normalization. Unnormalized operations are desirable, for example, in converting between floating point and binary formats (illustrated in a later section). Unnormalized add and subtract set the condition code, but omit use of the guard digit and the postnormalization step.

NAME	*OPERATION*	*OPERAND*
(symbol)	AU	R1,X2 or R1,D2(X2,B2)
	AW	R1,X2 or R1,D2(X2,B2)
	AUR	R1,R2
	AWR	R1,R2

NAME	*OPERATION*	*OPERAND*
(symbol)	SU	R1,X2 or R1,D2(X2,B2)
	SW	R1,X2 or R1,D2(X2,B2)
	SUR	R1,R2
	SWR	R1,R2

In these operations, U stands for single precision unnormalized and W (double-U) for double precision. Examples in Figure 17-5 are similar to those just given for normalized add and subtract and should be compared.

ADDFLTU illustrates single precision unnormalized addition. A doubleword is loaded into register-2. AU adds a short unnormalized constant to register-2. Another doubleword is loaded into register-4, and AUR adds the left half of register-2 to register-4. The right half of the registers are undisturbed and results are unnormalized. ADDFLTW is similar to ADDFLTU except that it uses double precision and all 64 bits engage in the addition.

SUBFLTU is also similar to ADDFLTU except that short unnormalized subtract is performed. SUBFLTW is similar to SUBFLTU, with double precision used. In this example, however, SWR shows a convenient way to clear a register to true zero—the characteristic and fraction are both set to zero.

COMPARE. The following operations compare two floating point fields:

NAME	*OPERATION*	*OPERAND*
(symbol)	CE	R1,X2 or R1,D2(X2,B2)
	CD	R1,X2 or R1,D2(X2,B2)
	CER	R1,R2
	CDR	R1,R2

The rules are:

1. The characteristics of the two operands are checked. The shorter one is incremented and its fraction shifted right, as for normalized subtract.

```
                       97  *    ------------------------------------------------
                       98  *        AU & AUR   ADD SINGLE-PRECISION UNNORMALIZED
                       99  *    ------------------------------------------------
0038E0  6820 3116     100 ADDFLTU   LD    2,AMTFLU1          REG-2: 427B7333 33333333
0038E4  7E20 311F     101           AU    2,AMTFLU2          REG-2: 44009AB6 33333333
0038E8  6840 3126     102           LD    4,AMTFLU3          REG-4: 435C0999 9999999A
0038EC  3E42          103           AUR   4,2                REG-4: 44065B4F 9999999A

                      105  *    ------------------------------------------------
                      106  *        AW & AWR   ADD DOUBLE-PRECISION UNNORMALIZED
                      107  *    ------------------------------------------------
0038EE  6820 3116     108 ADDFLTW   LD    2,AMTFLU1          REG 2: 427B7333 33333333
0038F2  6E20 311E     109           AW    2,AMTFLU2          REG-2: 44009AB6 04189375
0038F6  6840 3126     110           LD    4,AMTFLU3          REG-4: 435C0999 9999999A
0038FA  2E42          111           AWR   4,2                REG-4: 44065B4F 9DB22D0E

                      113  *    -----------------------------------------------------
                      114  *        SU & SUR   SUBTRACT SINGLE-PRECISION UNNORMALIZED
                      115  *    -----------------------------------------------------
0038FC  6820 3116     116 SUBFLTU   LD    2,AMTFLU1          REG-2: 427B7333 33333333
003900  7F20 311E     117           SU    2,AMTFLU2          REG-2: 44005C30 33333333
003904  6840 3126     118           LD    4,AMTFLU3          REG-4: 435C0999 9999999A
003908  3F42          119           SUR   4,2                REG-4: 44056469 9999999A

                      121  *    -----------------------------------------------------
                      122  *        SW & SWR   SUBTRACT DOUBLE-PRECISION UNNORMALIZED
                      123  *    -----------------------------------------------------
00390A  6820 3116     124 SUBFLTW   LD    2,AMTFLU1          REG-2: 427B7333 33333333
00390E  6F20 311F     125           SW    2,AMTFLU2          REG-2: 44005C30 624DD2F1
003912  2F44          126           SWR   4,4                REG-4: 00000000 00000000

003914  00000000
003918  427B733333333333  128 AMTFLU1  DC   D'123.45'         DOUBLEWORD NORMALIZED
003920  44001F42D0E56042  129 AMTFLU2  DC   DS2'31.261'       DOUBLEWORD UNNORMALIZED
003928  435C09999999999A  130 AMTFLU3  DC   D'1472.6'         DOUBLEWORD NORMALIZED
```

FIGURE 17-5 Floating point unnormalized add and subtract.

2. Operand-1 is compared algebraically to operand-2, including the sign, exponent, and fraction. However, if both fractions are zero, the result is equal regardless of sign and exponent.

3. CE and CER compare only the leftmost 32 bits.

4. For CE, operand-2 is an aligned fullword in storage. For CD, operand-2 is an aligned doubleword.

5. The condition is set for 0 (equal), 1 (low), and 2 (high).

In Figure 17-6 COMPE compares single precision and COMPD compares double precision.

HALVE. The Halve instructions permit convenient division of an operand by two.

NAME	OPERATION	OPERAND
(symbol)	HER	R1,R2
	HDR	R1,R2

```
                   134  *      ------------------------------------
                   135  *        CE & CER   COMPARE SINGLE-PRECISION
                   136  *      ------------------------------------
003930 7820 314E   137 COMPE    LE    2,COMP1
003934 7920 3156   138          CE    2,COMP2              427B7333 > 421F42D0
003938 7840 315E   139          LE    4,COMP3
00393C 3924        140          CER   2,4                  427B7333 < 435C0999

                   142  *      ------------------------------------
                   143  *        CD & CDR   COMPARE DOUBLE-PRECISION
                   144  *      ------------------------------------
00393E 6820 314E   145 COMPD    LD    2,COMP1
003942 6920 3156   146          CD    2,COMP2              427B7333 33333333 >
003946 6840 315F   147          LD    4,COMP3                       421F42D0 E5604189
00394A 2924        148          CDR   2,4                  427B7333 33333333 <
00394C 00000000                                                     435C0999 9999999A
003950 427B733333333333 150 COMP1  DC    D'123.45'            DOUBLEWORD
003958 421F42D0E5604189 151 COMP2  DC    D'31.261'            DOUBLEWORD
003960 435C09999999999A 152 COMP3  DC    D'1472.6'            DOUBLEWORD
```

FIGURE 17-6 Floating point compare operations.

The rules are:

1. Operand-2 references a register containing the dividend which is to be divided by two.
2. The operations move operand-2 to operand-1 and the fraction one bit to the right. The sign and characteristic are unaffected. Operand-2 is not changed.
3. HER references only the leftmost 32 bits.
4. The condition code is not set.
5. There is no normalization or test for zero fraction.

In Figure 17-7 a doubleword is loaded in register-6. HER shifts only the left 8 hex digits one bit to the right, and HDR shifts all 16 hex digits.

```
                   156  *      ------------------
                   157  *        HER & HDR  HALVE
                   158  *      ------------------
003968 6860 316E   159 HALVE    LD    6,AMTHALF            REG-6: 434D28F5 C28F5C29
00396C 3446        160          HER   4,6                  REG-4: 4326947A

00396E 2426        162          HDR   2,6                  REG-2: 4326947A E147AE14

003970 434D28F5C28F5C29 164 AMTHALF  DC    D'1234.56'          DOUBLEWORD
```

FIGURE 17-7 Floating point halve operation.

MULTIPLICATION. The following instructions multiply floating point fields.

NAME	*OPERATION*	*OPERAND*
(symbol)	ME	R1,X2 or R1,D2(X2,B2)
	MD	R1,X2 or R1,D2(X2,B2)
	MER	R1,R2
	MDR	R1,R2

The multiply operation prenormalizes the field if necessary. Then it adds the characteristics and multiplies the fractions. The rules are:

1. The operand-1 register specifies the multiplicand.
2. Operand-2 references the multiplier, either a storage address (ME and MD) or a register (MER and MDR).
3. The operation normalizes the product, which replaces the multiplicand. Regardless of the operation, the product is a *double precision value.*

In Figure 17-8 MULTE depicts single precision. A fullword multiplicand is loaded into register-2. Then ME multiplies the left half of register-2 by the fullword multiplier in storage. Although the fields are defined as doublewords, only the left half engages in the operations. Next, another fullword is loaded into register-4, and MER multiplies the contents of register-4 by register-2. The final product is in register-4. MULTD uses double precision. All 16 hex digits participate and provide a slightly more precise product.

```
                        168 *    -----------------------------------------
                        169 *        ME & MER   MULTIPLY SINGLE-PRECISION
                        170 *    -----------------------------------------
003978 7820 3196        171 MULTE   LE    2,MULTCAN1           REG-2: 4326D666
00397C 7C20 319F        172         ME    2,MULTPLER           REG-2: 445CB979
003980 7840 31A6        173         LE    4,MULTCAN2           REG-4: 441205B8
003984 3C42             174         MER   4,2                  REG-4: 476871CC

                        176 *    -----------------------------------------
                        177 *        MD & MDR   MULTIPLY DOUBLE-PRECISION
                        178 *    -----------------------------------------
003986 6820 3196        179 MULTD   LD    2,MULTCAN1           REG-2: 4326D666 66666666
00398A 6C20 319E        180         MD    2,MULTPLER           REG-2: 445CB97A E147AE13
00398E 6840 31A6        181         LD    4,MULTCAN2           REG-4: 441205B8 51EB851F
003992 2C42             182         MDR   4,2                  REG-4: 476871D0 639C0EBE

003994 00000000
003998 4326D66666666666 184 MULTCAN1 DC   D'621.4'             DOUBLEWORD
0039A0 4226333333333333 185 MULTPLER DC   D'38.2'              DOUBLEWORD
0039A8 441205B851EB851F 186 MULTCAN2 DC   D'4613.72'           DOUBLEWORD
```

FIGURE 17-8 Floating point multiplication.

DIVISION. The following instructions divide floating point fields:

NAME	OPERATION	OPERAND
(symbol)	DE	R1,X2 or R1,D2(X2,B2)
	DD	R1,X2 or R1,D2(X2,B2)
	DER	R1,R2
	DDR	R1,R2

The divide operation prenormalizes the fields if necessary. The rules are:

1. The operand-1 register specifies the dividend.
2. Operand-2 references the divisor, either a storage address (DE and DD) or a register (DER and DDR).
3. The operation normalizes the quotient, which replaces the dividend. For DE and DER the quotient is single precision; for DD and DDR the quotient is double precision.
4. There is no remainder.
5. A divisor containing a zero fraction causes a program interrupt.

In Figure 17-9, DIVIDE depicts single precision. An LE instruction loads a fullword dividend into register-2. Then DE divides the left half of register-2 by the fullword divisor in storage. Next, another fullword is loaded into register-4, and DER divides the contents of register-4 by register-2. The final quotient is in register-4. DIVIDD uses double precision. All 16 hex digits participate and provide a slightly more precise quotient.

```
                        190  *    -----------------------------------
                        191  *        DE & DER   DIVIDE SINGLE-PRECISION
                        192  *    -----------------------------------
0039B0 7820 31CE        193  DIVIDE  LE    2,DIVIDND1          REG-2: 4326D666
0039B4 7D20 31D6        194          DE    2,DIVSOR            REG-2: 4210445B
0039B8 7840 31DF        195          LE    4,DIVIDND2          REG-4: 441205B8
0039BC 3D42             196          DER   4,2                 REG-4: 4311B9FC

                        198  *    -----------------------------------
                        199  *        DD & DDR   DIVIDE DOUBLE-PRECISION
                        200  *    -----------------------------------
0039BE 6820 31CE        201  DIVIDD  LD    2,DIVIDND1          REG-2: 4326D666 66666666
0039C2 6D20 31D6        202          DD    2,DIVSOR            REG-2: 4210445B 24304055
0039C6 6840 31DF        203          LD    4,DIVIDND2          REG-4: 441205B8 51EB851F
0039CA 2D42             204          DDR   4,2                 REG-4: 4311B9FC E537151B

0039CC 00000000
0039D0 4326D66666666666 206  DIVIDND1 DC    D'621.4'          DOUBLEWORD
0039D8 4226333333333333 207  DIVSOR   DC    D'38.2'           DOUBLEWORD
0039E0 441205B851EB851F 208  DIVIDND2 DC    D'4613.72'        DOUBLEWORD
```

FIGURE 17-9 Floating point division.

CONVERSION FROM PACKED TO FLOAT

Although it is simple to define data in floating point format, it is somewhat difficult to convert packed or binary data into float. The standard practice is to use CVB to convert packed to binary in a general register, and there create the floating point number. Consider the decimal number 268,002. Converted to binary it is X'000416E2'. With the fraction to the right, the double precision float value is 4E000000 000416E2. You may load this number into an FPR and normalize the fraction with a float operation.

Because negative binary numbers are in two's complement form, you must first convert them to positive. For the packed number −268,002 the correct float value is CE000000 000416E2. Figure 17-10 gives the programming steps to convert −268,002 to normalized single precision floating point. When converted into binary in general register-8, −268,002 appears in two's complement as X'FFFBE91E'. But a floating point fraction is stored in absolute form. Therefore use LPR to adjust the binary number to its absolute value in register-10: X'000416E2'. Next load the characteristic X'4E' into register-9 and algebraically shift it left 32 bits into register-8. Now the sign bit of the original binary number is the leftmost bit of the characteristic, X'CE' or binary 1100 1110. With the characteristic loaded into register-9 and the fraction in register-10, the two registers are stored in a doubleword.

In order to normalize the floating point field, first clear the floating point register and then add the double precision value. The floating point number now contains the correct characteristic and normalized fraction in single precision: C5416E20.

```
                      212  *                            GENERAL REGISTERS:
0039E8 F875 3216 320A 213  PACKFLOT ZAP DBLWD,AMTPK        8:          9:          10:
0039EE 4F80 3216      214           CVB 8,DBLWD        FFFBE91E
0039F2 10A8           215           LPR 10,8           FFFBE91E                000416E2
0039F4 5890 322A      216           L   9,CHAR         FFFBE91E    4E000000    000416E2
0039F8 8F80 0020      217           SLDA 8,32          CE000000    00000000    000416E2
0039FC 1898          218           LR  9,8            CE000000    CE000000    000416E2
0039FE 909A 321E      219           STM 9,10,SAVEUNOR
                      220  *                            FLOATING-POINT REG-4:
003A02 2F44           221           SWR 4,4            00000000    00000000
003A04 6A40 321E      222           AD  4,SAVEUNOR     C5416E20    00000000
003A08 7040 3226      223           STE 4,SAVENORM

003A0C 00000268002D   225  AMTPK   DC  PL6'-268002'    PACKED FIELD
003A18                226  DBLWD   DS  D               DOUBLEWORD AREA
003A20                227  SAVEUNOR DS D               DOUBLEWORD AREA
003A28                228  SAVENORM DS F               FULLWORD   AREA
003A2C 4E000000       229  CHAR    DC  X'4E000000'     CHARACTERISTIC
```

FIGURE 17-10 Conversion of packed to floating point format.

CONVERSION FROM FLOAT TO PACKED

Because of the great magnitude of floating point numbers, you must be careful in converting to packed format. If the absolute floating point value is greater than $2^{31}-1$ (or 2,147,483,647), then its binary equivalent will exceed the capacity of a 32-bit general register. You may make use of a unique short cut in the conversion. Consider a normalized float value, 45416E20. Its correct unnormalized hexadecimal value is X'416E2', or decimal 268,002. You can use an unnormalized add operation, AW, with an operand containing a characteristic of 4E to shift the radix point from the left to the right as follows:

$$
\begin{array}{r}
4E000000\ 00000000 = 4E000000\ 00000000 \\
+45416E20\ 00000000 = \underline{4E000000\ 000416E2} \\
4E000000\ 000416E2
\end{array}
$$

The rightmost 8 hex digits now contain the correct binary value, which you can next convert to packed. If the float number had contained any significant digits to the right, the operation would have shifted them out.

If the float value is negative, convert it to two's complement in binary. A minor adjustment to the preceding routine gives correct results for either positive or negative values. The AW operation adds X'4E00000100000000. The "1" in the fraction has no effect on positive numbers, but forces two's complement on negative numbers. Assume a float value of C5416E20:

$$
\begin{array}{r}
4E000001\ 00000000 = 4E000001\ 00000000 \\
+C5416E20\ 00000000 = \underline{CE000000\ 000416E2} \\
CE000001\ FFFBE91E
\end{array}
$$

The rightmost 8 hex digits now contain the correct two's complement value which you can now translate to packed.

Figure 17-11 converts normalized single precision float to packed format. The float value is the one just discussed, C5416E20, and is loaded into floating point register-4. The first step checks that the value does not exceed $2^{31}-1$. Next, AW unnormalizes the number, STD stores the entire 64-bit register in DOUBLE. Finally, the rightmost four bytes of DOUBLE are converted into packed.

```
003A30 7840 3262            233 FLOTPACK LE    4,FLOAT                   FLT REG-4: C5416E20
003A34 3064                 234          LPER  6,4                       FLT REG-6: 45416E20
003A36 7960 325E            235          CE    6,MAXVAL                  IF EXCEEDS MAXIMUM,
003A3A 47B0 3266            236          BNL   B10PASS                   THEN BYPASS
003A3E 6E40 3256            237          AW    4,ADJUST                  FLT REG-4: 4E000000 FFFBE91E
003A42 6040 324E            238          STD   4,DOUBLE                  STORE FLOAT DOUBLEWORD
003A46 5890 3252            239          L     9,DOUBLE+4                GEN REG-9: FFFBE91E BINARY
003A4A 4E90 324E            240          CVD   9,DOUBLE                  DOUBLE:    -268,002 PACKED

003A50                      242 DOUBLE   DS    D                         DOUBLEWORD AREA
003A58 4E00000100000000     243 ADJUST   DC    X'4E00000100000000'       ADJUSTMENT FACTOR
003A60 48800000             244 MAXVAL   DC    E'2147483648'             MAXIMUM VALUE
003A64 C5416E20             245 FLOAT    DC    E'-268002'                FLOAT VALUE TO BE CONVERTED
```

FIGURE 17-11 Conversion of floating point to packed format.

Conversion rules can be much more complicated. The examples given process only single precision with integers—that is, the implicit decimal point for the number is to the right. The binary or decimal number may be mixed, that is with a binary or decimal point not to the right, such as 123.45. If so, then the integer portion must be separated from the fraction portion.

• *The remaining problems should now be attempted.* •

PROBLEMS

17-1. Under what circumstances should you consider the use of floating point?

17-2. Why is the characteristic represented in excess-64 notation?

17-3. Convert the binary numbers (represented in hex) to normalized single precision float: (a) X'1520'; (b) X'9A.312'; (c) X'6B3.F2'.

17-4. Convert the following decimal numbers to normalized single precision float: (a) 32,768; (b) 79.396; (c) 244.2166.

17-5. Code the decimal values in Problem 17-4 as DCs and assemble them. Compare the assembler object code to your own calculations (remember the USING directive).

17-6. Code the decimal value 412.673 as a floating point constant. Assemble and check the results: (a) Normalized single precision; (b) Normalized double precison; (c) With an exponent modifier E2 and double precision; (d) Unnormalized double precision with three hex digits preceding the first significant digit.

17-7. The slope m of a line joining two points (x_1, y_1) and (x_2, y_2) is $m = (y_2 - y_1)/(x_2 - x_1)$. Define four fields $X1$, $Y1$, $X2$, and $Y2$ containing single precision constants. Calculate and store the slope as float in M. Code, assemble, and take a storage dump of the results.

Warning: What if $X2 = X1$?

17-8. Convert m in Problem 17-7 to character format so that it may be printed normally.

17-9. Figure 9-15 calculated finance charge rebates in binary format. Rewrite the routine using float declares and instructions. Take a dump of the registers and storage to check the answers.

18

MACRO WRITING

The Greek word *makros* means "long." In programming, macro means a "long" instruction, one that causes the generation of several or many instructions. For each macro, the Assembler generates one or more instructions. Most programmers suppress the generated code, but the examples in this chapter print it by means of PRINT GEN. There are two sources of macros:

1. *Manufacturer-supplied Macros.* IBM macros facilitate the complex supervisor and input/output operations, and include OPEN, GET, EOF, DTFs, and DCBs. These macros simplify much difficult but repetitious coding. They are cataloged in the system library for assembling with source programs.

2. *User-defined Macros.* You may code as your own macro any routine commonly used in a program or in other programs. You may then include it with the source program at assembly-time or assemble and catalog it in the system library. Common examples include multiply, divide, program and base register initialization, and table look-up.

MACROS AND SUBROUTINES.   Subroutines covered earlier have a significantly different use from macros. In a subroutine, the program branches out of the main logic into a separately coded routine. This routine is performed identically each time it is executed. A macro, however, generates one or more Assembler instructions wherever it is coded. Depending on how the macro is coded, the generated instructions each time may be identical or different.

You will have to assess which technique is more efficient for any given situation. Subroutines are more easily coded and use less storage. Macros, however, are more versatile. High-level languages such as COBOL and PL/I use both subroutines and macros in converting their statements into Assembler language.

WRITING MACROS

There are three basic types of macros:

1. *Positional Macros.* For these, you code the entries or *parameters* in a predetermined sequence. An example is

        PUT PRTR,PRINT

    Depending on the way the macro has been defined, in some cases a parameter may be omitted, as PUT PRTR. Figure 18-1 illustrates a positional macro.

2. *Keyword Macros.* For these you code the entries in any sequence. The Assembler recognizes the presence of the parameter, followed by an equal sign (=). A familiar example is:

        FILEIN DTFCD   TYPEFLE=INPUT, +
                        WORKA=YES,   +   etc...

    TYPEFLE and WORKA may be in any sequence, and are recognized as keywords by the Assembler. In some cases you may omit keywords; the Assembler then assumes default values. Figure 18-3 depicts a keyword macro.

3. *Mixed.* A macro definition may combine both positional and keyword. Positional entries are specified first, in sequence. Figure 18-9 illustrates mixed types.

Certain rules govern writing and assembling macros. Figure 18-1 is a simple positional macro that performs packed divide, and shows the basic terminology for a *macro definition:*

				symbolic parameters	
(a)	Header	3	MACRO		
(b)	Prototype	4	DIVID	&QUOT,&DIVDEND,&DIVISOR	
(c)	Model	5	ZAP	&QUOT,&DIVDEND	MOVE DIVIDEND TO QUOT
	Statements	6	DP	&QUOT,&DIVISOR	DIVIDE BY DIVISOR
(d)	Trailer	7	MEND		

FIGURE 18-1 Definition of positional divide macro DIVID.

(a) The first statement of a macro definition is the *header* statement, containing the operation MACRO. This instruction tells the Assembler that a macro is being defined next.

(b) The *prototype* statement informs the Assembler the name of the macro (in this example DIVID), and how the macro-instruction will be coded. The operand contains three *symbolic parameters* (a name preceded by an ampersand (&)) for quotient, dividend, and divisor.

(c) The *model statements* are instructions that the Assembler uses to generate Assembler instructions. (There may also be comments and *Conditional Assembly* instructions, covered later.)

(d) The *trailer* statement, MEND, terminates the macro definition.

In the partial program in Figure 18-2, DIVID is the *macro-instruction* coded once for execution. DIVID was the only instruction coded; the ZAP and DP instructions are *generated code* or the *macro expansion.* The Assembler inserts a plus sign (+) beside the statement number in all the instructions that it generates. The Assembler generated these instructions based on (1) the macro definition, and (2) the operands coded in the macro-instruction.

14		DIVID	MILEAGE,MILES,GALS	MACRO-INSTRUCTION
15+		ZAP	MILEAGE,MILES	MOVE DIVIDEND TO QUOT
16+		DP	MILEAGE,GALS	DIVIDE BY DIVISOR
17	*	*		
18	*	*		
19	MILEAGE	DS	PL6	QUOTIENT — MILES/GAL
20	MILES	DS	PL3	DIVIDEND — MILES
21	GALS	DS	PL3	DIVISOR — GALLONS

FIGURE 18-2 Use of positional DIVID macro-instruction.

There are three entries in the macro-instruction operand, MILEAGE, MILES, and GALS, for each of the three parameters in the prototype, &QUOT, &DIVDEND, and &DIVISOR. For a positional macro, the macro-instruction operands correspond exactly with the prototype. The Assembler replaces each parameter in the macro definition:

MACRO-INSTRUCTION		MACRO DEFINITION
MILEAGE	replaces	&QUOT
MILES		&DIVDEND
GALS		&DIVISOR

MILEAGE, MILES, and GALS must be defined in the source program. The Assembler uses their addresses and lengths when producing the generated code (see the ZAP and DP instructions generated).

You insert macro definitions before the main source program. Only comments and Assembler control directives EJECT, PRINT, SPACE, TITLE, ICTL, and ISEQ may precede the MACRO header. You may define more than one macro, one after another, but you may not define a macro within another macro. Also, a macro may be separately assembled and cataloged for use in other programs.

Within the program you may *use* the macro-instruction any number of times, using either the same labels or labels of any other valid fields. However, the Assembler performs no automatic checking for validity. For example, if a macro-instruction is wrongly coded with character instead of packed operands, the Assembler generates character operands. To check for validity, use *conditional assembly instructions,* covered later.

VARIABLE SYMBOLS.   In a macro definition, a variable symbol begins with an ampersand (&) followed by 1 to 7 letters or digits, the first of which must be a letter. Examples are &NAME and &DIVISOR. There are three types of variable symbols.

1. *Symbolic Parameters.* You may use these in the macro definition name field and operand. In the prototype DIVID, one symbolic parameter is &QUOT. The macro-instruction contained a value MILEAGE that the Assembler assigned to the symbolic parameter &QUOT.

2. *System Variable Symbols.* The Assembler automatically assigns values to these special symbols. There are three: &SYSECT, &SYSLIST, and &SYSNDX, covered later.

3. *Set Symbols.* These permit you to define temporary storage and work-areas to be used within a macro definition. They are defined and processed by *conditional assembly instructions,* covered later.

EXPLANATION OF THE MACRO DEFINITION.   The general format for the macro definition is as follows:

	NAME	*OPERATION*	*OPERAND*
Header:	blank	MACRO	blank
Prototype:	Symbolic parameter or blank	symbol	Symbolic parameter(s)
Model Statements:	Ordinary, sequence or variable symbol, or blank	Instruction or variable symbol	Ordinary or variable symbols
Trailer:	Sequence symbol or blank	MEND	blank

HEADER.   The MACRO header statement is blank in the name or operand fields. It tells the Assembler that a macro is to be defined.

PROTOTYPE. The *name field* may be blank, as in Figure 18-1, or it may contain a symbolic parameter (a name preceded by an ampersand (&) as explained earlier). The operation is a unique symbolic name, such as DIVID, that is not the name of another macro or Assembler instruction. The *operand* may contain zero to 100 symbolic parameters separated by commas. OS permits up to 200 parameters.

MODEL STATEMENTS. Model statements define the Assembler statements that are to be generated. There may be none or many model statements. Use any nonblank characer to indicate continuation in column 72. The *name field* may be blank (as in Figure 18-1), or it may contain an ordinary symbol, a variable symbol, or a sequence symbol (a name preceded by a period, explained later). The *operation* may contain an Assembler instruction, a macro-instruction, or a variable symbol. The *operand* may contain ordinary symbols (such as AMTPK) or variable symbols (such as &QUOT).

TRAILER. MEND is a required entry to terminate the macro definition. The name may be blank or may contain a sequence symbol (a name preceded by a period).

COMMENTS. Comments may begin anywhere after a blank following the operand. In Figure 18-1, model statement comments begin in column 41. Also, an entire line may be coded as a comment. You may include comment lines anywhere in a macro definition following the prototype statement. There are two ways: (1) An asterisk (*) in column 1 causes the Assembler to print the comment along with the generated code (see Figure 18-5 and 18-6); (2) A period in column 1 followed by an asterisk (.*) tells the Assembler not to print the comment with the generated code (see Figures 18-5 and 18-6).

KEYWORD MACROS. Keyword macros have two advantages over positional macros: (1) You may code keyword parameters in *any sequence;* (2) the symbolic parameters in the prototype statement may contain *standard values* allowing you to omit the parameter when using the macro-instruction. Other than the prototype statement, keyword macros are defined the same as positional macros. The parameters of a keyword prototype are immediately followed by an equal sign (=) and an optional standard value.

The macro in Figure 18-3 is similar to the one in Figure 18-1. The prototype is keyword, and is coded as

```
DIVID &QUOT=QUOTIENT,&DIVDEND= ,&DIVISOR=
```

Figure 18-4 uses the macro twice, depicting two ways to code keyword macros. The first operand, &QUOT=, is followed by a standard value, QUOTIENT. When using the macro-instruction, you may omit the parameter &QUOT. In this case, the Assembler assumes that the name to be used by &QUOT is always QUOTIENT (see B10DIV in Figure 18-4). Alternatively, you may override the standard value by coding a different label, such as QUOT=SPEED (see B20DIV in Figure 18-4).

```
1              MACRO
2              DIVID  &QUOT=QUOTIENT,&DIVDEND=,&DIVISOR=
3              ZAP    &QUOT,&DIVDEND              MOVE DIVIDEND TO QUOT
4              DP     &QUOT,&DIVISOR             DIVIDE BY DIVISOR
5              MEND
```

FIGURE 18-3 Definition of keyword divide macro DIVID.

The other prototype parameters, &DIVDEND and &DIVISOR, have no standard values. You must code the name to be used in the macro-instruction as

DIVDEND=DIST, etc.

(See Figure 18-4. Note that in B20DIV the operands are not coded in sequence.)

Except for operands that have standard values, keyword macros require coding the keyword each time they are used. Unless there are a number of standard values, a keyword macro-instruction could cause more coding for a programmer.

```
12 B10DIV     DIVID  DIVDEND=DIST,DIVISOR=TIME
13+           ZAP    QUOTIENT,DIST              MOVE DIVIDEND TO QUOT
14+           DP     QUOTIENT,TIME             DIVIDE BY DIVISOR

16 B20DIV     DIVID  DIVISOR=TIME,DIVDEND=DIST,QUOT=SPEED
17+           ZAP    SPEED,DIST                MOVE DIVIDEND TO QUOT
18+           DP     SPEED,TIME                DIVIDE BY DIVISOR
19 *          .
20 *          .
21 QUOTIENT   DS     PL7                       QUOTIENT
22 DIST       DS     PL4                       DIVIDEND - DISTANCE
23 TIME       DS     PL3                       DIVISOR  - TIME
24 SPEED      DS     PL7                       QUOTIENT - SPEED
```

FIGURE 18-4 Use of keyword DIVID macro-instruction.

CONCATENATION.   Concatenation means linking together, as a chain. In model statements it is possible to concatenate a symbolic parameter with another symbolic parameter or with characters.

1. *Concatenate Symbolic Parameters.* Figure 18-5 codes a load operation that varies according to the type of data to be loaded. You code L concatenated with a symbolic parameter, called here &TYPE, as

L&TYPE. If &TYPE contains blank, H, E, or D, the Assembler generates L, LH, LE, or LD, respectively.

2. *Concatenate Characters.* If a symbolic parameter is concatenated with
digits, letters, left bracket, or a period, there must be a period joining
the two fields. Assume a symbolic parameter &AREA. If it references
a label called FIELD, then &AREA.A results in generated code
FIELDA. Figure 18-5 illustrates concatenation with a bracket
&PRIN.(&LEN) to permit different length codes.

```
1                MACRO
2  &LABEL1  MPY     &REG1,&REG2,&MULTCAN,&MULTPLR,&TYP,&LEN,&PRIN
3  .*               LOAD REGISTERS WITH MULTIPLICAND & MULTIPLIER
4  &LABEL1  L&TYP   &REG2,&MULTCAN            LOAD MULTIPLICAND
5           L&TYP   &REG1,&MULTPLR           LOAD MULTIPLIER
6  *                MULTIPLY TWO REGISTERS
7           MR      &REG1,&REG1             MULTIPLY REGISTERS
8  .*               CONVERT PRODUCT TO DECIMAL
9           CVD     &REG2,DBLEWORD           STORE PRODUCT
10          UNPK    &PRIN.(&LEN),DBLEWORD    UNPACK IN PRINT AREA
11          MEND
```

FIGURE 18-5 Definition of multiply macro MPY with concatenation.

The macro in Figure 18-5 multiplies both binary fullword or halfword
fields and illustrates symbolic parameters, comments and concatenation. The
prototype, MPY, contains a symbolic parameter &LABEL1 in the name field.
When using MPY as a macro-instruction you may code a label such as
M10MULT, which the Assembler includes in the generated code. The symbolic parameters in the prototype operand are:

&REG1	the even-numbered register of an even-odd pair.
&REG2	the odd-numbered register.
&MULTCAN	the multiplicand field, full or halfword.
&MULTPLR	the multiplier field, full or halfword.
&TYP	the type of operation—blank for fullword and H for halfword.
&LEN	the length in the print area where the product is unpacked.
&PRIN	the name of the print area.

The first model statement contains the same symbolic parameter
&LABEL1 as the prototype, because the Assembler is to generate this label
for this statement. The operation loads the full or halfword multiplicand into
the odd register. The second model statement loads the full or halfword
multiplier into the even register. The third model statement multiplies the
contents of the two registers. (Operand-1 of MR is the even register of an
even-odd pair.)

The fourth statement converts the product in the odd register to decimal format in DBLEWORD, defined in the main source program. Finally,

the decimal product is unpacked in the print area. Note the concatenation &PRIN. (&LEN) to append the length code in operand-1.

```
19 M10MULT   MPY    8,9,FIELDH1,FIELDH2,H,6,PRINT+10
20+M10MULT   LH     9,FIELDH1                LOAD MULTIPLICAND
21+          LH     8,FIELDH2                LOAD MULTIPLIER
22+*                MULTIPLY TWO REGISTERS
23+          MR     8,8                       MULTIPLY REGISTERS
24+          CVD    9,DBLEWORD                STORE PRODUCT
25+          UNPK   PRINT+10(6),DBLEWORD      UNPACK IN PRINT AREA


27 M20MULT   MPY    0,1,FIELDF1,FIELDF2,,10,PRINT+25
28+M20MULT   L      1,FIELDF1                 LOAD MULTIPLICAND
29+          L      0,FIELDF2                 LOAD MULTIPLIER
30+*                MULTIPLY TWO REGISTERS
31+          MR     0,0                       MULTIPLY REGISTERS
32+          CVD    1,DBLEWORD                STORE PRODUCT
33+          UNPK   PRINT+25(10),DBLEWORD     UNPACK IN PRINT AREA
34 *         .
35 *         .
36 DBLEWORD  DS     D                         DOUBLEWORD PRODUCT
37 FIELDH1   DS     H                         HALFWORD MULTIPLICAND
38 FIELDH2   DS     H                         HALFWORD MULTIPLIER
39 FIELDF1   DS     F                         FULLWORD MULTIPLICAND
40 FIELDF2   DS     F                         FULLWORD MULTIPLIER
41 PRINT     DC     CL121' '                  PRINT AREA
```

FIGURE 18-6 Use of MPY macro-instruction.

The program in Figure 18-6 tests the macro-instruction twice. M10MULT designates H in the &TYP position. Note that LH is generated for L&TYP. M20MULT omits the &TYP position by means of two commas. The instruction L is generated for L&TYP.

This example is still relatively simple. The conditional assembly instructions in the next section test for validity and permit more variations.

• *Problems 18-1, 18-2, and 18-3 should now be attempted.* •

CONDITIONAL ASSEMBLY INSTRUCTIONS

Conditional assembly instructions permit you to test such attributes as data format, value, field length, and to define fields and change values. They do not generate any code in themselves; rather, they help determine which Assembler instructions to generate. There are two main groups:

1. *Branching and Testing.* AGO, ANOP, AIF, and ACTR permit testing attributes and branching to different locations within a macro definition.

2. *Defining Symbols (SET Symbols) and Varying Their Values.* Local set symbols, LCLA, LCLB, and LCLC, provide defining within a macro expansion. Global set symbols, GBLA, GBLB, and GBLC, enable symbols to be known in other macro expansions. The values in the SET symbols are modified by SETA, SETB, and SETC instructions.

ATTRIBUTES. For each Assembler constant or instruction, the Assembler assigns attributes such as field length and packed format. You may reference these attributes by conditional assembly instructions. There are six kinds of attributes:

	ATTRIBUTE	**NOTATION**
L ′	Length	Length of symbolic parameter.
I ′	Integer	Integer attribute of fixed point, float, or decimal number.
S ′	Scaling	Scale attribute of fixed point, float, or decimal number.
K ′	Count	Number of characters in a macro-instruction operand.
N ′	Number	Number of operands coded in the macro-instruction.
T ′	Type	Type of DC or DS, such as P, C, X, F, etc.

LENGTH. Only AIF, SETA, and SETB statements may reference the length of a variable symbol. For example &X SETA L'&Y means store the length of &Y in the field defined by the SET symbol &X.

INTEGER AND SCALING. A macro may check the defined integer and scaling attributes of fixed point (binary), floating point, and decimal numbers with AIF, SETA, and SETB. In the statement AMT DC P'1234.56' the integer attribute is 4 (4 digits left of the decimal point), and the scale is 2 (2 digits right of the decimal point). See the IBM Assembler manual for further details.

COUNT AND NUMBER. The count attribute refers to the number of characters in a macro-instruction operand. The number attribute refers to the number of operands in a macro-instruction. They may be referenced with AIF, SETA, and SETB. For example: DIVID MPG,MILES,GALS. The count attribute of GALS, having four characters, is four. The number attribute of the macro, having three operands, is three. See the IBM Assembler manual for further details.

TYPE. The type attribute refers to the type of DC, DS, or instruction. Among the types are:

A	A-type address	F	Fullword	P	Packed
B	Binary	H	Halfword	V	V-type address
C	Character	I	Machine instruction	X	Hexadecimal
D	Long float	M	Machine code	Y	Y-type address
E	Short float	0	Omitted operand	Z	Zoned

The type attribute may be referenced by AIF, SETC, and SETB. The next section under AIF and Figure 18-7 give examples.

```
 1              MACRO
 2  &LABEL2     DIVID  &QUOT,&DIVDEND,&DIVISOR
 3  .*                 TEST IF DIVIDEND & DIVISOR BOTH DEFINED PACKED
 4              AIF    (T'&DIVDEND NE T'&DIVISOR).NOTPAK
 5              AIF    (T'&DIVDEND NE 'P').NOTPAK
 6  .*                 TEST IF QUOTIENT LENGTH ADEQUATE
 7              AIF    (L'&DIVDEND+L'&DIVISOR GT L'&QUOT).WRONLN
 8              AGO    .DIVE            VALID PACKED FIELDS
 9  .NOTPAK     MNOTE  'PARAMETER NOT DEFINED AS PACKED'
10              MEXIT
11  .WRONLN     MNOTE  'LENGTH OF DIVIDEND + DIVISOR GREATER THAN QUOTIENT'
12              MEXIT
13  .*                 PERFORM DIVISION
14  .DIVE       ANOP
15  &LABEL2     ZAP    &QUOT,&DIVDEND         MOVE DIVIDEND TO QUOTIENT
16              DP     &QUOT,&DIVISOR         DIVIDE BY DIVISOR
17              MEND
```

FIGURE 18-7 Definition of divide macro DIVID with validity tests.

BRANCHING & TESTING—AGO, AIF. These instructions make use of *sequence symbols.* A sequence symbol begins with a period (.) followed by one to seven letters or digits, the first of which is a letter. Examples are .B25, .AROUND, and .P. Since a name field of a model statement may contain a sequence symbol, it is possible to branch to different statements. Branching is done by the following:

NAME	OPERATION	OPERAND
Sequence symbol or blank	AGO	Sequence symbol
Sequence symbol or blank	AIF	(logical expression) sequence symbol

AGO—UNCONDITIONAL BRANCH. AGO branches unconditionally to a statement with a sequence symbol for its name, as:

```
        AGO    .B25
         .
         .
         .
  .B25   MVC    P+25(8),DATE
```

AIF—CONDITIONAL BRANCH. AIF means "ask if." The operand consists of two parts: (1) A *logical expression* in brackets; and (2) Immediately following, a sequence symbol. The AIF logical expression may use the following *relational operators:*

EQ	equal	NE	not equal
LT	less than	LE	less than or equal
GT	greater than	GE	greater than or equal

Following are five AIF examples:

1. `AIF (T'&AMT EQ 'P').B25PAK`
   (If the type of &AMT equals packed, then branch to .B25PAK.)

2. `AIF (L'&AMT GT 16).E35ERR`
   (If the length of &AMT is greater than 16, then branch to .E35ERR.)

3. `AIF (T'&LINK NE 'I').R45ERR`
   (If the type of &LINK does not equal an instruction, branch to .R45ERR.)

   This testing occurs when the Assembler converts the macro to generated code. The first example tests if &AMT is *defined* as packed, not what the field actually contains. (This macro may be cataloged for use by other programmers.) The Assembler cannot test the contents of a field at execution-time.

   Logical operators AND, OR, and NOT combine terms in a logical expression:

4. `AIF ('&TAB' EQ' AND T'&ARG EQ 'O').R65`
   (If *contents* of &TAB are blank and &ARG is omitted, branch to .R65. The latter is a way of checking if a macro-instruction operand is omitted—intentionally or accidentally.)

   Finally, *arithmetic operators,* +(add), −(subtract), *(multiply), and /(divide) may combine terms of an expression:

5. `AIF (L'PROD GE (L'&MULTCD+L'&MPR+1)).VALID`
   (If the length of product is greater than or equal to the length of &MULTCD plus &MPR plus 1, branch to .VALID. This test ensures that the defined product area is large enough for an MP operation.)

Examine the AGO and AIF instructions in Figure 18-7. This example is similar to Figure 18-1, with the additional checks that the dividend and divisor are defined as packed, and that the quotient area is at least as large as the dividend plus divisor. Figure 18-8 tests the macro. D10DIV shows valid operands that generate the correct instructions. D20DIV and D30DIV illustrate invalid operands that generate error messages.

OTHER INSTRUCTIONS

There are as well three instructions not yet covered: ANOP, MNOTE, and MEXIT.

```
24 D1ODIV    DIVID MILEAGE,MILES,GALS          VALID DIVISION
25+D1CDIV    ZAP   MILEAGE,MILES               MOVE DIVIDEND TO QUOTIENT
26+          DP    MILEAGE,GALS                DIVIDE BY DIVISOR

28 D2ODIV    DIVID MILEAGE,MILES,PRINT         INVALID DIVISION
29+PARAMETER NOT DEFINED AS PACKED

31 D3ODIV    DIVID MILES,MILEAGE,GALS          INVALID DIVISION
32+LENGTH OF DIVIDEND + DIVISOR GREATER THAN QUOTIENT
33 *         .
34 *         .
35 MILES     DS    PL3                         DIVIDEND - MILES
36 GALS      DS    PL3                         DIVISOR  - GALLONS
37 MILEAGE   DS    PL6                         QUOTIENT - MILES PER GAL
```

FIGURE 18-8 Use of DIVID macro-instruction.

ANOP—NO OPERATION. ANOP is a convenience instruction. AGO and AIF require a sequence symbol as a branch operand. But AGO or AIF may require branching to an instruction whose name is an ordinary or variable symbol. If so, then AGO and AIF must branch to an ANOP immediately before the statement.

NAME	*OPERATION*	*OPERAND*
A Sequence Symbol	ANOP	blank

Figure 18-7 illustrates the use of ANOP, where AGO has to branch to &LABEL2. Since AGO cannot branch to a variable symbol, it goes to .MULT containing the ANOP operation, and immediately preceding &LABEL2.

MNOTE AND MEXIT. You may use these operations to print error messages and to exit from a macro.

NAME	*OPERATION*	*OPERAND*
Sequence symbol, variable symbol, or blank	MNOTE	any message, within apostrophes
Sequence symbol or blank	MEXIT	blank

MNOTE—MACRO ERROR MESSAGE. MNOTE is used to print programmer macro messages at assembly-time. The message is enclosed in apostrophes. In order to print an ampersand or an apostrophe as part of the message, you must code two adjacent ampersands or apostrophes. For example:

```
MNOTE 'CAIN && ABEL ''S'
```

Two MNOTE messages in Figure 18-7 warn that the dividend or divisor are not packed format and that the quotient length is too short. In Figure 18-8 when the error condition occurs, the Assembler statements are not generated. Before program execution, first check for and correct any assembly errors.

MEXIT—MACRO DEFINITION EXIT. MEXIT provides a convenient way to terminate processing of a macro. It acts like MEND, although MEND must be the last statement of the macro definition. Figure 18-7 shows exit and termination of the macro. The MEXIT could have been alternatively coded as:

```
            MNOTE  'message'
            AGO    .FINISH (or any sequence symbol)
              .
              .
              .
FINISH      MEND
```

• *Problem 18-4 should now be attempted.* •

SET SYMBOLS

SET symbols are variable symbols that define and assign values. You may then use them to test values and to build instructions. SET symbols are assigned values when you code SETA, SETB, or SETC conditional assembly instructions. They must first have been defined by an LCL or GBL instruction. Local or global instructions may define and assign an initial value. GBLs, and then LCLs, must be coded in the macro definition immediately following the prototype statement.

NAME	*OPERATION*	*OPERAND*
blank	LCLA LCLB LCLC	One or more variable (SET) symbols, separated by commas

LCLA is used to define a SETA symbol and creates a 32-bit field initialized with zero. LCLB defines a SETB symbol that creates a 1-bit field initialized with zero. LCLC defines a SETC symbol that creates a "null character value"—that is, a field with no length defined.

GBLA, GBLB, and GBLC similarly define SET symbols, for values that are to be known in other macro expansions in the same assembly. A later section discusses global instructions.

LCL instructions merely define and initialize SET symbols. The SET operations, SETA, SETB, and SETC, then assign values to SET symbols.

SETA—SET ARITHMETIC. SETA assigns an arithmetic value to a SETA symbol.

NAME	OPERATION	OPERAND
A SETA symbol	SETA	an arithmetic expression

The maximum and minimum values of the expression are $+2^{31}-1$ and -2^{31}. An expression consists of a term or an arithmetic combination of terms. Valid terms are:

Self-defining terms. Such a term has an inherent value, one that is not assigned a value by the Assembler. These may be decimal (as 11), hexadecimal (as X'B'), and binary (as B'1011').

Variable symbols, such as &AMT.

Attributes for count, integer, length, number, and scale. Examples of SETA arithmetic are:

```
            LCLA    &FLD1,&FLD2
&FLD1       SETA    15
&FLD2       SETA    &FLD1+L'&AMT+25
```

LCLA defines &FLD1 and &FLD2 as SETA symbols.

&FLD1: the value 15 (a self-defining term) is assigned to &FLD1.

&FLD2: the expression contains an arithmetic combination of terms. Assume that &AMT is defined elsewhere with a length of 6. The Assembler calculates the expression as:

TERM		VALUE
&FLD1	(variable symbol)	15
L'&AMT	(length attribute)	6
25	(self-defining term)	25
Value assigned to &FLD2		46

The maximum number of terms in the expression is 16. Also, brackets may contain terms in the expression, such as (&COUNT−X'1B')*3.

Figure 18-9 illustrates LCLA and SETA. In this mixed-type macro, the first two parameters are positional whereas the third and fourth are keyword. This macro prints a heading line containing a heading title, page number, and the date. The macro centers the heading title on a page.

PARAMETER	SPECIFIES	LENGTH IN BYTES
&HEAD	Heading	Up to 90 characters
&PAGE	Page number	2 Packed bytes
&DAT	Date	Not defined
&PRT	Print area	121

```
 3            MACRO
 4  &NAME     HEDNG   &HEAC,&PAGE,&CAT=DATE,&PRT=PRINT
 5            LCLA    &LEN,&MID                 LENGTH & MID-POINT
 6            LCLC    &LIT,&L1,&L2              AREA FOR CHARS.
 7  .*                TEST VALIDITY OF PARAMETERS
 8            AIF     (T'&PAGE NE 'P').ERRPACK
 9            AIF     (T'&HEAD NE 'C').ERRCHAR
10            AIF     (L'&HEAD GT 90).ERRSIZE  HEADING > 90 CHARS?
11  .*                SET VALUES
12  &LEN      SETA    L'&HEAC                   LENGTH OF HEADING
13  &MID      SETA    (120-&LEN)/2              CENTER HEADING
14  &LIT      SETC    '=C''PACE'''              LITERAL FOR 'PAGE'
15  &L1       SETC    'L'''                     LENGTH CODE
16  &L2       SETC    '&CAT'                    DATE
17  .*
18  &NAME     UNPK    &PRT+115(3),&PAGE         UNPK PAGE CTR.
19            OI      &PRT+117,X'F0'            CLEAR UNITS ZONE
20            MVC     &PRT+110(4),&LIT          MOVE PAGE LITERAL
21            MVC     &PRT+&MID.(&LEN),&HEAD    MOVE HEADING
22            MVC     &PRT+1(&L1&L2),&DAT       MOVE DATE
23            MEXIT
24  .*                ERROR MESSAGES
25  .ERRPACK  MNOTE   'PAGE COUNT NOT DEFINED AS PACKED'
26            MEXIT
27  .ERRCHAR  MNOTE   'HEADING NOT CEFINED AS CHARACTER'
28            MEXIT
29  .ERRSIZE  MNOTE   'LENGTH OF HEADING EXCEECS PRINT AREA'
30            MEND
```

FIGURE 18-9 Definition of heading macro HEDNG with conditional assembly instructions.

&LEN and &MID define two SETA symbols. AIF checks that the length of heading does not exceed 90 bytes. (Assume 120 print positions with space for date and page.) SETA assigns the length of &HEAD to &LEN. The title is centered by calculating the first print position of &HEAD. For example:

L'&HEAD	EXPRESSION	1ST POSITION
23	$(120-23)/2 = 97/2 =$	48
16	$(120-16)/2 = 104/2 =$	52
11	$(120-11)/2 = 109/2 =$	54

These lengths are used in Figure 18-10. Check that they cause centering of the heading and that the correct code is generated.

Figure 18-10 also illustrates the SETC symbol, covered next.

SETC—SET CHARACTER. SETC assigns a character value to a SETC symbol, up to eight characters enclosed in apostrophes. The operand generally defines a character expression.

NAME	OPERATION	OPERAND
A SETC symbol	SETC	one character operand

```
39 P10HED   HEDNG HEADG1,PAGEPK
40+P10HED   UNPK  PRINT+115(3),PAGEPK     UNPK PAGE CTR.
41+         OI    PRINT+117,X'F0'         CLEAR UNITS ZONE
42+         MVC   PRINT+110(4),=C'PAGE'   MOVE PAGE LITERAL
43+         MVC   PRINT+48(23),HEADG1     MOVE HEADING
44+         MVC   PRINT+1(L'DATE),DATE    MOVE DATE

46 P20HED   HEDNG HEADG2,PAGEPK,DAT=DATOT
47+P20HED   UNPK  PRINT+115(3),PAGEPK     UNPK PAGE CTR.
48+         OI    PRINT+117,X'F0'         CLEAR UNITS ZONE
49+         MVC   PRINT+110(4),=C'PAGE'   MOVE PAGE LITERAL
50+         MVC   PRINT+52(16),HEADG2     MOVE HEADING
51+         MVC   PRINT+1(L'DATOT),DATOT  MOVE DATE

53 P30HED   HEDNG HEADG3,PAGEPK,PRT=OUTAREA,CAT=CATOT
54+P30HED   UNPK  OUTAREA+115(3),PAGEPK     UNPK PAGE CTR.
55+         OI    OUTAREA+117,X'F0'         CLEAR UNITS ZONE
56+         MVC   OUTAREA+110(4),=C'PAGE'   MOVE PAGE LITERAL
57+         MVC   OUTAREA+54(11),HEADG3     MOVE HEADING
58+         MVC   OUTAREA+1(L'CATOT),DATOT  MOVE DATE

60 P40HED   HEDNG HEADG4,PAGEPK
61+LENGTH OF HEADING EXCEEDS PRINT AREA

63 *          .
64 *          .
65 PRINT    DC    CL121' '                  PRINT AREA
66 OUTAREA  DC    CL121' '                  PRINT AREA
67 PAGEPK   DC    PL2'0'                    PAGE COUNTER
68 HEADG1   DC    CL23'HOTROD CUSTOM IMPORTERS'
69 HEADG2   DC    CL16'ABC DISTRIBUTORS'
70 HEADG3   DC    CL11'BAKER CORP.'
71 HEADG4   DS    CL100                     LONG HEADING
72 DATE     DS    CL12                      DATE AREA
73 DATOT    DS    CL12                      DATE AREA
```

FIGURE 18-10 Use of HEDNG macro-instruction.

Examples of SETC character operations:

```
          LCLC   &CHAR1,&CHAR2,&CHAR3
&CHAR1    SETC   'SAM''S'
&CHAR2    SETC   '&TYPE.A'
&CHAR3    SETC   'L'FLOAT'
```

LCLC defines three SETC symbols:

&CHAR1: The character value SAM'S is assigned to the SETC symbol &CHAR1. Two apostrophes within the expression denote a single apostrophe.

&CHAR2: Assume that &TYPE contains the value FIELD. The expression concatenates FIELD with A and assigns FIELDA to &CHAR2.

&CHAR3: the value L'FLOAT is assigned to the SETC symbol &CHAR3.

In Figure 18-9 SETC defines three symbols, &LIT, &L1, and &L2. One SETC assigns &LIT with a character expression to be used as a literal. Note the literal, =C'PAGE', in the generated code in Figure 18-10. Instead of using &LIT in the macro definition, the example could have coded the literal itself:

```
MVC   &PRT+110(4),=C'PAGE'
```

&L1 and &L2 are used to create a symbolic length reference for moving the date to the print area. Note the macro definition and generated code for this example.

We have now covered all the features used in the macro HEDNG. Some remaining items, SETB symbols, system variable symbols, and global SET symbols, are covered next.

SETB—SET BINARY. SETB assigns the binary value 0 or 1 to a SETB symbol. SETB determines if a condition is false (0) or true (1). SETB is commonly used as a switch indicator in a macro definition.

NAME	*OPERATION*	*OPERAND*
A SETB symbol	SETB	0 or 1, or (0) or (1), or (a logical expression)

A logical expression, enclosed in brackets, consists of one term (arithmetic relationship, character relationship, or SETB symbol), or a logical combination of terms (connected by AND, OR, or NOT). In the following examples of SETB binary operations assume that &SYM1 is format C containing the value 6, &SYM2 is format C, and &SYM3 contains the word YES:

```
        LCLB   &B1,&B2,&B3,&B4
&B1     SETB   1
&B2     SETB   (&SYM1 LT 7)
&B3     SETB   ('&SYM3' EQ 'NO')
&B4     SETB   ('&SYM3' EQ 'YES' AND T'&SYM1 NE T'&SYM2)
```

LCLB defines four SETB symbols:

&B1: an arithmetic term (1 = true) is assigned to &B1.

&B2: the arithmetic relationship is true, so 1 is assigned to &B2.

&B3: the character relationship is false, so 0 is assigned to &B3.

&B4: the logical combination of terms is false, so 0 is assigned to &B4.

In Figure 18-11, SETB is a switch &ERRB that determines if any errors have

```
 1              MACRO
 2 &LOOK        LOOKP   &TABLE,                    ADDRESS OF TABLE              +
                        &SERARG,                   ADDRESS OF SEARCH ARGUMENT    +
                        &FUNCTN,                   ADDRESS TO STORE FUNCTION     +
                        &NOTFND                    ADDRESS IF ARG'T NOT FOUND
 3              GBLB    &SAVIND                    SAVE AREA INDICATOR
 4              LCLA    &LSER,&LENTRY              LENGTH OF SEARCH & ENTRY
 5              LCLB    &ERRB                      ERROR SWITCH INDICATOR
 6              LCLC    &H,&HALF                   HALFWORD LITERAL
 7 &ERRB        SETB    (1)                        SET ERROR INDICATOR TO 1
 8 .*                   TEST FOR VALIDITY
 9              AIF     (T'&NOTFND EQ 'I').A10     IS NOTFND A VALID ADDRESS?
10              MNOTE   'ADDRESS FOR NOTFOUND IS INVALID'
11 &ERRB        SETB    (0)                        SET ERROR INDICATOR TO 0
12 .A10         AIF     (T'&TABLE EQ 'C' AND T'&SERARG EQ 'C').A20
13              AIF     (T'&TABLE EQ 'P' AND T'&SERARG EQ 'P').A20
14              MNOTE   'TABLE && SEARCH NOT BOTH CHAR OR PACKED'
15 &ERRB        SETB    (0)                        SET ERROR INDICATOR TO 0
16 .A20         AIF     (&ERRB).A30                IS ERROR INDICATOR = 1?
17              MNOTE   'MACRO CANNOT BE RESOLVED - TERMINATED'
18              MEXIT
19 .*                   SET VALUES
20 .A30         ANOP
21 &LSER        SETA    L'&SERARG                  LENGTH OF SEARCH ARGUMENT
22 &LENTRY      SETA    &LSER+L'&FUNCTN            LENGTH OF SEARCH + FUNCTION
23 &H           SETC    '=H'                       SET UP HALFWORD
24 &HALF        SETC    '''&LENTRY'''              *  CONSTANT
25 &LOOK        ST      10,SAVREG                  SAVE REGISTER-10
26              LA      10,&TABLE                  LOAD ADDRESS OF TABLE
27              AIF     (T'&TABLE EQ 'P').B10      IS TABLE DEFINED AS PACKED?
28 .*                   COMPARE SEARCH TO TABLE ARGUMENT
29 R&SYSNDX     CLC     &SERARG,0(10)              COMPARE CHARACTER
30              AGO     .B20
31 .B10         ANOP
32 R&SYSNDX     CP      &SERARG,0(&LSER,10)        COMPARE PACKED
33 .B20         BE      T&SYSNDX                   *  EQUAL - FOUND
34              BL      S&SYSNDX                   *  LOW  - NOT IN TABLE
35              AH      10,&H&HALF                 INCREMENT NEXT ENTRY
36              B       R&SYSNDX
37 .*                   DEFINE SAVEAREA FIRST TIME ONLY
38              AIF     (&SAVIND).B30              HAS SAVIND BEEN DEFINED?
39 SAVREG       DS      F                          REGISTER SAVE AREA
40 &SAVIND      SETB    (1)                        SET INDICATOR ON (1)
41 .B30         ANOP
42 .*                   ARGUMENT NOT FOUND
43 S&SYSNDX     L       10,SAVREG                  RESTORE REG-10
44              B       &NOTFND                    GO TO ERROR ROUTINE
45 .*                   ARGUMENT FOUND
46 T&SYSNDX     MVC     &FUNCTN,&LSER.(10)         MOVE FUNCTION FROM TABLE
47              L       10,SAVREG                  RESTORE REG-10
48              MEND
```

FIGURE 18-11 Definition of table look-up macro LOOKP.

been encountered in a macro-instruction. If an error is found, the Assembler prints the appropriate message, and the switch is set. The macro then continues with the next test. Only after *all* validity testing does the macro terminate processing. In this way, you fully test the macro-instruction each time it is used.

Note: SETB symbols such as &ERRB can contain only 0 or 1. In an instruction AIF (&ERRB).A30, AIF branches to A30 if &ERRB contains 1.

SYSTEM VARIABLE SYMBOLS

The Assembler automatically assigns values to the three local system variable symbols, &SYSECT, &SYSLIST, and &SYSNDX. Because of its limited use &SYSECT is not covered.

&SYSLIST—MACRO-INSTRUCTION OPERAND. &SYSLIST may be used as an alternative way of referencing a positional macro operand. In the HEDNG macro in Figure 18-9, you could have coded the UNPK instruction as

```
UNPK&PRT+115(3),&SYSLIST(2)
```

The subscript (2) refers to the second parameter in the prototype (&PAGE).

&SYSNDX—MACRO-INSTRUCTION INDEX. For the first macro-instruction processed in an assembly, the Assembler initializes &SYSNDX with 0001. For each succeeding macro-instruction, the Assembler increments &SYSNDX by 1. In Figure 18-10 the macro HEDNG is used four times. Since this is the only macro-instruction in the assembly, at P10HED, &SYSNDX is set to 0001; at P20HED, &SYSNDX is set to 0002, etc.

&SYSNDX can prevent a macro from generating duplicate labels. This situation did not occur in any examples up to this point. However, in Figure 18-11, the macro LOOKP requires that the macro generate several labels. If the macro-instruction is coded more than once, the macro generates labels with the same name, causing Assembler error messages. To avoid such an error, the macro uses labels such as R&SYSNDX. In the generated code in Figure 18-12, this label becomes R0001 for L10LK, and R0002 for L20LK.

- *Problems 18-5, 18-6, and 18-7 should now be attempted.* •

GLOBAL SET SYMBOLS

LCLA, LCLB, and LCLC define local SET symbols for use within the same macro definition. GBLA, GBLB, and GBLC define Global SET symbols for communicating values between different macro definitions.

NAME	OPERATION	OPERAND
(blank)	GBLA GBLB GBLC	One or more variable (SET) symbols, separated by commas

Global operations define the same initial values as do local operations. However, they are initialized only once, the first time the Assembler encounters the GBLA, GBLB, or GBLC. You define global instructions immediately after the prototype statement. Figure 18-11 gives an example. GBLB defines and initializes &SAVIND to zero, and prevents SAVREG DS F from being defined more than once. The macro tests if &SAVIND contains zero. If so, it permits SAVREG to be defined and sets &SAVIND to 1. &SAVIND is now permanently set to 1, through all succeeding macro-instructions, and the Assembler, through the AIF statement, bypasses generating more than one DS for SAVREG. (Consider how &SYSNDX could achieve the same result.)

EXTENDED EXAMPLE—TABLE LOOK-UP MACRO

The table look-up macro, LOOKP, is defined in Figure 18-11 and used in Figure 18-12. LOOKP permits you to code in one statement a table look-up routine that:

- Initializes a register with the table address.
- Compares a search argument to the table argument.
- If equal, branches to an address where the table function is extracted.
- If low, branches to the address of an error routine.
- If high, increments for the next argument and returns to the compare.

The macro allows for either character or packed arguments. It requires that the table contain discrete arguments (unique numbers such as Job or Stock numbers, rather than table ranges as in income tax), in ascending sequence. The comments beside each parameter explain the symbolic parameters in the prototype operand. You code as the fourth parameter in the macro-instruction the address to which the look-up routine branches if the search argument cannot be found. The program must contain the address of this error routine. The routine should provide usual error handling, such as the printing of a message.

• *The remaining problems should now be done.* •

```
55 L1OLK      LOOKP JOBTABPK,JOBNOPK,RATEPK,R1ONOFND
56+L1OLK      ST    10,SAVREG        SAVE REGISTER-10
57+           LA    10,JOBTABPK      LOAD ADDRESS OF TABLE
58+R0001      CP    JOBNOPK,0(4,10)  COMPARE PACKED
59+           BE    T0001         *   EQUAL - FOUND
60+           BL    S0001         *   LOW   - NOT IN TABLE
61+           AH    10,=H'7'         INCREMENT NEXT ENTRY
62+           B     R0001
63+SAVREG     DS    F                REGISTER SAVE AREA
64+S0001      L     10,SAVREG        RESTORE REG-10
65+           B     R1ONOFND         GO TO ERROR ROUTINE
66+T0001      MVC   RATEPK,4(10)     MOVE FUNCTION FROM TABLE
67+           L     10,SAVREG        RESTORE REG-10


69 L2OLK      LOOKP JOBTABCH,JOBNCCH,RATECH,R1ONOFND
70+L2OLK      ST    10,SAVREG        SAVE REGISTER-10
71+           LA    10,JOBTABCH      LOAD ADDRESS OF TABLE
72+R0002      CLC   JOBNOCH,0(10)    COMPARE CHARACTER
73+           BE    T0002         *   EQUAL - FOUND
74+           BL    S0002         *   LOW   - NOT IN TABLE
75+           AH    10,=H'9'         INCREMENT NEXT ENTRY
76+           B     R0002
77+S0002      L     10,SAVREG        RESTORE REG-10
78+           B     R1ONOFND         GO TO ERROR ROUTINE
79+T0002      MVC   RATECH,5(10)     MOVE FUNCTION FROM TABLE
80+           L     10,SAVREG        RESTORE REG-10


82 L3OLK      LOOKP JOBTABPK,JOBNCCH,RATEPK,R2ONOFND
83+ADDRESS FOR NOTFOUND IS INVALID
84+TABLE & SEARCH NOT BOTH CHAR OR PACKED
85+MACRO CANNOT BE RESOLVED - TERMINATED


87 R1ONOFND MVC    PRINT+10(21),=C'ARGUMENT NOT IN TABLE'
88 *             .
89 *             .
90 PRINT     DC    CL121' '         PRINT AREA
91 JOBTABPK  DS    25PL7            TABLE OF PACK JOBS & RATES
92 JOBNOPK   DS    PL4              SEARCH ARG - JOB NUMBER
93 RATEPK    DS    PL3              TO STORE FOUND TABLE RATE

95 JOBTABCH  DS    15CL9            TABLE OF CHAR JOBS & RATES
96 JOBNOCH   DS    CL5              SEARCH ARG - JOB NUMBER
97 RATECH    DS    CL4              TO STORE FOUND TABLE RATE
```

FIGURE 18-12 Use of LOOKP macro-instruction.

PROBLEMS

18-1. Distinguish between a positional and a keyword macro.

18-2. What is the difference between the use of a variable symbol and a sequence symbol?

18-3. Revise Figures 18-5 and 18-6 so that the operation is DR (Divide Register). Changes the names to suit.

18-4. Revise Figures 18-7 and 18-8 as in the previous problem.

18-5. Revise Figures 18-9 and 18-10 for the following: Print area = 133 positions —change other lengths accordingly; Add '1' to the page counter; Edit (ED) the page counter.

18-6. Write a macro that provides for MP with round and shift to two decimal places.

18-7. Expand the macro in the previous problem to provide as well for M and MH.

18-8. Write a macro to initialize a program with three base registers.

18-9. Write a macro to test given character fields for blank positions. (Assume that the fields are input fields, to be packed.) Replace any blank position with a zero.

19

SUBPROGRAMS
AND OVERLAYS

This chapter covers the concept of writing and assembling programs as separate subprograms. This chapter uses the general term subprogram to mean a section of coding that comprises a separate part of the program, such as a control section (CSECT) or a phase. The link edit step combines the separate subprograms into a single executable program. You may want to code a program in more than one subprogram for the following reasons:

- Several programmers can work separately on subprograms.
- Breaking the program into logical components simplifies the problem.
- It is easier to debug smaller sections.
- There may not be enough base registers available for a large program.
- Main storage may be too small for the entire program. The use of "virtual storage," however, provides automatic program sectioning and overlays, and to a large degree reduces the need for programmers to design such programs.
- A program may involve linking two different languages such as COBOL and Assembler.

CSECT—CONTROL SECTION

Chapter 6 introduced the term *control section* (CSECT). A CSECT is *a block of coding that can be relocated without affecting the operating logic of the program.* Both the Assembler and Linkage Editor process control sections, not programs. You may code CSECTs as separate assemblies, each with its own unique base registers. Then you link edit the CSECTs into one or more phases, the Linkage Editor output. A program may consist of one or more phases, and a phase may consist of one or more control sections. Among the ways to section a program into subprograms are:

1. The program may consist of a single phase—one or more control sections. The CSECTs are assembled separately or together, and link edited into a single phase. For execution, the system loads the entire phase into storage.

2. The program may consist of more than one phase, each with one or more CSECTs. Each phase is separately assembled, then link edited together. At execution-time, the system loads the first *(root)* phase into storage. The root phase loads *(overlays)* the other phases into storage as required.

There are two main problems associated with the use of subprograms:

1. Some data is common to more than one subprogram, but data is defined in only one subprogram. Because subprograms are assembled separately, the Assembler treats each subprogram as a completely different program. Data defined in one subprogram is not therefore known in another. Among the ways of making data known between subprograms are the use of "DSECTs" and "passing parameters."

2. A subprogram must be able to link to another subprogram, its register contents must be saved (especially base registers), and there must be some means of returning and restoring the register contents. The Assembler macros that provide this linkage are CALL, SAVE, and RETURN. The Assembler requires a standard savearea for registers and a standard linkage convention.

We will first examine a simple case of how a DSECT works. Then we will see how to assemble and link together two CSECTs for execution. The last example combines three separately assembled phases into one program —a root phase and two overlay phases. Finally, we will explain how to link a COBOL program with an Assembler program.

DSECT—DUMMY SECTION

You may want to *describe* a data area without actually reserving any storage. For example, the main subprogram, SUBPROGA, contains the main data and certain other coding, including instructions to link to SUBPROGB. SUBPROGB is a separately assembled control section. Within SUBPROGB you want to reference the main data that is defined and exists in SUBPROGA. You may describe this main data in SUBPROGB so that when assembling SUBPROGB, the Assembler knows the names, lengths, formats, and relative position of each field in SUBPROGA. For this purpose there is a special Assembler directive, DSECT, Dummy Section.

NAME	OPERATION	OPERAND
Name	DSECT	blank

The name of the DSECT refers to the first (leftmost) byte of the section. Instead of reserving storage, DSECT gives the Assembler a mask or image of data defined elsewhere. Figure 19-1 illustrates a DSECT defined within a CSECT. The partial program reads records with two buffers and no work-area (IOREG=5). Rather than transfer the current buffer to a workarea with MVC RECDIN,0(5), the program processes input records directly in the buffer, and defines the fields.

Note the following: The DSECT, called DATAIN, generates no object code. The fields defined within the DSECT tell the Assembler the names and formats. The directive USING DATAIN,5 assigns register-5 as a base register for DATAIN. This is because the buffers for RECDIN are under register-5 (IOREG=5). Register-5 acts as a base register with respect to DATAIN. For the instruction CLC CODEIN,=C'03', the Assembler treats CODEIN under base register-5. The operand for CODEIN in object code is 5000 (base register-5 and no displacement, because CODEIN is the first byte within DATAIN). Assume that for the first input record, IOCS has loaded register-5 with the address of buffer-1 (INBUFF1). Since register-5 contains the address of INBUFF1, then a reference to CODEIN is to the first two bytes of INBUFF1. On the next read operation, IOCS loads the address of INBUFF2 into register-5, and a reference to CODEIN is now to the first two bytes of that buffer.

In this program, base register-5 is to apply only to the fields within the DSECT. The directive DROP 5 tells the Assembler to discontinue applying base register-5, and in this example the Assembler resumes addressing under base register-3. The CSECT following the DROP terminates the DSECT, and because the CSECT is named TESTA, tells the Assembler to resume with the initial CSECT named TESTA.

Under OS, Locate Mode involves register-1. The changes necessary to convert the DOS example to OS would be:

- OS linkage for initialization and return to the supervisor.
- A DCB specifying MACRF=(GL).
- After the GET, load the contents of register-1 into register-5, as in the example:

```
LOC      OBJECT CODE        ADDR1 ADDR2  STMT  SOURCE STATEMENT

                                           1         PRINT ON,NODATA,NOGEN
000000                                     3  TESTA  CSECT  ,               CONTROL SECTION
000000   0530                              4         BALR  3,0
                            00002          5         USING *,3
                            00000          6         USING DATAIN,5
                                           8         OPEN  FILEIN            READ A RECORD
                                          16         GET   FILEIN
00001E   D501 5000 3132    00000 00134    21         CLC   CODEIN,=C'03'    VALID RECORD?
000024   4770 303E               00040    22         BNE   R10CODE          *  NO - ERROR
000028   D205 303E 5002    00040 00002    24         MVC   PREVACCT,ACCTIN
                                          25  *
                                          26  *
                                          27  B10END CLOSE FILEIN
                                          35         EOJ
000040                      00040         39  R10CODE EQU   *               ERROR ROUTINE
000040   000000000000                     41  PREVACCT DC  XL6'00'          PREV ACCOUNT #
                                          43  FILEIN DTFCD BLKSIZE=80,               +
                                                          DEVADDR=SYSIPT,           +
                                                          DEVICE=1442,              +
                                                          EOFADDR=B10END,           +
                                                          IOAREA1=INBUFF1,          +
                                                          IOAREA2=INBUFF2,          +
                                                          RECFORM=FIXUNB,           +
                                                          TYPEFLE=INPUT,            +
                                                          IOREG=(5)
00007A   404040 404040404040               66  INBUFF1 DC  CL80' '          INPUT BUFFER-1
0000CA   404040404040404040                67  INBUFF2 DC  CL80' '          INPUT BUFFER-2
000000                                     69  DATAIN DSECT ,               DATA DUMMY SECTION:
000000                                     70  RECDIN DS   0CL80            *  INPUT RECORD
000000                                     71  CODEIN DS   CL2              *  RECORD CODE
000002                                     72  ACCTIN DS   CL6              *  ACCOUNT NO.
000008                                     73         DS   CL72             *  REST OF RECORD
                                           74         DROP  5
00011A                                     76  TESTA  CSECT ,               RESUME CTL SECTION
000120                                     77         LTORG
000120   5B5BC2D6D7C5D540                  78              =C'$$BOPEN '
000128   5B5BC2C3D3D6E2C5                  79              =C'$$BCLOSE'
000130   00000048                          80              =A(FILEIN)
000134   F0F3                              81              =C'03'
00000                                      82         END   TESTA
```

FIGURE 19-1 Example CSECT and DSECT.

486

```
GET    FILEIN
LR     5,1
```

It is also possible to use register-1 as the DSECT base register, *provided* the program executes no macro that destroys the base address while it is still required.

• *Problems 18-1 through 18-4 should now be attempted.* •

SUBPROGRAM LINKAGE

You may use DSECTs to make data known between separately assembled subprograms. Additionally, you use standard linkage and saveareas to link between subprograms and to save the contents of registers.

LINKAGE REGISTERS. The standard linkage registers are 0, 1, 13, 14, and 15:

REGISTER	USE
0 & 1	Parameter registers, used by the CALL macro to pass "parameters" (i.e., addresses of data) to the called program.
13	Savearea register—contains the address of the calling program's savearea, to be stored by the called program.
14	Return register—contains the address of the calling program, to which the called program is to return.
15	Entry point register—contains the address of the called program's entry point, where we want to link to begin executing.

THE STANDARD SAVEAREA. Each calling program requires definition of a savearea to preserve the contents of its registers. The savearea contains 18 fullwords (or 9 doublewords), aligned on a doubleword boundary. The savearea provides for an additional condition—one subprogram may call another subprogram, which in turn may call yet another subprogram. Figure 19-2 gives the savearea format.

LINKAGE MACROS. The following macros link between subprograms:

NAME	*OPERATION*	*OPERAND*
(name)	CALL	entrypoint[,(parameter, . . .)]
	SAVE	(r1,r2)
	RETURN	(r1,r2)

Assume that SUBPROGA is the main subprogram, loaded in storage and being executed. SUBPROGA *calls* SUBPROGB for execution (SUBPROGB

Word	Displacement	Contents of each fullword
1	0	Used by PL/I programs.
2	4	Address of the savearea of the calling program. The called program saves this in its own savearea.
3	8	*Address of the savearea of the called program.
4	12	*Contents of register-14, return address to the calling program.
5	16	*Contents of register-15, the address of the entry point to the called program.
6	20	*Contents of register-0.
7-18	24	*Contents of registers-1 through 12

*Called program stores these in calling program's savearea.

FIGURE 19-2 Standard savearea words.

must also be in storage). SUBPROGA is the *calling* program, and SUBPROGB is the *called* program.

THE CALL MACRO.   Use the CALL macro in the calling program to link to the called program. The operand 'entrypoint' is the name of the first executable instruction of the called program. (Following entrypoint is an optional parameter list. Parameters are symbolic addresses that you want known in the called program.) CALL loads the address of the next sequential instruction in register-14 and branches to the called program.

THE SAVE MACRO.   When linking to the called program, you must save the contents of the registers of the calling program. The calling program defines the standard savearea for this purpose. Before issuing the CALL macro, first load the address of the savearea in register-13. At the beginning of the called program, code SAVE (14,12) to save the contents of the registers, except 13.

THE RETURN MACRO.   In order to return to the calling program, code RETURN (14,12) to restore the original contents of the calling program's registers and to return to the calling program.

Next we examine the generated code for the macros and the additional instructions needed to complete the linkage.

LINKING TWO CONTROL SECTIONS

Figure 19-3 gives skeleton coding for two separately assembled CSECTs—a calling subprogram, PROGA, and a called subprogram, PROGB. The save area in PROGA is named SAVEA, and the savearea in PROGB is SAVEB. PROGA defines common data under DATA (immediately at the start). DATA is subject to base register-4, and the rest of the program following BEGINA is under base register-3. Before calling PROGB the program loads register-13 with the address of the savearea, SAVEA. For the macro CALL PROGB, the Assembler generates:

```
L      15,=V(PROGB)   Load address of PROGB in register-15
BALR   14,15          Load next instruction address in register-14 and
                      branch to PROGB
```

The literal =V(PROGB) is an *external address constant.* Since the Assembler does not know the address of PROGB, you tell it that this address is external to this assembly. The Assembler inserts an address of X'0000', and the Linkage Editor inserts the correct address. BALR loads the address of the next instruction, A10RTN, in register-14 and branches to PROGB. Immediately PROGB saves PROGA's registers. The SAVE macro here generates the following instruction:

```
              STM  14,12,12(13)
```

In effect, SAVE stores registers 14 through 12 beginning at SAVEA+12 (word 4 through 18).

Next, PROGB initializes base register-9. This could be any available register except register-4 which still contains the address of the common data area DATA, as loaded in PROGA. You still need this address in order to reference the fields in the common data area, which in PROGB is named DATAB. Since register-4 is already loaded, you need only code the directive

```
              USING  DATAB,4
```

to inform the Assembler to assign base register-4 to DATAB. For any subsequent reference to the fields within the DSECT for DATAB, the Assembler will assign base register-4.

PROGB must now save the contents of register-13 which contains the address of PROGA's savearea. You have to store the contents of register-13 in SAVEB+4 (word 2) because, before returning, you must reload PROGA's registers. The next three instructions store the address of SAVEB in SAVEA +8 (word 3). This is done because if there are other subprograms, you can refer to this field for debugging and tracing if the program does not work correctly. The linkage routine has now stored the following:

// EXEC ASSEMBLY,SIZE=64K

EXTERNAL SYMBOL DICTIONARY

SYMBOL	TYPE	ID	ADDR	LENGTH	LD-ID
PROGA	SD (CSECT)	001	000000	000090	
PROGB	ER (EXTRN)	002			

LOC	OBJECT CODE	ADDR1	ADDR2	STMT	SOURCE STATEMENT	
				1	PRINT ON,NOGEN	
000000				3 PROGA	CSECT ,	MAIN CONTROL SECTION
				4 *	COMMON DECLARATIVES:	
000000	125C			5 DATA	DS 0CL1	DATA AREA UNDER REG 3
000000	125C			6 HRSPK	DC PL2'12.5'	|XX|.XC|
000002	01125C			7 RATEPK	DC PL3'11.25'	|XX|X.X|XC|
000005				8 WAGEPK	DS PL5	|00|XX|XX.X|XC|
00000A	0530			10 BEGINA	BALR 3,0	INIT BASE REGISTER-3
		0000C		11	USING *,3	
		00000		12	USING DATA,4	ASSIGN BASE REG-4
00000C	5840 307C		0088	13	L 4,=A(DATA)	LOAD BASE REG-4
				14 *	.	
				15 *	.	
000010	F841 4005 4000	00005	00000	16	ZAP WAGEPK,HRSPK	SET UP MULTIPL'D
				17 *	.	
				18 *	.	
000016	41D0 3024		00030	19	LA 13,SAVEA	ADDR OF SAVEAREA
				20	CALL PROGB	LINK TO PROGB
		00020		24 A10RTN	EQU *	ANY INSTR'N HERE
				25 *	.	
				26 *	.	
				27 *	.	
				28	PDUMP DATA,BEGINA	
				34	EOJ	
000030				38 SAVEA	DS 9D	PROGA REG SAVEAREA
000078				39	LTORG	
000078	5B5BC2D7C4E4D4D7			40	=CL8'$$BPDUMP'	
000080	000000000000000A			41	=A(DATA,BEGINA)	
000088	00000000			42	=A(DATA)	
00008C	00000000			43	=V(PROGB)	
0000A				45	END BEGINA	

FIGURE 19.3 (partial).

```
// EXEC ASSEMBLY

LOC     OBJECT CODE        ADDR1  ADDR2   STMT  SOURCE STATEMENT
                                            1      PRINT ON,NOGEN

000000                                      3 DATAB   DSECT ,          PROGB COMMON DATA:
000000                                      4 HRSPK   DS   PL2          |XX|.XC|
000002                                      5 RATEPK  DS   PL3          |XX|X.X|XC|
000005                                      6 WAGEPK  DS   PL5          |00|XX|XX|X.|XC|

000000                                      8 PROGB   CSECT
                                            9         SAVE  (14,12)     SAVE REGS 14-12
000004 0590                      00006      12        BALR  9,0         INIT BASE REG-9
                                 00000      13        USING *,9
                                            14        USING DATAB,4     ASSIGN BASE REG-4

000006 50D0 902A                 00030      16        ST    13,SAVEB+4  SAVE ADDR OF SAVEA
00000A 18CD                                 17        LR    12,13
00000C 41D0 9026                 0002C      18        LA    13,SAVEB
000010 50DC 0008                 00008      19        ST    13,8(12)    SAVE ADDR OF SAVEB
                                            20 *      .
                                            21 *      .
                                            22 *      .
000014 FC42 4005 4002     00005  00002      23        MP    WAGEPK,RATEPK  MULT HOURS X RATE
00001A F045 4005 003F     00005  0003F      24        SRP   WAGEPK,63,5    SHIFT & ROUNDWAGE
                                            25 *.
                                            26 *.
000020 58D0 902A                 00030      27        L     13,SAVEB+4  ADDR OF SAVEA
                                            28        RETURN (14,12)    RETURN TO PROGA

00002C                                      33 SAVEB   DS   18F          PROGB SAVEAREA

000000                                      35        END   PROGB
```

FIGURE 19-3 Linkage between a main program and subprogram.

SAVEA			SAVEB		
Word	Displacement	Contents	Word	Displacement	Contents
1	0		1	0	
2	4		2	4	A(SAVEA)
3	8	A(SAVEB)	3	8	
4	12	A(A10RTN)	4	12	
5	16	A(PROGB)	5	16	
6–18	20	Contents of registers 0–12	6–18	20	

Now PROGB may perform required processing, and reference the fields defined in the DATAB DSECT (actually DATA in PROGA). In order to return to the calling program, PROGA, simply reload register-13 with SAVEB+4, the address of SAVEA.

The RETURN macro next generates:

```
LM  14,12,12(13)        Reload registers 14-12 starting with SAVEA+12
                        (Word 4)
BR  14                  Branch to A10RTN in PROGA
```

RETURN restores the original SAVEA registers (14 through 12). Since register-14 now contains the return address (A10RTN), BR branches to this address. You now resume normal processing in PROGA, with base registers reinitialized.

The question may arise: Why doesn't PROGA save its own registers in SAVEA before linking to PROGB? Assume that this is done, and PROGB then initializes its own register values. When PROGB returns to PROGA, PROGA's base registers are not loaded—and without a base register PROGA has no way to reload its own registers.

In this example, SAVEB does not require a full save area. This is the way you would define SAVEB if PROGB were to link to another subprogram. If so, then the called program would store PROGB's registers, linkage address, and savearea in SAVEB.

TECHNICAL NOTE ON USING.   One rule of the Assembler is "in calculating the base register to be used, the Assembler always uses the available register giving the smallest displacement." This rule sometimes causes the Assembler to override a DROP or another USING. Suppose, for example, that the program uses two base registers (3 and 4). The common data is under register-5 and is defined toward the end of the CSECT:

```
        BALR  3,0
        USING *,3,4     3 & 4 are base registers for program
        USING DATA,5    5 is base register for common data
          .
          .
          .
DATA    DS    0C          common data area
          .
          .
```

Depending on the size of the program preceding DATA, the Assembler may apply register-4 to DATA rather than the specified register-5. For this reason, the program in Figure 19-3 defines the common data before the BALR/USING where the Assembler is sure to apply the correct base register.

• *Problems 19-5 through 19-8 should now be attempted.* •

PASSING PARAMETERS

Another way to make data known between subprograms is through the use of "passing parameters." The CALL statement contains a parameter list of the address(es) to be passed to the called program:

```
CALL   subprogram,(parameter-list)
```

Each parameter generates a fullword address, one after the other. CALL loads into register-1 the address of the first parameter in the list. Since the parameter is itself an address, register-1 will contain the address of the first address. The called program can load the address of the first parameter into an available register.

Figure 19-4 provides the same simple example as the previous one, converted to parameters. In the calling program, the instruction

```
CALL   PROGB,(HRSPK)
```

loads the address of HRSPK's address into register-1 and links to PROGB. The code that the CALL generates is (in part) the following:

```
L      15,=V(PROGB)   Load address of PROGB in register-15
LA     14,*+10        Load return address in register-14
BALR   1,15           Load address of HRSPK address in register-1,
DC     A(HRSPK)         and link to PROGB
```

The called program uses this address to load the actual address of HRSPK into register-8: L 8,0(0,1). The program can use this address explicitly as a base address reference. In the instruction

```
MP  5(4,8),2(3,8)
```

```
// OPTION LINK,NOXREF,LOG,PARTDUMP
// EXEC ASSEMBLY,SIZE=64K                    EXTERNAL SYMBOL DICTIONARY

SYMBOL    TYPE          ID   ADDR   LENGTH  LD-ID

PROGA     SD (CSECT)    001  000000 000074
PROGB     ER (EXTRN)    002


LOC    OBJECT CODE   ADDR1  ADDR2   STMT   SOURCE STATEMENT

                                      1    PRINT ON,NODATA,NOGEN

000000                                3 PROGA  CSECT
000000 0530                           4        BALR  3,0
                             00002    5        USING *,3
                                      6 *         .
                                      7 *         .
000002 41D0 3016             00018    8        LA    13,SAVEA      ADDR OF SAVEAREA
                                      9        CALL  PROGB,(HRSPK) LINK TO PROGB
                                     19 *         .
                                     20 *         .
                                     21        EOJ

000018                               25 SAVEA  DS    18F           PROGA REG SAVEAREA
000060                               26 HRSPK  DS    PL2           |xx|.xc|
000062                               27 RATEPK DS    PL3           |xx|x.|xc|
000065                               28 WAGEPK DS    PL5           |00|xx|xx|x.x|xc|

000070                               30        LTORG
000070 00000000                      31        =V(PROGB)
                             00000   32        END   PROGA
```

FIGURE 19.4 (partial).

```
// EXEC ASSEMBLY,SIZE=64K

LOC     OBJECT CODE    ADDR1 ADDR2  STMT  SOURCE STATEMENT

                                      1      PRINT ON,NOGEN

000000                                3  PROGB  CSECT
                                      4         SAVE  (14,12)        SAVE REGS 14-12
000004 0590                           7         BALR  9,0            INIT BASE REG-9
                              00006    8         USING *,9
000006 50D0 9032              00038    9         ST    13,SAVEB+4    SAVE ADDR SAVEA
00000A 18CD                           10         LR    12,13
00000C 41D0 902E              00034   11         LA    13,SAVEB
000010 50DC 0008              00008   12         ST    13,8(12)

000014 5880 1000              00000   14         L     8,0(0,1)      LOAD ADDR WAGEPK
000018 F841 8005 8000  00005  00000   15         ZAP   5(5,8),0(2,8) HOURS IN PROD
00001E FC42 8005 8002  00005  00002   16         MP    5(5,8),2(3,8) MULT HOURS X RATE
000024 F045 8005 003F  00005  0003F   17         SRP   5(5,8),63,5   SHIFT & ROUNDWAGE
                                      18  *        .
                                      19  *        .
00002A 58D0 9032              00038   20         L     13,SAVEB+4    LOAD ADDR OF SAVEA
                                      21         RETURN (14,12)      RETURN TO PROGA

000034                        00000   26  SAVEB  DS    18F           PROGB SAVEAREA

                                      28         END   PROGB
```

FIGURE 19-4 Passing parameters.

495

operand-1 references WAGEPK (containing hours), and operand-2 references RATEPK (containing rate).

The example provides standard program linkage, although there are shortcut methods. For example, PROGB could assume register-15 as a base register, since it contains the starting address of PROGB. You could omit the standard BALR/USING and code USING *,15 at its start. Also, you need not store the contents of register-13 in the save area and reload it on return. These practices may be shortsighted, however, because any input/output or CALL executed in PROGB will destroy the contents of registers 13 and 15, causing a subsequent execution error.

• *Problem 19-9 should now be attempted.* •

LINKING PHASES

You may assemble and link edit one or more control sections, and may arrange the assembly so that the Linkage Editor output is one or more *phases.* Up to now our programs consist of only one phase. The Linkage Editor writes the object code phase into the Core Image or Load library. The job control command //EXEC causes the first or only phase to load into main storage and to begin execution. If you have organized the program into additional phases, the system does not load them into storage. Instead, you use the LOAD or FETCH macros to load subsequent phases. The purposes of organizing a program into phases are:

1. Some phases may be separately assembled and cataloged. A useful example is data common to many programs—file declarations and record definitions. You need not reassemble these phases each time you need them; you can use the INCLUDE command to link edit them into your program.

2. The entire program may not fit into main storage. You may arrange the program into separate logical phases.

   The main *(root)* phase is first, followed by as many additional *(overlay)* phases as required. After the link edit, the //EXEC job command loads the root phase into storage and begins its execution. The root phase generally contains the common data and the main program logic. It may load (with LOAD or FETCH) the various phases as they are required. (The system loads phases, not programs or CSECTs.) Such phases are called *overlays*—when they load into storage they may overlay previously loaded phases. The root phase generally remains intact and is not overlaid.

THE PHASE CONTROL STATEMENT. Linkage Editor control statements include PHASE, INCLUDE, ENTRY, and ACTION. The PHASE command tells the Linkage Editor that a section of coding is to link edit as a separate phase. If the code is to be assembled, insert the PHASE command ahead of // EXEC ASSEMBLY.

NAME	*OPERATION*	*OPERAND*
blank	PHASE	name,origin

The *name* gives the symbolic name of the phase, up to 8 characters. If the program consists of more than one phase, then the first four characters of each phase name must be identical. The *origin* gives the address of where the phase is to load at execute-time. Among the commonly used entries are:

PHASE name, ROOT: The name phase is the root phase, to be always in storage during execution of the program. Only the *first* phase may be ROOT. Under a simple operating system, the root phase begins at a doubleword address immediately following the supervisor. In a multiprogramming system, the root phase loads at the beginning of a partition.

PHASE name,*: The * references the Linkage Editor location counter (similar to that of the Assembler). If not the first phase, the Linkage Editor assigns it to begin at a doubleword address following the previous phase. If the first phase, it is assigned a starting location like the root phase.

PHASE name, symbol: You may instruct the Linkage Editor that at execute-time this phase is to be overlaid in storage beginning at the same address as a previously defined phase.

In Figure 19-5 there are three phases organized as follows:

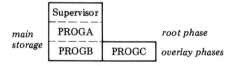

The PHASE statements are:

PHASE PROGA, ROOT defines PROGA as the root phase, always in storage during execution.

PHASE PROGB,* tells the Linkage Editor to begin the phase PROGB following the previous phase (PROGA).

PHASE PROGC,PROGB tells the Linkage Editor to assign the phase PROGC to begin at the same storage location as PROGB (an overlay).

```
// OPTION LINK,NOXREF,LOG
   ACTION MAP
   PHASE PHASA,ROOT
// EXEC ASSEMBLY,SIZE=64K

LOC      OBJECT CODE          ADDR1 ADDR2  STMT  SOURCE STATEMENT

000000                                       1        PRINT ON,NODATA,NOGEN
000000                                       3 PROGA  CSECT
000000                                       4 DATA   DS    0CL1            COMMON DATA:
000000 125C                                  5 HRSPK  DC    PL2'12.5'          |XX|.XC|
000002 01125C                                6 RATEPK DC    PL3'11.25'         |XX|X.X|XC|
000005                                       7 WAGEPK DS    PL5
00000A 0530                                  9 BEGINA BALR  3,0
                                            10        USING *,3
                                   0000C    11        USING DATA,4
00000C 5840 31FC                   00208    12        L     4,=A(DATA)        BASE REG FOR DATA
                                            13        OPEN  PRTR
                                   000A4    21        LOAD  PHASB             LOAD PHASB IN STORAGE
000026 5010 3098                   00000    26        ST    1,ADDRESB         SAVE ENTRY TO PHASB
                                            27 *
00002A F841 4005 4000 00005                 28        ZAP   WAGEPK,HRSPK      SET UP MULTIPLICAND
                                            29 *
000030 41D0 3050                   0005C    30        LA    13,SAVEA          LOAD ADDR OF SAVEAREA
000034 58F0 3098                   000A4    31        L     15,ADDRESB        LOAD ADDR OF PHASB
                                            32        CALL  (15)              LINK TO PHASB ENTRY
                                            35 *
                                            36 *
                                            37 *
                                            38        LOAD  PHASC             LOAD PHASC IN STORAGE
000042 18F1                                 43        LR    15,1              LOAD PHASC ENTRY POINT
000044 41D0 3050                   0005C    44        LA    13,SAVEA          LOAD ADDR OF SAVEAREA
                                            45        CALL  (15)              LINK TO PHASC ENTRY
                                            48 *
                                            49 *
                                            50        CLOSE PRTR
                                            58        EOJ
00005C                                      62 SAVEA  DS    18F               SAVEAREA FOR PHASE
0000A4                                      63 ADDRESB DS   F                 ADDR OF PHASEB ENTRY
                                            65 PRTR   DTFPR BLKSIZE=133,
                                                           CTLCHR=YES,
                                                           DEVADDR=SYSLST,
                                                           DEVICE=3203,
                                                           IOAREA1=IOARPRT1,
                                                           IOAREA2=IOARPRT2,
                                                           RECFORM=FIXUNB,
                                                           IOREG=(5)
```

+ + + + + + +

FIGURE 19.5 (partial).

```
0000D8 40404040404040      87 IOARPRTI DC   CL133' '          PRINT BUFFER-1
00015D 40404040404040      88 IOARPRT2 DC   CL133' '          PRINT BUFFER-2
                           89          ENTRY PRTR
0001E8                     90          LTORG
0001E8 5B5BC2D6D7C5D540    91               =C'$$BOPEN '
0001F0 D7C8C1E2C2404040    92               =CL8'PHASB'
0001F8 D7C8C1E2C3404040    93               =CL8'PHASC'
000200 5B5BC2C3D3D6E2C5    94               =C'$$BCLOSE'
000208 00000000            95               =A(DATA)
              0000A        96          END   BEGINA
```

          PHASE PHASB.*
// EXEC ASSEMBLY,SIZE=128K

```
                            1          PRINT ON,NODATA,NOGEN          COMMON DATA:
000000                      2 DATAB    DSECT ,                        |XX|.XC|
000000                      3 HRSPK    DS    PL2                      |XX|X.X|XC|
000002                      4 RATEPK   DS    PL3
000005                      5 WAGEPK   DS    PL5

000000                      7 PROGB    CSECT
                            8 BEGINB   SAVE  (14,12)                  SAVE REGS IN SAVEA
000004 0530                11          BALR  3,0                      INIT PROGB BASE REG
00006                      12          USING *,3
00000                      13          USING DATAB,4

000006 50D0 302A           15          ST    13,SAVEB+4              SAVE ADDR OF SAVEA
00000A 18CD                16          LR    12,13
00000C 41D0 3026           17          LA    13,SAVEB
000010 50DC 0008           18          ST    13,8(12)                STORE ADDR OF SAVEB

000014 FC42 4005 4002 00005 00005  20  MP    WAGEPK,RATEPK           MULT HOURS X RATE
00001A F045 4005 003F 00005 003F   21  SRP   WAGEPK,63,5             SHIFT & ROUND

000020 58D0 302A           23          L     13,SAVEB+4              LOAD ADDR OF SAVEA
                           24          RETURN (14,12)                RETURN TO PROGA

00002C                     29 SAVEB    DS    18F                     PROGB SAVEAREA
00000                      30          END   BEGINB
```

          PHASE PHASC,PHASB
// EXEC ASSEMBLY,SIZE=128K

```
                            1          PRINT ON,NODATA,NOGEN          COMMON DATA:
000000                      2 DATAC    DSECT ,                        |XX|.XC|
000000                      3 HRSPK    DS    PL2                      |XX|X.X|XC|
000002                      4 RATEPK   DS    PL3
000005                      5 WAGEPK   DS    PL5
```

FIGURE 19.5 (partial).

```
000000                      7 PROGC  CSECT
000004 0530                 8 BEGINC  SAVE  (14,12)          SAVE REGS IN SAVEA
00006                      11         BALR  3,0               INIT PROGC BASE REG
00000                      12         USING *,3
                           13         USING DATAC,4
000006 50D0 303A           15         ST    13,SAVEC+4        SAVE ADDR OF SAVEA
00040
00000A 18CD                16         LR    12,13
00003C 41D0 3036           17         LA    13,SAVEC          STORE ADDR OF SAVEC
000010 50DC 0008           18         ST    13,8(12)
0008
000014 D209 3093 307E 00099  20       MVC   WAGEPR,EDWORD
000084
00001A DE09 3093 4006 00099  21       ED    WAGEPR,WAGEPK+1   MOVE TO BUFFER
000006
000020 D284 5000 3088 00000  22       MVC   0(133,5),PRINT   PRINT WAGE
00008E
                           23         PUT   PRTR
000032 58D0 303A           29         L     13,SAVEC+4        LOAD ADDR OF SAVEA
00040
                           30         RETURN (14,12)          RETURN TO PROGA
00003C                     35 SAVEC   DS    18F               SAVEC SAVEAREA
000084 402020212048202060  36 EDWORD  DC    X'402020212048202060'
00008E                     37 PRINT   DS    0CL133            PRINT LINE:
00008E 09                  38         DC    XL01'09'          *
00008F 40404040404040      39         DC    CL10' '           *
404040
000099                     40 WAGEPR  DS    ZL10              *
0000A3 40404040404040      41         DC    CL112' '          *
404040
                           43         EXTRN PRTR
                           44         LTORG
000118                     45               =A(PRTR)
000118 00000000            47         END   BEGINC
```

// EXEC LNKEDT

23/02/86	PHASE	XFR-AD	LOCORE	HICORE	DSK-AD	LABEL	LOADED	REL-FR	OFFSET	INPUT
ROOT	PHASA	7CE082	7CE078	7CE2E7	00225169	PROGA	7CE078	7CE078	00000	SYSLNK
						+PRTR	7CE120			
						IJDFYZIZ	7CE288	7CE288	000210	IJDFYZIZ
	PHASB	7CE2E8	7CE2E8	7CE35B	00225171	PROGB	7CE2E8	7CE2E8	000270	SYSLNK
	PHASC	7CE2E8	7CE2E8	7CE403	00225173	PROGC	7CE2E8	7CE2E8	000270	SYSLNK

// EXEC ,SIZE=64K
140.63

FIGURE 19-5 Linkage between three phases.

THE LOAD AND FETCH MACROS. The LOAD and FETCH macros are used to load a phase into storage during program execution.

NAME	*OPERATION*	*OPERAND*
(name)	LOAD	phasename or (1)
(name)	FETCH	phasename or (1)

THE LOAD MACRO. The operand of LOAD contains the name of the phase to be loaded. You may use the phase name or load the phase name into register-1. LOAD causes the phase to load into storage and returns control to the calling phase. LOAD also stores in register-1 the entry point address of the called phase. This address is required because you later use it to CALL the overlay phase for execution. Place LOAD in the program so that the overlay phase does not erase it.

THE FETCH MACRO. The operand of FETCH contains the name of the phase to be loaded. You may use the phase name or load the phase name into register-1. FETCH loads the phase into storage and branches to its entry point address. In effect, FETCH acts as a combined LOAD and CALL, but with no automatic return.

THE LINKAGE EDITOR MAP. In Figure 19-5, each phase name begins with the same first four characters, PROG. At the end of the sample program is the *Linkage Editor Map.* You may cause this map to print with the DOS control command ACTION MAP. The map lists the starting address of each phase and CSECT in the program. In large programs, the map is a useful debugging and tracing device.

In the map, REL-FR means "relocation factor." PROGA loaded for execution beginning at location X'7CE078', PROGB loaded beginning at X'7CE2E8', and PROGC overlayed PROGB also at X'7CE2E8'.

OFFSET signifies the displacement of a module from the initial load point, PROGA. Thus, the offset for PROGA is 000000. PROGB and PROGC are offset X'270' bytes from PROGA, as follows:

Load point of PROGA:	X'7CE078'
Offset of PROGB and PROGC:	X'000270'
Load point of PROGA and PROGB:	X'7CE2E8'

Following the map is the EXEC job statement that causes the supervisor to load and execute the linked program, and following this statement is the output for the program: 140.63.

The CSECT beginning IJD in the Linkage Editor Map represents the module that IOCS generated for the DTFPR macro for the file PRTR in the program. The module is called PRMOD. Details are in the IBM Supervisor and I/O Macro manual. Other DOS modules include the following:

FILE	DTF MACRO	IBM MODULE	
Card	DTFCD	CDMOD	IJCxxxxx
Printer	DTFPR	PRMOD	IJDxxxxx
Magnetic Tape	DTFMT	MTMOD	IJFxxxxx
Sequential Disk	DTFSD	SDMOD	IJGxxxxx
Indexed Seq'l	DTFIS	ISMOD	IJHxxxxx
Direct Access	DTFDA	DAMOD	IJIxxxxx

OVERLAY PROGRAM.   Figure 19-5 illustrates a simple overlay program that links three phases. The first phase initializes hours (HRSPK) in a product field (WAGEPK) and links to the second phase. This phase multiplies hours by rate-of-pay (RATEPK) to calculate wage, and returns to phase-1. Next, phase-1 loads phase-3 over phase-2, and links to phase-3, which prints the wage.

DETAILED EXPLANATION.   After assembly and link edit, the //EXEC job command loads the first phase, PHASA, into storage. The first statements define the common data area. At BEGINA, base register-3 for the program and register-4 for the common data area are loaded. Then LOAD causes PHASB, the second phase, to load into storage, following PHASA. LOAD also places in register-1 the address of the entry point to PHASB. The program stores this entry point in ADDRESB for later use. The program then initializes WAGEPK with HRSPK, and links to PHASB.

PHASB saves the registers of PHASA and initializes its own registers. Then it multiplies WAGEPK by RATEPK (DSECT entries, defined in PHASA), and returns to PHASA.

PHASA next loads and links to PHASC, which saves the registers, prints WAGEPK, and returns to PHASA. At this point, PHASA, and the program, terminate.

Note: PHASA contains the definition of the DTFPR macro, PRTR, which PHASC also uses. The Assembler directive ENTRY PRTR makes PRTR known outside PHASA. In PHASC, EXTRN PRTR tells the Assembler that PRTR is defined outside this phase. The Link Editor completes the address linkage.

Under OS, the relative location of each CSECT appears in the "CROSS REFERENCE TABLE" following the last assembled CSECT. Look for "CONTROL SECTION" that could appear with such entries as:

CONTROL NAME	SECTION ORIGIN	LENGTH
PHASA	00	. . .
PHASB	6D8	. . .
PHASC	6D8	. . .

If the entry-point address (EPA) of the first CSECT, PHASA, is 99080, then the entry-point of both PHASB and PHASC in this case is:

EPA of PHASA	99080
Origin of PHASB & PHASC	6D8
EPA of PHASB & PHASC	99758

You can locate any field in a storage dump through use of the EPA plus the contents of the location counter (LOC) on the program printout.

Note also that execution diagnostics show the contents of the registers under "SA" (save area) in the same 18 fullword format as explained in this chapter.

OVERLAY CONSIDERATIONS

LOAD brings a phase into storage, where it remains until overlaid by another phase. Therefore, *once you LOAD a phase, you may CALL it any number of times.* To load and immediately execute a phase once, you may use FETCH. If there is insufficient storage, large programs may require loading and reloading phases as needed. A common use of overlays is the following:

1. The ROOT phase contains all common declaratives and basic main logic. It loads (or fetches) the initialize phase.
2. The initialize phase contains routines executed only once, such as OPEN files, handle a date record, and extract the date from the communications region.
3. The ROOT phase then overlays the initialize phase with the general processing phase, which includes calculations, and input/output. (Storage restrictions may require overlaying some of these phases as required.)
4. At the end of the run, the ROOT phase overlays the general processing phase with an end-of-file phase. This phase includes final totals and CLOSEs the files.

There are countless ways to handle program overlays. However, in all programming problems, *the simplest way is generally the best way.* And simpler may include dividing a problem not into phases but into completely separate programs.

LINKING COBOL AND ASSEMBLER

Linking between a COBOL program and an Assembler program is similar to linking between two Assembler programs. Of course, you have to be already familiar with COBOL! Figure 19-6 provides an example, for brevity once again defining hours, rate, and wage, and multiplying hours times rate. After compilation of the COBOL program and assembly of the Assembler program, both are linked into one executable module.

The COBOL program defines hours, rate, and wage in a group-item named COMMON-DATA. Its format is COMP-3, which is equivalent to packed format in Assembler. Understandably, the sequence and format of common data items must be identical, although their names need not be. Remember, also, that the data in this example exists only in the COBOL program which passes its address to the Assembler program.

The CALL statement in the COBOL program is the following:

```
CALL 'PROG15D' USING COMMON-DATA.
```

PROG15D happens to be the name of the CSECT in the Assembler program —it could be any valid Assembler name. COMMON-DATA is the name of the COBOL group-item (any valid COBOL name) that is to be known to the called Assembler program. The COBOL CALL generates an address constant for COMMON-DATA, inserts its address in register-1, and transfers to the specified CSECT address, PROG15D. This procedure is similar to passing parameters between two Assembler programs, as you saw in the previous section, PASSING PARAMETERS.

The COBOL program needs to make known only the address of the defined data area. The Assembler program defines the common data as a DSECT with the name DATAB. Hours, rate, and wage are in the same sequence and format as in the COBOL program. A USING directive assigns register-4 as base register for DATAB and loads the address constant of the common data into register-4:

```
USING   DATAB,4
L       4,0(1)
```

It may help (or then again it may not) to examine a pictorial representation of the above Load (L) instruction:

The Assembler program performs the usual business about saving regis-

```
// JOB ABEL
// OPTION LINK,LOG,NOSYM,ERRS,NOXREF
   ACTION MAP
// EXEC FCOBOL,SIZE=128K


   1  IBM DOS VS COBOL                              REL 2.5 + PTF53 PP NO. 5746-CB1


CBL SEQ,LAGW,NOSUP,ACE1,NOLVL,NOCLI,NOSTX,APO,TRU              CBL 0030
CBL ZWB,NOSYN,SXR,NOOPT,STA,NOCATALR,NOLIB,NOVER,NOCOU         CBL 0040
```

```
 00002              IDENTIFICATION DIVISION.
 00003              PROGRAM-ID. COBLINK.
 00004              REMARKS.    LINKS COBOL WITH ASSEMBLER PROGRAM.

 00006              ENVIRONMENT DIVISION.

 00008              DATA DIVISION.
 00009              WORKING-STORAGE SECTION.

 00011              77  WAGE-OUT         PIC ZZZZZZ9.99- USAGE DISPLAY.

 00013              01  COMMON-DATA                  USAGE COMP-3.
 00014                  03  HOURS        PIC S99V9     VALUE +12.5.
 00015                  03  RATE         PIC S999V99   VALUE +11.75.
 00016                  03  WAGE         PIC S9(7)V99.

 00018              PROCEDURE DIVISION.
 00019          *
 00020          *
 00021          *
 00022              MOVE RATE TO WAGE.
 00023              CALL 'PROG15D' USING COMMON-DATA.
 00024              MOVE WAGE TO WAGE-OUT.
 00025              DISPLAY 'AMOUNT OF WAGE  ', WAGE-OUT.
 00026          *   ...
 00027              STOP RUN.
```

```
    2       COBLINK        19.04.32        23/02/86


                              CROSS-REFERENCE DICTIONARY


DATA NAMES                    DEFN      REFERENCE


COMMON-DATA                   000013    000023
HOURS                         000014
RATE                          000015    000022
WAGE                          000016    000022    000024
WAGE-OUT                      000011    000024    000025

END OF COMPILATION
```

FIGURE 19-6 (partial).

505

```
// EXEC ASSEMBLY

    LOC   OBJECT CODE    ADDR1 ADDR2  STMT    SOURCE STATEMENT
                                       1               PRINT ON,NOGEN
  000000                               3 DATAB  DSECT  ,             PROGB COMMON DATA:
  000000                               4 HRSPK  DS     PL2           |XX|.XC|
  000002                               5 RATEPK DS     PL3           |XX|X.X|XC|
  000005                               6 WAGEPK DS     PL5           |0X|XX|XX|X.X|XC|

  000000                               8 PROG15D CSECT
                                       9               SAVE   (14,12)      SAVE REGISTERS 14-12
  000004 0590                         12               BALR   9,0          INIT BASE REGISTER-9
                          00006       13               USING  *,9
                          00000       14               USING  DATAB,4      BASE REG-4 FOR DATAB
  000006 5841 0000        00000       15               L      4,0(1)       ADDR OF COMMON DATA

  00000A 50D0 902E        00034       17               ST     13,SAVEB+4   SAVE ADDR OF SAVEA
  00000E 18CD                         18               LR     12,13
  000010 41D0 902A        00030       19               LA     13,SAVEB
  000014 50DC 0008        00008       20               ST     13,8(12)     STORE ADDR OF SAVEB
                                      21 *        .
                                      22 *        .
                                      23 *        .
  000018 FC41 4005 4000  00005 00000  24               MP     WAGEPK,HRSPK  MULT HOURS X RATE
  00001E F045 4005 003F  00005 0003F  25               SRP    WAGEPK,63,5   SHIFT & ROUND
                                      26 *        .
                                      27 *        .
  000024 58D0 902E        00034       28               L      13,SAVEB+4   LOAD ADDR OF SAVEA
                                      29               RETURN (14,12)       RETURN TO PROGA

  000030                              34 SAVEB  DS     18F           PROGB SAVEAREA

                          00000       36               END    PROG15D
```

FIGURE 19-6 Linkage between COBOL and Assembler.

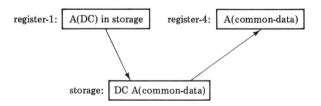

ters, multiplies hours times rate, rounds the result, and performs the usual return operation.

Figure 19-7 displays the Link Editor map for this program. The two CSECT entries COBLINK and PROG15D designate the starting locations of each of these modules. The CSECT entries beginning with ILBD are modules that the COBOL compiler has included, in the extravagant manner of a typical compiler. Note that the resulting executable module is considerably larger than one comprised of two Assembler programs.

```
// EXEC LNKTST
// EXEC LNKEDT

PHASE    XFR-AD   LOCORE   HICORE   DSK-AD    LABEL    LOADED   REL-FR OFFSET INPUT

PHASE*** 867078   867078   86937B   00191507
                                             COBLINK   867078   867078 000000 SYSLNK
                                             PROG15D   867520   867520 0004A8 SYSLNK
                                             IJJCPDV   867598   867598 000520 IJJCPDV
                                            +IJJCPDV1  867598
                                            *IJJCPDV2  867598
                                             ILBDDBG0  867948   867948 0008D0 ILBDDBG0
                                            +ILBDDBG4  867F64
                                            +ILBDDBG3  867F5A
                                            *ILBDDBG1  867B18
                                            *ILBDDBG2  867C86
                                            *ILBDDBG5  867EE0
                                            *ILBDDBG6  867F74
                                            *STXITPSW  86804C
                                            +ILBDDBG7  867FB4
                                            *SORTEP    8681FC
                                            +ILBDDBG8  867F86
                                             ILBDDSP0  8684A0   8684A0 001428 ILBDDSP0
                                            +ILBDDSP1  8688B0
                                             ILBDDSS0  8689E8   8689E8 001970 ILBDDSS0
                                            +ILBDDSS1  868C40
                                            +ILBDDSS2  868C38
                                            +ILBDDSS3  868CF8
                                            +ILBDDSS4  868A0E
                                            +ILBDDSS5  868ABE
                                            +ILBDDSS6  868B12
                                            +ILBDDSS7  868AE8
                                            +ILBDDSS8  868A3E
                                             ILBDMNS0  868D08   868D08 001C90 ILBDMNS0
                                             ILBDSTN0  868D60   868D60 001CE8 ILBDSTN0
                                             ILBDTC20  869288   869288 002210 ILBDTC20

UNRESOLVED EXTERNAL REFERENCES               WXTRN    ILBDFLW0
                                             WXTRN    ILBDFLW2
                                             WXTRN    ILBDSRT0
                                             WXTRN    ILBDTEF3
                                             WXTRN    ILBDTC00
                                             WXTRN    ILBDTC01
                                             WXTRN    ILBDTC30

UNRESOLVED ADCON  AT OFFSET 008681EC
UNRESOLVED ADCON  AT OFFSET 008680A8
UNRESOLVED ADCON  AT OFFSET 008680AC
UNRESOLVED ADCON  AT OFFSET 008680A0
UNRESOLVED ADCON  AT OFFSET 008681F0
UNRESOLVED ADCON  AT OFFSET 008681F4
UNRESOLVED ADCON  AT OFFSET 00869340
UNRESOLVED ADCON  AT OFFSET 00869344
UNRESOLVED ADCON  AT OFFSET 0086933C

009 UNRESOLVED ADDRESS CONSTANTS

// EXEC

AMOUNT OF WAGE      146.88
```

FIGURE 19-7 Link Editor map.

The alarming entry indicating "unresolved external references" as WXTRN ("weak externals") does not in this case indicate a true linkage error. The statement at the bottom, "009 unresolved address constants" also refers to these non-errors. The Linkage Editor signals a true error as EXTRN, not WXTRN; your program would generate such an error if the Linkage Editor cannot find a required module. One cause would be if the COBOL program calls the Assembler program using the wrong name, such as PROG14D instead of PROG15D.

Following the map is the EXEC job command and output from the program.

● *The remaining problems should now be attempted.* ●

PROBLEMS

19-1. For what reasons would it be useful to organize a program into subprograms?

19-2. What is the difference (if any) between a CSECT and a DSECT?

19-3. USING tells the Assembler to apply a base register to a particular section of code. What directive tells it to discontinue applying the base register?

19-4. Recode and test a previous program using Locate Mode for input and output, with buffers defined under a DSECT.

19-5. Why is it an especially dangerous practice to use register-13 as a base register?

19-6. For subprogram linkage, what is the purpose of registers 0, 1, 13, 14, and 15?

19-7. What are the three macros, and their purpose, required to link to another subprogram, to preserve register contents, and to return?

19-8. Revise and test any previous program into two separately assembled CSECTs. Use a DSECT for common data.

19-9. Revise Problem 19-8, changing the common data from a DSECT to passing parameters.

19-10. What is the difference between the LOAD and CALL macros? Between LOAD and FETCH?

19-11. Revise any previously written program into 4 phases. Phase-1 (ROOT) calls Phase-2 for initialization and OPEN. Phase-1 then overlays Phase-2 with Phase-3 for processing. At end-of-job, Phase-1 overlays Phase-3 with Phase-4 for final processing.

20

OPERATING SYSTEMS

The topic of operating systems is large and complex. This chapter introduces material that is useful for advanced Assembler programming. The first section examines general operating systems and its various support programs, including the Assembler and the Linkage Editor. The following sections examine the functions of the supervisor, the program status word, and the interrupt system. Finally, there is a discussion of channels, physical IOCS, the channel program, and the input/output system.

A knowledge of these features can be a useful asset when serious bugs occur and where the solution requires a more intimate knowledge of the system. For the serious student, these topics are a useful introduction to *systems programming* and the relationship between the computer hardware and manufacturer-supplied software.

OPERATING SYSTEMS

IBM supplies various programs ("software") to support the computer system. These include language translators such as Assembler, COBOL, and PL/I, and "utility" programs to facilitate disk and tape processing. The levels of programming support depend on the size of the CPU and the needs of the user.

On earlier and on smaller computers the operators were very much involved in operating the computer. For example, to assemble and execute a program, the operator would have done the following:

- Load the Assembler translator program into storage.

- Load the source program into storage for translation into machine language object code onto punched cards.
- Load the punched object program into the computer storage.
- Load the data into storage for the object program to execute.

Each step is separate, time-consuming, and prone to errors. In a large system such operator intervention is too costly. Therefore, *operating systems* were devised to minimize operator intervention in the processing of programs. An operating system is a collection of related programs that provides for the preparation and execution of our programs. The operating system is stored on disk, and part of it, the supervisor program, is kept in the lower part of main storage. Under a typical operating system you provide *job control commands* to tell the system what you want it to do. For example, you may want to assemble and execute a program. In simple terms the operating system could work as in Figure 20-1.

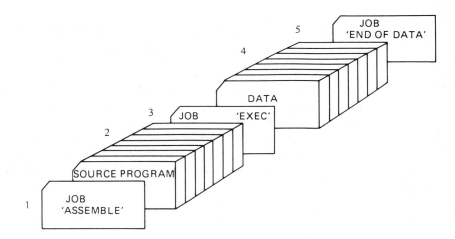

FIGURE 20-1 Job control for an operating system.

1. Preceding the job is a job control command that tells the operating system to assemble a program. The Assembler program is stored (cataloged) in a library on disk. The system loads the Assembler program from the disk library into storage.

2. The Assembler reads and translates the source program. It writes the object program onto another library on disk.

3. Following the source program is a job control command telling the system to execute the assembled object program. The system then

loads the object program from the disk library into storage.

4. The program executes the data.

5. Following the data is a job command telling the system that there is no more data. The operating system is now ready to process the next job.

An operating system involves little manual operating, but a complex system is required to perform the preceding and other necessary tasks. There are various operating systems, depending on the user's requirements. They differ in services offered and the amount of main storage they require. The systems include:

SYSTEM		TYPICAL USER
Basic Operating System	BOS	Smaller systems
Disk Operating System	DOS	Medium systems with disk
Disk Operating System	DOS/VS	Medium systems with "virtual storage"
360 Operating System	OS/MFT	Large 360, "Fixed number of Tasks"
360 Operating System	OS/MVT	Large 360, "Variable number of Tasks"
370 Operating System	OS/VS1	Large 370, equivalent to OS/MFT
370 Operating System	OS/VS2	Large 370, equivalent to OS/MVT

The computer central processing unit (CPU), main storage, and input/output devices are called the *hardware*. IBM "customer engineers" install the hardware and service breakdowns. The operating system is a group of IBM-supplied programs, and is called *software*. IBM "system engineers" help install and maintain the software. Large installations have their own "systems programmers" who are responsible for maintaining these complex operating systems. An operating system is composed of several interrelated parts. Disk Operating System (DOS), on which this text is mostly based, is organized as in Figure 20-2. The three main parts are *Control Program, System Service Programs, and Processing Programs.*

CONTROL PROGRAM. The control program controls all other programs that are processed. It consists of the supervisor, job control, and initial program load (IPL). Under OS, the functions are data management, job management, and task management.

The supervisor is the nucleus of the operating system. At all times part of the supervisor resides in lower storage. The system loads user programs (yours) in storage after the supervisor area. Therefore there are always two (or more) stored programs in storage: the supervisor program and your program(s). Only one is executed at one time, but control passes between them. The supervisor's functions include the handling of "interrupts" (such as your program asking to use an input or output device), fetching required routines

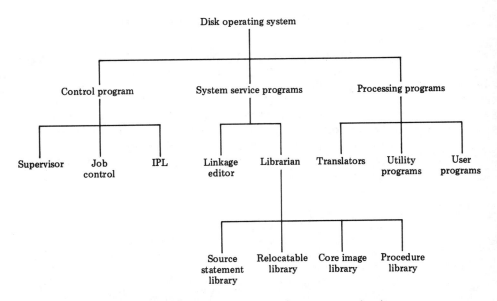

FIGURE 20-2 Disk Operating System organization.

from the program library, and handling program execution errors. An important part of the supervisor is the *Input/Output Control System (IOCS)* to handle the complex input/output. IOCS handles such items as checking for valid tape and disk files, and data transfer between I/O units and storage. A later section covers the supervisor in detail.

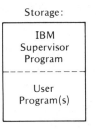

Job Control handles the transition between jobs run in the system. When required, the supervisor loads job control into storage. You provide job control commands with your job to tell the system what you want to do next.

Initial program load (IPL) is a program that the operator uses to load the supervisor into storage (done daily or whenever required).

SYSTEM SERVICE PROGRAMS. These include the *Linkage Editor* and the *Librarian.*

THE LINKAGE EDITOR.   The Linkage Editor has two main functions:

1. To include input/output modules. An installation catalogs I/O modules in the system library (covered next). When you code and assemble a program, it does not yet contain the complete instructions for handling input/output. On completion of assembly, the Linkage Editor includes all the required I/O modules from the library.

2. To link together separately assembled programs. You may code and assemble a number of subprograms separately, and then link-edit these subprograms into one executable program. The Linkage Editor enables data in one subprogram to be recognized in another, and at execution-time facilitates transfer of control between subprograms.

THE LIBRARIAN.   The operating system contains libraries on a SYSLNK disk to catalog both IBM programs and the installation's own commonly used programs and subroutines. Under DOS/VS there are four libraries:

1. *The Source Statement Library (SSL)* catalogs as a "book" any program, macro, or subroutine still in source code. You can use the Assembler directive COPY to include cataloged code into your source program for subsequent assembling.

2. *The Relocatable Library (RL)* catalogs frequently used "modules" that are assembled but not yet ready for execution. The Assembler directs the Linkage Editor to automatically include I/O modules, and you can use the INCLUDE command to direct the Linkage Editor to include your own cataloged modules in with your own assembled programs.

3. The *Core Image Library (CIL)* contains "phases" in executable machine code, ready for execution. The CIL contains, for example, the Assembler, COBOL, PL/I, and other translator programs, various utility programs such as LINK and SORT, and your own production programs ready for execution. To request the supervisor to load a phase from the CIL into main storage for execution, use the job control command

/ /   E X E C

4. *The Procedure Library (PL)* contains cataloged job control to facilitate automatic processing of jobs.

The OS libraries vary by name according to the version of OS, such as OS/MFT and OS/MVT, but basically the OS libraries equivalent to the DOS Source Statement, Relocatable, and Core Image are respectively Source Library, Object Library, and Load Library, and serve the same functions.

PROCESSING PROGRAMS. Processing programs are cataloged on disk in three groups:

1. *Language translators* that IBM supplies with the system include Assembler, PL/I, COBOL, and RPG.
2. *Utility programs* that IBM supplies include such special purpose programs as disk initialization, copy file-to-file, and sort/merge.
3. *User-written programs* that users in an installation write and that IBM does not support. All the programs in this text are user-written programs.

For example, the job command

```
// EXEC ASSEMBLY
```

causes the system to load the Assembler from the CIL into an available area ("partition") in storage and begins assembling a program. The job command

```
// OPTION LINK
```

directs the Assembler to write the assembled module on SYSLNK in the Relocatable Library.

Once the program is assembled and stored on SYSLNK, the job command

```
// EXEC LNKEDT
```

tells the Linkage Editor to load the module from SYSLNK into storage, to complete addressing, and to include I/O modules from the RL. Assuming that there was no job command to catalog it, the Linkage Editor writes the linked phase in the CIL in a *noncatalog area.* If the next job command is

```
// EXEC
```

with no specified phase name, the supervisor loads the phase from the noncatalog area into storage for execution. The next program that the Linkage Editor links overlays the previous one in the CIL noncatalog area.

The job command

```
// OPTION CATAL
```

instead of

```
OPTION LINK
```

tells the system both to link the program and to catalog the linked phase in the catalog area of the CIL. You normally catalog production programs in the CIL and for immediate execution use the job command

```
// EXEC phasename.
```

MULTIPROGRAMMING

Multiprogramming is the concurrent execution of more than one program in storage. Technically, a computer executes only one instruction at a time, but because of its extremely fast speed and relative slowness of I/O devices, the computer is able to service a number of programs at the same time, making it appear that processing is simultaneous. For this purpose, an operating system that supports multiprogramming divides storage into various partitions, and is consequently far more complex than a single-job system.

The three partitions in a DOS multiprogramming system are Foreground 1 and 2 (F1 and F2) and Background (BG). DOS/VSE provides for up to 12 partitions.

Supervisor (low storage)
F1
F2
BG (higher storage)

When an operator "boots" the system (the IPL procedure), the supervisor is loaded from the CIL into low storage. The supervisor next loads job control from the CIL into F1, F2, and BG. The supervisor then scans the system reader(s) and terminals for job control commands.

OS supports more and larger partitions. OS/MFT supports 15 partitions with fixed length established by the system programmer; OS/MVT runs programs under variable length regions that each job can establish via a job command, such as

```
REGION=128K
```

VIRTUAL STORAGE

In a multiprogramming environment, a large program may not fit entirely in a partition. As a consequence, both DOS/VS and OS/VS support a *virtual storage* system that divides programs into 2K or 4K *pages.* On disk, the entire program is contained as pages in a *page data set,* and in storage, VS arranges a *page pool* for as much of the program as it can store.

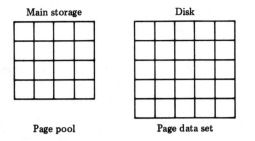

Main storage   Disk

Page pool   Page data set

As a consequence, a program that is 100K in size could run for example in a 64K partition. If the executing program references an address for a part of the program that is not in storage, VS swaps an unneeded page into the page data set on disk and pages in the required page from disk into the page pool in storage. (Actually, VS swaps *onto* disk only if the program has not changed the contents of the page.)

Since a page from disk may map into any page in the pool, VS has to change addresses; this process is known as *dynamic address translation* (DAT).

If you are running a "real time" application such as process control, a data communications manager, or an optical scan device, you may not want VS to page it out. It is possible to assign an area of nonpageable (real) storage for such jobs, or use a "page fix" to lock certain pages into real storage.

THE SUPERVISOR

The size of the operating system and of the supervisor vary considerably according to their complexity and functions they must perform. A small sized supervisor under DOS typically requires some 10,000 bytes of main storage, whereas under a large system the supervisor often requires over 100,000 bytes.

Although the supervisor program resides permanently in lower main storage, the first section up to X'200' is allocated for use by the CPU. These "fixed storage locations" are listed in Figure 20-3. Some of the locations are explained in the later section, Program Status Word.

The supervisor loads operating system routines stored on disk into main storage as required. The section of storage that the supervisor uses for temporary routines is the *"transient area."* Figure 20-4 illustrates the layout of the supervisor in main storage (not an exact representation).

1. *Communication Region.* This area contains the current date as well as other fields shown in the diagram. (There is one communication region for each partition under multiprogramming.)

FIXED STORAGE LOCATIONS

AREA, dec.	Hex addr	EC only	Function
0– 7	0		Initial program loading PSW, restart new PSW
8– 15	8		Initial program loading CCW1, restart old PSW
16– 23	10		Initial program loading CCW2
24– 31	18		External old PSW
32– 39	20		Supervisor Call old PSW
40– 47	28		Program old PSW
48– 55	30		Machine-check old PSW
56– 63	38		Input/output old PSW
64– 71	40		Channel status word (see diagram)
72– 75	48		Channel address word (0–3 key, 4–7 zeros, 8–31 CCW address)
80– 83	50		Interval timer
88– 95	58		External new PSW
96–103	60		Supervisor Call new PSW
104–111	68		Program new PSW
112–119	70		Machine-check new PSW
120–127	78		Input/output new PSW
132–133	84		CPU address assoc'd with external interruption, or unchanged
132–133	84	X	CPU address assoc'd with external interruption, or zeros
134–135	86	X	External interruption code
136–139	88	X	SVC interruption (0–12 zeros, 13–14 ILC, 15:0, 16–31 code)
140–143	8C	X	Program interrupt (0–12 zeros, 13–14 ILC, 15:0, 16–31 code)
144–147	90	X	Translation exception address (0–7 zeros, 8–31 address)
148–149	94		Monitor class (0–7 zeros, 8–15 class number)
150–151	96	X	PER interruption code (0–3 code, 4–15 zeros)
152–155	98	X	PER address (0–7 zeros, 8–31 address)
156–159	9C		Monitor code (0–7 zeros, 8–31 monitor code)
168–171	A8		Channel ID (0–3 type, 4–15 model, 16–31 max. IOEL length)
172–175	AC		I/O extended logout address (0–7 unused, 8–31 address)
176–179	B0		Limited channel logout (see diagram)
185–187	B9	X	I/O address (0–7 zeros, 8–23 address)
216–223	D8		CPU timer save area
224–231	E0		Clock comparator save area
232–239	E8		Machine-check interruption code
248–251	F8		Failing processor storage address (0–7 zeros, 8–31 address)
252–255	FC		Region code*
256–351	100		Fixed logout area*
352–383	160		Floating-point register save area
384–447	180		General register save area
448–511	1C0		Control register save area
512†	200		CPU extended logout area (size varies)

*May vary among models: see system library manuals for specific model

†Location may be changed by programming (bits 8–28 of CR 15 specify address)

FIGURE 20-3 Fixed storage locations.

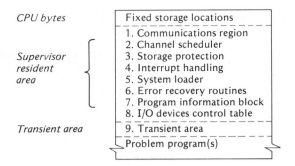

FIGURE 20-4 Supervisor routines.

Date Mo/Day/Yr or Day/Mo/Yr	Reserved	User Area — set to zero when JOB statement is read. (Communication within a job step or between job steps)	Program Switches (UPSI)	Job Name (Entered from Job Control)	Address: Uppermost Byte of Problem Program Area	Address: Uppermost Byte of Current Problem Program Phase	Address: Uppermost Byte of phase with highest ending address	Length of Problem Program Label Area
Bytes → 0 7	8 11	12 22	23	24 31	32 35	36 39	40 43	44 45

2. *Channel Scheduler.* The channels provide a path between main storage and the input/output devices, and permit overlapping of program execution with I/O operations. The channel scheduler routine handles all I/O. If the requested channel, control unit, and device are available, the channel operation begins. If busy, the channel scheduler places its request in a queue to wait until the device is available. The channel notifies the channel scheduler when the I/O operation is complete, or that an error has occurred (these are "I/O interrupts").

3. *Storage Protection.* Storage protection is an optional feature that prevents a problem program from erroneously moving data into the supervisor area and destroying it. Under a multiprogramming system, storage protection is required to prevent a program in one partition from erasing a program in another partition.

4. *Interrupt Handling.* An interrupt is a signal that informs the system that special action is required, to interrupt the program currently being executed, and to give control to the appropriate supervisor routine. This topic is covered in detail in the next section, PSW.

5. *System Loader.* This routine is responsible for loading programs into main storage for execution.

6. *Error Recovery.* For each I/O device (or class of devices) there is a special routine to handle device error-recovery. When an error is sensed, the channel scheduler invokes the required routine which attempts to correct the error.

7. *Program Information Block (PIB).* The PIB contains information tables required by the supervisor about the current program(s) in storage.

8. *I/O Devices Control Table.* This area contains the table of I/O devices that relate physical unit addresses (X'nnn') with logical units (SYSxxx).

9. *Transient Area.* This area provides temporary storage for routines that the supervisor loads as required: OPEN/CLOSE, DUMP, computer operator messages, end-of-job handling, some error recovery, and "checkpoint" routines.

THE PROGRAM STATUS WORD—PSW

The PSW is a doubleword of data stored in the control section of the CPU. The PSW controls an executing program and indicates its status. There are two PSW modes that provide control and status information: *basic control (BC) mode* and *extended control (EC) mode.* Both the 360 and 370 use BC mode, and the mode is indicated by a 0 in the PSW bit-12. EC mode was made available on the 370 for "virtual storage," with the "extended-control" facility. When in EC mode, PSW bit-12 contains a 1. For each mode the PSW format is the same in only certain positions. The charts next show the two modes (bits are numbered from left to right zero through 63):

Fields that programmers may find useful include:

PROGRAM STATUS WORD (BC Mode)

Channel masks	E	Protect'n key	CMWP	Interruption code
0 6	7	8 11	12 15	16 23	24 31

ILC	CC	Program mask	Instruction address
32	34	36 39	40 47	48 55	56 63

0–5 Channel 0 to 5 masks	32–33 (ILC) Instruction length code
6 Mask for channel 6 and up	34–35 (CC) Condition code
7 (E) External mask	36 Fixed-point overflow mask
12 (C–0) Basic control mode	37 Decimal overflow mask
13 (M) Machine-check mask	38 Exponent underflow mask
14 (W–1) Wait state	39 Significance mask
15 (P–1) Problem state	

PROGRAM STATUS WORD (EC Mode)

0R00 0TIE	Protect'n key	CMWP	00	CC	Program mask	0000 0000
0 7	8 11	12 15	16	18 20	23	24 31

0000 0000	Instruction address
32 39	40 47	48 55	56 63

1 (R) Program event recording mask	15 (P-1) Problem state
5 (T-1) Translation mode	18–19 (CC) Condition code
6 (I) Input/output mask	20 Fixed-point overflow mask
7 (E) External mask	21 Decimal overflow mask
12 (C-1) Extended control mode	22 Exponent underflow mask
13 (M) Machine-check mask	23 Significance mask
14 (W-1) Wait state	

BIT 15: STATE In both modes, 0 = Supervisor state and 1 = Problem state (the computer always functions in one or the other state). When the computer is executing the supervisor program, the bit is 0, and all instructions are valid. When in the problem state, the bit is 1, and certain *privileged* instructions (such as Start IO and Load PSW) cannot be executed.

BITS 16–31: PROGRAM INTERRUPT CODE (BC mode only). The computer sets these bits according to the type of program interrupt when one occurs. The following list of interrupt codes shows the hex representation of the 16-bit code:

PROGRAM INTERRUPTION CODES

0001	Operation exception	000C	Exponent overflow excp
0002	Privileged operation excp	000D	Exponent underflow excp
0003	Execute exception	000E	Significance exception
0004	Protection exception	000F	Floating-point divide excp
0005	Addressing exception	0010	Segment translation excp
0006	Specification exception	0011	Page translation exception
0007	Data exception	0012	Translation specification excp
0008	Fixed-point overflow excp	0013	Special operation exception
0009	Fixed-point divide excp	0040	Monitor event
000A	Decimal overflow exception	0080	Program event (code may be combined with another code)
000B	Decimal divide exception		

BITS 34–35: CONDITION CODE (BC mode only. Under EC mode, the condition code is in bits 18–19). Certain arithmetic and logical instructions set this code.

BITS 40–63: INSTRUCTION ADDRESS (both modes). This area contains the address of the next instruction to be executed. The CPU accesses the designated instruction from main storage, decodes it in the control section, and then executes it in the arithmetic/logical section. The first two bits of every machine code instruction indicate its length. Assume an RR-format instruction, two bytes long; when executing the RR instruction, the CPU increments the instruction address in the PSW by two, and this now indicates the address of the next instruction. In the case of a "branch" instruction, the branch address may replace the PSW instruction address.

INTERRUPTS

An interrupt occurs when it is necessary for the supervisor to perform some special task. There are six main classes of interrupts:

1. *Program Interrupt.* This is caused by an operation that the computer cannot execute, such as an attempt to perform arithmetic on invalid arithmetic data. This is the common type of interrupt when a program terminates abnormally (sometimes called "bombing"). Appendix B lists the various types of program interrupts that can occur during execution.

2. *Supervisor Call Interrupt.* A transfer from the problem program to the supervisor requires a "supervisor call" (SVC) operation and causes an interrupt. For example, your program may issue a request for input/output or to terminate processing. Control is passed to the supervisor by means of a supervisor call (SVC).

3. *External Interrupt.* An external device may need attention. For example, the computer operator may press the request key on the console, or there may be a request for telecommunications.

4. *Machine Check Interrupt.* The machine-checking circuits may detect a hardware error, such as a byte not containing an odd number of bits (odd parity).

5. *Input/Output Interrupt.* Completion of an I/O operation making the unit available or malfunction of an I/O device (such as damaged tape) cause this interrupt.

6. *Restart Interrupt* permits the operator or another CPU to invoke execution of a program.

For every interrupt, the system alters the PSW as required, and stores the PSW in a fixed storage location, where it is available to any program for testing.

The PSW referenced to this point is often called the "current" PSW. When an interrupt occurs, the computer stores the current PSW and loads a "new" PSW that controls the new program (usually the supervisor program). The current PSW is in the control section of the CPU, but the "old" and "new" PSWs are stored in main storage.

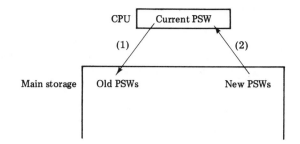

The interrupt replaces the current PSW: (1) It stores the current PSW into main storage as the "old" PSW, and (2) It fetches a "new" PSW from main storage, to become the "current" PSW. (The old PSW will therefore contain in its instruction address the location following the instruction that caused the interrupt.) The computer stores PSWs in 12 doubleword locations in fixed storage; six are for "old" PSWs and six for "new" PSWs, depending on the class of interrupt:

	OLD PSW	NEW PSW		OLD PSW	NEW PSW
Restart	0008	0000	Program	0040	0104
External	0024	0088	Machine	0048	0112
Supervisor	0032	0096	Input/Output	0056	0120

The following illustrates the sequence of events following a supervisor interrupt. Assume that the supervisor has stored in each of the six *new* PSWs the address of each of its interrupt routines (the old PSWs are not yet required). Remember also that when any instruction executes, the computer updates the current PSW—the instruction address, and the condition code as required.

1. Assume that your program requests input from disk. The input macro-instruction, GET or READ, contains a supervisor call to link to the supervisor for I/O. This is a *supervisor interrupt.*

2. The Instruction address in the current PSW contains the address in your program immediately following the SVC that caused the interrupt. The CPU stores this current PSW in the *old* PSW for supervisor interrupt, location 32. The *new* PSW for supervisor interrupt, location 96, contains supervisor state bit = 0 and the address of the supervisor interrupt routine. The CPU moves this new PSW to the current PSW, and is now in supervisor state.

3. The PSW instruction address contains the address of the supervisor I/O routine, which now executes. The channel scheduler requests the channel for disk input.

4. To return to your program, the supervisor loads the old PSW from location 32 back into the current PSW. The instruction "goes to" the PSW instruction address, which is the address in your program following the original SVC that caused the interrupt. The system switches from supervisor state back to problem state.

In the case of a *program check interrupt,* the computer sets the cause of the program check in PSW bits 16–31, the program interrupt code. If the problem program attempts arithmetic on invalid data, the computer senses a Data Exception, and stores X'0007' in PSW bits 16–31 (i.e., B'111' in bits 29–31). The computer then stores the current PSW in old PSW location 0040, and loads the new PSW from 0104 into the current PSW. This PSW contains the address of the supervisor's program check routine, which tests the old PSW to determine which type of program check caused the interrupt.

The supervisor prints the contents of the old PSW in hexadecimal and the cause of the program check, "DATA EXCEPTION," "flushes" the interrupted program, and begins processing the next job. Suppose that the invalid operation is an MP at location X'6A320'. Since MP is six bytes long, the instruction address in the PSW and the one printed will be X'6A326'. You can tell from the supervisor diagnostic message first, that the error is a Data Exception, and second, that the invalid operation immediately precedes the instruction at X'6A326'.

CHANNELS

Channels direct data between devices and main storage. A channel is a component that functions as a separate computer operated by "channel commands" to control input/output devices. Channels permit attaching a great variety of I/O devices. There are two types of channels:

1. *The multiplexor channel* is designed to handle low-speed devices, such as a printer and terminals. It permits simultaneous operation of more than one device. Early model 370s had only one multiplexor channel on a system, although current IBM computers have more than one.

2. *The selector channel* is designed to handle high-speed devices, such as magnetic tape and disk. However, data can be transferred from only one device at a time (burst mode). Depending on the model, there may be up to six selector channels.

In a simple system, each channel has a four-bit address coded as follows:

CHANNEL	ADDRESS	TYPE	CHANNEL	ADDRESS	TYPE
0	0000	Multiplexor	4	0100	Selector
1	0001		5	0101	channels
2	0010	Selector	6	0110	
3	0011	channels			

To interface a device with a channel requires a *control unit.* Since many devices may be attached, the control unit is specific to the device. For example, a magnetic tape control unit connects tape drives with a selector channel. The control unit also has a 4-bit address. Further, each *device* has a 4-bit address, and is known to the system by a *physical address*—a 12-bit code that specifies channel/control unit/device, as 0CCC UUUU DDDD (C = channel, U = control unit, D = device). This physical address permits the attaching of 2^8 or 256 devices. Figure 20-5 illustrates one possible configuration.

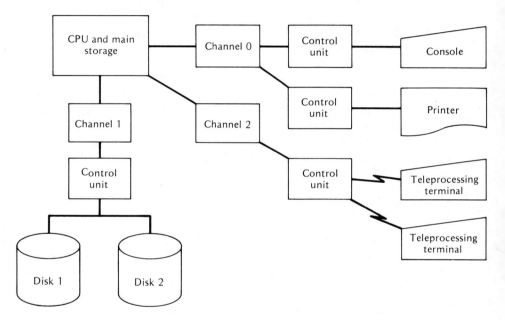

FIGURE 20-5 Channels and I/O devices.

For example, a printer device number is 1110, and is attached to channel 0, control unit 1. To the system, the physical address of the printer is 0000 0001 1110, or X'01E'. Assume that the two disk devices are numbered 0000 and 0001; if they are both attached to channel 1, control unit 9, their physical addresses are respectively X'190' and X'191'.

SYMBOLIC ASSIGNMENTS.   Although the supervisor references I/O devices by their physical numbers, your programs use symbolic names. You can assign a symbolic name "permanently" or temporarily to any device, and a device may have assigned more than one symbolic name. The system control program uses certain names, called *system logical units,* including the following:

SYSIPT The terminal, card reader, tape, or disk device used as input for programs.

SYSRDR The terminal, card reader, tape, or disk device used as input for job control for the system.

SYSIN The system name to assign both SYSIPT and SYSRDR to the same terminal, card reader, tape, or disk device.

SYSLST The printer, tape, or disk used as the main output device for the system.

SYSPCH The card punch, tape, or disk used as the main device for "punching."

SYSOUT The system name to assign both SYSLST and SYSPCH to the same output device.

SYSLNK The disk area used as input for the Linkage Editor.

SYSLOG The console (or printer) used by the system to log operator messages and job control statements.

SYSRES The disk or tape device where the operating system resides.

SYSRLB and SYSSLB The devices for the relocatable and system libraries.

In addition, there are *programmer logical units,* SYS000–SYSnnn. A user may assign any valid symbolic name to a device, such as assigning a disk drive, physical address X'160', with a logical address SYS002. The supervisor stores these physical and logical addresses in a table in order to relate them. The table is called I/O Devices Control Table, and in simplified form could contain the following:

I/O DEVICE	PHYSICAL ADDRESS	LOGICAL UNIT(S)
reader	X'00C'	SYSIPT, SYSRDR
printer	X'00E'	SYSLST
disk drive	X'160'	SYSLNK, SYSRES, SYS002
tape drive	X'280'	SYS026, SYS035

For example, a reference to SYSLST is to the printer, and the disk device, X'160', is known as SYSLNK, SYSRES, and SYS002, depending on its particular use. You may assign a logical address permanently or temporarily, and may change logical addresses from job to job. For instance, you could use an ASSGN job control statement to reassign SYS035 from tape output for a program to disk output on X'160'.

I/O LOGIC MODULES

Assume that a program reads a tape file named TAPEFL. It would require a DTFMT or DCB file definition macro to define the characteristics of the file and tape device to generate a link to a logic module. The Assembler determines which particular logic module based on (1) the kind of DTF, and (2) the specifications within the file definition, such as device number, an input or output file, the number of buffers, and whether processing is in a workarea (WORKA) or a buffer (IOREG). In the following example, the Assembler has generated a logic module named IJFFBCWZ (the name would vary depending on specifications within the DTFMT).

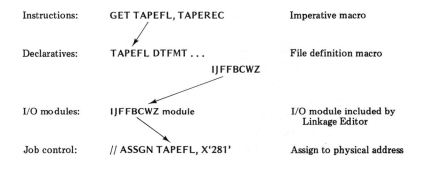

Instructions:	**GET TAPEFL, TAPEREC**	Imperative macro
Declaratives:	**TAPEFL DTFMT . . .**	File definition macro
	IJFFBCWZ	
I/O modules:	**IJFFBCWZ module**	I/O module included by Linkage Editor
Job control:	**// ASSGN TAPEFL, X'281'**	Assign to physical address

When linking a program, the Linkage Editor searches for addresses in the External Symbol Dictionary that the Assembler generates. For this example, the ESD would contain entries at least for the program name and IJFFBCWZ. The Linker accesses the named module cataloged on disk (assuming that it was ever cataloged), and includes it at the end of the assembled object program. One role of a system programmer is to define and catalog these I/O modules.

On execution of the program, the GET macro links to the specified file definition macro, DTFMT. This macro contains the address of the I/O logic module at the end of the object program where Link included it. The module, combined with information from the DTFMT, contains all the necessary instructions to notify the supervisor as to the actual type of I/O operation, device, block size, and so forth.

The only remaining information is which tape device; the supervisor derives it from the job control entry that in this example assigns X'281' as the physical address. The supervisor then (at last) delivers the physical request for input via a channel command.

As an example, the printer module, PRMOD, consists of three letters (IJD) and five option letters (abcde), as IJDabcde. The options are based on the definitions in the DTFPR macro, as follows:

a RECFORM: FIXUNB (F), VARUNB (V), UNDEF (U).

b CTLCHR: ASA (A), YES (Y), CONTROL (C).

c ERROPT=YES and PRINTOV=YES (B), PRINTOV=YES and ERROPT not specified (Z), plus 14 other options.

d IOAREA2: defined (I), not defined (Z).

e WORKA: YES (W), YES and RDONLY=YES (V), neither specified (Z).

A common printer module for IBM control character, two buffers, and a workarea would be IJDFYZIW. For one buffer, the module would be IJDFYZZW.

PHYSICAL IOCS

PIOCS, the basic level of IOCS, provides for channel scheduling, error recovery, and interrupt handling. When using PIOCS, you must write a "channel program" (the channel command word), and synchronize the program with completion of the I/O operation. You must also provide for testing the command control block for certain errors, checking wrong-length records, switching between I/O areas where two are used, and, if records are blocked, for blocking and deblocking. PIOCS macros include CCW, CCB, EXCP, and WAIT.

(name)	CCW	Command code, Data address, Flags, Count field
Blockname	CCB	SYSnnn, Command-list-name
(name)	EXCP	Blockname or (1)
(name)	WAIT	Blockname or (1)

CHANNEL COMMAND WORD—CCW. The CCW instruction causes the Assembler to construct an 8-byte Channel Command Word that defines the I/O command to be executed.

COMMAND CODE Defines the operation to be performed, such as 1 = Write, 2 = Read, X'09' = Print, and space one line.

DATA ADDRESS The storage address of the first byte where data is to be read or written.

FLAGS When the channel completes an operation defined in a CCW, it determines its next action from these flag bits, and you can set flag bits to '1' to vary the channel's operation (explained in detail later).

COUNT FIELD An expression that defines the number of bytes in the data block that is to be processed.

COMMAND CONTROL BLOCK—CCB. There must be a CCB for each I/O device that PIOCS macros reference. The CCB comprises the first 16 bytes of most generated DTF tables. The CCB communicates information to PIOCS to cause required I/O operations, and receives status information after the operation.

BLOCKNAME The symbolic name associated with this CCB, used as an operand for the EXCP and WAIT macros.

SYSnnn The symbolic name of the I/O device associated with this CCB.

COMMAND-LIST NAME The symbolic name of the first CCW used with the CCB.

THE EXECUTE CHANNEL PROGRAM (EXCP) AND WAIT MACROS. The operand of both EXCP and WAIT gives the symbolic name of the CCB macro to be referenced. The EXCP macro requests physical IOCS to start an I/O operation, and PIOCS relates the blockname to the CCB to determine the device. When the channel and the device become available, the channel program is started. Program control then returns to your program. The WAIT macro synchronizes program execution with completion of an I/O operation, since the program normally requires its completion before it can continue execution. For example, you have issued EXCP to read a data block—you must now WAIT for delivery of the entire data block before you can begin processing it. (When bit-0 of byte-2 of the CCB for the file is set to '1', the WAIT is completed and processing continues.)

CCW FLAG BITS.   The flag bits in the CCW may be set and used as follows:

BIT 32 "Chain Data flag," set by X'80'. This bit specifies "data chaining." When the CCW has processed the number of bytes defined in its Count field, the I/O operation does not terminate if this flag bit is set. The operation continues with the *next* CCW in storage. You can use data chaining to read or write data into or out of storage areas that are not necessarily adjacent. In the following three CCWs, the first two specify data chaining with X'80' in the Flag bits, operand-3. An EXCP and CCB may then reference the *first* CCW, and as a result, the chain of three CCWs causes the contents of an 80-byte input record to be read into three separate areas in storage—20 bytes in NAME, 30 in ADDRESS, and 30 in CITY.

```
DATACHAIN CCW  2,NAME,X'80',20      Read 20 bytes into NAME, then
                                    chain.
          CCW  ,ADDRESS,X'80',30    Read 30 bytes into ADDRESS,
                                    then chain.
          CCW  ,CITY,X'00',30       Read 30 bytes into CITY, no
                                    chain (stop).
```

BIT 33, "Chain Command flag," set by X'40'. This bit specifies "command chaining" to enable the channel to execute more than one CCW before terminating the I/O operation. Each CCW applies to a *separate I/O record*. The following set of CCWs could provide for reading three input blocks, each 100 bytes long.

```
COMCHAIN   CCW  2,INAREA,X'40',100          Read   record-1  into
                                            INAREA, then chain.
           CCW  2,INAREA+100,X'40',100      Read   record-2  into
                                            INAREA+100, chain.
           CCW  2,INAREA+200,X'00',100      Read   record-3  into
                                            INAREA+200, stop.
```

BIT 34, "Suppress Length Indication flag," set by X'20', is used to suppress an error indication that occurs when the number of bytes transmitted differs from the count in the CCW.

BIT 35, "Skip flag," set by X'10', is used to suppress transmission of input data. The device actually reads the data, but the channel does not transmit the record.

BIT 36, "Program Controlled Interrupt flag," set by X'08', causes an interrupt when this CCW's operation is complete (used when one supervisor SIO instruction executes more than one CCW).

BIT 37, "Indirect Data Address flag." This flag as well as other features about physical IOCS are covered in the IBM Principles of Operation manual and in the appropriate supervisor manual.

EXAMPLE PHYSICAL IOCS PROGRAM

The program in Figure 20-6 performs the following:

- At initialization, prints three heading lines by means of command chaining (X'40').
- Reads input records one at a time containing salesman name and company.
- Prints each record.
- Terminates on reaching end-of-file.

Note that the program defines a CCB/CCW pair for each type of record, and the EXCP/WAIT operations reference the CCB name—INDEVIC for the reader, OUTDEV1 for heading lines, and OUTDEV2 for sales detail lines. Each CCB contains the name of the I/O device, SYSIPT or SYSLST, and the name of an associated CCW: INRECD, TITLES, and DETAIL respectively.

```
LCC    OBJECT CODE          ACCR1 ADCR2   STMT  SOURCE STATEMENT

CCCCCO                                       1  PICCSPRG PRINT NOCATA,NOGEN       INITIALIZATION
CCCCCO 053C                       00002      2           START 0                 *
                                             3           BALR  3,0               *
                                             4           USING *,3
                                             6           EXCP  OUTDEV1           PRINT TITLES
                                            10           WAIT  OUTDEV1           *
C0002A D501 3076 3332  00078 00334          17  A1CCREAD EXCP  INDEVIC           READ A RECORD
C0C030 478C 305C             CCC5E          21           WAIT  INDEVIC           *
                                            28           CLC   RECORD(2),=C'/*'   END OF FILE?
C00034 D21C 3288 3076  0028A 00078          29           BE    A9OOEND           YES- TERMINATE
CC03A  D213 32D7 3094  C2D9  00096          31           MVC   SURNOUT,SURNAME   LOAD PRINT LINE
CCC040 D21D 32EC 3CAE  32EE  0CCAA          32           MVC   GIVENOUT,GIVENAME
                                            33           MVC   COMPOUT,COMPANY
                                            35           EXCP  OUTDEV2           PRINT DETAIL LINE
                                            39           WAIT  OUTDEV2           *
00005A 47F0 3014             CCC16          45           B     A1OOREAD          RETURN TO READ NEXT
                                            47  A9CCENC  EOJ                     END OF JCB
                                            51  **********************
                                            52  *  C E C L A R A T I V E S  *
                                            53  **********************
                                            54  INDEVIC  CCB  SYSIPT,INRECRD     INPUT DEVICE
COCC70 C2CC00782CC00050                     65  INRECRD  CCW  X'02',RECORD,X'20',80
000078                                      67  RECORD   DS   OCL80              INPUT RECORD
C00078                                      68  SURNAME  DS   CL30               *
CCC096                                      69  GIVENAME DS   CL20               *
C000AA                                      70  COMPANY  DS   CL30               *
                                            72  OUTDEV1  CCB  SYSLST,TITLES      OUTPUT DEVICE
CCCCD8 8BCCCCD86CCCC01                      84  TITLES   CCW  X'8B',*,X'60',1
C000E0 110000F84CCCCCE5                     85           CCW  X'11',PRIMARY,X'40',133
C000E8 190001704C000085                     86           CCW  X'19',SECONDRY,X'40',133
CCCCF0 110002020C0C0085                     87           CCW  X'11',TERTIARY,X'00',133
C000F8 4040404040404040                     89  PRIMARY  DS   OCL133             FIRST TITLE LINE
C00F8  E340D6440D7404C40                    90           DC   CL47' '            *
000127 E24CD440C540D540                     91           DC   CL16'TOP  SALE'    *
000137                                      92           DC   CL70'SMEN OF'       *
C0017D 404C4C4040404040                     94  SECONDRY DS   OCL133             SECOND TITLE LINE
0001A9 E34CC840C54C4C40                     95           DC   CL44' '            *
0001B7 E34CC54CD940D540                     96           DC   CL14'THE WES'      *
0001C5 C740C940D640D540                     97           DC   CL14'TERNRE'       *
                                            98           DC   CL61'GION'         *
```

FIGURE 20.6 (partial)

```
LCC    OBJECT CODE       ADDR1 ADDR2   STMT   SOURCE STATEMENT

                                       100    TERTIARY  DS    0CL133                      SUBHEADING LINE
C00202 4C4C4C4C4C4C4C4C                101              DC    CL26' '                      *
00021C E2E4D9D5C1D4C540                102              DC    CL31'SURNAME'                *
000238 C7C9E5C5D54005C1                103              DC    CL21'GIVEN NAME'             *
0C0250 C3D6D4D7C1D5E840                104              DC    CL55'COMPANY'                *

CCC297 00                              106    OUTDEV2   CCB   SYSLST,OUTRECRD             OUTPUT DEVICE
000298 09C002A02C000085                118    OUTRECRD  CCW   X'09',DETAIL,X'20',133

0002A0                                 120    DETAIL    DS    0CL133                      DETAIL LINE
0002A0 4C4C4C4040404C040              121              DC    CL26' '                      *
00028A                                 122    SURNOUT   DS    CL30                        *
0002D8 40                              123              DC    CL01' '                      *
0002D9                                 124    GIVENOUT  DS    CL20                         *
0002ED 40                              125              DC    CL01' '                      *
0002EE                                 126    COMPOUT   DS    CL30                         *
C0030C 404040404040404040             127              DC    CL25' '                      *

                                       129              LTORG ,
000328 0CC000C8                        130                    =A(OUTDEV1)
00032C 0C0CC060                        131                    =A(INDEVIC)
000330 0C00287                         132                    =A(OUTDEV2)
000334 615C                            133                    =C'/*'
                        00000          134              END   PIOCSPRG
```

Output:-

```
                    T O P   S A L E S M E N   O F
                  T H E   W E S T E R N   R E G I O N

   SURNAME          GIVEN NAME             COMPANY

   RUTH             GEORGE HERMAN          LASER CORP.
   JOHNSON          WALTER                 AMX ELECTRONICS
   COLLINS          EDDIE                  B M I
   COBB             TYRUS RAYMOND          AUDIO SHACK
   SPEAKER          TRIS                   PACKLETT HEWARD
   SIMMONS          AL                     VIDEO DUMP
   SISLER           GEORGE                 COMPUTER HEAP
   WAGNER           HANS                   DIGITAL CORP.
```

FIGURE 20.6 Example physical IOCS program.

PROBLEMS

20-1.   What is the purpose (if any) of an operating system?

20-2.   Where is the supervisor program located?

20-3.   What are the two main features of the Linkage Editor?

20-4.   In what libraries are the following stored (a) phase, (b) module, (c) book?

20-5.   What is dynamic address translation?

20-6.   What do the first 512 bytes of main storage contain?

20-7.   What is the purpose and contents of the supervisor "transient area?"

20-8.   What are the two modes of the PSW? The two states?

20-9.   Where in the PSW (the name and bit positions) is the next sequential instruction located?

20-10.   What are the classes of interrupts and their causes?

20-11.   What is the purpose of channels? What are the two types and their differences?

20-12.   A printer, number 1101, is attached to control unit 0010 and a multiplexor channel. What is the printer's physical address in hex?

20-13.   Distinguish between physical address and logical address.

20-14.   What are system logical units and programmer logical units?

20-15.   Revise some simple program and substitute physical IOCS for input/output.

APPENDICES

APPENDIX A

HEXADECIMAL AND DECIMAL CONVERSION*

Hexadecimal and Decimal Integer Conversion Table

	HALFWORD								HALFWORD						
	BYTE				BYTE				BYTE				BYTE		
BITS: 0123		4567		0123		4567		0123		4567		0123		4567	
Hex	Decimal	Hex	Decimal	Hex	Decimal	Hex	Decimal	Hex	Decimal	Hex	Decimal	Hex	Decimal	Hex	Decimal
0	0	0	0	0	0	0	0	0	0	0	0	0	0	0	0
1	268,435,456	1	16,777,216	1	1,048,576	1	65,536	1	4,096	1	256	1	16	1	1
2	536,870,912	2	33,554,432	2	2,097,152	2	131,072	2	8,192	2	512	2	32	2	2
3	805,306,368	3	50,331,648	3	3,145,728	3	196,608	3	12,288	3	768	3	48	3	3
4	1,073,741,824	4	67,108,864	4	4,194,304	4	262,144	4	16,384	4	1,024	4	64	4	4
5	1,342,177,280	5	83,886,080	5	5,242,880	5	327,680	5	20,480	5	1,280	5	80	5	5
6	1,610,612,736	6	100,663,296	6	6,291,456	6	393,216	6	24,576	6	1,536	6	96	6	6
7	1,879,048,192	7	117,440,512	7	7,340,032	7	458,752	7	28,672	7	1,792	7	112	7	7
8	2,147,483,648	8	134,217,728	8	8,388,608	8	524,288	8	32,768	8	2,048	8	128	8	8
9	2,415,919,104	9	150,994,944	9	9,437,184	9	589,824	9	36,864	9	2,304	9	144	9	9
A	2,684,354,560	A	167,772,160	A	10,485,760	A	655,360	A	40,960	A	2,560	A	160	A	10
B	2,952,790,016	B	184,549,376	B	11,534,336	B	720,896	B	45,056	B	2,816	B	176	B	11
C	3,221,225,472	C	201,326,592	C	12,582,912	C	786,432	C	49,152	C	3,072	C	192	C	12
D	3,489,660,928	D	218,103,808	D	13,631,488	D	851,968	D	53,248	D	3,328	D	208	D	13
E	3,758,096,384	E	234,881,024	E	14,680,064	E	917,504	E	57,344	E	3,584	E	224	E	14
F	4,026,531,840	F	251,658,240	F	15,728,640	F	983,040	F	61,440	F	3,840	F	240	F	15
	8		7		6		5		4		3		2		1

*Reprinted by permission from *Introduction to IBM Data Processing Systems,* © 1960, 1967, by International Business Machines Corporation.

TO CONVERT HEXADECIMAL TO DECIMAL

1. Locate the column of decimal numbers corresponding to the left-most digit or letter of the hexadecimal; select from this column and record the number that corresponds to the position of the hexadecimal digit or letter.

2. Repeat step 1 for the next (second from the left) position.

3. Repeat step 1 for the units (third from the left) position.

4. Add the numbers selected from the table to form the decimal number.

EXAMPLE	
Conversion of Hexadecimal Value	D34
1. D	3328
2. 3	48
3. 4	4
4. Decimal	3380

TO CONVERT DECIMAL TO HEXADECIMAL

1. (a) Select from the table the highest decimal number that is equal to or less than the number to be converted.
   (b) Record the hexadecimal of the column containing the selected number.
   (c) Subtract the selected decimal from the number to be converted.

2. Using the remainder from step 1(c) repeat all of step 1 to develop the second position of the hexadecimal (and a remainder).

3. Using the remainder from step 2 repeat all of step 1 to develop the units position of the hexadecimal.

4. Combine terms to form the hexadecimal number.

EXAMPLE	
Conversion of Decimal Value	3380
1. D	-3328
	52
2. 3	-48
	4
3. 4	-4
4. Hexadecimal	D34

To convert integer numbers greater than the capacity of table, use the techniques below:

HEXADECIMAL TO DECIMAL

Successive cumulative multiplication from left to right, adding units position.

Example: $D34_{16} = 3380_{10}$

DECIMAL TO HEXADECIMAL

Divide and collect the remainder in reverse order.

Example: $3380_{10} = X_{16}$

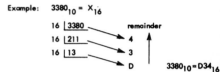

$3380_{10} = D34_{16}$

POWERS OF 16 TABLE

Example: $268,435,456_{10} = (2.68435456 \times 10^8)_{10} = 1000\ 0000_{16} = (10^7)_{16}$

16^n	n
1	0
16	1
256	2
4 096	3
65 536	4
1 048 576	5
16 777 216	6
268 435 456	7
4 294 967 296	8
68 719 476 736	9
1 099 511 627 776	10 = A
17 592 186 044 416	11 = B
281 474 976 710 656	12 = C
4 503 599 627 370 496	13 = D
72 057 594 037 927 936	14 = E
1 152 921 504 606 846 976	15 = F

Decimal Values

APPENDIX B

PROGRAM INTERRUPTS BY CODE

A program interrupt occurs when a program attempts an operation that the CPU cannot execute. The following lists the various program interrupts by code.

1. *Operation Exception.* The CPU has attempted to execute an invalid machine operation, such as hexadecimal zeros. Possible cause: (1) missing branch instruction—the program has entered a declarative area; (2) the instruction, such as a floating point operation, is not installed on the computer; (3) during assembly, an invalid instruction has caused the Assembler to generate hexadecimal zeros in place of the machine code. For a 6-byte instruction such as MVC, the computer generates six bytes of hex zeros. At execute-time, the computer tries to execute the zero operation code, causing an operation exception. (Since the computer will attempt to execute two bytes at a time, some systems may generate three consecutive operation exceptions.) See, also, the causes for an addressing exception.

2. *Privileged-Operation Exception.* An attempt has been made to execute a "privileged instruction" that only the supervisor is permitted to execute. Possible causes: see Addressing and Operation exceptions. There are many possible causes, and it may be necessary to take a hexadecimal dump of the program to determine the contents of I/O areas and other declaratives to discover at what point during execution the error occurred.

3. *Execute Exception.* An attempt has been made to use the EX instruction on another EX instruction.

4. *Protection Exception.* Many computer models have a useful "storage protection" device that prevents the program from erroneously moving data into the supervisor area (or into the areas of other programs under multiprogramming). Such attempts (for example, by MVC and ZAP) cause the computer to signal the error. Possible cause: (1) the program has erroneously loaded data into one of the program's base registers; (2) improper explicit use of a base register.

5. *Addressing Exception.* The program is attempting to reference an address that is outside available storage. Possible causes: (1) a branch to an address in a register containing an invalid value; (2) an instruction, such as MVC, has erroneously moved a data field into program instructions; (3) improper use of a base register, for example, loaded with a wrong value; (4) a BR instruction has branched to an address in a register and the wrong register was coded or its contents were changed.

6. *Specification Exception.* There are many causes. (1) An attempt has been made to execute an instruction that does not begin in an even storage address (possibly an incorrect base register). (2) For packed operations, a multiplier or divisor exceeds eight bytes, or the length of the operand-1 field is less than or equal to that of operand-2. (3) For binary operations, the instruction violates the rule of integral boundaries—halfword, fullword, or doubleword (e.g., operand-2 of binary multiply (M) should align on a fullword location, and that of CVB should align on a doubleword location). Also, operand-1 of the operation (such as M or D) must specify an even-numbered register. (4) For floating point, there may be a reference to a register other than 0, 2, 4, or 6, or failure to address on the proper single or double precision boundary.

7. *Data Exception.* An attempt has been made to perform arithmetic on an invalid packed field. Possible causes: (1) an input field contained blanks or other non-digits that pack invalidly; (2) failure to pack, or an improper pack; (3) improper use of relative addressing; (4) an MVC has erroneously destroyed a packed field; (5) the multiplicand field for an MP is too short; (6) improper explicit use of a base register; (7) an AP has added to an accumulator that was not initialized to valid packed data.

8. *Fixed-Point—Overflow Exception.* A binary operation (add, subtract, shift) has caused the contents of a register to overflow, losing a leftmost significant digit. The maximum value in a register is, in decimal notation, $+2,147,483,647$.

9. *Fixed-Point—Divide Exception.* A binary divide (D or DR) or a CVB has generated a value that has exceeded the capacity of a register.

Common cause for divide operations: dividing by a zero value. Remember that the maximum value that a register can contain, in decimal notation, is $+2,147,483,647$.

A. *Decimal-Overflow Exception.* The result of a decimal (packed) operation is too large for the receiving field. Solution: redefine the receiving field so that it can contain the largest possible value, or perform a right shift to reduce the size of the amount.

B. *Decimal-Divide Exception.* The generated quotient/remainder for a DP is too large for the defined area. Possible cause: (1) failure to follow the rules of DP; (2) the divisor contains a zero value.

C. *Exponent-Overflow Exception.* A floating point arithmetic operation has caused the exponent to overflow (exceed $+63$).

D. *Exponent-Underflow Exception.* A floating point arithmetic operation has caused the exponent to underflow (less than -64).

E. *Significance Exception.* A floating point add or subtract has caused a zero fraction. All significant digits are lost, and subsequent computations may be meaningless.

F. *Floating-Point—Divide Exception.* An attempt has been made to divide in floating point using a zero divisor.

In each case, the system issues an error message, giving the type of program interrupt and the address where the interrupt occurred. Sometimes a programming error causes the program to enter a declarative area or some other invalid area outside the program. (The computer may even find some valid machine operation, such as X'3C', Multiply Float!) In debugging, determine *how* the program arrived at the invalid address. In many cases, a dump of the program's registers and storage area will be essential in tracing the cause of the error.

INVALID STATEMENT. Another common error, although not a program interrupt, is one that the operating system generates: INVALID STATEMENT. The reason: the system is trying to read a job control statement that is invalid. Usually, this is a data record on the system reader—the program has gone to its end-of-file routine before all the data was read. Possible causes: (1) missing branch instruction causing the program to enter the EOF routine; (2) branching to the EOF routine, such as on an error condition, without flushing remaining input data.

370 INSTRUCTION SET

MACHINE INSTRUCTIONS

NAME	MNEMONIC	OP CODE	FORMAT	OPERANDS
Add (c)	AR	1A	RR	R1,R2
Add (c)	A	5A	RX	R1,D2(X2,B2)
Add Decimal (c)	AP	FA	SS	D1(L1,B1),D2(L2,B2)
Add Halfword (c)	AH	4A	RX	R1,D2(X2,B2)
Add Logical (c)	ALR	1E	RR	R1,R2
Add Logical (c)	AL	5E	RX	R1,D2(X2,B2)
AND (c)	NR	14	RR	R1,R2
AND (c)	N	54	RX	R1,D2(X2,B2)
AND (c)	NI	94	SI	D1(B1),I2
AND (c)	NC	D4	SS	D1(L,B1),D2(B2)
Branch and Link	BALR	05	RR	R1,R2
Branch and Link	BAL	45	RX	R1,D2(X2,B2)
Branch on Condition	BCR	07	RR	M1,R2
Branch on Condition	BC	47	RX	M1,D2(X2,B2)
Branch on Count	BCTR	06	RR	R1,R2
Branch on Count	BCT	46	RX	R1,D2(X2,B2)
Branch on Index High	BXH	86	RS	R1,R3,D2(B2)
Branch on Index Low or Equal	BXLE	87	RS	R1,R3,D2(B2)
Clear I/O (c,p)	CLRIO	9D01	S	D2(B2)
Compare (c)	CR	19	RR	R1,R2
Compare (c)	C	59	RX	R1,D2(X2,B2)
Compare and Swap (c)	CS	BA	RS	R1,R3,D2(B2)
Compare Decimal (c)	CP	F9	SS	D1(L1,B1),D2(L2,B2)
Compare Double and Swap (c)	CDS	BB	RS	R1,R3,D2(B2)
Compare Halfword (c)	CH	49	RX	R1,D2(X2,B2)
Compare Logical (c)	CLR	15	RR	R1,R2
Compare Logical (c)	CL	55	RX	R1,D2(X2,B2)
Compare Logical (c)	CLC	D5	SS	D1(L,B1),D2(B2)
Compare Logical (c)	CLI	95	SI	D1(B1),I2
Compare Logical Characters under Mask (c)	CLM	BD	RS	R1,M3,D2(B2)
Compare Logical Long (c)	CLCL	0F	RR	R1,R2
Convert to Binary	CVB	4F	RX	R1,D2(X2,B2)
Convert to Decimal	CVD	4E	RX	R1,D2(X2,B2)
Diagnose (p)		83		Model-dependent
Divide	DR	1D	RR	R1,R2
Divide	D	5D	RX	R1,D2(X2,B2)
Divide Decimal	DP	FD	SS	D1(L1,B1),D2(L2,B2)
Edit (c)	ED	DE	SS	D1(L,B1),D2(B2)
Edit and Mark (c)	EDMK	DF	SS	D1(L,B1),D2(B2)
Exclusive OR (c)	XR	17	RR	R1,R2
Exclusive OR (c)	X	57	RX	R1,D2(X2,B2)

MACHINE INSTRUCTIONS (Contd)

NAME	MNEMONIC	OP CODE	FORMAT	OPERANDS
Exclusive OR (c)	XI	97	SI	D1(B1),I2
Exclusive OR (c)	XC	D7	SS	D1(L,B1),D2(B2)
Execute	EX	44	RX	R1,D2(X2,B2)
Halt I/O (c,p)	HIO	9E00	S	D2(B2)
Halt Device (c,p)	HDV	9E01	S	D2(B2)
Insert Character	IC	43	RX	R1,D2(X2,B2)
Insert Characters under Mask (c)	ICM	BF	RS	R1,M3,D2(B2)
Insert PSW Key (p)	IPK	B20B	S	
Insert Storage Key (p)	ISK	09	RR	R1,R2
Load	LR	18	RR	R1,R2
Load	L	58	RX	R1,D2(X2,B2)
Load Address	LA	41	RX	R1,D2(X2,B2)
Load and Test (c)	LTR	12	RR	R1,R2
Load Complement (c)	LCR	13	RR	R1,R2
Load Control (p)	LCTL	B7	RS	R1,R3,D2(B2)
Load Halfword	LH	48	RX	R1,D2(X2,B2)
Load Multiple	LM	98	RS	R1,R3,D2(B2)
Load Negative (c)	LNR	11	RR	R1,R2
Load Positive (c)	LPR	10	RR	R1,R2
Load PSW (n,p)	LPSW	82	S	D2(B2)
Load Real Address (c,p)	LRA	B1	RX	R1,D2(X2,B2)
Monitor Call	MC	AF	SI	D1(B1),I2
Move	MVI	92	SI	D1(B1),I2
Move	MVC	D2	SS	D1(L,B1),D2(B2)
Move Long (c)	MVCL	0E	RR	R1,R2
Move Numerics	MVN	D1	SS	D1(L,B1),D2(B2)
Move with Offset	MVO	F1	SS	D1(L1,B1),D2(L2,B2)
Move Zones	MVZ	D3	SS	D1(L,B1),D2(B2)
Multiply	MR	1C	RR	R1,R2
Multiply	M	5C	RX	R1,D2(X2,B2)
Multiply Decimal	MP	FC	SS	D1(L1,B1),D2(L2,B2)
Multiply Halfword	MH	4C	RX	R1,D2(X2,B2)
OR (c)	OR	16	RR	R1,R2
OR (c)	O	56	RX	R1,D2(X2,B2)
OR (c)	OI	96	SI	D1(B1),I2
OR (c)	OC	D6	SS	D1(L,B1),D2(B2)
Pack	PACK	F2	SS	D1(L1,B1),D2(L2,B2)
Purge TLB (p)	PTLB	B20D	S	
Read Direct (p)	RDD	85	SI	D1(B1),I2
Reset Reference Bit (c,p)	RRB	B213	S	D2(B2)
Set Clock (c,p)	SCK	B204	S	D2(B2)
Set Clock Comparator (p)	SCKC	B206	S	D2(B2)

MACHINE INSTRUCTIONS (Contd)

NAME	MNEMONIC	OP CODE	FORMAT	OPERANDS
Set CPU Timer (p)	SPT	B208	S	D2(B2)
Set Prefix (p)	SPX	B210	S	D2(B2)
Set Program Mask (n)	SPM	04	RR	R1
Set PSW Key from Address (p)	SPKA	B20A	S	D2(B2)
Set Storage Key (p)	SSK	08	RR	R1,R2
Set System Mask (p)	SSM	80	S	D2(B2)
Shift and Round Decimal (c)	SRP	F0	SS	D1(L1,B1),D2(B2),I3
Shift Left Double (c)	SLDA	8F	RS	R1,D2(B2)
Shift Left Double Logical	SLDL	8D	RS	R1,D2(B2)
Shift Left Single (c)	SLA	8B	RS	R1,D2(B2)
Shift Left Single Logical	SLL	89	RS	R1,D2(B2)
Shift Right Double (c)	SRDA	8E	RS	R1,D2(B2)
Shift Right Double Logical	SRDL	8C	RS	R1,D2(B2)
Shift Right Single (c)	SRA	8A	RS	R1,D2(B2)
Shift Right Single Logical	SRL	88	RS	R1,D2(B2)
Signal Processor (c,p)	SIGP	AE	RS	R1,R3,D2(B2)
Start I/O (c,p)	SIO	9C00	S	D2(B2)
Start I/O Fast Release (c,p)	SIOF	9C01	S	D2(B2)
Store	ST	50	RX	R1,D2(X2,B2)
Store Channel ID (c,p)	STIDC	B203	S	D2(B2)
Store Character	STC	42	RX	R1,D2(X2,B2)
Store Characters under Mask	STCM	BE	RS	R1,M3,D2(B2)
Store Clock (c)	STCK	B205	S	D2(B2)
Store Clock Comparator (p)	STCKC	B207	S	D2(B2)
Store Control (p)	STCTL	B6	RS	R1,R3,D2(B2)
Store CPU Address (p)	STAP	B212	S	D2(B2)
Store CPU ID (p)	STIDP	B202	S	D2(B2)
Store CPU Timer (p)	STPT	B209	S	D2(B2)
Store Halfword	STH	40	RX	R1,D2(X2,B2)
Store Multiple	STM	90	RS	R1,R3,D2(B2)
Store Prefix (p)	STPX	B211	S	D2(B2)
Store Then AND System Mask (p)	STNSM	AC	SI	D1(B1),I2
Store Then OR System Mask (p)	STOSM	AD	SI	D1(B1),I2
Subtract (c)	SR	1B	RR	R1,R2
Subtract (c)	S	5B	RX	R1,D2(X2,B2)
Subtract Decimal (c)	SP	FB	SS	D1(L1,B1),D2(L2,B2)
Subtract Halfword (c)	SH	4B	RX	R1,D2(X2,B2)
Subtract Logical (c)	SLR	1F	RR	R1,R2
Subtract Logical (c)	SL	5F	RX	R1,D2(X2,B2)
Supervisor Call	SVC	0A	RR	I
Test and Set (c)	TS	93	S	D2(B2)
Test Channel (c,p)	TCH	9F00	S	D2(B2)
Test I/O (p)	TIO	9D00	S	D2(B2)
Test under Mask (c)	TM	91	SI	D1(B1),I2
Translate	TR	DC	SS	D1(L,B1),D2(B2)
Translate and Test (c)	TRT	DD	SS	D1(L,B1),D2(B2)
Unpack	UNPK	F3	SS	D1(L1,B1),D2(L2,B2)
Write Direct (p)	WRD	84	SI	D1(B1),I2
Zero and Add Decimal (c)	ZAP	F8	SS	D1(L1,B1),D2(L2,B2)

Floating-Point Instructions

NAME	MNEMONIC	OP CODE	FORMAT	OPERANDS
Add Normalized, Extended (c,x)	AXR	36	RR	R1,R2
Add Normalized, Long (c)	ADR	2A	RR	R1,R2
Add Normalized, Long (c)	AD	6A	RX	R1,D2(X2,B2)
Add Normalized, Short (c)	AER	3A	RR	R1,R2
Add Normalized, Short (c)	AE	7A	RX	R1,D2(X2,B2)
Add Unnormalized, Long (c)	AWR	2E	RR	R1,R2
Add Unnormalized, Long (c)	AW	6E	RX	R1,D2(X2,B2)
Add Unnormalized, Short (c)	AUR	3E	RR	R1,R2
Add Unnormalized, Short (c)	AU	7E	RX	R1,D2(X2,B2)
Compare, Long (c)	CDR	29	RR	R1,R2
Compare, Long (c)	CD	69	RX	R1,D2(X2,B2)
Compare, Short (c)	CER	39	RR	R1,R2
Compare, Short (c)	CE	79	RX	R1,D2(X2,B2)
Divide, Long	DDR	2D	RR	R1,R2
Divide, Long	DD	6D	RX	R1,D2(X2,B2)
Divide, Short	DER	3D	RR	R1,R2
Divide, Short	DE	7D	RX	R1,D2(X2,B2)
Halve, Long	HDR	24	RR	R1,R2
Halve, Short	HER	34	RR	R1,R2
Load and Test, Long (c)	LTDR	22	RR	R1,R2
Load and Test, Short (c)	LTER	32	RR	R1,R2
Load Complement, Long (c)	LCDR	23	RR	R1,R2
Load Complement, Short (c)	LCER	33	RR	R1,R2
Load, Long	LDR	28	RR	R1,R2

Floating-Point Instructions (Contd)

NAME	MNEMONIC	OP CODE	FORMAT	OPERANDS
Load, Long	LD	68	RX	R1,D2(X2,B2)
Load Negative, Long (c)	LNDR	21	RR	R1,R2
Load Negative, Short (c)	LNER	31	RR	R1,R2
Load Positive, Long (c)	LPDR	20	RR	R1,R2
Load Positive, Short (c)	LPER	30	RR	R1,R2
Load Rounded, Extended to Long (x)	LRDR	25	RR	R1,R2
Load Rounded, Long to Short (x)	LRER	35	RR	R1,R2
Load, Short	LER	38	RR	R1,R2
Load, Short	LE	78	RX	R1,D2(X2,B2)
Multiply, Extended (x)	MXR	26	RR	R1,R2
Multiply, Long	MDR	2C	RR	R1,R2
Multiply, Long	MD	6C	RX	R1,D2(X2,B2)
Multiply, Long/Extended (x)	MXDR	27	RR	R1,R2
Multiply, Long/Extended (x)	MXD	67	RX	R1,D2(X2,B2)
Multiply, Short	MER	3C	RR	R1,R2
Multiply, Short	ME	7C	RX	R1,D2(X2,B2)
Store, Long	STD	60	RX	R1,D2(X2,B2)
Store, Short	STE	70	RX	R1,D2(X2,B2)
Subtract Normalized, Extended (c,x)	SXR	37	RR	R1,R2
Subtract Normalized, Long (c)	SDR	2B	RR	R1,R2
Subtract Normalized, Long (c)	SD	6B	RX	R1,D2(X2,B2)
Subtract Normalized, Short (c)	SER	3B	RR	R1,R2
Subtract Normalized, Short (c)	SE	7B	RX	R1,D2(X2,B2)
Subtract Unnormalized, Long (c)	SWR	2F	RR	R1,R2
Subtract Unnormalized, Long (c)	SW	6F	RX	R1,D2(X2,B2)
Subtract Unnormalized, Short (c)	SUR	3F	RR	R1,R2
Subtract Unnormalized, Short (c)	SU	7F	RX	R1,D2(X2,B2)

c. Condition code is set.
n. New condition code is loaded.
p. Privileged instruction.
x. Extended precision floating-point.

EXTENDED MNEMONIC INSTRUCTIONS[†]

Use	Extended Code* (RX or RR)	Meaning	Machine Instr.* (RX or RR)
General	B or BR	Unconditional Branch	BC or BCR 15,
	NOP or NOPR	No Operation	BC or BCR 0,
After	BH or *BHR*	Branch on A High	BC or BCR 2,
Compare	BL or *BLR*	Branch on A Low	BC or BCR 4,
Instructions	BE or *BER*	Branch on A Equal B	BC or BCR 8,
(A:B)	BNH or *BNHR*	Branch on A Not High	BC or BCR 13,
	BNL or *BNLR*	Branch on A Not Low	BC or BCR 11,
	BNE or *BNER*	Branch on A Not Equal B	BC or BCR 7,
After	BO or *BOR*	Branch on Overflow	BC or BCR 1,
Arithmetic	BP or *BPR*	Branch on Plus	BC or BCR 2,
Instructions	BM or *BMR*	Branch on Minus	BC or BCR 4,
	BNP or *BNPR*	Branch on Not Plus	BC or BCR 13,
	BNM or *BNMR*	Branch on Not Minus	BC or BCR 11,
	BNZ or *BNZR*	Branch on Not Zero	BC or BCR 7,
	BZ or *BZR*	Branch on Zero	BC or BCR 8,
After Test	BO or *BOR*	Branch if Ones	BC or BCR 1,
under Mask	BM or *BMR*	Branch if Mixed	BC or BCR 4,
Instruction	BZ or *BZR*	Branch if Zeros	BC or BCR 8,
	BNO or *BNOR*	Branch if Not Ones	BC or BCR 14,

*Second operand not shown; in all cases it is D2(X2,B2) for RX format or R2 for RR format.

[†]For OS/VS and DOS/VS, source: GC33-4010.

EDIT AND EDMK PATTERN CHARACTERS (in hex)

20—digit selector	40—blank	5C—asterisk
21—start of significance	4B—period	6B—comma
22—field separator	5B—dollar sign	C3D9—CR

CONDITION CODES

Condition Code Setting	0	1	2	3
Mask Bit Value	8	4	2	1
General Instructions				
Add, Add Halfword	zero	<zero	>zero	overflow
Add Logical	zero, no carry	not zero, no carry	zero, carry	not zero, carry
AND	zero	not zero	—	—
Compare, Compare Halfword	equal	1st op low	1st op high	—
Compare and Swap/Double	equal	not equal	—	—

CONDITION CODES (Contd)

Compare Logical	equal	1st op low	1st op high	—
Exclusive OR	zero	not zero	—	—
Insert Characters under Mask	all zero	1st bit one	1st bit zero	—
Load and Test	zero	<zero	>zero	—
Load Complement	zero	<zero	>zero	overflow
Load Negative	zero	<zero	—	—
Load Positive	zero	—	>zero	overflow
Move Long	count equal	count low	count high	overlap
OR	zero	not zero	—	—
Shift Left Double/Single	zero	<zero	>zero	overflow
Shift Right Double/Single	zero	<zero	>zero	—
Store Clock	set	not set	error	not oper
Subtract, Subtract Halfword	zero	<zero	>zero	overflow
Subtract Logical	—	not zero, no carry	zero, carry	not zero, carry
Test and Set	zero	one	—	—
Test under Mask	zero	mixed	—	ones
Translate and Test	zero	incomplete	complete	—

Decimal Instructions

Add Decimal	zero	<zero	>zero	overflow
Compare Decimal	equal	1st op low	1st op high	—
Edit, Edit and Mark	zero	<zero	>zero	—
Shift and Round Decimal	zero	<zero	>zero	overflow
Subtract Decimal	zero	<zero	>zero	overflow
Zero and Add	zero	<zero	>zero	overflow

Floating-Point Instructions

Add Normalized	zero	<zero	>zero	—
Add Unnormalized	zero	<zero	>zero	—
Compare	equal	1st op low	1st op high	—
Load and Test	zero	<zero	>zero	—
Load Complement	zero	<zero	>zero	—
Load Negative	zero	<zero	—	—

CONDITION CODES (Contd)

Load Positive	zero	—	>zero	—
Subtract Normalized	zero	<zero	>zero	—
Subtract Unnormalized	zero	<zero	>zero	—

Input/Output Instructions

Clear I/O	no oper in progress	CSW stored	chan busy	not oper
Halt Device	interruption pending	CSW stored	channel working	not oper
Halt I/O	interruption pending	CSW stored	burst op stopped	not oper
Start I/O, SIOF	successful	CSW stored	busy	not oper
Store Channel ID	ID stored	CSW stored	busy	not oper
Test Channel	available	CSW stored	interruption pending	burst mode	not oper
Test I/O	available	CSW stored	busy	not oper

System Control Instructions

Load Real Address	translation available	ST entry invalid	PT entry invalid	length violation
Reset Reference Bit	R=0, C=0	R=0, C=1	R=1, C=0	R=1, C=1
Set Clock	set	secure	—	not oper
Signal Processor	accepted	stat stored	busy	not oper

CNOP ALIGNMENT

DOUBLEWORD							
WORD				WORD			
HALFWORD		HALFWORD		HALFWORD		HALFWORD	
BYTE	BYTE	BYTE	BYTE	BYTE	BYTE	BYTE	BYTE
0,4		2,4		0,4		2,4	
0,8		2,8		4,8		6,8	

APPENDIX D

DOS AND OS JOB CONTROL

This appendix provides some typical examples of job control under DOS and OS.

DOS JOB CONTROL

Figure D-1 illustrates an example of conventional job control to assemble and execute a program under the Disk Operating System.

// JOB job-name	Job-name may be 1–8 characters.
// OPTION DECK,DUMP,LIST, LOG,XREF	DECK: Punch an assembled object deck (or NODECK).
	DUMP: Print contents of storage on abnormal execute error (or NODUMP).
	LIST: List the assembled program (or NOLIST).
	LOG: Print the job control statements (or NOLOG).
	XREF: Print a cross-reference of symbolic names after the assembly (or NOXREF).
ACTION MAP	Print a map of the "link-edited" program (NOMAP).
// EXEC ASSEMBLY	Load Assembler program into storage, begin assembly.

```
      .
      ·   (source program here)
      .
```

FIGURE D-1 (partial).

/*	Denotes end of assembly.
// EXEC LNKEDT	Perform link-edit—include input/output routines.
// EXEC	Load assembled program into storage, begin execution.
· (test data here)	
/*	Denotes end of data.
/&	Denotes end of job, return control to supervisor.

FIGURE D-1 Conventional DOS job control.

Larger DOS systems provide for cataloging commonly used job control on disk in the "Procedure Library." The preceding example of job control could be cataloged, for example, to provide for automatic assembly, link-edit, and execute, through the use of only a few job commands, as in Figure D-2.

* $$ JOB jobname	Job-name may be 1–8 characters.
// EXEC PROC=ASSEMBLY	The cataloged procedure "Assembly" contains assembly, link-edit and execute job statements.
· (source program here)	
·	Denotes end of assembly.
/*	
· (test data here)	
/*	Denotes end of data.
/&	Denotes end of job.
* $$ EOJ	

FIGURE D-2 DOS job control under cataloged procedure.

DOS JOB CONTROL FOR MAGNETIC TAPE

The job commands for magnetic tape are similar to those for the system reader and printer. However, tape files require additional information to provide greater control over the file. Under DOS, two additional job commands are LBLTYP and TLBL, and appear in the following sequence:

```
// LBLTYP TAPE
// EXEC LNKEDT
// TLBL filename . . .
```

The command / / LBLTYP TAPE informs the Linkage Editor to reserve 80 bytes ahead of the assembled object program for processing tape file labels. If your program normally loads at location X'8800', then with LBLTYP the first instruction will be at X'8850'.

The TLBL job command provides details of your file to IOCS, as follows:

/ / TLBL filename, 'file-ID', date, file-serial-number, volume-sequence number,

      (a)   (b)   (c)   (d)   (e)

file-sequence-number, generation-number, version-number

       (f)   (g)   (h)

(a) filename	The name of the DTFMT, the only required entry for TLBL.
(b) 'file-ID'	The file identifier in the file label, 1–17 characters.
(c) retention date	One of two formats: (1) yy/ddd—the date of retention, e.g. 95/030 tells IOCS to retain the file until Jan. 30, 1995; (2) dddd—for output files, you may code a retention period in days.
(d) file serial number	1–6 characters, the volume serial number for the first or only volume of the file.
(e) volume sequence number	1–4 digits for the volume number in a multi-volume file.
(f) file sequence number	1–4 digits for the file number in a multi-file volume.
(g) generation no.	1–4 digits for the generation number.
(h) version number	1–2 digits for the version number.

If you omit the entry for e, f, g or h, IOCS assumes '1' if output, and ignores if input.

FIGURE D-3 DOS job control for magnetic tape.

DOS JOB CONTROL FOR DIRECT ACCESS STORAGE DEVICES

Each extent for a DASD file requires two job control commands, DLBL and EXTENT, equivalent to the magnetic tape TLBL job command. Note that you may store a file on more than one extent. DLBL and EXTENT follow the LNKEDT command, coded as follows:

```
// EXEC LNKEDT
// DLBL filename . . .
// EXTENT symbolic-unit . . .
```

Following are the details for the DLBL and EXTENT commands:

// DLBL filename, 'file-ID', date, codes
          (a)   (b)   (c)   (d)

(a) filename	The name of the DTFSD, 1–7 characters.
(b) 'file-ID'	File-ID (within apostrophes), 1–44 characters. This is the first field of the format-1 label. You can code file-ID and optionally generation and version number. If you omit this entry, IOCS uses the filename.
(c) retention date	One of two formats: (1) dddd = retention period in days; and (2) yy/ddd = the date of retention, e.g., 95/030 means retain file until January 30, 1995. If you omit this entry, IOCS assumes 7 days.
(d) codes	The type of file label: SD—Sequential Disk; ISC—Index Sequential Create; ISE—Index Sequential Extend; DA—Direct Access. If you omit this entry, IOCS assumes SD.

// EXTENT symbolic-unit, serial-no., type, sequence-no., relative-track,
             (a)   (b)   (c)   (d)   (e)

number of tracks, split-cylinder track
          (f)   (g)

(a) symbolic unit	The symbolic unit SYSnnn for the file. If you omit this entry, IOCS assumes the unit from the preceding EXTENT, if any.
(b) serial number	The volume serial number for the volume. If you omit this entry, IOCS uses the number from the preceding EXTENT, if any.
(c) type	The type of extent. If omitted, IOCS assumes type 1. 1—Data area with no split cylinder; 2—Independent overflow area for IS; 4—Index area for IS; 8—Data area, split cylinder.
(d) sequence number	The sequence number (0–255) of this extent in a multi-extent file. Not required for SD and DA, but if used the extent begins with 0. For IS with a master index, the number begins with 0; otherwise IS files begin with extent 1.
(e) relative track	1–5 digits to indicate the sequential track number, relative to 0, where the extent begins. The formula to calculate the relative track is: $RT = \text{tracks per cylinder} \times \text{cyl. no} + \text{track no.}$ Example for a 3350 (30 tracks/cylinder), on cylinder-3, track-4: $RT = (30 \times 3) + 4 = 94$.
(f) number of tracks	1–5 digits to indicate the number of tracks allocated for the file on this extent.
(g) split cylinder track	Digits 0–19 to signify the upper track number for split cylinders in SD files. (There may be more than one SD file within a cylinder.)

Note: The LBLTYP job control entry used for tape is also required for *non-sequentual* disk. For example, if there are two non-sequential disk files in the program, the entry is // LBLTYP NSD(2).

FIGURE D-4 DOS job control for DASD.

OS JOB CONTROL

There are different versions of OS job control language. The following illustrates one version, providing for assembly, link-edit, and execution of test data. The program uses the system reader and a printer file, both of which require a DD (data definition) job command.

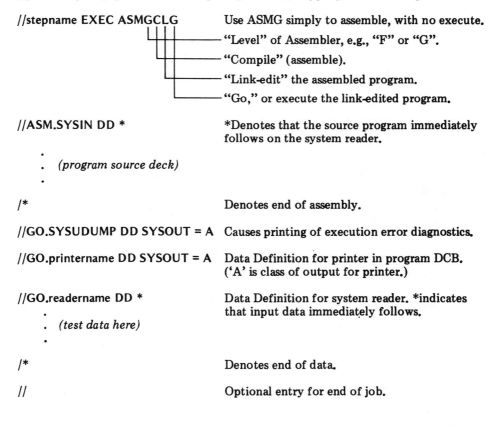

//jobname JOB [optional account#, acctg information, programmer name]

//stepname EXEC ASMGCLG   Use ASMG simply to assemble, with no execute.

            "Level" of Assembler, e.g., "F" or "G".

            "Compile" (assemble).

            "Link-edit" the assembled program.

            "Go," or execute the link-edited program.

//ASM.SYSIN DD *   *Denotes that the source program immediately follows on the system reader.

   .
   . *(program source deck)*
   .

/*   Denotes end of assembly.

//GO.SYSUDUMP DD SYSOUT = A   Causes printing of execution error diagnostics.

//GO.printername DD SYSOUT = A   Data Definition for printer in program DCB. ('A' is class of output for printer.)

//GO.readername DD *   Data Definition for system reader. *indicates that input data immediately follows.
   .
   . *(test data here)*
   .

/*   Denotes end of data.

//   Optional entry for end of job.

FIGURE D-5 Simple OS job control.

Following are descriptions of the OS EXEC and DD commands. As a convention, braces { } indicate a choice of one entry, square brackets [ ] indicate an optional entry from which you may choose one entry or none, and round brackets ( ) where they appear must be coded.

THE OS EXEC COMMAND. The general format for the OS EXEC command is the following:

```
//[stepname] EXEC  (PGM=programname
                   )PGM=*.stepname.ddname
                   )PGM=*.stepname.procstepname.ddname
                   ([PROC=]procedure-name
```

Other options for EXEC include ACCT (accounting information), COND, DPRTY (for MVT), PARM (parameter), RD (restart definition), REGION (for MVT), ROLL (for MVT), and TIME (to assign CPU time limit for a step).

```
ACCT[.procstepname]=(accounting information)

COND[.procstepname]=([(code,oper'r)
                      (code,oper'r,stepname)
                      (code,oper'r,stepname.procstepname)]

DPRTY[.procstepname]=(value1,value2)

PARM[.procstepname]=value

RD[.procstepname]=R or RNC or NC or NR

REGION[.procstepname]=(valueK[,value1K])

ROLL[.procstepname]=( (YES( (,YES( )
                      (NO ( (,NO  (

TIME[.procstepname]=(mins,secs)
```

THE OS DD COMMAND. The DD (data definition) command defines the name and property of each device that the program requires. Its general format is the following:

```
//ddname    DD operand
   procstepname. ddname
```

The operand for DD permits a variety of options, as follows:

```
[*    ]                                Define a data set in the
[DATA]                                     input stream.

[DCB=(attributes)                    ]  Completion of data
 DCB=(dsname[,attributes])              control block.
 DCB=(*.ddname[,attributes])
 DCB=(*.stepname.ddname[,attributes])
[DCB=(*.stepname.procstep.ddname[,attributes])]
```

```
[DDNAME=ddname]                          Postpones definition of
                                             data set

[DISP=( ⎡NEW⎤ ⎡,DELETE⎤ ⎡,DELETE ⎤ )     Assigns status, disposition,
        ⎢OLD⎥ ⎢,KEEP  ⎥ ⎢,KEEP   ⎥           and conditional
        ⎢SHR⎥ ⎢,PASS  ⎥ ⎢,CATLG  ⎥           disposition of the
        ⎣MOD⎦ ⎢,CATLG ⎥ ⎣,UNCATLG⎦           data set.
              ⎣,UNCATLG⎦

[DSNAME=⎧dsname                          ⎫ Abbreviated as DSN.
        ⎪dsname(areaname)                ⎪ Assign name to new or
        ⎪dsname(membername)              ⎪     existing data set.
        ⎪dsname(generation#)             ⎪
        ⎨&&dsname                        ⎬
        ⎪&&dsname(areaname)              ⎪
        ⎪&&dsname(membername)            ⎪
        ⎪*.ddname                        ⎪
        ⎪*.stepname.ddname               ⎪
        ⎩*.stepname.procstepname.ddname  ⎭

[FCB=(image-id ⎡,ALIGN ⎤)]               Forms control for 3211
               ⎣,VERIFY⎦                     printer.

[LABEL=([data set seq#][parameters]      Label information (see
                                             below).

[SPACE=(parameters)]                     Allocate space on a DASD
                                             for a new data set
                                             (see below).
[SYSOUT=(classname ⎡,programname⎤[,form#])[OUTLIM=no.]]
                   ⎣            ⎦         Route a data set through
                                             output job stream.

[UNIT=(parameters)]                      Unit information.

[VOLUME=(parameters)]                    Also VOL.  Provide
                                             information re the
                                             volume (see below).
```

The following describes in detail the parameters for LABEL, UNIT, and VOLUME.

```
LABEL=([dataset seq#]⎡,SL ⎤⎡,PASSWORD⎤⎡,IN ⎤ [,]⎡EXPDT=yymmdd⎤)
                     ⎢,SUL⎥⎣,NOPWREAD⎦⎣,OUT⎦    ⎣RETPD=nnnn  ⎦
                     ⎢,AL ⎥
                     ⎢,AUL⎥                        (EXPDT is expiry
                     ⎢,NSL⎥                        date and RETPD is
                     ⎢,NL ⎥                        retention period)
                     ⎣,BLP⎦

SPACE=( ⎧TRK      ⎫(,prim'y⎡,sec'y⎤⎡,dir'y⎤) ⎡,RLSE⎤⎡,CONTIG⎤[,ROUND])
        ⎨CYL      ⎬        ⎣,    ⎦⎣,index⎦ ⎣,   ⎦⎢,MXIG ⎥
        ⎩blocksize⎭                              ⎣,ALX  ⎦
```

```
SPACE=(ABSTR,(primary qty,address ,directory ))
                                 ,index

UNIT=(┌unit-address┐ ┌,count┐[,DEFER][,SEP=(ddname1, ...)]
      │device-type │ │,P    │
      └group-name  ┘ └,     ┘

UNIT=AFF=ddname

VOLUME=([PRIVATE] ┌,RETAIN┐ ┌,volseq#┐[,volcount][,]┌SER=serial#,...)┐)
(or VOL)          └,      ┘ └,       ┘                │REF=dsname       │
                                                     └REF=*.ddname     ┘
```

For REF, other entries are:

```
┌REF=*.stepname.ddname                 ┐
│REF=*.stepname.procstepname.ddname    │
└                                      ┘
```

Other DD operands are DUMMY (bypass I/O on a data set under BSAM and QSAM), DYNAM (request dynamic allocation under MVT with TSO), AFF=ddname (request channel separation), OUTLIM=number (limit the number of logical records to be included in an output data set), SPLIT= operand (assign space for a new data set on a DASD and to share cylinders), SUBALLOC=operand (request part of the space on a DASD that the job assigned earlier), and TERM=TS (inform the system that data is transferring to or from a time-sharing terminal).

SPECIAL MACROS: INIT, PUTPR, DEFIN, DEFPR, EOJ

Included in this appendix are the special macros used at the beginning of this text: INIT, PUTPR, DEFIN, and DEFPR. The macros are simple to implement and to use, and anyone is free to catalog them. Beginners often have trouble coding the regular full macros, making punctuation and spelling errors and omitting entries. The use of macros such as the ones in this appendix can avert a lot of initial coding mistakes and can free the beginner to concentrate on programming logic.

The INIT macro (used to establish base register addressability) requires versions for both DOS and OS (Figure E-1 and E-2). A further refinement (recommended) could include the DOS STXIT or OS SPIE macro for error recovery.

PUTPR (Figure E-3) generates two instructions, of the form:

```
MVI    PRINT,X'nn'    Insert control character
PUT    PRTR,PRINT     Print line
```

If the control character supplied is invalid, the macro-instruction generates write/space one line.

```
          MACRO
&INITZE   INIT
&INITZE   BALR   3,0                LOAD BASE REGISTER 3
          USING  *,3,4,5            ASSIGN BASE REGS 3,4 & 5
          LA     5,2048             LOAD X'800' (1/2 OF X'1000')
          LA     4,2048(3,5)        LOAD BASE PEG 4
          LA     5,2048(4,5)        LOAD BASE REG 5
          MEND
```

FIGURE E-1 DOS INIT macro.

```
          MACRO
&INITZE   INIT
&INITZE   SAVE    (14,12)                   SAVE REGS FOR SUPERVISOR
          BALR    3,0                       LOAD BASE REGISTER 3
          USING   *,3,4,5                   ASSIGN BASE REGS 3,4 & 5
          ST      13,SAVEAREA+4             SAVE ADDRESSES FOR RETURN
          LA      13,SAVEAREA                  TO SUPERVISOR
          LA      5,2048                    LOAD X'800' (1/2 OF X'1000')
          LA      4,2048(3,5)               LOAD BASE REG 4
          LA      5,2048(4,5)               LOAD BASE REG 5
          B       SAVEAREA+18*4
          SPACE
SAVEAREA  DC      18F'0'                    SAVEAREA FOR INTERRUPTS
          MEND
```

FIGURE E-2 OS INIT macro.

```
          MACRO
&WRITE    PUTPR   &FILE,&PRAREA,&CTLCHR
          LCLC    &CTL
.*
.VALAREA  AIF     ('&CTLCHR' NE 'WSP1').NEXT1    PRINT & SPACE 1?
&CTL      SETC    'X''09'''
          AGO     .NEXT9
.*
.NEXT1    AIF     ('&CTLCHR' NE 'WSP2').NEXT2    PRINT & SPACE 2?
&CTL      SETC    'X''11'''
          AGO     .NEXT9
.*
.NEXT2    AIF     ('&CTLCHR' NE 'WSP3').NEXT3    PRINT & SPACE 3?
&CTL      SETC    'X''19'''
          AGC     .NEXT9
.*
.NEXT3    AIF     ('&CTLCHR' NE 'SP1').NEXT4     SPACE 1, NO PRINT?
&CTL      SETC    'X''0B'''
          AGO     .NEXT9
.*
.NEXT4    AIF     ('&CTLCHR' NE 'SP2').NEXT5     SPACE 2, NO PRINT?
&CTL      SETC    'X''13'''
          AGO     .NEXT9
.*
.NEXT5    AIF     ('&CTLCHR' NE 'SP3').NEXT6     SPACE 3, NO PRINT?
&CTL      SETC    'X''1B'''
          AGO     .NEXT9
.*
.NEXT6    AIF     ('&CTLCHR' NE 'SK1').NEXT7     SKIP TO NEW PAGE?
&CTL      SETC    'X''8B'''
          AGO     .NEXT9
.*
.NEXT7    AIF     ('&CTLCHR' NE 'WSP0').NEXT8    PRINT & SPACE 0?
&CTL      SETC    'X''01'''
          AGO     .NEXT9
.*
.NEXT8    MNOTE   1,'INVALID PRINT CONTROL - DEFAULT TO WSP1'
&CTL      SETC    'X''09'''
.*
.NEXT9    ANOP
&WRITE    MVI     &PRAREA,&CTL              MOVE CTL CHAR TO PRINT
          PUT     &FILE,&PRAREA            *    & PRINT
.NEXT10   ANOP
          MEND
```

FIGURE E-3 PUTPR macro.

DEFIN and DEFPR define the system reader and the printer respectively, and assume a workarea for PUT and use of IBM machine code rather than the ASA control characters. DEFIN checks the validity of the supplied end-of-file address, a useful test. The DOS versions (Figure E-4 and E-5) generate DTFIN and DTFPR, and the OS versions (Figure E-6 and E-7) generate DCBs. The particular entries may vary slightly by installation.

```
          MACRO
&FILEIN   DEFIN &EOF
          AIF   (T'&EOF EQ 'I' OR T'&EOF EQ 'M').A10   EOF ADDRESS VALID?
          MNOTE 1,'EOF ADDRESS NOT DEFINED'   NO -
&EOF      CLOSE &FILEIN                      *   GENERATE EOF ROUTINE
          EOJ
.A10      ANOP
&FILEIN   DTFCD BLKSIZE=80,               DEFINE INPUT FILE            +
                DEVADDR=SYSIPT,        .                               +
                DEVICE=1442,                                           +
                EOFADDR=&EOF,                                          +
                IOAREA1=INBUFF1,                                       +
                IOAREA2=INBUFF2,                                       +
                TYPEFLE=INPUT,                                         +
                WORKA=YES
          SPACE
INBUFF1   DC    CL80' '                  INPUT BUFFER-1
INBUFF2   DC    CL80' '                  INPUT BUFFER-2
          MEND
```

FIGURE E-4 DOS DEFIN macro.

```
          MACRO
&PRFILE   DEFPR
&PRFILE   DTFPR BLKSIZE=133,             DEFINE OUTPUT FILE            +
                CTLCHR=YES,                                           +
                DEVADDR=SYSLST,                                       +
                DEVICE=3203,                                          +
                IOAREA1=PRBUFF1,                                      +
                IOAREA2=PRBUFF2,                                      +
                WORKA=YES
          SPACE
PRBUFF1   DC    CL133' '                 OUTPUT BUFFER-1
PRBUFF2   DC    CL133' '                 OUTPUT BUFFER-2
          SPACE
          MEND
```

FIGURE E-5 DOS DEFPR macro.

```
          MACRO
&INFILE   DEFIN &EOF
          AIF   (T'&EOF EQ 'I' OR T'&EOF EQ 'M').A10   VALID EOF ADDRESS?
          MNOTE 1,'EOF ADDRESS NOT DEFINED'   NO -
&EOF      CLOSE &INFILE                     *   GENERATE EOF RTNE
          EOJ
.A10      ANOP
&INFILE   DCB   DDNAME=SYSIN,            DEFINE INPUT FILE            +
                DEVD=DA,                                              +
                DSORG=PS,                                             +
                EODAD=&EOF,                                           +
                MACRF=(GM)
          MEND
```

FIGURE E-6 OS DEFIN macro.

```
            MACRO
&OUTFILE DEFPR
&OUTFILE DCB     DDNAME=SYSPRINT,      DEFINE OUTPUT FILE        +
                 DEVD=DA,                                        +
                 DSORG=PS,                                       +
                 RECFM=FBSM,                                     +
                 MACRF=(PM)
SYSPRINT EQU     &OUTFILE
            ENTRY SYSPRINT
            MEND
```

FIGURE E-7 OS DEFPR macro.

DOS already has a simple EOJ macro. The OS EOJ macro included in Figure E-8 is to generate the load savearea and return, to tie in with the OS INIT macro.

```
            MACRO
&LABEL   EOJ
&LABEL   L       13,SAVEAREA+4         END-OF-JOB,
            RETURN (14,12)             RETURN TO SUPERVISOR
            MEND
```

FIGURE E-8 OS EOJ macro.

APPENDIX F

370 CODE REPRESENTATION

CODE TRANSLATION TABLE

Dec.	Hex	Instruction (RR)	BCDIC	EBCDIC(1)	ASCII	EBCDIC Card Code	Binary
0	00			NUL	NUL	12-0-1-8-9	0000 0000
1	01			SOH	SOH	12-1-9	0000 0001
2	02			STX	STX	12-2-9	0000 0010
3	03			ETX	ETX	12-3-9	0000 0011
4	04	SPM		PF	EOT	12-4-9	0000 0100
5	05	BALR		HT	ENQ	12-5-9	0000 0101
6	06	BCTR		LC	ACK	12-6-9	0000 0110
7	07	BCR		DEL	BEL	12-7-9	0000 0111
8	08	SSK			BS	12-8-9	0000 1000
9	09	ISK			HT	12-1-8-9	0000 1001
10	0A	SVC		SMM	LF	12-2-8-9	0000 1010
11	0B			VT	VT	12-3-8-9	0000 1011
12	0C			FF	FF	12-4-8-9	0000 1100
13	0D			CR	CR	12-5-8-9	0000 1101
14	0E	MVCL		SO	SO	12-6-8-9	0000 1110
15	0F	CLCL		SI	SI	12-7-8-9	0000 1111
16	10	LPR		DLE	DLE	12-11-1-8-9	0001 0000
17	11	LNR		DC1	DC1	11-1-9	0001 0001
18	12	LTR		DC2	DC2	11-2-9	0001 0010
19	13	LCR		TM	DC3	11-3-9	0001 0011
20	14	NR		RES	DC4	11-4-9	0001 0100
21	15	CLR		NL	NAK	11-5-9	0001 0101
22	16	OR		BS	SYN	11-6-9	0001 0110
23	17	XR		IL	ETB	11-7-9	0001 0111
24	18	LR		CAN	CAN	11-8-9	0001 1000
25	19	CR		EM	EM	11-1-8-9	0001 1001
26	1A	AR		CC	SUB	11-2-8-9	0001 1010
27	1B	SR		CU1	ESC	11-3-8-9	0001 1011
28	1C	MR		IFS	FS	11-4-8-9	0001 1100
29	1D	DR		IGS	GS	11-5-8-9	0001 1101
30	1E	ALR		IRS	RS	11-6-8-9	0001 1110
31	1F	SLR		IUS	US	11-7-8-9	0001 1111
32	20	LPDR		DS	SP	11-0-1-8-9	0010 0000
33	21	LNDR		SOS	!	0-1-9	0010 0001
34	22	LTDR		FS	"	0-2-9	0010 0010
35	23	LCDR			#	0-3-9	0010 0011
36	24	HDR		BYP	$	0-4-9	0010 0100
37	25	LRDR		LF	%	0-5-9	0010 0101
38	26	MXR		ETB	&	0-6-9	0010 0110
39	27	MXDR		ESC	'	0-7-9	0010 0111

CODE TRANSLATION TABLE (Contd)

Dec.	Hex	Instruction (RX)	BCDIC	EBCDIC(1)	ASCII	EBCDIC Card Code	Binary
40	28	LDR			(	0-8-9	0010 1000
41	29	CDR			)	0-1-8-9	0010 1001
42	2A	ADR		SM	*	0-2-8-9	0010 1010
43	2B	SDR		CU2	+	0-3-8-9	0010 1011
44	2C	MDR			,	0-4-8-9	0010 1100
45	2D	DDR		ENQ	-	0-5-8-9	0010 1101
46	2E	AWR		ACK	.	0-6-8-9	0010 1110
47	2F	SWR		BEL	/	0-7-8-9	0010 1111
48	30	LPER			0	12-11-0-1-8-9	0011 0000
49	31	LNER			1	1-9	0011 0001
50	32	LTER		SYN	2	2-9	0011 0010
51	33	LCER			3	3-9	0011 0011
52	34	HER		PN	4	4-9	0011 0100
53	35	LRER		RS	5	5-9	0011 0101
54	36	AXR		UC	6	6-9	0011 0110
55	37	SXR		EOT	7	7-9	0011 0111
56	38	LER			8	8-9	0011 1000
57	39	CER			9	1-8-9	0011 1001
58	3A	AER			:	2-8-9	0011 1010
59	3B	SER		CU3	;	3-8-9	0011 1011
60	3C	MER		DC4	<	4-8-9	0011 1100
61	3D	DER		NAK	=	5-8-9	0011 1101
62	3E	AUR		SUB	>	6-8-9	0011 1110
63	3F	SUR			?	7-8-9	0011 1111
64	40	STH	Sp	Sp	@	no punches	0100 0000
65	41	LA			A	12-0-1-9	0100 0001
66	42	STC			B	12-0-2-9	0100 0010
67	43	IC			C	12-0-3-9	0100 0011
68	44	EX			D	12-0-4-9	0100 0100
69	45	BAL			E	12-0-5-9	0100 0101
70	46	BCT			F	12-0-6-9	0100 0110
71	47	BC			G	12-0-7-9	0100 0111
72	48	LH			H	12-0-8-9	0100 1000
73	49	CH			I	12-1-8	0100 1001
74	4A	AH	¢	¢	J	12-2-8	0100 1010
75	4B	SH	.	.	K	12-3-8	0100 1011
76	4C	MH	)	<	L	12-4-8	0100 1100
77	4D		[	(	M	12-5-8	0100 1101
78	4E	CVD	<	+	N	12-6-8	0100 1110
79	4F	CVB	‡	|	O	12-7-8	0100 1111

FIGURE F-1 (partial).

CODE TRANSLATION TABLE (Contd)

Dec.	Hex	Instruction and Format	BCDIC	EBCDIC(1)	ASCII	EBCDIC Card Code	Binary
80	50	ST	& +	&	&	P	12	0101 0000
81	51					Q	12-11-1-9	0101 0001
82	52					R	12-11-2-9	0101 0010
83	53					S	12-11-3-9	0101 0011
84	54	N				T	12-11-4-9	0101 0100
85	55	CL·				U	12-11-5-9	0101 0101
86	56	O				V	12-11-6-9	0101 0110
87	57	X				W	12-11-7-9	0101 0111
88	58	L	.			X	12-11-8-9	0101 1000
89	59	C				Y	11-1-8	0101 1001
90	5A	A		!	!	Z	11-2-8	0101 1010
91	5B	S	$	$	$	[	11-3-8	0101 1011
92	5C	M	•	•	•	\	11-4-8	0101 1100
93	5D	D	]	)	)	]	11-5-8	0101 1101
94	5E	AL	;	:	:	¬ ^	11-6-8	0101 1110
95	5F	SL	Δ	¬	¬	_	11-7-8	0101 1111
96	60	STD	-	-	-	`	11	0110 0000
97	61		/	/	/	a	0-1	0110 0001
98	62					b	11-0-2-9	0110 0010
99	63					c	11-0-3-9	0110 0011
100	64					d	11-0-4-9	0110 0100
101	65					e	11-0-5-9	0110 0101
102	66					f	11-0-6-9	0110 0110
103	67	MXD				g	11-0-7-9	0110 0111
104	68	LD				h	11-0-8-9	0110 1000
105	69	CD				i	0-1-8	0110 1001
106	6A	AD		!		j	12-11	0110 1010
107	6B	SD	,	,	,	k	0-3-8	0110 1011
108	6C	MD	%(	%	%	l	0-4-8	0110 1100
109	6D	DD	Y	_	_	m	0-5-8	0110 1101
110	6E	AW	\	>	>	n	0-6-8	0110 1110
111	6F	SW	⋆⋆	?	?	o	0-7-8	0110 1111
112	70	STE				p	12-11-0	0111 0000
113	71					q	12-11-0-1-9	0111 0001
114	72					r	12-11-0-2-9	0111 0010
115	73					s	12-11-0-3-9	0111 0011
116	74					t	12-11-0-4-9	0111 0100
117	75					u	12-11-0-5-9	0111 0101
118	76					v	12-11-0-6-9	0111 0110
119	77					w	12-11-0-7-9	0111 0111
120	78	LE				x	12-11-0-8-9	0111 1000
121	79	CE		`		y	1-8	0111 1001
122	7A	AE	⊃	:	:	z	2-8	0111 1010
123	7B	SE	# •	#	#	{	3-8	0111 1011
124	7C	ME	@ '	@	@	!	4-8	0111 1100
125	7D	DE	:	'	'	}	5-8	0111 1101
126	7E	AU	>	=	=	~	6-8	0111 1110
127	7F	SU	√	"	"	DEL	7-8	0111 1111
128	80	SSM -S					12-0-1-8	1000 0000
129	81			a	a		12-0-1	1000 0001
130	82	LPSW -S		b	b		12-0-2	1000 0010
131	83	Diagnose		c	c		12-0-3	1000 0011
132	84	WRD }SI		d	d		12-0-4	1000 0100
133	85	RDD		e	e		12-0-5	1000 0101
134	86	BXH		f	f		12-0-6	1000 0110
135	87	BXLE		g	g		12-0-7	1000 0111
136	88	SRL		h	h		12-0-8	1000 1000
137	89	SLL		i	i		12-0-9	1000 1001
138	8A	SRA }RS					12-0-2-8	1000 1010
139	8B	SLA			{		12-0-3-8	1000 1011
140	8C	SRDL			≤		12-0-4-8	1000 1100
141	8D	SLDL			(		12-0-5-8	1000 1101
142	8E	SRDA			•		12-0-6-8	1000 1110
143	8F	SLDA			+		12-0-7-8	1000 1111
144	90	STM					12-11-1-8	1001 0000
145	91	TM		j	j		12-11-1	1001 0001
146	92	MVI }SI		k	k		12-11-2	1001 0010
147	93	TS -S		l	l		12-11-3	1001 0011
148	94	NI		m	m		12-11-4	1001 0100
149	95	CLI		n	n		12-11-5	1001 0101
150	96	OI }SI		o	o		12-11-6	1001 0110
151	97	XI		p	p		12-11-7	1001 0111
152	98	LM -RS		q	q		12-11-8	1001 1000
153	99			r	r		12-11-9	1001 1001
154	9A						12-11-2-8	1001 1010
155	9B				}		12-11-3-8	1001 1011

CODE TRANSLATION TABLE (Contd)

Dec.	Hex	Instruction (SS)	BCDIC	EBCDIC(1)	ASCII	EBCDIC Card Code	Binary
156	9C	SIO, SIOF }SI		¤			12-11-4-8	1001 1100
157	9D	TIO, CLRIO			)		12-11-5-8	1001 1101
158	9E	HIO, HDV }S		±			12-11-6-8	1001 1110
159	9F	TCH		▪			12-11-7-8	1001 1111
160	A0			-			11-0-1-8	1010 0000
161	A1		~	°			11-0-1	1010 0001
162	A2		s	s			11-0-2	1010 0010
163	A3		t	t			11-0-3	1010 0011
164	A4		u	u			11-0-4	1010 0100
165	A5		v	v			11-0-5	1010 0101
166	A6		w	w			11-0-6	1010 0110
167	A7		x	x			11-0-7	1010 0111
168	A8		y	y			11-0-8	1010 1000
169	A9		z	z			11-0-9	1010 1001
170	AA			L			11-0-2-8	1010 1010
171	AB			L			11-0-3-8	1010 1011
172	AC	STNSM }SI		⌐			11-0-4-8	1010 1100
173	AD	STOSM		[			11-0-5-8	1010 1101
174	AE	SIGP -RS		≥			11-0-6-8	1010 1110
175	AF	MC -SI		▪			11-0-7-8	1010 1111
176	B0			°			12-11-0-1-8	1011 0000
177	B1	LRA -RX		1			12-11-0-1	1011 0001
178	B2	See below		2			12-11-0-2	1011 0010
179	B3			3			12-11-0-3	1011 0011
180	B4			4			12-11-0-4	1011 0100
181	B5			5			12-11-0-5	1011 0101
182	B6	STCTL }RS		6			12-11-0-6	1011 0110
183	B7	LCTL		7			12-11-0-7	1011 0111
184	B8			8			12-11-0-8	1011 1000
185	B9			9			12-11-0-9	1011 1001
186	BA	CS }RS		⌐			12-11-0-2-8-9	1011 1010
187	BB	CDS		⌐			12-11-0-3-8-9	1011 1011
188	BC			¬			12-11-0-4-8-9	1011 1100
189	BD	CLM		]			12-11-0-5-8-9	1011 1101
190	BE	STCM -RS		±			12-11-0-6-8-9	1011 1110
191	BF	ICM }RS		▬			12-11-0-7-8-9	1011 1111
192	C0		?	{	{		12-0	1100 0000
193	C1		A	A	A		12-1	1100 0001
194	C2		B	B	B		12-2	1100 0010
195	C3		C	C	C		12-3	1100 0011
196	C4		D	D	D		12-4	1100 0100
197	C5		E	E	E		12-5	1100 0101
198	C6		F	F	F		12-6	1100 0110
199	C7		G	G	G		12-7	1100 0111
200	C8		H	H	H		12-8	1100 1000
201	C9		I	I	I		12-9	1100 1001
202	CA						12-0-2-8-9	1100 1010
203	CB						12-0-3-8-9	1100 1011
204	CC			ʃ			12-0-4-8-9	1100 1100
205	CD						12-0-5-8-9	1100 1101
206	CE			¥			12-0-6-8-9	1100 1110
207	CF						12-0-7-8-9	1100 1111
208	D0		!	}			11-0	1101 0000
209	D1	MVN	J	J	J		11-1	1101 0001
210	D2	MVC	K	K	K		11-2	1101 0010
211	D3	MVZ	L	L	L		11-3	1101 0011
212	D4	NC	M	M	M		11-4	1101 0100
213	D5	CLC	N	N	N		11-5	1101 0101
214	D6	OC	O	O	O		11-6	1101 0110
215	D7	XC	P	P	P		11-7	1101 0111
216	D8		Q	Q	Q		11-8	1101 1000
217	D9		R	R	R		11-9	1101 1001
218	DA						12-11-2-8-9	1101 1010
219	DB						12-11-3-8-9	1101 1011
220	DC	TR					12-11-4-8-9	1101 1100
221	DD	TRT					12-11-5-8-9	1101 1101
222	DE	ED					12-11-6-8-9	1101 1110
223	DF	EDMK					12-11-7-8-9	1101 1111
224	E0		+	\			0-2-8	1110 0000
225	E1						11-0-1-9	1110 0001
226	E2		S	S	S		0-2	1110 0010
227	E3		T	T	T		0-3	1110 0011
228	E4		U	U	U		0-4	1110 0100
229	E5		V	V	V		0-5	1110 0101
230	E6		W	W	W		0-6	1110 0110
231	E7		X	X	X		0-7	1110 0111

FIGURE F-1 (partial).

CODE TRANSLATION TABLE (Contd)

Dec.	Hex	Instruction and Format	Graphics and Controls BCDIC	EBCDIC(1)	ASCII	EBCDIC Card Code	Binary
232	E8		Y	Y	Y	0-8	1110 1000
233	E9		Z	Z	Z	0-9	1110 1001
234	EA					11-0-2-8-9	1110 1010
235	EB					11-0-3-8-9	1110 1011
236	EC				⊣	11-0-4-8-9	1110 1100
237	ED					11-0-5-8-9	1110 1101
238	EE					11-0-6-8-9	1110 1110
239	EF					11-0-7-8-9	1110 1111
240	F0	SRP	0	0	0	0	1111 0000
241	F1	MVO	1	1	1	1	1111 0001
242	F2	PACK	2	2	2	2	1111 0010
243	F3	UNPK	3	3	3	3	1111 0011

CODE TRANSLATION TABLE (Contd)

Dec.	Hex	Instruction (SS)	Graphics and Controls BCDIC	EBCDIC(1)	ASCII	EBCDIC Card Code	Binary
244	F4		4	4	4	4	1111 0100
245	F5		5	5	5	5	1111 0101
246	F6		6	6	6	6	1111 0110
247	F7		7	7	7	7	1111 0111
248	F8	ZAP	8	8	8	8	1111 1000
249	F9	CP	9	9	9	9	1111 1001
250	FA	AP				12-11-0-2-8-9	1111 1010
251	FB	SP				12-11-0-3-8-9	1111 1011
252	FC	MP				12-11-0-4-8-9	1111 1100
253	FD	DP				12-11-0-5-8-9	1111 1101
254	FE					12-11-0-6-8-9	1111 1110
255	FF			EO		12-11-0-7-8-9	1111 1111

FIGURE F-1 370 code representation.

SUMMARY OF ASSEMBLER DECLARATIVES

Type	Format	Implied length	Maximum length	Alignment	Truncation/ padding
A	address	4	4	word	left
B	binary digits	—	256	byte	left
C	character[1]	—	256	byte	right
D	floating-point — — long	8	8	doubleword	right
E	floating-point — — short	4	8	word	right
F	fixed-point binary	4	8	word	left
H	fixed-point binary	2	8	halfword	left
L	floating-point — — extended	16	16	doubleword	right
P	packed decimal	—	16	byte	left
Q	symbol naming a DXD or DSECT[2]	4	4	word	left
S	address in base/ displacement format	2	2	halfword	—
V	external defined address	4	4	word	left
X	hexadecimal digits[1]	—	256	byte	left
Y	address	2	2	halfword	left
Z	zoned decimal	—	16	byte	left

[1]For DS, C and X type declaratives may have a defined length up to 65,535. [2]Q-type declaratives are available only for F-level Assembler.

SUMMARY OF ASSEMBLER DIRECTIVES

The following lists the various Assembler directives according to general category. Directives indicated by an asterisk (*) are available only under OS/VS or VM.

Program sectioning and linking:

COM	Identify beginning of a common control section.
CSECT	Identify start or resumption of a control section.
CXD*	Cumulative length of an external dummy section.
DSECT	Identify start or resumption of a dummy control section.
DXD*	Define an external dummy section.
ENTRY	Identify an entry point, referenced in another assembly.
EXTRN	Identify an external symbol, defined in another assembly.
START	Define start of the first control section in a program.
WXTRN	Identify a weak external symbol (suppresses search of libraries).

Base register assignment:

DROP	Discontinue use of a base register.
USING	Indicate sequence of base register(s) to use.

Listing Control:

EJECT	Start assembled listing on next page.

PRINT	Control assembled listing (operands are ON/OFF, GEN/NOGEN, and DATA/NODATA.
SPACE	Space n lines in the assembled listing.
TITLE	Provide a title at the top of each page of listing.

Program control:

CNOP	Conditional no-operation (see the section following).
COPY	Copy code from an Assembler source library.
END	Signal end of an assembly module.
EQU	Equate name or number to a symbol.
ICTL	Define the format of following source statements.
ISEQ	Start or end sequencing of source input statements.
LTORG	Begin literal pool.
OPSYN*	Equate a name operation code with an operand op-code.
ORG	Set the location counter.
POP*	Recover status of PRINT/USING directives saved by last PUSH.
PUNCH	Provide output on cards.
PUSH*	Save current PRINT/USING status.
REPRO	Reproduce the following card.

Macro definition:

MACRO	Begin a macro definition.
MEND	Terminate a macro definition.
MEXIT	Exit from a macro definition.
MNOTE	Display a macro note.

Conditional assembly:

ACTR	Set loop counter for conditional assembly.
AGO	Branch to sequence symbol.
AIF	Conditional branch to sequence symbol.
ANOP	Assembly no-operation.
GBLA	Define global SETA symbol.
GBLB	Define global SETB symbol.
GBLC	Define global SETC symbol.
LCLA	Define local SETA symbol.
LCLB	Define local SETB symbol.
LCLC	Define local SETC symbol.
SETA	Set an arithmetic variable symbol.
SETB	Set a binary variable symbol.
SETC	Set a character variable symbol.

Relevant IBM reference manuals:

GC33-4010 OS/VS-DOS/VS-VM/370 Assembler Language
GC24-3414 DOS Assembler Language

Following is a description of the CNOP Assembler directive which is included here for convenience.

CNOP—Conditional No-Operation. The purpose of CNOP is to enable you to align instructions on integral boundaries. You would most likely use CNOP where you have local declaratives defined at the end of a subroutine, and want to ensure that the first instruction for the next subroutine begins on an even boundary.

There are six variations on CNOP depending on whether you want alignment based on fullword or doubleword boundaries. Operand-2 designates fullword (4) or doubleword (8) alignment. Operand-1 determines the particular location in the fullword or doubleword. To force the correct alignment, CNOP generates from one to three NOP instructions, each two bytes long.

Fullword alignment:

```
CNOP  0,4        On fullword boundary.
CNOP  2,4        On address aligned on halfword boundary in middle of
                 aligned fullword.
```

Doubleword alignment:

```
CNOP  0,8        On doubleword boundary.
CNOP  2,8        On second halfword immediately following doubleword
                 boundary.
CNOP  4,8        On fullword boundary in middle of aligned doubleword.
CNOP  6,8        On fourth halfword boundary in aligned doubleword.
```

A common requirement for alignment on a fullword boundary is simply CNOP 0,4. If the Assembler location counter was at X'762', then this CNOP would generate one NOP so that the following instruction begins at X'764'. Note, however, that if the location counter is at an odd-numbered address, the Assembler forces normal alignment before processing the CNOP.

ANSWERS TO SELECTED PROBLEMS

```
0-5.   (a) 14.
0-14.  (a) E;      (c) B3.
0-15.  (a) A;      (c) 18;     (e) 113.
0-16.  (a) 15;     (c) 45;     (e) 128.
0-17.  (a) 24      (c) AAA     (e) 437B
            6          555         2A4B
           2A         FFF         6DC6
```

1-2.   An asterisk in column 1 means a comment and in column 72 would mean continuation.

1-3.   The following are invalid: (b) no hyphen; (c) maximum is eight characters; (e) no blanks; (f) asterisk; (g) leading digit.

1-4.   The START Directive.

1-5.   During assembly.

1-8.   With PRINT GEN.

1-11. Location counter.

2-3.   Condition code is 1 for minus.

```
2-4.   (a) 370   F3F7F0   11110011 11110111 11110000
       (c) Sam   E28194   11100010 10000001 10010100 (lowercase)
       (e) PAT   D7C1E3   11010111 11000001 11100011
```

```
3-1.   (a) OUT     DS    CL80
       (b)         DS    0CL100
3-2.   (a) ASTER   DC    C'*'
       (c)         DC    C'SAM''S'
3-3.   (a)         MVC   B+1(2),C
       (c)         MVC   B+2(3),A
       (e)         MVC   A(6),A+1
3-4    (a)         CLC   E,F
                   BNH   G40
```

3-5.   (a) low; (c) low; (e) high.

```
4-1.   (a)         MVN  HAM,TOAST      hex = C9C2D4, char = IBM.
4-2.   (a) P = 12 3C
       (c) Q = 01 02 3C
       (g) Q = 00 12 3D
       (j) Q = 01 23 9C (same as i)
```

4-3.   (a) low; (c) data exception.

```
5-1.   Any character.

5-2.   (a) ED2    DC   X'4020205B2020214B202060'
              MVC  PRINT+20(L'ED2),ED2
              ED   PRINT+20(L'ED2),AMT2

5-5.   (a) PROD   DS   PL5
              ZAP  PROD,A
              MP   PROD,B
              AP   PROD,PROD+4(1)      } or SRP PROD,63,5
              MVO  PROD,PROD(4)        }

       (c) PROD   DS   PL6
              ZAP  PROD,B
              MP   PROD,D
              SRP  PROD,62.5           (or MVO/AP/MOV)

5-6.   (a) RESULT DS   PL5
              ZAP  RESULT,B
              SRP  RESULT,1,0          (or MP by =P'10')
              DP   RESULT,A            (two decimal places)
              SRP  RESULT(3),63,5      (or AP/MVO)

       (c) RESULT DS   PL6
              ZAP  RESULT,D
              DP   RESULT,A            (3 decimal places)
              SRP  RESULT(4),62,5      (or MVO/AP/MVO)
```

6-4.   (a) 05 9A; (c) 95 E7 2226; (e) F8 10 2A2D 2C44.

6-5.   (a) Since a reference in machine code to a register is four bits long, the range is 0 through F (0 through 15).

6-6.   START simply sets the location counter at assembly-time, and has no effect on the execution loading point.

```
6-11.  (a)          BE   C90
       (c)          BNL  E90
6-12.  (a)          B    B30          47 F0 3A38
       (c)          BAL  5,B30        47 50 3A38
```

6-14. BALR loads the address of the next instruction (BR) in register-8. BR then branches to the address in register-8 -- to itself. The BR becomes an endless loop.

7-2.   Only the Supervisor can execute a privileged instruction.

7-3.   Permits overlapping input/output with processing.

```
7-5.             MVI  PRINT,X'19'
                 PUT  PRTR,PRINT
```

8-3.   BAL 3,P10PAGE destroys the address in base register-3.

8-4.   The subroutine returns to the address in the base register, causing the program to restart at its initialization.

```
9-1.   (a) 00110   (c) 01000
           00101       11011
           -----       -----
           01011       00011
           -----       -----
```

9-3.   (a) Loads contents of BINA into register-6.
       (b) Operand-2 should reference a doubleword.
       (d) Operand-2 is a displacement, as 5000(0,0), but the maximum displacement is 4095.

(h) Operand-1 is a displacement that references storage
location 12 -- the result is a protection exception on
computers with that feature.
(l) Loads the first two bytes of BINA into register-8.

9-4. (a) Subtracts 9 from register-8.
(c) Subtracts the contents of register-9 from register-8.
(e) Compares the contents of register-9 to the contents of
BINB.
(f) Subtracts the first two bytes of BINB from register-8.
(j) Multiplies the contents of register-9 by register-9.
(l) Shifts left nine bits the contents of registers 8 and 9.

9-6. (a) Multiplies the contents of register-5 by itself -- the
result is 225.
(c) Shifts the contents of BINA two digits to the left -- in
effect, multiplies by 4.

9-7. (a) Divides the contents of BINA into the contents of
register-9.

10-1. 4500 + 4000 + 7 = X'8507'.
10-2. Adds AMOUNT to TOTAL.
10-5. (a) Loops 20 times; register-4 contains 40.
10-6. (a) Decrements register-5 by 1 (becomes 9), and since the
result is nonzero, branches to W30.
(b) Executes the BCT 25 times until register-8 is
decremented to zero.

11-2. (a) AND BYTE,=X'0F'
(b) OR BYTE,=X'F0'

11-4. The following defines the name, address, and city:

```
NAMADDR   DS     0CL63
          DC     X'0D'                      Length of name
          DC     C'JP PROGRAMMER'
          DC     X'13'                      Length of address
          DC     C'3700 WILLINGDON AVE'
          DC     X'07'                      Length of city
          DC     C'BURNABY'

PRINT     DC     CL133' '
          SR     1,1                        Clear register-1
          LA     9,NAMADDR                  Init address of
          LA     10,PRINT+20                name & print area
LOOP      IC     1,0(0,9)                   Get length
          LR     8,1                        Save length
          BCTR   1,0                        Decrement length
          STC    1,MOVE+1                   Set length of MVC
          LA     9,1(0,9)                   Increment address
MOVE      MVC    0(0,10),0(9)               Move field to print
          AR     9,8                        Add length to addr
          AH     10,=H'30'                  Incr print address
          C      10,=A(PRINT+30)            Past 3rd field?
          BNH    LOOP                       yes -- print
```

```
11-6.    TRANTAB   DC    75X'40',X'4B'
                   DC    31X'40',X'63'
                   DC    85X'40',X'313283348586878889'
                   DC    07X'40',X'919293949596979899'
                   DC    08X'40',X'A2A3A4A5A6A7A8A9'
                   DC    06X'40',X'F0F1F2F3F4F5F6F7F8F9'
                   DC    06X'40'
```

11-9. Assume that register-9 contains eight hex digits to be
converted and printed.

```
         BYTE      DS    C
         TABLE     DC    X'F0F1F2F3F4F5F6F7F8F9'
                   DC    X'C1C2C3C4C5C6'

                   LH    10,=H'8'            Initialize count
                   LA    7,PRINT+11          & address of PRINT
         LOOP      SR    8,8                 Clear register-8
                   SLDL  8,4                 Shift digit into 8
                   STC   8,BYTE              Store digit as 0n
                   TR    BYTE,TABLE          Translate to char
                   MVC   0(1,7),BYTE         Move to print
                   AH    7,=H'1'             Incr print address
                   BCT   10,LOOP             Loop if not 8 times
```

12-2. (a) Number of bytes per inch; (c) a gap that separates
        blocks of records; (d) number of records per block.
12-3. Advantage: more records on tape and faster input/output;
disadvantage: larger program space for buffer(s).
12-5. (a) EOV indicates end of data on the reel and continues on
another reel; EOF indicates end of the data file.
12-8.   total:
```
Block 1: |4|4|  325   |4|  414   |                          752
Block 2: |4|4|    502 |4|  334   |4|  293   |              1195
Block 3: |4|4|    504 |                                     512
```

13-3. Reduces the disk access motion for sequential processsing.
13-5. CKD stores records of any length by tracks and cylinder;
FBA stores records in fixed length blocks.
13-9. The Volume Table of Contents (VTOC).
13-10. (a) Blocks per track = $\dfrac{19{,}254}{185 + 6(300)} = \dfrac{19{,}254}{1{,}985} = 9.69 = 9.$

Records per track = 9 x 6 = 54.

(b) Blocks per track = $\dfrac{19{,}254}{185 + 82 + 10 + 1800} = 9.27 = 9.$

Records per track = 9 x 6 = 54.

14-1. (a) If the cylinder index occupies more than four tracks, a
master index reduces the time required to search the
cylnder index.

15-1. KSDS permits sequential and direct processing by key; ESDS
permits sequential and direct processing by RBA; RRDS
permits sequential and direct processing by relative record
number.
15-3. (a) 285/315 and 380/495.

```
15-5.  DEFINE CLUSTER
          (NAME(CUSTOMER.FILE) -
          BLOCKS(no.) -
          VOLUME(name) -
          NONINDEXED -
          RECORDSIZE(100) ) -
        DATA (NAME(data.name) )
15-7.  CUSVSIN  ACB  DDNAME=CUSTVS,            +
                     EXLST=EOFCUS,             +
                     MACRF=(ADR,SEQ,IN)
15-8.  RPLCUSIN RPL  ACB=CUSVSIN,              +
                     AREA=CUSVSREC,            +
                     AREALEN=100,              +
                     OPTCD=(ADR,SEQ,NUP)
```

16-1. (a) The literal should be =CL5' '.
     (b) The literal should be =5C'0'.
     (c) Tests only the first byte of HOURSIN; change to (a).
     (d) Needs an explicit length: HOURSIN+3(2).

16-2. (a) Data Exception; HOURTOT should be a DC.
     (b) Decimal Overflow: PAGENO should be PL3.
     (c) Data Exception: To test a zoned field, use CLC and a character literal.
     (d) Use CP.
     (e) Decimal Divide Exception (divides by zero).

16-3. The BAL to C10CALC loads register-6 but returns via register-5. Since register-5 contains the return address for the BAL to H10HDG, the program executes C10CALC endlessly.

16-4. (a) OPEN should specify PRTR.

16-5. (a) Operand-2 of PACK should specify an explicit length.

16-6. (a) X'004C'.
     (b) X'368C2' and X'368C7'.
     (c) TOTAL contains hex zeros and VALUE contains packed blanks. Either will cause a Data Exception.

17-2. To enable both positive and negative characteristics.

17-3. (b) X'9A.312' = 42 9A3120

17-4. (b) X'4F.6560' = 42 4F6560

19-1. The program may be extremely large, or the subprograms may be common to a number of other programs.

19-3. DROP reg.

19-5. The system uses register-13 for linkage.

19-7. CALL: call the subprogram; SAVE: save the calling program's registers; RETURN: return to the calling program.

19-10. LOAD loads a module from disk into storage whereas CALL links to the module for execution; FETCH both loads a module and links to it for execution, but does not provide a path for return.

20-2. During execution, in lower main storage.

20-3. Includes any required IOCS modules into the assembled program and links together separate subprograms.

20-4. (a) CIL; (b) RL; (c) SSL.

20-6. The Fixed Storage Locations.

20-8.   The two PSW modes are Basic Control (BC) and Extended
        Control (EC). The two PSW states are Supervisor and
        Problem state.
20-9.   In the instruction address, bits 40-63.
20-11. Channels provide a path between main storage and input/
        output devices. The types are multiplexor for slow devices
        and selector for fast devices.
20-12. X'02D'.
20-13. A physical address is the actual hex address by which an
        operating system accesses a device; a logical address is a
        name such as SYSLST by which a programmer can reference a
        device. The Supervisor relates the devices by means of its
        I/O Devices Control Table.

INDEX

&SYSLIST, 479
&SYSNDX, 479

A

A (add fullword), 248
A-format (address constant), 238
ABEND macro, 208
Abnormal termination, 208
ACB macro, 397
Access Method Services (AMS), 394
Access motion, 359
ACTION command, 429
ACTR conditional assembly instruction, 468
AD, ADR (add float), 451
Addition:
    binary, 234, 248
    floating point, 450
    packed, 114
ADDR1, ADDR2 on program listing, 33, 67
Address, 29, 34, 239
Address constant (A-type), 238
Address marker, 361
Addressability error, 99
Addressed accessing (VSAM), 391, 396
Addressing, 34, 166, 418
Addressing exception, 538
AE, AER (add float), 451
AGO conditional assembly instruction, 468, 470
AH (add halfword), 248
AIF conditional assembly instruction, 468, 470

AL, ALR (add logical), 308
Alignment of data, 239
Alternate track, 358
AMS (see Access Method Services)
AND (Boolean operation), 311
ANOP conditional assembly instruction, 468, 472
AP (add packed), 114
AR (add register), 248
Argument:
    in table, 277
    in TR, 321
    in TRT, 324
Arithmetic:
    binary, 234, 248
    decimal (packed), 103
    floating point, 450
Array (see table)
ASA control character, 195
ASCII code, 321
Assemble, 20, 30, 182, 509, 545
Assembler, 20
Assembler listing, 31
Assigning a base register, 177
Asterisk total indication, 141
Attributes for conditional assembly, 469
AU, AUR, AW, AWR (add unnormalized), 453

B

B (unconditional branch), 50, 185
B-format (binary), 235

BAL (Basic Assembler Language) (see Assembler)
BAL (branch and link), 122
BALR (branch and link register), 42, 178
Base of number, 9, 442
Base register:
    addressing, 36, 42, 166, 177
    defined, 36, 167
    explicit use, 205, 244, 269
    initialize multiple, 169, 243, 245
    initialize one, 167, 178
BC (branch on condition), 85, 185
BCR (branch on condition register), 123, 185
BCT (branch on count), 281
BCTR (branch on count register), 281
BE (branch equal), 85, 186
BH (branch high), 85, 186
Binary:
    arithmetic, 234, 248
    comparisons, 249
    constant (B-type), 235
    data, 13, 16, 233
    data packing, 309
    numbers, 9
    point, 10
    search, 292
    shift, 255, 309
Bit, 10
BL (branch low), 85, 186
Blank, 55, 71, 112
Block, 197, 200, 203
Block control word, 350
Block count, 346
Blocked records, 190, 337
Blocking factor, 337
BM:
    branch minus, 115, 186
    branch mixed, 315
BO:
    branch overflow, 115, 186
    branch ones, 315
Book, 513
Boolean logic, 311
Boundary alignment, 239
BP (branch plus), 115, 186
Bpi (bytes per inch), 336
BR (branch register), 122, 185
Branch on condition, 85, 115, 185
Branching, 50, 85, 185
Buffer (I/O area), 189, 191, 194, 204
BXH (branch index high), 281
BXLE (branch index low/equal), 281

Byte, 10, 13
BZ (branch zero), 115, 186, 315

C

C (compare fullword), 249
C-format (character), 66
CALL macro, 487
CALL, SAVE, and RETURN, 487
CANCEL macro, 209
Card, 8
Carriage control tape, 195
CATAL option, 524
Catalog in a library, 524
CCB (command control block), 190, 527
CCW (channel command word), 190, 527
CD, CDR, CE, CER (compare float), 453
Central processing unit (CPU), 4, 12, 521
CH (compare halfword), 249
Channel command word (CCW), 190, 527
Channel for carriage control tape, 195
Channel for input/output, 189, 523
Channel scheduler, 518
Character format, 13, 54, 66
Character instructions, 73, 415
Characteristic (float), 443
CKD (count-key-data architecture), 359, 360
CL (compare logical), 309
CLC (compare logical character), 82
CLCL (compare long), 264
CLI (compare logical immediate), 87
CLM (compare characters under mask), 327
CLOSE macro, 44, 192, 401
CLR (compare logical register), 309
CNOP (conditional NOP), 565
CNTRL macro, 195
COBOL, linkage to, 504
COCR (cylinder overflow control record), 374
Codes, 54
Coding, 29
Coding form, 21
Command control block (CCB), 190, 529
Comments, 23, 24, 465
Communication region, 275, 516
Compare:
    binary (algebraic), 249
    binary (logical), 309
    character, 82, 87, 264
    floating point, 453
    packed, 117
Completion code, 423
COMRG macro, 275
Concatenation (for macros), 466

Condition code, 55, 83, 115, 117
Conditional assembly instruction, 468
Conditional branch, 83, 115
Connector on flowchart, 58
Constant (see DC)
Continuation, 24
Continuous forms, 9
Control character, 69, 195, 200
Control interval, 390
Control program, 4, 511
Control section (see CSECT)
Control unit, 6, 524
Conventions for coding, 29
Conversion of:
    binary to decimal, 240, 261
    decimal to binary, 240
    double precision binary, 261
    float to packed, 458
    packed to float, 458
Core image library (CIL), 513
Count area (disk), 361
Count attribute (macros), 469
Count-key-data format, 359
CP (compare packed), 117
CPU (see Central processing unit)
CR (compare register), 249
Cross reference listing, 52
CSECT (control section), 21, 175, 483, 489
CVB (convert to binary), 240
CVD (convert to decimal), 240
Cylinder, 360
Cylinder index, 374
Cylinder overflow area, 376

D

D (divide register), 258
D-format (doubleword), 240
DASD (direct access storage device), 357
DASD capacity, 369
DATA (entry in PRINT directive), 27
Data exception, 116, 117, 416, 538
Data management, 190
Data set, 9, 53
Data transfer rate (disk), 359
Date from communication region, 275
DC (define constant):
    address (A), 236
    address (V), 489
    binary (B), 235
    character (C), 66, 70
    definition, 27, 65
    floating point (D, E), 240

DC *(Contd.)*
    fullword (F), 236
    halfword (H), 236
    hexadecimal (X), 103
    packed (P), 108
    zoned (Z), 106
DCB (data control block), 191, 201
DD (data definition job command), 201, 203, 550
DD, DDR, DE, DER, (divide float), 457
DDNAME (job entry), 550
Debugging, 415
Decimal data (see Packed data)
Decimal precision, 143, 153
Decimal-divide exception, 417, 539
Decimal-overflow exception, 417, 539
Declaratives, 21, 23, 27, 65, 561
DEFIN macro, 43, 553
DEFINE CLUSTER command, 394
Define constant (see DC)
Define storage (see DS)
DEFPR macro, 43, 553
Delete code for ISAM, 384
Device independence, 207
Diagnostic messages, 34
Digit selector, 138
Direct access storage device (DASD), 357
Direct file organization, 363
Direct table addressing, 286
Directive, 21, 23, 25, 563
Disk labels, 366
Disk operating system (see DOS)
Disk pack, 357
Displacement, 36, 167
Division:
    binary, 258
    floating point, 457
    packed, 151
DLBL job command, 364, 547
Documentation, 214
DOS, 14, 61, 545
Double precision,
    addition, 308
    binary, 261, 307
    floating point, 446
Doubleword format (D-type), 240
DP (divide packed), 151
DR (divide register), 258
DROP macro, 485, 490
DS (define storage), 27, 65
DSECT (dummy section), 484
DSNAME job entry, 550
DTFCD macro, 197

DTFCN macro, 209
DTFDI macro, 207
DTFDR macro, 209
DTFDU macro, 209
DTFIS macro, 377, 381
DTFMR macro, 209
DTFMT macro, 339
DTFOR macro, 209
DTFPR macro, 191, 200
DTFSD macro, 364
Dummy section (see DSECT)
DUMP macro, 208
Dump of storage (see Storage dump)
Duplication factor, 66, 68, 70
Duplicating characters, 79
Dynamic address translation (DAT), 516

E

E-format (floating point), 446
EBCDIC code, 13, 557
ED (edit), 137
Edit word, 137
EDMK (edit and mark), 272
EJECT directive, 26
END directive, 21, 27, 47
End-of-file:
    card, 43, 194, 197, 203
    disk, 362
    tape, 348, 349
End-of-tape marker, 337
End-of-volume (EOV), 346, 348
ENDFL macro, 377
Endless loop, 418
Entry point address (EPA), 183, 423
Entry sequenced data set (ESDS), 389, 390, 408
ENTRY statement, 497, 502
EOJ macro, 46, 556
EPA (see Entry point address)
EQU directive, 91
ERASE macro, 397, 401
ESD (see External symbol dictionary)
ESDS (see Entry sequenced data set)
ESETL macro, 386
EX (execute), 317
Excess-64 notation, 443
EXCP (execute channel program), 190, 527
EXEC job command, 15, 60
Execute exception, 537
EXLST macro, 397, 403
Explicit length, 75
Explicit use of base register, 205, 244, 269
Exponent, 443
Exponent modifier, 446

Exponent-overflow exception, 539
Extend an ISAM file, 377
Extended mnemonics, 85, 185
Extended precision floating point, 446
Extent on disk, 364
External address constant (V-type), 489
External symbol dictionary (ESD), 31, 183
EXTRN statement, 502

F

F-format (fullword), 236
FBA (see Fixed block architecture)
FETCH macro, 501
Field, 41
File:
    card, 43, 197
    definition, 41, 53
    disk, 363
    input, 43, 53, 203
    output, 203
    printer, 45, 200
    tape, 343
File definition macro, 43, 191, 197
File label, 343, 368
FilenameC, 378
Fill character, 138
Fixed block architecture (FBA), 362
Fixed length record, 200
Fixed point data (see binary data)
Fixed-point-divide exception, 538
Fixed-point-overflow exception, 538
Fixed storage locations, 517
Floating point format, 13, 441
Floating point register, 447
Flowchart, 56, 124
Format-1 label (disk), 368
Fraction for floating point, 443
Fullword format (F-type), 236
Function for table, 277, 321, 324

G

GBLA, GBLB, GBLC (global), 480
GEN (entry in PRINT directive), 27
General purpose register (see Register)
Generations of computers, 3
GET macro, 28, 68, 193, 402
Global SET symbol, 479
Guard digit, 451

H

H-format (halfword), 236
Halfword format (H-type), 236
HALT I/O, 190

HDR, HER (Halve float), 454
Header label, 345
Header statement (macro), 463
Hexadecimal:
    arithmetic, 16
    conversion, 535
    format (X-type), 15, 103
Hierarchy chart, 213
High-level language, 20
Home address (disk), 361

I

IBG (interblock gap), 338
IC (insert character), 316
ICM (insert character under mask), 327
IDCAMS, 394
Identification sequence (ISEQ), 24
Immediate operand, 87, 171
Imperative macro, 191, 192
Implicit length, 75
INCLUDE statement, 497
Independent overflow area, 376
Index point, 361
Index register, 166, 175, 245
Index set (VSAM), 392
Indexed sequential access method (ISAM), 363, 373
INIT macro, 42, 553
Initial program load (IPL), 512
Initialization under OS, 181
Input, 44, 53, 68, 193, 197, 203
Input/output, 7, 12, 189, 419
Input/Output Control System (IOCS), 190
Input/output errors, 210, 419
Input/output modules, 201, 421
Instruction, 4, 13, 23, 541
Instruction alignment, 77
Instruction format, 37, 170
Interblock gap (IBG), 338
Interrupts, 15, 521, 537
INVALID STATEMENT (diagnostic), 539
I/O area (see buffer)
IOCS (Input/Output Control System), 190, 339, 347, 512
IOCS modules, 201, 502, 526
IOREG macro entry, 204
ISAM (see Indexed sequential access method)
ISEQ directive, 27

J

JCL (job control language) see Job control
Job control, 15, 60, 510, 545
JOB command, 60, 545

K

K (measurement of storage size), 12
Key, 362, 373
Key area, 362
Key sequenced data set (KSDS), 389, 391
Keyed accessing (VSAM), 396
Keyword macro, 197, 462, 463
KSDS (see Key sequenced data set)

L

L (load), 241, 242
L-format (floating point), 446
LA (load address), 241, 243
Label (see name)
LBLTYP command, 546
LCDR, LCER (load complement float), 449
LCLA, LCLB, LCLC (locals), 473
LCR (load complement), 246
LD, LDR, LR, LER (load float), 448
Length indication, 66, 70
LH (load halfword), 241, 242
Libraries, 513
Link edit, 61, 183, 201, 513
Link edit map, 201, 429, 501
Linkage:
    between COBOL and Assembler, 504
    between phases, 496
    between subprograms, 487
    between subroutines, 122
Linkage editor control statement, 497
Linkage register, 487
LIOCS (logical IOCS), 190
Literal, 33, 90
Literal pool, 90
LM (load multiple), 241, 242
LNDR, LNER (load negative float), 449
LNKEDT command, 61, 546
LNR (load negative), 246
Load:
    a base register, 167, 243, 245
    a program, 19
    a table, 278, 292
    an ISAM file, 377, 384
LOAD macro, 501
Load point address (see Entry point address)
Load point marker (tape), 337
Load register operations, 241, 246
Loader program, 183
LOC (see Location counter)
Local SET symbol, 473
Locate mode, 204
Location counter, 30, 31, 67, 93

Logic, 6
Logical expression, 471
Logical IOCS (LIOCS), 190
Logical operation, 307
Logical operators, 471
Logical record, 190
Looping, 50
Low-level language, 20
LPDR, LPER (load positive float), 449
LPR (load positive), 246
LR (load register), 241, 242
LTDR, LTER (load and test float), 449
LTORG directive, 33, 91
LTR (load and test register), 246

M

M (multiply fullword), 252
Machine language, 19, 170
MACRF entry, 398
Macro:
    definition, 462
    expansion, 463
    instruction, 20, 463
    writing, 461
Magnetic tape, 335
Main logic section, 212
Main storage (see storage)
Mask:
    Boolean operation, 311
    branch instruction, 185
    masked byte operations, 327
Master index, 375
MD, MDR, ME, MER (multiply float), 456
Memory (see storage)
MEND directive, 464
MEXIT directive, 472
MH (multiply halfword), 252
Minus sign:
    binary, 234
    packed, 107
    zoned, 106
Mixed-type macro, 462
MNOTE statement, 472
Model statement, 463
Module, 201, 513
MP (multiply packed), 142
MR (multiply register), 252
Multi-file volume, 343
Multi-volume file, 343
Multiplexor channel, 523
Multiplication:
    binary, 252
    floating point, 456
    packed, 142

Multiprogramming, 169, 515
MVC (move characters), 74
MVCL (move characters long), 264
MVI (move immediate), 87
MVN (move numerics), 104
MVO (move with offset), 147
MVZ (move zones), 104

N

N (Boolean AND), 311
Name (label), 23, 28
NC (Boolean AND character), 311
NI (Boolean AND immediate), 311
NOP (no-operation), 86, 186
Normalization, 445
NR (Boolean AND register), 311
Numeric portion of byte, 13, 104

O

O (Boolean OR), 311
Object code, 33, 49, 60, 71
Object program, 30, 61, 183
OC (Boolean OR character), 311
OI (Boolean OR immediate), 311
OPEN macro, 43, 192, 400
Operand, 6, 24
Operating system, 14, 509
Operation, 24
Operation exception, 537
Operator's guide, 217
OPTION command, 209, 546
OR (Boolean OR register), 311
ORG directive, 93
OS (Operating System), 14, 61, 181, 549
Output, 12, 69, 194, 200, 203
Overflow:
    binary, 234
    packed, 115
Overflow area (ISAM), 375
Overlay phase, 496, 503

P

P-format (packed), 107
PACK instruction, 109
Packed data, 13, 107
Packed format (P-type), 13, 108
Packed operations, 114
Page in VS, 515
Page overflow, 121
Parameter, 197, 493
Parity bit, 10
Partition, 515
Pass a parameter, 493
PDUMP macro (partial dump), 429

Phase, 484, 496, 513
PHASE statement, 497
Physical address, 524
Physical IOCS (PIOCS), 190, 527
PIOCS (see Physical IOCS)
POINT macro, 401
Positional macro, 462
Primary track, 358
Prime data area, 373
PRINT directive, 26
Printer, 9, 195
Printer file, 43, 191, 200
Printing lines, 45, 47, 121
Privileged instruction, 190, 520
Privileged-operation exception, 537
Problem program, 189
Procedure library, 513
Product length, 143
Program information block (PIB), 519
Program interrupt, 15, 537
Program organization chart (see Hierarchy chart)
Program relocatability, 169
Program status word (PSW), 11, 14, 178, 190, 423, 519
Programmer logical unit, 525
Programming style, 211
Protection exception, 538
Prototype statement (macro), 463
PSW (see Program status word)
Punched card, 8
PUT macro, 194, 402
PUTPR macro, 45, 69, 553
PUTR macro (PUT with reply), 209
PUTX macro, 386

Q

Quotient:
    binary, 258
    packed, 152

R

Radix point, 444
Random retrieval, 379
RBA (relative byte address), 390
READ macro, 379
Record, 41, 47
Record control word, 350
Record overflow, 362
Reflective marker (see tape marker)
Register:
    floating point, 11, 447
    general purpose, 11, 14, 165, 233
Register restrictions, 166

Relational operators, 470
Relative addressing, 36, 69, 76
Relative record data set (RRDS), 389, 391
Relocatable library (RL), 513
Relocation dictionary (RLD), 183
Relocation factor, 184, 423, 501
Remainder:
    binary, 258
    packed, 152
Representation in storage, 127, 237
RETURN macro, 182
RLD (relocation dictionary), 183
ROOT phase, 497, 503
Rotational delay (disk), 359
Rounding:
    binary, 259
    packed, 143, 145, 148, 153
RPL macro, 397, 399
RR-format, 37, 170, 173
RS-format, 37, 170, 174
RX-format, 37, 170, 174
RRDS (see Relative record data set)

S

S (subtract fullword), 248
S-format, 37, 171
SAVE macro, 181, 487
Savearea for registers, 181, 487
Saving registers, 248
Scale modifier (floating point), 446
Scan (see TRT)
SD, SDR, SE, SER (Subtract float), 451
Search argument (tables), 277
Selector channel, 523
Sequence set (VSAM), 392
Sequence symbol (macro), 470
Sequence-checking, 53, 56, 94, 125
Sequential file organization (disk), 363, 364
Sequential processing of an ISAM file, 384, 385
SET symbol, 464, 473
SETA (macro), 474
SETB (macro), 477
SETC (macro), 476
SETFL macro, 377
SETL macro, 385
SH (subtract halfword), 248
Shift:
    binary number, 255, 309
    decimal number, 143, 145, 147, 153, 275
SHOWCB macro, 397, 404
SI-format, 37, 73, 87, 170
Sign:
    binary number, 234
    decimal number, 107

Sign *(Contd.)*
  floating point number, 443
  zoned number, 106
Significance exception, 539
Significance starter, 138
Single precision float, 446
SL (subtract logical), 308
SLA (shift left algebraic), 255
Slash/asterisk (/*) job command, 43, 196
SLDA (shift left double algebraic), 255
SLDL (shift left double logical), 309
SLL (shift left logical), 309
SLR (subtract logical register), 308
SNAP macro, 429, 432
Sort:
    table entries, 288
    VSAM, 409
Source document, 9
Source program, 29
Source statement library (SSL), 513
SP (subtract packed), 114
SPACE directive, 26
Specification exception, 538
SPIE macro, 438
SR (subtract register), 248
SRA (shift right algebraic), 255
SRDA (shift right double algebraic), 255
SRDL (shift right double logical), 309
SRL (shift right logical), 309
SRP (shift and round packed), 145, 275
SS-format, 37, 74, 170
ST (store register), 246
Standard file label, 343, 366
Standard tape label, 343
START directive, 21, 26, 176
START I/O instruction, 190
Status condition, 378, 383
STC (store character), 316
STCM (store character under mask), 327
STD, STE (store float), 450
STH (store halfword), 246
STM (Store multiple), 246
STMT (on listing), 33, 67
Storage, 5, 12
Storage dump, 16, 127, 421
Storage immediate (see SI-format)
Storage protection, 518
Storage-to-storage (see SS-format)
Store register operations, 246
Stored program, 5
Structured programming, 212
STXIT macro, 437
SU, SUR (subtract unnormalized float), 453

Subject instruction (for EX), 317
Subprogram, 483
Subroutine, 122
Sum of digits, 119, 251, 257, 263
Supervisor, 14, 189, 511, 516
SVC (supervisor call), 190
SW, SWR (subtract unnormalized float), 453
Switch, 314
Symbol length attribute, 77
Symbolic assignment, 524
Symbolic language, 20
Symbolic parameter, 464
SYS address (see System logical unit)
SYSIN, 203, 525
SYSIPT, 197, 525
SYSLNK, 514, 525
SYSLOG, 209, 525
SYSLST, 200, 525
SYSRDR, 197, 525
SYSRES, 525
System logical unit, 525
System service programs, 512
System variable symbol, 464, 479
SYSUDUMP job command, 423, 549

T

Table (array):
    define, 277
    load, 278, 292
    look-up, 278
    sort, 288
Tape:
    labels, 343
    mark, 347
    marker, 337
    programming, 339, 341
Target (Boolean operation), 311
Terminal I/O, 209
Terminate a program, 46
Test channel, 190
TEST I/O, 190
TIME macro, 275
TITLE directive, 25, 73
TLBL job command, 546
TM (test under mask), 314
TR (translate), 320
Track:
    descriptor record, 361
    format, 358, 360
    index, 373
Trailer label, 345
Trailer statement, 463
Transient area, 516, 519

Translate (see TR and TRT)
TRT (translate and test), 324
True zero, 446
Two's complement representation, 145, 234
TXT entry, 183

U

Unconditional branch, 86
UNPK (unpack), 112
USING directive, 42, 177, 492
Utility program, 410, 514

V

V-type constant, 183, 489
Variable-length field, 316, 319, 320, 327
Variable-length record, 338, 349
Variable symbol, 464
Video display terminal (VDT), 7·
Virtual storage, 515
Virtual storage access method (VSAM), 363, 389
Volume label:
    disk, 368
    tape, 344
Volume table of contents (VTOC), 366

VSAM (see Virtual storage access method)
VSAM sort, 409
VSAM utility print, 410
VTOC (see Volume table of contents)

W

WAIT macro, 527
WAITF macro, 379
Workarea, 200, 201, 347
WRITE macro, 377, 379
WXTRN, 508

X

X, XC, XI, XOR, XR (Boolean exclusive OR), 311
X-format (hexadecimal), 103

Z

Z-format (zoned), 106
ZAP (zero and add packed), 114
Zero duplication factor, 68, 69
Zero suppression, 138
Zone portion of byte, 13, 104
Zone punch, 8, 108
Zoned format (Z-type), 106